The Literary Companion
to Parliament

THE LITERARY
COMPANION
TO PARLIAMENT

Edited by

CHRISTOPHER SILVESTER

SINCLAIR-STEVENSON

First published in Great Britain in 1996
by Sinclair-Stevenson
an imprint of Reed International Books Ltd
Michelin House, 81 Fulham Road, London SW3 6RB
and Auckland, Melbourne, Singapore and Toronto

A CIP catalogue record for this book
is available at the British Library

ISBN 1 85619 460 4

Phototypeset in 10 on 12 point Goudy Old Style
by Intype London Ltd
Printed and bound in Great Britain
by Clays Ltd, St Ives plc

Lord Maynard was the person who said
of the H. of Commons, 'Is that going on still?'

Thomas Moore, Journal, October 27, 1827

Contents

Acknowledgements

I wish to thank Christopher Sinclair-Stevenson for commissioning this anthology and my agent, Caradoc King, for championing it.

Otherwise, the following persons have offered assistance and encouragement: Bill Cash MP, Maurice Cowling, Michael Foot, Stephen Fry, George Galloway MP, Simon Heffer, Matthew Parris, Robin Reeve, Tom Utley, Alan Watkins, Francis Wheen, Michael White and A. N. Wilson.

The structure of this anthology is arbitrary. There are items in each chapter which could just as easily appear in another chapter or chapters. I make no apology for this, but trust that readers will appreciate the reason for my preference in each case.

I have chosen to modernise spellings and have expanded abbreviations in the main—for example, banishing the ampersand. I hope this will make for a more easily readable text.

The preparation of this anthology has been arduous and time-consuming: I have been working at it, off and on, for five years. Nevertheless, I have found the experience both enriching and enjoyable.

The editor and the publishers wish to thank the following for permission to use copyright material: Edward Arnold Ltd for an extract from Stephen Gwynn, *John Redmond's Last Years*, copyright © renewed 1969, Stephen Gwynn (1919); Lady Bonham-Carter, for an extract from Margot Asquith, *More Memories*, copyright © Lady Bonham-Carter, 1933; The Rt Hon. Paul Channon, MP, for extracts from the papers of Sir Henry Channon, copyright © the Estate of Sir Henry Channon; Artemis Cooper, for an extract from the diary of Alfred Duff Cooper, and for the use of a letter to his wife Diana, copyright © the Estate of Sir Alfred Duff Cooper; Curtis Brown Group Ltd for an extract from *My Early Life* by Winston S. Churchill, and an extract from a letter from Winston S. Churchill to Clementine Churchill, reproduced with permission of Curtis Brown Ltd, London on behalf on The Estate of Sir Winston S. Churchill. Copyright © Winston S. Churchill; The *Guardian* and *Observer* newspapers for extracts from articles by Harry Boardman; HarperCollins*Publishers* Ltd for extracts from *Harold Nicolson Diaries* by Harold Nicolson; David Higham Associates, for an extract from Malcolm MacDonald, *Titans and Others*, copyright © Malcolm MacDonald, 1972; and an extract from Aneurin Bevan, *In Place of Fear*, copyright © Aneurin Bevan, 1952; and an extract from Hugh Dalton, *Call Back Yesterday: Memoirs 1887–1931*, copyright © Hugh Dalton, 1953; and for an extract from Tom Driberg, *The Best of Both Worlds: A Personal Diary, 1953,* copyright © Tom Driberg, 1953; Hodder Headline plc for an extract from the diary of John Colville, copyright © John Colville, 1940; Lawrence & Wishart Ltd, for an extract from William Gallacher, *The Last Memoirs of William Gallacher,* copyright © William Gallacher, 1966; Little, Brown & Co. (UK), for an extract from Jack and Bessie Braddock, *The Braddocks,* copyright © Little, Brown & Co. (UK), 1963; John Murray (Publishers) Ltd for an extract from *Whippingham to Westminster: The Reminiscences of Lord Ernle* by Rowland Prothero (Lord Ernle) and for an extract from *Years of Endeavour* by George Leveson-Gower, copyright © George Leveson-Gower; The National Library of Wales for the use of extracts from the papers of Lloyd-George of Dwyfor; Peters, Fraser & Dunlop Group Ltd, for an extract from a letter from Hilaire Belloc to Maurice Baring, copyright © the Estate of Hilaire Belloc; *Punch,* for 'Essence of Parliament', copyright © *Punch,* 1925; the Society of Authors as the literary representative of the Estate of Virginia Woolf for Virginia Woolf, 'This is the House of Commons'; the *Spectator,* for Harold Nicolson, 'An atmosphere of comradely vivacity', copyright © *Spectator,* 1939 and 'Taper' (Bernard Levin), 'The dog days', copyright © *Spectator,* 1959; Thames & Hudson Ltd, for an extract from Peter de Mendelssohn, *The Age of Churchill,* copyright © Peter de Mendelssohn, 1961; Tribune Publications Ltd for two articles by J. P. W. Mallalieu, copyright © Tribune Publications Ltd; A. P. Watt Ltd, on behalf of The Literary Executors of the Estate of H. G. Wells, for an extract from *The New Machiavelli* by H. G. Wells, and on behalf of Crystal Hale and Jocelyn Herbert for an extract from *Independent Member* by A. P. Herbert.

Every effort has been made to trace the copyright holders of the quoted material. If there are any inadvertent omissions, however, these can be rectified in any future editions.

Introduction

The British Parliament at Westminster, St Stephen's, has often been incorrectly described as 'the Mother of Parliaments', whereas the actual quotation, from the nineteenth-century Radical MP John Bright, is that 'England is the Mother of parliaments'.[1] It was the peculiar nature of the English polity which gave birth to parliamentary government and guaranteed its evolution and development. In the seventeenth century, when absolutist monarchies were the norm in Europe, the English Parliament was a singular achievement.[2] However, when politicians and pundits repeat the misquotation that Westminster is the mother of parliaments, they are nonetheless uttering a bastard truth, since most parliaments have to some extent followed the Westminster model, perhaps not in the physical arrangement of their chambers but frequently in their procedural arrangements.

'A desire to serve the nation in Parliament is an Englishman's ambition,' wrote George Savile, Marquis of Halifax, in 1695, adding that this is 'always to be encouraged and never to be disapproved'.[3] Trollope puts a similar sentiment into the mouth of one of the characters in his 1864 novel *Can You Forgive Her?*: 'I have told myself, in anger and in grief, that to die and not to have won that right of way, though but for a session,—not to have passed through those lamps [on either side of the St Stephen's entrance],—is to die and not to have done that which it most becomes an Englishman to have achieved.'[4] Nor has this high opinion been confined to native observers. In 1874 a Frenchman named Auguste Laugel, private secretary to the Duc d'Aumale, wrote that there 'is no more august assembly than the English parliament; its name ranks with that of the Roman senate'. These are classic statements of enthusiasm for parliamentary life.

In a letter to Gilbert Murray, H. A. L. Fisher wrote: 'The mere atmosphere of the House of Commons, contributing to the general opinion, is so much higher and more serious than it is in a university, that is, if one considers the men who matter in the House.'[5] Richard Monckton Milnes, too, was impressed by his colleagues, though he found the experience more inhibiting than enabling. 'The worst effect on myself resulting from listening to the debates in Parliament', he said, 'is that it prevents me from forming any clear political opinion on any subject.'[6] Others have found it frustrating for different reasons. The most famous of the earls of Chesterfield, author of *Letters to his Son*, lamented the lack of intellectual calibre among MPs. When Sir Philip Yorke's friend and correspondent James Harris took his seat in the House of Commons,

Charles Townshend enquired who he was and was informed that he had written on the subject of logic and grammar. 'Why does he come here,' Townshend replied, 'where he will hear nothing of either?'[7] Another confirmed cynic, the Scottish Labour MP 'Don Roberto' Cunninghame Graham, scorned Parliament, dismissing it as 'this dreary waste of mud and stucco', as the 'Great Thieves' Kitchen, manned with magnolia-scented cooks, too fine to cook', as the 'National Gas Works' and as 'the Asylum for Incapables'.[8]

For some MPs, however, being away from it all is worse than being kept there in a state of perpetual frustration. Edward Gibbon, who never overcame his fear of speaking in the House, wrote to a friend in 1783 that life at Lausanne was 'more conducive to happiness than five nights in the week passed in the House of Commons', yet in his *Autobiography* he admitted, 'I never found my mind more vigorous nor my composition more happy, than in the winter hurry of society and Parliament.'[9] These sentiments were later echoed by C. F. G. Masterman who declared in a letter to his sweetheart Lucy Lyttelton in September 1907: 'I am having an easy time now Parliament is up, though I feel like a watch whose main spring has suddenly stopped.'[10] Austen Chamberlain, in a letter to his stepmother in 1912, also expressed how the House exercised its spell on him: 'I dined last night with George Wyndham and had no intention of going back to the House, but seeing the light burning as I crossed Hyde Park Corner I was attracted to it like a moth to the candle.'[11] It was the immense variety of human emotions to which parliamentary life gave rise, according to the Edwardian parliamentary correspondent Frank Dilnot, which enchanted those who were a part of it:

> Those electric feelings which set members shouting like thrilled schoolboys, or reduce them to a palpitating silence, those feelings which turn the House sometimes into a solemn court of justice, sometimes into an arena where brilliant wits battle against each other mercilessly and tenaciously, sometimes into a mystic temple from the altar of which political high priests of the time deliver eagerly-awaited announcements which may alter some portion of a nation's life—those feelings are not to be found reflected in any of the prints of the time. Yet they are the great human feature of Parliamentary life. With their many variations they give that fascination to Westminster which every member feels in some degree or other, and which once it has touched a man never leaves him.[12]

For those who had departed the Westminster scene, a prod to the memory could have an enlivening effect. Hannah Macaulay told the retired Sir William Wilberforce, with whom she was staying, that she had received a letter from her brother in the House of Commons: 'He was silent for a moment and then his mobile face lighted up, and he slapped his hand to his ear and cried: "Ah! I hear that shout again! Hear, hear! What a life it was!" '[13]

Even Irish Home Rulers could be gripped by the ways of the House. Joseph Biggar was an arch-obstructionist who used ancient procedural rules to block business—such as the spying of strangers, which necessitated a division, or the counting out and adjourning of the House, if there were fewer than forty MPs in the Chamber. After the 41½-hour sitting in 1881, although he was exhausted, Biggar attended mass at St George's Cathedral, Southwark, and fell asleep. When the sermon began, he woke with a start and, imagining himself still in the House of Commons, exclaimed: 'Mr Speaker, I beg to call your attention to the fact that there are not forty members present.'[14]

John Morley described parliamentary life as 'having the singular peculiarity of being neither business nor rest'.[15] But then Morley was a minister throughout most of his career. On the other hand, Harold Nicolson, writing to his son Nigel in May 1945, observed: 'I have loved my ten years at Westminster, and have found there that combination of genial surroundings with useful activity which is the basis of all human happiness.'[16] A decade or so later, Nigel Nicolson was himself an MP and reached a similar conclusion: 'There is no place where a man can occupy himself more intensively or usefully, and no place where he can hold down his job by doing so little.'[17]

A parliamentary career, according to Lord Macaulay, was one 'in which the most its combatants can expect is that by relinquishing liberal studies and social comfort, by passing nights without sleep and summers without one glimpse of the beauties of nature, they may attain that laborious, that invidious, that closely watched slavery which is mocked with the name of power'. Macaulay's nephew and biographer, Sir George Trevelyan, who also sat as an MP, concurred: 'Waiting whole evenings to vote and then walking half a mile at a foot's pace round and round the crowded lobbies; dining amidst clamour and confusion, with a division twenty minutes long between two of the mouthfuls; trudging home at three in the morning through the slush of a February thaw; and sitting behind Ministers in the centre of a closely packed bench during the hottest week of the London summer.'[18] On the other hand, Winthrop Mackworth Praed, a man of weak constitution, praised this way of life for its therapeutic qualities: 'Losing a dinner now and then and listening to Mr Hume till 5 in the morning are things which do as much good to me as air and exercise and natural *materia medica* to wiser and soberer men.'[19]

Robert Cecil, later to become 3rd Marquis of Salisbury and a Tory prime minister, described the 'sorrows of a poor MP' in an article for the *Saturday Review* in 1859, comparing them unfavourably to the privations of monastic life:

> If any ancient ascetic had ventured to prescribe what a modern senator pays heavily to be allowed to do, a monastic mutiny would have been the certain consequence. What is fasting compared to feeding on Bellamy's beef? What are vigils compared to seven hours of Committee of Supply? It may be painful to flesh and blood to get up for Lauds at three in the morning, but it is luxury compared to sitting up till three in order to listen to Mr Vincent Scully. Imprisonment in a convent may be dreary work, even though it be on a green hill-side and close by a rippling trout-stream; but what is it to imprisonment in the lowest flats of Westminster, on the banks of the foetid Thames? People may vaunt the asceticism of St Simeon

Stylites, but the idea of sitting on a pillar where there is no Thames and no counsel is Elysium itself to the wretch who is sitting on an Election Committee. The rank and file of the House of Commons, who, without hope of office or of fame, ruin their fortunes, shatter their healths, squander their lives, and submit to be set up as targets for the thick-flying abuse of county politics, in order that they may be at liberty to subject themselves to this super-monastic maceration, is an enigma to the student of humanity. Spring and summer bloom for them in vain—it is to no purpose that night offers sleep to their weary eyes. What is it that can induce them still, with whitening faces and more and more haggard eyes, to go on crowding to the green benches of their punishment at mid-day, and shuffling away from them three hours after midnight? Is it possible that they are credulous enough to believe they are of any use?[20]

The curious contrast between the working environment of Parliament and its working practices, that strange combination of comforts and tortures, has elicited criticism from many MPs. In 1796 William Lambton was warned 'against an attendance in Parliament, from which late hours, a corrupt atmosphere and much anxiety to all who really feel for their country are inseparable'.[21] Macaulay complained of 'bad air and bad speeches'. Yet the sketch-writer Edward Michael Whitty was the first to dub it in print as 'the best club in London', while George Pryme recalled that his MP, Hope Vere,[22] had called it the 'best and pleasantest Club',[23] and the phrase was taken up by Mr Twemlow in Dickens's *Our Mutual Friend* (1864–5). One of the first Labour MPs, Frederick Jowett, found this contrast between material luxuries and inefficient arrangements absurd:

The nation will go to great lengths in providing for the convenience and comfort of private members, but it gives very little assistance to the working member. As many as wish to play chess or draughts can be accommodated. In addition to the ordinary members' dining rooms, for instance, a large dining hall and a number of smaller ones opening on to the Terrace are set apart for swell dinner parties, and they are in daily use while Parliament is sitting. Dressing rooms are also provided for the convenience of members who 'dress for dinner'. Here the valets attend and assist their masters to get into their boiled shirts. If your own valet is not at hand, or you do not happen to employ one, the dressing-room attendant paid by the State will hand you your clean things and put the discarded ones away for you. But if you require any assistance in drafting an amendment to a Bill which is under consideration, or in drafting a new Bill, there is not a single person to whom you can go for guidance. The Statute Book has been strewed by generations of lawyer members of Parliament with pitfalls for the unwary plain man, and unless you can afford to pay for expert assistance you must flounder as best you can.[24]

T. P. O'Connor believed that 'the great object of the House of Commons is not how to do business, but how not to do it; that it consists of men who, for the most part, unless for a couple of hours each day, avoid the place as if it were infected with the pestilence; and that, of those who remain in the House and take a part in its proceedings, the majority are wearied, disillusioned men, who have lost nerve and hope and the freshness of their energies'. He put this down to the hours kept by the House of Commons: 'In these hours, I see the unhappy origin of the enervating and disheartening atmosphere of the place, and of many of the other phenomena which make it one of the most unbusiness-like and ineffective legislative instruments in the world.'[25]

Influence

The influence of Parliament was at its height in the second half of the nine-teenth century. Ironically, as the power of the press increased along with its immediacy and its right to report parliamentary proceedings was recognised, its own direct influence on public opinion declined while that of Parliament was extended. Looking back on the mid-eighteenth century from the vantage point of the mid-nineteenth century, Lord Macaulay considered how oratorical skill had overtaken literary skill as the appropriate tool for parliamentary leadership:

> At present, the best way of giving rapid and wide publicity to a fact or an argument is to introduce that fact or argument into a speech made in Parliament ... A speech made in the House of Commons at four in the morning is on thirty thousand tables before ten. A speech made on the Monday is read on the Wednesday by multitudes in Antrim and Aberdeenshire. The orator, by the help of the shorthand writer, has to a great extent superseded the pamphleteer. It was not so in the reign of Anne. The best speech could then produce no effect except on those who heard it. It was only by means of the press that the opinion of the public without doors could be influenced; and the opinion of the public without doors could not but be of the highest importance in a country governed by parliaments, and indeed at that time governed by triennial parliaments. The pen was therefore a more formi-dable political engine than the tongue. Mr Pitt and Mr Fox contended only in Parliament. But Walpole and Pulteney, the Pitt and Fox of an earlier period, had not done half of what was necessary, when they sat down amidst the acclamations of the House of Commons. They had still to plead their cause before the country, and this they could do only by means of the press.[26]

The influence of Parliament burgeoned during the reign of George III, when party feeling began to manifest itself with a greater intensity and the willingness of the Opposition to challenge the policies of the monarch became more unashamed. From 1760 to 1818, the changes in parliamentary hours affected the entire life of London society, as Lady Susan O'Brien reflected at the end of that period:

> Hours—They are so changed that the change has occasioned many others. The Houses of Parlt. met early and when no particular business was expected, were up time enough for the dinner-hour, universally four o'clock. This allowed for going easily to the Play, Opera or to card-parties, and for keeping early hours at night; long speeches were very rare, even with the great orators.
>
> Now Parlt. does not meet till 4 or 5 o'clock; long speeches are in daily practice on every topic, and by every body. All are orators. This mania has occasion'd the lateness of every amusement and every topic and family transaction—dinner 7 or 8 o'clock, parties beginning at ten, balls at eleven or twelve. Thus everything is done by candle-light, which adds greatly to the expense in large families, is hurtful to the health of young persons, and the morals of the lower classes.[27]

A pamphlet of 1824 stated that 'the chapel of St Stephen's forms for half the year the leading topic of conversation with the whole British public', but added that few had seen it at work. 'Supposing the cock-loft which is opened to the public by the silver key of half-a-crown, to be filled every night by a fresh audience, it would take about a hundred years before all the full-grown male population could get a sight of it; and then when the women and children are added, the quantity of ungratified curiosity is immense.'[28] Those who were fortunate to gain admittance as strangers and to watch the proceedings were frequently disappointed. Thomas Carlyle pronounced Parliament a waste of time and was contemptuous of its influence,[29] while the historian G. M. Young has pinpointed the 1830s as the period when this frustration reached its height:

> The procedural history of Parliament is a struggle between an old principle (freedom of debate) and a new one (to make a programme and get through it). In the thirties, freedom, exercised through (a) a multitude of formal stages, (b) irrelevant amendments on going into Committee or adjourning, was in the ascendant. The public, intensely interested in Parliament, was in consequence often baffled to know what Parliament was doing and why.[30]

Indeed, the 1830s was the decade in which for the first time parliamentary papers were put on sale (1835) and division lists published (1836). The twenty years following the 1832 Reform Act were an important period for parliamentary development: business grew, scrutiny in the form of parliamentary questions multiplied, MPs tended to vote independently of party to a greater extent than before or since, and Parliament formalised arrangements for press coverage of its proceedings. Gladstone later reflected that 'as a whole our level of public principle and public action were at their zenith'.[31] Yet there were dissenting voices. In 1853 E. M. Whitty expressed the opinion that 'the plan of the French Chamber to class secondary "subjects" into large committees, is very preferable to the system of talking about everything and effecting very little, which we continue to adopt'; by discussing the lighting and ventilation of the Chamber at length, he wrote, the 'House had devoted a large share of the week to silly drivel, all about itself'.[32]

Notwithstanding this criticism of Parliament, Richard Cobden, the free trader, believed that the floor of the House of Commons was the best platform from which to address the nation.[33] Disraeli's biographers, Monypenny and Buckle, wrote that:

> ... while Disraeli was numbered among its members the House of Commons was at the height of its power and reputation and preserved all its traditional liberties. The place which it then held in the mind and esteem of the country may be gauged by the amount of space which the newspapers accorded to the reports of debates. Those who search the files of *The Times* during these years will find that, in the session, the Parliamentary reports not only occupied the most conspicuous pages, but filled, every day, half or three-quarters of the total news columns,

crowding most other matter into short paragraphs and obscure corners. The luminaries of the cricket-field and the river, of the stage and the turf, had not then risen to the rank of popular heroes; and an oration by Macaulay or Bright, a tussle between Disraeli and Peel, or a serious debate in which Palmerston, Russell, Cobden, and Gladstone put forth all their powers, excited the universal interest among newspaper readers which has subsequently, in times of peace, only been secured by visits of Australian cricketers or the successes of royal horses at Epsom. It was on this wide and universal theatre and among these Parliamentary giants that Disraeli played his striking part, battling with spirit and distinction against succeeding generations of orators and statesmen from O'Connell and the elder Stanley at the beginning to Hartington and Harcourt at the close.[34]

However, it was not only changes in Parliament itself which brought about this new-found interest in its activities, but also changes in the nature of journalism and the technology of communications. In 1857 two English engineers were arrested at sea and put on trial in Naples for their alleged involvement in a conspiracy to liberate some prisoners of the monarchical regime. The British Government considered that their arrest had been illegal and demanded compensation for the engineers. They were soon released and compensation paid to them, and one MP pointed out that their release had followed closely upon the telegraphing to Naples of statements in Parliament.[35] Indeed, Henry Lucy emphasised the advances wrought by the electric telegraph:

> Whatever may be the effect on the intelligence of the public wrought by the cheapening of telegraph rates, there is no doubt it has served appreciably to lengthen Parliamentary proceedings. Most of the wealthy provincial daily papers have their special wire, over which are transmitted full reports of speeches delivered by local members. Formerly these gentlemen, being dismissed with curt paragraphs of the reports in the London papers, and having no special provision made for them by the local journals, did not find it worth while to insist on contributing weighty speeches to current debates. It is different now, and the altered circumstances are responsible for much loquacity in the dinner-hour at Westminster.[36]

In 1853 one MP complained that too much time in the summer was given over to trivial questions: 'A Member reads a paragraph in a newspaper and asks a question on the subject—one about a dispute with a cabman and another about the soldiers getting wet at the encampment at Chobham.'[37] A few years later a Minister responded to a question from a backbencher thus: 'Certainly very singular questions are asked in this House, but I never expected that we should descend to such trifling matters as the chimney-pots of Somerset House.'[38] By the early 1870s, however, Parliament was still being misused, according to one sketch-writer, William Hale White, writing in the *Nonconformist*:

> Private members can hardly wonder at the impatience of the public at the Tuesday and Friday evening's exercises, when time is wasted so egregiously as it was the other evening by Lord Elcho. His lordship once more brought before the House that wretched business of Mr Tribe and the 9th Lancers, which has already occupied us to exhaustion and sickness. Hour after hour the legislature of this great country has spent in discussing a miserable regimental squabble involving no principle, and

not of the slightest importance except to the half-dozen persons immediately concerned. The thoroughly aristocratic constitution of the club which calls itself the House of Commons has never been more strikingly proved than by these Tribe debates. The military gentlemen who sit in the House seem to imagine that it exists for the purpose of discussing their small personal grievances, which really are hardly worth a column in one of their service newspapers, and that anything which touches them is of such supreme importance as to justify its shutting out the consideration of all other matters. Imagine the conceit which could induce the officers of the 9th Lancers to get Lord Elcho to propose that Parliament should spend the best part of one entire night upon their domestic affairs![39]

T. P. O'Connor, trying to explain the 'absurdities' of Parliament to the readers of an American magazine in 1900, argued that the procedural arrangements tended to favour an inversion of priorities:

... if it should happen that the business under discussion is of vast importance, and yet presents no hope of picturesqueness or general interest, the House again empties. For instance, the Navy estimates, the Army estimates, dealing as they do with the defence of the country—one of its supreme interests, involving expenditure by tens of millions—are always debated in a House that is practically empty. I have seen millions of money voted by a House consisting at most of ten or fifteen members. Indeed, one might almost venture on the paradox, with regard to the House of Commons, that its attendance and its interest are in inverse proportion to the importance of the subjects which it is debating. A small personal squabble between two members will often bring to the House a crowded, excited and interested audience, while the interests of the Empire will leave the House cold and empty.[40]

Nonetheless, even the most radical of MPs understood how influential Parliament could be. C. J. O'Donnell, an Irish London MP, lamented that Irish independence, rather than devolution or Home Rule, had deprived Ireland of a powerful platform: 'Personally my chief regret is that Ireland has lost the position in the Empire and in the world that once was hers,' he wrote in 1932. 'The British House of Commons was the most effective rostrum in the world. From that mighty pulpit it was possible to send forth appeals for justice or tidings of great joy or sorrow to the nations of the world.'[41] John Wheatley, one of the Red Clydesider MPs, described the House of Commons as 'the best broadcasting station in the world, which could be used for socialist propaganda more effectively than any other agency'.[42] Harold Macmillan once explained that 'if you can impress upon the House of Commons that the Government is strong and the Prime Minister is in control ... then gradually ... it begins to go out into the country as the Members go back to their constituencies. Then gradually the Press begin to show a certain surprise at the success of the Government in overcoming one obstacle or another.'[43]

Rhetoric
Sir Henry Crabb Robinson once declared that 'a senate of orators is a symptom of material decay ... Neither the Habeas Corpus Act, nor the Bill of Rights,

nor Magna Carta originated in eloquence.'[44] Lord Macaulay was also critical of what he regarded as a system too readily dominated by eloquence:

> Parliamentary government is government by speaking. In such a government, the power of speaking is the most highly prized of all the qualities which a politician can possess; and that power may exist in the highest degree without judgement, without fortitude, without skill in reading the characters of men or the signs of the times, without any knowledge of the principles of legislation or of political economy, and without any skill in diplomacy or in the administration of war. Nay, it may well happen that those very intellectual qualities which give a peculiar charm to the speeches of a public man may be incompatible with the qualities which would fit him to meet a pressing emergency with promptitude and firmness. It was thus with Charles Townshend. It was thus with Windham. It was a privilege to listen to those accomplished and ingenious orators. But in a perilous crisis they would be found far inferior in all the qualities of rulers to such a man as Oliver Cromwell, who talked nonsense, or as William the Silent, who did not talk at all.[45]

Yet the popularity among MPs of Robert Harley, Speaker during the last three Parliaments of William III, was not the result of eloquence but of what Forster called 'House of Commons tact'.[46] If parliamentary rhetoric in the eighteenth century was for the most part an aberration, there was a definite change in rhetorical style in the nineteenth century. 'Speeches were very long,' the historian G. M. Young has written, 'but the contentions over the currency and the fiscal system had created a new style, of which Huskisson was the first exponent, Peel the most specious master, and which Mr Gladstone wielded like a Tenth Muse: knowledge of the facts and an apt handling of figures was now the surest proof of capacity, and among the most memorable feats of Victorian oratory are speeches on finance.'[47] The need to do business was paramount. The House 'admires intensely Mr Macaulay delivering an essay; but they admire more, because it is "business", even a Mr Walpole delivering a *plan*'.[48] Justin McCarthy, too, agreed: 'Even with Bright, even with Gladstone, the best speeches were, above all else, business speeches—speeches directed to the practical work of persuading and convincing the House; and therefore, no matter how exquisite in style, noble in thought, and persuasive in argument, were yet addressed to the level of the average common-sense and delivered in the language that came home to the ordinary intelligence of the listeners.'[49]

Lord Brougham blamed the practice of making long speeches, which had prevailed by the early nineteenth century, on William Pitt, Earl of Chatham, who had held sway in Parliament in the 1750s and 1760s: 'He was prolix in the whole texture of his discourse, and he was certainly the first who introduced into our Senate the practice, adopted in the American War by Mr Burke, and continued by others, of long speeches—speeches of two and three hours—by which oratory has gained little, and business less.'[50] Sheridan's celebrated oration on the spoliation of the Begums of Oude, part of the impeachment of Warren Hastings, lasted for five hours and forty minutes. Sylvester Douglas remembered

George III saying in 1802 that 'long speeches in Parliament had come in about 20 or 25 years ago; that Lord North ("but," says he, "I may be partial to that quarter") never even on his budget spoke above an hour and a half, and always made an apology when he did. He said he told him he never spoke from notes and that he never wrote down more than mere heads; that Lord Grenville told him that he almost always wrote the full speech he was to make down at length, but did not try to get it by heart.'[51] During a debate on the business of the House of Commons in 1833 one MP suggested that the printing of debates and the consequent need to impress consituents was the principal cause of speeches becoming longer.

'Is Parliament more talkative?' asked the journalist Alexander Mackintosh in 1945. 'Well, yes. More members desire to speak and more speak fluently. The Victorian squires took little part in debate. Some, like Mr Speaker Lowther's grandfather, who was fifty years in the House, never addressed it . . . Nowadays an MP will seek to catch the Speaker's eye after less than a week in the House.'[52] One reason for increased talk in the nineteenth century had been the realisation that talk could act as a drag on business which the Opposition regarded as undesirable. No sooner had Parliament developed instruments for dealing with this than the gain in dispatch was matched by the pressure of business generated by a collectivist state. 'It is true that in old times their only hope of escape from obstructive talk lay in the fatigue of the talkers, and now they are relieved by the closure, the guillotine and the kangaroo,' explained Mackintosh, 'but these devices do not compensate for the load imposed by the expansion of State activities.'[53]

Lord Brougham himself was no slouch when it came to making long speeches: his 1831 speech on Law Reform lasted six hours. Other speeches notable for their length were Palmerston's defence of his Government's role in the Don Pacifico affair in 1851, Gladstone's five-hour Budget statement in 1853, and Lloyd George's Budget statement of 1909, which ran to four hours and fifty-one minutes, excluding a thirty-minute interval so that he could regain his vigour.[54]

Regardless of their tendency to brevity or prolixity, what made certain speakers great? In explaining the reason why William Pitt (the Elder) and Mr Murray (later Lord Chancellor as Lord Mansfield) 'alone can inflame or quiet the House', Lord Chesterfield told his son: 'Is it that their matter is better, or their argument is stronger, than other people's? Does the House expect extra-ordinary information from them? Not in the least; but the House expects pleasure from them, and therefore attends; finds it, and therefore approves.'[55] Sir Thomas Fowell Buxton explained to a friend in 1819 that 'the House likes good sense and joking, and nothing else'. The House even had its own term for the joking element, namely 'chaff'. John Bright passed judgement on Benjamin Disraeli's rhetorical skills: 'his chaff is excellent,' he said, 'but his wheat is abominable!'[56] Robert Cecil described the disappointment of Members when one of their favourite clowns, Sir Robert Peel, son of his more famous namesake, failed to perform his customary role:

> ... the House looked for an abundance of bad jokes and personal chaff. Great was their disappointment when nothing came of it but a dignified and sensible speech. The House was baulked of its amusement; but the public will infinitely prefer unpolished and unstudied good sense to a whole week's accumulation of well-prepared and elaborated buffoonery.[57]

But buffoonery was not always intentional. Some came by it accidentally. Try as he may, Richard Monckton Milnes was never able to obtain the recognition that he sought as a man of business. Disraeli, who was his friend, left a memorandum in which he proffered a harsh though doubtless accurate judgement of why this was the case:

> He never caught the House of Commons tone ... Too easy and familiar in Society, the moment he was on his legs in St Stephens he was nervous, took refuge in pomposity and had no flow; a most elaborate style and always recalling his words ... [His face was] like a Herculaneum mask or a countenance cut out of an orange ... [His speaking had] the effect of some celebrated droll ... and before he had proceeded five minutes, though he might be descanting on the wrongs of Poland or the rights of Italy, there was sure to be a laugh.[58]

Despite Macaulay's objection to government by speaking, there have been times when rhetoric has persuaded the House to take a particular course. In 1680 George Savile, Viscount Halifax, spoke against the Exclusion Bill (to disbar the Catholic-inclined Duke of York from acceding to the throne) in the House of Lords, after it had sailed through the Commons on a Whig majority. 'Deserted by his most important colleagues, and opposed to a crowd of able antagonists, he defended the cause of the Duke of York in a succession of speeches which, many years later, were remembered as masterpieces of reasoning, of wit, and of eloquence. It is seldom that oratory changes votes. Yet the attestation of contemporaries leaves no doubt that, on this occasion, votes were changed by the oratory of Halifax.'[59]

Sheridan once asked Burke, who usually found himself in a minority, why he 'took so much pains, knowing for certain it will have no effect, not one vote gained by it'. Burke felt that speaking was worthwhile, for 'though not one vote is gained, it has effect. We see, though an Act passes, it is modified, it is softened in such a manner that we see plainly the Minister has been told that Members are so sensible of its injustice and absurdity from what they have heard that it must be altered.' Dr Johnson, also present at this exchange, added that 'there is a gratification of pride. Though we cannot out-vote them, we'll out-argue them. They shall not do wrong without its being shown both to themselves and to the world.'[60]

It is a truism that no parliamentary speech ever persuaded listeners to change their minds and vote differently. With modern party discipline, this nostrum may have gained credence, but in the nineteenth century MPs were often swayed by skilful speakers. Lord Plunket saved the Cabinet from destruction in the wake of the Peterloo massacre in November 1819. 'He assailed the fabric of his adversary,' wrote Lord Dudley, 'not by an irregular damaging fire that left parts of its standing, but by a complete rapid process of demolition that did not let one stone continue standing upon another.' Plunket is also credited with having persuaded as many as six MPs to vote in support of Catholic Emancipation, despite their previously held convictions.[61] 'Over and over again I have listened to speeches which have had a conclusive effect in the division lobbies,' wrote Herbert Gladstone in his memoirs. 'It is perhaps the exception when they do not,' he added, challenging the conventional view. He cited as an instance the debate about the alleged mistreatment of an old civil servant of the Indian Government. 'The whole House was against the Government. Then Gorst [Under-Secretary for India] rose and mercilessly taunted the House for its sentimental weakness and ignorance. Having infuriated everyone, he replied deliberately and conclusively to every point that had been made. The House melted away.'[62]

The sketch-writing tradition

The tradition of parliamentary sketch-writing was initiated in the 1830s, by James Grant, a Whig journalist, who also published his sketches in book form. The torch was taken up for a single session, 1852–3, by Edward Michael Whitty; then by William White in the mid-1850s, and by his son, William Hale White, in the late 1860s. Thereafter, there was a steady growth in the number of practitioners of this peculiar craft. While the interest in verbatim reports of MPs' speeches gradually declined, the fondness for the parliamentary sketch grew: 'newspaper readers have developed a greater liking for that new departure in journalism—the vivid, impressionist, descriptive sketch of the proceedings of the House, which, as a rule, amply satisfies the desires of the public for Parliamentary intelligence; and if they turn at all to the report, it is only to ascertain more fully what has been said by the leading statesmen, or perhaps to peruse a more detailed account of a "scene", or a heated wrangle across the floor of the House'.[63] Also, the descriptive writers took great liberties. Whitty was probably the most scathing. He had little reverence for Parliament as it was then conducted, and his satirical powers were highly developed. 'He describes the ways and doings of Parliament in a spirit of utter irreverence, and he criticises the measures and the men and even the manners in the style of one who is much more inclined to mockery than to adulation.'[64] In particular, he treated Parliament as essentially a theatrical enterprise, dubbing it his 'favourite public amusement'.[65] On another occasion he complained that 'it is indeed a session of work; but may we never have another; for Parliament is our principal amusement'.[66] A former Prime Minister, George Canning, once described the House of Commons as 'one of the highest entertainments that can be conceived',[67] and Joseph Biggar called it the 'best theatre in London'.[68] When

Norman Shrapnel wrote a book reflecting on his experience as a sketch-writer during the 1950s and 1960s, he called it *The Performers: Politics as Theatre*. 'Parliament as theatre is a conception that some find ... distasteful,' he wrote, nonetheless judging his subjects to be 'a famous but ever-struggling repertory company'.[69]

Referring in 1897 to the activities of the descriptive writers, Michael Mac-Donagh wrote that the 'audacity of these gentlemen's comments on the peculiarities, characteristics and eccentricities of members, in manner, speech and apparel, is sometimes almost sublime'.[70] Disraeli, who had complained that the *Times*'s reports of his early parliamentary speeches were inadequate, nonetheless was wary of the later mania for descriptive writing. ' "Our own Reporter" has invaded it [Parliament] in all its purlieus. No longer content with giving an account of the speeches of its members, he is not satisfied unless he describes their persons, their dress, and their characteristic mannerisms. He tells us how they dine, even the wines and dishes which they favour, and follows them into the very mysteries of their smoking-room.'[71]

Yet while Disraeli dismissed the sketch-writer as superficial and impertinent, the Irish Nationalist MP T. P. O'Connor, himself a sketch-writer, was convinced of the historical value of this burgeoning genre:

> They display haste, inaccurate estimates of men, falsified predictions of events. On the other hand, impressions noted at the moment ought to have a freshness and a trustworthiness that cannot belong to accounts written from memory some time after ... an effort was made at impartiality ...[72]
>
> ... the reporting columns of a newspaper do not always give an accurate and rarely a vivid picture of what really takes place in a legislative body. Columns appear of speeches which have been delivered to empty benches, and which, therefore, have influenced the fortunes of debate little, if at all ... The speech that reads convincing and eloquent may, owing to the physical defects of the orator, have not been listened to at all. Equally a speech which appears dull and cold in print may have produced wild outbursts of enthusiasm or of anger. It is assuredly as important that there should be some record of how the speeches influenced the assemblies to which they were addressed as of the mere words of the speeches themselves. Nor can any account of a speech be entirely complete which does not convey some idea of the man who makes it, his manner of speaking, his appearance, his character, his career.[73]

The task of the sketch-writer was by no means an easy one. William Hale White apologised for curtailing a sketch in 1872, telling his readers: 'I ought to say something about the subsequent course of the debate, but writing at 9 o'clock in the morning after sitting up half the night, is not easy work.'[74] 'A good part of my letters to the [Rochdale] *Observer* has been written in the House while speeches were being made, while obstructiveness was roaring its wort, while the blunders of which even the best of leaders must at time be guilty were being committed, while impatience was at its height.'[75] Another sketch-writer, John Foster Fraser, agreed:

The conscientious descriptive writer has a constant nightmare that he may miss something. The temper of Parliament is as uncertain as the English climate. You may sit for three solid hours waiting, like Mr Micawber, for something to turn up that will lend itself to dramatic treatment, and get nothing. In lowness of spirits you go off to have a cup of tea, or a chop, and—as a perverse providence watches over the journalist—you will be sighing there is nothing to write about when a man will come in and carelessly remark there has been no end of a shindy between Mr Chamberlain and Mr Lloyd George, or that an extremely humorous thing has just happened to one of the Irishmen. You've missed it, and you are angry . . . But here the comradeship of the Gallery again comes in, and you soon hunt up a friend who has seen it all, and he describes the scene to you, knowing you will do the same for him should occasion arise. It is only by this means a parliamentary descriptive writer can be omnipresent. Personally, however, I make a point of being in the Gallery whenever I can. There is always something that lends itself, and yet which all helps to make a particular impression on the mind and produce a particular atmosphere throughout one's article.[76]

It was even worse for those MPs who were foolish enough to make their living as journalists. 'During my first years of Parliamentary life I had often to sit down at four o'clock in the morning to write my Parliamentary sketch, and that after I had been speaking constantly during a hot sitting,' T. P. O'Connor explained to the Authors' Club in 1921. 'Parliamentary chronicling tends to paralyse Parliamentary effectiveness; it is a horrible kill-joy. When one is enjoying an amusing or exciting scene and tingling with a desire to join in it, one suddenly remembers another half-column of description is required and has to rush off and write it.'[77] T. W. Russell, the Liberal Unionist MP for South Tyrone from 1886, wrote a 'Parliamentary Letter' for the *Manchester Examiner* in the late 1880s.[78] Charles Masterman MP took over the *Daily News* sketch from H. W. Massingham in 1906, but was soon swept up into the ministerial ranks. Later MP sketch-writers have included Tom Driberg and Maurice Edelman (for the *New Statesman* in the 1940s), and J. P. W. Mallalieu (for *Tribune* in the late 1940s and early 1950s).

From the mid-nineteenth century, the power of the sketch-writer increased remorselessly. William Hale White wrote parliamentary reports (not sketches) for the weekly *Aberdeen Herald* and was Parliamentary Correspondent of the *Morning Star* ('Below the Gangway'), and of the *Rochdale Observer* from the mid-1860s until 1872. After that, he wrote a sketch (called 'How It Strikes a Stranger') for Edward Miall's weekly paper, *The Nonconformist*. Bernard Bussey wrote a descriptive summary for the *Glasgow Herald* from 1870 to 1900; Harry Y. Bussey was chief of the *Morning Post*'s staff and its sketch-writer; the *St Stephen's Gazette*, a weekly magazine, carried a regular, anonymous sketch in the 1890s (under the now familiar title 'Below the Gangway'). Henry Lucy was omnipresent: in addition to writing 'The Diary of Toby MP' in *Punch* for thirty years, he contributed a monthly column ('Behind the Speaker's Chair') to the *Strand Magazine*, wrote 'Pictures in Parliament' for the *Daily News* and was the parliamentary representative of the *Daily Express*. H. W. Massingham took over his sketch at the *Daily News*, while Charles T. King succeeded him at the *Daily Express*. Harold Spender wrote 'Sketches from Parliament' (later, 'Sketches from Westminster') for the *Manchester Guardian*. In the 1900s, however, it was Massingham who reigned supreme. 'His influence was certainly greater than that of most of the Ministers and ex-Cabinet Ministers of the time,' Masterman later wrote. 'Everybody who mattered in the world round Westminster read the Parliamentary sketch which he wrote night by night; and those who knew nothing of the actual debate very largely took their opinions from it.' His qualities were 'a complete fearlessness, a brilliance of phrasing, a disinterestedness, and that sudden seizing of the effect of the events at the moment, with all their implications, which make the difference between a first-class and second-class journalist in the extraordinarily rapid hour-by-hour changes in the discussions of Parliament.'[79]

Speaking at the Reporters' Gallery dinner of 1911, Lloyd George stated that:

> ... the sketch-writer has become the real terror of the Parliamentarian. He is universally read, and therefore is dangerous. (Laughter.)
> Since my younger days in Parliament the sketch-writer has developed his functions enormously, and people depend for their impressions of Parliament on his writings. I think, on the whole, an impression is created which rather underestimates the capacity of Parliament.[80]

This was a theme echoed by James Johnston, the *Yorkshire Post*'s parliamentary correspondent for several years, who wrote regular profiles of MPs in the late 1920s. When these were published as a collection, he ventured that it would prove 'the amount of character and capacity which is contained in the House of Commons' and he dismissed 'the current chatter about Parliamentary degeneration'. It may contain 'fewer great men than it did a generation ago, and there are many ordinary men in it, but it includes among its members a large number of men and women of distinctive personality and real accomplishment'.[81]

Since World War II, the influence of Parliament has declined. The reputation of MPs in general is now at its lowest ebb, although the institution of parliamentary democracy is regarded as unsurpassable. Newspapers have reduced their coverage of Parliament to a minimum: debates are rarely reported in detail. However, sketch-writers have continued to ply their trade and there have been many distinguished practitioners of this craft: Harry Boardman, Norman Shrapnel, Michael White, Andrew Rawnsley and Simon Hoggart for the *Guardian*; Colin Welch, John O'Sullivan, Frank Johnson, Edward Pearce and Godfrey Barker for the *Daily Telegraph*; Andrew Alexander for the *Daily Mail*; Craig Brown and Matthew Parris for *The Times*; and Mark Lawson for the *Independent*.

The strength of the sketch-writing tradition is that it is primarily concerned with the human dimension and a true professional does not allow politics to get in the way of portraying the idiosyncrasies of Parliament. 'The daily spectator of Parliament cannot fail to acquire emotional attitudes to the politicians whom he constantly sees and hears,' wrote James Johnston. 'The admirations, the affections, the likings, the repulsions which he comes to entertain towards them are, however, the result of accumulated impressions, and of nothing else. In the formation of these impressions political kinships play only a small part, and are outweighed by other potent considerations of an entirely aesthetic or emotional nature.'[82] That is why writings about Parliament bear such similarities across the centuries—the themes of frustration and disillusionment, the emotional charge arising from a historic debate, the spectacle of a great man brought down or a little man making his mark, the quaint procedures and the bores continue to fascinate the sketch-writer and his audience. Broadcasting has brought about the decline of the Chamber[83] and Parliament has, of course, been overtaken as our 'principal public amusement' by other sources of entertainment. Yet, like a much-loved soap opera, it is 'going on still'.

1. John Bright, Speech, Birmingham, January 18, 1865; H. H. Asquith referred to the 'vulgar error' of so describing the English Parliament in a chapter on political catchwords contained in his *Fifty Years of Parliament* (1926), Vol. II, p. 228.
2. There was a Scottish Parliament in Edinburgh until 1707 and an Irish Parliament in Dublin until 1801.
3. George Savile, Marquis of Halifax, *Some Cautions Offered* (1695); Halifax, *Complete Works* (Penguin edition, 1969), p. 167.
4. Anthony Trollope, *Can You Forgive Her?* (1953), Vol. I, p. 53.
5. Quoted in David Ogg, *Herbert Fisher 1865–1940* (1947), pp. 122–3.
6. Quoted in Michael MacDonagh, *The Pageant of Parliament* (1921), Vol. II, p. 76.
7. Quoted in George Henry Jennings, *An Anecdotal History of the British Parliament from the Earliest Periods to the Present Time* (1880), p. 130.
8. Quoted in A. F. Tschiffely, *Don Roberto: Being the Account of the Life and Works of R. B. Cunninghame Graham, 1852–1936* (1937), pp. 204 and 263.
9. Parliament met for a mere six or seven months a year, usually between the end of January and the end of July.
10. C. F. G. Masterman, Letter to his sweetheart, Lucy Lyttelton, September 3, 1907.
11. Austen Chamberlain, Letter to his stepmother, Mrs Chamberlain, March 23, 1912.
12. Frank Dilnot, *The Old Order Changeth* (1911), pp. 36–7.
13. Quoted in MacDonagh, op. cit., Vol. I, p. 87.
14. Michael MacDonagh, *Irish Life and Character* (1898), pp. 282–3.
15. John Morley, *Recollections*, Vol. I, p. 190.
16. Harold Nicolson, Letter to Nigel Nicolson, May 27, 1945.
17. Nigel Nicolson, *People and Parliament* (1958), p. 65.
18. Quoted in Michael MacDonagh, *The Book of Parliament* (1897), pp. 51–2.
19. Quoted in Derek Hudson, *A Poet in Parliament: The Life of Winthrop Mackworth Praed 1802–1834* (1939), p. 177.
20. Robert Cecil, 3rd Marquis of Salisbury, 'Pity the Sorrows of a Poor MP', *Saturday Review*, August 20, 1859.
21. William Lambton, Letter to Charles Grey, August 5, 1796; quoted in R. G. Thorne (ed.), *The Commons 1790–1820* (1986), Vol. IV, p. 373.
22. James Joseph Hope Vere (?–1843), a landowner in Ireland and Scotland, and MP for Newport, Hampshire.
23. Alicia Bayne (ed.), *Autobiographic Recollections of George Pryme Esq., MA* (1870), p. 220.
24. *Clarion*, July 24, 1908.
25. T. P. O'Connor, 'Some Absurdities of the House of Commons', *North American Review*, August 1900.
26. T. B. Macaulay. 'The Life and Writings of Addison', *Edinburgh Review*, July 1843.
27. Memorandum by Lady Susan O'Brien, 'Changes between 1760 and 1818'; quoted in *The Life and Letters of Lady Sarah Lennox* (1901), Vol. II, p. 291.

28. *The Collective Wisdom: or, Sights and Sketches of the Chapel of St Stephen's* (1824), pp. 1–2.
29. Thomas Carlyle, *Latter-Day Pamphlets* (No. 6: *Parliaments*) (1898).
30. G. M. Young, *Portrait of an Age* (1936), p. 29 n.
31. Patrick Howarth, *Questions in the House: The History of a Unique British Institution* (1956), p. 101.
32. E. M. Whitty, *Leader*, August 6, 1853.
33. Howarth, op. cit., p. 100.
34. W. F. Monypenny and G. E. Buckle, *The Life of Benjamin Disraeli, Earl of Beaconsfield* (1910–12), Vol. II, p. 840.
35. Howarth, op. cit., pp. 143–4.
36. Henry W. Lucy, *Later Peeps at Parliament* (1904), pp. 442–3.
37. Quoted in Howarth, op. cit., p. 132.
38. ibid.
39. 'How It Strikes a Stranger', *Nonconformist*, February 19, 1873.
40. O'Connor, op. cit.
41. C. J. O'Donnell, *Outraged Ulster* (1932), p. 23.
42. Gordon Brown, *Maxton* (1986), p. 126.
43. Interviewed on the BBC, April 23, 1971: quoted in Alistair Horne, *Macmillan 1957–1986* (Vol. II of the Official Biography) (1989), p. 20.
44. T. Sadler (ed.), Sir Henry Crabb Robinson, *Diary, Reminiscences and Correspondence* (1869), Vol. I, p. 330.
45. Quoted in Jennings, op. cit., pp. 284–5.
46. J. Forster on De Foe; quoted in Jennings, op. cit., p. 92.
47. Young, op. cit., p. 32.
48. E. M. Whitty, *St Stephen's in the Fifties: The Session 1852–3, A Parliamentary Retrospect* (1906), p. 25; the Walpole referred to is Spencer Walpole, Home Secretary under Derby in 1852.
49. Justin McCarthy, *Reminiscences* (1899), pp. 174–5.
50. Henry Brougham, *Historical Sketches of Statesmen Who Flourished in the Time of George III* (1839), Vol. I, pp. 32–3.
51. Sylvester Douglas (Lord Glenbervie), Journal, August 19, 1802.
52. ibid.
53. Alexander Mackintosh, *Echoes of Big Ben: A Journalist's Parliamentary Diary, (1881–1940)* (1945), p. 165.
54. Strathearn Gordon, *Our Parliament* (1952), p. 210.
55. Quoted in Jennings, op. cit., p. 123.
56. Sir James T. Agg-Gardner, *Some Parliamentary Recollections* (1927), p. 224.
57. Robert Cecil, 3rd Marquis of Salisbury, *Saturday Review*, March 3, 1860.
58. James Pope-Hennessy, *Monckton Milnes: The Years of Promise 1809–1851* (1949), pp. 99–100.
59. T. B. Macaulay, *The History of England from the Accession of James II* (1849), Vol. I, p. 259.
60. *Boswell in Extremes, 1776–8* and *Life of Johnson*; quoted in Paul Johnson (ed.), *The Oxford Book of Political Anecdotes* (1986), p. 80.
61. Jennings, op. cit., p. 186.
62. Herbert Gladstone, *After Thirty Years* (1928), p. 174.
63. MacDonagh, *The Book of Parliament*, p. 315.
64. Justin McCarthy, Introduction to Whitty, op. cit., p. xxi.
65. Whitty, op. cit., p. 118.
66. ibid., p. 99.
67. George Canning, Letter journal to the Rev. William Leigh and family, January 21, 1794.
68. Harry Graham, *The Mother of Parliaments* (1911), p. 50.
69. Norman Shrapnel, *The Performers: Politics as Theatre* (1978), pp. 7 and 9.
70. MacDonagh, *The Book of Parliament*, p. 317.
71. Quoted by Mackintosh, op. cit., p. 14.
72. T. P. O'Connor, *Gladstone's House of Commons* (1885), p. v.
73. ibid., p. vi.
74. Catherine Macdonald Maclean, *Mark Rutherford: A Biography of William Hale White* (1955), pp. 198–9.
75. ibid., p. 199.
76. Michael MacDonagh, *The Reporters' Gallery* (1913), p. 54.
77. Hamilton Fyfe, *T. P. O'Connor* (1934), p. 102.
78. Interview with T. W. Russell, *Young Man*, July 1902.
79. Lucy Masterman, *C. F. G. Masterman: A Biography* (1939), p. 78.

80. MacDonagh, *The Reporters' Gallery*, p. 45.
81. James Johnston, *A Hundred Commoners* (1931), p. 15.
82. ibid., p. 14.
83. Simon Hoggart, 'The Silent Chamber', *Spectator*, February 10, 1996.

1 Arrivals and Departures

> I also saw little Baumann in the Lobby who was rather
> disconsolate as he will pretty surely lose his seat at the
> Elections. It is pretty hard, he said, after having been six
> months in heaven to be pitched out.[1]
>
> Wilfred Scawen-Blunt, Diary, June 4, 1886

First and last impressions of Parliament tend to be powerful ones. Yet, while early days in the House and the experience of delivering a maiden speech are things common to almost all Members, there are fewer testaments to the final moments of a parliamentary career and fewer descriptions of a last glimpse of the Chamber. This is quite simply because the majority of Members who do not retire tend either to die while away from the environs of the House or find themselves turfed out unceremoniously, and often against their expectations, at a general election. In the case of distinguished parliamentarians whose deaths are marked by a Commons tribute, it is a case of the House paying its respect to their memories. Those who retire willingly, whether from the Commons to the Lords, or from Westminster altogether, are able to indulge in a conscious moment of leave-taking, of discreetly and informally bidding the House farewell. It is these moments which are the most poignant, when the subject is overwhelmed by a sense of impending loss.

Once departed, the Member may look back on his Commons life with elegiac yearning: 'We are living out our quiet life here in a manner for which a reasonable mortal ought to feel very thankful to the destinies,' wrote Justin McCarthy from retirement. 'But when I read of the great political struggles going on, I am often in a mood to lament my later London life and the House of Commons and the keen excitement of my days . . . I sometimes feel as if I were looking back on that life out of a world of dull, grey shadows.'[2]

Perhaps it is better to die while still a Member, as Henry Grattan did, on the eve of a new parliamentary initiative; and as Richard Cobden did, the day after a sterling performance in the House. Some, of course, fade away while still Members. This was the fate of Joseph Chamberlain who suffered a stroke in July 1906, only a few days after celebrating his seventieth birthday and his thirtieth year as an MP. Nevertheless, despite his inability to attend the House of Commons thereafter, he was elected unopposed at the two general elections of 1910. Following this second contest, he was sworn and he signed the roll for the last time. To spare him the indignity, since he had to be carried into the Chamber by his son Austen and Arthur Lee, he was sworn after the other MPs. 'For a few moments he sat, piteously but proudly motionless, whilst his eye surveyed the empty benches and galleries, and then he indistinctly repeated the oath after the clerk,'

1

witnessed Sir Edward Clarke. 'To sign the roll was, for him, a physical impossibility, but Austen guided his hand sufficiently to make a shaky cross, and then after another poignant pause we carried him out again.'[3] A similar fate befell T. P. O'Connor, who died, as Father of the House, in his eighty-first year. 'Returned, as a matter of course at the General Election [1929],' recorded his biographer, 'he was in June wheeled into the House of Commons to take the oath, but he made no other appearance there.'[4]

Others have taken final bows while overtaken by infirmity. In 1778 the Earl of Chatham (Pitt the Elder) had a seizure while speaking in support of a motion in favour of a peace settlement with the American colonies. Although suffering from ill health, he had come up to Westminster from his country seat especially to speak, and though he recovered from the attack he died a month later. Daniel O'Connell made his last speech to the Commons in 1847, on the subject of the Irish potato famine. 'There was something infinitely forlorn and piteous in the drooped and dejected form of O'Connell, and his tottering gait, which filled members universally, and those especially who could recall him in his prime, with a dumb, helpless rush of sympathy,' wrote one biographer. 'He was imperfectly heard, for gone, too, was all his old power and melody of utterance . . . He sat down amid cheers from both sides of the House . . . Never has there been a more pathetic leave-taking of the House of Commons.'[5]

Disraeli left the House of Commons while still Prime Minister, in 1876. Ill health meant that constant attendance at the House, always an arduous task, had become an intolerable burden. Queen Victoria suggested that, if Disraeli were to feel 'that the fatigue of the House of Commons is too great, she would be happy to call him up to the other House, where the fatigue would be *far less* and where he would be able to *direct* everything'.[6] He took an earldom and retained the premiership. Nevertheless, the wrench away from the House of Commons life that he had enjoyed for so many years caused Disraeli a 'pang', as he told Mr Speaker Brand, and on the night of his last speech in the Commons a colleague noticed him weeping. The sense of bereavement was as great for his Commons colleagues as it was for Dizzy. On the morning that Disraeli's move to the House of Lords was announced, Viscount Barrington recorded: 'Small groups are dotted about here and there, talking with bated breath, as though there were a coffin within the precincts of the House.'[7] A year later, Disraeli visited the Commons for the first time since his departure as an MP. 'The House gave him a cheer when he appeared in the gallery,' as Disraeli himself explained in a letter to Queen Victoria, 'and the cheer commenced on the Liberal benches, which first observed him.'[8]

First appearances have occasionally struck awe into observers. Two such examples are those of Robert Jenkinson, who later inherited his father's title as the Earl of Liverpool and served as Prime Minister for fifteen unbroken years, and F. E. Smith, who later became Lord Chancellor as the Earl of Birkenhead. Jenkinson 'did not rise in the house till he had been for above a year a member of it; though it is no slight proof how great was the expectation which was already formed of him that, on the occasion of Mr Whitbread moving a censure on the Government on the question known as the Russian Armament, Pitt selected him to open the debate on his side. Our parliamentary annals have recorded no maiden speech which made so great an impression. Pitt himself began his own harangue by pronouncing it "not only a more able first speech than had ever been heard from a young member, but one so full of philosophy and science, strong and perspicuous language, and sound and convincing arguments, that it would have done credit to the most practised debater and most experienced statesman that ever existed" . . .'[9] F. E. Smith's début was, if anything, even more distinguished. 'Light badinage and cutting sarcasm came with equal dexterity in that even magnetic voice which never faltered or failed,' wrote G. D. Faber. 'It was a long, sustained *tour de force*, which captivated and held friend and foe alike.'[10]

Joseph Chamberlain had acquired a reputation as a 'wild Republican' during his time as Radical Mayor of Birmingham, so it surprised MPs to discover that he was fastidious in his costume and grooming and that he even wore a monocle. Justin McCarthy recalled the impression Chamberlain made when he delivered his maiden speech: ' "He looks like a ladies' doctor," one stout Tory murmured. "Seems like the model of a head clerk at a West End draper's," observed another . . . the quiet, self-possessed delivery greatly astonished those who had expected to see and hear a mob orator.'[11]

Some new arrivals are themselves star-struck. 'I am a very new Member of Parliament and it is still exciting to bump into Winston Churchill in the members' lavatory, as I did the other day,' wrote Anthony Wedgwood Benn in 1951. 'It is still pleasant to be called by my Christian name by Aneurin Bevan and to call him Nye.'[12] For most, however, whether they have arrived with an established reputation or not, the pattern has been similar. The nervousness, the gradual summoning of confidence, the sense of camaraderie as friends and even opponents seek to welcome one; and yet, at the same time, the gradual realisation that parliamentary life is for the most part drudgery and obedience to the collective will of one's party.

The excitement of arriving in the House after an electoral contest is often the prelude to disappointment and frustration, as Nigel Nicolson has explained: 'As I stood at the bar of the House, on February 19th, 1952, ready to take my seat after a by-election which had aroused no more than ordinary interest, a senior Member whispered in my ear, "In a few minutes you will walk behind the Speaker's chair into the obscurity from which you should probably never have emerged." It was my first lesson in parliamentary deflation. To come from the concentrated arc-lights, the excitement, the triumph, of an election, to the goal of your ambition, and find that the size of your majority is better known than your name, is an immediate reminder that you are of so little significance that when you die or lose your seat, you will probably be replaced as easily as a broken window-pane.'[13] Some are never able to get over this feeling of their bubble having burst. Others knuckle down to business.

Some MPs have started out as observers and only later become participants. Edmund Burke, as the Marquis of Rockingham's political secretary, was a keen visitor to the Strangers' Gallery, like 'the young eagle accustoming his eye to the sun before it soared aloft'. He told a friend that some MPs 'talk like Demosthenes or Cicero; and I feel when I am listening to them as if I were in Athens or Rome'.[14] Justin McCarthy reported Gladstone's budgets of 1854 and 1856 for a Liverpool paper and entered the House as an Irish Nationalist MP in 1879. John Campbell (ultimately Lord Chancellor) and Sir Edward Clarke, both great advocates and later MPs, did spells in the Reporters' Gallery (for the *Morning Advertiser* and the *Standard* respectively). Lord Russell of Killowen, too, the Lord Chief Justice, in a conversation with Henry Lucy 'dropped the remark that his first acquaintance with the House of Commons was made from the Press Gallery'. He would not elaborate, but Lucy surmised 'he must have gone either to report speeches or to write leading articles'.[15] The journalist Spencer Leigh Hughes became a Liberal MP in 1910 having served in the Reporters' Gallery for almost eighteen years.[16] J. P. W. Mallalieu was taken to the House by his father and during 'the twenties, whenever I was in London, I homed on the public gallery, rather than a West End theatre or Twickenham or even Lords'; as lobby correspondent for the *Financial News* from 1934 till the outbreak of war, he 'was able to go in whenever I wanted' and 'spent far more time in the chamber than was necessary for my job'; and after serving in the Royal Navy during the war he was returned as a Labour MP at the 1945 general election.

Arrivals vary enormously in their circumstances. Some new Members are remembered for their impetuosity. In 1708 Nicholas Lechmere 'turned round and addressed the House immediately after he had taken the oaths. A country gentleman, however, interrupted his speech, objecting to his right to be heard, inasmuch as he could not be considered a "sitting member", not having sat down since he had entered the house.' Mr Cowper spoke three times on the day he took his seat, while 'Orator' Hunt spoke six times on different questions.[17] William Cobbett, who arrived in the Commons in his sixties, felt that there was no time to lose and delivered his maiden speech on the choice of a Speaker, in the course of which he had the temerity to berate his audience thus: 'It appears to me that since I have been sitting here, I have heard a great deal of vain and unprofitable conversation.'[18] In more recent times, the prize for impetuosity went to Robert Maxwell. In 1964 he made the first maiden speech of the new Parliament during the debate on the Address.

By contrast, the Marquis of Hartington, heir to the Duke of Devonshire, was well into his second session as a Member when he was encouraged by Mr Speaker Denison to take the plunge and speak. The Speaker had wanted him to speak, but complained 'you are very wild and keep at a distance, out of shot. I wish to persuade you to enter the arena and to descend like a Young Eagle in *reluctantes dracones* ... I am very confident about it, and I think, after a little while, you will like the sport in my forest as well as that on the Scotch hills.' Once Hartington had ventured forth, the Speaker reported to his father that 'it was done in good taste, and just in such a way as to please the House and to make a favourable impression, which it did most completely'.[19] Sir William Fraser recalled in the closing years of the nineteenth century that: 'In former days it was not necessary for a member to attempt to take the House by storm. The best speakers waited until they had studied the House. Lord Palmerston sat thirteen years in the House before he addressed it. A Parliamentary life is too short in these days for those wise and gradual approaches.'[20]

John Horne Tooke arrived in the House at the age of sixty-five as the Member for Old Sarum, a pocket borough. When he shook hands with the Speaker it 'attracted the particular notice of the house and the gallery: for but a very short space of time had elapsed, since the late solicitor-general, who now occupied the chair [Sergeant Mitford], had been obliged to labour officially to convict the new member of treason; and, in a speech of several hours' duration, had actually endeavoured to subject him to all the penalties incident to that crime'.[21] Sir Herbert Watkin Williams-Wynn arrived in the House after a by-election only to take part in a single division which resulted in a dissolution and his subsequent defeat at the polls, while John Redmond arrived in time to join his Irish Nationalist brothers in being suspended *en masse* for their obstructionist tactics.

Returned in 1935 as one of the burgesses for Oxford University, A. P. Herbert devoted his maiden speech to a complaint about the fact that Mr Baldwin's Government had taken for its own purposes a Friday normally given over to private Members' business. Herbert proposed his own Matrimonial Causes Bill 'to reform the indecent, hypocritical, cruel and unjust marriage laws of this country'—an endeavour in which he was eventually to succeed. His bid on this occasion to reclaim the time of the House for private Members failed, however. He mustered the votes of three Independent Labour Party MPs and one other University Member, but the Government had 232 votes. 'Alone of the swells,' Herbert later recalled, 'Mr Churchill sought out the naughty boy and complimented me on my "composure and aplomb". It was right, he said, for a young Member to take advantage of the chances of procedure to say what was in him. He finished, with a characteristic chuckle: "Call that a maiden speech? It was a brazen hussy of a speech. Never did such a painted lady of a speech parade itself before a modest Parliament." '[22]

Some have found themselves thrust into high office the moment they arrived or even beforehand. The gifted barrister John Somers, later Lord Chancellor, was appointed chairman of the parliamentary committee set up to draft the Declaration of Right in 1688, only ten days after had given his maiden speech. Oliver Lyttelton was appointed president of the Board of Trade by Churchill in 1940, and only became an MP a year later, thus joining 'the small and select club of those who made their maiden speeches from the Front Bench. In those days it included Anderson, Duncan, Bevin, Grigg and me in the Commons, and Woolton, Leathers and Cherwell in the Lords.'[23] Those circumstances were unique to World War II and the years immediately following (Harold Wilson, too, delivered his maiden speech from the front bench), although parliamentary law officers had often in the past sought election as the final endorsement of a *fait accompli.*

Comparisons of the new environment of the Commons to one's early schooldays have been commonplace. Gladstone referred to his schoolboy bashfulness and was as nervous of approaching the Speaker as he had been of approaching his headmaster at Eton, the legendary disciplinarian Dr Keate: 'I remember the revival in me bodily of the frame of mind in which a schoolboy stands before his master.'[24] The House reminded Albert Pell of Rugby, while T. P. O'Connor, George Leveson-Gower and W. J. Brown each compared it to school. The Wykehamist Hugh Gaitskell recorded his arrival in his diary: 'On Tuesday I went to the House for the first time. Evan [Durbin] says it is like going back to school, but I pointed out that everybody is much politer, especially the policemen.'[25] As a result of a by-election in June 1914, Rowland Prothero entered a House of Commons that had already been sitting for four years. He compared his 'feelings to those which I experienced when I was launched as a solitary small boy into the strange world of a great public school . . . Indeed the feeling of loneliness was less acute at school than in the House of Commons.' Matters were made worse for him by the fact that he was much older than the average new Member: 'The demigods of my new world—the parliamentary veterans who commanded the ear of the House—were my juniors . . . In entering a new society, such as that of the House of Commons, youth is a valuable asset. If it is frank and natural, it brings out the kindlier feelings of others. Years and experience make no such appeal; on the contrary, they put men on their guard.'[26]

The young Churchill looked precociously self-assured, as did Ramsay MacDonald. According to Bruce Glasier, 'MacDonald lay back on the bench, his legs outstretched, listening with a bored expression and without looking at the Member speaking, just as if he were a Cabinet Minister of twenty years' standing.'[27] However, initial humility is no indication of an MP's later disposition, as is illustrated by an anecdote of Sir William Fraser's: 'I heard an old member relate to Disraeli; at the beginning of a new Parliament; that a feeble individual had said to him, "If you please, Sir, where do the Members for Boroughs sit?" Disraeli was diverted by this; he said, "Yes! and in three months we shall have him bawling, and bellowing, and making such a row, there will be no holding him!" '[28]

❖

Chatham's last speech

William Pitt the Elder (1708–78), 1st Earl of Chatham, was educated at Eton, at Trinity College, Oxford, and at Utrecht. He joined the Army in 1731 and became MP for Old Sarum, a pocket borough controlled by his family, in 1735. Thereafter, he held a variety of seats in succession until he was elevated to the peerage as Prime Minister in 1766. He had already served as Prime Minister in 1756 and again, in coalition with the Duke of Newcastle, from 1757 to 1761.

Charles Pratt (1714–95), 1st Baron Camden and later Earl Camden, was also educated at Eton, where he befriended Pitt, and at Cambridge. He was called to the bar in 1738, became a KC in 1755, and was Lord Justice of the Court of Common Pleas from 1761 to 1766. He sat as a Whig MP for Downton from 1757 to 1762 and was Lord Chancellor from 1766 to 1770. Like his friend Pitt, he was sympathetic to the cause of the American colonists.

Lord Camden, Letter to the Duke of Grafton, April 1778

I cannot help considering the little illness which prevented your Grace from attending the House of Lords last Tuesday to have been a piece of good fortune as it kept you back from a scene that would have overwhelmed you with grief and melancholy as it did me, and many others that were present: I mean Lord Chatham's fit that seized him as he was attempting to rise and reply to the Duke of Richmond; he fell back upon his seat and was to all appearance in the agonies of death. This threw the whole House into confusion; every person was upon his legs in a moment, hurrying from one place to another, some sending for assistance, others producing salts, and others reviving spirits. Many crowding about the earl to observe his countenance; all affected; most part really concerned; and even those who might have felt a pleasure at the accident, yet put the appearance of distress, except only the Earl of M.: who sat still almost as much unmoved as the senseless body itself. Dr Brocklesby was the first physician that came but Dr Addington in about an hour was brought to him. He was carried into the prince's chamber, and laid upon the table supported by pillows. The first motion of life that appeared was an endeavour to vomit, and after he had discharged the load from his stomach that probably brought on the seizure, he revived fast ... I saw him in the prince's chamber before he went into the house, and conversed a little with him, but such was the feeble state of his body, and indeed the distempered agitation of his mind, that I did forebode that his strength would certainly fail him before he had finished his speech ... The earl spoke but was not like himself; his speech faltered, his sentences broken, and his mind not master of itself. His words were shreds of unconnected eloquence, and flashes of the same fire which he, Prometheus like, had stolen from heaven, and were then returning to the place from whence they were taken. Your grace sees even I, who am a mere prose man, am tempted to be poetical while I am discoursing of this extraordinary man's genius. The Duke of Richmond answered him, and I cannot help giving his Grace the commendation he deserved for his candour, courtesy, and liberal treatment of his illustrious adversary.

William Pitt the Younger

William Pitt the Younger (1759–1806) was the second son of William Pitt, 1st Earl of Chatham. He was educated privately and at Pembroke College, Cambridge, and was called to the bar in 1780. He was MP for Appleby, 1781–4; and for Cambridge University,

1784–1806. Within two years of entering the House, in 1782, he was made Chancellor of the Exchequer under Shelburne. At the age of twenty-five, when the Lord North–Fox coalition fell in 1783, he became Prime Minister and remained in that office until 1801, holding it again from 1804 until his death.

Lord John Russell (1792–1878), later Earl Russell, was the third son of the 6th Duke of Bedford and was educated at Westminster for a while, then privately by tutors, and later at the University of Edinburgh. He was Whig MP for Bandon, 1826–30; Devon, 1831; Devon South, 1832–5; Stroud, 1841; and London, 1841–61. One of the key proponents of the Great Reform Bill, he introduced the Bill into the Commons and led the Whigs in the Commons after Althorp's retirement in 1834, serving as Prime Minister from 1846 to 1852. Having been created an earl in 1861, he briefly served again as Prime Minister in 1865–6. Apart from his biography of Fox, he also edited Thomas Moore's *Memoirs, Journal and Correspondence*.

Earl Russell, *Life of Charles James Fox* (1866)

On the 26th of February (1781), Mr Burke's renewed Bill for the Reduction of the Civil List was rejected by 233 to 190. On this occasion Mr Sheridan [the dramatist] and Mr John Townshend made their first speeches. But, above all, Mr William Pitt spoke with a fluency, a precision, a dignity, and a method which are usually the acquirements of many years of practice. Lord North declared it was the best *first* speech he had ever heard. The effect appears to have been prodigious. By no one was Mr Pitt's success more warmly greeted than by Mr Fox. Lord Holland has related an anecdote which illustrates the presence of mind of the young orator. 'As Mr Fox hurried up to Mr Pitt to compliment him on his speech, an old member, said to be General Grant, passed by and said, "Ay, Mr Fox, you are praising young Pitt for his speech. You may well do so; for, excepting yourself, there's no man in the house can make such another; and, old as I am, I expect and hope to hear you both battling it within these walls as I have done your fathers before." Mr Fox, disconcerted at the awkward turn of compliment, was silent, and looked foolish; but young Pitt, with great delicacy, readiness, and felicity of expression, answered, "I have no doubt, general, you would like to attain the age of Methuselah." Before long Mr Fox had an opportunity of testifying in public the admiration he had avowed in private; and early in the following year, in praising a speech of Mr Pitt, he said "he could no longer lament the loss of Lord Chatham, for he was again living in his son, with all his virtues and all his talents".'

George Selwyn, Letter to Lord Carlisle, June 13, 1781

I heard yesterday young Pitt; I came down into the House to judge for myself. He is a young man who will undoubtedly make his way in the world by his abilities. But to give him credit for being very extraordinary upon what I heard yesterday would be absurd. If the oration had been pronounced equally well by a young man whose name was not of the same renown, and if the matter and expression had come without that prejudice, all which could be said was that he was a sensible and promising young man.

Lord Erskine

Thomas Erskine (1750–1823), 1st Baron Erskine, was born in Edinburgh and was sent to sea in 1764. Four years later he bought a commission in the Army and studied law. He soon acquired a reputation as a brilliant advocate and in 1783 became a KC and Whig MP for Portsmouth. His parliamentary oratory did not match his forensic skills, which he deployed to defend clients in political prosecutions in the early 1790s. He became Lord Chancellor in 1806, but resigned the following year and retired from public life.

George Croly, *The Life and Times of His Late Majesty, George the Fourth* (1830)

Erskine was returned to Parliament for Portsmouth, November 20th, 1783, and delivered his maiden speech on Fox's India Bill. Pitt sat, evidently intending to reply, with pen and paper in his hand, prepared to catch the arguments of this formidable adversary. He wrote a word or two. Erskine proceeded; but with every additional sentence Pitt's attention to the paper relaxed, his look became careless, and he obviously began to think the orator less and less worthy of his attention. At length, when every eye in the house was fixed upon him, with a contemptuous smile he dashed the pen through the paper, and flung them on the floor. Erskine never recovered from this expression of disdain. His voice faltered, he struggled through the remainder of his speech, and sank into his seat dispirited, and shorn of his fame.

George Canning

George Canning (1770–1827) was the son of a barrister and was educated at Eton and at Christ Church, Oxford. He never qualified for the bar, but instead became a professional politician. He was elected MP for Newport, Isle of Wight, in 1793, and during his long career sat for seven seats and supported Pitt, who quickly made him a Minister. Having served as Ambassador to Lisbon in 1814 and president of the Board of Control, 1816–20, he was Foreign Secretary from 1822 until 1827, when he became Prime Minister at the head of a Tory–Whig coalition which favoured Catholic Emancipation and reform of the Corn Laws. However, he died in the same year. His great friend Robert Jenkinson, later Earl Liverpool (under whose premiership he held office from 1812 to 1827), had entered the House four years before him, while his Whig arch-enemy Grey (later Earl Grey and also Prime Minister) had become an MP eight years earlier. Despite his own self-satisfaction, Canning's début was generally pronounced a failure.

Letter journal to the Revd William Leigh and his family, February 1794

This was the important day. I got up with I know not how many odd feelings about me, and could not sit still for a moment till it was time to go down to the House. About three I went and took my station under the gallery (till I had been sworn in I had no right in the *body* of the House), then attended the Speaker to the House of Lords to hear the King's Speech, then returned to the House of Commons and took the oaths and my seat. I can not describe you with what emotions I felt myself walking about the floor which I had so often contemplated in my youth from the Gallery, and wondered when I should have a right to tread upon it—I sat down too upon the Treasury Bench, just to see how it felt, and from that situation met the grinning countenance of half my acquaintance who were in the gallery. I was all in a flutter for some minutes, but however I bowed to the chair, and shook hands with the Speaker, and went through all the Ceremonies down to that of paying my fees with the utmost decorum and propriety. At 4 o'clock the debate began and lasted, as you will have seen by the papers, for thirteen hours, that is till 5 in the morning. It was to me one of the highest entertainments that can be conceived. I had no notion that there had been such a difference, as I find there is, in the interest with which one hears a debate, when merely a spectator in the gallery, and that which one feels, as a member, with the consciousness of having a right to join in it, if one pleases, and to give one's vote upon the decision.

Later entry, Letter journal, February 1794

I really tremble when I look back and consider what I undertook on this day. When I recollect that on three quarters of an hour in this day, depended perhaps the whole colour and character of my future fortune, condition, and reputation—that if I had many people, who were anxious that I should do well, there was not wanting some, to whom my failure would have been a matter of triumph—and that the chances of my doing well, or of my failure, on whatever other circumstances they might depend, were rendered not a little more precarious by the circumstances of the public expectation having been raised so high not only by the solicitous puffings of my friends, but by the designing and feigned ardour of those who wished to prejudice me, that it was no improbable thing, but rather the most likely in the world, that *they* would find opportunity of saying with apparent *candour* and fairness, but with a more fatal effect to my reputation than could arise from downright abuse, 'that it was *pretty well*, to be sure; but nothing like what they had been taught to *expect* etc.'—There is but one man who has said this. I will tell you who, by and by. Let me now begin by telling you, dear Leigh, and dear Fan, and dear Bess, and dear Tish, that my success has been equal to—nay beyond my most sanguine expectations. When I proceed to explain this to you I feel that this will be a *vain* sheet, that when I have written it, I shall be inclined to burn it. But I am sure your delight in hearing particulars will be so much more, in proportion, than the backwardness which I ought to feel in relating them (if I were properly modest) that I will get the better of all my feelings, and go through the task manfully from beginning to end.

On Friday morning then I was scarcely up, when Frere and Sturges, and Bobus Smith came to tell me, that they were setting off to get places in the Gallery—Frere and Sturges succeeded, and placed themselves just opposite to the situation from which I spoke. Bobus, to his great regret, and mine also, was detained by his good-natured attentions to his poor *Emigré* [Talleyrand], till he was too late to get in. As soon as they were gone, I walked up and down my room, in an agitation something like what I should suppose a man to feel who is going to be hanged, but who dying innocent has hopes of salvation. I argued the Sardinian Treaty over with great success in my own mind—and was going on very satisfactorily to myself—when Charles Ellis called by appointment to tell me that it was time to dress, and go down to the House. I dressed therefore, and sent for a bit of cold meat, and a glass of white wine, for Jenkinson and all wise people had told me that it was necessary to have some support, to prevent a sensation of sinking and emptiness. Then off I set with Charles Ellis, got to the House, in a sort of anguish fever, took a place immediately behind Pitt and Dundas on the second Bench (for I did not think it decorous to speak from the floor the first time) and sat myself down to wait the beginning of the Debate. In the Gallery, besides Sturges and Frere, before mentioned, I spied the two Legges, Edward and Augustus, Adderley, and two or three Christ Church faces, who might have come there by chance, but looked shrewdly as if they had smelt out the probability of my speaking, and were come to hear me. I whispered to Pitt, 'If there comes on a Debate, I have thoughts of speaking.' Mr P., 'You cannot chuse a better time.' C., 'If Fox opens, I think I will not speak immediately after him, but wait for Grey, or some other young one.' P., 'I think you judge very rightly—and I think I can augur from Grey's looks that he will probably give you an opportunity.' C., 'Pray have you the dates, and minutes of all the old Sardinian Treaties about you? I want to look at them again.' P., 'No, really I have not—but here comes Ryder—he has them I know, and he shall let you see them.' C., 'I have another Treaty, which strikes me as being much more completely analogous, than even any of the former Sardinian ones—It is the Prussian Subsidy of 1758—what do you think of it?' P., 'Good God-aye-it is exactly in point, it will do admirably. £670,000 if I recollect right—I am glad of it—it is the very thing.' The Order of the Day—Fox began, and spoke for about 20 minutes, or half an hour. At this time the House was not very full I was afraid it would not fill, but was glad to see people come flocking.

I took no notes, being resolved not to get a habit of using them, but I committed to my memory as many of Fox's arguments, as I could, and was lucky enough to retain them when I came to speak. I had always determined that my first speech should be in reply, that it might not be said 'aye this will do as a speech—but it does not promise a Debater' and it is my business, you know, if

I would get forward, to be useful. After Mr Fox rose Mr Powys, and very luckily for me, took up the question in the point of view in which I had resolved to consider it—as connected with the subject of the whole war—very luckily, I say, because, he is not the sort of speaker to anticipate one's arguments, but is the sort of man, of weight and consequence in the House, to justify any man who follows him, in taking up the subject in a point of view different from other people, which but for such an authority, might have looked like lugging foreign matter into discussion. After Powys, Ryder spoke and confined himself solely to the consideration of the Treaty, and to the justification of it by the other Sardinian Treaties. After Ryder Grey, in answer to him, and on precisely the same grounds of the Treaty and its precedents. Oh! what I felt while Grey was speaking! What I felt when I saw him retreating towards his seat! What I felt, when I found myself, standing bolt upright, and saw the Speaker pull off his hat towards me, and heard him cry and the House echo 'Mr Canning'! It was not fear—it was tumult. I began—Shall I tell you how I began? It must have been nearly as follows—'Mr Speaker'. A long interruption of Hear-Hear-Order-Places—during which I adjusted myself and pulled out my handkerchief and put it in my hat, which Lord Bayham who sat by me, held—Pitt and Dundas sat immediately below me, and next to them Ryder and Jenkinson. Wallace stood a good way to my left hand, near the Speaker's chair. Lord Hobart was immediately behind me, and Ch. Ellis behind me, but a good way to the left. I began somehow in this manner.

'If, Sir, I could consider the question in the same point of view, in which it has been considered by the Hon. Gent. (Grey) who spoke last—as a single, insulated, and independent question, standing on its own narrow grounds, and to be argued solely on its own limited and appropriate principles—I should have sat contentedly by, while Gentlemen, possessed of more official information, and every way of better ability than myself for such a purpose, had given the proper answers to such objections as have been urged against this Treaty. I should [have] sat by contented, with the answer which an Honble. Gent. below me (Ryder) has already given to every objection of that kind, in a most ample, and able, and to my mind satisfactory manner.

'But, Sir, as I do much rather agree with the Hon. Gent. who spoke second in this Debate (Powys) in viewing this question, as a question of much wider references, connexions, and dependencies—in viewing it not as a matter of mere mercantile bargain and sale, not as an investigation of the *quid pro quo*, which we may or may not have gained by this Treaty, not as a tradesmanlike prudential enquiry whether or no we may have been extravagant or over-reached—but as an extensive important political question, growing out of, and inseparable from, a great, connected and comprehensive system—Sir—as upon this system, and upon this Treaty as forming a part of this System, I have found little difficulty, nor can I conceive how any Gent. can have found much in *forming* an opinion—so—Sir—I trust, that I shall stand excused from the charge of presumption if I attempt to *deliver mine*.'

I then went on to argue the Treaty itself, and to defend it against Fox's objections. I did intend to have fought against Grey rather, but he disappointed my intention by wholly omitting any thing like an argument that was worth consideration. In answering Fox, I triumphantly produced my Prussian Treaty, which being new to the House had a great effect, and put me in spirits. Finding after a certain time, that I had been attacking Fox only and continually, I thought it decent, even if I had not known him, or liked, or admired him, or his connection as I do, yet simply as a young man, commenting on what a great and established character had said, to make some little apology for what, I modestly styled my presumption, and to assure him that if I treated his arguments, as I found them in my way, it was not from any want of admiration for his talents, or of respect and esteem for his person. While I was doing this, I necessarily looked, where I had not much looked before to the Opposition Bench, and saw how they were situated. Sheridan was behaving perfectly well, sitting quiet and attentive, looking neither to the right nor to the left. Fox was, as is his usual custom, turning round and talking over what I said, as I was going on—this was a little embarrassing but he meant nothing uncivil. But there was one person, who did mean and did shew much incivility. If I forgive him till I have revenged myself may—But I will not swear—This person was Grey. Agitated as I was, it did not require much to put me in still greater agitation. Once, for half a minute, or a minute, I was nearly overcome. But I summoned all my resolution. The thoughts of the great game that I was playing, that I had staked my all, and must win or lose through life, by the event of this night—anger too, and indignation against the person who was playing his anticks to perplex me—all conspired at once. I made one effort, regained my breath, drew myself up as undauntedly as I could. The House supported me nobly, and I got triumphantly to the end. During the latter part of my speech, I know no pleasure (sensual pleasure I had almost said) equal to that which I experienced. I had complete possession of all that I meant to say, and of myself, and I saw my way clear before me. The House was with me to a degree that was most comfortably assuring and delightful. I ventured to look boldly round me, and before me, and on each side, and met goodnatured, chearing countenances—and there were Pitt and Dundas—as I was afterwards informed by those who saw them in front, with their countenances, smirking, and glittering, rubbing their hands, and beating time to the sentences, and nodding to each other—and it was during this period, that Dundas exclaimed in the way, that I told you yesterday, 'By God, this will do.' All this, as you may suppose, was rapture to me—should [you] like to see some of my concluding topics?

'Sir, we are told this is a war of *passion*. If by a war of passion Honourable Gentlemen mean, that we have been hurried into a war, contrary to justice, to humanity and to sound policy, by the indulgence of some blameable propensity in our dispositions—if they mean to prove this, Sir, they appear to have undertaken a very difficult task indeed—They must arraign Nature, and confute instinct:—for they must prove that *self-preservation* is a passion, which it is criminal to indulge. But if by a war of passion they intend no more than that in addition to all the acknowledged and legitimate causes of war, for which we contend we have been forced into *this*—in addition to the necessity of repelling unprovoked aggression, of extending our assistance to our allies, of preserving Europe, of saving ourselves—that in addition to all this, Sir, it is a war, in which the best feelings and instincts of our nature are engaged, Sir (pause) to own that in *this* sense, it may be called a war of passion—and if ever from this dignified character it should be degraded to war of interest and aggrandisement, I, Sir, for one should cease to be its warm defender.

'But when our feelings cannot be convinced they attack our prudence. They ask us—what are we to get by the war? Sir, in the first place, I would ask to what species of war such a question fairly applies—to a war, which I contend this *not* to be of aggrandisement and speculation—or to *one* which I contend this to be—of self-defence and self-preservation? Sir, if Ministry had come down to this House, and said, we have an opportunity of gaining from the French, some accession of Commerce, some enlargement of Territory, if you will but support us in a war for that purpose; and if upon these grounds this House had agreed to support them in that war—then I admit this question might fairly have been put—then I admit that it would have been conclusive and the issue of the whole debate between Ministers in this House would be—Well what are we, after all, to get by this War? But in a war forced upon us by necessity no such issue is fair. We are proud to say—It was not the first question asked—I should be ashamed to be an advocate for a war, in which it was the only question that could be answered. And yet, Sir, I would not have it supposed that we have gained nothing—Sir—that we have still a government and constitution—Sir, that when we are now assembled there is not assembled in our room a Corresponding Society or a Scotch Convention—Sir—that instead of sitting to debate here whether or no we shall subsidise the King of Sardinia—we are not discussing the means of raising a forced loan to satisfy the rapaciousness of some proconsular deputy, whom the Banditti of Paris might have sent to receive our contributions—Sir, that we *sit here at all*, These are the fruits of the war.'

Then came my French madness—and my Strumpets and Calendar, all of which took amazingly.[29] The Strumpets indeed tickled everybody, and I assure you I have had very pretty and very chaste mouths beginning to say to me since, 'Oh, but what you said about the Str—— I mean about the *women* in oak leaves.'

Well, I sat down at last in an agitation great indeed, but of a very different kind, from that in which I had risen. Must I tell you all that was said to me? No, that I cannot do—you must guess—I will only say that everybody whom I did know and many whom I did not came up and shook hands, and thanked and complimented, and so on, and—what Jenkinson had long ago warned me to consider as a sure test of a speech having succeeded, and made an impression—there was a general buzz, and stir, and changing of places and going out, and no disposition to hear the person who got up after—by which— by the bye I lost a very fine compliment which Mr Stanley, if they had heard him, was about to pay me. Burke came across the House and said, 'I lament that the Debate upon this subject is at an end. I want to say *aloud* to tell the House what I think of you. I would get up on purpose to do so, but that I think that would look as if I thought you *wanted* help. It is more dignified to let you *go alone.*'

As soon as it was decent to go down the House I withdrew, and Jenkinson and Wallace and Ch. Ellis from the House, and Edward Legge and Augustus from the Gallery came and we dined up stairs—and the Bumpers of port wine that I swallowed—and the mutton chops that I devoured—and the sensations that I felt, are not to be described.

I find I was about 3 qrs. of an hour upon my legs—and my faults are—that I speak too rapidly, so much so as to run myself entirely out of breath, and louder than is necessary for filling the House—of which however I could not judge the first time—and that I use too violent and theatrical action, insomuch that people about me are apprehensive of some mischief from me. Lord Bayham I did once hit a plaguey hard blow on the shoulder—Pitt who was beneath me, *sidled* a little out of the way and Dundas was obliged to *bob* to save his *wig* from confusion. All this was told me as well by friends, as by some utter strangers among the Members, who very goodnaturedly came up to me for the purpose, and whose interference in this manner, I looked upon as an instance of as much kindness as the most flummery compliments could have been.

Henry Grattan

Henry Grattan (1746–1820) was born in Dublin and educated at Trinity College. While training as a barrister at Middle Temple, he fell under the influence of Henry Flood, a man with populist political views, and was disinherited by his father as a result. In 1775 he was elected to the Irish Parliament and became leader of the independence move- ment. After the Act of Union, which he was powerless to prevent, he sat in the Westminster Parliament until his death.

Charles Phillips, *Curran and his Contemporaries* (1850)

When he rose every voice in that crowded house was hushed—the great rivals, Pitt and Fox, riveted their eyes on him. He strode forth and gesticulated—the hush became ominous—not a cheer was heard—men looked in one another's faces and then at the phenomenon before them, as if doubting his identity; at last, and on a sudden, the indication of the master spirit came. Pitt was the first generously to recognise it; he smote his thigh hastily with his hand—it was an impulse when he was pleased—his followers saw it and knew it, and with a universal burst they hailed the advent and the triumph of the stranger.

Lord Byron, Detached thoughts, October 15, 1821–May 18, 1822

I have heard that when Grattan made his first speech in the English House of Commons, it was for some minutes doubtful whether to laugh or cheer him. The début of his predecessor Flood had been a complete failure, under nearly similar circumstances; but when the ministerial part of our senators had watched Pitt (their thermometer) for the cue and saw him nod repeatedly his stately nod of approbation, they took the hint from their huntsman, and broke out into the most rapturous cheers. Grattan's speech, indeed, deserved them; it was a *chef d'oeuvre*.

Charles Butler, *Reminiscences of Charles Butler, Esq.* (1822)

At the end of May 1820, Mr Grattan came, for the last time to London:—On the first day of the following June, the writer of these pages called upon him; and, being informed, that he was extremely ill, was retiring, without having seen him; but Mr Grattan, having heard that he was in the house, sent for him. It was evident that he touched the moment of his dissolution:—but the ethereal vigour of his mind was unsubdued, and his zeal for the Catholic cause, unabated. He pressed the writer by the hand:—'It is,' he said, 'all over!—Yes,—all over:—but I will die in the cause.—I mean to be carried to the house of commons tomorrow:—to beg leave of the speaker to take the oaths sitting,—and then, to move two resolutions.' These he mentioned to the writer; but spoke so indistinctly, that the writer could only perceive generally, that they were substantially the same as the clauses which he had prefixed to the bill, which, in 1812, he brought into parliament for the relief of the Catholics. He again pressed the writer by the hand, repeated the intention of being carried to the house, and desired the writer to attend him to it:—But—he died in the ensuing night!

❖

Sir James Graham

Sir James Graham, Bt. (1792–1861), was the eldest son of the 1st baronet. He obtained an LLD at Cambridge in 1835 and was made Lord Rector of the University of Glasgow in 1840. He sat for various seats during his career: Hull (1818–20), Carlisle (1826–9), Cumberland East (1830–7), Pembroke district (1838–41), Dorchester (1841–7), Ripon (1847–52) and Carlisle again (1852–61). He held office as a Whig First Lord of the Admiralty (1830–4), resigning in opposition to Reform of the Irish Church, and served as a Tory Home Secretary (1841–6) and as First Lord of the Admiralty again in the Aberdeen Coalition (1852–5).

William Torrens McCullagh Torrens (1813–94) was educated at Trinity College, Dublin, and called to the Irish bar in 1836. A historian and biographer, he was Liberal

15

MP for Dundalk, 1848–52; for Yarmouth, briefly, in 1857 (as plain Mr McCullagh); and for Finsbury from 1865 to 1885.

W. McCullagh Torrens, *Life of Sir James Graham* (1863)

Mr Graham wished to know if a member who sat for a borough of which he was neither an inhabitant nor freeman would come within the mischief of the Act? He paused to listen for the report of his shot; but few were attending, and nobody cried 'Hear.' He looked to see if it had hit, but the under-secretaries were talking to one another on the Treasury bench, and Lord Castlereagh was occupied in smelling the hot-house flower in his button-hole. Mr Graham repeated his question in other words, but with no better effect. He felt half vexed with himself at having got up, but was up, and must go on; so he thought he would argue the point. The case was not an imaginary one, he said, for it was his own, as he happened to sit for a borough of which he was neither a freeman nor an inhabitant, and of which he was not likely to become either, having no connection with the place. At this unlucky proffer of irrelevant information he heard, or thought he heard, something like a suppressed laugh. He felt himself getting confused, a little at first, and then very much so. For a few minutes he rambled on through commonplace and reiteration, but no timely cheer came to his rescue, and he sat down without any distinct recollection of what he had said or what he had intended to say. Mr Henry Lascelles, who sat opposite, whispered to a mutual friend, 'Well, there is an end of Graham; we shall hear no more of him.'

❖

Sir Thomas Fowell Buxton, Bt.

Sir Thomas Fowell Buxton, Bt. (1786–1845), was a member of the Norfolk gentry. His business interests embraced brewing and insurance, and he was a Whig. He was a philanthropist, a prominent campaigner for the abolition of slavery and an opponent of the Corn Laws, as well as a prison reformer. MP for Weymouth from 1818 until 1837 when he was defeated, Buxton was created a baronet in 1840. John Gurney, of the famous Norwich merchant-banking family, was his father-in-law and Elizabeth Gurney (later Elizabeth Fry, the prison reformer) his sister by marriage.

Letter to J. J. Gurney, February 25, 1819

When I last spoke (on the state of convict ships) there was no cry of question, but, on the contrary, marked attention; but alas! most undeserved, for, like a blockhead, I rose, having nothing to say, without a moment's premeditation. This has mortified me, which proves that my motives are not purified from selfish desires of reputation; and that all my anxiety is, not eagerness for the reform of prisons and the penal code, but, in truth, debased and alloyed by a desire for the reputation of T.F.B. I despise this vanity. On Monday next comes on the question of prisons; on Tuesday, the question of the penal code. On the latter I shall speak with my arguments and facts clearly before me. If I then fail, the failure is final—I may serve the cause as a labourer, but neither this, nor any other, as an advocate—and we must be satisfied. I endeavour to divest my mind of too much carefulness about the matter, persuaded that, whatever the event may be, that event is right both for me and for the cause.

Letter to J. J. Gurney, March 4, 1819

Well, the effort is over. Last night came on the grand question. I spoke for nearly an hour. I was low and dispirited, and much tired (bodily) when I rose. I cannot say I pleased myself. I could not, at first, get that freedom of language which is so essential, but I rose with the cheers of the House.

❖

Winthrop Mackworth Praed

Winthrop Mackworth Praed (1802–39) was the sixth son of a barrister with a Chancery practice, Serjeant Praed, and grandson on his mother's side of a Governor of the Bank of England. He was educated at Eton (where he founded *The Etonian*) and at Trinity College, Cambridge. He became a barrister and entered Parliament in 1830 as Conservative MP for St Germain's. He stood unsuccessfully for St Ives in 1832 and held a government post, as Secretary to the Board of Control, for a few months in 1835 before winning the seat of Great Yarmouth, for which he sat until 1837, thereafter sitting as MP for Aylesbury until his death from consumption in 1839. He was renowned as a witty and mildly satirical versifier, and his *Poems* were published in 1864.

Letter to Derwent Coleridge

The House appears to me day by day more awful. I begin to find that, after all, I must have recourse to the trite old motive, the hope of doing good . . . personal distinction or profit, even if either were of probable acquirement in the road I travel, would scarcely support me through the horrors of a début.

Letter to his sister Susan, February 1831

I have been engrossed by gratulatory notes, visits and meetings. My common greeting from old college acquaintances is 'How d'ye do? Pray where did you know all that about cotton?' . . . I can only say I wish I had succeeded less, for I shrink from the expectations I seem to have excited. I do my best to bear my praises meekly, saying every half hour, 'You overrate what I have done.' 'I owe it all to the kindness of the House.' 'It was an isolated question. I have not information enough for general debate,' and so on . . . It is to be hoped all this will not intoxicate me.

George Kinloch

George Kinloch (1775–1833), born in Dundee, was a member of the gentry from the Strathmore Valley. His father died within days of George's birth, and his mother died of tuberculosis when he was seven. His guardians decided to send George and his elder brother John (who was already showing signs of tuberculosis) to Europe in the company of a tutor. He later studied at Edinburgh University, though without graduating, and learnt a little Law in a writing chambers before settling down to farm his estate in Perthshire and marrying. While in his early twenties he became a Captain in the Volunteers and a JP, and made earnest efforts to develop the harbour at Dundee, receiving civic recognition for this work.

A passionate Reformer, he was declared an outlaw at the Cross of Edinburgh in 1819 (for his strongly voiced opinions about the Peterloo massacre at a public meeting in Dundee) and escaped to France before returning to England in 1822 and living on the run for several months. In 1823 he sneaked back to his estate before being granted a pardon. He was a prime mover in establishing a local railway linking Strathmore with Dundee, the first passenger railway in Scotland. On the anniversary of his being declared an outlaw in 1832 he was elected as Radical MP for Dundee. He died early the following year.

Letters to his wife Helen, February 1, 1832

I went down to the House at twelve today, and it came to my turn to be sworn in, about one. The Scotch and Irish members turned out very ill, for Wales, Scotland and Ireland were all called at the same time, and only about sixteen answered. I, of course, got a shake of the Speaker's hand, and a gracious bow, and having no more to do there, I went in quest of lodgings, and fixed on one in Parliament Street, that is the street which leads down from the Horse Guards, Whitehall, etc. towards Westminster Hall, from which last it is not above 300 yards distant; so that I shall be very near the *workshop*. It is at a gunsmith's, No. 55 a comfortable parlour and small bedroom within it, at 31/6d. week, and free to quit at a week's notice. A good eating house hard by, and the landlady offered to cook any plain victuals when required.

February 6. I took possession of my lodging yesterday forenoon, and find it very comfortable. A parlour with two windows to the street, and a small bed-room within it with one, also a large dark closet and a large pantry within the room. The street is macaddamed, so the noise, tho' great, is nothing to what it would have been with the old pavement.

At a little after twelve yesterday, I went to the House, and took my seat with Cobbett on my left, and my *friend* Peel, second from me, on the right. We had prayers, as usual. Then swearing in members till a little after two, when the guns announced the approach of King *Bill*. Then came the Usher of the Black Rod, as fine as a peacock, to summon us to the Lords, and then such a rush as I never witnessed

February 10. As to public matters, here we are, after four tedious debates, just where we were. Ministers have provoked it by their abominable speech, and we were determined to show them we would not submit to be treated like their slaves under the old system, but that we would discuss their measures 'ere we voted either for or against them.

I have taken a hasty dinner, each day, a little after three and been in the House always before four, when the Speaker comes in. Then we have prayers for about eight minutes, and all those who have previously put their names on their seats, and who are present at prayers are entitled to retain them for the night. Then goes on the private Bill business, the presenting of petitions, and so forth, till nearly six, when the Speaker calls on the Member who had moved the adjournment to continue the debate.

❖

Benjamin Disraeli

Benjamin Disraeli (1804–81), 1st Earl of Beaconsfield, was Jewish, the son of Isaac D'Israeli, the man of letters, who had him baptized in 1817. He was educated privately by a Unitarian minister and became a solicitor before achieving fame as a novelist in 1826 with *Vivian Grey*. He went on the Grand Tour and fought four electoral contests before winning Maidstone as a Conservative in 1837. With Lord George Bentinck he led a guerrilla campaign from the Tory back benches against the Tory leader, Sir Robert Peel, over the repeal of the Corn Laws. He soon emerged as leader of the protectionist Tories in the Commons and when the Earl of Derby formed a short-lived administration in 1852 Disraeli served as his Chancellor of the Exchequer. After another brief term of office with Derby in 1858, he proved himself a formidable Opposition leader and in 1866 he again served as Chancellor of the Exchequer under Derby and successfully piloted a Reform Bill through Parliament in 1867. He was briefly Prime Minister in 1868, though he lost the general election that year. He again served as premier from 1874 to 1880 (as the Earl of Beaconsfield from 1876).

Disraeli's maiden speech is famous for having been a failure, though some contemporaries thought this assessment exaggerated and attested that the barracking and ridicule had come from the unruly Irish. 'From the eastern, and more appreciative portion of the House, he was cheered: and from curiosity, from interest, and good nature, the leading men of both sides approved; and applauded,' claimed Sir William Fraser. 'His voice was, however, finally drowned by the Irish Members; who had but one object; to destroy him.'[30] Even so, as Disraeli himself explains below, he adapted his style of speaking to the methods of parliamentary business.

Letter to his sister Sarah, November 15, 1837

I took my seat this morning: I went down to the House with Wyndham [Lewis] at two, and found it very full, the members standing in groups and chatting. About three, there was a cry of 'Order, order,' all took their seats (myself on the second bench, behind Sir Robert Peel), and a messenger summoned the Commons. The Government party was very strong in consequence of an article in *The Times* about two days back, which spread a panic through their ranks, but which I think was a hoax. Shaw Lefevre proposed, and Strutt of Derby seconded, Abercromby. Both were brief, the first commonplace, the other commonplace and coarse; all was tame. Peel said a very little, very well. Then Abercromby, who looked like an old laundress, mumbled and moaned some dullness, and was then carried to the chair, and said a little more amid a faint, dull cheer. To me of course the scene was exciting enough, but none could share my feelings except new members.

Peel came to the Carlton yesterday, and was there a great deal. He welcomed me very warmly, but all indeed noticed his cordial demeanour; he looks very well, and shook hands with me in the House. He asked me to join a small dinner at the Carlton on Thursday. 'A House of Commons dinner purely,' he said; 'by that time we shall know the temper of the House.'

December 8. I made my maiden speech last night, rising very late after O'Connell, but at the request of my party and the full sanction of Sir Robert Peel. As I wish to give you an *exact* idea of what occurred, I state at once that my début was a *failure*, so far that I could not succeed in gaining an opportunity of saying what I intended; but the failure was not occasioned by my breaking down or any incompetency on my part, but from the physical powers of my adversaries. I can give you no idea how bitter, how factious, how unfair they were. It was like my first début at Aylesbury, and perhaps in that sense may be auspicious of ultimate triumph in the same scene. I fought through all with undaunted pluck and unruffled temper, made occasionally good isolated hits when there was silence, and finished with spirit when I found a formal display was ineffectual. My party backed me well, and no one with more zeal and kindness than Peel, cheering me repeatedly, which is not his custom. The uproar was all organised by the Rads and the Repealers. They formed a compact body near the bar of the House and seemed determined to set me down, but that they did not do. I have given you a most impartial account, stated indeed against myself.

In the lobby at the division, Chandos, who was not near me while speaking, came up and congratulated me. I replied that I thought there was no cause for congratulations, and muttered 'Failure!' 'No such thing!' said Chandos; 'you are quite wrong. I have just seen Peel, and I said to him, "Now tell me exactly what you think of D." Peel replied, "Some of my party were disappointed and talk of failure. I say *just the reverse*. He did all that he could do under the circumstances. I say anything but failure; he must make his way." '

The Government and their retainers behaved well. The Attorney-General,[31] to whom I never spoke in my life, came up to me in the lobby and spoke to me with great cordiality. He said, 'Now, Mr Disraeli, could you just tell me how you finished one sentence in your speech, we are anxious to know—"In one hand the keys of St Peter, and in the other——"?' 'In the other the cap of liberty, Sir John.' He smiled, and said, 'A good picture.' I replied, 'But your friends will not allow me to finish my pictures.' 'I assure you', he said, 'there was the liveliest desire to hear you from us. It was a party at the bar, over whom we had no control; but you have nothing to be afraid of.' Now I have told you all.

December 11. I dined with Bulwer on Saturday, and, strange enough, met Sheil. I should have been very much surprised, had I not arrived first and been apprised. It thus arose: on Saturday, Bulwer walked into the Athenaeum; Sheil, who has just recovered from the gout, was lounging in an easy chair reading the newspaper; around him was a knot of low Rads (we might guess them) abusing me and exulting in the discrimination of the House. Probably they thought they pleased Sheil. Bulwer drew near, but stood apart. Suddenly Sheil threw down the paper and said in his shrill voice, 'Now, gentlemen, I have heard all you have to say, and, what is more, I heard this same speech of Mr Disraeli, and I tell you this: if ever the spirit of oratory was in a man, it is in that man. Nothing can prevent him from being one of the first speakers of the House of Commons (great confusion). Ay! I know something about that place, I think, and I tell you what besides, that if there had not been this interruption, Mr Disraeli might have made a failure; but I don't call this a failure, it is a crush. My début was a failure, because I was heard, but my reception was supercilious, his malignant. A début should be dull. The House will not allow a man to be a wit and an orator, unless they have the credit of finding it out. There it is.' You may conceive the sensation that this speech made: I heard of it yesterday, from Eaton, Winslow, and several other quarters. The crowd dispersed, but Bulwer drew near, and said to Sheil: 'D. dines with me today; would you like to meet him?' 'In spite of my gout,' said Sheil, 'I long to know him; I long to tell him what I think.'

So we met: there were besides only D'Eyncourt, always friendly to me, Mackinnon, a Tory, and one Quin of the Danube. Sheil was most charming, and took an opportunity in conversation with me of disburthening his mind of the subject with which it was full. He insisted continually on his position that the clamorous reception was fortunate, 'for,' said he, 'if you had been listened to, what would have been the result? You would have done what I did; you would have made the best speech that you ever would have made: it would have been received frigidly, and you would have despaired of yourself. I did. As it is, you have shown to the House that you have a fine organ, that you have an unlimited command of language, that you have courage, temper and readiness. Now get rid of your genius for a session. Speak often, for you must not show yourself cowed, but speak shortly. Be very quiet, try to be dull, only argue and reason imperfectly, for if you reason with precision, they will think you are trying to be witty. Astonish them by speaking on subjects of detail. Quote figures, dates, calculations. And in a short time the House will sigh for the wit and eloquence, which they all know are in you; they will encourage you to pour them forth, and then you will have the ear of the House and be a favourite.'

December 18. Nothing daunted, and acting on the advice of Sheil (a strange parliamentary mentor for me after all), I spoke again last night and with complete success. It was on the Copyright Bill. The House was not very full, but all the Cabinet Ministers and officials were there, and all our principal men. Talfourd, who had already made a long speech (his style flowery, with a weak and mouthing utterance), proposed the Copyright Bill very briefly, having spoken on it last session. Bulwer followed him, and confined himself to the point of international copyright, which called up Poulett Thomson. Then Peel on the copyright of art; and then I rose.

I was received with the utmost curiosity and attention. As there had been no great discussion I determined not to be tempted into a speech, which everyone expected of course I rose to make. All I aimed at was to say something pointed and to the purpose. My voice, in spite of our doings at Maidstone, was in perfect condition. I suggested a clause to Talfourd, with the idea of which I had been furnished by Colburn. I noticed that the subject had already been done so much justice to on other occasions that I should not trouble the House, but I had been requested to support this Bill by many eminent persons interested in its success. Thus far I was accompanied by continual 'hear, hears', and I concluded thus: 'I am glad to hear from her Majesty's Government that the interests of literature have at length engaged their attention. It has been the boast of the Whig party, and a boast not without foundation, that in many brilliant periods of our literary annals they have been the patrons of letters ("Hear, hear" from John Russell & Co.). As for myself, I trust that the age of literary patronage has passed ("Hear, hear" from leader of the Rads), and it will be honourable to the present Government if, under its auspices, it be succeeded by that of legislative protection.' I sat down with a general cheer.

Talfourd, in reply, noticed all the remarks of the preceding members, and when he came to me said he should avail himself of 'the excellent suggestion of the honourable member for Maidstone, himself one of the greatest ornaments of our modern literature'. Here Peel cheered loudly, and indeed throughout my remarks he backed me. So on the whole there was glorification. Everybody congratulated me. Colonel Lygon said, 'Well, you have got in your saddle again, and now you may ride away.' Even Granville Somerset said, 'I never heard a few sentences so admirably delivered. You will allow me to say so, after having been twenty-five years in Parliament.' But all agree that I managed in a few minutes by my voice and manner to please everyone in the House. I don't care about the meagre report, for I spoke to the House and not to the public . . . it is my firm opinion that the next time I rise in the house, which will be very soon in February, I shall sit down amid loud cheers, for I really think, on the whole, though I have not time now to give you reasons, that the ·effect of my début, and the circumstances that attended it, will ultimately be favourable to my career. Next to my undoubted success the best thing is to make a great noise, and the many articles that are daily written to announce my failure only prove that I have not failed. One thing is curious, that the opinion of the mass is immensely affected by that of their leaders. I know a hundred little instances daily, which show me that what Peel, and Sheil, and other leading men have said, have already greatly influenced those who are unable to form opinions for themselves.

Richard Cobden

Richard Cobden (1804–65) was born in Sussex and became a cotton printer in Lancashire. He was a director of the Manchester Chamber of Commerce, one of the leading members of the Anti-Corn Law League and the principal intellectual advocate of Free Trade in Parliament. He sat for Stockport from 1841 to 1847, for the West Riding of Yorkshire from 1847 to 1857, and for Rochdale from 1859 until his death.

Letters to Francis Cobden

August 24, 1841. Yesterday, I went down to the House to be sworn to renounce the Pope and the Pretender. Then I went into the Treasury, and heard Lord John deliver his last dying speech and confession to his parliamentary minority. He gave us the substance of the Queen's speech, which is in the *Chronicle* today. I cannot learn what the Tories intend to do tonight, but I suppose they will try to avoid committing themselves against the Free Trade measures. It is allowed on all sides that they fear discussion as they do death. It is reported that the old Duke advises his party not to force themselves on the Queen, but to let the Whigs go on till the reins fairly drop out of their hands. The Queen seems to be more violently opposed than ever to the Tories.

August 26. I was induced to speak last night at about nine o'clock. We thought the debate would have been brought to a close. The Tories were doggedly resolved from the first not to enter upon any discussion of the main question, and the discussion, if it could be called one, went on as flat as possible. My speech had one good effect. I called up a booby who let fly at the manufacturers, very much to the chagrin, I suspect, of the leader of his party. It is now thought that the Tories must come out and discuss in self-defence the Free Trade question, and if not, they will be damaged by the arguments on the other side. All my friends say I did well. But I feel it very necessary to be cautious in speaking too much. I shall be an observer for some time.

William White (1807–82) was born in Bedford and was educated at the town's grammar school. He became a bookseller, but in 1854 Lord Charles Russell appointed him assistant-doorkeeper to the House of Commons. He soon graduated to doorkeeper, and in 1855 he started writing sketches for the *Illustrated Times* (which later became the *Illustrated London News*). These sketches—as his son, William Hale White, also a sketch-writer, wrote—were notable for their 'pure idiomatic English' and 'pictorial fidelity'. When White retired in 1875, he received a gift subscribed by 100 Members.[32]

William White, *Illustrated Times*, April 8, 1865

The scene in the House of Commons on Monday night, when the public tribute was paid to the dead Cobden, was to us painful rather than gratifying. We felt as a man feels when he arrives at the house in which a dear friend lies dead, and sees at the door professional mutes and similar griefmongers with their trappings, upholsteries, and other mockeries of woe. For the speakers here, except, of course, Mr Bright, were professional eulogisers. They were not hired by money, but neither were they inspired by love or grief. It was a 'right thing to do' this lauding the dead statesman, and therefore they did it. It is questionable whether Lord Palmerston was moved even by this faint inspiration. It was not in his mind at first to say a word, but he was urged to consent to the adjournment of the House, and, as he could not do this because the Government wanted some votes in Supply, he compromised by giving, instead of an adjournment, a speech; and, this being settled, a note was dispatched to Mr Disraeli to inform him of the arrangement, that he too, if he felt inclined, might contribute his meed of eulogy of the deceased statesman. This was, then, no burst of grief, no spontaneous expression of sorrow, but a thing got up. All this we knew when we entered the House, and, knowing it, the scene could give us no pleasure. However, it was not wanting in solemnity; unquestionably, the sorrow of the majority of the members was profound and their homage sincere.

Lord Palmerston rose to perform his stipulated task at a quarter to five, and as he rose the House at once hushed into profound silence and attention. Of his Lordship's speech little need be said, as all our readers will have seen and read it. The noble Lord did his work, on the whole, neatly enough, and this is all that can be said in his praise. He was not inspired. The light that he threw upon Mr Cobden's character and achievements was 'a dry light'—*lumen siccum*. There was little or no warmth in it. And what a blunder he made when he described the eloquence of Cobden as Demosthenic! Had we not been too much distressed by our loss we should have laughed at this strange, inappropriate epithet. But the noble Lord made a worse mistake than this when he named the allies of Richard Cobden and forgot to mention Bright. But no matter. The nation knows, and all the world knows, and history will record that, whilst Villiers prepared the way for the fight for free trade, and Peel, after long and pertinacious opposition, turned round when resistance had become hopeless and headed the last grand assault, 'Cobden and Bright' were the foremost soldiers in that protracted and arduous war. Men say—but no! just now we will not record what men say, but rather charitably hope that, strange as this omission was, it was merely a mistake.

Mr Disraeli's speech was far the more impressive of the two. His manner was more solemn, his thoughts more appropriate, his estimate of the great statesman more just. And how solemn the House was whilst Mr Disraeli was speaking! There was silence that might be felt. The attention was rapt. Every man seemed to be holding his breath lest his struggling emotions should break forth into expression and disturb the speaker. And when the orator told us that the deceased statesman had joined that great band of members who, though not present in the body, are still here, there burst forth from many parts of the House deep sighs and low but unusually expressive murmurs of applause. That was a beautiful figure of Disraeli's: nothing more beautiful was ever presented to the House. It was borrowed, as we all know; but it was none the less beautiful because St Paul used it before.

Of Mr Bright's speech we will not say a word. It is a speech to be read, and felt, and not to be talked about. Nor will we describe his appearance as he delivered it. It would be an intrusion into the sanctuary of sorrow—something very much like a profanation—to do this. When Mr Bright sat down Sir Morton Peto rose. For a moment the members listened, thinking that possibly he, too, was going to say something about Mr Cobden; but when the words 'Board of Admiralty' fell upon their ears, up rose the crowd,

'And all the pent-up stream of life
Dashed downward in a cataract.'

Yes; it was all over. The drama had been performed; and that crowd, lately so solemn and silent, was now rushing out, gabbling and cackling as if nothing had happened. For a few short minutes the current of business had been stopped; but now the dam is broken down, and on rushes the mighty, impetuous river in its course again, apparently as heedless of the solemn event which had occurred as the roaring sea is of the wrecks which it casts upon the shore.

Edmund Lechmere Charlton

Edmund Lechmere Charlton (b. 1789) was a landowner and barrister. He served as MP for Ludlow from January 1835 until his retirement in 1837.

The Hon. George Charles Grantley Fitz-Hardinge Berkeley (1800–81) was a younger son of Earl Berkeley. Formerly a lieutenant in the army, he sat as MP for Gloucestershire West from 1832 until 1852, when he was defeated.

Grantley Berkeley, *My Life and Recollections* (1866)

The late Mr L. Charlton tried to make a maiden speech, and rising in his place with a very bald head, known too as he was to everybody, as one of the oldest stagers in all the ways of the world, he began with great affectation of inexperience, and with an exceedingly mild voice—

'Mr Speaker—I am but a young member.'

On hearing this assertion from so well known and crafty a man, possessing so venerable a pate, the entire House roared with laughter. Twice he stopped, and three times he commenced with these words; but it was useless; the House would not listen, and he never to my knowledge essayed to speak again, or if he did, the sight of his bald head set his audiences in a roar.

Henry Fawcett

Henry Fawcett (1833–84) was blinded in a shooting accident in 1858. He was appointed professor of political economy at Cambridge in 1863, and in 1865 was elected to Parliament as a Liberal. He was a committed reformer, even advocating women's suffrage. As Gladstone's Postmaster-General from 1880, he presided over such developments as parcel post and sixpenny telegrams.

Letter to his father, February 1, 1866

I have just returned from my first experience of the House of Commons. I went there early in the morning, and soon found that I should have no difficulty in finding my way about. I walked in with Tom Hughes about five minutes to two,[33] and a most convenient seat close to the door was at once, as it were, conceded to me; and I have no doubt that it will always be considered my seat. Every one was most kind, and I was quite overwhelmed with congratulations. I am glad that my first visit is over, as I shall now feel perfect confidence that I shall be able to get on without any particular difficulty. The seat I have is as convenient a one as any in the House, and a capital place to speak from. I walked away from the House of Commons with Mill. He sits on the bench just above me, close to Bright. I sit next but one to Danby Seymour. White (his colleague for Brighton) is three or four places from me.

Arthur Kavanagh

Arthur MacMurrough Kavanagh (1831–89) was High Sheriff of the counties of Kilkenny in 1855 and Carlow in 1857 and sat as a magistrate in the counties of Carlow and Wexford. He was Conservative MP for the County of Wexford from 1866 to 1868, thereafter sitting for the County of Carlow until 1880, when he was defeated.

William White, *Illustrated Times*, February 9, 1867

On Wednesday there was no small curiosity to see Mr Kavanagh—the gentleman born without arms or legs—take the oaths; and this curiosity was satisfied, for soon after the House met the hon. member for the county of Wexford made his appearance. He entered the House through the door at the back of the Speaker, seated in a chair, which, by an ingenious contrivance, he can wheel about himself. Mr Powell used to do this; but then he did it in a common way, by turning the wheels of the chair with his hands. Mr Kavanagh has no hands, but only short stumps; but necessity is the mother of invention, and some clever mechanic has contrived a simple piece of machinery by which

Mr Kavanagh can propel his chair as easily as Mr Powell could his. On each side of his chair there is a cup; in these cups Mr Kavanagh places his stumps, and, by a circular motion, he turns a perpendicular rod, which, by means of two cog-wheels, turns the axle of the greater wheels, and thus propels the chair forward; and, as there is in the front of the chair a guiding wheel, he can, obviously, steer which way he pleases. Mr Kavanagh, of course, took the oaths sitting, holding the Testament between his stumps. He signed the book as easily as any other member could, holding the pen as he held the Testament. It is the custom of every new member, after he has taken the oath, to shake hands with the Speaker. Mr Kavanagh, of course, could not do that. He therefore only bowed to the Speaker as he passed out. Where he will sit, and how he will speak—for speak he will, we may be sure, as he is an able man—the Speaker has not yet decided.

❖

Albert Pell

Albert Pell (1820–1907) was educated at Rugby and at Trinity College, Cambridge. He was a magistrate for Leicestershire and the Isle of Ely, and Deputy-Lieutenant of Cambridgeshire. He sat for South Leicestershire from December 1868 until his retirement in 1885.

The Reminiscences of Albert Pell (1908)

On February 15, 1869, was the opening of Parliament—a most beautiful spring day. I walked to the House in good time for the Queen's Speech. There was a great crush, and all seemed strange and almost riotous to me. It was public-school life over again. I fell in with no acquaintance in the central lobby, but was struck with the civility and attentions of the police. At last the procession started from the Commons, headed by the Speaker in his robes and his train-bearer. I joined in the rush pursuing him, giving him, as a witty little paper, *The Owl*, reported, very little 'law'. I got a good start, elbowing, I make no doubt, many distinguished persons, and was brought up with much vehemence of Mr Speaker. As her Majesty was not on the throne, I paid no attention to the speech, but looking round, found an old schoolfellow—'Little Glyn' we called him at Rugby—at my elbow. He had been our 'hare' at 'hare and hounds', and a happy thought came into my mind. I was so pinned by the Speaker on one side and Glyn on the other that I could not shake hands with him. Thirty years, however, had not effaced the recollection of his running powers and the breathless chases I had made after him, so I said to him, 'Here we are again, and I will run you for sixpence back to the door of the Commons.' 'Done!' was his cheerful reply. So, giving time for Mr Speaker and his crew to get back to the House, we started fair, and tore like pickpockets through the crowd of gazing strangers; the police had not time nor presence of mind to shout 'Make way for members' till we pulled up with a jerk at the door of the House, startling the old white-haired guardian out of his senses. From that moment, however, I was known to the officials and the police as the new member. I took my seat that day below the gangway, but next to it.

T. P. O'Connor

Thomas Power O'Connor (1848–1929) was educated at Queen's College, Galway. He sat as a Nationalist MP for Galway from 1880 to 1885 and for the Scotland division of Liverpool from 1885 until his death. A prolific journalist, he wrote sketches for the *Pall Mall Gazette* and the *Weekly Sun*, which were published in collected form in the 1880s and 1890s. He was Father of the House of Commons from 1918 to 1929.

Memoirs of an Old Parliamentarian (1929)

I returned to London Member for Galway, and my shyness and self-distrust will be demonstrated by the fact that I stood in the Lobby afraid or ashamed to enter the House, after nearly every other elected member had entered.

My awe of the House was immense. A few days after this I was present at a debate; a rather wild type of Irishman named Lysaght Finigan, who by this time was a veteran of a few months, made me jump when he called out, 'Hear, hear'. It seemed to me an act of shameless daring. And yet the first appearances of a new House of Commons are by no means awe-inspiring. The immediate task is to swear the members in, and this is done in a haphazard and almost riotous form. Members, in their eagerness to have the job over, hustle, rush, and form long queues, all amid a scene of merriment quite characteristic of the House of Commons.

John Redmond

John Edward Redmond (1856–1918) was the son of William Archer Redmond, MP for Wexford borough, 1872–80. He was educated at Trinity College, Dublin, and was called to the bar at Gray's Inn in 1866 (as well as to the Irish bar in 1887). He sat as a Nationalist MP for New Ross, 1881–5; for North Wexford, 1885–91; and for Waterford City, 1891–1918. From 1891 to 1900 he was Leader of the Parnellite Nationalists, and from 1900 until his death he led the reunited Nationalist Party.

'Fifteen Years in the House of Commons', lecture in New York, November 29, 1896

At the moment when the Sheriff declared me duly elected, the House of Commons had already been sitting continuously for some twenty-four hours. The brunt of the fight against the Coercion Bill was being borne by some dozen of Mr Parnell's most active supporters; and they were looking anxiously for my election to send them a recruit. I received a wire urging me not to lose an hour in crossing to Westminster. I started at once, and travelled all night to London. On my way I received another wire saying the House was still sitting. I reached London about seven o'clock on a dark and cold winter's morning. I drove straight from the station to the House of Commons, and it was thus, travel-stained and weary, that I first presented myself as a member of the British Parliament. The House was still sitting, it had been sitting without a break for over forty hours, and I shall never forget the appearance the Chamber presented. The floor was littered with paper. A few dishevelled and weary Irishmen were on one side of the House, about a hundred infuriated Englishmen upon the other; some of them still in evening dress, and wearing what once were white shirts of the night before last. Mr Parnell was upon his legs, with pale cheeks and burning face, his hands clenched behind his back, facing without flinching a continuous roar of interruption. It was now about eight o'clock. Half of Mr Parnell's followers were out of the Chamber snatching a few moments' sleep in chairs in the library or smoke-room. Those who remained had each a specified period of time allotted to him to speak, and they were wearily waiting their turn. As they caught sight of me standing at the bar of the House of Commons there was a cheer of welcome. I was unable to come to their aid, however, as under the rules of the House I could not take my seat until the commencement of a new sitting. My very presence, however, brought, I think, a sense of encouragement and approaching relief to them, and I stood there at the bar with my travelling coat still upon me, gazing alternately with indignation and admiration at the amazing scene presented to my gaze. This, then, was the great Parliament of England! Of intelligent debate there was none. It was one unbroken scene of turbulence and disorder. The few Irishmen remained quiet, too much amused, perhaps, or too much exhausted to retaliate. It was the English—the members of the first assembly of gentlemen in Europe, as they love to style it—who howled and roared, and almost foamed at the mouth with rage at the calm and pale-featured young man who stood patiently facing them, and endeavouring from time to time to make himself heard. The galleries were filled with strangers every whit as excited as the members, and even the Ladies' Gallery contained its dozen or so of eager spectators. No one knew what was going to happen. There was no power under the rules of the House to stop the debate, consequently it had resolved itself into a question of physical endurance, and it seemed as if the Irishmen battling for the liberties of their country were capable of resisting until the impotence of the House of Commons had covered it with the contempt and ridicule of Europe.

At last the end came suddenly and unexpectedly. At eight o'clock Mr Speaker Brand, from a sense of duty, as he said, and acting on his own responsibility, and in defiance of the rules of the House, ordered the debate to cease . . .

The Irish members endeavoured to protest by speech against this proceeding, and failing in the attempt, they rose in their seats, and left the Chamber in a body shouting 'Privilege', a cry not heard in that place since Charles I attempted to invade the liberty of Parliament. So ended the first battle over this Coercion Bill, the net result being that England found, in order to suspend the constitution of Ireland, she was obliged to destroy the most cherished tradition and most precious possession of her Parliament: the freedom of speech of its members!

The following day my membership of the House of Commons actually commenced, and I had an experience, I believe, absolutely unique in Parliamentary history. I took my oath and my seat, made my maiden speech, and was suspended and expelled from the House for the rest of the sitting—all in the same evening! It was not of my choosing; I had the distinction thrust upon me. It occurred in this way. The excitement of the previous day had been intensified by the news of the arrest of Mr Davitt in Ireland. Mr Dillon had endeavoured to extract some explanation from the Government and had been named and suspended, and then Mr Parnell, on the Prime Minister rising to speak, moved: 'That Mr Gladstone be not heard.' [The Speaker ruled that Gladstone was in possession of the House, Parnell persisted and was named, and Gladstone moved his suspension. Parnell's followers refused to vacate seats for the ensuing division.] . . .

For this refusal to vote thirty-seven Irish members were suspended, myself among the number. Having been suspended, we each in turn refused to leave the Chamber, and, addressing the Speaker, protested against the entire proceeding, and intimated that unless superior force was employed, we should resist. That was my maiden speech! Superior force, in the shape of the Sergeant-at-Arms and his merry men, was then applied, and eventually each one of us was escorted under arrest from our seats, and thus, as I have said, my Parliamentary career opened with the unique experience of taking my seat, making my maiden speech, and being expelled by force from the Chamber on the same evening.

❖

'Don Roberto'

Born Robert Bontine in London, R. C. Cunninghame Graham (1852–1936), known as 'Don Roberto', learnt Spanish as his first language (he had a Spanish grandmother). He was educated at Harrow, but left at the age of sixteen to live on an Argentine cattle ranch belonging to relatives. Having assumed his father's old family name of Cunninghame Graham, he lived the life of an adventurer in South America for fifteen years, marrying a Chilean mystical poet, working as a fencing master in Mexico City and as a cowboy in Texas. In 1884 he inherited his father's debt-ridden Scottish estate, and from 1886 to 1892 he was Labour MP for North Lanarkshire, often riding to Parliament on his mustang. He was imprisoned for two months after leading the workers against the police in the Trafalgar Square riots, and helped Keir Hardie organise the Scottish Labour Party. (Years later, at the age of seventy-six, he helped set up the Scottish National Party.) After losing his seat and various subsequent electoral contests, he embarked on a new career as a writer of travel books and short stories, and befriended Joseph Conrad, W.

H. Hudson and George Bernard Shaw—Conrad once described him as 'a grand seigneur born out of his time'. During World War I he travelled to South America to buy horses for the British Army. He later died in Buenos Aires. With his exotic background, his radicalism was that of a buccaneer who was scornful of bourgeois morality.

A. F. Tschiffely, *Don Roberto: Being the Account of the Life and Works of R. B. Cunninghame Graham, 1852–1936* (1937)

On the 1st of February 1887, Don Roberto made his maiden speech in Parliament. The opportunity was an ideal one for a man such as he was, and he took full advantage of it, rising with an elegant gesture to make his address in answer to Queen Victoria's Speech. With unique courage and conviction he spoke, his stentorian voice ringing through the House, and his words startling and shocking the Members who had rarely heard such an eloquent flow of language. It can easily be imagined what the effect must have been when he started:

'A debate on the Queen's Speech forms the best occasion for a new Member to lose his political virginity, and, therefore, I cast myself at once on the forbearance and the generosity of the House.

'On glancing over the Queen's Speech, I am struck with the evident desire which prevails in it to do nothing at all. There is a similarity in its paragraphs to the *laissez-faire* school of political economy. Not one word is said in the Speech about lightening the taxation under which Her Majesty's lieges suffer; not a word to bridge over the awful chasm existing between the poor and the rich; not one word of kindly sympathy for the sufferers from the present commercial and agricultural depression—nothing but platitudes, nothing but views of society through a little bit of pink glass ... It is not to be expected that Her Majesty's Government will vouchsafe to the House any idea of when the British troops might be withdrawn from Egypt ...'

Continuing his startling speech he proceeded to attack what he styled 'our latest filibustering exploit in Burma ... with arms of precision shooting down naked savages'. Then he went on, sarcastically: 'When telegrams come from Burma we slap our hands on our chests—quite regardless of damage to our shirts—and talk of British gallantry, and laugh like parrots at a bagpiper, when we look at the sketches in the illustrated papers depicting natives running away from our troops ...'

Going on, probably smiling inwardly at the expressions on the faces looking at him, he referred to Liberals as 'crutch-and-toothpick gentlemen', and then, sweeping a pointing finger at the assembly, at the same time looking round the House, he said that this Government reminded him of Pope's flies in amber:

'Things in themselves, though neither rich nor rare,
One wonders how the devil they got there.'

31

Then, referring to the resignation of Lord Randolph Churchill, he continued: 'The noble Lord's resignation has saddened me as children are saddened when they see a rocket spout up, and are all unaware that it will fall down a stick as well said by Ben Johnson:

'He was a child that so did thrive in grace and feature
As Heaven and nature seemed to strive which owned the creature.'

'Where is the noble Lord now?' Don Roberto exclaimed. 'Yesterday he was, today he is not—gone like the froth on the licensed victualler's beer . . .'

Touching on the Irish Home question he astonished his listeners by saying: 'With regard to Ireland, I have eminent qualifications for dealing with that subject, for many reasons. First of all, I have never been there, second, because I am sitting next to Nationalist Members, and then because I have once known an Irish commercial traveller who imparted to me various facts quite unattainable by the general public . . .'

Raising his voice more and more, and looking, sometimes even pointing at Members, who wriggled with indignation, he wound up his speech by attacking society in general:

' . . . The society in which one man works and another enjoys the fruit— the society in which capital and luxury makes Heaven for 30,000 and a Hell for 30,000,000, that society whose crowning achievement is this dreary waste of mud and stucco—with its misery, its want and destitution, its degradation, its prostitution, and its glaring social inequalities—the society we call London—that society which, by a refinement of irony, has placed the mainspring of human action, almost the power of life and death, and the absolute power to pay labour and to reward honour, behind the grey tweed veil which enshrouds the greasy pocket of the capitalist.'

What effect this maiden speech must have had upon the assembly is best left to the imagination. Before the bewildered Members had finished staring at each other, he strode out, leapt on his mustang 'Pampa', and cantered towards his London home to attend to his many new duties.

❖

James Keir Hardie

James Keir Hardie (1856–1915) was a coal-miner who became Secretary of the Miners' Union in 1879 as well as a journalist (he edited the *Miner* and, later, the *Labour Leader*). He sat for West Ham, 1892–5, and for Merthyr Tydfil, from 1900 until his death. He was chairman of the Independent Labour Party, 1893–1900, and Leader of the Labour Party in the House of Commons, 1906–8.

Sir Henry William Lucy (1845–1924) was educated at the Crescent School, Liverpool. He was apprenticed to a Liverpool merchant, but joined the *Shrewsbury Chronicle* as Chief Reporter in 1864, leaving in 1869 to study French language and literature in Paris for a year. On his return he joined the staff of the new morning edition *Pall Mall Gazette*.

Then in 1873 he became Special Correspondent, Chief of Gallery Staff, and writer of the parliamentary sketch for the *Daily News*. He edited the paper in 1886, but returned to the Reporters' Gallery in 1887. From 1880 onwards he wrote the Cross Bench article for the *Observer* and from 1881 wrote 'The Diary of Toby MP' for *Punch*. He contributed articles about Parliament to several newspapers and magazines, and wrote numerous books on the subject, drawn from his journalism.

Henry W. Lucy, Strand Magazine, June 1899

He came in in 1892 as member for West Ham, numbered among the narrow majority of forty that placed Mr Gladstone in precarious power. From the first he made it clear that he was no hack—like Mr Burt, for example—but would let bloated patricians know that the working man is their master. To that end he wore the Cap of Liberty, of somewhat dingy, weather-worn cloth. Also he sported a short jacket, a pair of trousers frayed at the heel, a flannel shirt of dubious colour, and a shock of uncombed hair. On the day of the opening of Parliament he drove up to Westminster in a break, accompanied by a brass band. His first check was received at the hands of the police, who refused to allow the musical party to drive into Palace Yard. So the new member was fain to walk.

His appearance on the scene kindled keen anticipation in the breast of Lord Randolph Churchill, who saw in him a dangerous element in the Ministerial majority. The member for West Ham did his best to justify that expectation. At the outset the House listened to him with its inbred courtesy and habitual desire to allow every member, however personally inconsiderable, full freedom of speech. It soon found out that Mr Keir Hardie was as sounding brass or tinkling cymbal. His principal effort to justify his appearance on the Parliamentary stage was a motion made in his second Session to discuss the widespread destitution among members of the working classes. He rose after questions, claiming to have the matter discussed as one of urgent public importance. When the Speaker asked if he were supported by the statutory number of forty, only thirty-six rose. The bulk of members, not unmindful of the prevalent condition of the working man or unwilling to help him, did not care to march under Mr Keir Hardie's flag. His six months of probation were over, and he had shrunk to his proper dimensions. When the dissolution came he, almost unobserved, sank beneath the Parliamentary horizon.

❖

The House makes a gesture to a dying Charles Bradlaugh

Charles Bradlaugh (1833–91) was a lecturer, president of the Secular Society, and proprietor of the *National Reformer*, a Radical periodical. He stood unsuccessfully for Northampton borough in 1868 and twice in 1874 before being elected in April 1880. The Court of Appeal ordered another election because he insisted on affirming rather than swear the oath. Voted back four times before he finally swore an amended oath in 1885. He sat for the next five years, during which he emerged as an opponent of socialism.

T. P. O'Connor, *T.P.'s Weekly*, August 21, 1903

The House of Commons, which had been so unjust to Bradlaugh—with that readiness to undo a wrong and to make atonement which is one of an Englishman's best characteristics—showed an almost pathetic eagerness to beat death in the race, and to soothe Bradlaugh's spirit before it had ceased to be. When the news came to the House that he was dying, at once and spontaneously from all quarters the motion was made and adopted that there should be expunged from the Journals of the House the record of his expulsion; and a messenger was sent to convey what it was felt would be joyful news to the dying man. The messenger came too late. Bradlaugh was not yet dead, but the mighty mind was already hidden in the clouds and mists of coming death. He went out into what he believed was eternal night, ignorant of the tardy reparation: already he was beyond praise or blame, or all the other things that make up our lives, that are so enormous in ordinary existence, and shrink into such nothingness when they stand under the awful and gigantic shadow of death.

David Lloyd George

David Lloyd George (1863–1945) was the son of a schoolteacher. He was educated at church schools and privately and became a solicitor in 1884. He was Liberal MP for Caernarvon district from 1890 until 1945 when he was created Earl Lloyd George of Dwyfor shortly before his death. He first held office in 1905, as President of the Board of Trade, and from 1908 to 1915 he was Chancellor of the Exchequer. During World War I he was consecutively Minister of Munitions, Secretary of State for War, and Prime Minister, a post which he held until 1922 as head of a coalition. He was also Leader of the Liberal Party from 1926 to 1931 and of the Independent Liberal Group from 1931 to 1935. From 1929 to 1945 he was Father of the House of Commons.

Diary, November 12, 1881[34]

Went to the Houses of Parliament, very much disappointed with them—great buildings outside, but inside they are crabbed, small and suffocating, especially the House of Commons. I will not say that I eyed the Assembly in a spirit similar to that in which William the Conqueror eyed England on his visit to Edward the Confessor as the region of his future domain. Oh! Vanity.

Letters to his wife Margaret, April 17, 1890

This is the first letter which I write as an introduced member of the House of Commons and I dedicate it to my little darling.

I snatch a few minutes during the delivery of Goschen's budget to write her. I was introduced amid very enthusiastic cheers on the Liberal side . . .

Cymru Fydd [Welsh nationalists] came to the station to meet us. Mr Alfred

Davies a member of the London County Council had his carriage ready to drive us to the House. A very small 'landau'.

Sir John Puleston[35] came up to me and very kindly invited me to dine with him at 7.30 . . .

June 14. Shortly after I wrote my letter of yesterdays [*sic*] to you I got up and spoke for the first time in the House of Commons . . . there is no doubt I scored a success and a great one. The old man and Trevelyan, Morley and Harcourt appeared delighted. I saw Morley shortly afterwards and he said it was 'a capital speech—*first rate*' and he said it with marked emphasis. He is such a dry stick that he wouldn't have said anything unless he thoroughly believed it.

I have been overwhelmed with congratulations both yesterday and today. I was in the Library of the House getting up statistics . . . and several Irish members who happened to be there came up . . . and said my speech was all the talk. Tom Ellis—who is *genuinely* delighted because one of his own men has succeeded—told me that several members had congratulated Wales upon my speech. Stuart Rendel said I had displayed 'very distinguished powers' . . . There is hardly a London Liberal paper or even provincial paper which does not say something commendatory about it. I send you some of them . . .

Mrs Verney, 'Town and Country Notes', *Caernarvon Herald*, May 2, 1890

It was a striking sight, the closely packed benches, the Chancellor of the Exchequer with many little volumes of notes, bracing himself up for a grand effort; while immediately below the venerable figure of Lord Cottesloe stood the young MP for the Caernarvon Boroughs, nearly seventy years his junior, pale with excitement and the thoughts of the career opening before him, waiting for the last answer to be given before taking his seat.

He had plenty of time to study the scene of his future labours and to weave golden dreams if he chose, for the Boulak Museum, the Portuguese Imbroglio and the Indian Factory Law still blocked the way.

When at last the young Member, with his sensitive face and slight, boyish figure, advanced to the Table, between Mr Stuart Rendel and Mr Arthur Acland, the cheers were loud and hearty; and they had scarcely subsided when Mr Goschen had risen and was congratulating the House upon the state of the national balance-sheet . . .

❖

The arrival of a great Liberal majority

Josiah Wedgewood (1872–1943), Baron Wedgewood, was educated at Clifton College and the Royal Naval College, Greenwich. He became a naval architect, served as an artillery officer in the Boer War and afterwards as a Resident Magistrate in the Transvaal, and became MP for Newcastle-under-Lyme from 1906 to 1942, sitting as a Liberal from 1906 to 1919, as a Labour MP from 1919 to 1931, and as an Independent Labour MP from 1931 to 1942. He had a remarkably diverse record in World War I, serving in

Flanders, at Gallipoli (where he was awarded a DSO), in East Africa and in Siberia, and attaining the rank of colonel. He was Chancellor of the Duchy of Lancaster in the short-lived Labour Government of 1924 and became chairman of the Committee on House of Commons Records in 1929.

Josiah Wedgewood, *Memoirs of a Fighting Life* (1940)

There had never been, since the Great Reform Bill, such an overwhelmingly Liberal House of Commons as that which met in February 1906. Appropriately a dozen of us met on the eve at the house in Great College Street of Macaulay's great-nephew.[36] As midnight approached we filed out, clad in top-hats and morning coats, and guided by Trevelyan past strange gateways and boilers by secret ways into the lobby. As the clock struck the doors were unbolted, and some forty rushed in to secure their seats by depositing their head-dress on the chosen spot.

Now that Austen Chamberlain and Sir Nicholas Grattan Doyle are gone none wear the silk top-hat. It went out in the war. But in those days only Keir Hardie wore a Scotch cap, though George Peabody Gooch, with sublime innocence, represented Beau Brummel's Bath in a bowler, a frock coat and brown boots—or so we said in that gay spring-time. The top-hat was a perfect nuisance. Till prayers it remained on your seat; thereafter it was glued to your head until you lost it. At half-past eleven the search began;—bands of hat-hungry Members prowled around tea-room, lavatories and libraries to find a hat exactly like six hundred others. In the chamber itself, unless you swung off your hat with a flourish on rising to address the House, the Speaker never 'saw' you; and the most splendid peroration was destroyed as you sat on it. I miss, however, the courtly grace wherewith, in older times, any Hon. Member referred to by another in debate acknowledged the compliment by raising his hat.

There sat Joe Chamberlain, hat over eyes, seeking whom he might devour, the vitriol of whose tongue has never since been matched. Two rows behind him was Frederick Edwin Smith, now rising all silky, and with velvet paws, starting that maiden speech which dared to scratch right across the face of the immense majority. The front Opposition bench was nearly empty, with Talbot asleep in the corner; and Sir Gilbert Parker 'climbing, climbing, climbing', ensconced in the front corner seat below the gangway. Dilke was in the opposite seat, alive to his finger-tips—left out by the younger rulers, but knowing more about it than all on our front bench—still, at seventy, walking with that quick, sharp step about the lobbies, or sculling vigorously up the Thames. He led the little group of independent radicals who met daily in the terrace tea-room at 2.15—Joe King, P. W. Wilson, Percy Alden, Chiozza Money, Athelstan Rendel, Ellis Davies, Henry Dalziel sometimes, and myself. We agreed on nothing— (How could Money and I agree?)—save that we loved and respected Dilke, who had been a great man before we were born.

Charles Trevelyan, then Charity Commissioner, sat behind Ministers—a thorn in the flesh of Sir Edward Grey. Three elderlies—'Radical' Pickersgill, 'Profit-sharing' Taylor and 'Chinese' Walton—came almost to blows, competing for the corner seat behind Ministers. In the corner behind the immaculately clothed Gilbert Parker, sat Keir Hardie and his small band of the Labour Representation Committee—George Barnes, best of them, beside him. Back of that, two solid ranks of Irishmen—John Redmond like Jove, John Dillon with leanings towards the radicals but never allowed to stray, the boy orator, Joe Devlin, and Willie Redmond, who knew how to die. I think O'Connor sat in front of Redmond, for Tim Healy was not yet back, and William O'Brien alone was hardly powerful enough to compete for a corner seat with the Labour Representation Committee. Possibly Carson refused to sit on the Opposition front bench, for I seem to remember the two giants Redmond and Carson, heads averted, on either side of the gangway. The Redmonds always sat through all the session immovable. When Carson was away Craig was as mute, whereas Moore would bandy asides with the extremely responsive Irishmen. Redmond, however, never smiled and never partook under any provocation.

On the front Opposition bench below the gangway soon gathered the imitation Fourth Party—Lord Castlereagh, Hemsley & Co. Eddie Winterton then sat as Lord Turnour behind Chamberlain, a boisterous leading juvenile of twenty-four.

❖

C. F. G. Masterman

Charles Frederick Gurney Masterman (1873–1927) was educated at Weymouth and at Christ's College, Cambridge. He was President of the Cambridge Union in 1896 and became a Fellow of Christ's in 1900. A regular contributor of articles to the *Nation*, the *Athenaeum* and the *Daily News*, he published several books of social reportage, including *From the Abyss* and *The Condition of England*. From 1906 to June 1911 he was Liberal MP for West Ham North, and from July 1911 to February 1914 he represented South-West Bethnal Green. During this time he held several ministerial posts: Parliamentary Secretary to the Local Government Board; Under-Secretary of State, Home Department; Financial Secretary to the Treasury; and Chancellor of the Duchy of Lancaster. He stood unsuccessfully for Ipswich in 1914 and lost contests in 1918 and 1922. In December 1923 he won the Rusholme division of Manchester, only to lose it at the 1924 General Election. He was chairman of the National Insurance Commission, and briefly director of the Literature Department of the Ministry of Information in 1918.

'First Impressions', *Daily News*, February 14, 1906

It is not easy to put into words precisely what is this strange sensation that overwhelms a new member when he finds himself in the House of Commons upon the opening day of a new Parliament. One had imagined that it would be so difficult to reach this far, far distant goal, yet here are the doors flung wide open for all who desire to enter. You approach the gates at Palace Yard, inform a policeman that you are the member for a certain division and discover that the constable actually takes your word for it. He at once salutes, directs you to the next constable upon an unaccustomed route, who also salutes, and so you pass from hand to hand to the innermost shrine of constitutional liberty. At this moment I have no single word of documentary evidence that I am a member of the new Parliament, nor has anyone else on either side of the House that he is a member . . . In practice it is the police who decide the matter, and they are chiefly guided by the rather pathetic knowledge that as a rule old faces must not be re-admitted . . .

In the next place it does not seem to be quite the same House of Commons when viewed from the inside. The old figures are conspicuous by their absence. To us who sit behind the Government this is especially noticeable, since we cannot see our leaders, huddled behind their front bench, while the opposite side of the House, with its gaps, is an open landscape. No Balfour, no Chamberlains—for they did not put in an appearance—no Hugh Cecil, no Gibson Bowles, no Lyttelton—all are gone, the old familiar faces. And when the Prime Minister spoke in his usual exquisitely chosen phrases about this ancient assembly and referred to its glorious traditions, one felt instinctively that the characteristic of this Parliament is not that it is old, but that it is new. We have turned a page in the history of the nation . . .

It is interesting to hear the applause of the House of Commons, but believe me, it is far more interesting to be among those who produce that applause. Whatever may have been true of the old House, this present assembly is at this moment a kind of instrument keenly sensitive to the lightest emotion. Here is an audience which in its mood of today ought to produce great oratory. The personal courtesy, the studious respect of man for man, the good humour, and, underlying all, the sense of a splendid opportunity, lend meaning to the simplest and most obvious commonplaces; while the serried ranks of the Labour members have today evoked general attention and much comment, doubtless varied, according to the point of view.

It has been held—in the old trite phrase—that the House of Commons is the best club in London; but I am not quite sure that this is the true way of putting it. Everything is doubtless very comfortable; the doors swing upon noiseless hinges; the view from the library window over the river and away to the bridge, with its roar of distant traffic, is peaceful as the drift of the barges with the tide—all in a grey light. But the charm is not the charm of luxury or of display. I am not partial to the late gothic of the Tudor age. Still less do I admire the imitation of a former architecture by an age which ought to have some new message of its own to deliver. But the least imaginative of persons must admit that upon every detail of the Palace of Westminster and its furniture is stamped the unmistakable seal of supreme authority. To express the truth in a sentence, here is a palace, a real palace, not a municipal building nor a Government office.

Everywhere the eye is greeted by sumptuous panelling and a multiplicity of those rigid lines in which the Tudors delighted. What we are seeing today is Mr Keir Hardie in the environment of Henry VIII—that is the splendid and characteristic contradiction which lends such piquant meaning to the new democracy. Here is an edifice now teeming with popular ideals, yet designed in the style of pure royalism. You cannot sit on a chair without leaning against a portcullis. The moulding on the panels is broken by double rose and *fleur de lys*. The division lobbies are everywhere emblazoned—perhaps appropriately— with the sign manuals of Tyranny, fit emblem of a whip. You expect to meet Queen Elizabeth, and lo! it is John Burns . . .

It is a splendid place for a game of hide and seek. There are secret passages, winding staircases, strange galleries and mysterious corridors. Members set forth to explore the labyrinth and never meet again. At every corner policemen head the unwary off dangerous preserves, like the House of Lords or the Speaker's private residence. One walks for miles through ever varied country, with a surprise at every step, and then one suddenly discovers someone is less experi- enced than oneself, for here is another new member wanting to know where he can hang his coat, and whether all the lockers are taken, and how he is to ballot for the ladies' gallery, and who gives out the handbooks of procedure, and why all the seats in the House are taken.

Then again there are the meetings of the groups, called to discuss points of policy upon which the best of all governments may require a little uninvited assistance. Suddenly one discovers that politicians are not plain black and white, but there are shades and differences of complexion, especially among progressives. We have in fact a complex because living organism, palpitating with conflicting ambitions, opinions and prejudices. A party is the greatest common factor, that, and nothing more. Inside the House conversation is far freer than in the constituencies. It is not a question of pledge and promise, to be carefully and publicly entered into. It is a confidential informal discussion of the best way to arrive at the result we wish, of the forces which help and the forces which hinder, inside the government and outside the government. A new and unaccustomed function commences which suddenly becomes baffling and complicated. To make speeches about the destinies of Empire is doubtless an imposing task. But here the destinies of Empire provide the small-talk of the tea-table. The most stupendous possibilities are mentioned in the same breath as the latest anecdote. We pass rapidly from talking about the price of lunch to talking about the probability of a Kaffir rising—all in excellent good feeling, yet without finding it possible adequately to differentiate the trivial and the vital—which doubtless is the real peril and pitfall of Parliamentary life.

Hilaire Belloc

Hilaire Belloc (1870–1953), the journalist, poet, historical biographer and Roman Catholic polemicist, was born in France, the son of a French barrister and his English wife. The family moved to England during the Franco-Prussian War and Belloc was educated at the Oratory School, Birmingham (which was founded and presided over by John Henry Newman), and at Balliol College, Oxford. He had already gained public attention as a writer when he entered Parliament as the MP for South Salford at the general election of 1906. He was marked down as a maverick from the moment he arrived in the House. He was a Radical in small things and had no enthusiasm for the mainstream reforms advocated by Lloyd George, for whom he conceived a profound dislike. His friends in the House were two Tories, George Wyndham and Henry Cavendish-Bentinck, and the Liberal John Poynder. Belloc quickly became disillusioned with Parliament and in 1910 decided not to stand again. He wrote two satirical novels about British politics: *Mr Clutterbuck's Election* (1908) and *A Change in the Cabinet* (1909).

Letter to Maurice Baring, February 27, 1906

I have made my maiden speech. After it I was sick. This is true and not an exaggeration. My maiden speech lasted eight minutes. It was intensely Radical and would have pleased you. I said that if the Government made any pretence to be liberal it would (a) deport the first batch of Chinese labourers from South Africa in the next three months; (b) fix the rate at which the deportation was to continue (I suggest five thousand a month); and (c) make the whole cost fall upon the mine owners. The *Morning Post*, naturally trying to hurt the Government, said that I alone of the Liberals had shown courage. *The Times* said in a leader that what I had said was 'dangerous rant'. The Liberal papers keep an ominous silence—being cowardly, but I, my dear Maurice, continue to dance in the sunlight and to sing like the gaslight. For instance, even today I leaped up in my seat and asked a question of the Government which gave them the greatest possible annoyance, to wit, whether it was not a fact that Kaffir labour was increasing steadily until the Chinese labour was brought in, and has since then been decreasing. It is a fact.

A fleeting acquaintance

Sir Herbert Watkin Williams-Wynn (1860–1944) was Conservative MP for County Denbigh, in Wales, from May to December 1885. He contested the same seat without success in 1885, 1886 and 1892.

Sir Henry Morris-Jones, *Doctor in the Whips' Room* (1955)

Sir Herbert Watkin Williams-Wynn, seventh baronet, chairman of the committee [for local celebrations for the Jubilee], was a 'character'. He visited me more than once at the House of Commons to discuss the arrangements. Entering the empty Chamber one Friday afternoon, dressed in his thick corduroy breeches and mackintosh, this interesting old country squire—one of the largest landowners in Britain—gazed ruminatively around the benches.

'That is where Labouchere sat in 1885,' he pointed out.

'Were you a Member?' I asked.

'Yes, for a few weeks,' he replied. 'But it came to an end quickly. Catching the four o'clock train from Ruabon after the day's hunt, I arrived in the House while a Division was in progress. I did not know what it was about. I was pushed into the Lobby. The vote defeated Gladstone on the Home Rule Bill, the Government resigned, and I was not elected afterwards.'

Alfred Duff Cooper

Sir Alfred Duff Cooper (1890–1954), 1st Viscount Norwich, was educated at Eton and Oxford, and married Lady Diana Manners, daughter of the Duke of Rutland. Elected to Parliament in 1924 as a Conservative, he later served as Secretary for War (1935–7). He resigned as First Lord of the Admiralty over Munich, then served as Churchill's Minister of Information (1940–2) and later as Ambassador to France (1944–7). Lord Curzon, with whom Cooper had worked at the Foreign Office, congratulated him on his maiden speech, calling it a 'brilliant achievement', while a newly elected Labour MP, E. Rosslyn Mitchell, wrote to him thus: 'You were direct, fluent, a wee bit rhetorical at times, but above all things courageous, for much that you said was at complete variance from the opinions expressed by your friends in earlier speeches . . . Except for breaks for meals, I have sat in the House all the time since Parliament met. Yours is the first speech that has gripped the House. You perhaps didn't notice it, but no one went out, there was no conversation, no moving about.'[37]

Diary, December 10, 1924

All the afternoon I had to hang about in a fever of excitement and uncertainty. I went through the ordeal of standing up to catch the Speaker's eye and saw it hovering over me. I could have spoke in the dinner hour when the House was empty but I was strongly advised not to. Sidney was very kind to me and took me to dine at the St Stephen's Club. When we came back the House was still empty and I finally decided not to speak. The Speaker has practically promised to put me on on Monday next, which in many ways will be a better day for me, as it will be especially devoted to the discussion of Egypt. I am glad now that I didn't speak. I think I can improve what I was going to say.

Letter to his wife Diana, December 15, 1924

All the afternoon I waited anxiously. Trevelyan spoke first, then Austen Chamberlain spoke for an hour and a half. I thought he would never stop. Then Ramsay MacDonald spoke. I had got a good place by then and towards the end of his speech I saw Curzon (Mary's husband, who is now a Whip) nodding at me from behind the Speaker's chair, so I realised that I was probably going to be put on next, and yet I could hardly believe it when I heard my name called. I felt really nervous and a thing happened to me which has never happened before: my mouth became perfectly dry. However, the sound of my own voice encouraged me and I gathered confidence. What was still more encouraging was that as I went on people kept dribbling in instead of dribbling out, as usually happens. It was a wonderfully fortunate moment to get put on, as Ministers and ex-Ministers hadn't left the House. Ramsay was one of the few who left while I was speaking. Lloyd George was there throughout and so was Baldwin. Austen came in after I had been going about five minutes and I heard him say to Baldwin as he sat down, 'I hear he's very good.' H. A. L. Fisher, who spoke after me, congratulated me on 'a really brilliant and successful maiden speech, perfect in form and distinguished by liberality and generosity of spirit and by a width of outlook that the whole House has appreciated'. Arthur Ponsonby spoke next and said it 'was one of the most brilliant maiden speeches he had heard in the House'. Lady Astor, who was sitting near me, said it was the best she had ever heard and asked for your address to telegraph to you. I hope she did. Sidney said he would too. I had a letter of congratulation from the Speaker, which I gather is rather an unusual honour—and also one from Winston and one from Archie Sinclair. All the evening people whom I didn't know were coming up to me and congratulating me, including members of the Labour Party, and finally Philip Sassoon asked me what I was doing for Christmas.

Harold Balfour

Harold Harington Balfour (1897–1988), Baron Balfour of Inchrye, was educated in Dover and at the Royal Naval College, Osborne. He served from 1914 to 1923 in the Army and the RAF and was Conservative MP for the Isle of Thanet division of Kent from May 1929 until his retirement in 1945, whereupon he was made a peer. He thereafter became a businessman, principally in the aviation industry. He was Parliamentary Under-Secretary of State for Air from May 1938 to November 1944 and for the rest of World War II was Minister Resident in West Africa.

Wings over Westminster (1973)

The day before Parliament met after the '29 election, an uncle, who had been a member, took me round the House. In the lobby where members leave their coats and hats an old gentleman with a beard came in at the same time. He looked round, turned to me and said, 'I haven't been here since Gladstone's last Parliament.'

This was true for he had just been returned for an outer London seat.

'Who are you? A new member?'

I replied, 'Yes, sir.'

He asked me my constituency. I told him it was the Isle of Thanet. He grunted. 'Do you want a happy political life?'

'Yes, sir. I always like good advice.'

'Well, my boy, remember two things. If you are a little drunk after dinner follow the white waistcoats and you'll be in the right lobby, and always leave the Chamber when a Liberal speaks.'

Good counsel for in those days in the Harcourt Room it was always evening dress, black tie or tail coat for those dining, while the moral turpitude of the Liberal Party in the months following the '29 Parliament had to be seen and heard to be believed. Their voices might be voices of criticism and protest but their votes were always votes to keep the Labour Government in office. Almost daily we watched the prostitution of political principles in the interest of saving their political skins from defeat at the polls. It was in this Parliament that we watched the discordant Liberals under Herbert Samuel's leadership dig their grave, filled with wreaths of political dishonour. They knew we saw their despicable behaviour. Most of the bunch hated the Tories as much and more than the Labour Party, except for the special hate they reserved for Jowitt, KC, returned as Liberal candidate one day, and, beating the conversion of St Paul, appeared next day on the Government Front Bench as Attorney General. From the back Tory benches we chanted almost daily, 'Portugoose, Portugoose!', unfairly labelling them, as was the Portuguese Expeditionary Force in France who in the 1918 attack allegedly left that section of our front line allotted to them and, seizing the bicycles of a British Cyclist battalion, pedalled westwards away from the war as fast as they could go. It was after this probably false accusation that Haig is said to have issued the order (I cannot claim to have seen it myself), 'The attention of all ranks is drawn to the fact that the Portuguese Expeditionary Force must not be referred to as "the bloody Portugoose" but "Our brave little Portuguese ally" ' . . .

Maiden speeches can be put into two categories. There is the set occasion for the new Member, arranged through the whips. The Speaker will call the embryo, probably immediately after the Front Bench speeches. The House is polite. Compliments are showered in profusion by succeeding speakers. The new member is told how well he has done. Everyone says that they hope to hear him again and often. He feels a satisfied glow of contentment and pride. Alas; this is all forgotten and all too soon. After sixteen years in the House of Commons listening to dozens of maiden speeches I do not think I can remember one except that of Ralph Assheton, now Lord Clitheroe. The set occasion is the first and usual way for the new Member to get rid of his political virginity. The second way is one that Gerard Lymington, now Earl of Portsmouth, and I both followed. It was dinner time: the House was in Committee, and the Chamber was virtually empty, for Baldwin was speaking at a party rally at the Albert Hall. I may have been a little drunk. Gerard and I both got up, first he and then I. We were on some new unemployment regulations. I can remember using the phrase 'the prostitution of the principles of insurance', but nothing much beyond that. In *The Times* Parliamentary Report next day it said, 'the debate was continued by——' and that was all the notice ever taken of our maiden speeches.

William Gallacher

Better known as 'Willy' Gallacher (1881–1965), he was educated at the Elementary School, Paisley, just outside Glasgow. From 1914 to 1918 he was Chairman of the Clyde Workers Committee, and from 1920 onwards he was a leading member of the Communist Party and the Communist International. He sat as the Communist MP for the Western Division of Fife from 1935 to 1950, and was later president of the Communist Party (1956–63).

The Last Memoirs of William Gallacher (1966)

First, with a new Parliament, all members have to line up and take the oath or make an affirmation. I did the latter. Then there's the Chair: every member on entering or leaving the Chamber is expected to bow to the Chair. Some make quite an occasion if it. I often admired the elegant demonstration of Sir Alexander Sinclair; coming in or going out, he was the best of the lot. Somehow I could never quite get myself to bow, not once in all the time I was there. An old member remarked on this one day and asked me why. 'I've a very stiff back,' I replied. 'It won't bend.'

Once in and seated I had to arrange, like the other new members, with the Speaker for a day and a time to make my maiden speech. The day having been settled, I let Harry Pollitt know. The evening before I was to make my speech, he came down to see me, accompanied by John Strachey. This latter gentleman had considerately come down to advise me on how I should prepare and deliver my maiden speech.

For this I thanked him, but said that it was already written out. I went over it with Harry, and at one point I said: 'They will interrupt me here.'

'They won't,' said Strachey, 'they never interrupt a maiden speech.'

The following day, at the appointed time, I 'caught the Speaker's eye' and made my first contribution in the House of Commons. When I got to the part to which I had drawn Harry's attention I got the response I expected, maiden speech or no maiden speech. With emphasis I declared:

'On this side of the House we represent and speak for the workers of the country, the men who toil and sweat . . .' (Hon. Members: 'So do we!') 'All right. We'll see. The leaders of the miners say that mining is the hardest, most dangerous and poorest paid job in the country. Is there anyone who will deny that? The miners are demanding two shillings a day increase on their present miserable wage, and we who speak for the workers support that demand—two shillings a day increase for the miners. We demand it from these benches. Now it is your turn. Speak, you who claim to speak for the workers.'

Not a murmur from them. Dead silence on the other side, while the Labour members laughed and jeered.

Sir Henry 'Chips' Channon

Sir Henry Channon (1897–1958) was the only son of a wealthy Chicago businessman with English roots. 'Chips' was educated at Christ Church, Oxford, and, although primarily homosexual, he married a Guinness by whom he had a son, Paul (who inherited his father's parliamentary seat). 'Chips'—his nickname is thought to stem from the fact that he once shared a bachelor residence with a friend known as 'Fish'—was elected as Conservative MP for Southend in 1935 and held the seat until 1950, thereafter sitting as MP for Southend West until his death in 1958. He was PPS to R. A. Butler when 'Rab' was Parliamentary Under-Secretary of State for Foreign Affairs from 1938 to 1941. His *Diaries*, which were published posthumously in 1967, are an invaluable chronicle of parliamentary life over thirty-three years.

Diary

November 26, 1934. After luncheon at Emerald's to meet the Kents, I drove at breakneck speed to the House of Commons, and hurried into 'The House'—no clerk, no policeman asked me my name. The Chamber was crowded, and I stood up in the gangway. Everyone was nice to me, but I, ever over-intuitive, felt less so than usual; there was a touch of the old boy, and the new frightened freshman. Only I wasn't in the least frightened, and only bored, a bit amused and desperately self-possessed.

November 28. I went to the House of Commons and joined the queue to take my oath, and in a few moments found myself swearing and signing and then shaking hands with the Speaker, who is Honor's cousin. He looks so ordinary in morning clothes; but today, aloof and bewigged, he seemed terrific. I wrote my first note on House of Commons paper to Paul reigning in Yugoslavia, and then left. I have time enough . . . months, perhaps years to be spent in 'The House'.

December 5. I do not really think the House of Commons 'My Cup of Tea', I am too much of an individualist, and also, too self-centred and set in my ways. Enough if I remain a mute, just adequate back-bencher, but frankly most of the problems that so excite 'the Hon. Members' leave me quite cold and indifferent.

December 9. In the House of Commons I was struck by David Margesson's changed attitude; for years he has been my firm friend; but now he seems aloof and pre-occupied. Is he being the big boy . . .? Perhaps it is the House of Commons manner.

I roamed about the House of Commons and I have learned the geography; that is something.

December 10. Most of the day at the House of Commons. Today for the first time I really liked it; boredom passed and a glow of pleasure filtered through me. But I wish I sometimes understood what I was voting for, and what against.

Harold Nicolson

Sir Harold George Nicolson (1886–1968), the son of a diplomat, was educated at Wellington College and Balliol College, Oxford. After a thirty-year career as a diplomat, he devoted his energies to journalism and books. He was elected as National Liberal MP for West Leicester in 1935 and sat until 1945. He married Vita Sackville-West, the writer and gardener, in 1913. The official biographer of George V, he stood again for Parliament at the Croydon North-West by-election in 1948, but failed to get in. His *Diaries*, edited by his son Nigel Nicolson, contain some wonderful evocations of parliamentary experience.

Letter to Vita Sackville-West, December 4, 1935

Yesterday the House was opened at 12 noon. I went down and stood in the lobby. There was a crowd of visitors and the wail echoing from the recesses of the House, 'Speaker! Speaker!' impressed them almost as much as it did me. Then came the mace and everybody bowed low and the Speaker followed. After which the doors were locked and poor old Black Rod tottered across and struck with his staff on the doors. At which they all poured across to the House of Lords and I climbed up to the Members' gallery. It was a poor show and the Lord Chancellor read the speech and then we all went back again. Poor Wakefield had to move the Address and he sat there looking very wretched in an airman's uniform with his white gloves twisting themselves. But when the moment came he spoke very well and modestly and quite captured the affection of the House. Then rose Attlee—such a poor speaker, so precise and school-maidish. And then Baldwin, experienced and sedate. There is something very strange about Stanley Baldwin. At first sight he is a solid English gentleman, but then one observes odd nervous tricks. He has an extraordinarily unpleasant habit of smelling at his notes and licking the edges slightly as if they were the flap of an envelope. He scratches himself continuously. There are russet patches across his head and face. And a strange movement of the head, with half-closed eyes, like some tortoise half-awake smelling the air—blinking, snuffy, neurotic. Thereafter rose Archie Sinclair as Liberal Leader and shortly after that I had to run away.

Diary, December 19, 1935

After questions Sam Hoare comes in with his nose plastered and sits on the third bench below the gangway. He makes his statement in a precise voice. It is excellent. His voice just breaks at the end: 'I trust that my successor will have better luck than myself.' Then Attlee moves the vote of censure, and while he does so Hoare creeps out a broken man. I do not like him but my whole sympathy went out to him. After Attlee, Baldwin makes one of his take-you-into-my-confidence speeches admitting that a mistake has been made. He says the time is past for platitudes and that we now come back to stark realities. Yet he goes on with platitude after platitude, and by the end the House is no wiser than before. Then Archie Sinclair makes a magnificent fighting speech.

The Speaker's Secretary taps me on the shoulder and says that I will be called after Macpherson and Maxton. It is getting near the dinner-hour. I must confess that waiting is torture to me and I am afraid that my knees will knock together when I rise. But eventually Maxton finishes his speech and I find myself on my feet and beginning, 'I crave the indulgence . . .' It all goes well enough and members crowd in from the dining-rooms. Baldwin remains on the front bench and leans forward appreciatively. Very friendly of him. When I sit down there is much applause and Eustace [Percy] comes and says it is the best maiden speech he has ever heard. He is followed by J. H. Thomas who sits down beside me: 'You did fine, Harold, you did fine!' Thereafter many Members cross the House and congratulate me, and one way or another it is rather a sort of demonstration. Duff Cooper is particularly polite. Yet I know that I could have done better if I had been less nervous. The manner was right enough but the matter was too thin. But it is good enough for a start. I then go out and dine.

My speech had lasted sixteen minutes. Austen Chamberlain congratulates me and I get a message from Baldwin and a note from Ramsay MacDonald. The debate ends up with a good speech by Dalton and a poor speech by Neville Chamberlain. We divide and the Government is saved. Drinks afterwards with Bob Boothby, Aneurin Bevan and Seymour Cocks. Then to bed at last. What a day!

Diary, June 15, 1945

To the House at 11. We have prayers, and then just sit chatting till 11.20 when Black Rod knocks on the door. We all crowd into the House of Lords, but the entrance is too narrow to see anything and we stand and chatter outside. We then stroll back to the House. Finally the Speaker returns without the mace. He sits down at the Clerks' table and we file past him and shake hands. I go to the smoking-room where I have a final drink with Jim Thomas and Florence Horsbrugh. I then sadly leave the building. The police are very affectionate. My special friend who calls me taxis bids me a fond farewell: 'Good luck, sir, and by God, you will need all of it in Leicester!' I shake his hand and leave the House, perhaps for ever. How happy I have been there these ten years!

The death of Austen Chamberlain

Sir Joseph Austen Chamberlain (1863–1937), the eldest son of Joseph Chamberlain, was educated at Rugby; at Trinity College, Oxford; at the École des Sciences Politiques, Paris; and at Berlin. He sat for East Worcestershire from 1892 to 1914 and for West Birmingham from 1914 until his death. He was Chancellor of the Exchequer from 1903 to 1906, and later served as Secretary of State for India (1915–17), Leader of the House (1921–2) and Foreign Secretary (1924–9).

Harold Nicolson, Diary, March 17, 1937

Proceedings in the House are delayed by speeches on the death of Austen Chamberlain. The Prime Minister makes an adequate oration but rather spoils it by introducing at the end a somewhat unsuccessful play on the phrase 'Who Goes Home?' Attlee follows with a very nice little speech, and is succeeded by Archie Sinclair who for once is short and to the point. Then old Lloyd George gets up and makes one of the most effective speeches I have ever heard. For whereas the other funeral orations might have been written in *The Times* second article, Lloyd George's speech could only have taken place in the Chamber itself. He reminded us of that famous day on which Austen made his maiden speech and when Gladstone congratulated Joseph Chamberlain on his son. This was the only occasion when Joseph Chamberlain is known to have shown emotion, and it was most effective as told by Lloyd George, since he pointed with his pince-nez at the place in the House where the protagonists of that sentimental drama were sitting at the time. The younger members felt that they had been carried back through Lloyd George to Gladstone away to the battlers of the Reform Bill and the administration of the Duke of Wellington.

Baldwin retires

Harold Nicolson, Diary, May 27, 1937

I arrive at the House just in time to hear Baldwin make his last statement amid loud applause. With characteristic subtlety he does it in the form of an answer to a question on Parliamentary salaries, so that his final words are to give us all £200 a year more. This means a lot to the Labour members and was done with Baldwin's usual consummate taste. No man has ever left in such a blaze of affection.

George Thomas

George Thomas (b. 1909) was brought up a Methodist and educated at University College, Southampton. He worked as a schoolmaster before World War II. He was MP for Cardiff Central from 1945 to 1950 and for Cardiff West from 1950 until he retired in 1983. He became a PPS (to the Minister for Civil Aviation) in 1950 and thereafter served in the Home Office, the Welsh Office and the Commonwealth Office, returning to the Welsh Office as Secretary of State from 1968 to 1970. He was Deputy Speaker and chairman of Ways and Means from 1974 to 1976, and Speaker from 1976 to 1983. He received numerous honorary degrees and, as a bachelor without issue, was created 1st Viscount Tonypandy on his retirement.

Mr Speaker (1985)

I felt eight feet tall when I walked through the great Carriage Gates into Palace Yard, Westminster, for the first time as a newly elected Member of Parliament. I thought of Palmerston and Pitt, of Gladstone and Disraeli, and all the other giants of our parliamentary history. I never lost that deep sense of the privilege of being an MP.

During the war, the Chamber of the House of Commons had been completely destroyed by a bomb, but because the damage was invisible from the road, it was a well-kept secret. The rebuilding and repairs went on for several years, and it was actually in the House of Lords—arranged to look like the Commons—that I took my seat for the first time.

The Chamber was absolutely packed. Members were standing below the Bar, around the Speaker's Chair, and sitting in the aisles. I sat next to Jim Callaghan and a man with a streaming cold, which I was afraid I would catch. He turned out to be Michael Foot. I was a great admirer of his radical father, Isaac, and remarked, 'Your father is a great Methodist—and a teetotaller.' Michael smiled and replied, 'My father is a good man; but I don't share his views.'

During parliamentary sessions, I used to lodge throughout the week at a friendly little Welsh hotel called the Harlingford, near Russell Square. It suited me because it was completely temperance, and other members from the same sort of background stayed there too.

I went to the House of Commons first thing in the morning to collect my mail, and take it to the library. Sometimes I received between thirty and forty letters in one day, and had to write all my replies in longhand as I could not afford a secretary. In those days members had no allowance for expenses, and all office and accommodation bills had to come out of our low salaries. We had no special room to work in, and if the library was full, members had to sit in the corridors. So we did get to know each other well.

I particularly remember the always courteous Anthony Eden, who called me 'Tommy', which I rather liked. Once when we met just outside the library, he said, 'Hello, Tommy. Have you settled down yet?' When I replied, 'This is a wonderful place, Mr Eden, and there are some wonderful people here,' he laughed outright. Then he said, 'You are quite right, Tommy. There are wonderful people here, but there are also some of the other sort. The good thing is that we can choose our friends. You be careful in your choice.'

❖

Bevin's look of death

Ernest Bevin (1881–1951) was the General Secretary of the Transport and General Workers' Union from 1922 to May 1940, when he became Minister of Labour and National Service and a member of Churchill's War Cabinet. He was Labour MP for Central Wandsworth from June 1940 to February 1950 and for East Woolwich from 1950 until his death. He was Foreign Secretary under Attlee from 1945 to 1951, dying during the month after he left office.

(James) Arthur Salter (1881–1975), 1st Baron Salter, was the son of a boat-builder and a Mayor of Oxford. He was educated at the Oxford City High School and at Brasenose College, Oxford. In 1904 he became a civil servant and from 1911 to 1915 worked for the National Health Insurance Commission. He was in charge of Ship Requisitioning during World War I and worked for the secretariat of the League of Nations throughout much of the following decade. In 1934 he was appointed Gladstone Professor of Political Theory and Institutions at Oxford and he was elected a Fellow of All Souls. From 1937 until the abolition of the university Members in 1950 he sat as the Independent Member for Oxford University, and between April 1951 and September 1953 (when he was elevated to the peerage) he sat as Conservative MP for the Ormskirke division of Lancashire. He held various ministerial posts during World War II and also during Churchill's second premiership.

Arthur Salter, *Slave of the Lamp: A Public Servant's Notebook* (1967)

One of the legacies left by Greek medicine of the fifth century BC is Hippocrates' description of the look of death in a man's face when he is so stricken that the end must soon come. This description is still known clinically as *Facies Hippocratica* . . .

. . . I once saw this same look of death in the face—and so at the same moment did Winston Churchill, near whom I was sitting in the House of Commons.

Churchill was then Leader of the Opposition while Ernest Bevin was Foreign Secretary and he introduced a major debate on various aspects of current foreign policy. After he had been speaking for a few minutes his back-benchers began to say, 'Where is the Foreign Secretary?' (It was obviously incumbent on the Foreign Secretary to be present on such an occasion.) Churchill looked across to the Government Bench and repeated the same question himself. Then Ernest Bevin suddenly appeared and walked towards his seat. As Churchill and myself looked at him we each saw the look of death in his face. Churchill paused for a moment in shocked silence. Then he resumed his speech. But he began by saying that, before continuing the argument about certain aspects of current policy, he would like to say how great was the debt which he and his supporters felt that the country owed to Ernest Bevin for what he had done in its service. It was a momentary but moving interlude of a rare kind in an otherwise normal parliamentary debate.

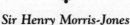

Sir Henry Morris-Jones

Sir (John) Henry Morris-Jones (1884–1972) was educated at Menai Bridge Grammar School and St Mungo's College, Glasgow. He served as a soldier overseas in World War I, then practised as a doctor for twenty years in Colwyn Bay. He was elected as Liberal MP for the Denbigh division of Denbighshire in May 1929, joining the National Liberals in 1931. He served as their Assistant Whip from 1932 to 1937 and as Junior Lord of the Treasury from 1935 to 1937. Knighted in 1937, he sat until his retirement in 1950. He was part of a parliamentary delegation to the Buchenwald Concentration Camp in 1945.

Doctor in the Whips' Room (1955)

My last day as a Member—in February 1950—was the saddest day of my life. In the Dining-Room were several others who were leaving, amongst them Wilson Harris, Vernon Bartlett, Captain Marsden, RN, Sir Frank Sanderson and Sir Stanley Reed. The expression on the faces of some of us at lunch reminded me of Asquith's remark on being told that a gloomy, cadaverous-looking Member had for many years been a Coroner. 'He looks as if he had been sitting on dead bodies.'

My devoted Irish waitress, Mrs Goddard, was in tears. Saying good-bye to Mr Mumford, our perfect Dining-Room supervisor, was hard. The officers of the House, the commissionaires, the wonderful police, the Gallery and Lobby journalists—a friendly, knowledgeable, loyal and trustful fraternity who never divulge a confidence. Emptying my locker—a few treasures; so much that was worthless. Handing in a key; walking under Big Ben, perhaps only to be heard again on the wireless; the traffic held up in Whitehall, for a last shake of the hand. Good-bye.

Earl Winterton

Edward Turnour (1883–1962), Earl Winterton, was educated at Eton and New College, Oxford. He succeeded his father as 6th Earl Winterton in the Peerage of Ireland in 1907. A Tory, he represented Horsham (through modest boundary alterations) from 1904 until 1951, when he retired. He held ministerial office as Under-Secretary of State for India, 1922–4, and as Chancellor of the Duchy of Lancaster, 1937–9. He was briefly in the Cabinet, 1938–9, and throughout World War II he chaired the Intergovernmental Committee. He sat in Churchill's Shadow Cabinet after the 1945 election and was also Father of the House for the last six years of his career in the Commons, thereafter going to the Lords as Baron Turnour.

Orders of the Day (1953)

It was October 4, 1951, the last day of the 1950 Parliament—the day of Prorogation. Normally there is only formal business, and no speeches, when the House prorogues. But on this occasion there were expressions of congratulations to King George VI on his recovery from his illness—a recovery which unhappily proved only temporary. They came from Leaders of Parties and lastly from myself as 'Father of the House'. It thus came about that I made the closing speech of the 1950 Parliament and of my career as an MP at one and the same time—nearly forty-seven years after I had first been elected. I was received as I rose with a long low murmur of sympathetic cheers from all parts of the House, in which both the Prime Minister and Mr Churchill joined; it is a tribute which the House pays to those who have been for a long time familiar figures in it and who are about to retire from it. Afterwards I sat down on the corner-seat on the front Opposition bench which I customarily occupied to await my turn to walk past the Speaker and shake hands with him, as is the custom on the day of Prorogation.

As I sat there, feeling somewhat emotional, alike because of the occasion and the kindness which the House had just shown to one who had been in the past one of its most turbulent members, a flashback was suddenly projected on to the screen of my memory.

I was in the 1900 Parliament again. Mr Speaker Gully was back in the Chair in place of Mr Speaker Clifton Brown; Sir Courtenay Ilbert had taken the Clerk of the House's seat at the Table instead of Sir Frederick Metcalfe. The new, rebuilt Chamber had disappeared, and I was in the old one with its dark varnished oak and its dark green benches instead of the pale grey oak and the pale green benches in the modern House. There was a grille in front of the Ladies' Gallery for the very proper purpose of preventing members from being distracted by female beauty when making their speeches. All the present members of the House had vanished except Mr Churchill and myself, for we two alone had then been members. In their place were a number of men whose features seemed so familiar to me that I forgot they were ghosts and that most of them had died a quarter of a century ago or even earlier. The vast majority of them were in morning or frock coats with high stiff collars and wore top-hats on their heads; but there were some deviations from the normal; two or three of the Irish Nationalists were in lounge suits and without hats, and Mr Keir Hardie was in his well-known tweeds. Mr Arthur Balfour had a turn-down white collar like that worn by Eton boys; Mr Joseph Chamberlain was more orthodox—he had a wing collar and, of course, an orchid in his button-hole and a monocle in his eye. There they were, the men of fame and distinction who then sat on the two front benches—Asquith, Haldane, Austen Chamberlain, Grey, Brodrick, Birrell, Morley, Long, Campbell-Bannerman, Lyttelton. And behind and below the gangway were many others whose names were very familiar to every newspaper reader of the day—Mr Wyndham, Mr John Redmond, Mr Healy, Sir Wilfred Lawson, Mr Gibson Bowles, Sir Charles Dilke, Mr Labouchere and Colonel Mark Lockwood, for example.

I reflected sadly that most of them had long been forgotten, and that mention of them would mean nothing to my colleagues of the 1950 Parliament. But I noticed with pleasure that Mr Churchill was sitting below the gangway; he was a younger and slimmer Mr Churchill than the one on the bench beside me a few seconds earlier, but had not altered in many respects very much. He was pugnaciously cheering a young Welsh member, Mr Lloyd George, who was angrily asking Mr Balfour, the Prime Minister, if he did not think the answer he had just given was an insult to the House. Mr Balfour remained seated with the look of amused indifference which he habitually wore on such an occasion. There were shouts of 'Answer' from the Liberal and Opposition side of the House and 'Sit down' from the Conservatives; and that noise of the past brought me back to the present and to reality: so my daydream ended.

I rose to pass the Chair and shake hands with Mr Speaker whose last day it also was in the House of which he had been so long a popular member. And my chief feeling, as I left the Chamber, was pride in having been a member of this great assembly for nearly half a century and in having seen it survive, with its essence and spirit unimpaired, when freedom of action and discussion had vanished from half the Parliaments of Europe.

The death of Aneurin Bevan

Aneurin Bevan (1897–1960) was born in Tredegar, Wales. He became a miners' agent and was involved in local and county council politics before entering Parliament in 1929, as MP for the Ebbw Vale division of Monmouthshire. He held the seat until his death. He was editor of *Tribune* from 1942 to 1945 and during his tenure as Minister of Health from 1945 to 1951 he pushed through the legislation which established the National Health Service. He was Minister of Labour from January to April 1951, when he resigned in protest at Gaitskell's budget. He was later Shadow Foreign Secretary and Deputy Leader of the Labour Party.

Norman Shrapnel (b. 1912) was educated at King's School Grantham and became a journalist in 1930. He joined the *Manchester Guardian* in 1947 as a reporter and did a brief stint as a theatre critic before being appointed as the paper's Parliamentary Correspondent in 1947, a post which he held until 1975.

Norman Shrapnel, *Guardian*, July 8, 1960

'I regret to have to inform the House,' the Speaker told the Commons when it met yesterday, 'of the death of the Right Honourable Aneurin Bevan, the member for Ebbw Vale.'

It is a frequent sort of announcement, usually applying to some devoted back-bencher of whom the public has scarcely heard. Its very formality, its acknowledgement that all men are equal at this point in their career, its traditional air of bringing the news to us as though for the first time, made it almost the most poignant moment of all this mourning day. The silence was like a groan.

The House was mourning Nye Bevan, but in one sense it was also mourning itself. Something more has died than a great political figure and a well-loved man. An entire Parliamentary era ruled by the golden tongue and the flamboyant personality has now put out its last light.

Bevan's greatest gift to the Commons, as it turned out, was a posthumous one. Fine speaker that he had been, he was now the cause of fine speaking in others. The tributes paid to his memory by Mr Macmillan and Mr Gaitskell, followed by others from Mr Clement Davies and Mr James Griffiths—fellow Welshmen both—added up to a vivid portrait that Bevan himself would have been proud to recognise. One could pay no higher tribute to a tribute than that.

Fine speaking in this context meant emotionally honest speaking, and the Prime Minister set the tone in a frank, affectionate appraisal that moved at least one Labour member to unashamed tears. 'He was a genuine man,' he said. 'There was nothing fake or false about him.'

And here quite naturally to his hand were whole sets of those paradoxes that Mr Macmillan so loves, all embodied in this dead man under whose lash, as he now almost proudly confessed, he had himself smarted. Revolutionary, but a patriot; ebullient, yet deeply serious; a man who moved in a wide circle, yet kept his simplicity; a politician—and this sounded the most paradoxical of all—who never played at politics.

So the Prime Minister went on about his old antagonist of the Back and Front Benches with a lively sadness that struck exactly the right note in mourning such a man. It was in saying that he expressed, in his personality and his career, some of the deepest feelings of humble people throughout the land that Mr Macmillan came to the heart of the matter.

Both he and Mr Gaitskell emphasised a side of Bevan that has not been made much of by the obituary writers. He was a cultivated man. (Lord Alexander of Hillsborough went still further in the Lords and called him, in no derogatory sense, an intellectual.) Nobody denied that he was a difficult man.

Mr Gaitskell, indeed, was outspoken on this theme. A fire had gone out, he said—'a fire which we sometimes found too hot, by which we were sometimes scorched, a fire which flamed and flickered unpredictably, but a fire which warmed us, cheered us, and stimulated us, a fire which affected the atmosphere of our lives here and which illuminated all our proceedings'.

He did not flinch from recalling how very much at odds he and Bevan were for several years after 1951, and how strained were their personal relations— an unhappy period, he called it, followed by a loyal and fruitful partnership.

Another part of his speech that particularly gripped the attention was about their Russian visit last summer. Bevan was in great form, in spite of, as Mr

Gaitskell told us, 'the shadow of his approaching illness'. He was utterly frank with the Russians and laughed at what he called their bourgeois puritanism.

So the last portrait was built up, stroke by stroke. Staunch, gay, courageous, dominant, Mr Gaitskell called him. Upright, downright, forthright, Mr Clement Davies added. In every mining village, Mr Griffiths softly put in, they would be saying to each other, 'Our Nye is gone.'

The tributes over, the House virtually emptied itself as though, just then, it had no heart for routine business. But Sir Winston sat on a little, alone with his memories. The remarkable thing was that so much that had been truly said about Aneurin Bevan will have to be said again, one day, about him.

Macmillan's exit

(Maurice) Harold Macmillan (1894–1986), 1st Earl of Stockton, was educated at Eton and at Balliol College, Oxford. He served in the Grenadier Guards during World War I and was wounded three times. He sat as a Conservative for Stockton-on-Tees from 1924 to 1929, and again from 1931 to 1945 (although he had the Conservative Whip withdrawn from June 1936 to July 1937). He was MP for Bromley from November 1945 until 1963, when he retired. He first became a minister in 1940 and later held Cabinet office as Minister of Defence, Foreign Secretary, and Chancellor of the Exchequer, and as Prime Minister from 1957 to 1963.

Norman Shrapnel, *The Performers: Politics as Theatre* (1978)

. . . The Great Macmillan could still give us one more gaudy night.

It came at 11 o'clock on 26 July 1963 when Macmillan stalked into the crowded house to make a statement. At that time of night, a prime ministerial announcement could hardly fail to be sensational. Nerves were more than usually raw; we were at the end of a bad-tempered day near the close of a gruelling session. The Profumo disaster was five weeks behind. There comes a point in every administration where the parliamentary Opposition senses that the time has come to gather for the kill, and they may be aided by a contagious death-wish on the ruling side. There are times when they strike too early, other times when—perhaps lacking any real stomach for taking the stage them-selves—they delay too long. This time it looked almost as though getting rid of the Government would be a humane act. Never had the time looked riper for a new show, under fresh management.

Yet what happened? Far from shambling off as quietly as a fallen star decently should, here was Supermac making one last triumphal appearance. He was announcing nothing less—nothing more, to be sure, but certainly nothing less—than that very same nuclear test ban promised by Aneurin Bevan four years earlier for when the Socialists should come to power. But the Socialists had not yet come to power, and here was Macmillan providing not promise but performance—achieved, moreover, by international agreement.

So the man they had been calling the Lost Leader was now, for one last night, the Conquering Hero. He loved it, and his cooling supporters loved it, and who could wonder? Conservatives who had long given up any hope of finding themselves with a success on their hands, and who would have been in the mood to applaud any of their leading actors who could manage to keep going for five minutes on end without falling over, were delirious with joy. All the Tories, and some Labour men, too, were on their feet and cheering. They were even fluttering their programmes at him, like flags. A standing ovation, no less. This was the parliamentary accolade, the equivalent of a dozen curtain-calls.

Mac made the most of every heady moment. He walked slowly along the Treasury bench, past his cheering ministerial colleagues—the survivors and successors of his notorious sacrificial orgy not so many months before. Even his victims, one might have thought, no longer held it against him. Then, reaching the Speaker's Chair, he did an unheard of thing. Instead of disappearing from view behind the Chair in the conventional way, he turned and bowed to his ecstatic audience. He bowed again, and the cheers re-echoed.

'This success is deeply moving to us all.' That had been the curtain-line, and evidently it was right. Though eccentric by House of Commons standards, Macmillan's behaviour seemed perfectly normal and even modest in the context he had provided for it. Sir John Martin-Harvey could hardly have done it more gracefully. The applause even continued after he had gone, leaving us wondering, for some incredulous minutes, whether he would actually come back and take another unassuming curtain. But enough was enough: this master of the grandiloquent gesture knew when to stop.

Sydney Silverman

(Samuel) Sydney Silverman (1895–1968) was educated at the Liverpool Institute and at Liverpool University. He became a solicitor in 1921 and spent some years as a lecturer at the National University of Finland before being elected as Labour MP for Nelson and Colne, a seat which he held until his death. He was a member of the National Executive Committee of the Labour Party from 1956 and was chiefly associated with the campaign to abolish capital punishment. He was recognisable from cartoons as an energetic man of diminutive stature who always wore a pointed beard (facial hair being a rarity among MPs during the post-World War II years).

Emrys Hughes (1894–1969) was the son of a priest and married a daughter of Keir Hardie. A teacher and journalist by profession, he sat for the South Ayrshire division of Ayrshire and Bute from February 1946 until his death. He twice had the Labour Whip withdrawn.

Emrys Hughes, *Sydney Silverman: Rebel in Parliament* (1967)

He was obviously a very sick man and had not fully recovered from a stroke which had attacked him some time before. He had been told to take it easy and he sat there in his corner seat unusually silent.

Although Sydney felt that he could no longer take part in a debate he would come into the House, sit in his corner seat below the gangway and listen attentively to what went on . . .

One afternoon during question time, he slumped in his seat and lost consciousness. Tom Swain, the burly miner, picked him up and carried him out as he would have carried a child.

Some thought that this was the last time they would ever see Sydney Silverman. But, no! Just as questions were drawing to a close, twenty minutes later, in walked Sydney. 'Even the ranks of Tuscany could scarce forbear to cheer.'

Tom Swain told me afterwards, 'I carried him out into the lobby and laid him down on a bench, and like an old ambulance man, I looked in his breast pocket for the tablet that I knew would be there. I put it in his mouth and he opened his eyes and asked, "Where am I?" "You are in the lobby," I said, "you collapsed during questions." He seemed dazed for a moment and then got on to his feet and asked, "Are questions still on?" I looked at the clock and said, "Yes, I think so." He then moved towards the lobby. "Where are you going?" I asked. "Back in there," he said. I knew better than to try to argue with him and in he went.'

Although he did not attempt to speak much, he continued to keep a vigilant eye on current events. He was always on the alert when any matter arose in which the death penalty was involved. When a British soldier was condemned to death by the authorities in Aden, he questioned their right to hang the soldier, and when the Speaker ruled that this was not then under the jurisdiction of the British Government he took the extreme step of putting down a motion of censure on the Speaker in order to question his ruling.

But in February he had another stroke and was taken into Hampstead Hospital, where he died on February 9th, 1968.

It was a Friday and on that afternoon a few of us were discussing the political situation in the corner of the House of Commons smoke-room where the rebels had so often met. Someone came in and said, 'Sydney's gone, the news is on the tape.'

There was dead silence. It seemed incredible. I looked up at the indicator which shows the name of the speaker who is addressing the House. It moved to 'House Adjourned'. The proceedings of the day were over.

I looked up at the indicator again on which the familiar name had so often appeared and a feeling of sadness and loss came over me as I realised that we would never see his name there again.

Jack Ashley

Jack Ashley (b. 1922) was educated at Ruskin College, Oxford, and at Caius College, Cambridge. He was President of the Cambridge Union and later became a BBC radio and television producer. He has been Labour MP for Stoke-on-Trent South since 1966 and served as a PPS to Michael Stewart and subsequently to Barbara Castle. A childhood infection had left him with a partial loss of hearing owing to a perforated left eardrum, while the hearing in his other ear had deteriorated badly. After almost a year-and-a-half in the House, an operation to repair the left ear went wrong, leaving him deaf. When he returned to the House he had to start all over again and, despite his personal victory over his disability, he found that some of the magic had vanished for ever.

Journey into Silence (1973)

Returning to the House of Commons without any hearing was a hazardous undertaking. On the last occasion I had clung to a wisp of sound; this time I had nothing to cling to. I was enveloped in a shroud of silence from which there was no escape. My previous attempt to return to the House had ended in disaster and left its mark. Now I was about to try again—with even less confidence . . .

At least this time Members would be aware of my disability. They all knew I was totally deaf and dependent on lip-reading—yet they wanted me to return. But did they fully appreciate the enormity of the problem? Despite their letters of encouragement urging me to return, would they be shocked when confronted with a colleague who required painstaking patience before being able to understand a limping dialogue? Would I be able to establish any semblance of ordinary relationships with my colleagues and officials of the House?

Understanding debates was important, but other occasions, previously taken for granted, would now present major problems. To check a point made in debates I could always read *Hansard*, the Official Report, but there is no report of those informal discussions in corridors and tea-rooms which are as important to political understanding as formal debates. Discussions over a meal would be difficult, partly because of inadequate lip-reading but also because I had to look at my plate to eat and this could cause me to lose the tenuous thread of comprehension. I might become an albatross around the necks of my colleagues, or an odd man out on my own.

As I left for the House, Pauline and I smiled reassurance to each other. We had discussed every detail of the problems, but now I was on my own. I drove through uncannily silent traffic in a subdued mood, as if reserving my energies for what lay ahead; I felt like a spring coiled for action, without any idea what action would be required. As I walked through the Members' entrance I was approached by a policeman with a thick, bushy moustache. Normally no one would be more difficult to lip-read, but he said slowly and clearly, 'Welcome back, sir.' They were the first words spoken to me on my return and, because of his consideration, I understood them.

In the Members' Lobby I was surrounded by friends and well-wishers. I did not pretend to understand all they said and no one launched into a detailed conversation. It was a unique atmosphere compounded of extraordinary warmth, a little bewilderment and the faintest suggestion of embarrassment. Everyone wanted to welcome me yet no one knew how to say it other than in the simplest terms. I dallied for only a few moments before going into the Chamber.

There is no ideal seat for a lip-reader in the House of Commons. Long benches facing each other along the Chamber are divided by a gangway. The front benches above the gangway are for Ministers on one side and Opposition leaders on the other. Those behind them, and below the gangway, including the front bench, are for backbenchers. I thought my best position would be at the far end of our front bench below the gangway; I could then pivot round and see both sides. The redoubtable Bessie Braddock, who had visited me in the Liverpool hospital, always sat there but when I wrote to her about it she assured me there would be no problem.

It was Question Time when I walked in and the front bench was full so I stood undecided at the Bar of the House. Until a Member crosses this line near the end of the Chamber he is technically not in the House and unable, therefore, to take part in the proceedings. The usual fusillade of questions was being fired at Ministers and I was anxious to avoid interrupting by trying to squeeze on to the crowded bench. I was uncomfortably aware that many Members from both sides were beginning to look at me, but the moment Bessie Braddock spotted me she turned to the crowded bench and called, 'Push up.' She gave them a friendly shove as she spoke and as she weighed at least fifteen stone the effect was dramatic. A space was provided where she had been sitting a moment ago. She patted it in welcome and I thankfully slid into it, shielded to some extent by her massive maternal frame from the full gaze of the House.

After a few moments I tried to lip-read. I had not expected to understand much but the reality was a chilling experience. I understood very little of what was said and, to add to my discomfort, I had no idea where to look. By the time I had swivelled round to locate a speaker he would be halfway through his question; a brief one would be finished before I could start to make any sense of it.

This did not seem like the Chamber where I had vigorously interrupted other speakers and impatiently waited my turn to speak. It was transformed into a mysterious, menacing arena where I could be trapped into misunderstanding the arguments and passions which swiftly ebbed and flowed. It would be all too easy to make a fool of myself: somehow I had to make sense out of this silence and as I sat there I reflected on the daunting prospect.

I became conscious for the first time of the shifting patterns of light in the Chamber. The high windows above the Distinguished Strangers' Gallery caught and reflected the slightest change of sunlight on this fitfully cloudy day. As shadows flitted across the faces I was trying to lip-read they made a difficult task nearly impossible. I tried to dispel the thought that it seemed symbolic of the sun setting on my political career.

Soon my spirits drooped and my eyes grew tired; I left the Chamber and went into the tea-room. There, touched by warmth and friendship, I felt my depression lifting, despite the problems. Conversation was not easy but it was not impossible, because colleagues were mainly enquiring about my personal situation and if they had to repeat themselves they were ready to do so. The House of Commons is a remarkable institution; its Members are individually diverse but collectively they act in subtle unity. Crushing to anyone who offends against their canons, they can sometimes lavish affection which is powerful and moving. I was the fortunate recipient of this immense goodwill at a time when I needed it most . . .

Some problems were more easily solved than I anticipated. I had expected to miss important Divisions because of being unable to hear the bell, but this never happened; I could usually detect a surge of movement in any part of the Palace of Westminster. As soon as three or four Members moved briskly in the direction of the Division Lobbies I would check the television prompters and confirm there was a Division. Sometimes colleagues working nearby would see that I was reading or writing and had failed to notice the movement of Members. They invariably let me know, and Conservative Members often smiled as they nudged me to go and vote against them.

Parliamentary questions posed difficulties since failure to lip-read replies would result in asking the wrong supplementary question. I therefore arranged to receive from Ministers a draft of their initial answer, though this still meant I had to lip-read the reply to my supplementary. It was more difficult when I intervened in other Members' questions. If I missed a question or answer I could easily misconstrue the situation or be repetitious, so I occasionally asked colleagues to make a note for me before I intervened, but this created almost as many difficulties as it solved. Question time requires speedy reflexes, as nine or ten Members may jump up the moment a Minister sits down. While I was reading the note of the Minister's reply, my colleagues were on their feet and one would be called by the time I looked up. I had to draw a fine line between glancing at notes and swift lip-reading, with a preference for the latter if I could manage it.

The difficulty of making telephone calls and receiving messages was solved by the perceptive kindness and efficiency of Miss Kay Andrews of the Library staff. She recognised the problem and volunteered to help me because she realised I was reluctant to ask. If she happened to be otherwise engaged, other members of the Library staff or the police would assist me.

No matter how kind people were, the shock of total deafness reverberated daily for many months and shook me every day I entered the House of

Commons. Whenever I walked into the Chamber I was struck by the absolute silence of the greatest debating forum in the land. I had no alternative but to join in as best I could, though my contribution was more limited than in earlier days. I felt at this time that I was only on the periphery of Parliament. I was slowly and hesitantly trying to understand this remarkable state of affairs and come to terms with it.

But one day, out of the blue, I was invited to propose a Ten-Minute-Rule Bill. This is a Parliamentary device which enables a Member to present the case for a change in the law. A Bill is prepared by the Member; supporters who may have campaigned on the subject or shown a special interest add their names, and it is then advocated by the chief sponsor in a ten-minute speech. Although such Bills are rarely enacted, because they lack Government support, they focus Parliamentary and public attention on a particular issue. The Bill offered to me proposed a Commission to examine the problems of disabled people. It was prepared by David Owen, who had just been appointed a Minister; knowing my interest he suggested I should present it. This was just a few weeks after my return and I had not yet spoken in the Chamber.

A traditional ritual has to be followed in the presentation of such a Bill. When the proposer has made his speech, he is asked by the Speaker for the names of the sponsors; he announces these, then he goes to the Bar of the House and bows, walks three paces and bows again. He hands a copy of the Bill to the Speaker, who formally invites him to state when the Bill will next be discussed. The standard reply of 'Tomorrow' indicates an indeterminate date in the future but it is part of the ritual.

I was delighted with the opportunity but there were hazards to be faced. If I missed any of the questions, or made an error of procedure, it would be difficult for anyone to correct me on such a formal occasion. Another problem was my voice. As I was totally deaf to sound of any kind I was unable to hear my own voice and it was sometimes difficult to control the volume. The tendency was to shout—perhaps a subconscious effort to hear what I was saying—and when I did so the modulation and pitch could be adversely affected. But lowering my voice sometimes made it inaudible. When I spoke I did so from memory and the only guidance was the delicate vibration of my throat muscles. At that time this was inadequate and my clearest indication of shouting occurred when people beyond my own circle suddenly looked across . . .

The day I was to present the Bill I arranged to meet a fellow Member, Eric Ogden, in the empty Chamber before the House sat at 2.30 p.m. I explained the problem I might have with my voice. In the Chamber, while Eric sat nearby, within my range of vision, we arranged and practised a series of unostentatious signals. If my voice was satisfactory he would sit still and upright with his hands on his lap. If I spoke too loudly he would raise his hand to his face and rest his chin on it, whereas if my voice was too quiet he would lean forward attentively. No one would notice these natural movements but they would provide important guidance for me. When we had completed and rehearsed these arrangements I waited with mounting anxiety for the summons to speak. Pauline went to the visitors' gallery with Jean and Peter Thorpe, who had done so much to help me learn lip-reading.

The House was full, as is usual at the end of Question Time; Members who are not interested in a particular Ten-Minute-Rule Bill, or who have other engagements, generally leave immediately at 3.30 p.m. This is no mark of disrespect to anyone but simply the way the Commons usually works. But on this occasion, as I rose to speak, nearly everyone remained in their seats, including the Prime Minister and the Leader of the Opposition.

As the minutes ticked by I knew I was winning the House. I told them of the Trafalgar Square demonstration and what it meant to the disabled. The bleak, impersonal word 'disablement' was a synonym for personal and family tragedy, and I tried to explain the need for urgent assistance, pointing out that the disabled had no powerful trade union or pressure group to fight for them. As I moved from specific examples to the national problem and so on to international comparisons, I occasionally glanced at Eric Ogden. Not moving a muscle, he sat like a statue, eyes on me, hands in his lap. The Prime Minister looked up at Pauline in the gallery and smiled his approval at her. Well before the end I knew that the House was with me and I lost my fears. As I sat down I could sense the cheers although I could not hear them; then the Speaker rose to ask for the names of the sponsors of the Bill, which I read aloud before moving to the Bar of the House. From there, I walked in the traditional manner through the Chamber to the Speaker's Chair and on my way I passed the Prime Minister sitting near the Dispatch Box. He touched my arm and I lip-read, 'Well done, Jack.' I was conscious of Pauline watching, and I was delighted that she was sharing this moment.

We went out into the sunshine on the terrace with our friends Jean and Peter Thorpe. As we enjoyed a celebration drink, Members from all parties crowded over, offering congratulations. In the excitement, I found it difficult to lip-read, but it did not matter. I had returned to the House of Commons without any hearing and my first speech in the Chamber had been warmly accepted. It was a significant day and, in its own way, a landmark; to my knowledge it was the first speech by a totally deaf man in any legislature in the world. For me it was also a happy day. I was in the company of those who understood and had helped me to return; I noticed that the Thames no longer looked bleak and cold but seemed to reflect a new sparkle in the air.

In the House of Commons the Speaker's attitude was important; if he had lacked understanding my difficulties would have been greater. Speaker King was a firm and sometimes impatient man who allowed no one to delay Parliamentary business. Fortunately for me he proved to be also a most thoughtful man who took great trouble to ease my way back. I met him for the first time after my return at a formal reception in his palatial apartments. I joined the queue to be received and when I reached him he dropped protocol and substituted for the formal handshake a warm and long embrace. It was the first time I had ever been embraced by a man but I greatly appreciated the gesture. He promised to let me know in advance whether I was to be called in debates, so that I could avoid the eye-strain of sitting watching and waiting from mid-afternoon until late at night. On the occasions when he told me I would not be called I did not know whether to be pleased to have avoided eye-strain or sorry I had prepared a speech in vain.

Some difficult situations were unavoidable. I found the crowded Division Lobby the loneliest place in the Commons. It was always packed with Members but in those early days few came to talk to me. Apart from the inadequacy of my lip-reading, the noise level was high in the Lobby and it was difficult to adjust my voice, which hardly made for relaxed conversation. I usually passed through, trying to look at ease, while moving forward slowly with the drifting crowd. There can be no more demoralising sense of isolation than to be alone in a crowd.

These incidents had a desolating effect in the months after my return to the House; there were others which under normal circumstances I could have brushed aside as of no consequence. The warmth had vanished. I missed it more deeply and more sadly than I cared to show.

1. Baumann's fear was misplaced: he actually sat for a further six years until the general election of 1892. He later grew disillusioned with the House of Commons (see Chapter 2).
2. Justin McCarthy, Letter to Mrs Campbell Praed, February 25, 1906.
3. Sir Edward Clarke, *The Story of My Life* (1918); quoted in Robert Rhodes James, *The British Revolution*, Vol. I: *From Gladstone to Asquith 1880–1914* (1976), p. 253.
4. Hamilton Fyfe, *T. P. O'Connor* (1934), p. 337.
5. Michael MacDonagh, *Daniel O'Connell and the Story of Catholic Emancipation* (1929), pp. 362–3.
6. Queen Victoria, Letter to Benjamin Disraeli, June 5, 1876.
7. W. F. Monypenny and G. E. Buckle, *The Life of Benjamin Disraeli, Earl of Beaconsfield* (1910–12), Vol. II, p. 837.
8. Benjamin Disraeli, Letter to Queen Victoria, August 1, 1877.
9. Quoted in Charles Duke Yonge, *The Life and Administration of Robert Banks, Second Earl of Liverpool, KG* (1868), Vol. I, pp. 17–18.
10. Quoted in Paul Johnson (ed.), *The Oxford Book of British Political Anecdotes* (1986), p. 187.
11. Justin McCarthy, *British Political Portraits* (1903), pp. 79–80.
12. Anthony Wedgwood Benn, Diary, January 1951.
13. Nigel Nicolson, *People and Parliament* (1958), p. 62.
14. Peter Burke, *The Public and Domestic Life of the Rt Hon. Edmund Burke* (1853); quoted in George Henry Jennings, *An Anecdotal History of the British Parliament from the Earliest Periods to the Present Time* (1880), p. 150.
15. Henry W. Lucy, *Strand Magazine*, November 1900.
16. Spencer Leigh Hughes, *Press, Platform and Parliament* (1918), p. 22.
17. Jennings, op. cit., p. 445.
18. ibid., p. 201.
19. Quoted in B. H. Holland, *The Life of Spencer Compton, Eighth Duke of Devonshire, 1833–1908* (1911), Vol. I, pp. 30–1.
20. Sir William Fraser, *Disraeli and his Day* (1891), pp. 450–1.
21. Alexander Stephens, *Memoirs of John Horne Tooke* (1813), pp. 238–9.

22. A. P. Herbert, *Independent Member* (1950), p. 38.
23. Oliver Lyttelton (Viscount Chandos), *The Memoirs of Lord Chandos* (1962), p. 209.
24. John Morley, *The Life of William Ewart Gladstone* (1903), p. 100.
25. Hugh Gaitskell, Diary, August 6, 1945.
26. Rowland Prothero (Lord Ernle), *Whippingham to Westminster: The Reminiscences of Lord Ernle* (1938), p. 264.
27. *Labour Leader*, April 13, 1906.
28. Fraser, op. cit., pp. 396–7.
29. This was a satirical figure. Canning said he would not have wanted to interfere with the French if they had kept their lunacy to themselves and contented themselves with 'dressing up strumpets in oak leaves, and inventing nicknames for the calendar'.
30. Fraser, op. cit., p. 186.
31. The Attorney-General was Sir John Campbell.
32. Justin McCarthy, Introduction to William White, *The Inner Life of the House of Commons* (1897), p. xxii.
33. Thomas Hughes (1823–96) was educated at Rugby (about which he wrote a famous novel, *Tom Brown's School Days*) and at Oriel College, Oxford, and called to the bar in 1848. He sat as a Liberal for Lambeth from July 1865 to December 1868, and for Frome from then until his retirement in 1874. He was made a County Court Judge in 1882.
34. Lloyd George was in London for his Intermediate examination.
35. Puleston was a Welsh aristocrat who had been Tory MP for Devonport since 1874; at the 1892 general election he stood against Lloyd George for the Caernarvon Boroughs seat and was defeated.
36. Sir Charles Philips Trevelyan, Bt. (1870–1958), was a Liberal MP for the Elland division of Yorkshire, 1899–1918; and Labour MP for Newcastle-upon-Tyne Central division from 1922 until 1931, when he was defeated as an Independent Labour candidate.
37. Quoted in Alfred Duff Cooper, *Old Men Forget: The Autobiography of Duff Cooper* (1953), pp. 139–40.

2 The Essence of Parliament

Sir J. Glynne: I have often thought of a comparison for
the House of Commons; it is most like a dunghill, made
up of many heterogeneous particles; after they have
undergone a state of fermentation and corruption, they
naturally produce everything that you can wish—
mushrooms, fruits of the earth etc. But plants raised in
the hot-bed of the House of Commons, whether, once
planted, they can ever be rooted out, there lies the
question.

Sir Henry Cavendish, Journal, February 3, 1763

During the reign of Elizabeth I, shortly after Parliament had been prorogued in 1580,
when there had been much discussion in the House of Commons but little business had
been concluded, the Queen asked the Speaker, Mr Popham: 'Now, Mr Speaker, what
hath passed in the Lower House?' 'If it please your Majesty, seven weeks,' was his dry
answer.[1] Complaints about the time-wasting, frustration and tedium of parliamentary
life have a respectable tradition. 'The tide of talk rolls on,' wrote T. P. O'Connor in one
of his parliamentary sketches.[2] John Buchan compared the House of Commons to that
'impossible form of art' Grand Opera: whenever something happened, the hero 'sings a
long song about nothing in particular'.[3]

Endless talk has a stultifying or, at the very least, an inhibiting effect. Henry Fairlie
commented in the late 1960s that 'politics are primarily concerned with getting things
done. Speech and debate are merely the instruments of action.'[4] The Scottish Labour
MP 'Don Roberto' Cunninghame Graham had little faith in the ability of Parliament
to get anything done. '*Something must be done*. Ill-omened phrase to whisper to a
Parliament—People's Parliament. If it had been, *something must be SAID*, or better still,
left unsaid, then, indeed, there would be probability enough of Parliament attending.
But done! perish the thought; a *fico* for it; done, done, no do's in Parliament.'[5] Other
radicals have warned against the perils of parliamentary life, its lethal combination of
inertia and perquisites. 'Sometimes I remark that I have spent three years in prison and
three years in Parliament,' wrote Fenner Brockway, 'and that I saw character deteriorate
in Parliament more than in prison. It is true. The conditions of Parliamentary existence
are fatal to the average man unless he has compelling interests or activities.'[6] A. P.
Herbert's modest ambition was rather 'to try to get a few small things done than to
vapour vainly about the woes of the world'.[7] But in this he was not typical. The
inclination of MPs to keep talking rather than actually do something was epigrammati-
cally captured by Walter Bagehot: 'If you want to raise a certain cheer in the House of

Commons, make a general panegyric on economy; if you want to invite a sure defeat, propose a particular saving.'[8]

The insufficiency of Parliament in getting things done has been both the cause and effect of the passivity and pliant nature of most MPs. 'You know the nature of that assembly,' wrote Bolingbroke in a letter to Windham; 'they grow, like hounds, fond of the man who shows them game, and by whose loud halloo they are encouraged.'[9] At least Bolingbroke's hounds were following his lead as an orator, whereas MPs followed the lead of Sir Robert Walpole because he was an adept at buying votes with the King's money. It is no wonder that Walpole was able to tell Sir Horace Mann: 'Our unanimity is prodigious. You would as soon hear "No" from an old maid as from the House of Commons.'

The realisation on the part of most MPs that, despite their best efforts, they are lobby-fodder, is naturally a depressing one. 'All that is required of a man, in order to make him an efficient Member of Parliament,' said R. B. Cunninghame Graham, 'is that he has a good pair of legs to enable him to trot in and out of the Division Lobby at the call of the Party Whip.'[10] Lord Rosebery condemned 'the waste of time and character' engendered by the House of Commons: 'You take the best men you can in the nation and you keep them kicking their heels for eight months in the lobbies and smoking rooms, doing nothing but being ready to vote when the division bell rings.'[11] Churchill, in his biography of his father, wrote that the 'earnest man becomes a silent drudge, tramping at intervals through lobbies to record his vote, and wondering why he comes to Westminster at all';[12] and Christopher Hollis suggested 'it would really be simpler and more economical to keep a flock of tame sheep and from time to time drive them through the division lobbies in the appropriate numbers'.[13]

As well as having an essential role (or anti-role), Parliament also has an essential nature as a body of men. Sir James Mackintosh recorded in his journal in 1817: 'F—— said it was delightful to see how completely the currycomb of the House of Commons had taken off all the gilding and lackering that Castlereagh had brought from the Congress.'[14] Sir Henry Morris-Jones wrote in 1955: 'Character tells. I know of no assembly like the House of Commons for quickly sifting the sham from the real.'[15] Nigel Nicolson, writing a couple of years later, observed that it is 'not only the antiquity of Parliament which cuts a man down to size. It is its terrible power to sum up character and detect fraud.'[16] In the same year, Woodrow Wyatt reached a similar judgement: 'Members of the House of Commons individually are fallible in their estimates of each other. Collectively they rarely make a mistake. The combined judgement of the House of Commons on a man's character and abilities contains a high element of accuracy. No assembly can be more forgiving, more charitable, more shrewd, or fairer. It searches out all a man's qualities and weaknesses as they show up in good fortune and in bad, in the interplay of debates, and in the association of many years with his colleagues.'[17]

However, some have felt that the House has a tendency to go too far and to indulge in cruelty. Francis Horner could hardly bear to attend the House following Sir John Moore's retreat at Corunna: 'When I think of the flippant sneers we shall have from Canning, and the cold malignity of Castlereagh, both of whom hated Moore, and intrigued against him. These are the things which often make attendance at the House of Commons painful to me, and have repeatedly sent me home disgusted and saddened.'[18] 'Chips' Channon felt a similar disgust at the way a 'poisonous' House rounded on Neville Chamberlain in 1940.

Along with the capacity for making 'the best man look silly, and the greatest man afraid',[19] the House is given to effusions of immense pathos and sentimentality. Sincerity is much admired and the admiration cuts across party lines. There is a division, according to Oliver Lyttelton, between 'the smart Members whom no one is willing to listen to, and the solid, sincere bores, who will always get a hearing because the House likes sincerity'.[20] The House hates a lecturer, says an imaginary ex-MP in H. G. Wells's *The New Machiavelli*, echoing Sir Thomas Fowell Buxton's observation in 1819 that the House 'loves good sense and joking, and nothing else', while it hates 'that species of eloquence which may be called Philippian'. Self-deprecation finds favour, whereas bombast tends to meet with a frosty reception. Self-immolation is a special virtue, as Margot Asquith once explained: 'There is nothing more popular in the House of Commons than to blame yourself. "I have killed my mother. I will never do it again," is certain to raise a cheer.'[21]

Above all, the House is a changeling, a creature of unpredictable moods and tempers. Consequently, one who has a talent for spotting such changes is said to have 'a great eye for parliamentary weather', a quality that can outweigh many others. T. P. O'Connor referred to the infectious crowd psychology of the House and Oliver Lyttelton wrote that 'it is necessary to grow the antennae which enable you to guess the mood of this changeable and chameleon-like assembly. One day it will take a joke, on another the slightest levity will be greeted with a snarl.'[22] Harold Macmillan described thus the advice he would give a new, young minister:

> You have to sympathise with the House, and like it . . . rather like those Italian lakes, one moment it's calm, the next moment there is suddenly a tremendous storm . . . you have to study it closely . . . usually when the press would say that something big was going to happen, it always petered out . . . you have to know the man who is your questioner . . . like a prep school, there are boys who are popular, whom you must *never* slap down, even if they are asking a silly question, on the other side . . . then there are the unpopular, the tiresome, and the House rather enjoys their being slapped down . . . You must remember that, like a school, on the whole it dislikes the front bench (the masters) . . . often you can turn an enemy into a friend, by some slight recognition.[23]

Another master of the House, at least in his pre-SDP days, was Roy Jenkins. 'I think of it rather as if I were in a bullfight,' he once explained to his Cabinet colleague Tony Crosland: 'I try to feel the House, to play the House, like a matador playing a bull, for if you slip, it's very difficult to get up again.'[24]

Sometimes particular Parliaments have had distinctive characteristics. Compare the Parliament of 1795, which the Whig Member William Lambton thought was 'dwindling into a mere registering office', assuring his correspondent that 'you would be astonished as well as indignant at the perfect apathy of most of our worthy Members to whom I believe the establishment of a *bastille* or the *lettres de cachet* would not be unacceptable'.[25] Or the Parliament of the late 1880s which reminded R. B. Cunninghame Graham 'with all the bald heads, crowded together . . . of a huge ostrich nest; with the only difference that these "eggs" were either empty or addled'.[26] Or the Parliament elected in 1906, dominated by a Liberal majority, as portrayed by C. F. G. Masterman and H. G. Wells; or the Parliament that followed World War I, described by Willie Gallacher as 'profiteers and money-grabbers who would have stolen the coppers from the eyes of a corpse'.[27] During a dinner in 1919 Balfour (who had been away at the Versailles Conference) asked Lloyd George what the new House of Commons was like:

> 'I'll tell you,' said Lloyd George, his eyes sparkling with fun and a smile spreading rapidly over his face. 'I made a speech to them. I addressed myself at first to the Opposition benches in front of me. They were very cold and hostile; I couldn't get a cheer. This, said I to myself, is not the House of Commons; it's the Trades Union Congress. So I turned as one does in such circumstances to the benches behind

me, but neither was that the House of Commons; it was the Associated Chambers of Commerce.[28]

And then there was the Parliament of 1945, dominated by a Labour majority about which a 'good old Tory is said to have said: "Who *are* these people? They look like a lot of damned constituents." '[29]

Parliaments dominated by landslide majorities—as were those of 1906 and 1945—have been subject to hubris. Oliver Lyttelton reflected on this when he arrived in the Chamber a little late in August 1945 to find that the massed ranks of Labour MPs were singing the Red Flag: 'Any party returned with a large majority usually exhibits bad manners: men who have never administered anything bigger than a bazaar find themselves charged with great offices of state. The members of the victorious party usually jeer and interrupt and think they are as permanent as the benches they sit on. The Liberal Party after their victory in 1906 would not give Arthur Balfour a hearing. In 1945, the socialists greeted Winston with derisive cheers and volleys of rather childish interruptions.' Fortunately, it is an essential characteristic of Parliament to counteract this tendency. Not only does parliamentary procedure play its part, but the ancient surroundings, the rituals, the ancestor-worship that so appalled Aneurin Bevan, or 'the churchy smell of the place' as A. P. Herbert put it, all contribute to assert a sense of continuity with what has gone before. Triumphalism is gradually and inexorably humbled. 'The House of Commons soon pricks some of these bladders,' Lyttelton continued. 'Since legislation has to be got through the House on a time-table, back-benchers in a party with a large majority are restrained by the Whips from speaking. Arguments to which they have not an immediate answer begin insidiously to enter their heads. It begins to dawn on them that there may be two sides to most questions. Moreover, so closely knit is the British race that it is impossible to confine more than 600 Britons within the precincts of Westminster without tolerance beginning to spread. Many incongruous friendships are formed and although bitterness and abuse and disorder may come to the surface any day, they certainly do not on most days.'[30]

The same process affects the awkward individual with demagogic tendencies. 'I have never seen a demagogue', said George Canning, 'who did not shrink to his proper dimension after six months of Parliamentary life.'[31] Indeed, Parliament is a leveller. It can discipline the noisome, it can flail the pretentious, it can institutionalise the bore, and it can douse the firebrand. The Red Clydesider MP James Maxton was one such firebrand. Early on, he got himself suspended from the House for calling Tory Members murderers, but soon the House came to love him in spite of his extreme beliefs. Kingsley Martin complained that Maxton had allowed himself to be made into 'a House of Commons character'[32] and thus emasculated. 'He is their raven-haired pirate, a Captain Hook who waves his finger but who everyone knows is really the most lovable of fellows. They treat him as an institution and entertainment. It is a point of honour among them to appreciate Maxton's burning sincerity.' In recent times, the same fate of becoming a House of Commons character has befallen Dennis Skinner, who, like Maxton, has eschewed the society of Tories. Shortly before Maxton died, Winston Churchill wrote him a letter, saying: 'I have been thinking a lot about you lately. I always say of you, "The greatest gentleman in the House of Commons" . . .'[33]—a deadly compliment to Maxton the radical, but a glowing compliment to the essence of Parliament.

During the 1926 General Strike, the restraint of Labour MPs earned the admiration of the young Tory MP Duff Cooper, who noted that 'they have at any rate become during the crisis Parliament men and have behaved in a manner worthy of the traditions of Parliament'.[34] This realisation was anathema to those left-wing Labour Members who were desperately trying to keep their Labour colleagues up to the mark. 'It was an inferiority complex, together with a hankering after the fleshpots of life, which undermined the fighting quality of certain Labour MPs,' wrote Fenner Brockway, ever scornful of Parliament's power to bewitch its inmates. 'To them parliamentary life and its associations became a vested interest.'[35] Those who have succeeded in this forum have invariably been those who have paid tribute to it. 'The House of Commons is a jealous mistress and will not grant success without due attention,' wrote Sir William Fraser in 1891. 'The greatest compliment you can pay to a woman is to give to her your time, and it is the same with our Senate. A man who is always in his place becomes a sort of favourite.'[36] This, of course, is what happened to Maxton.

Sorrowful reflection

The Hon. Roger North (1653–1734) was the sixth son of Sir Dudley North, 4th Lord North. He was a barrister, a member of Middle Temple, and served as MP for Dunwich during James II's Parliament. He was Solicitor-General in turn to the Duke of York (before he became King) and to Queen Mary, and thereafter, from October 1685 to 1688, he was her Attorney-General. He served on twenty parliamentary committees, and in his capacity as chairman of the Committee of Ways and Means, he carried three Bills through to the Upper House. He took no part in the Glorious Revolution, and stood successfully for re-election in 1689, although he was asked to withdraw from the Convention. He thereafter retired from public life, acquired an estate in Norfolk, married a wealthy lady, and wrote several books, including his autobiography and biographies of his brothers (his brother Francis became Chief Justice of the Common Pleas in 1675).

Roger North, *The Autobiography of Roger North* (1887)

The chief occurrence in this time wherein I was concerned was the Parliament. I had the opportunity to be elected for the borough of Dunwich, to serve in the Parliament first summoned by King James after his accession to the Crown . . .

In that Parliament, as much a courtier as I was, I joined with the Church of England, partly to maintain laws and religion established. I voted with those who were against the Court in the article of the dispensing power. But in the matter of money, which was but a trifle—½d. per lb. on tobacco and ¼d. on sugar—I was tooth and nail for the King. And I was altogether against the affronting set of men, who had not much power there, but aimed to overturn the Crown, and had shewed by a series of trouble given to it, they meant nothing less, and that nothing would content them which should leave the Crown power to keep its own or peace among others. In short the Parliament, that is a great majority, was unanimous, and I was cordially with them to defend the Crown and the laws.

I cannot forbear remarking some things that occurred to my observation there. As how apt the gentlemen of England are to be wheedled and deceived. There was a division of the Court party: some were for all the Kings' purposes whatever: others were for the Crown, but the laws also. But our friends and relations out of the country look on us who were of the latter sort to be as bad as the worst, and we had no sort of credit with them. Once a motion was for leave to bring in a Bill which should oblige all foreign churches to use the Liturgy, as the French, Dutch, etc. This aimed to get the King to confirm the Liturgy by Act of Parliament, though it was feared, after all, he would not do it. The arguments were plain, and spoke by Sir Thomas Meers. If you indulge one sort of dissenters, how can you blame the Crown indulging another, as Papists for instance, etc. The mere courtiers, as I may call them, all spoke against it, as H. Savill, the Lord Antrim, etc. They had travelled, and knew the Vaudois, Walloons, etc., all to be good Protestants, and so jargoned the word Protestant that the ears of the country gentlemen were tickled, and they divided with them against us; for which we rallied them sufficiently in our private recesses, when they had nothing but ignorance to extenuate the shame of such a mistake.

And really it appeared strange to me that the most indifferent of the English gentry were perpetually hunting projects to make their estates richer to themselves without regard to others: some to have wool dear, others corn, and the like. One cannot without the very thing imagine the business that was in all their faces. All this came from their clubs, where those of a country and interest usually met and plotted projects for their private interest. I had at the desire of my neighbours the conduct of a Bill about corn, and carried it through, but some suspecting a trick of the city of London, whose friend (or rather retainer) they took me to be, gave me trouble, which the interest soon removed. But I was so angry as almost to resolve not to meddle any more in such matters, but my friends not being spokesmen, set me upon the part as belonging to my trade. And truly it is a most useful education we have that are bred to speak in public, else we could not, as I did, being young, and bashful in nature, as well as not gifted to public oratory, instantly fall to speaking and managing in a public assembly, where is so much noise and confusion as there often will be.

Once upon the Money Bill I was put in the chair of the committee of the whole House. Mr Finch was absent, which made me, though a novice, called to the service. There was much noise and importunity upon the wording of the questions, which I always took as the Court party worded, and then would be the noise of a bear garden on the other side. But I carried it through, and was well backed, and though I did not this with so much art as an old Parliament stager would, yet it pleased the managers for the Court, who loved to see their measures advanced, right or wrong. I was for the Bill, and sided as much as I could with those that promoted it, and had no ear for those that obstructed and puzzled it, which made the Court rally and say I was the best chairman they had, as men will always say of those who serve their turns.

I opposed the Bill against hawkers and pedlars. I perceived it was brought in by men that solicited for corporations, who would have no buying or selling out of their shops, whereas a world of honest dealers in the country go from house to house, especially with their own or neighbours' manufactures, and many buy such things when laid open, as ribbons, gloves, etc., who would not lay out money at all if it must be sent to a market town; so it promoted trade and helped poor people, as well buyers as sellers, with most convenience to each other. I had a great cry upon me from corporation members, but that did not discourage me, but I battled the Bill in every instance, and at the engrossing and last reading I brought in a clause to answer the colours of the Bill (which were that Scotchmen and vagrant thieves went about spying in men's houses), that Justices at sessions might license housekeepers to travel and sell within ten miles; but this would not do, my clause was rejected, reasonable as it was, and the only argument was, this set up a shop of licences; and Mr Finch took my part, and rallied very handsomely on that subject. But I was not wanting to acquaint the lords of my acquaintance, and particularly my brother, of what was coming, who was against it, and the House of Lords threw it out, which much angered my opponents, who ascribed more influence in the matter to me than I was guilty of, though I confess I did all I could within and without the House to prevent them, and was moved in it by pure zeal for poor men, and the benefit of ordinary housekeepers who were to be oppressed by corporations. But on the other side, I found solicitors for the Bill, even members who paid fees at the office for all things, as for a private Bill.

I had often been angered at the insinuations against the lawyers, as if they had no regard to anything but fees. It was usual for members to say, the lawyer speaks for his fee. I have expostulated if they knew a member that did not consider the interest of his own estate, country, or borough, apart from the good of England. That it was so usually, witness the prohibition of Irish cattle, and the many projects even then on foot of like intent. I condemned with them all scent of a fee in parliament, but it was hard to be so reflected upon at random, when nothing appeared of it, by those who visibly promoted their private interests every day. If a lawyer took a fee to present a petition, it was not so bad as to give a vote against the public for the sake of a paltry private advantage to themselves. If the matter be well weighed, it will be found the former is less corruption and breach of trust than the latter. It happened that a gentleman of the long robe presented a petition thus: '—— hath a considerable estate, but it is all settled for children, so is not able to raise money upon his estate for payment of his debts, and desires that a bill may be received to enable him.' 'What!' said some, 'are we here to give away the children's estates to pay the father's foolish debts? No!' and the petition was rejected. I knew the person and his circumstances, but nothing of this attempt, and out of mere respect to him endeavoured to soften the matter, but it would not do. Afterward the gentleman was advised to re-offer his petition, but not by the same hand. He came to me and offered a fee (I guess he had given the other), desiring I would, having appeared for him, present it. I refused his fee, and undertook it with some civil reproof for his offensive manner in coming with a fee. I told the House that the estate was settled upon children by way of contingent remainder, but he had been married many years and had no child, and now it was next to impossible he should have any, and it was the opinion of all friends, as well his wife's as his own, that it was the interest of both, and the family in general, that he had such a power if the House should think fit. I believe the story of the fee had been told, which made his friends give an applause upon the motion, as the use is there, and the leave was given and the Bill passed . . .

I promoted a Bill for the stopping further divisions of the fens. It was found that the dividing the commons depopulated the fens; for a house was kept up for the sake of its right of common, which as soon as an allotment was made of a share to it in severalty was mortgaged, sold, and let fall, being a charge, and the land better manageable without it. In the agitation of this matter some mistakes were strangely supine. Sir Wm. Killigrew had a Bill for the enclosing some fens in Lincolnshire, which had been offered every session since the restoration of the late King Charles II, and being a project had been always rejected, yet constantly brought in, and as an omen of ill luck commonly towards the latter end of the session, so it used jestingly to be said 'the session is not long-lived, for Sir Wm. Killigrew's Bill is come in'. Some members took the Bill to be that, having heard or at least minded only the words 'fen', 'inclose', 'common', etc., and rose up upon it with such fury that we wondered whence the opposition should come, and it cost us some time and attention to find out the mistake, but more pains to correct it. So the Bill was to be heard a second time. Then we ourselves found a danger that some persons might be surprised who had sued decrees for inclosing, but had them not actually signed by the commissioners, whereby the Act referring to decrees of the commissioners might hinder their suing out their decrees. Wherefore a proviso was offered to give a time for so doing. This was taken to be a trick, and opposed with great earnestness, as a manifest surprise intended to be put upon those people. I endeavoured to satisfy them it was not so intended, but the contrary, for their very sakes, and to prevent a surprise which too large a construction of the words of the Act might infer, but I was not so happy to be understood. And offering to be more explained I was taken down to order because I had spoken before in the debate; but Sir Joseph moved I might be heard, which being granted I convinced the House, and the proviso was received. These and many such blundering passages would make one sick of public business there. It must be a warm zeal for the common good that must inspire a good man to act in those walls honestly. So many rubs, affronts, and scratches will meet with him as shall make his heart ache. Nay, it is strange, considering how disorderly Bills pass, that common sense comes out. Everyone offers his conceit for wording clauses, and many without much attention to the connexion, and others as supine to let it pass. But enough of this sorrowful reflection.

The management of the House

Henry Pelham (1695–1754), son of an MP and peer, was educated at Westminster and at Hart Hall, Oxford. He served as a volunteer in the 1715 rebellion and was MP for Seaford from 1717 to 1722; and for Sussex from 1722 until his death. The chief protégé of Sir Robert Walpole, he inherited Walpole's system of managing the Commons by bribing MPs on behalf of the King (he lamented that he had few 'cordials' to dispense, as the Prince of Wales was busy bribing Opposition MPs). As Chancellor of the Exchequer and Prime Minister from 1743 until his death, he was an adept manager of the public finances and was never corrupt himself, dying in comparative poverty.

Sir Nathaniel Wraxall, Bt. (1751–1831) was the son of a Bristol merchant and from 1780 to 1794 sat as MP successively for Hindon, Ludgershall and Wallingford. A follower of Pitt's, he enjoyed an estimation of his own abilities which was not shared by others, and he proved unrelenting though unsuccessful in his importunacy. As one person put it whom he approached for support in his bid for a diplomatic appointment, 'he is as fit for a foreign minister as he is to command the fleet but this he will not see'.[37] However, his *Historical Memoirs* (1815) and *Posthumous Memoirs* (1836) contain vivid and memorable descriptions of political life. Lord St Helens encountered him shortly after the publication of the *Historical Memoirs* had caused a stir and described him as exhibiting a certain air of triumph, 'like a monkey, grinning and chattering over the havoc which he has been committing in a china closet'.[38]

Sir Nathaniel Wraxall, Bt., *Historical Memoirs of My Own Time* (1815)

A friend of mine, a man of high rank and high character, whom I do not name, because, being still alive, I consider myself not at liberty to divulge it, but whose name would at once stamp the veracity and authenticity of whatever he relates, has frequently assured me that about the year 1767 he was personally acquainted with Roberts, who had been Secretary of the Treasury under Mr Pelham, but who was then old, infirm, and near his end. He lies buried in Westminster Abbey, in Poets' Corner, where his epitaph describes him as 'the most faithful secretary of the Right Honourable Henry Pelham'. This gentleman conversing with Roberts upon the events of those times when he held a place under Administration, and particularly on the manner in which the House of Commons was then managed, Roberts avowed, without reserve, that while he remained at the Treasury there were a number of members who regularly received from him their payment or stipend at the end of every session in banknotes. The sums, which varied according to the merits, ability, and attendance of the respective individuals, amounted usually from £500 to £800 per annum. 'This largess I distributed,' added Roberts, 'in the Court of Requests on the day of the prorogation of Parliament. I took my stand there, and as the gentlemen passed me in going to or returning from the House, I conveyed the money in a squeeze of the hand. Whatever person received the Ministerial bounty in this manner thus related, I entered his name in a book, which was preserved in the deepest secrecy, it being never inspected by any human being except the King and Mr Pelham. On the decease of that minister in 1754, his brother, the Duke of Newcastle, Mr Fox, afterwards Lord Holland, and others of the Cabinet who succeeded to power, anxious to obtain an accurate knowledge of the private state of the House of Commons, and particularly to ascertain the names of all the individuals who received money during Mr Pelham's life, applied to me for information. They further demanded of me to surrender the book, in which, as they knew, I was accustomed to enter the above particulars. Conceiving a compliance to be dishonourable, I peremptorily refused to deliver it up, except by the King's express command, and to his Majesty in person. In consequence of my refusal, they acquainted the King with the circumstance, who sent for me to St James's, where I was introduced into the closet, more than one of the above-mentioned Ministers being present. George II ordered me to return him the book in question, with which injunction I immediately complied. At the same time, taking the poker in his hand, he put it into the fire, made it red hot, and then, while we stood round him, he thrust the book into the flames, where it was immediately reduced to ashes. He considered it, in fact, as too confidential a register to be thus transferred over to the new Ministers, and as having become extinct with the Administration of Mr Pelham.'

Good sense and joking, and nothing else

Sir Thomas Fowell Buxton, Bt., Letter to J. H. North, April 19, 1819

A report has reached me that you are likely to get a seat in Parliament. Is there a bit of truth in it? Is there the remotest probability of so joyful an event? Pray do not conceal it from me a moment, for I speak only truth when I say it would materially add to my happiness. I have plenty of acquaintance, but hardly a familiar friend in the House, and this is a very needful thing. I much want some one with whom I can freely communicate, and who would honestly tell me when I am right and when I am in error; and I need not tell you how fully my wishes would be satisfied if we were there together. Perhaps you will like to hear the impression the House makes upon me. I do not wonder that so many distinguished men have failed in it. The speaking required is of a very peculiar kind: the House loves *good sense and joking*, and nothing else; and the object of its utter aversion is that species of eloquence which may be called Philippian. There are not three men from whom a fine simile or sentiment would be tolerated; all attempts of the kind are punished with general laughter. An easy flow of sterling, forcible, plain sense is indispensable; and this, combined with great powers of sarcasm, gives Brougham his station. Canning is an exception to this rule. His reasoning is seldom above mediocrity; but then it is recommended by language so wonderfully happy, by a manner so exquisitely elegant, and by wit so clear, so pungent, and so unpremeditated, that he contrives to beguile the House of its austerity. Tierney has never exerted himself much in my hearing. Wilberforce has more native eloquence than any of them, but he takes no pains, and allows himself to wander from his subject: he holds a very high rank in the estimation of the House.

And now let me tell you a secret; these great creatures turn out, when viewed closely, to be but men, and men with whom you need not fear competition. I again, therefore, say 'Come among us,' and I shall be greatly deceived if you do not hold a foremost place.

My line is distinctly drawn. I care but little about party politics. I vote as I like; sometimes pro, and sometimes con; but I feel the greatest interest on subjects such as the Slave Trade, the condition of the poor, prisons, and Criminal law: to these I devote myself, and should be quite content never to give another vote upon a party question. I am upon the Jail and Criminal law committees, and devote three mornings in the week to one, and three to the other; so I am contented, and feel as little inclination, as ability, to engage in political contentions. My body is strong enough, but any stress upon my mind, just now, deranges me instantly. 'Indolent vacuity of thought' is my only remedy; but it is not a very convenient medicine for one who has such a magnitude of engagements. How fares the law? Is Ireland blessed with abundant litigation, or does poverty deny this, the chief of luxuries?

Never mind discouragements. If you live and labour, you must stand in the front of that society in which you may be placed, be it the Dublin Courts, or St Stephen's. So I have always thought and said, and so I still think and say. I wish you were with us. I know you will be a Tory: you always were one in heart, and your wife will make you still worse: but we will contrive to agree together, for I am not a Whig. I am one of those amphibious nondescripts called Neutrals; but how can I be anything else? I cannot reconcile to myself the doctrine of going with a party right or wrong. I feel with you that my objects would prosper much better if I sat behind the Treasury Bench; but then I must often vote against my convictions; i.e., do wrong that right may come; and I do not feel this to be my duty, even for prisons and Criminal law. Has Wyndham Quin's business made much noise in Ireland? It occupied about a week of our time, and the House were so amused they would do nothing else. Smith's evidence was excellent, and true; for Gould's there are more appropriate phrases. Plunkett made a speech which did not please the House: it was special pleading which they hate.

❖

A mob of lords and gentlemen

William Hazlitt (1778–1830), the essayist, was the son of a Unitarian minister, who took him to America for a couple of years before sending him to college to study for the ministry himself. In 1796 he met Samuel Taylor Coleridge, who encouraged him to become an author of essays, such as *Principles of Human Action* (1805), *Free Thoughts on Public Affairs* (1806) and his *Reply to Malthus* (1807). His first journalistic job, starting in 1812, was as a reporter of parliamentary speeches, at four guineas a week, for the *Morning Chronicle*, the Whig London daily. His opinion of contemporary orators was already low. Parliament, he felt, had degenerated from the 'representative and depositary of the collective sense of the nation' in the seventeenth century into a 'regular debating society' under the Whig supremacy of Walpole. He had already written an essay on *The Eloquence of the British Senate* in 1807, and his experiences in the press gallery led him to contribute two articles on this subject to the *London Magazine* in 1820.

William Hazlitt, 'On the Difference between Writing and Speaking', *London Magazine*, July 1820

It may appear at first sight that here are a number of persons got together, picked out from the whole nation who can speak at all times upon all subjects . . . but the fact is they only repeat the same things over and over on the same subjects . . . Read over the collections of old Debates, twenty, forty, eighty, a hundred years ago; they are the same *mutatis mutandis* as those of yesterday. You wonder to see how little has been added; you grieve that so little has been lost. Even in their own favourite topics, how much are they to seek! They still talk gravely of the Sinking Fund in St Stephen's Chapel, which has been for some time exploded as a juggle by Mr Place of Charing-Cross; and a few of the principles of Adam Smith, which every one else had been acquainted with long since, are just now beginning to dawn on the collective understanding of the two Houses of Parliament. Instead of an exuberance of sumptuous matter, you have the same meagre standing dishes for every day in the year. You must serve an apprenticeship to a want of originality, to a suspension of thought and feeling. You are in a go-cart of prejudices, in a regularly constructed machine of pretexts and precedents. You are not only to wear the livery of other men's thoughts, but there is a House of Commons jargon which must be used for every thing. A man of simplicity and independence of mind cannot easily reconcile himself to all this formality and mummery; yet woe to him that shall attempt to discard it! You can no more move against the stream of custom, than you can make head against a crowd of people; the mob of lords and gentlemen will not let you speak or think but as they do. You are hemmed in, stifled, pinioned, pressed to death,—and if you make one false step, are 'trampled under the hoofs of a swinish multitude'! Talk of mobs! Is there any body of people that has this character in a more consummate degree than the House of Commons? Is there any set of men that determines more by acclamation, and less by deliberation and individual conviction? That is moved more *en masse*, in its aggregate capacity, as brute force and physical number? That judges with more Midas ears, blind and sordid, without discrimination of right and wrong? The greatest test of courage I can conceive, is to speak truth in the House of Commons. I have heard Sir Francis Burdett say things there which I could not enough admire; and which he could not have ventured upon saying, if, besides his honesty, he had not been a man of fortune, of family, of character,—aye, and a very good-looking man into the bargain! Dr Johnson had a wish to try his hand in the House of Commons. An elephant might as well have been introduced there, in all the forms: Sir William Curtis makes a better figure. Either he or the Speaker (Onslow) must have resigned. The orbit of his intellect was not the one in which the intellect of the house moved by ancient privilege. *His* common-places were not *their* common-places.—Even Horne Tooke failed, with all his tact, his self-possession, his ready talent, and his long practice at the hustings. He had weapons of his own, with which he wished to make play, and did not lay his hand upon the established levers for wielding the House of Commons. A succession of dry, sharp-pointed sayings, which come in excellently well in the pauses or quick turns of conversation, do not make a speech. A series of drops is not a stream. Besides he had been in the practice of rallying his guests and tampering with his subject; and this ironical tone did not suit his new situation. He had been used to 'give his own little Senate laws', and when he found the resistance of the great one more than he could manage, he shrunk back from the attempt, disheartened and powerless. It is nothing that a man can talk (the better, the worse it is for him) unless he can talk in trammels; he must be drilled into the regiment; he must not run out of the course! The worst thing a man can do is to set up for a wit there—or rather (I should say) for a humorist—to say odd out-of-the-way things, to ape a character, to play the clown or the wag in the House. This is the very forlorn hope of a parliamentary ambition. They may tolerate it till they know what you are at, but no longer. It may succeed once or twice, but the third time you will be sure to break your neck. They know nothing of you, or your whims, nor have they time to look at a puppet-show. 'They look only at the stop-watch, my Lord!' We have seen a very lively sally of this sort which failed lately. The House of Commons is the last place where a man will draw admiration by making a jest of his own character. But if he has a mind to make a jest of humanity, of liberty, and of common sense and decency, he will succeed well enough.

❖

Preliminary business

Anon. (A Member of the Upper Benches), *The Collective Wisdom: or, Sights and Sketches of the Chapel of St Stephen's* (1824)

You are now all impatience, or rather all expectation for the mighty display, on account of which you squeezed yourself into the house; but such mighty matters come not at once. A petition, the size of a piece of calico or bolt of canvas, is brought up, praying for an abolition of the monopoly of alehouse licences, which after a few words from Mr Brougham in its favour, and Mr Buxton against it, is pushed quietly under the table. To this succeed other prayers for other matters, which meet with similar attention and meet a similar fate. Colonel Davies next, 'seeing a right honourable gentleman opposite, in his place', puts a question about the importation of 'French kid gloves', which he says is a very important matter; and the right honourable gentleman nods without rising. Sir James Graham next brings in a bill for the draining of a mill-pond in Cumberland, which meets with no opposition. A bill to amend an act passed in the session before that, for regulating the solemnisation of marriages, is then moved to be read a second time. It is read as far forth as these words, 'Whereas great inconveniences have in many instances arisen from marriages.' Upon which some very significant looks are exchanged; and Dr Phillimore, after making a speech of three quarters of an hour's length, to which few listen, and which gives the pens and pencils of the reporters a jubilee, moves that the said bill be committed for Monday se'nnight. Mr Hume, then, after stating the number of men, women, and children in the four provinces of Ireland, and placing Leinster in the west, and Connaught in the east,—in the former of which he is set right by Mr Spring Rice, and in the latter by Mr Richard Martin, moves for a return of the number of Hibernians in the parish of St Giles in the Fields, which is opposed by Sir John Newport, and ultimately refused. Mr Baring then puts a question to the Chancellor of the Exchequer, about the sinking fund; and Mr Hobhouse recommends that the King's Mews should be made a library and not a barrack. The honourable Henry Grey Bennet makes an able attack upon the tread-mill, which is defended in a similar style by Mr Holme Sumner. An attack is made by Mr Brougham upon the practice in the Court of Chancery, which Sir John Copley parries. At this stage of business, you hear a pattering above the ceiling which you conclude is occasioned by rats; but the Speaker glances his eye upward in such manner as to inform you that some ladies, as not being permitted to hear the debate in the gallery, have posted themselves over the ventilator. Serjeant Onslow next presents a petition from some Jews, against the usury laws, which is violently opposed by the country gentlemen upon both sides of the house, but ultimately received, read, laid upon the table, and ordered to be printed; the learned Serjeant makes a long speech upon the occasion, which shares the same fate with that of Dr Phillimore. Mr Martin, of Galway, awakens the sympathy and admiration of the 'Collective', by recounting a most piteous tale of the beating of a jack-ass in the Lambeth Road, opposite the Asylum, to which he had fortunately put a stop, by bribing the cudgelling costermonger with a 'fi'penny'; and how he had been glorious at Smithfield, in triumphing over a butcher, who had struck a bullock in the pith to save the beef, and who, by the honourable member's grappling with him, had been himself kicked into the kennel, and had, in his fall, upset a great basket of potatoes, which had been scattered over the place, and picked up by certain emigrants from Connemara, who called out 'Long life and the blessings of a red cow to your honour!' all the time. At this stage of the proceedings, Mr Dennis Browne and the honourable W. Maule, as being the largest men on their respective sides of the House, are so far melted, that they at the same instant take out their handkerchiefs and wipe their faces. The handkerchiefs appear to be India silk, which calls forth a remark against the smuggling of them, from Mr Ellice of Coventry, in which he is supported by Mr Peter Moore. Mr Secretary Peel makes some jokes about the donkey, the costermonger, the butcher, and the bullock; and Mr Canning plays off his wit upon the subject of the handkerchiefs. Mr Alderman Wood presents a petition from Mr Hunt, praying that his roasted corn may be used at the public breakfasts given by the Speaker. The petition is supported by Mr Gooch, upon the score of agricultural relief; but violently opposed by Sir Charles Forbes, as an invasion of the East India Company's charter, and by Mr Rose Ellis, as injurious to West India interests. An animated discussion ensues, which ends in the petition being withdrawn. Eight o'clock approaches; the benches and the side-galleries fill, and the Speaker calls upon Sir James Mackintosh. It is some time ere Sir James makes his appearance; but he comes at last, presents a petition from a place, the name of which you cannot hear, praying for a committee to enquire into the conduct of the law officers of the crown, and for the revision of the criminal code. After a remark or two, the petition lies upon the table.

Lord Byron scorns Parliament

George Gordon Byron (1788–1824), 6th Baron Byron of Rochdale, was the son of a Captain 'Mad Jack' Byron. He was educated at Aberdeen grammar school; privately at Dulwich; at Harrow School (in the same class as Peel); and at Trinity College, Cambridge. He inherited his title on the death of his great-uncle in 1798; took his seat in the Lords in 1809, declaring his independence from party; and gave his maiden speech in favour of the rioting stocking weavers of Nottingham during the second reading of a Bill to apply the death penalty for frame-breaking. 'I spoke very violent sentences with a sort of modest impudence, abused every thing and every body, and put the Lord Chancellor [Lord Eldon] very much out of humour: and if I may believe what I hear, have not lost any character by the experiment.'[39] He soon lost interest in Parliament and embarked on a grand tour, finding fame as a poet in 1812 with *Childe Harold*. He spent much of his subsequent life engaged in womanising and dissipation as well as composing poetry, though he remained committed to the cause of political liberty. He died of marsh fever at Missolonghi while fighting alongside those Greeks who were seeking independence from the Turks.

Lord Byron, Detached thoughts, October 15, 1821–May 18, 1822

I have never heard any one who fulfilled my ideal of an orator. Grattan would have been near it but for his Harlequin delivery. Pitt I never heard. Fox but once, and then he struck me as a debater, which to me seems as different from an orator as an *improvisatore* or a versifier from a poet. Grey is great, but it is not oratory. Canning is sometimes very like one. Windham I did not admire though all the world did—it seemed sad sophistry. Whitbread was the Demosthenes of bad taste and vulgar vehemence, but strong and English. Holland is impressive from sense and sincerity. Lord Lansdowne good, but still a debater only. Grenville I like vastly, if he would prune his speeches down to an hour's delivery. Burdett is sweet and silvery as Belial himself, and I think the greatest in Pandemonium—at least I always heard the country gentlemen and ministerial devilry praise his speeches upstairs, and run down from Bellamy's when he was upon his legs. I heard Bob Milnes make his second speech—it made an impression. I like Ward, studied but keen and sometimes eloquent. Peel, my school and form-fellow (we sat within two of each other), strange to say I have never heard, though I often wished to do so, but from what I remember of him at Harrow, he is or should be among the best of them. Now I do not admire Mr Wilberforce's speaking—it is nothing but a flow of words—'words—words alone'.

I doubt greatly if the English have any eloquence, properly so called, and am inclined to think that the Irish had a great deal, and that the French will have, and have had in Mirabeau. Lord Chatham and Burke are the nearest approach to oratory in England. I don't know what Erskine may have been at the Bar, but in the House I wish him at the Bar once more. Lauderdale is shrill, and Scotch, and acute. Of Brougham, I shall say nothing as I have a personal feeling of dislike to the man. But amongst all these good, bad, and indifferent, I never heard the speech that was not too long for the auditors, and not very intelligible, except here and there. The whole thing is a grand deception, and as tedious and tiresome as may be, to those who must be often present. I heard Sheridan only once, and that briefly, but I liked his voice, his manner, and his wit—he is the only one of them I ever wished to hear at greater length . . .

The impression of Parliament upon me was that its members are not formidable as speakers, but very much so as an audience; because in so numerous a body there may be little eloquence (after all, there were but two thorough orators in all antiquity, and, I suspect, still fewer in modern times), but there must be a leaven of thought and good sense sufficient to make them know *what* is right, though they can't express it nobly.

Horne Tooke and Roscoe both are said to have declared that they left Parliament with a higher opinion of its aggregate integrity and abilities than that with which they entered it. The general amount of both in most Parliaments is probably about the same, as also the number of speakers and their talent. I except orators, of course, because they are things of ages, and not septennial or triennial reunions. Neither House ever struck me with more awe or respect than the same number of Turks in a divan, or of Methodists in a barn, would have done. Whatever diffidence or nervousness I felt (and I felt both in a great degree) arose from the number rather than the quality of the assemblage, and the thought rather of the public without than the persons within, knowing (as all know) that Cicero himself, and probably the Messiah, could never have alter'd the vote of a single Lord of the Bedchamber or Bishop. I thought *our* house dull, but the other animating enough upon great days.

Macaulay is captivated by the House of Commons

Thomas Babington Macaulay (1800–59) was the son of the philanthropist Zachary Macaulay. He was educated at Trinity College, Cambridge, where he became a Fellow upon graduating in 1822. He was called to the bar in 1826 and worked as a civil servant in India for several years. While he is best known for his essays, principally for the *Edinburgh Review*, and his *History of England from the Accession of James II*, he was also Whig MP for Calne (1830–2), Leeds (1832–4), and Edinburgh (1840–7; and again 1852–6). He twice held office, as Secretary at War from 1839 to 1841 and as Paymaster General of the Forces from 1846 to 1848.

William Whewell (1794–1866) was Second Wrangler at Trinity College, Cambridge, in 1816. Although principally a mathematician, he became Professor of Mineralogy and Moral Philosophy in Cambridge and Master of Trinity.

T. B. Macaulay, Letter to William Whewell, February 1831

I am impatient for Praed's début. The House of Commons is a place in which I would not promise success to any man. I have great doubts even about Jeffrey. It is the most peculiar audience in the world. I should say that a man's being a good writer, a good orator at the bar, a good mob-orator, or a good orator in debating clubs, was rather a reason for expecting him to fail than for expecting him to succeed in the House of Commons. A place where Walpole succeeded and Addison failed; where Dundas succeeded and Burke failed; where Peel now succeeds and where Mackintosh fails; where Erskine and Scarlett were dinner-bells; where Lawrence and Jekyll, the two wittiest men, or nearly so, of their time, were thought bores, is surely a very strange place. And yet I feel the whole character of the place growing upon me. I begin to like what others about me like, and to disapprove what they disapprove. Canning used to say that the House, as a body, had better taste than the man of best taste in it, and I am very much inclined to think that Canning was right.

❖

'Stanzas to the Speaker Asleep'

Winthrop Mackworth Praed, *Morning Post*, March 6, 1833

> Sleep, Mr Speaker! it's surely fair,
> If you don't in your bed, that you should in your chair;
> Longer and longer still they grow,
> Tory and Radical, Aye and No;
> Talking by night, and talking by day:
> Sleep, Mr Speaker—sleep, sleep while you may!
>
> Sleep, Mr Speaker! slumber lies
> Light and brief on a Speaker's eyes;
> Fielden or Finn, in a minute or two,

Some disorderly thing will do;
Riot will chase repose away:
Sleep, Mr Speaker—sleep, sleep while you may!

Sleep, Mr Speaker! Cobbett will soon
Move to abolish the sun and the moon;
Hume, no doubt, will be taking the sense
Of the House on a saving of thirteen-pence:
Grattan will growl, or Baldwin bray:
Sleep, Mr Speaker—sleep, sleep while you may!

Sleep, Mr Speaker! dream of the time
When loyalty was not quite a crime;
When Grant was a pupil in Canning's school;
When Palmerston fancied Wood a fool:
Lord! how principles pass away!—
Sleep, Mr Speaker—sleep, sleep while you may!

Sleep, Mr Speaker; sweet to men
Is the sleep that comes but now and then;
Sweet to the sorrowful, sweet to the ill,
Sweet to the children who work in the mill;
You have more need of sleep than they:
Sleep, Mr Speaker—sleep, sleep while you may!

The tactics of the House of Commons

Sir Samuel Egerton Brydges (1762–1837) was educated at Maidstone; at King's College, Canterbury; and at Queen's College, Cambridge. He was called to the bar in 1787, but never practised, preferring to be a literary man and a publisher. He was obsessed with genealogy and particularly with his own futile claim to the Chandos peerage. As MP for Maidstone from 1812 until 1818, when he was defeated, he was essentially a supporter of the Tory Government. He also wrote an autobiographical novel, *Arthur Fitz-Albini* (1798).

Sir Egerton Brydges, *The Autobiography of Sir Egerton Brydges, Bt.* (1834)

But the tactics of the House of Commons depend on party combinations. No one can carry business through by his own sole power, because he cannot get attendances. The greater part of members are too lazy to be present at what they are not forced to wait upon; and this no individual can, merely as an individual, command. He can only be carried on by the tide of faction.

It was often wearisome to hear the dull ill-expressed speeches of unintellectual men, and, on these occasions, I was too apt to get on one of the back seats and go to sleep. The attendance on these occasions, often till four in the morning, required both health and patience, when at the close one had a long walk to the upper part of the town. It is said that many may have good judgements who cannot explain themselves; and it is well known that ministers want a vote rather than a speech.

A conglomeration of noise and confusion

Charles Dickens (1812–70), the novelist, was the son of John Dickens, who was a parliamentary reporter during the 1820s and was later involved on the production side of the *Mirror of Parliament*, a quasi-rival to *Hansard* that was owned by his sister's husband. Charles Dickens learned shorthand as a solicitor's clerk in the Law Courts, and at nineteen he became a parliamentary reporter for the *True Sun*, a new evening paper, in the year of the Great Reform Act. In 1833 he joined the *Mirror of Parliament*. 'He used to relate that he was compelled to lay down his pencil so moved was he by the pathos of the orator's descriptions of a widow seeking her only son among the peasants killed by the military in a tithe riot, and of a young girl shot, on another occasion, while leading her blind grandfather along a country lane.' In 1834 Dickens joined the *Morning Chronicle*, a Whig newspaper, and stayed in the Reporters' Gallery until 1836, when his sketches were collected and he was busy writing *Pickwick Papers*. His fellow parliamentary reporter James Grant said that 'literary abilities of a high order with reporting capacity of a superior kind are seldom found in conjunction' and that they were combined in Dickens 'in a measure which I venture to say they never were before known in any other man since parliamentary reporting was known'.[40]

Charles Dickens, 'The House', *Evening Chronicle*, March 7, 1835

By dint of patience, and some little interest with our friend the constable, we have contrived to make our way to the Lobby, and you can just manage to catch an occasional glimpse of the House, as the door is opened for the admission of Members. It is tolerably full already, and little groups of Members are congregated together here, discussing the interesting topics of the day.

That smart-looking fellow in the black coat with the velvet facings and cuffs, who wears his D'Orsay hat so rakishly, is 'Honest Tom', a metropolitan representative; and the large man in the cloak with the white lining—not the man by the pillar; the other with the light hair hanging over his coat collar behind—is his colleague. The quiet gentlemanly-looking man in the blue surtout, grey trousers, white neckerchief, and gloves, whose closely buttoned coat displays his manly figure and broad chest to great advantage, is a very well-known character. He has fought a great many battles in his time, and conquered like the heroes of old, with no other arms than those the gods gave him. The old hard-featured man who is standing near him is really a good specimen of a class of men, now nearly extinct. He is a county Member, and has been from time whereof the memory of man is not to the contrary. Look at his loose, wide, brown coat, with capacious pockets on each side; the knee-breeches and boots, the immensely long waistcoat, and silver watch-chain dangling below it, the wide-brimmied brown hat, and the white handkerchief tied in a great bow, with straggling ends sticking out beyond his shirt-frill. It is a costume one seldom sees nowadays, and when the few who wear it have died off, it will be quite extinct. He can tell you long stories of Fox, Pitt, Sheridan, and Canning, and how much better the House was managed in those times, when they used to get up at eight or nine o'clock, except on regular field-days, of which everybody was apprised beforehand. He has a great contempt for all young Members of Parliament, and thinks it quite impossible that a man can say anything worth hearing, unless he has sat in the House for fifteen years at least, without saying anything at all. He is of opinion that 'that young Macaulay' was a regular impostor; he allows, that Lord Stanley may do something one of these days, but 'he's too young, sir—too young'. He is an excellent authority on points of precedent, and when he grows talkative, after his wine, will tell you how Sir Somebody Something, when he was whipper-in for the Government, brought four men out of their beds to vote in the majority, three of whom died on their way home again; how the House once divided on the question, that fresh candles be now brought in; how the Speaker was once upon a time left in the chair by accident, at the conclusion of business, and was obliged to sit in the House by himself for three hours, till some Member could be knocked up and brought back again, to move the adjournment; and a great many other anecdotes of a similar description.

There he stands, leaning on his stick; looking at the throng of Exquisites around him with most profound contempt; and conjuring up, before his mind's eye, the scenes he beheld in the old House, in days gone by, when his own feelings were fresher and brighter, and when, as he imagines, wit, talent, and patriotism flourished more brightly too.

You are curious to know who that young man in the rough great-coat is, who has accosted every Member who has entered the House since we have been standing here. He is not a Member; he is only an 'hereditary bondsman', or, in other words, an Irish correspondent of an Irish newspaper, who has just procured his forty-second frank from a Member whom he never saw in his life before. There he goes again—another! Bless the man, he has his hat and pockets full already.

We will try our fortunes at the Strangers' gallery, though the nature of the debate encourages very little hope of success. What on earth are you about? Holding up your order as if it were a talisman at whose command the wicket would fly open? Nonsense. Just preserve the order for an autograph, if it be worth keeping at all, and make your appearance at the door with your thumb and forefinger expressively inserted in your waistcoat-pocket. This tall stout man in black is the door-keeper. 'Any room?' 'Not an inch—two or three dozen gentlemen waiting down-stairs on the chance of somebody's going out.' Pull out your purse—'Are you *quite* sure there's no room?'—'I'll go and look,' replies the door-keeper, with a wistful glance at your purse, 'but I'm afraid there's not.'

He returns, and with real feeling assures you that it is morally impossible to get near the gallery. It is of no use waiting. When you are refused admission into the Strangers' gallery at the House of Commons, under such circumstances, you may return home thoroughly satisfied that the place must be remarkably full indeed.

Retracing our steps through the long passage, descending the stairs, and crossing Palace-yard, we halt at a small temporary doorway adjoining the King's entrance to the House of Lords. The order of the serjeant-at-arms will admit you into the Reporters' gallery, from whence you can obtain a tolerably good view of the House. Take care of the stairs, they are none of the best; through this little wicket—there. As soon as your eyes become a little used to the mist of the place, and the glare of the chandeliers below you, you will see that some unimportant personage on the Ministerial side of the House (to your right hand) is speaking, amidst a hum of voices and confusion which would rival Babel, but for the circumstance of its being all in one language.

The 'hear, hear', which occasioned that laugh, proceeded from our warlike friend with the moustache; he is sitting on the back seat against the wall, behind the Member who is speaking, looking as ferocious and intellectual as usual. Take one look around you, and retire! The body of the House and the side galleries are full of Members; some, with their legs on the back of the opposite seat; some going out, others coming in; all talking, laughing, lounging, coughing, oh-ing, questioning, or groaning; presenting a conglomeration of noise and confusion, to be met with in no other place in existence, not even excepting Smithfield on a market-day, or a cock-pit in its glory.

❖

For the sake of usefulness

Richard Cobden, Letter to George Combe, March 7, 1846

I might add as a motive for leaving Parliament a growing dislike for House of Commons life, and a distaste for mere party political action. But this applies to my present views only in as far as it affects my health and temporary purposes. It is a repugnance which might and ought to be overcome for the sake of usefulness; and there are enough good men in Parliament to sacrifice private convenience for public good, to compensate for the society of the herd who are brought there for inferior objects.

❖

A great debate night

Edward Michael Whitty (1827–60) was born in London, the son of an Irishman, Michael James Whitty, who later founded the *Liverpool Daily Post*. He trained as a reporter in the provinces before writing the 'Parliamentary Summary' for *The Times* from 1846 to 1849, and subsequently wrote a series of parliamentary sketches for the *Leader* covering the session of 1852–3. These were published in collected form as *A Parliamentary Retrospect* (1854), as were his *Political Portraits*. In 1857 he published a novel called *Friends of Bohemia or Phases of London Life* (Whitty was a self-styled Bohemian) and in the same year he went to Belfast to edit a paper called the *Northern Whig*. He returned to London for a brief time before emigrating to Australia, where he died in Melbourne.

E. M. Whitty, 'Hints to New MPs', the *Leader*, September 1852

You have been at Lady Dedlock's party, out Chelsea way. You have danced or played whist, or heard songs, or flirted, or been bored in some other way; and at about eleven you discover that, having undergone sufficient of the horrors of English society, there is to be a division down at 'the House', and you impetuously get away, convincing the hon. Misses Dedlock that you are a martyr to your public duty. You leap into your brougham or your hansom, and drive to the Reform or to the Carlton, to ask what is going on at the bottom of Parliament Street. You meet somebody shirking Mr Hayter or Mr Mackenzie, avoiding the 'whip' over a late cutlet or an early cigar; and they tell you that they left at ten, when that 'solemn ass' So-and-so was on his legs—'his hind ones, of course'—but that 'Dizzy' or Lord John was expected to be 'up' every minute. You hasten out of the club back to your cab. 'To the House.' You whirl along dark Pall Mall, and past deserted Charing Cross, and down empty Whitehall. It is an odd contrast:—the silent streets, and the busy bustling scene, alive with light and life even at midnight, to which you are hurrying, and which you have already pictured on your brain, exciting you as the colours mingle. Mighty London is putting its pulses to rest; but the heart—the Senate— is pumping away the sustaining blood of the nation, in the far corner, on the Thames; and you—is it not strange that the policemen do not bend as you rush by?—are going to lend a hand. The Horse Guards strike twelve as you pass—the strokes reverberating through the still air; and it is an effort of the parliamentary imagination to credit that the Imperial Legislature can be at work, and the Imperial People of the capital—having gone to bed—so utterly indifferent to it. But as your vehicle hastens on by the bridge, you meet a couple of cabs galloping eastward; you see that they are carrying the familiar faces of reporters; and you judge by the mad speed they are going at, there is something 'important' in progress. It is a sign of life, and you are now glad you left Lady Dedlock's in such good time. You turn into Palace Yard, crammed with four-wheelers, and horses, and grooms, and porters; the new House and the old Hall are a blaze of gas; and you are excited, and even begin to wonder how the division will go. You thread the well-lighted but silent hall of Rufus and Hastings, and get into the lobby—empty, but ghastly with excess of glare. Hayter receives you with a wink, or Mackenzie with a grin. You haul down your white vest, and square your tie, and make your curls all taut; lift your hat, slide along the vestibule, and enter the House. As you have gone on, since you alighted from your cab, you have heard, from porter, policemen, messengers, stray members, and the whippers-in, that 'Mr Disraeli is up'; and hints have flown about your ears that he is making a 'great speech'. As you reach the vestibule, you hear swelling cheers; and your fancy, in spite of your experience, if you have any, will insist that there is a fervent orator within, consuming his hearers with burning eloquence, and wielding fierce MPdom with overwhelming power. Your blood tingles through your veins with expectation; and as you push open the green door, your every nerve is throbbing with eagerness.

The House of Commons is before you, and your sensations undergo an instantaneous collapse. Your eye takes in the scene: a full House, listening, but lazily and loungingly; the cheer you have heard having been made up of an aggregate half laugh, half sneer. You see the orator, there at the top. His body is half thrown across the table, one hand resting behind him, flirting with a laced cambric, the other white hand tapping gently a red box. And is he making a great speech? He is talking to Lord John, whose arms are crossed carelessly, whose thin lips are parted with an easy smile, and who seems to think the eloquence rather amusing. Mr Disraeli has a most exquisite voice, and he is using only its gentlest modulations. He is quite colloquial, and his tone is friendly and familiar,—especially when he comes to a bitter innuendo, when he turns his head to the country gentlemen, that they may hear it and laugh— a low, simmering chuckle, that just agitates the surface for a moment only, Lord John and the Whigs and Radicals smiling, too, as though the sarcasm were a good-natured joke. Mr Disraeli is getting near the end of his speech, and is now recapitulating and fastening all the points (not mathematical ones) together, as is his wont; and this is his argumentative style. He approaches the peroration— his forte; and here he raises his head; he throws back his collar; he puts by his cambric; he turns from Lord John and faces the House. He speaks slower; he ceases his affected stammer; he is more serious and more solemn, but still quiet and unpretending. Talking now to the many, and not to one or two, he becomes more oratorical, and he fixes attention. What he is now saying is the manifesto of a party; and not a syllable is lost. He is nearing a meaning, and his articulation is elaborate; and there is a dead silence. But he is still unexcited; dexterously and quietly he eludes the meaning—soars above it, in one or two involuted closing sentences, delivered with a louder voice and with more vehement gestures; and having got the cheer at the right spot, this great orator, concluding, sinks into his seat, as nonchalant as though he had been answering a question about Fahrenheit, and immediately (Mackenzie having told him how the division will be) turns to ask Lord Henry Lennox whether Grisi was in good voice that night! . . .[41]

❖

Bad air and long speeches

Richard Cobden, Letter to a friend, 1857

I don't know whether you feel yourself similarly affected by the air of the House, but after sitting there for two or three hours I find my head useless for any other purpose but aching. I find my brain throbbing, as though it were ready to burst; and the pain returns upon me as soon as I awake in the morning. It seems as if the air were dried and cooked to such an extent as to rob it of its vital properties. My reasoning powers are in abeyance while under the roof of the House, and if the symptoms continue and no remedy be called for by others, likely to effect a change, I shall seriously consider whether I ought to continue to hold a trust which I am rendered physically and mentally incapable of fulfilling . . .

I came away on Tuesday after listening for two hours and a half to Disraeli. I wish there could be some Bessemer's powder invented for shortening the time of speaking in the House. My belief, after a long experience, is that a man may say all that he ought to utter at one 'standing' in an hour, excepting a budget speech or a government explanation, when documents are read. The Sermon on the Mount may be read in twenty minutes; the Lord's Prayer takes one minute to repeat; Franklin and Washington never spoke more than ten minutes at a time.

❖

The House of Commons mare's-nesting

Robert Cecil (1830–1903), 3rd Marquis of Salisbury, was educated at Eton and at Christ Church, Oxford, and was elected a Fellow of All Souls in 1853. He sat as Conservative MP for Stamford from August 1853 (first as Lord Robert Cecil, then as Viscount Cranborne following the death of his elder brother in 1865) until he succeeded his father in 1868. For many years he worked as a journalist, writing unsigned articles, including numerous parliamentary sketches, for the *Quarterly Review* and the *Saturday Review*. He was Secretary of State for India in 1866, but resigned over the 1867 Reform Bill. He was later Secretary of State for Foreign Affairs, 1878–80, and was three times Prime Minister, June 1885–February 1886, June 1886–92 and 1895–1902.

Robert Cecil, 3rd Marquis of Salisbury, *Saturday Review*,
February 14, 1857

Tuesday was a gala day for the House of Commons. On Monday there was nothing but a discussion on the best securities for life and property; and the audience hardly consisted of more than those gentlemen who intended to speak, the Government and Opposition leaders, and Mr Spooner—who, having attended Protestant meetings for half a century, is warranted bore-proof, and sits through every debate. But on Tuesday, there was that green oasis in the desert of legislation—that dainty morsel in the sessional banquet—a personal explanation, which, in Mr Disraeli's hands, was pretty sure to include also a personal attack. The House mustered in force. All the leaders of all the parties were there—Ministers and their backers, warm with 'the lively sense of antici-pated favours'—the Opposition chiefs and those who *were* their backers—the mutinous squires, whose single tie to Mr Disraeli is their hatred of Mr Glad-stone—the 'bench of talents', where Manchester is linked to Oxford in the common dilemma of supporting a Government which they detest, where the wolf lies down with the lamb, and Mr Robert Phillimore sits between Mr Cobden and Mr Milner Gibson—and the troops of Free Lances, who almost form a majority in the House, and whose fickle allegiance is the nightmare of the whips.

The galleries, too, were full. There was Lord Derby, evidently not without a sense of the ridiculous position into which his colleague's excessive taste for startling dramatic situations had led him. There was Lord Eglintoun, with that unruffled serenity which, under the most adverse circumstances, never deserts him, and which Prince Talleyrand himself might have envied. There was Lord Stanhope, with a full sense of the historic import of the conjuncture, but with a strong tendency to go to sleep. And there was that now well-known statesman, the Marquis of Bath, in a pair of pink gloves. All were in rapt attention, such as has scarcely been seen since the last Layard-bait. But, unhappily, Mr Disraeli has of late years discovered a narcotic for the most resolute attention. His novels first opened to him a path to fame; but that he was ever a novelist is the most unfortunate thing for his career as a politician. Judging, we presume, from his opponents, he thinks it absolutely necessary to his character as a statesman to be generally dull; and his efforts in this direction have been so portentously successful that he is considered almost as great a bore as the Chancellor of the Exchequer himself. On the present occasion, he was not wanting to this sinister reputation. He began with a weary rigmarole, touching his success in some debate which took place eight years ago. He proceeded to recite the object of his charges against the Government, then the motive which dictated them, then the nature of them, then the nature of the Government rejoinder, and then the terms in which it had been couched—and all this with an iteration and a reiteration which could only have been excused in a village schoolmaster lecturing a form of ploughboys. After the narcotic had been applied for about half an hour it began to tell. The members of note put on that look of helpless wretchedness which men generally wear at a charity dinner. The *profanum vulgus* began to talk, and some to murmur, and some even to call out, 'Question.' The lines of care deepened on Lord Derby's brow, Lord Stanhope was fast asleep, Lord Eglintoun still looked imperturbably polite, and Lord Bath as intellectual as usual. The House was reduced to the amusement of laughing at the solitary sonorous cheers with which the single voice of Mr Bowyer continued to encourage the censor of our Italian policy. At last, the weary preamble was over, and the actual 'explanation' commenced. The sole fact which Mr Disraeli added to his former statement was a contradiction of it. On the first night of the session, he had alleged that the Secret Treaty had been executed during the Ministry of Lord Palmerston. He now gave the date— Dec. 22, 1854—before Lord Palmerston's Government was formed. Besides this addition, his explanation was a barren reiteration of his previous allegations, without any sort of proof, beyond a challenge to print all the correspondence in the archives of Downing-street, during December, 1854.

Whoever duped Mr Disraeli into believing this fable was, in addition to the moral qualifications evinced by the exploit, a very blundering artist. If he had selected any date later than 1854, Mr Disraeli might have relinquished the discussion, pitting his own assertion against that of the Prime Minister, and, on the strength of the traditional mendacity of Governments, leaving a film of doubt over the real solution of the contradiction. But, by placing his myth in the days of the Aberdeen Government, he enabled Lord Palmerston to appeal to his 'right honourable friends' who sat by him then, but love him not now, and who, by their eloquent silence, endorsed the assertions of the Premier. Lord Palmerston's refutation seemed overwhelming. There had been a convention, which, after all, he said, was never signed, and which was limited entirely to a promise on the part of France to abstain from offensive operations against Lombardy, in case Austria should withdraw her troops from Italy to aid the allies in the Crimea. His speech was, like all his speeches, short enough to be effective. He sat down in triumph; and Major Reed stood up to slay the Income-tax. The apparition scattered the pleasure-loving legislators like chaff before the wind. In two minutes, the House was reduced to that knot of all-enduring *habitués* to whom is practically left the business of the nation.

But the drama was not over yet—perhaps it is not over now. On Thursday, the House was gayer still. It began by enjoying a quarter of an hour's laugh at the strange gesticulations of a post-prandial artist—kept by the Government apparently for the low comedy parts—and at the comical comments which he gave to his Birmingham buffoonery. As soon as he had retired to more fitting obscurity behind the Speaker's chair, Lord Palmerston came forward, and bluntly announced that the 'military convention' *had* been signed. What, on the first night of the session, was dismissed parenthetically as 'communications', on Tuesday became an unsigned convention, on Thursday a signed convention. Lord Palmerston's drawn face, hurried manner, and loss of temper, showed how keenly he felt the disadvantage of the retraction. His adversaries felt it too, for they received him with a perfect roar of ironical cheering. The disadvantage was, however, more apparent than real; for the marrow of Mr Disraeli's original charge lay in the existence of a permanent guarantee, not in the nature of the instrument by which it was conveyed. But the Opposition, by apparent exultation, gave the best colour they could to their assumed triumph. Some sharp sparring followed, echoed by savage cheers and counter cheers. Mutual interruptions, flat contradictions, interjected with scant courtesy of tone or manner, showed that both leaders were smarting under the discredit of their respective blunders. But the Speaker, who has no taste for these disrespectable scenes, put a stop to the fray at the first available opening, by hastily calling on Mr Napier, whose name stood first on the paper; and that amiable man, whose deafness enables him to go on with unflagging spirit, no matter how loud his auditors may talk, at once plunged into an elaborate disquisition on the English law, which speedily sent the excited multitude to their dinners.

An intellectual Paradise

Sir William Augustus Fraser, Bt. (1826–98), was educated at Eton and Christ Church, Oxford, and served as a captain in the Life Guards. He sat as the Tory MP for Barnstaple in 1852 and 1857, for Ludlow in 1863, and for Kidderminster from 1874 to 1880. He was one of Disraeli's greatest fans, as is borne out by his published collection of anecdotes about the Tory leader and the period of his prominence.

Sir William Fraser, *Disraeli and his Day* (1891)

On entering those doors you felt the exhilaration of success: but far deeper was the intoxication which soon affected everyone possessing a sensitive organisation, and an appreciative brain. To find oneself day after day breathing an atmosphere of good sense; to hear each important topic of the day freshly discussed by the first minds in the country; to listen to those, whose fame was world-wide; to meet daily in the charming companionship of Intelligence, and Patriotism; to feel sure that ultimate success was certain, should you deserve it, within those walls.

It was the same delicious sensation as breathing air containing an increased proportion of oxygen; such as we enjoy on the mountains of Switzerland.

Every power of the mind was stimulated: thoughts that would lie dormant elsewhere here came to the surface; and, at that time, one felt that the House of Commons was an intellectual Paradise.

Some advice for aspirants

Sir William Fraser, *Disraeli and his Day* (1891)

As regards the House of Commons, I may say a word to those who have an ambition to excel there. I should advise an aspirant, if he can, to act upon the following suggestions; Never, under any circumstances, to speak on a subject with which he is not thoroughly acquainted. To be content to see the points, which he has carefully prepared, taken, one after another, by previous speakers; and should they all be exhausted, to sit still. Not to attempt to learn a speech by heart, but, on a great occasion, when he wishes to earn distinction, to write out what he intends to say, each day for five consecutive days; in each case destroying, and not copying, nor learning by heart, the previous draught. On rising, to pause, if he can, for ten seconds: he will find this a very long time: to begin in rather a low voice; and very slowly; not an easy task. Not to look at any one: should he do so, an imaginary change of countenance may check the current of his ideas completely. He will fancy ridicule and contempt in the face of one who is, very possibly, not listening to him: for in the House of Commons you may hear for an hour without listening. To give the House the impression that his rising is nothing extraordinary: that it is a matter of course. Not to attempt to address the House when it is impatient; just before a Division, etc. Not to be bullied by the 'Whips' into shortening his speech because they want to get into Committee: and, if he can persuade himself to do it, to sit down immediately on making a good point. To have fifty good words prepared, with which he can finish up at any time. Not, if it can be avoided, to speak soon after a meal; to eat plain food, and not too much, at two or three o'clock p.m., if he intends to address the House that evening. Never to be tempted, under any circumstances, to stimulate his intellect, nor to nerve himself, by wine nor spirits. To acquire fluency, it is good practice to take up a French book, or newspaper, and read it out in English. If it be natural to you to gesticulate, it is wise to do so: I do not think that the gestures which are taught do a man any good. A pointed quotation enhances a speech: search Dryden's 'Absalom and Achitophel': 'Hudibras': Canning's 'New Morality': and Young's 'Night Thoughts'. Finally, make the Rules of the House your constant study.

Justin McCarthy (1830–1912) was born in Cork and became a journalist for the provincial press in the early 1850s. He later wrote numerous books of popular history as well as several novels (including three political novels in collaboration with Mrs Campbell-Praed). He was a Nationalist MP for Longford County, 1879–85; for North Longford, 1885–6; for Londonderry, 1886–92; and for Longford North, 1892–1900. When Parnell was deposed as Leader of the Irish Nationalist Party in 1890, McCarthy succeeded him (although some members of the party formed a breakaway group).

Justin McCarthy, *Reminiscences* (1899)

I remember that in one of my earliest speeches in the House of Commons I ventured to give point to some lesson which I was endeavouring to impress upon the House by a line or two quoted from the second part of *Faust*. Let not the reader think too badly of my audacity and my literary display; I did not quote the words in the language of Goethe, but only gave their meaning in an extemporaneous rendering of my own. Next day I received a letter of playful remonstrance and rebuke from Lord Houghton. He warned me in his own humorous way that if I really meant to get on in the House of Commons, or even to stand well with it, I positively must not endeavour to get the House to accompany me on excursions into the second part of *Faust*. With the first part he cheerfully admitted something might possibly be done: most Members had seen Gounod's Opera, and might therefore put up with a passing allusion to something in the drama; but to expect men to endure any citation from the second part was to ask too much of average respectability. Lord Houghton set off his good advice with so many happy and humorous turns of expression that I felt quite proud of having received such a letter; and I need hardly say that I never again intruded on the House of Commons even the slightest reference to the second part of *Faust*.

Never be absent

Sir William Fraser, *Disraeli and his Day* (1891)

I always found that the way to enjoy the House of Commons was never to be absent. I never knew two hours pass there without something amusing or interesting: if you were away, and missed your attendance for a day or two, or even for a few hours, something would be sure to happen at which you particularly wished to be present. I am told that the House of Commons has become very dull: I can only say that my experience of it was exactly the contrary: whether it was that the ludicrous, which mixes in every human affair, was strongly contrasted with the outward solemnity of the proceedings or not, I do not know: but a more diverting and amusing place I never was in.

Mr Gladstone's estimation

W. E. Gladstone, Speech at a dinner of the Institution of Civil Engineers,
April 6, 1878

I may speak of the House as a school of discipline for those who enter it. In my opinion it is a school of extraordinary power and efficacy, and I am qualified to say so from having sat there, I believe, longer, as a man actively engaged in a political career and in official life, than any one who has sat within those walls, with the single exception of Lord Palmerston. It is a great and noble school for the creation of all the qualities of force, suppleness, and versatility of intellect. And it is also, permit me to say, a great moral school. It is a school of temper; for if in Parliament any one unhappily goes astray in a point of temper, rely upon it he will not be five minutes older before he has found out his mistake. (Laughter.) If any of you are so unfortunate as to know a member of the House of Commons who has taken a leading part in its business whose temper is not good, depend upon it if he had not been in the House of Commons it would have been a great deal worse. (Laughter.) It is also a school of patience. A man who is disposed to learn patience there will find plenty of opportunities when, having been smitten on one cheek, he may turn the other cheek to the smiter if he is so disposed. It is a school of honour; for it is a place in which many small, mean, shabby advantages may be taken from the circumstances of the moment, though, perhaps, to be afterwards regretted. And it is a school of justice; for no one can be engaged in the constant exercise of political controversy without being exposed to the constant temptation to abate somewhat of the sanctifying integrity and homage which is due from us all to truth, and, with more or less wilfulness, more or less unconsciousness, to deviate from justice in stating his own argument and in dealing with that of his opponent. The House of Commons has stood hitherto at a very high level, and I trust the level will be maintained. I speak not now of its power, which I look upon as placed beyond all question, dispute, or doubt. Its power never can be brought, except by its own faith, into a situation of peril or uncertainty.

A variety of men

Joseph Chamberlain (c. 1888)[42]

I have never known the House of Commons without a funny man. Then there is the House of Commons bore—of course, there is more than one, but there is always one *par excellence*; he is generally a man who is very clever, a man of encyclopaedic information which he has been unable to digest himself and which, therefore, he is always ready to impart to everybody else. Then you have the weighty man, and the gravity of the weighty man of the House of Commons is a thing to which there is no parallel in the world. You have the foolish man, you have the man with one idea, you have the independent man, you have the man who is a little cracked.

Good humour

T. P. O'Connor, *Memoirs of an Old Parliamentarian* (1929)

There is no mistake more generally made, especially by foreigners, with regard to the general demeanour of the House of Commons than to think of it as an always sober, staid, and reticent assembly. It could better be compared to the sea on an uncertain day, quiet and sunny at one moment, the very next vociferous and stormy; for in the House good-humour constantly lies in the wake of the fiercest passions. I have ventured to compare it to a boarding-school of boys, when it did not resemble even more a boarding-school of girls.

It is a wonderful demonstration of crowd psychology; its emotions rush from breast to breast with lightning rapidity; a small joke, which in private would scarcely raise a smile, leads to a hurricane of laughter. The great masters of the House of Commons are those who realise this mutability and this infectiousness of crowd psychology, and know how to play, as Gladstone could do so consummately, on its varying moods, from grave to gay, from passion to good nature. To all Parliamentarians who are striving to make their way, I would give the counsel never to forget that the House has a lighter and essentially good-humoured side.

❖

A funny place

George Granville Leveson-Gower (1858–1951) was the son of a former MP. He was educated at Eton and at Balliol College, Oxford, and was Assistant Private Secretary to Gladstone during his 1880–5 administration. He was a Home Ruler and sat as a Liberal MP for Staffordshire North-West from November 1885 to June 1886, when he was defeated, and for Stoke-upon-Trent from March 1890 until he was again defeated in 1895. He was European Editor of the *North American Review* from 1899 to 1908 and a Commissioner of Woods and Forests from 1908 to 1924, thereafter serving as the chairman of two local London railway companies.

George Leveson-Gower, Letter to a friend, February 23, 1886

The House is a funny place, rather like a grown-up school; with plenty of jokes and fun under the upper current of serious business. Many of the new Members seem possessed with an earnestness and a dullness which is quite appalling but we must hope that the former, if not the latter, will wear off in time . . . We are not so busy tonight as it is not a Government night, but as a rule we all squash about the Lobby to prevent sleepy or hungry men going home to bed or to dinner. It is like the demons who get no rest themselves but make up for it by letting no one else get any.

❖

The life of the House

Justin McCarthy, Letter to Mrs Campbell Praed, April 10, 1890

I am going up to London tomorrow, chiefly for a dinner-party, come down again on Saturday and go back on Monday for good—or ill. Then the life of the House sets in again. I am glad of it. I yearn for it, with its vividness, its rush, its crowds, its passion and its storm—yes, even its long lapses of dullness—all—all combine to make one feel what a small unimportant creature he is, unless in so far as he is part of a great moving whole. We shall have some important debates—and it will be like living.

It's Heart-break House for the young MP

Arthur Anthony Baumann (1856–1936) was born in Glasgow and educated at Wellington College and at Balliol College, Oxford. He was called to the bar in 1880 and practised at the parliamentary bar until 1895, when he went into the City. Entering the House at the age of twenty-nine, he was Conservative MP for the Peckham division of Camberwell from 1885 until 1892. He later edited the *Saturday Review*, 1919–21; and wrote articles for the *Evening Standard* under the by-line 'A. A. B'.

A. A. Baumann, *Evening Standard*, April 15, 1931

The Whips disliked me, and somehow contrived that I always missed the Speaker's eye. I prepared an elaborate and excellent speech—much better than those that were delivered—against the Home Rule Bill of 1886, and went down night after night with my sheaf of notes. Weeks passed, and my carefully pinned bundle of notes began to wear thin and greasy.

After my thirteenth unsuccessful attempt I threw them in the fire and, like Sir William Jowitt, consoled myself with tobacco.

In the next Parliament things were a little better, not much. The Speaker had learnt my name, and I was called once or twice in the dinner hour. I observed that the sparse occupants of the front benches took advantage of my rising to indulge in the luxury of good stories, old Harcourt being particularly offensive with his loud Rabelaisian anecdotes. As for the other stragglers scattered about the green benches, I discovered that they were only there to shoot up when I sat down, and I could hear them counting and cursing the strokes of Big Ben.

When one addresses a public meeting you know that everybody, whether 300 or 1000, wants to hear you, otherwise they would not be there. What can be more heart-breaking than to speak to an audience of whom the majority are eagerly waiting for you to sit down? These are the annoyances and discouragements inseparable from initiation into parliamentary life . . .

If the young man is clever enough to realise that he will never get office, then, unless he has some clear mission, such as to legalise gambling or to abolish the female police, he had better reconcile himself to paying periodically the heavy entrance fee to the worst club in London, where bad air is only compensated by the inexhaustible amusement of watching the rise and fall of individuals.

. . . being very fresh, I asked for my marching orders from the Conservative Central Office. I was given a triple legend to inscribe on my banner, 'No central municipality for London, no free schools, no loans from British taxpayers to Irish tenants.'

Alas, and alack a day! Before the end of that Parliament in '92 I had voted for

1. An Act to establish the London County Council.

2. An Act to abolish the school pence.

3. An Act to raise a large loan to help Irish tenants to buy their farms.

These are the experiences which sour the milk of enthusiasm and turn it into cynicism.

❖

A sense of manliness and fair play

John Redmond, Lecture in New York, November 29, 1896

The House of Commons throughout its long and chequered history has most of the time been a true reflex of the mind of the British nation, and its attitude at different periods towards different men and towards events has been the attitude which the nation at large has eventually assumed. During even my short time I have seen it change again and again in its way of regarding and feeling towards certain men and certain events, and I have seen the British nation invariably follow, or at least keep up with, its varying phases . . .

In the main the House of Commons is, I believe, actuated by a sense of manliness and fair play. Of course, I am not speaking of it as a governing body, in that character it has been towards Ireland always ignorant and always unfair; I am treating it simply as an assembly of men, and I say of it, it is a body where sooner or later every man finds his proper level, where mediocrity and insincerity will never permanently succeed, and where ability and honesty of purpose will never permanently fail.

❖

The 'full-dress debate'

Sir Richard Temple, Bt. (1826–1902), was educated at Rugby and at Haileybury College and entered the Bengal Civil Service in 1847. He ascended to the positions of Prime Minister of India, 1868–73; Lieutenant-Governor of Bengal, 1874–7; and Governor of Bombay, 1877–80. He sat as a Conservative MP for the Evesham division of Worcestershire, his native county, from 1885 to 1892; and for the Kingston-upon-Thames division of Surrey from 1892 until 1895, when he retired. He was created a baronet in 1876. Throughout his parliamentary career he kept a private journal of an average of four pages for each day in the form of letters addressed to his wife; he also wrote character sketches of many MPs and in 1912 his son published a selection from both sources. He wore a peculiar beard with moustachios and was regarded as one of the ugliest Members of the House.

Sir Richard Temple, Bt., *The Story of My Life* (1896)

I was laid up by illness when Mr Gladstone introduced his Home Rule Bill for Ireland. After Easter I listened to the debate on the Second Reading of the Bill, the grandest discussion that occurred in the present generation. I then gathered the meaning of a 'full-dress debate', which was a set performance for each evening arranged between the opposite Parties. There was oratorical cannonading, musketry, sharpshooting in nearly a fixed order, according to the rules of the 'Kriegspiel'. The evening began by a cannon of first-rate calibre being let off, reply being made by a cannon of equal weight. Then musketry rattled till near the dinner hour. Thereon sharpshooting would play till about ten o'clock. Then guns of heavier sound would fire again, till the night's performance was wound up by fresh cannons going off and answering shot for shot. The arguments were soon worked out by this riddling process, but still the roar of artillery went on; so I wondered what all this was for. I soon perceived that many lesser Members indulged in this wild shooting for the satisfaction of their constituents. The people at large outside did indeed complain of there being an excess of speaking in Parliament. But then the constituencies, if taken one by one, were but too often apt to insist on their Members speaking inside the House. Naturally the consequence was the very excess complained of. Happily my constituents, in their wisdom, refrained from putting any pressure upon me in this respect. So I sat still during the six weeks of this debate. I listened to the mighty performance much as the audience does in the theatre.

'What am I doing here?'

Herbert George Wells (1866–1946) came from humble origins in Kent. He was a draper's apprentice before teaching science and turning to literature, writing both science fiction novels and social comedies. *The New Machiavelli* falls into the latter category, and its protagonist is among the landslide Liberal majority elected in 1906.

H. G. Wells, *The New Machiavelli* (1911)

I found the next few weeks very unsatisfactory and distressing. I don't clearly remember what it was I had expected; I suppose the fuss and strain of the General Election had built up a feeling that my return would in some way put power into my hands, and instead I found myself a mere undistinguished unit in a vast but rather vague majority. There were moments when I felt very distinctly that a majority could be too big a crowd altogether. I had all my work still before me, I had achieved nothing as yet but opportunity, and a very crowded opportunity it was at that. Every one about me was chatting Parliament and appointments; one breathed distracting and irritating speculations as to what would be done and who would be asked to do it. I was chiefly impressed by what was unlikely to be done and by the absence of any general plan of legislation to hold us all together. I found the talk about Parliamentary procedure and etiquette particularly trying. We dined with the elder Cramptons one evening, and old Sir Edward was lengthily sage about what the House liked, what it didn't like, what made a good impression and what a bad one. 'A man shouldn't speak more than twice in his first session, and not at first on too contentious a topic,' said Sir Edward.

'No.'

'Very much depends on manner. The House hates a lecturer. There's a sort of airy earnestness—'

He waved his cigar to eke out his words.

'Little peculiarities of costume count for a great deal. I could name one man who spent three years living down a pair of spatterdashers. On the other hand— a thing like that—if it catches the eye of the *Punch* man, for example, may be your making.'

He went off into a lengthy speculation of why the House had come to like an originally unpopular Irishman named Biggar . . .

The opening of Parliament gave me some peculiar moods. I began to feel more and more like a branded sheep. We were sworn in in batches, dozens and scores of fresh young men, trying not to look too fresh under the inspection of policemen and messengers, all of us carrying new silk hats and wearing magisterial coats. It is one of my vivid memories from this period, the sudden outbreak of silk hats in the smoking-room of the National Liberal Club. At first I thought there must be a funeral. Familiar faces that one had grown to know under soft felt hats, under bowlers, under liberal-minded wide brims, and above artistic ties and tweed jackets, suddenly met one, staring with the stern gaze of self-consciousness, from under silk hats of incredible glossiness. There was a disposition to wear the hat too far forward, I thought, for a good Parliamentary style.

There was much play with the hats all through; a tremendous competition to get in first and put hats on coveted seats. A memory hangs about me of the House in the early afternoon, an inhumane desolation inhabited almost entirely by silk hats. The current use of cards to secure seats came later. There were yards and yards of empty green benches with hats and hats and hats distributed along them, resolute-looking top hats, lax top hats with a kind of shadowy grin under them, sensible top hats brim upward, and one scandalous incontinent that had rolled from a back Opposition bench right to the middle of the floor. A headless hat is surely the most soulless thing in the world, far worse even than a skull . . .

At last, in a leisurely muddled manner we got to the Address; and I found myself packed in a dense elbowing crowd to the right of the Speaker's chair; while the attenuated Opposition, nearly leaderless after the massacre, tilted its brim to its nose and sprawled at its ease amidst its empty benches.

There was a tremendous hullaboo about something, and I craned to see over the shoulder of the man in front. 'Order, order, order!'

'What's it about?' I asked.

The man in front of me was clearly no better informed, and then I gathered from a slightly contemptuous Scotchman beside me that it was Chris Robinson who had walked between the honourable member in possession of the house and the Speaker. I caught a glimpse of him blushingly whispering about his misadventure to a colleague. He was just that same little figure I had once assisted to entertain at Cambridge, but grey-haired now, and still it seemed with the same knitted muffler he had discarded for a reckless half-hour while he talked to us in Hatherleigh's rooms.

It dawned upon me that I wasn't particularly wanted in the House, and that I should get all I needed of the opening speeches next day from *The Times*.

I made my way out, and was presently walking rather aimlessly through the outer lobby.

I caught myself regarding the shadow that spread itself out before me, multiplied itself in blue tints of various intensity, shuffled itself like a pack of cards under the many lights, the square shoulders, the silk hat, already worn with a parliamentary tilt backward; I found I was surveying this statesmanlike outline with a weak approval. 'A member!' I felt the little cluster of people that were scattered about the lobby must be saying.

'Good God!' I said in hot reaction, 'what am I doing here?'

It was one of those moments, infinitely trivial in themselves, that yet are cardinal in a man's life. It came to me with extreme vividness that it wasn't so much that I had got hold of something as that something had got hold of me. I distinctly recall the rebound of my mind. Whatever happened in this Parliament, I at least would attempt something. 'By God!' I said, 'I won't be overwhelmed. I am here to do something, and do something I will!'

But I felt that for the moment I could not remain in the House.

Addressing the House of Commons is like no other public speaking in the world. Its semi-colloquial methods give it an air of being easy, but its shifting audience, the comings and goings and hesitations of members behind the chair—not mere audience units, but men who matter—the desolate emptiness that spreads itself round the man who fails to interest, the little, compact, disciplined crowd in the strangers' gallery, the light, elusive, flickering movements high up behind the grille, the wigged, attentive, weary Speaker, the table and the mace and the chapel-like Gothic background with its sombre shadows, conspire together, produce a confused, uncertain feeling in me, as though I was walking upon a pavement full of trapdoors and patches of uncovered morass. A misplaced, well-meant 'Hear, Hear!' is apt to be extraordinarily disconcerting, and under no other circumstances have I had to speak with quite the same sideways twist that the arrangement of the House imposes. One does not recognise one's own voice threading out into the stirring brown. Unless I was excited or speaking to the mind of some particular person in the House, I was apt to lose my feeling of an auditor. I had no sense of whither my sentences were going, such as one has with a public meeting well under one's eye. And to lose one's sense of an auditor is for a man of my temperament to lose one's sense of the immediate, and to become prolix and vague with qualifications.

The frustration of waiting

C. F. G. Masterman, 'Still Waiting', *Daily News*, March 1906

Still expecting. That, in a word, is the attitude of the new House of Commons. We have enjoyed a month of prologue. There is some impatience for the curtain to rise upon the actual progress of the play.

It has all been talk up till the present. A few supplementary estimates and a Navy vote represent the actual work accomplished. Otherwise we have formed the audience of a large debating society. The debates are continued in a heated, oppressive atmosphere for eight hours every day. There is no time-limit. It is an assertion and reassertion of arguments. There are occasional breaks when we occupy a jolly half-hour in wedging ourselves through the narrow, crowded alleys which are called the Division Lobbies. Then the flow of talk is resumed again. Members, as they bivouac on the green benches, gaze dismally at the speakers, and wonder what relation all this bears to the passion and hopes of the elections in the country some incredible ages ago.

The thing would perish of mere tedium but that each orator is speaking under a sounding board, with the nation for listeners.

It is all quaintly reminiscent of Union days at Cambridge. There is the same type of audience—an audience of would-be speakers alternately sympathetic and scornful. There are all the old recognised Union types of speaker—the well-informed, the pretentious, the pushful, the brilliant, the intolerably dull. There are the same explosions of elaborately prepared 'impromptus'; the same fluency with uncertain success or failure; the same dim sense of the unreality of it all.

We proceed by Resolutions, for which we ballot. There is an assumption that by such methods the nation, listening just outside, will become fired with enthusiasm for the measures which are proposed. There is a similarity at present about all our evenings. The member who has been favoured by chance proposes his motion—of the general type that in the opinion of this House it is desirable that every man and woman and child in this country should enjoy happiness and comfort. This is proposed (perhaps) by a Labour member, who will plead in fervent, rugged accents for the justice and desirability of universal happiness and comfort. A Liberal member will second the motion, congratulating his honourable friend on the moderation of his demands, and assuring him that beneath many Liberal breasts beat hearts at unison with the beating of the heart of Labour. Eighteen men rise on his conclusion, each desirous of exhibiting before the world his longing for universal happiness and comfort. Specialists reveal to an astonished audience that remote countries such as Denmark and New Zealand have already attained happiness and comfort. Protectionist members indignantly, if slightly inarticulately, assert that the Tory Party has always been in the forefront of the struggle for happiness and comfort. They add that it is absurd to expect any universal happiness and comfort except through the beneficent action of a Protective Tariff. At the end of the debate a Cabinet Minister rises. He assures the House of the complete sympathy of the Government with the motion. The Government's sole desire is immediately to promote universal happiness and comfort. For his part his heart bleeds whenever he thinks of the comparative absence of happiness and comfort. Unfortunately happiness and comfort cost money. The Government has no money. The disorganised state of national finance, due to wild extravagance, prevented the Government having any money. It would be idle to hold out to the House any immediate hope of the Government obtaining money. The debate hastily closes. The question is put by the Speaker. We unanimously vote for universal happiness and comfort. Then in the small hours of the morning we wend our way homewards—pondering.

I have said that the new members are showing an impatience at this state of affairs. The old members assure them that this impatience will soon die away. Some take this to mean that the methods of the House of Commons will become congruous with the ideals of the new members. Others—and those the wisest—are inclined to think that the new members will become congruous with the methods of the House of Commons. A similar impatience has been known in the earlier stages of imprisonment. 'They do make a lot of noise at first,' said the warder of Wormwood Scrubs, 'but most of 'em get quiet and 'appy before the end.' It would appear that after each General Election such impatience is manifest before the end of the first month. It has always become soothed before the end of the first Session. Since our fathers fell asleep all things have continued until now. They are also cheered by the information that if they had only known the last Parliament they would never complain of the atmosphere of the present one.

A breath of this last Parliament entered indeed with Mr Balfour. For the first time in the new Session the House understood what it was that England had repudiated. For the first time also the House was really angry. Mr Balfour has spoken every day last week. The sentiment is one of deepening bewilderment and repugnance. I have heard language concerning his method and attitude incomparably more violent than that directed toward any other prominent figure in the House. Mr Chamberlain is listened to with respect and attention. Mr Balfour, if he continues his present methods, will, I am afraid, be listened to not at all. Mr Chamberlain's political position is entirely repudiated; but members seem to feel that he is fighting about real things, and that he cares. Mr Balfour may care also, and he may be fighting about real things. But he has not succeeded in conveying that impression to the House of Commons. Two remarks one hears repeated everywhere: The first, 'How did this man manage to retain the leadership of the House for ten years?' The second, 'Now for the first time, the history of the past ten years becomes explicable.'

'But it was not *this* House of Commons,' was the reply of a Tory member to the first of these assertions. Both speakers found consolation in the thought.

Meantime we await tomorrow. Everything is coming tomorrow. We challenge the Navy estimates. Reductions, we are told, will be considered tomorrow. We propose a definite retrenchment on the Army. The Government is pledged to such action tomorrow. Mr Bryce, in what, perhaps, was the finest speech of this session, has pleaded for the remedying of the most obvious Irish grievances, and for the government of Ireland by Irish ideas. The Irish members are waiting for the proposals—tomorrow. The Chinese are to leave South Africa—tomorrow. There is to be social legislation when finance permits—tomorrow. There is a rumour that an Education Bill is to be presented—tomorrow.

So we wait, vaguely wondering how any body of men could have continued the clumsy methods of Procedure, the unnatural hours and days and seasons of meeting, the horrors of division lobbies, the general archaic system of keeping just alive the organism of Parliament.

Meantime, the universal if somewhat watery harmony no doubt tends to lessen the general interest. The Opposition practically have ceased to oppose. They are torn by internal dissensions and penned up in a quarter of the House which they occupy but scantily. A second quarter is filled by the Irish and Labour members, whose aims and purposes are clear. A third is retained by the Government and their most faithful supporters. It is the fourth quarter which provides the incalculable element. Amongst the 'Radicals' below the gangway are those forces whose development no man can foresee. It is a centre of energy—explosive, disorganised, set upon action. It is nearly all new; unused to Parliamentary ways. No one knows its mind. It does not know its own mind. It knows it was not sent to the House of Commons to debate academic resolutions. The very weakness of the Tory Opposition is a cause of danger lest the work of criticism should suddenly flame out in the ranks of the Government supporters.

No one blames the Government. No one blames anybody. All are simply waiting—for tomorrow.

❖

Success in the House

Robert Farquharson (1837–1918) was born in Edinburgh and studied medicine at Edinburgh University before becoming Assistant Surgeon Coldstream Guards, Medical Officer to Rugby School, and later Assistant-Physician and a lecturer at St Mary's Hospital London. He was the Liberal MP for Aberdeenshire from 1880 until his retirement in 1906.

Robert Farquharson, *The House of Commons from Within and Other Memories*
(1912)

The most fatal thing for success in the House of Commons is to be a prig,
which has been described as an animal overstuffed for its size. Definition is
difficult, but we all know this type in St Stephen's or elsewhere, and although
the old Oxford manner is nearly extinct, traces of it survive, and occasionally
we meet the high flute-like voice, the aggressive nose, the eyes beaming with
sweetness and light, and the supercilious gaze and pitying smile with which he
surveys those mortals who have not shared his assured advantages. The House
of Commons is an absolutely democratic place, snobbery is unknown, people
are taken entirely on their merits, without much heed to rank, position, or
prestige; and if you wish to make a good impression at the start, suppress any
trace of intellectual superiority, even if you think you are entitled to show it.
My observation is that people about half-way across the journey of life, men of
affairs, who have been working at something definite, and have been trained
in what John Burns suggestively calls the University of the World, are most
successful. They know something at first-hand, and can tell it simply and
practically to their listeners, and that is the real way to obtain and retain the
ear for such a fastidious yet sympathising assembly. And what is even of greater
importance; that is the way to catch the Speaker's and the Chairman of
Committees' eye, for these judicial and judicious officials with admirable tact
choose from the covey of ambitious speakers who spring into the air when some
one sits down, the competitor whom they believe the House wishes to hear,
and who has something really useful to add to the debate. Chamberlain, Bright,
Cobden, H. Fowler, John Burns, and some of the leading Labour members, who
are always heard with respect, had received no definite academic training, but
had been intimately mixed up with public affairs, in which they played a
conspicuous part.

A heart-breaking place

Oliver Ridsdale Baldwin (1899–1958), Viscount Corvedale, was the son of Stanley
Baldwin, 1st Earl Baldwin of Bewdley. He was educated at Eton and served in France
from 1916 to 1919. While his father was Tory leader, he was Labour MP for Dudley from
1929 to 1931, and he lost contests for other seats in both 1931 and 1935. During World
War II he was a major in intelligence in the Middle East and North Africa and he was
Labour MP for Paisley from 1945 until 1947, when he inherited his father's earldom.
He was also Governor of the Leeward Islands, 1948–50.

Oliver Baldwin, *The Questing Beast: An Autobiography* (1932)

The House of Commons is a heart-breaking place. The wasted hours; the old-
fashioned machinery of government; the opposition for the sake of opposition;

the interminable talking that has not the slightest effect, and the pile of legislation that need never come to us for decision throws a pall on all and sundry. The deadening effect of the comfort and warmth so easily enable one to forget the purpose of one's presence, and the vain endeavours to seek justice for a constituent make one wonder at the life one is leading, and deplore the ineffectiveness of one's labours.

No other audience

L. S. Amery, *My Political Life* (1953)

It is the most critical of audiences, critical, not only of the substance and manner of speech, but, even more, of the character of the speaker himself. No body of men listens more respectfully and sympathetically to real knowledge and sincerity, however inadequately expressed. But no other audience is so quick to discount a speech mainly got up for the occasion, or to see through self-seeking ambition. Nor is it always easy to make sure exactly what combination of qualities will enable a member to gain what is known as the 'ear of the House'. All that can be said is that there is no satisfaction equal to that feeling that you are carrying the House with you on some subject about which you care deeply. For no other audience in the world has such power to influence the mainsprings of action.

A barometer

Sir Henry 'Chips' Channon, Diary, April 12, 1937

Oh, the House of Commons and its joys. Everyone was charming to me today and greeted me vigorously. How one's stock rises and falls in this most barometric of buildings. My speech on Thursday seems to have been well received after all, and Baldwin smiled at me with one half of his face in the division lobby. His smiles are porcine but warm for all that.

The cruelty of the pack

Sir Henry 'Chips' Channon, Diary, May 8, 1940

The cataclysmic day has drawn to a welcome close and I am worn out, revolted by the ingratitude of my fellow-men, nauseated by the House of Commons, which I really think ought, though I love it, to be abolished.

When I got there the atmosphere of the House was definitely excited and it intensified as the long hours passed. Herbert Morrison opened the debate with vituperation, and announced that the Opposition would challenge the

Government into a division. The PM, angry and worn out, intervened to say that the Government accepted the challenge, and he called upon his friends to rally round and support him. Possibly he was tactless, but I do not quite see what other course he could have followed. We then knew that it was to be war. Samuel Hoare, the pet aversion of the Labour Party, made a boring contribution in defence of the Government, which did not help. The temperature rose, hearts hardened, tempers sharpened, and I came to the conclusion that there is nothing so revolting as the House of Commons on an ugly night. Little Neville seemed heartbroken and shrivelled (as Lady Halifax said) but remained courteous and patient. I sat behind him, hoping to surround him with an aura of affection. From time to time I looked up into Mrs Fitzroy's[43] gallery and several times I caught the eye of poor Mrs Chamberlain, who has hardly left the House for two days: she is a loyal, good woman. She was in black—black hat—black coat—black gloves—with only a bunch of violets in her coat. She looked infinitely sad as she peered down into the mad arena where the lions were out for her husband's blood.

For hours the issue was in doubt. Duff Cooper made a damaging speech in which he said that he hoped we should get on more actively with the war . . . good advice from someone who has just returned from four months in America . . .

The whispering in the lobbies was unbearable. Ham Kerr offered to bet that 100 Government supporters would vote against the regime; I scoffed. Mrs Tate offered to bet me £5 that over fifty would do so, but refused to take up the challenge, when I agreed. Lady Astor rushed about, intriguing and enjoying the fray and the smell of blood: she has joined hands with the insurgents, probably because she must always be in the limelight, and also because I think she is seriously rattled by the 'Cliveden Set' allegations which were made against her before the war, and now wants to live them down.

At last the atmosphere became so horrible that I decided I must leave for a few minutes—when I came back Alexander was speaking,[44] winding up for the Opposition. The real issue of the debate—Norway—had long since been forgotten: speakers attacked us on any possible ground, and still the doubt was in everybody's mind, would Winston be loyal! He finally rose, and one saw at once that he was in bellicose mood, alive and enjoying himself, relishing the ironical position in which he found himself: i.e. that of defending his enemies, and a cause in which he did not believe. He made a slashing, vigorous speech, a magnificent piece of oratory. I was in the gallery behind him, with Rab, who was, several times, convulsed with laughter. Winston told the story of the Norwegian campaign, justified it, and trounced the Opposition, demolishing Roger Keyes, etc. How much of the fire was real, how much ersatz, we shall never know, but he amused and dazzled everyone with his virtuosity. He taunted the Opposition and accused Shinwell of skulking: a Labour MP—rather the worse for drink—had never heard the word and thought that he had said skunking. There was laughter, but somehow the tension was increased and poor Healy, the new Deputy Sergeant-at-Arms, was quite nervous lest he be called on to eject an unruly member. It was like bedlam.

I asked Roy Wise how many would vote against the Government—and he said that he would, for one: it was the only way to shock us out of our complacency, he said. I told him that he was playing with dynamite: then Charles Taylor ('Cow and Gate' and looks like a calf) came up to me and said: 'We are trying to get your Government out tonight.' Feeling grew, still we thought we would survive. At last the Speaker called a division which Winston nearly talked out. I went into the Aye Lobby, which seemed thin for a three-line Whip, and we watched the insurgents file out of the Opposition Lobby (Teenie Cazalet could not make up his mind and abstained). 'Quislings,' we shouted at them, 'Rats.' 'Yes-men,' they replied. I saw all the expected ones, and many more—Herbert [Duggan] among them and my heart snapped against him for ever. Then I voted, as usual everyone wondered how many had dared to vote against us: so many threaten to do so, and funk it at the last moment. Anthony Eden and Jim Thomas in our Lobby looked triumphant, and I saw Winston and his PPS Brendan Bracken there. I went back to the Chamber, and took my seat behind Neville. 'We are all right' I heard someone say, and so it seemed as David Margesson came in and went to the right, the winning side of the table, followed by the other tellers. '281 to 200' he read, and the Speaker repeated the figures. There were shouts of 'Resign—Resign' . . . and that old ape Josh Wedgewood began to wave his arms about and sing 'Rule Britannia'. Harold Macmillan, next to him, joined in, but they were howled down. Neville appeared bowled over by the ominous figures, and was the first to rise. He looked grave and thoughtful and sad: as he walked calmly to the door, his supporters rose and cheered him lustily and he disappeared. No crowds tonight to cheer him, as there were before and after Munich—only a solitary little man, who had done his best for England.

What can Neville do now? He can reconstruct his Government: he can resign: but there is no doubt that the Government is seriously jarred and all confidence in it is gone. Hitler will be quick to take advantage of our divided councils.

What changes does that fatal division portend? Neville may survive but not for long: Oh, the cruelty of the pack in pursuit . . . shall I too crash when the Chamberlain edifice crumbles?

I am disgusted by politics and human nature and long to live like Walpole, a semi-social, semi-literary life in a Strawberry Hill (only not Gothic) of my own.[45] Perhaps one day I will.

A *curious spell of fascination*

William John Brown (1894–1960) was educated at an elementary school in Margate and at a grammar school in Sandwich. He was Secretary of the Civil Service Clerical Association from 1919 to 1942 and fought several seats for Labour before being elected as MP for West Wolverhampton in 1929. He resigned the Labour Whip in early 1931, joining with Sir Oswald Mosley's New Party for a single day, then sitting as an Independent Labour Member until October 1931 when he was defeated. He later sat as an Independent for the Rugby division of Warwickshire from April 1942 until he was again defeated, in 1950. He was a journalist and author as well as an MP.

W. J. Brown, So Far . . . (1943)

It is a curious place, the House of Commons—a combination of Church and Public School! The character of the building, the elaborate formal ritual of the proceedings, give to it a quasi-ecclesiastical atmosphere. (I remember George Lansbury when, as a youngster of twenty-two or so, I 'lobbied' him on some Civil Service question, remarking to me how difficult it was to feel revolutionary in it.) It has, too, something of the character of the Public School. There is the bewigged Speaker in the part of Schoolmaster! There are the Upper Sixth—on the Front Bench there! There are the Monitors, in the shape of the Whips! There are the Old Boys, only too ready to sit on the New Boys who don't know the rules! Here, too, are the New Boys, muttering darkly about the privileges of the Old Boys! And the analogy goes further. If the Speaker cracks a joke we dutifully laugh heartily at it, just as we used to do at the heavy witticisms of our Schoolmaster; heartily, whether the joke be good or bad! At the end of the session we 'break up' for the holidays, very like a crowd of schoolboys. And we re-assemble after a vacation full of experiences of the holiday, just as we did at school—Lord! how many years agone! And the humour of the House is very much 'schoolboy humour'—excised from *Hansard* when it gets too broad!

It is a difficult place to speak in, and some Members never do their best in the House. People who make great reputations on the platform, where they addressed packed, silent and attentive audiences, often fail miserably in the House. Here there is, save on rare occasions, no packed House. For the greater part of the day—except at Question Time—it is very sparsely occupied indeed. And—make no mistake about it—most of those who are there don't particularly want to hear you! Their major interest in you, when you are speaking, is when you will sit down—so that they may leap to their feet in an attempt to catch the Speaker's eye, and so get their contribution off their chests, and on to the pages of *Hansard* and (most important) into the columns of the papers which circulate in their constituencies! There is constant movement of Members, going in and out—to meals, to appointments, to see constituents who have sent in green cards for them. And when you are speaking you are liable to a good deal of interruption, which is capable of putting the nervous speaker (and, despite appearances to the contrary, we are pretty well all nervous when speaking here) right off his carefully prepared theme! Yet the place weaves a curious spell of fascination about you. It tames the exuberant into propriety, humbles the proud into comparative humility, knocks the rough edges off all and sundry, and withal provides high drama and rich comedy. It is liable to swift bursts of temper, rollicking fits of humour, and moods of exaltation and despair. In short it is a stage on which the actors portray, in scenes rehearsed and unrehearsed, all the complex and conflicting qualities and emotions of which our humanity (at once glorious and contemptible) is compounded.

Above all, it is a place where men find their true level. It is a place at once utterly undemocratic, and yet perhaps the most democratic in the world. Policy does not spring from the thoughts of free men, freely debating great issues. Policy is determined on by the Party caucuses, then imposed on the Parties by their Whips—using the twin weapons of bullying and bribery—and so upon the country at large. In this sense there is very little democracy about the House. On the other hand, its rules (however abused they sometimes are) are utterly democratic, and a rough democracy characterises the personal life—the collective personal life—of the place. Neither money, nor achievement outside the House, nor title, is any passport, by itself, to the regard and esteem of the House. Character and capacity alone wear well here.

❖

An atmosphere of comradely vivacity

Harold Nicolson, *Spectator*, June 2, 1939

It is a truism to liken the House of Commons to a public school, and in truth I find the boyishness of the Mother of Parliaments most rejuvenating. It's natural, I suppose, that human beings, when segregated from their domestic or social surroundings and herded in one building for purposes both of work and play, should develop similar patterns of behaviour. Yet it often strikes me as strange and interesting that our elderly legislators should, even in the smallest quirks of conduct and of gesture, repeat so accurately the manners and customs of their own puberty. One recognises the same preference for 'character' (which is the house-master's phrase for 'convenient conformity') as against imagination or independence (which are classed as symptoms of the 'crank' or 'freak'). There is an identical tendency to laugh a little too loudly at the Headmaster's jokes; the same propensity towards herd-giggling when any untoward incident occurs; the same overt desire to address the Captain of Cricket by his Christian name . . .

Even as at school, the head-boy passes through the admiring throng with rapid strides of busy importance: the gait of the junior whips takes upon itself the self-conscious lilt of the newly appointed prefect. At no time does this similarity impress itself so forcibly upon one as on the last day of term. The sense of impending release, the imminence of other and gentler standards of social behaviour, the approaching interruption of our communal existence, create an atmosphere of comradely vivacity. Old animosities are discarded with our school clothes; the shout of derision, the obviously averted eye, give place to polite enquiries regarding the approaching holidays; the grey suits, the neat checks of the last day of term give to our school-fellows the adornment and the glamour of some other and some unknown world; even the head prefect has discarded his flowing tails in favour of a neat green suit. Amity abounds.

The beehive

Sir Alan Patrick Herbert (1890–1971) was the son of an India Office civil servant and he was educated at Winchester and at New College, Oxford. Called to the bar, he nonetheless made his name as a journalist and humorous author. He sat as an Independent MP for Oxford University from 1935 to 1950 and was a champion of Private Members' legislation. During World War II he held the rank of petty officer and was in charge of the *Water Gypsy*, a Thames patrol vessel jointly maintained by the Royal Navy and the Port of London Authority, which he would occasionally anchor off the Speaker's Stairs.

A. P. Herbert, *Independent Member* (1950)

There is, of course, almost every possible ingredient of unease in that place. An after-dinner speaker or a platform speaker may reasonably expect to have the attention of most of his audience. They are in front of him, and they cannot easily get away. He has a table, or desk, for his notes and papers. Even the 'front-bencher' commands the length of the House and can use the Dispatch Box for his notes and papers—and thumping fist, if necessary. He has a fort; he has a field of fire. The back-bencher, clutching his notes, is like a lonely man standing up in the middle of a public meeting. His audience is all round him, some in front, some behind, some above him, some below—and a great many high up in galleries in a building not highly meritorious for 'acoustics'. An interruption, a sneer, an ironical laugh may hit him from any quarter. And, if he rounds upon the interrupter to the south-west, or the sneerer to the east, he may be reminded that he must address his remarks to the Chair, which lies north. More, unless he is very good, or fairly important—and even if he is— his audience is moving and changing all the time. Members, good friends, it may be, receive urgent telephone messages or 'green cards', bow to the Speaker, and march out as he approaches his principal, or only, joke. The Minister whom he hopes to convert, or intends to shatter with a deadly jest, is relieved by another Minister and goes out for a cup of tea, just before the unanswerable argument or the crushing quip is reached. The Front Opposition Bench, in the same way, are constantly coming and going. There is a procession of Members to the Table, putting down Questions and getting advice from the Clerks.

Others go up to the Speaker and engage him in conversation. There is movement everywhere. It is like making a speech in a beehive. And those who remain motionless are not necessarily attentive, or even silent. Ministers and Whips must confer upon the course of the debate, check facts and figures, read documents about something quite different. A Member will come in with a resolution or an amendment to another Bill, to which he is seeking signatures. He goes from friend to friend, and there is a whispered colloquy with each. All this is quite legitimate. Then there will be a few couples having private conversations about their holiday plans, about the party meeting, about the latest scandal, or the by-election, or the pretty girl in the Speaker's Gallery. Behind the orator may be one of those Members who have the habit of muttering a running commentary—'Quite right, too'—'Not with this Government'—'They're *afraid*'—quite friendly, maybe, but maddening. Then there are the professional interrupters, who, if they do not like the speaker or the speech, make it their business to snap at him from time to time—'Nonsense!' 'Rubbish!' 'What about 1926?' 'All very well for you!' and so on. But these may be an advantage to the speaker since they revive the languishing interest of others. Then there is the formal interruption. No two Members may be on their feet at the same time: but any moment a Member, half-rising, with his rump just airborne, may say: 'May I——?' or 'If I may——?' The speaker is not bound to 'give way' and sit down—it is a matter of courtesy: but it is generally best, and it is generally done. Again, if he has a telling answer to the interjection, it may assist him. At least, it shows that someone is awake and listening. But the interjection, question, or comment may well be devastating, knocking or seeming to knock his whole case from under him. And if he has not got a good answer, though he completes the course with a confident air and does a jaunty jump or two, he will be uneasily aware that he knocked down the big fence in the middle. Here is perhaps the fundamental cause of alarm. Whatever jokes may be made about it, the House of Commons is a formidable body, drawn from every class and corner. They may not all be philosophers or senior wranglers, which is just as well: but you could hardly mention any subject, they say, without some Member shyly coming forward and confessing that he knows all about it, whether it is the Battle of Waterloo, the keeping of hens, the geography of Malaya, or the running of a coal-mine. For many years you may have maintained without much contradiction (in clubs and pubs) that all cows have five legs. But when you rise to make the same assertion in the House of Commons you have to recognise that there are 638 other Members, each of whom may rise, politely or not, to say that he knows more about cows than you do.

The easy answer to all this is that a man should not get up at all unless he is sure of his subject and can speak so well as to command attention. That is a little too easy. The beehive is a tyrant: it has the shifting incalculable moods of a tyrant, and is seldom in the same mood two days running. You may catch it in a sunny mood at tea-time, half-asleep at dinner-time, alive but angry an hour or two later.

Playing the game

Joseph Percival Mallalieu (1908–80), known as 'Curly', was the son of a woollen manufacturer and Liberal MP, and was educated at Cheltenham; at Trinity College, Oxford; and at Chicago University. He covered Parliament as a reporter during the 1930s and served in the Navy during World War II. He was Labour MP for Huddersfield from 1945 to 1950 and for the East division of Huddersfield from 1950 until his retirement in 1979. For a couple of years he wrote a weekly parliamentary sketch for *Tribune*. His elder brother, Edward, also sat in the House—as a Liberal before the war and as a Labour MP from 1948 to 1974.

J. P. W. Mallalieu, *Tribune*, July 7, 1950

When, nowadays, a Member of Parliament wishes to address the House of Commons he first writes a polite little note to the Speaker.

'Dear Mr Speaker' (he writes):

'I would like to speak in next Thursday's debate on films. I have been connected with the film industry for fifteen years. I haven't spoken in the House since the General Election. I only want ten minutes.'

Next he prepares his speech, putting on paper his own ideas, picking other people's brains for theirs, looking up the figures, maybe practising the finished article in front of a mirror. By Thursday he is all teed-up. On Friday the papers will be full of him.

Towards the end of Questions on Thursday he enters the Chamber with elaborate casualness, dryness in his throat and an uncomfortable quickening in his pulse. He gets as near as he can to his favourite seat.

By and by the Minister rises to open the debate for the Government. The Member listens to him, in the intervals of shuffling his notes, just to see if there is something really startling in the speech. There seldom is.

After a lapse of time—an inordinate lapse of very lightfooted time, it seems—the Minister sits down, the spokesman of the Opposition rises, and the Member stops shuffling his notes and gets out his fountain pen.

Who knows? He may be called to speak next, to answer the Opposition case. He begins to shape an opening for his own speech, full of biting satire and withering retort, a sentence which will demolish the Opposition and leave nothing to be said by subsequent speakers. He also listens to the argument to see if something particularly fatheaded is said. There seldom is.

After another lapse of time—an interminable lapse of uncountable time, it seems—the Opposition Front Bench speaker sits down and the Member leaps, glowing-eyed, to his own feet. So do a hundred of his colleagues. Fifty of them have leaped to their feet because they've done their duty listening to all this stuff. They can now have a cup of tea. They leave the Chamber thankfully and noisily. The other fifty have leaped to their feet because they, too, have written polite little notes beginning 'Dear Mr Speaker . . .' They too have worked out a devastating opening sentence, they too have listened to some of the arguments.

The Member and his fifty colleagues stand erect, eyeing the Speaker with friendly confidence. The Speaker calls on someone who has already spoken six times that week and everyone but he sits down again.

As the new speaker is one of his own side, the Member ignores him. Someone from the other side will be called next anyhow and by the time it is the Government's turn again no one will remember what the previous Government-side speaker has said.

The Member shuffles his notes, half listens to see whether 'this fellow is pinching any of my points', then strolls round to the Chair. 'What are the chances this afternoon, Mr Speaker?' he asks. Mr Speaker says the chances are pretty good provided some of the others don't talk too long. Back to his seat goes the Member with renewed hope. He stands perfunctorily when his own colleague sits down, then hastily finds out what constituency the Opposition speaker represents.

Then he listens carefully and frames a new opening sentence which will knock hell out of everyone. As the Opposition speaker goes into his peroration, the Member gets ready to spring and, at a split second's notice, is on his feet, glowing-eyed. Mr Speaker calls another of his colleagues from the Government side.

It is now 4.45 p.m. and the Member could do with a cup of tea himself. But he dare not leave the Chamber. He might miss his turn. He shuffles his notes and wonders 'why this blatherer doesn't sit down. Must get his half column in the local paper, I suppose.'

At this point he notices that Mr Speaker has himself left the Chamber to get a cup of tea. So the Member strolls round to the Chair. 'What are the chances this afternoon, Jim?' he asks. Jim Milner, the Deputy-Speaker, says the chances are pretty good provided some of these others don't talk too long. Back to his seat goes the Member, with considerable hope. His colleague at last sits down, another Opposition speaker is called and the Member begins to devise a new devastating opening sentence.

At 5.45 the Member desperately wants a smoke. But he dare not leave the Chamber. Further, he notices that Jim Milner has now left the Chamber for a smoke. So the Member strolls round to the Chair. 'What are the chances, Sir Charles?' he asks. Sir Charles McAndrew, deputising for Jim Milner, says the chances are pretty good provided some of these others don't talk too long.

Back to his seat goes the Member, still with some hope but with increasing hatred of all his colleagues—'long-winded so-and-so's. Why don't they get to hell out of this.' Savagely he prepares a new still more devastating opening sentence. That done, he pays no attention to the debate but instead concentrates upon glaring at his colleagues. 'Dear Sirs and Brothers. You're a set of bastards. Yours fraternally.'

It is 7.45 p.m. The Member is gasping for a cigarette. He is thirsty. He is famished. He is exhausted by all these opening sentences. But he dare not leave the Chamber. Moreover, there is Mr Speaker again. The Member strolls round to the Chair. 'What are the chances tonight, Mr Speaker?' he asks. What, says Mr Speaker, haven't you been called yet? Well, I've promised to call Foot next. Then there'll be a Tory. But I will call you after him. But you mustn't be more than five minutes. Lyttelton wants three-quarters of an hour to wind up and Harold Wilson the same.

Back to his seat goes the Member, cursing Foot, and Lyttelton and Wilson and the Speaker and Jim and Sir Charles, but with hope suddenly rising into certainty. At the next break, he rises to his feet, as of routine, and without disappointment or rancour hears the Speaker say, 'Mr Michael Foot'. Mr Michael Foot then proceeds to make every point which the Member had in his notes.

All this happens to a Member of Parliament at some stage in his career and the suffering is terrible. It happened to me last week. But I have forgotten about it now because on Tuesday I played my first game of cricket for twenty years, not just watching it or talking about it, but actually playing it.

In the Lords and Commons game against Westminster, I did not actually bat. I did not actually bowl. I did not actually make a catch. I did not actually drop one. But I played. And if your reaction to that is 'So what?' I hope you want to get into the Korean debate and that it keeps fine for you.

Ancestor worship

Aneurin Bevan, *In Place of Fear* (1952)

'The past lies like an Alp upon the human mind.' The House of Commons is a whole range of mountains. If the new Member gets there too late in life he is already trailing a pretty considerable past of his own, making him heavy-footed and cautious. When to this is added the visible penumbra of six centuries of receding legislators, he feels weighed to the ground. Often he never gets to his feet again.

His first impression is that he is in a church. The vaulted roofs and stained-glass windows, the rows of statues of great statesmen of the past, the echoing halls, the soft-footed attendants and the whispered conversation, contrast depressingly with the crowded meetings and the clang and clash of hot opinions he has just left behind in his election campaign. Here he is, a tribune of the people, coming to make his voice heard in the seats of power. Instead, it seems he is expected to worship; and the most conservative of all religions—ancestor worship.

The first thing he should bear in mind is that these were not his ancestors. His forebears had no part in the past, the accumulated dust of which now muffles his own footfalls. His forefathers were tending sheep or ploughing the land, or serving the statesmen whose names he sees written on the walls around him, or whose portraits look down upon him in the long corridors. It is not the past of his people that extends in colourful pageantry before his eyes. They were shut out from all this; were forbidden to take part in the dramatic scenes depicted in these frescoes. In him his people are there for the first time, and the history he will make will not be merely an episode in the story he is now reading. It must be wholly different; as different as is the social status which he now brings with him.

To preserve the keen edge of his critical judgement he will find that he must adopt an attitude of scepticism amounting almost to cynicism, for parliamentary procedure neglects nothing which might soften the acerbities of his class feelings. In one sense the House of Commons is the most unrepresentative of representative assemblies. It is an elaborate conspiracy to prevent the real clash of opinion which exists outside from finding an appropriate echo within its walls. It is a social shock absorber placed between privilege and the pressure of popular discontent.

The new Member's first experience of this is when he learns that passionate feelings must never find expression in forthright speech. His first speech teaches him that. Having come straight from contact with his constituents, he is full of their grievances and his own resentment, and naturally, he does his best to shock his listeners into some realisation of it.

He delivers himself therefore with great force and, he hopes and fears, with considerable provocativeness. When his opponent arises to reply he expects to hear an equally strong and uncompromising answer. His opponent does nothing of the sort. In strict conformity with parliamentary tradition, he congratulates the new Member upon a most successful maiden speech and expresses the urbane hope that the House will have frequent opportunities of hearing him in the future. The Members present endorse this quite insincere sentiment with murmurs of approval. With that, his opponent pays no more attention to him but goes on to deliver the speech he had intended to make. After remaining in his seat a little longer, the new Member crawls out of the House with feelings of deep relief at having got it over, mingled with a paralysing sense of frustration. The stone he thought he had thrown turned out to be a sponge.

I would not have bothered to describe this typical experience of a working man speaking in the House of Commons for the first time were it not characteristic of the whole atmosphere. The classic parliamentary style of speech is understatement. It is a style unsuited to the representative of working people because it slurs and mutes the deep antagonisms which exist in society.

The dog days

(Henry) Bernard Levin (b. 1928) was educated at Christ's Hospital and at the London School of Economics and has worked as a journalist since 1953, principally with *The Times*, and as a broadcaster. He wrote a series of sketches for the *Spectator* under the pseudonym 'Taper' (a character from Disraeli's *Coningsby*) during the Macmillan years.

'Taper' (Bernard Levin), *Spectator*, May 15, 1959

The hot weather is affecting my nerves. Figure to yourself: there I was the other day, sitting with a Member in the tea-room, idly sipping a cup of something that I presume was piped direct from the Thames two yards away. Through the open door we could see the sun on the terrace (the strawberries and cream do not begin until after Whitsun), the pigeons strutting self-importantly about like so many Junior Government Whips, the funnel of a passing ship or two. We could hear the gentle slap of the waves against the stonework, the murmur of voices from outside, the chimes of Big Ben. It was an incredibly peaceful English scene, and sorted well with the scene I had just left—the Chamber. There, some half-dozen Members a side had been dragging themselves to their feet from time to time to deploy all the cut-and-thrust of debate on such grave constitutional questions as the determination of Messrs Harold Wilson, Patrick Gordon Walker, Douglas Jay and Hector Hughes to carry an amendment to the Finance Bill (Page 12, Clause 12, line 33) to leave out the word 'and', and the equal determination of the Government that the Opposition should not harm a hair of an and's head.

We spoke, my friend and I, of the only subject anybody at Westminster discusses these days at all: the rigid catalepsy that from Left to Right holds almost undisputed sway within the precincts of the Palace of Westminster. Zombie-like, they go back and forth about their duties, even past praying for death or Mr Macmillan to release them from a travail that the Flying Dutchman and the Wandering Jew, not to mention Sisyphus, would never have dreamed of exchanging for their own. The other day there were forty-seven Tories away from a Division unpaired; nobody paid the slightest attention. (A mere few months ago there would have been a row of such proportions that they would not have needed to take away the statue of Sir William Harcourt that the one of Mr Balfour is to replace; it would have fallen off its pedestal without anybody lifting a finger.) There is no subject in sight, or indeed conceivable, that could cause anybody to get excited or even interested; Mr Profumo's statement about arms for Iraq passed with no more than a perfunctory gibe or two from the Opposition, though this time last year they would have torn the place down around Mr Profumo's sleek ears. Once it was the custom for Members not wishing to attend morning Committees to dream up elaborate excuses; now they have taken to telling the Whips bluntly that they have no intention of turning up, and their names are meekly struck off the lists. If some enterprising lead-swinger should summon up the energy, during the Whitsun recess, to circularise all his fellow-Members with a suggestion that they should none of them come back at all when it was over, the chances are that they would accept the suggestion with joy and unanimity, and that when they put it into effect nobody would notice.

Well, there we were, talking of such matters with many a drowsy pause, when suddenly a bell began to ring; it rang with a loud and ugly clangour, harsh and alarming. I regret to say that I lost my head; assuming that the Palace of Westminster was on fire, I leaped to my feet and, seizing the milk jug, was about to hurl its contents over the Parliamentary Secretary to the Minister of Pensions and National Insurance (who was sitting at the next table) when I was gently restrained. The bell, I was told, was the Division Bell. Collapsing, all a-quiver, into my seat, I digested this news as my companion went off to register his vote. When he came back, I was careful not to ask him on what he had been voting (I know better than *that*), but he genially volunteered the information that neither he, nor anyone he had met on the day, had any idea. When the figures ticked up on the wall a moment later, I was astonished to see that no fewer than 384 Members had been present, not counting the Tellers, to vote upon an amendment that had been forced to a Division by the Opposition (though the two Conservative sponsors had wished to withdraw it), the effect of which, I later learned, would have been to change the provision for duty payable on club liquor licences so that instead of 'five pounds' it would read 'five pounds or duty of threepence for every pound's worth of purchases of intoxicating liquor whichever is the less'.

As Mr Belloc[46] once asked, what *is* the use of going on like this! How can the time of even 384 grown men and women be justifiably occupied in this way, with the temperature 80 degrees in the shade and the rhododendrons out at Kew! Why do they not go now into recess and not come back until the prorogation! There is an amendment to the Finance Bill which seeks to exempt parking meters from income tax; there is another to omit the word 'otherwise' from a passage which admittedly makes no sense as it stands but which will not be affected in the slightest by the omission of the word 'otherwise' or for that matter two-thirds of the other words it contains. These amendments will be discussed; they may be voted on; for all I know there may be 484 or even 548 members willing to troop through the lobbies when the bell (oh, my heart! it is thumping still!) goes. What, as I say, is the use!

I do not know; I simply do not know. And what is more to the point, I do not propose to stay and find out. I am going away, and I am not coming back until the Finance Bill has been dealt with, parking meters, otherwise and all. I am going, if you must know, to Elba, where I shall amuse myself by sending picture-postcards of Napoleon to Mr Butler with offensive messages on the back signed 'Talleyrand'.

1. Francis Bacon, *Apophthegms*; quoted in Paul Johnson (ed.), *The Oxford Book of Political Anecdotes* (1986), p. 11.
2. T. P. O'Connor, *Mr Gladstone's House of Commons* (1885), p. 397.
3. John Buchan, Speech to Federation of University Conservative Associations, January 9, 1933.
4. Henry Fairlie, *The Life of Politics* (1968), p. 18.
5. Quoted in A. F. Tschiffely, *Don Roberto: Being the Account of the Life and Works of R. B. Cunninghame Graham, 1852–1936* (1937), pp. 206–7.
6. Fenner Brockway, *Inside the Left: Thirty Years of Platform, Press, Prison and Parliament* (1942), p. 220.
7. A. P. Herbert, *Independent Member* (1950), p. 6.
8. Walter Bagehot, *The English Constitution* (1867), p. 136.
9. Viscount Bolingbroke, *A Letter to Windham* (1753 edition), p. 33.
10. Quoted in Tschiffely, op. cit., p. 204.
11. In an unpublished interview with W. T. Stead; quoted in J. W. Robertson Scott, *The Life and Death of a Newspaper* (1932), p. 172.
12. Winston Churchill, *Life of Lord Randolph Churchill* (1906), Vol. I, p. 69.
13. M. C. Hollis, *Can Parliament Survive?* (1949), p. 64.
14. Sir James Mackintosh, Journal, March 22, 1817.
15. Sir Henry Morris-Jones, *Doctor in the Whips' Room* (1955), p. 164.
16. Nigel Nicolson, *People and Parliament* (1958), p. 62.
17. Woodrow Wyatt, *Distinguished for Talent* (1958), pp. 198–9.
18. Quoted in R. G. Thorne, *The Commons 1790–1820* (1986), Vol. IV, p. 240.
19. Herbert, op. cit., (1950), p. 48.
20. Oliver Lyttelton (Viscount Chandos), *The Memoirs of Lord Chandos* (1962), p. 337.
21. Margot Asquith, *Off the Record* (1943), p. 87.
22. Lyttelton, op. cit., p. 211.
23. Quoted in Alistair Horne, *Macmillan 1957–1986* (Vol. II of the Official Biography) (1989), p. 154.
24. Susan Crosland, *Tony Crosland* (1982), p. 165.
25. William Lambton, Letter to an unknown Durham friend, November 19, 1795; quoted in R. G. Thorne (ed.), *The History of Parliament: The House of Commons 1790–1820* (1986), Vol. IV, p. 372.
26. Tschiffely, op. cit., p. 204.
27. William Gallacher, *The Last Memoirs of William Gallacher* (1966), p. 285.
28. Austen Chamberlain, *Down the Years* (1935), p. 243.
29. Sir Alan Herbert, *A. P. H., His Life and Times* (1970), pp. 186–7.
30. Lyttelton, op. cit., p. 329.
31. Letter to William Gregory, *Mr Gregory's Letter Box*; quoted in Henry W. Lucy, *Later Peeps at Parliament Taken from Behind the Speaker's Chair* (1905), p. 283.
32. Quoted in Gordon Brown, *Maxton* (1986), pp. 311–12.
33. Letter from Churchill to Maxton, in Maxton Papers; quoted in Brown, op. cit., p. 306.
34. Alfred Duff Cooper, *Old Men Forget: The Autobiography of Duff Cooper* (1953), p. 154.
35. Brockway, op. cit., p. 223.
36. Benjamin Disraeli, from an unfinished novel printed as an appendix to W. F. Monypenny and G. E. Buckle, *The Life of Benjamin Disraeli, Earl of Beaconsfield* (1910–12), Vol. II, pp. 1521–50.
37. *The Correspondence of George, Prince of Wales, 1770–1812* (1963), Vol. V, p. 2150.
38. *The Croker Papers* (1884), Vol. II, p. 297.
39. Lord Byron, Letter to Francis Hodgson, March 5, 1812.
40. James Grant, *The Newspaper Press: Its Origin, Progress, and Present Position* (1871–2), Vol. I, p. 298.
41. Giulia Grisi (1811–69), the great Italian soprano.
42. Quoted in Alexander Mackintosh, *Echoes of Big Ben: A Journalist's Parliamentary Diary, 1881–1940* (1945), pp. 8–9.
43. The wife of Speaker FitzRoy—related to Channon by marriage.
44. A. V. Alexander (1885–1965) was Labour MP for the Hillsborough division of Sheffield from 1922 until his defeat in 1931 and again from 1935 to 1950, when he was created Viscount Alexander of Hillsborough.

He served under Attlee as a Minister of Defence and later led the Labour Party in the Lords for nine years.

45. Horace Walpole, 4th Earl of Orford (1717–97), was the youngest son of Sir Robert Walpole. He was an MP but derived his fame from his letters, essays and verse. Strawberry Hill was the former coachman's cottage near Twickenham which he transformed into a pseudo-Gothic castle.

46. Hilaire Belloc, the writer, was a Liberal MP from 1906 to 1910 (see Chapter 1).

3 Ceremony, Ritual and Procedure

> Ceremony keeps up all things; 'tis like a penny glass to
> a rich spirit, or some excellent water; without it the
> water will be spilt, the spirit lost.
>
> John Selden, *Table Talk* (1689)

Several of the ancient ceremonies and rituals of Parliament remain to this day: the State Opening of Parliament, the prayers that mark the beginning of business, the election of a new Speaker, the debate on the Address, the pairing of MPs, the reverencing of the Father of the House, the all-night sitting, and that familiar and versatile exclamation of 'Hear! Hear!'

The State Opening has often been attended by an unseemly scramble. In 1604 the Yeomen of the Guard closed the doors of the Lords in the faces of the charging MPs. 'Goodmen burgesses,' said the Sergeant of the Guard, 'ye come not here!' In 1832, Sir Augustus Clifford, then Black Rod, was injured and lost his hat.[1] John O'Connell compared the summoning of the Commons to the Lords for the King's speech to schoolboys rushing from the classroom; they tend to drive the Speaker before them like a sacrificial ox being borne to the horns of the altar. Throughout the nineteenth century, the ceremony was often accompanied by chaotic and even violent scenes and it was to avoid such scrimmages that the authorities decided in 1860 that MPs should ballot for the seats. 'The faithful Commons being elected by ballot,' reported *The Times*, 'not now as formerly rushing in like gods in the gallery on Boxing Night; on the contrary, they came steadily up to the Bar, the Speaker leading, and on his right Lord Palmerston.'[2] During Queen Victoria's declining years the State Opening was dispensed with and in 1901 a new king presided over the first State Opening for several years, which also followed upon a general election. There was, accordingly, much excitement and, despite the presence of eighty extra policemen, the crowd proved difficult to control: several MPs were injured and several policemen lost their helmets.[3] The ceremony continues to this day, though it is much more sedate and subject to the occasional mockery of radicals such as Richard Crossman, who likened the State Opening in 1967 to 'the *Prisoner of Zenda* but not nearly as smart or well done as it would be in Hollywood. It's more what a real Ruritania would look like—far more comic, more untidy, more homely, less grand.'[4]

The late hours kept by the House of Commons have been a perennial feature of the last three centuries and the all-night sitting has been one of the most abiding of parliamentary rituals. 'The winding-up speeches in a debate—and long speeches they were—began on normal occasions about 10.30, when members in evening dress were back from dinner,' wrote the journalist Alexander Mackintosh, whose career in the

Reporters' Gallery stretched from the 1880s to the 1940s. 'Sometimes the speeches were even later. I remember an occasion when Hartington, as a member of the Liberal Government, spoke after midnight for an hour-and-a-half and Northcote replied at equal length. Members as a rule did not complain of being kept out of bed. "We should have been sitting up somewhere else, had we not been in the House of Commons," said Francis Scrope in the time of *Endymion*.'[5]

However, not all have been as proud as Francis Scrope in their reminiscence of these nocturnal ordeals. 'In the 1886 Parliament practically every night was an all-night sitting,' recalled Lord Frederic Hamilton. 'Under the old rules of Procedure, as the Session advanced, we were kept up night after night till 5 a.m. Some Members, notably the late Henry Labouchere, took a sort of impish delight in keeping the House sitting late. Many Front-Bench men had their lives shortened by the strain these late hours imposed on them, notably Edward Stanhope and Mr W. H. Smith.'[6] The ILP Member Fenner Brockway was another who was indignant at the perils of the all-night sitting for some frailer Members: 'In the early hours of one morning I found the frail figure of Sir Norman Angell beside me in the division lobby; his expression, never robust, was weary and drawn. How stupid, I thought, requiring a man of his weak physique but brilliant mind to spend the night tramping the division lobbies so that the revenue of the country should be assured!'[7]

Yet there was camaraderie to be found in this peculiar adversity. Spencer Leigh Hughes noted that in the early hours of an all-night sitting MPs were 'bad-tempered and defiant, and they became worse, ill-humoured and more defiant, until about four in the morning', but that thereafter 'tempers began to improve, and as time goes on men become more and more genial, until at length they are boisterously friendly'. Fresh troops who turn up at breakfast-time are 'ashamed of their spruce appearance' while the 'all-night heroes' are 'proud of their unshaven chins, and their crushed shirt-front put on with their dinner-dress the night before'.[8] There is another consolation. Looking back on his brief period in the House during the 1950s, Nigel Nicolson pointed out that 'if occasionally the House is a prison for an evening or a night, it is a prison from which no visitors are barred'.[9]

Otherwise, Parliament has evolved its own curious procedures and rules, such as the one whereby a Member can count out the House if there are fewer than the quorum of forty, or the one requiring a Member wishing to make a point of order during a division to remain seated and to obtain a covering for his head. 'The House conducts both its business and its manners', wrote Sir Reginald Palgrave, a Clerk of the House, 'according to chance remarks, or casual rules, recorded in the Journals of about three centuries ago; which rules were, in their turn, founded upon custom and usage of immemorial antiquity.'[10]

❖

The State Opening

Anchitell Grey, *Debates of the House of Commons*, May 23, 1678

Sir Winston Churchill complained that we cannot follow the Speaker to the Lords' House without hazard of our lives—the disorder is so great, by reason of overcrowding.

Benjamin Disraeli, Letter to his wife Sarah, November 21, 1837

Thence again to the House, where we were summoned to the Lords at two o'clock. The rush was terrific; Abercromby himself nearly thrown down and trampled upon, and his mace-bearer banging the members' heads with his gorgeous weapon, and cracking skulls with impunity. I was fortunate enough to escape, however, and also to ensure an entry. It was a magnificent spectacle. The Queen looked admirably, no feathers but a diamond tiara; the peers in robes, the peeresses, and the sumptuous groups of courtiers rendered the affair most glittering and imposing. The Speech was intentionally vague, that no division might possibly occur. All was mystery until five o'clock. From the Lords I escaped, almost at the hazard of our lives, with Mahon, who is now most cordial, and we at length succeeded in gaining the Carlton, having several times been obliged to call upon the police and military to protect us as we attempted to break the line, but the moment the magical words 'Member of Parliament' were uttered all the authorities came to our assistance, all gave way, and we passed everywhere. You never saw two such figures, our hats crushed and covered with mud, and the mobocracy envying us our privileges, calling out 'Jim Crow' as we stalked through the envious files.

Charles Dickens, 'Ten Minutes with Her Majesty', *Household Words*, March 1, 1851

The Speaker of the House of Commons answers the summons of his liege lady the Queen, as if he were a schoolmaster with a mob of unmannerly boys at his heels; and is propelled to the bar of the House with the frantic fear of being knocked down and trampled upon by the rush of MPs. A transient cloud passes over the Royal countenance, but is rapidly succeeded by a prolonged smile at the ludicrous efforts of a couple of hundred of eager Commons to squeeze themselves into a space only ample enough for a hundred. The account of a sufferer in the scramble is amusing: 'I happened,' said Mr Joseph Hume, in his place in Parliament on the following evening, 'to be the twenty-fifth from the Speaker; but both sides of the bar were so filled, that I neither saw the Queen nor heard her voice. I was knocked against a corner; my head was knocked against a post, and I might have been much injured if a stout member, to whom I am much obliged, had not come to my assistance. (Hear, hear, and laughter.) It was no laughing matter.' Mr Hume recollected, moreover, that on a similar occasion the coat of a member of the House who now fills a high office abroad, had been torn, and that his shoulder was dislocated.

In 1876 the first State Opening that Queen Victoria had attended for many years was bound to excite more than the average interest among parliamentarians, but nobody expected the mêlée that occurred. It was said that Disraeli vowed never to take part in this dangerous ceremony as a Commoner again, but Henry Lucy called this 'Smoking-room humour'.[11] Fortunately, Dizzy was elevated to the peerage before he had to undergo any further indignity. 'At the same ceremony the next year,' noted one observer, 'he carried the Sword of State immediately before the Queen.'[12]

Benjamin Disraeli, Letter to Queen Victoria, February 9, 1876

He offers his congratulations to your Majesty on yesterday: without sun, without joy-bells, everybody seemed excited and happy. He himself followed the Speaker to the House of Lords, that he might have the satisfaction of seeing your Majesty in your state, but the throng was so tumultuous, and so violent, that he could not enter the House, and, in attempting to guard the Speaker, who was at one moment nearly overcome, Mr Disraeli himself was nearly borne down, when he must have been trampled on. He believes that the mob, which he never saw equalled in violence since the old Westminster elections, was, if not entirely, mainly of members of the House of Commons. He saw the respectable Mr Bass absolutely fighting with a Conservative giant, the member for Plymouth. And yet all this turmoil was, in a certain sense, satisfactory; for it was occasioned by a desire to see your Majesty, and indicates what an immense influence your Majesty's occasional presence can produce.

Duff Cooper, Letter to his wife Diana, December 11, 1924

Have you ever been to the opening of Parliament? If not you mustn't miss it next time. The scene in the House of Lords is the most delightful thing in the world, the most like a fairy story. The King and Queen sitting on their thrones with their crowns on, the King reading the speech extremely well, the Prince of Wales on a smaller throne in the robes of the Garter, looking most like a fairy prince, his pink face and golden hair rising out of ermine, beautiful as an angel, the Peers looking like chessmen. F. E.[13] looking very fine standing on the left of the throne carrying the sword of office, never moving a muscle— and best of all, saintly Bob Cecil wearing some wonderful robes and carrying something, standing on the right of the throne and looking incredibly wicked and scheming, like the evil counsellor in the fairy tale, or the bad uncle of a mediaeval king.

Hugh Todd Naylor Gaitskell (1906–63) was educated at Winchester and at New College, Oxford. From 1928 to 1939 he was a University Lecturer and Reader and during World War II he was a civil servant. He was elected as Labour MP for South Leeds in 1945 and held the seat until his death. He obtained office within a year of arriving in Parliament and was Chancellor of the Exchequer from October 1950 to October 1951. He led the Labour Party in opposition, from 1955 until his death

The State Opening which took place on VJ [Victory over Japan] Day in 1945 failed to make much of an impression on the newly elected Gaitskell.

Hugh Gaitskell, Diary, August 13–24, 1945

I was lucky to draw a seat in the ballot for viewing the ceremony of the opening of Parliament. We Members of the House of Commons were stuck up in the gallery of the House of Lords, facing the throne, while down below were sitting the Peers and Peeresses. It seems to me all wrong that the seats on the floor should be occupied not merely by the members of the House of Lords but also by their families, while we were tucked up in the background. The ceremony itself was not particularly impressive, but that may be because the full peacetime splendour had not been restored. The King read the speech in a very flat monotonous tone, but I imagine that this is because it is the only way he can get through without stammering. However, the speech itself has made an excellent impression, containing as it does such a large number of first-class measures—about half the Labour Party election programme.

Later in the day there was a procession to St Margaret's Church for a service of thanksgiving. I walked along with Chris Mayhew. There were large crowds in Parliament Square, but very orderly and only cheering and shouting occasionally when they recognised an MP. Chris and I felt rather lonely because we represented divisions far from London. However, on the way back somebody started waving to me and I had the pleasure of waving back to a genuine constituent.

❧

Announcing the death of a monarch

Thomas Edward Neil Driberg (1905–76) was educated at Lancing College and at Christ Church, Oxford, and worked as a journalist on the *Daily Express* from 1928 to 1943. He was elected for the Maldon division of Essex as an Independent in June 1942 and took the Labour Whip in January 1945, retiring from the seat in 1955. However, he returned as Labour MP for Barking in 1959 and remained in the House until he retired again in 1974. He was made a life peer as Baron Bradwell the following year.

Tom Driberg, *The Best of Both Worlds: A Personal Diary* (1953)

February 7, 1952. By remarkable coincidence, it has fallen to Winston Churchill twice in his life—but with a lapse of forty-two years between the two events—to announce the King's death in the House of Commons. The words that he used were by no means the same on both occasions.

On 7th May 1910, when Edward VII had died, Churchill was Home Secretary in Asquith's Liberal administration. Both Asquith and the Speaker and Deputy-Speaker of the House happened to be away. Churchill, 'addressing himself', says *Hansard*, 'to the Clerk (who, standing up, pointed to him and then sat down), said: "Sir Courtenay Ilbert, the House is assembled this afternoon in pursuance of the Statute of Anne, which regulates the proceedings of the

Crown. There being no business before us, and in the unavoidable absence of Mr Speaker, it is my duty to move that this House do now adjourn." '

Commons procedure grows gradually more informal. Yesterday's *Hansard*—a slim ninepenceworth—shows that, altho' the Lords retain the old legal phrase, *Demise of the Crown* (no doubt because the House of Lords is a court of law), Churchill in the Commons was able to voice the 'spontaneous expression of our grief' from which he had been debarred by the statelier manners of the Edwardian age.

No doubt all the party leaders will speak with eloquence when Parliament pays tribute to the memory of King George VI. None, nowadays, not even Churchill, would essay the sonorous and rolling rhythm in which Asquith addressed the Commons of his day—in such phrases as: 'By the unsearchable councils of the Disposer of Events, he has been called, suddenly and without warning, to his account.' The end of the Edwardian age marked the beginning of the end of the Augustan style in English public oratory: its successor is, I suppose, the Celtic style.

It is a sobering reminder of the onrush of old age, a useful *memento mori*, to reflect that in the natural course this is the last change of monarch that I shall see. The new Queen is the fifth monarch in my lifetime: she may well be not only a second Elizabeth but a second Victoria—good for another fifty or sixty years.

Prayers

Robert Cecil, 3rd Marquis of Salisbury, *Saturday Review*, March 5, 1859

The religious 'function' with which the House of Commons inaugurates its daily labours, and in which Ministerialists and Opposition, standing opposite each other, gravely pray that their deliberations may not be 'partial', is generally a very dreary rite. The congregation is as scanty as in the pews of a City church. There are official suppliants, of course, who take it in the day's work—the Speaker and the Clerks, and the motionless Sergeant-at-arms, who is condemned to do nothing all the night long but sit, like Patience in an arm-chair, smiling at bores. But, beyond these, the attendance is generally confined to half-a-dozen of Mr Wilson Patten's myrmidons, who give themselves up to roads and waterworks. The ceremony has a ritual all of its own. As soon as the Speaker arrives at the table, he bows to the Chaplain; the members stand up and turn towards the wall, like schoolboys in disgrace; those who are devout among them put one knee on the bench and look into their hats; and the Chaplain proceeds to mumble through a Psalm and some State Prayers. The Clerks do not consider that saying the responses comes in their day's pay; and generally the apparent connexion between the figure mumbling at the table and the members adoring the wall is so very slight, that it looks more like a

Quaker's meeting with one unruly worshipper than any other known religious observance.

But on Monday, 'Prayers' were a much more animated scene. Long before the Speaker came in, the benches were crowded to excess. There had not been so devoutly-minded a House of Commons since the days of Barebones.[14] Even Alderman Salomons did not disdain the Christian ritual. Whence this sudden fever of devotion? Was it fear of the scourge of Bright, or thankfulness at the disappearance of Walpole? Alas, that it should bear a more sordid significance! The secret of it lay in a premium of prayerfulness, which the House of Commons, distrusting its own much-impugned piety, has been sagacious enough to offer. It is a standing order that any member who shall be self-denying enough to come to Prayers shall have, as a reward, his seat secured to him the whole evening, all interlopers notwithstanding. The result is, that the popularity of Prayers is in exact proportion to the liveliness of the very mundane party scuffle which is expected to follow them. On Monday, when the House of Commons was to hear its fate, the attendance was naturally large; and, owing to the admirable calculations of Sir Charles Barry, who has provided 400 seats for 654 senatorial carcasses, the House was absolutely crammed. Even the punctual Mr Ayrton was wandering about discomfited on the floor; and Mr H. Berkeley, just when his pet question was about to come on, was fain, for support, to twine himself round a pillar in a distant corner. Lord Palmerston, whose religious position relieves him from the necessity of attending Prayers, did not arrive till just before the debate began, and could only be accommodated by that painful process of wedging, to which the occupants of official benches, as a set-off to their honours, have occasionally to submit.

T. P. O'Connor, 'The House of Commons, its Structure, Rules, and Habits',
Harper's New Monthly Magazine, December 1893

There are, it will be thus easily understood, two peculiarities under these circumstances, about the attendance at prayers. First, the gentlemen usually present are not always those most distinguished for their piety. The caustic editor of *Truth* has taken, in recent years, to laying the foundation stones of nonconformist places of worship, but nobody would be less likely to set up a claim for special piety than Mr Labouchere. Nevertheless, every night of the week Mr Labouchere listens with pious attention to the ministrations of the chaplain. The secret reason is that the first seat on the front bench below the gangway . . . is a place peculiarly well suited for the guerilla that is ever on the watch for the moment to make an onslaught on a wicked adminis-tration; and Mr Labouchere, as the chief of the guerillas, is especially fond of this seat, and has occupied it for years. This incumbency, though sanctified by so many years of usage, has still to be won by regular attendance at every evening's prayers; the rule is inflexible—except in the cases already mentioned—

that a seat can be held only for one night, and that then it shall be won by attendance at prayers. The second peculiarity is that the men who are most in want of assistance of prayers, as having the heaviest responsibility upon their shoulders—the members of the administration and the leaders of the parties—are always conspicuously absent. During prayer-time the front benches are always a yawning desert, unbroken by the form of a single member of the administration, great or small.

The late Mr Bradlaugh was, it is well known, an avowed agnostic, but he was particularly attached to a certain seat on the benches below the gangway. He used to get over the difficulty by waiting outside the House until prayers were ended, and then hurrying in, he placed his card on the particular seat of which he was so fond. It was slightly irregular, but nobody cared to interfere.

The debate on the Address

Robert Cecil, 3rd Marquis of Salisbury, *Saturday Review*, January 28, 1860

The debate on the Address is a dreary solemnity both to senator and spectator. The mover and seconder are always enough to throw a damp upon the most promising debate. They are a traditional Ministerial device, ingeniously contrived for cooling the ardour with which hungry opponents advance to the attack, and candid supporters undertake the painful task of friendly admonition. First, two men are selected, just good enough not absolutely to break down, but not good enough to be insulted by the offer. They are then coached by the junior whip in such fragmentary revelations of the Ministerial mind as it may please the great men to drop from the Cabinet table. The scanty points having been equitably divided between the two, their speeches are composed and learned. When the House opens, everything looks much the same as at an ordinary debate, except that just behind the Prime Minister are seen two stiff, pale figures, in gay colours, looking the pictures of abject and ghastly misery. Unless they are lucky enough to belong to some rifle corps or archery club, they are probably deputy-lieutenants—an office which has about as much real existence as that of the Great Mogul, but which the sagacious vestimentary regulations of our Court have made an object of no small ambition; for a deputy-lieutenant is allowed to wear a hideous combination of red and silver, which at a distance bears a remote resemblance to a military uniform. He is, moreover, permitted to cover the nakedness of his calves; whereas any ordinary unofficial subject of Her Majesty who wishes to appear before her gracious eyes must do so—to his own utter confusion and the great amusement of his friends—in footman's legs. We trust that, if Mr Danby Seymour introduces a Bill for the abolition of chasubles, he will insert a clause extending the prohibition to knee-breeches—which, we are certain, is much the more unpopular garment of the two. In whatever masquerade, however, the two helpless backers of the Ministry are condemned to exhibit, it is not to be expected that their oratory will be otherwise than embarrassed by the unwonted and ill-fitting garments. Every time the trembling orator raises his arm to enforce some pet period which cost much midnight oil to compose, those vile epaulettes get in his way and distract his thoughts. Every time he bends his head to get a glance at some furtive notes, his collar, stiff with an uncouth *bas-relief* of silver acorns, runs into his windpipe and chokes him. This eloquence in difficulties is naturally not very exciting to the House, especially as its only theme is the hypothetical praise of possible measures, which the praiser not only has not helped to draw up, but has never even seen. Mr St Aubyn, by a modest acquiescence in the impossibility of excelling, performed his task as well as it could be done. Lord Henley, appreci-ating with a complacent smile the grandeur of a Radical Lord's position, tried to give a flavour of novelty to the necessary panegyrics by a fulsome eulogy on the Emperor of the French—at the expense even of so moderate and sensible a ruler as Louis XVIII—and by an expression of unbounded confidence in the foreign policy of two noble Lords, who, when last there was a division on foreign policy in the House of Commons, were found in opposite lobbies. By the time Lord Henley had finished his speech the House had sufficiently examined the attire of himself and his colleague, pity was exhausted, and ennui began to take its place. It was necessary, as a matter of form, that the Opposition should oppose, and that the Ministry should defend. Mr Disraeli accordingly, in the most accommodating spirit, found a mare's-nest on the spot, and presented it, with many flourishes and full details of the discovery, to the acceptance of his admiring friends. Lord Palmerston, recognising it as a pastime of debate, scarcely did more than gently kick it to pieces. But his speech, though short, was weighty. It contained an exposition of the policy of England towards the Italian States, fatal to Austrian or Papal pretensions, and yet expressed in terms of such inimitable irony that no Power can possibly complain. By the time he had finished, it was half-past seven—the crisis had arrived which is fatal to the constitution of a weakly debate. The next day showed that there was no lack of speakers, charged up to the muzzle; but no one was bold enough to face the outcry of 400 legislators roaring for their dinners.

❖

The Book of Remembrance

Sir Henry 'Chips' Channon, Diary, March 20, 1951

As I walked past the House of Commons Book of Remembrance—its pages are turned daily—I happened to look at it, and saw there inscribed in blue and gold letters the names of six MPs killed in the war. I was startled, for one I had known well and long, though never intimately, both at Oxford and here; another was a Commons acquaintance; and all the others I had known well. How full my life has been, and how I wish that I were not on the last lap.

Pairing

Joseph Pearson was for many years the principal door-keeper of the House of Commons. In that post he not only admitted Strangers to the galleries in return for the gratuity of half a crown, but was able to observe the characters of MPs at close quarters—he was politically inclined towards Fox and the cause of liberty. His satirical *Political Dictionary* was published after his death.

Joseph Pearson, *Pearson's Political Dictionary* (1793)

PAIRING OFF—Two sneaking scoundrels, not worth a piece of dog's meat to either party.—N.B. Bamber Gascoyne was a d—mn'd lazy fellow this way.

J. L. Garvin, *The Life of Joseph Chamberlain* (1933), Vol. II

Later, when Harcourt is Chancellor of the Exchequer, he [Chamberlain] pleads confidentially and with success that in spite of general orders for economy, the Treasury may find the money for completing the Temperate House at Kew.

That House had remained uncompleted for thirty years. Then, one day during the session of 1893, Harcourt when Chancellor of the Exchequer invited Chamberlain to pair with him for the evening.

J.C. 'I am afraid I cannot do that as I am going to speak in this debate.'

W.V.H. 'Oh, don't do that, for if you speak I shall have to stay to reply. But I have an old engagement to preside this evening at the annual banquet of the Civil Service.'

J.C. 'Well, I will make a bargain with you. If you will put the money into next year's Estimates to complete the Temperate House at Kew, I will pair with you for as long as you like.'

W.V.H. 'That's a bargain.'

And so it was done.

Tom Driberg, *The Best of Both Worlds: A Personal Diary* (1953)

May 25, 1952. The Parliamentary practice of 'pairing' seems to cause some mystification in the country. No doubt this is because—perhaps unfortunately—there is no public official record of pairs. A pair, tho' in present circumstances it usually has to be authorised by the Whips, is essentially a private arrangement between two MPs on opposite sides who both happen to want to be away from the House on the same evening.

A government with a small majority has to be stricter in keeping all its MPs at Westminster than a government with a large majority or an opposition. Tory MPs, having on the whole more outside interests in London—both business and social—than Labour MPs, find this discipline particularly irksome.

So, increasingly as the summer wears on, and Epsom and Ascot and the debutante balls come round and Court mourning ends, Tory MPs are to be seen hovering in lobbies and corridors with a questing look in their eyes and a smile so ingratiating that one might almost suppose that there were constituents around.

Never have so many Tory MPs called so many Labour MPs by their Christian names. The common formula is: 'I say, Bill, old boy, you don't want to be away next Monday, do you?' (or Wednesday or Thursday).

Hardest of all is the task of those MPs who are Parliamentary private secretaries to Ministers. They have to beg these favours on behalf of their chiefs, who may have to be away on official duty.

Labour MPs react variously to these blandishments. Some take the view that this is an ordinary courtesy of public life, and occasionally, anyway, useful to themselves. Others, more austerely, say: 'I'm d——d if I'll do anything to help those so-and-sos. Look what they did to us.'

It is said that a Tory MP recently approached a group of three Labour MPs and asked each of them in turn if he would like to pair.

'No,' said the first. 'I'm paired already.'

'No,' said the second. 'I'm paired already.'

'No,' said the third. 'I'm a liar too.'

The office of Speaker

Earl Winterton, *Orders of the Day* (1953)

The holder of the great office of Speaker has to repress his feelings, at least in public, but every Speaker, in my experience, has his own method of expressing approval or disapproval of the content of speeches. Mr Speaker Lowther's took the pleasant form of telling young or new members, in private, if and when they went to talk to him, whether he thought they had spoken well or badly, and how the debate in which they had spoken had gone. Both Mr Speaker Fitzroy and Mr Speaker Clifton Brown had their particular methods of showing disapproval of bad, tedious and too lengthy speeches. Mr Fitzroy would remark to himself in a voice audible at least to the two front benches 'What a speech,' or 'When is this boring fellow going to sit down?' Returning to the Chair after his dinner he once said to the Deputy-Speaker of the time, 'You might have called this dreary woman as I asked you as soon as I left the Chair to have my dinner. Now I suppose I shall have to listen to fifteen minutes of the invariable nonsense which she talks!' Mr Speaker Clifton Brown drummed angrily and repetitively with his fingers on the sides of the chair when he thought a speech had lasted too long—a frequently effective method of unofficial closuring. It is a tribute to the fairness of Speakers of the House of Commons that they give the male and female bores, of which that assembly contains, as is natural, a proportion, their reasonable share of speaking. Sometimes I have suspected them of deliberately 'calling' a bore after a stormy scene in order that he or she may empty the House and give members a chance of cooling down.

A Father of the House

Sir John Robert Mowbray, Bt. (1815–99), was educated at Westminster and at Christ Church, Oxford. He was called to the bar in 1841 and joined the Western Circuit, twice serving as Judge-Advocate-General. He was Conservative MP for Durham city from 1853 to 1868; and for Oxford University from 1868 until his death. From 1874 he was chairman of the Standing Orders and Selection Committees, and he was created a baronet in 1880. He became Father of the House—the honorary title bestowed on the longest-serving MP for a particular constituency—shortly before he died.

Sir John Mowbray, Diary, first day of session of 1898

Things have been very pleasant and amusing. First the policeman's greeting, 'Hope you are quite well, Sir John; you have quite recovered your colour.' Then the chorus in the House and lobbies is 'How well you look!' Cohen said, 'You want to be the Father of the House, but I shall vote against you on one ground only—you look too young; you look younger than you did last year.' The Speaker's greeting was very pleasant, and I hope significant: as he shook me by the hand he said, 'I suppose I must greet you as Father of the House in spite of what I read to the contrary.' Men of all shades of opinion seem to take the same view, and if I may draw any conclusion, the feeling of the House is very much in my favour. Dr Tanner said, 'Now you are the Father, we must look after your health.' The three Clerks all greeted me in a row. Palgrave said something on saluting the Father, Milman followed, and said 'Undoubtedly,' and then Jenkinson joined in chorus.

An MP counting himself out

Sir William Fraser, *Disraeli and his Day* (1891)

The Speaker is obliged, whenever his attention is called to the fact, or alleged fact, that forty Members are not present, to count the House, after waiting for two minutes.

On one occasion, the Member for the North Riding of Yorkshire, W. Morritt of Rokeby, was addressing the House on the subject of the Agricultural Interest. The House was obviously very thin: he said, 'I am very sorry that I have not a larger audience. I am sorry that, when I go back to the North Riding, I shall have to tell the farmers of Yorkshire that when I addressed the House of Commons on a subject interesting to them, there were only, let me see! how many Members present': he then began to count. The Speaker, rising immediately, said, 'Order! Order! My attention has been called to the number of

Members present in the House.' After two minutes he proceeded to count. The House adjourned: and Morritt, being a man of most exceptional sharpness, found that he had done what I believe had not been done before in the history of the House of Commons, 'counted himself out'.

Outmanoeuvring the other side

David Lloyd George, Letters to his brother William George

June 26, 1891. You will be surprised, perhaps, to find that I spoke last night upon the refusal of the Government to sanction the establishment of a Volunteer Corps at Ffestiniog. It was only a clever piece of Parliamentary manoeuvring. My Motion on the employment of the military at tithe sales was next on the Paper. It was within half an hour of midnight when the debate would stand adjourned. If I had gone on then, I should have had to fire away my speech at midnight. There would have been no time for a reply and the Government would have had a month wherein to communicate with the authorities down below about my statements. D'ye see? And besides, my speech would have been lost at that late hour. It would not have appeared in the papers, so I raised some sort of hare. This kept the ball rolling until within five minutes of midnight. I then got up to move to 'report progress' before they took up another vote and the Government had to consent. Go *dda ynte* [Quite good, wasn't it?]. The Welshmen laughed consumedly at the sudden interest I had developed on Military questions!

February 23, 1904. I got a good word in during the Debate yesterday after I had written to you. Poured a little sulphuric into them. Government only escaped defeat this afternoon by withdrawing a motion. We found they were in a minority and although it was the usual motion about taking the time of the House on Financial business, we opposed it—they withdrew it—we refused to allow them to withdraw and challenged a Division. They allowed it to be defeated without a Division. Nasty knock for them. That is the sort of thing that may happen one day.

July 21, 1905. The unexpected does happen—sometimes. And yet it was not altogether unexpected. It had been arranged, very cleverly. Our usual tactics are to come back after Dinner and surprise them. Last night our tactics were not to turn up until a quarter to twelve. Lure their men away by our absence— and then overwhelm them when it was too late for them to beat up any more men. We beat them by four not three. Balfour looked sick—vexed. No one can tell what he'll do. I wired you my impression last night.

August 7. Done my part of the work as far as this afternoon is concerned. My duty was to keep the Unemployed Bill going until 4.30 or 5 if possible— without quarrelling with the Labour Members. I carried it on till 6.30. I moved 4 Amendments, all of which were accepted. Drew three Tory MPs to attack the Bill. So now we are assured of a late sitting on Naval Works Bill unless Balfour, realising his danger, throws part of it over until tomorrow. That I don't mind.

❖

A new Speaker

Harold Nicolson, Letter to his sons Ben and Nigel, March 9, 1943

I came up for the election of the new Speaker. It was clear that the only possible candidate was Clifton Brown. The Serjeant at Arms, with the mace at his shoulder, stalked into the House as the clock struck 11, and laid the mace under the table. The Senior Clerk thereupon rose and darted out an arm and accusing finger at Anthony Eden. The latter informed us that His Majesty had been pleased to signify his assent to our electing a new Speaker. Clifton Brown meanwhile was sitting all careless on a back-bench, dressed in a very neat morning coat. So his name was proposed and seconded, and when the proposer and seconder advanced towards him, he made defensive gestures, indicative of reluctance. Firmly they grasped him by the arm and propelled him, resisting slightly, to the Chair. He stood there, looking very small and thin, and said a few words of thanks. He then tucked his tails under his arms and sat down. Since then he has appeared in his gown and wig. For all these years I have been accustomed to see that wig, that throne, framing the Carolean features of Fitzroy; saturnine he was, and sallow, and tall. Clifton Brown is pink and gay and white. The effect is strange. It is like seeing the fireman's nephew, on holiday from Wolverhampton, putting on his uncle's helmet.

Sir Henry 'Chips' Channon, Diary, March 9, 1943

Clifton-Brown has won the Speaker stakes, and I went to the House to watch his election as the new Speaker... Clifton-Brown is well-liked: has good manners, is simple and straightforward: is audible (perhaps a disadvantage as a Speaker) and a good House of Commons man. He is only 63, and now goes practically into purdah for the remainder of his days. No more intimacies: no more smoking-room colloquies. After luncheon, I brought Emerald back to see his Installation, and as we arrived the sirens sounded. We bombed Berlin heavily last night: this was probably the reprisal. I went into the Chamber, and saw Clifton-Brown in Court dress and wearing a short clerk's wig. At that moment Black Rod knocked, entered, bowed several times and summoned us to the Lords. We marched in solemn procession through the Princes' Gallery, but the little Robing-Room, the present abode of the Lords, was too small to admit any of us. I stayed outside with Emerald and, joined by Max Beaverbrook, we listened to the very short proceedings, and Emerald was soon surrounded by Peers of the Realm... The procession returned, and somewhere *en route*

Clifton-Brown must have changed his wig, for when I reached the Chamber he was already be-gowned and be-wigged in full Speaker's paraphernalia. There were a few perfunctory remarks from Anthony Eden, the new Speaker then rose, and declared the House adjourned. As he walked out with dignity, with his train-bearer and secretary, I heard him turn to the attendants and Serjeant and say—as if he had done it all his life—'Usual time tomorrow.' All this quaint, rather Alice-in-Wonderland ceremony went on whilst a severe air-raid was in progress.

The all-night sitting

During his tenure as Prime Minister, Stanley Baldwin assumed the traditional role of reporter to the monarch of proceedings in the House. The occasion of his description was the Committee Stage of the Widows', Orphans' and Old Age Pensions Bill, which was taken on the floor of the House. The Labour Party obstructed proceedings for two nights in succession. The King, through Lord Stamfordham, objected to the light-hearted tone of Baldwin's letter and regarded the conduct of the MPs as 'hardly decorous, or worthy of the tradition of the Mother of Parliaments'.[15]

Stanley Baldwin, Letter to King George V, July 2, 1925

After midnight a change gradually came over the proceedings. In the early hours of the morning the House bore many resemblances to St James's Park at midday. Members were lying about the benches in recumbent positions, some being overcome with sleep oblivious of their surroundings, while others occasionally feigned an interest in the proceedings by making interruptions from a sleepy and recumbent posture. The Labour Party's attempts at obstruction became intensified, and there was a tendency for the weariness of the flesh to be exhibited by signs of temper and irritation. Mr Wheatley especially showed himself to be an expert in obstructive tactics. On one amendment he actually spoke for an hour and a quarter without transgressing the rules of order—a very striking and masterly performance but one with which Members at that stage of the night would willingly have dispensed.

Sydney Silverman, *Nelson and Colne Gazette*, February 1936[16]

I suppose I may now consider myself fully-fledged. I have sat—certainly not in silence—through an all-night sitting. On Thursday morning last, at 11 a.m., I attended a meeting of the Cotton Spindles Bill. That lasted till 11 p.m. The actual session of the House began, as usual, at 2.45 p.m. That session continued without intermission until 12.43 on Friday. I had therefore actually been in the House of Commons for a few minutes short of 26 hours. It had all blown up very suddenly. It was not until about one in the morning that it became clear there was no other way out. People have an idea that all-night sittings are due to the inordinate desire of MPs to make speeches and the impossibility of restraining them, or cutting them short. That is not the case at all. Most MPs speak in the House but rarely. Indeed the criticism of most Tory MPs is that they do not speak at all, and that they regard the House just as a first-class club. No, the real reason for all-night sessions is quite different. It is in the nature of a demonstration or stay-in strike, a fight to the death. On this occasion it was designed to put an end to a particularly obnoxious habit which the Government had adopted. It succeeded in that object. The Government will not repeat the practice for a long time . . .

I was proud of the party that night. Throughout the night the bulk of the party remained on the benches showing the utmost ingenuity in discerning new points to attack and the utmost pertinacity on following every hare raised to the kill. It was good-humoured enough, but quite relentless. The Government game of course was to exhaust us. Their supporters, therefore, did not speak. We managed so to prolong discussion, that by seven o'clock next morning only two Supplementary Estimates had gone through. The outstanding heroes of the stricken field were Cripps, Aneurin Bevan, Shinwell and Garro Jones. I need hardly say that I endeavoured to do my own small share.

Tom Driberg, *The Best of Both Worlds: A Personal Diary* (1953)

June 8, 1951. Still dazed after twenty-nine hours at a stretch in the Palace of Westminster without, as they say, 'a wink', I look back over a yawning eternity to 12.30 a.m. during this past night.

An all-night sitting wouldn't be its traditional self if one of the Tory front-bench spokesmen didn't get up at about that time to move that the chairman 'do report progress and ask leave to sit again'—in other words that the debate be adjourned just after most of London's public transport has closed down and most of the MPs, especially the Labour MPs, are stuck at Westminster for the night anyway.

Much as most of us detest this archaic legislative technique, once we are past 11.30 p.m. or midnight we would rather stay and see it through till the tubes and buses start again.

The Tory spokesman usually suggests that we should go home 'at a reasonable time'—perhaps an hour or two later; that we are approaching several clauses of great importance; that we should debate them 'with fresh minds'; that our debates on these important matters will necessarily be reported inadequately by the Press, and so on . . .

The Government spokesman replies that ample legislative talent is evidently available; that (as Ede said this time) the Attorney-General 'seems to shine brighter the smaller the hours of the morning'; that it 'would not be for the general convenience of the Committee' to adjourn now; and that 'we hope therefore to make substantial progress' for 'some hours'.

Sometimes he indicates the point in the Bill it is hoped to reach, thus giving the Opposition, if they really want to get on with it and pack up, some incentive not to talk too time-wastingly.

We vote. The Government wins. The debate proceeds. It is all part of the Parliamentary tourney.

On this occasion Winston Churchill himself, in high good humour, was Tory spokesman. There was, of course, no conscious humbug or hypocrisy in his choice of the time for moving to report progress. Just as he genuinely believed that hundreds of millions of Indians could and should remain subject to our rule, so it is genuinely difficult for him to grasp the fact that most Labour MPs do not have a town house within a few minutes' stroll of St Stephen's or cars to take them home. His heart and his subconscious mind are still in the golden age in which the world and Parliament were ruled by his class.

During the long wearisome stretches of this night—when listening to the debate palled, and the skylon[17] was dark, and dawn was not yet a pale promise above Westminster Bridge, and one had eaten the special all-night 3s. 6d. breakfast (egg, bacon, sausage, cup of tea or coffee: as things are, not bad value, but hardly 'subsidised by the taxpayer')—in those purgatorial hours MPs had time to brood and gossip on that extraordinary story, the mystery of the missing Foreign Office men.

Few remembered that they had once known one of them quite well (for there are always many people around whom one knows by sight, and even to speak to, but not by name). Before he went to the Foreign Office, Guy Burgess worked for the Talks Department of the BBC. His job took him constantly into the lobby of the House of Commons; for he had to help choose, and to groom for the air, MPs doing the well-known *Week in Westminster* series. So he was at one time a fairly close friend of many MPs, including a number of Tory MPs—for instance, the present Tory Chief Whip, Patrick Buchan-Hepburn.

They recall him as a curly-headed, untidy young man, with a twinkling, mischievous face, scholarship laced with wit, and an engaging streak of the *enfant terrible*. Those who knew him best couldn't help feeling, and hoping, that the story had been played up disproportionately, and that the whole escapade might turn out to be just a trip for fun, with no ideological implications.

Sir Henry 'Chips' Channon, Diary, June 11, 1951

All afternoon, all evening, I have been cooped up here at the House, with divisions to break the boredom of the Debates, which are also occasionally enlivened by wrangles about procedure, though the Government have been dictatorial and ridiculous. But Winston has been tactless too. Many scenes and now the corridors, the lobbies, the little rooms, the libraries are all filled with supine, ungainly, snoring men. Some look dead. Our minority is usually 9 or

10 . . . towards six a.m. as the dawn broke over the Thames the rumour that we were not to rise at all but to continue on until midnight was confirmed. I am half-hysterical with exhaustion. Attlee is waspish . . . I talked with both Anthony Eden and Winston, both elegant and spruce; and later—such strange things happen during all-night sittings—I had a cup of coffee with Aneurin Bevan.

Later—Tuesday morning—12.6.51 at 10.15 I realised the hopelessness of the Parliamentary position, and had to send a message to the Duchess of Kent that I would be unable to give her luncheon as I arranged at Buck's Club at Ascot . . . it just cannot be helped—I am stuck. The world here is now divided into two camps: those who have shaved and are tidy; and those who look 'frosty'. I sent for fresh clothes, shirt and a carnation and now look extremely elegant, though I felt hungry and hysterical. What a farce it all is. These Hitler tactics on the part of the Prime Minister (whose personal decision I am told it is) to keep us going for 36 hours or so will do him no good. Though, so far, nobody has collapsed, except Clifton-Brown.

William Francis Deedes (b. 1913) was educated at Harrow and joined the *Morning Post* in 1931 and the editorial staff of the *Daily Telegraph* in 1937. During World War II he attained the rank of major and won the Military Cross. He was the Conservative MP for the Ashford division of Kent from 1950 to 1974. He first became a minister in 1954 and held Cabinet office as Minister without Portfolio, July 1962–October 1964. He was Editor of the *Daily Telegraph* from 1974 to 1986.

W. F. Deedes, *Sunday Telegraph*, June 27, 1952

And where else, it may be asked, might Members be? All Ministers have rooms and so the option of a settee. These objects, on which it is possible to sleep only on your back, give rise to some of the worst nightmares I have experienced.

An increasing number of MPs have rooms of their own and can rest there. I do not recommend lonely catnaps, broken by bells, in these cells. Nothing lowers morale faster.

For the rest, there are a dozen deep armchairs in the library, which for some curious reason attract all those who snore loudest; seating for 50 in the smoke room; for another 30 or so in the tea room. The rest of the place is furnished exactly like a railway station waiting-room.

To nap or not to nap? It is a hard question. To eat or not to eat? that is even harder. From midnight onwards the canteen will offer eggs and bacon. The tea room does a roaring trade in a particular brand of night drink. Tea and coffee too, of course . . .

Deepest depression comes to me not in the small hours before dawn, but at 1 a.m. This is a common experience. A canvass on the prospects then invariably draws dismal forebodings. Even the police and badge messengers, apostles of the disciplined approach to all-night sittings, look forlorn.

It is, of course, the hour when those of normal habits should be dropping into deepest sleep and are most missing it. If dinner has not been digested, it makes this known about 1 a.m.

By 3 a.m. one feels better. Fading hope has given way to certainty and resolve. Soon after, in high summer, the new Member sees his first dawn from the terrace, the equivalent of being blooded while fox-hunting.

Tony Benn was born Anthony Wedgwood-Benn in 1925, the second son of the 1st Viscount Stansgate (who had been a Labour MP and Cabinet Minister). He was educated at Westminster and at New College, Oxford, and served in the air force and navy volunteer reserves from 1943 to 1946. He was Labour MP for Bristol South-East from 1950 until 1961, when he was disqualified following his father's death (his elder brother having predeceased him). He won a by-election in May 1961, but his opponent took the seat. However, after the law was changed he renounced his peerage and was elected for the same seat in 1963. He became a front-bencher in 1964 and remained one until 1979. Although he was defeated in 1983, he returned as Labour MP for Chesterfield in 1984. At the time of writing this diary entry he was Opposition Spokesman on Trade and Industry.

Tony Benn, Diary, January 28, 1971

To the Party meeting at 6 which was absolutely packed. Bob lectured those of us who had been absent from votes in a general sense and then Douglas Houghton said we had set up an Action Committee made up of himself, the Leader and Deputy-Leader of the Party, the Chief Whip and Barbara Castle to plan our work for the next week. He produced a code of conduct under which we pledged ourselves not to be away unpaired for the week and not to give any hints to our opposite numbers as to what might be happening—really to declare parliamentary war. He said that at the end of the debate at midnight tonight, when the guillotine falls, there would be something like twenty-one clauses and fourteen amendments that wouldn't have been debated and we could therefore have up to thirty divisions. He asked the Party to agree to trust the decision entirely to the Action Committee and that there would be no private enterprise at all. This was accepted. Shirley Summerskill, who is a doctor, got up and commented on the possible health implications of this, but there wasn't much discussion . . .

Anyway it came to midnight, and when the guillotine fell the voting began and we voted twenty-two times. It was a great psychological experience. Here was the Party purging itself of Government in a way because, although it has long since been forgotten because it has happened so often in the past few weeks, it was the final occasion on which we ate our words as a Government and as Ministers on industrial relations, and we went through the lobby time after time after time. We must have spent five hours actually locked in the lobby and it was interesting to see people talking to each other. There was a game of chess going on between Douglas Jay and John Stonehouse. Members began reading the old *Hansards* on the bookshelves. At the end I persuaded a few people to start singing the 'Red Flag'. In the final division as we went through the lobbies, we sang the 'Red Flag', 'Cwm Rhondda' and 'We Shall Overcome' and we filed back into the Chamber and stood and sang. Harold came in and we all threw our order papers in the air. It was ridiculous in a sense and anybody from outside would have thought we were mad but the Tories were very dispirited and we were encouraged. I think it did the Party good.

❖

A House of Commons Committee

Robert Cecil, 3rd Marquis of Salisbury, *Saturday Review*, July 4, 1857

We were lingering about the hallowed precincts of St Stephens, on the way to the great hall, contemplating the fathers of English liberty with whose images a grateful posterity lines the passages, and puzzling over the apparent phenomenon that all great men have small heads, when we found ourselves in the centre of a stream of human beings hotly careering in one direction. There were counsel in wigs, attorneys dandling huge briefs, oppressed-looking clerks groaning under blue bags, and a nondescript crowd of keen eager-looking faces, panting and steaming as they elbowed each other through the splendid hall. We suffered our steps to follow the rush, which was indeed making a virtue of necessity, and after a desperate struggle up a gorgeous but somewhat ill-smelling staircase, we found ourselves in a huge square room hung round with maps. There was a bar in front of us, and beyond that a horse-shoe table, round which five weary-looking gentlemen were seated. It was that awful tribunal, a Committee of the House of Commons. In the centre was the chairman, whom we recognised as Sir Tunbelly Turnbull, MP for an agricultural county in the west, noted for his success in fatting pigs, and a great connoisseur in middens. On one side was Mr O'Blunderbuss, Dr M'Hale's representative on the principle of universal opposition, and Mr Muddle, a small country grocer, whom the late apotheosis of town clerks had exalted into a senator. On the other side sat a scamp of a Life-Guardsman, whom his aristocratic mother had sent into the House as the sole chance of making him steady, and a Yellow Admiral, who has a strong opinion on the peculiar construction of scuppers, but has never been known to express any opinion on any other subject whatever.

We wondered what these sages could possibly have met to discuss, and what human being could pay the slightest deference to their decision. But on listening to Mr Hope Scott and Serjeant Wrangham, who were arguing at the bar, we discovered that the disposal of several millions turned on their sentence. Indeed there were many witnesses in the room who loudly asseverated that, if the project under discussion were sanctioned, they would be utterly ruined. The matter just then at issue was a nice point of conveyancing, which at that moment was still *sub judice* in the Court of Chancery. Serjeant Wrangham had succeeded in convincing the Life-Guardsman that the fee-simple of land had no connexion with a lawyer's fee; but he had been compelled to do so with the greatest delicacy, for his young lordship was very sulky at being supposed to be ignorant of anything, and was very much inclined to swear. The argument proceeded. The counsel flung cases at each other, which certainly the Committee, and probably no one else, had ever heard of, and overwhelmed the tribunal with legal terms which, warned by the fate of his fellow-ignoramus, the Life-Guardsman, Sir Tunbelly was too prudent to ask the meaning of. The rest of the Committee took the infliction in various ways. Mr O'Blunderbuss kept shaking his head knowingly at all the points, to make believe he understood, and would occasionally interject a joke, at which counsel, agents, witnesses, and public roared 'in counterfeited glee'. Mr Muddle appeared to be taking notes; but his papers being afterwards found on the table, it appeared that he had been calculating the effect of the Budget on the prices of tea. The Life-Guardsman gave himself up unreservedly to sandwiches; and the Yellow Admiral, wisest of all, fairly snored.

In our innocence, we inquired of a friend close by, who we knew was an ardent admirer of the constitution, how this strange collection of varieties had been set in a position to dispose at will of the property of their fellow-subjects. We were told in answer, that they had been elected by sundry communities of publicans, small tradesmen, or small farmers, to give effect to certain political opinions on the Ballot, Church Rates, and other like matters. But why, we asked, was that supposed to fit them to adjudicate on legal points, and to adjust the claims of those to whose detriment railways or other works might have to be carried out? The only answer we could obtain was, that the House of Commons was an ancient body, and was loth to part with its privileges. But we had been often told by the *Times*, in which we are implicit believers, that this House of Commons contained some of the best men of business in the country. 'Oh!' answered our informant, 'none of the members are employed on this work except those who have nothing else to do. None of the great politicians are employed, because they have Blue-books and such matters to study, and great speeches to get up. The lawyers have quite enough of law cases without listening to their brethren in a committee-room; and the great merchants and bankers and railway directors, whose time is money, cannot afford to throw it away in meting out justice to their fellow-countrymen. And therefore these committees, which within the last few years have disposed of money more than equal to half the national debt, are almost invariably composed only of men whose time is worth nothing to themselves and whose opinion is worth nothing to the political world.' We further learned, that these sapient judges are irresponsible—that their power extends over all property, and to the abrogation of any title and any law—that they are bound by no code or precedent, except their own views of equity and policy—that their sentence, if it be against a project, is without appeal, and that, if in its favour, there is no appeal for those whom its operation may injure, except to a tribunal nearly as bad in the House of Lords. We were moreover informed that the management of these judges, to whom legal acumen appeals in vain, is so delicate a matter, and requires such peculiar talents, that the fortunate few who possess them are able to charge the luckless suitors, whose all depends upon their aid, as much as fifteen guineas for every four hours. We thought to ourselves that it was idle to talk of the House of Commons being unchristianised; for verily it is the only body in Christendom whose zeal goes so far that it carries out to the letter the Apostle's ironical precept, to 'set them to judge who are least esteemed'. But while we were communicating this original thought to our friend, the Yellow Admiral awoke and called us to order, to show that he had been attending all the while.

Hear! Hear!

Joseph Pearson, *Pearson's Political Dictionary* (1793)

HEAR! HEAR!—A note of approbation used by one side or the other of the House, whenever any thing is said to please it by its respective friends. Sometimes Hear! Hear! is vociferated on one side upon something being said on the other; not that it likes it, but merely to pin it down to the words used. And sometimes both sides will roar out Hear! Hear! at what has fallen, both thinking it in their favour, and tending to serve them.—*Mem.* I have often thought it rather puzzling to determine which side had most right to call out Hear! Hear!

T. P. O'Connor, *Harper's New Monthly Magazine*, December 1893

'Hear, hear!' is the one form of expressing emotion which the House of Commons knows. Usually, of course, it means the intellectual assent to some proposition which is being stated by the speaker, and in that sense it is frigid and quiet. But if the House of Commons wishes to signify not merely intellectual assent, but also depth of emotion, the 'Hear, hear!' is, of course, louder, but it is still 'Hear, hear!' Again, the House of Commons, or a portion of it, wishes to be ironical, and 'Hear, hear!' is uttered in as rasping a voice as its utterers can command. The words also get transformed in all kinds of ways, according to the idiosyncrasies, the accents, and the education of the persons who use them. The late Sir Robert Fowler, an ex-Lord Mayor, and a Tory of the old true-blue order, for instance, was famous as a shouter of 'Hear, hear!' but it became in his mouth 'Yah, yah!' Often, 'Hear, hear!' becomes transformed into "Ear, 'ear!'

The reader of Parliamentary debates must understand in the light of these observations the reports in our newspapers. When they read that a certain sentence has been received with cheers, they must understand that a certain number of members have together called out 'Hear, hear!' for, say, ten seconds. When the report announces 'loud and prolonged cheers', it simply means that the 'Hear, hear!' has been uttered in somewhat louder tones than usual, and for a period more prolonged—perhaps to thirty seconds. There is something ludicrous, and yet there can be something very expressive, in this strange method the House of Commons has of expressing emotions.

Charles T. King (b. 1868) succeeded Henry Lucy as the Parliamentary representative of the *Daily Express*. He held the post from 1906 to 1919.

Charles T. King, *The Asquith Parliament (1906–1909)* (1910)

There is a rule in the House of Commons against every form of expression in chorus by way of applause or blame other than by the phrase 'Hear! Hear!' This seems at first glance a very scanty instrument of expression. It is the reverse. Members are not allowed to applaud. They are not allowed to clap their hands. They are forbidden to stamp their feet. However much they revel in the perorations of their leader, the only phrase they may use by way of showing it is 'Hear! Hear!' But this is a wonderful flexible expression. If members agree enthusiastically with something said by a member they may only say 'Hear! Hear!' If they disagree with it they can only say 'Hear! Hear!' When a new member walks up the floor after winning a seat for his party, the only cry that party has at its command for the expression of its gladness and the roar of its triumph is 'Hear! Hear!'

But in reality this severe restriction means no poverty of expression. The House of Commons has extended the shouting, the wailing, the crying, the roaring or bawling of that phrase 'Hear! Hear!' into the most comprehensive vocal expression ever emitted from the lips of man.

It is the foundation of cries narrowly articulate as to words, but prodigal with expression of sound. Sometimes it will sweep forth as a paean of victory from a mighty chorus of throats. Now it is a high, a sort of Gaelic skirl. Now it is a low or fierce in anger, or it is a soft drone or a tender note of sympathy. A great leader on one side or the other will strike his chorus as one striking a vast sounding-board. Never did the seasoned soldiers of a well-drilled infantry regiment hit the ground with the butts of their rifles with more simultaneous sharpness than will a great party roar out a volume of sound at the word of a leader or an opponent.

The minds of the men who make up the House of Commons are quick minds. It seems to hit them all at the same moment, the same second . . .

The cry of sudden pain, the shout of party anger, the rattle of mocking, laughing exultation, the skirl of political victory, of party triumph, are all expressed on the foundation of the one phrase, 'Hear! Hear!'

But there is another time when it has another sound. Now it runs on a minor key; it knows no party now. A broad sweep of sympathy has united the House of Commons as one man. I shall never forget sitting in the Press gallery gazing down at the House of Commons in the late days of the Premiership of Sir Henry Campbell-Bannerman. For some time he had been absent from the House of Commons. He came back to the House. He rose, a bowed, grey figure, shaken with age and personal sorrow. He had come back from the sick-room where he had hovered a week or so between hope and fear. He began a word or two as of passing apology to the House. A broad, low sound of sympathy went up, tender and soft, and long and deep. It came, not from a party, but from the House of Commons.

'Who goes home?'

Charles T. King, *The Asquith Parliament (1906–1909)* (1910)

We will pause a moment while the cry of 'Who goes home?' is ringing through the halls and corridors of the Palace of Westminster. That cry has been ringing here nightly for long centuries, relic of a time when members, before leaving the House, banded themselves together for their mutual protection against highwaymen, cut-throats and footpads who infested the way. 'Home!' cries a messenger every night now when the Speaker pronounces the magic words 'This House now stands adjourned.' 'Who—o— go—O—oes ho—o—me!' cry the policemen along the corridors, while the Serjeant-at-Arms lifts the Mace from the table and the last glint of the silver buckles and the last flutter of the flowing robes of Mr Speaker Lowther vanish in the shadows behind the great chair.

1. Harry Graham, *The Mother of Parliaments* (1911), pp. 153–4.
2. *The Times*, January 25, 1860.
3. Graham, op. cit., p. 154.
4. Richard Crossman, Diary, October 31, 1967.
5. Alexander Mackintosh, *Echoes of Big Ben: A Journalist's Parliamentary Diary, 1881–1940* (1945), p. 14.
6. Lord Frederic Hamilton, *The Days Before Yesterday* (1920), p. 213.
7. Fenner Brockway, *Inside the Left: Thirty Years of Platform, Press, Prison and Parliament* (1942), p. 224.
8. Spencer Leigh Hughes, *Press, Platform and Parliament* (1918), pp. 144–7.
9. Nigel Nicolson, *People and Parliament* (1958), p. 64.
10. Sir Reginald Palgrave, *The House of Commons* (1878), p. 9.
11. Henry W. Lucy, *Memories of Eight Parliaments* (1908), p. 285.
12. Sir William Fraser, *Disraeli and his Day* (1891), p. 323.
13. F. E. Smith, as the Earl of Birkenhead, was now Lord Chancellor.
14. The Barebones Parliament was the Nominated or Little Parliament, July–December 1653, whose membership was chosen by Cromwell and his council; its nickname derived from the fanatical MP Praise-God Barebon.
15. Montgomery Hyde, *Baldwin* (1973), pp. 248–9.
16. Emrys Hughes, *Sydney Silverman: Rebel in Parliament* (1967), p. 57.
17. The skylon was a cigar-shaped object that was erected on the south bank of the Thames as part of the Festival of Britain.

4 Great and Terrible Occasions

> I have tried all forms of excitement, from tip-cat to tiger-shooting; all degrees of gambling, from beggar-my-neighbour to Monte Carlo; but have found no gambling like politics, and no excitement like a big division in the House of Commons.
>
> Lord Randolph Churchill[1]

The central drama of parliamentary life has been the great struggle for power, first between King and Commons and later between King and Opposition, and later still between the parties. In this chapter can be found accounts of Cromwell's dissolution of parliament; of the only assassination of a British prime minister, within the precincts of Parliament; of crucial motions of censure and votes of confidence which led to the fall of administrations, such as those of Melbourne in 1841, Peel in 1845, and MacDonald in 1924; although sometimes the fall of an administration can be bathetic in the extreme. When Rosebery's administration fell in 1895 over the issue of the supply of cordite to the Army, the Ministers and Whips were caught napping: 'Harcourt was on the Terrace chatting with friends and rejoicing that they were having a quiet evening without a crisis when the division bells rang, and some unsuspecting Liberals, like Labouchere, after voting, hurried home to dinner without waiting to hear the result of the division.'[2]

Budgets have often been great occasions, of course, but none are found here: Gladstone's great budgets are described in another chapter, while Lloyd George's 1909 statement, known as 'The People's Budget', is excluded. Some obviously terrible occasions, such as instances of grave disorder in the House, or of Irish obstruction, are also reserved for later chapters. Instead, there are announcements of war, by Grey in 1914 and Chamberlain in 1939, and of the Normandy Landings in 1944. There is the struggle to bring about that landmark of constitutional change, the Reform Act of 1832; and those fundamental legislative measures such as the Repeal of the Corn Laws and the 1886 Home Rule Bill, each of which split a party for more than a generation. Finally, there are rare moments of collective emotion, as when Parliament formally recognised the plight of the Jews during World War II. Among the notable omissions are King Charles I's attempt to arrest the five Members; the Don Pacifico debate in 1851 (there is no particularly vivid description); the debate on J. A. Roebuck's motion censuring the conduct of the Crimean War; the debates on the creation of the National Health Service; the debates on steel nationalisation in 1947, in which Churchill rekindled the spirit of the Opposition against the Attlee Government; and the Profumo debate, which proved a turning-point in the life of the Macmillan administration.

'It has been said that the most striking happenings at Westminster are the unexpected happenings,' wrote the *Daily Mail*'s Frank Dilnot in 1911. 'This is not absolutely correct. Sometimes a long-looked-forward-to event, a great political revealment, comes with all the more effect when its secrets have been guessed at for months, when all the world has been agog to get a hint of those secrets, and when on the appointed day, the announcement, full, definite, and clear, is made in the presence of the House of Commons, which has come together especially for that purpose. That was the position with regard to Mr Lloyd George's Budget of April 29th, 1909.'[3] Indeed, as well as the usual crush in the Chamber and galleries, there was an unprecedented break in the proceedings at half-past six, after the Chancellor had been speaking for three-and-a-half hours. A half-hour interval followed and Lloyd George resumed his task at seven o'clock, speaking until eight-thirty.

Tiny details, too, may add to the drama of a great occasion. Sir Henry Morris-Jones observed the demeanour of Mr Speaker FitzRoy on Abdication Day in 1937, noting that 'as Mr Baldwin handed him the Message from the King, which he had walked up with from the Bar of the House, the hand that took the paper visibly shook, and there was a tremor in his voice as he read its contents to the hushed House'.[4] Yet the occasion was still susceptible to a different interpretation. Aneurin Bevan, for example, viewed the parliamentary reaction to the Abdication as one of hollow melodrama.[5]

'What constitutes a great debate?' one parliamentary journalist has asked. 'There are, I suggest, only two constant factors: the Chamber must be packed, and there must be no triviality about the theme. No debate can be great if it is conducted in the presence of twenty or thirty Members. Similarly, crowded benches may howl and bay to the moon without lending one iota of significance to a petty occasion.'[6]

An attempt to infect John Pym with the plague

John Pym (1584–1643) was educated at Broadgates Hall (now Pembroke College), Oxford, and studied law at the Middle Temple. He entered Parliament as MP for Calne in 1614. He soon became identified with the party that opposed the King and in the Short Parliament of 1640 he emerged as the effective leader of the House of Commons.

John Forster, *The Debates on the Grand Remonstrance* (1860)

Pym was sitting in his usual place on the right hand, beyond the members' gallery, near the bar, on the 25th of October, 1641, when, in the midst of debate on a proposition he had submitted for allowance of 'powder and bullet' to the City Guard, a letter was brought to him. The sergeant of the House had received it from a messenger at the door, to whom a gentleman on horseback in a grey coat had given it that morning, on Fish Street Hill—with a gift of a shilling, and injunction to deliver it with great care and speed. As Pym opened the letter, something dropped out of it on the floor; but without giving heed to this he read to himself a few words, and then, holding up the paper called it a scandalous libel. Hereupon it was carried up to the lately appointed clerk's assistant, Mr John Rushworth, who, in his unmoved way, read aloud its abuse of the great leader of the House, and its asseveration that if he should escape the present attempt, the writer had a dagger prepared for him. At this point, however, young Mr Rushworth would seem to have lost his coolness, for he read the next few lines in an agitated way. They explained what had dropped from the letter. It was a rag that had come from a plague wound, sent in the hope that infection might by such means be borne to him who opened it. Whereupon Rushworth, having read so far, threw down the letter into the house, and so it was spurned away out of the door.

Cromwell dissolves Parliament

In 1651 Cromwell began to grow impatient with the Rump of the Long Parliament, which had been sitting since 1640. It had become a self-perpetuating body given to endless talking and procrastination, reluctant to proceed with legal reforms or to contemplate its own dissolution. The Army had wanted a dissolution for some years now. A Bill of Elections, to determine the nature of the electorate for a new Parliament, was introduced, but when Cromwell and the Army objected, the Rumpers agreed to delay consideration of the Bill until other matters were resolved. In April 1653 Cromwell heard that the Rump was in the process of passing an Act for its prolongation. Wearing but a plain black coat and grey worsted stockings and with a party of musketeers behind him, he descended on the House of Commons in a fury.

Edmund Ludlow (c.1617–92) was the son of Sir Henry Ludlow, MP for Wiltshire in the Long Parliament, and distinguished himself as a soldier fighting in the parliamentary cause in the Civil War. A keen republican, he was elected as MP for Wiltshire in 1646 and was later one of the King's judges and Regicides. He was elected as one of Cromwell's Council of State and served in Ireland as a Lieutenant-General and a Civil Commissioner. He later fell out with Cromwell over the latter's assumption of dictatorial powers. After 1660 he went into exile in Switzerland, returning briefly in 1689 until an order for his arrest forced him to flee to Holland and back again to Switzerland. The principal figure present on this occasion, from whom Ludlow gleaned most of the details, Major-General Thomas Harrison, was not so fortunate as his friend. A fanatical Puritan, he was one of the Regicides who was tried for high treason after the Restoration. He was hanged, drawn and quartered along with others of the Regicides at Tyburn, in the presence of Charles II.

The Memoirs of Edmund Ludlow (1698)

The Parliament now perceiving to what kind of excesses the madness of the army was like to carry them, resolved to leave as a legacy to the people the Government of a Commonwealth by their representatives, when assembled in Parliament, and in the intervals thereof by a Council of State, chosen by them, and to continue till the meeting of the next succeeding Parliament, to whom they were to give an account of their conduct and management. To this end they resolved, without any further delay, to pass the Act for their own dissolution; of which Cromwell having notice, makes haste to the House, where he sat down and heard the debate for some time. Then calling to Major-General Harrison, who was on the other side of the House, to come to him, he told him, that he judged the Parliament ripe for a dissolution, and this to be the time of doing it. The Major-General answered, as he since told me; 'Sir, the work is very great and dangerous, therefore I desire you seriously to consider of it before you engage in it.' 'You say well,' replied the General, and thereupon sat still for about a quarter of an hour; and then the question for passing the Bill being to be put, he said again to Major-General Harrison, 'this is the time I must do it'; and suddenly standing up, made a speech, wherein he loaded the Parliament with the vilest reproaches, charging them not to have a heart to do any thing for the public good, to have espoused the corrupt interest of the Presbytery and the lawyers, who were the supporters of tyranny and oppression, accusing them of an intention to perpetuate themselves in power, had they not been forced to the passing of this Act, which he affirmed they designed never to observe, and thereupon told them, that the Lord had done with them, and had chosen other instruments for the carrying on of his work that were more worthy. This he spoke with so much passion and discomposure of mind, as if he had been distracted. Sir Peter Wentworth stood up to answer him, and said, that this was the first time that ever he had heard such unbecoming language given to the Parliament, and that it was the more horrid in that it came from their servant, and their servant whom they had so highly trusted and obliged: but as he was going on, the General stepped into the midst of the House, where continuing his distracted language, he said, 'Come come, I will put an end to your prating'; then walking up and down the House like a mad-man, and kicking the ground with his feet, he cried out, 'You are no Parliament, I say you are no Parliament; I will put an end to your sitting; call them in, call them in': whereupon the serjeant attending the Parliament opened the doors, and Lieutenant-Colonel Worsley with two files of musketeers entered the House; which Sir Henry Vane observing from his place, said aloud, 'This is not honest, yea it is against morality and common honesty.' Then Cromwell fell a railing at him, crying out with a loud voice, 'O Sir Henry Vane, Sir Henry Vane, the Lord deliver me from Sir Henry Vane.' Then looking upon one of the members, he said, 'There sits a drunkard'; and giving much reviling language to others, he commanded the mace to be taken away, saying, 'What shall we do with this bauble? here, take it away.' Having brought all into this disorder, Major-General Harrison went to the Speaker as he sat in the chair, and told him, that seeing things were reduced to this pass, it would not be convenient for him to remain there. The Speaker answered, that he would not come down unless he were forced. 'Sir,' said Harrison, 'I will lend you my hand'; and thereupon putting his hand within his, the Speaker came down. Then Cromwell applied himself to the members of the House, who were in number between 80 and 100, and said to them, 'It's you that have forced me to do this, for I have sought the Lord night and day, that he would rather slay me than put me upon the doing of this work.' Hereupon Alderman Allen, a member of Parliament, told him, that it was not yet gone so far, but all things might be restored again; and that if the soldiers were commanded out of the House, and the mace returned, the public affairs might go on in their former course: but Cromwell having now passed the Rubicon, not only rejected his advice, but charged him with an account of some hundred thousand pounds, for which he threatened to question him, he having been long treasurer for the army, and in a rage committed him to the custody of one of the musketeers. Alderman Allen told him, that it was well known that it had not been his fault that his account was not made up long since; that he had often tendered it to the House, and that he asked no favour from any man in that matter. Cromwell having acted this treacherous and impious part, ordered the guard to see the House clear'd of all the members, and then seized upon the records that were there, and at Mr Scobell's house. After which he went to the clerk, and snatching the Act of Dissolution, which was ready to pass, out of his hand, he put it under his cloak, and having commanded the doors to be locked up, went away to Whitehall.

The assassination of Spencer Perceval

Spencer Perceval (1762–1812), the seventh son of the 2nd Earl of Egmont, was educated at Harrow and at Trinity College, Cambridge. He was called to the bar in 1786 and became Deputy Recorder of Northampton. He was MP for Northampton from 1796 until his death, and although he never called himself a Tory he served mainly in Tory administrations. He held office as Solicitor-General under Addington in 1801 and as Attorney-General the following year. He was Chancellor of the Exchequer and Leader of the House from 1807 until 1809, when he became Prime Minister. He was admired for his talents and very popular, though some scorned him for his bitter opposition to Catholic Emancipation (he was an Evangelical). 'Nothing could be so gentlemanlike or fair as his management of the House of Commons,' declared John William Ward.[7]

William Jerdan (1782–1869) was born in Scotland, the son of a small landowner, and after working briefly as a clerk in a counting-house and in the office of a writer to the signet, he moved to London in 1806 and worked as a reporter for various newspapers, covering parliamentary proceedings for three sessions for the *British Press*. He was editor of the *Sun*, a High Tory daily paper, from 1813 to 1817, and editor of the *Literary Gazette* from 1817 to 1850, becoming its sole proprietor in 1842. He retired with a civil list pension and settled down to write his four-volume *Autobiography*.

The murder of Perceval occurred on May 11, 1812, the trial of the murderer took place on the 15th, and his execution followed on the 18th. Jerdan, who gave evidence at the trial, kept the opera-glass that had belonged to the murderer. As he explained: 'it had frequently been seen, during the fortnight before, in the assassin's hands in the gallery of the House of Commons, whence he surveyed the members below, and ascertained surely by asking the reporters which was Mr Perceval. There can, however, be no doubt but that he had long fixed upon his victim; and given up the idea, if he ever entertained it, of murdering Lord Leveson Gower, whom he accused of traversing his commercial course in Russia.'

The Autobiography of William Jerdan, Vol. I (1852)

About 5 o'clock of the tragical day referred to, I had walked down to the House to listen, in my turn, to the interminable debates in Committee on the Orders in Council, which were very briefly reported in the newspapers. On ascending the broad flight of steps which led to the folding door of the lobby, I perceived the minister, with whom I had the honour of a slight acquaintance, immediately behind me, with his light and lithesome step following in the same direction. I saluted him, and was saluted in return, with that benevolent smile which I was so instantly destined to see effaced for ever, and pushing open and holding back the half door, to allow the precedence of entering, I of course made way for him to go in.

He did enter, and there was an instant noise, but as a physical fact it is very remarkable to state that, though I was all but touching him, and if the ball had passed through his body it must have lodged in mine, *I did not hear* the report of the pistol. It is true it was fired in the inside of the lobby, and I was just out of it; but considering our close proximity, I have always found it difficult to account for the phenomenon I have noticed. I saw a small curling wreath of smoke rise above his head, as if the breath of a cigar; I saw him reel back against the ledge on the inside of the door; I heard him exclaim, 'Oh God!' or 'Oh my God!' and nothing more or longer (as reported by several witnesses), for even that exclamation was faint; and then making an impulsive rush, as it were, to reach the entrance to the house on the opposite side for safety, I saw him totter forward, not half way, and drop dead between the four pillars which stood there in the centre of the space, with a slight trace of blood issuing from his lips.

All this took place ere with moderate speed you could count five! Great confusion, and almost as immediately great alarm ensued. Loud cries were uttered, and rapidly conflicting orders and remarks on every hand made a perfect Babel of the scene; for there were above a score of people in the lobby, and on the instant no one seemed to know what had been done, or by whom. The corpse of Mr Perceval was lifted up by Mr William Smith, the member for Norwich, assisted by Lord Francis Osborne, a Mr Phillips, and several others, and borne into the office of the Speaker's Secretary, by the small passage on the left hand, beyond and near the fire-place.—It must have been, pallid, and deadly, close by the murderer; for in a moment after Mr Eastaff, one of the clerks of the Vote Office, at the last door on that side, pointed him out, and called 'that is the murderer!' Bellingham moved slowly to a bench on the hither side of the fire-place, near at hand, and sat down. I had in the first instance run forward to render assistance to Mr Perceval, but only witnessed the lifting of his body, followed the direction of Mr Eastaff's hand, and seized the assassin by the collar, but without violence on one side, or resistance on the other. Comparatively speaking, a crowd now came up, and among the earliest Mr Vincent Dowling, Mr John Norris, Sir Charles Long, Sir Charles Burrell, Mr Henry Burgess, and, in a minute or two, General Gascoigne from a committee room up stairs, and Mr Hume, Mr Whitbread, Mr Pole, and twelve or fifteen members from the House. Meanwhile, Bellingham's neckcloth had been stripped off, his vest unbuttoned, and his chest laid bare. The discharged pistol was found beside him, and its companion was taken, loaded and primed, from his pocket. An opera-glass, papers, and other articles were also pulled forth, principally by Mr Dowling, who was on his left, whilst I stood on his right hand; and except for his frightful agitation, he was as passive as a child. Little was said to him. General Gascoigne on coming up and getting a glance through the surrounding spectators observed that he knew him at Liverpool, and asked if his name was Bellingham, to which he returned no answer, but the papers rendered farther question on this point unnecessary. Mr Lynn, a surgeon in Great George Street, adjacent, had been hastily sent for, and found life quite extinct, the ball having entered in a slanting direction from the hand of the tall assassin, and passed into the victim's heart. Some one came out of the room with this intelligence, and said to Bellingham, 'Mr Perceval is dead! Villain, how could you destroy so good a man, and make a family of twelve children orphans?' To which he most mournfully replied, 'I am sorry for it.' Other observations and questions were addressed to him by by-standers; in answer to which he spoke incoherently, mentioning the wrongs he had suffered from government, and justifying his revenge on similar grounds to those he used, at length, in his defence at the Old Bailey.

I have alluded to Bellingham's 'frightful agitation' as he sat on the bench, as all this dreadful work was going on; and I return to it to describe it as far as words can convey an idea of the shocking spectacle. I could only imagine something like it in the overwrought painting of a powerful romance writer, but never before could conceive the physical suffering of a strong muscular man, under the tortures of a distracted mind. Whilst his language was cool, the agonies which shook his frame were actually terrible. His countenance wore the hue of the grave, blue and cadaverous; huge drops of sweat ran down from his forehead, like rain on the window-pane in a heavy storm, and coursing his pallid cheeks, fell upon his person where their moisture was distinctly visible; and from the bottom of his chest to his gorge, rose and receded, with almost every breath, a spasmodic action, as if a body, as large or larger than a billiard-ball, were choking him. The miserable wretch repeatedly struck his chest with the palm of his hand to abate this sensation, but it refused to be repressed.

Lord John Russell introduces the Reform Bill

In the eighteenth century the King's Government used patronage to buy the support of aristocratic borough-owners and their nominee MPs, a system which the Radicals called 'Old Corruption'. The Whigs had been split over the issue of parliamentary Reform and Pitt the Younger's attempt to introduce a set of mild proposals had foundered in 1785. Reform became popular with the working classes, who believed that it would bring an end to their economic difficulties; while the middle classes by 1830 had also embraced Reform, because they thought it would stave off revolution. Instead of producing a mild measure as expected, such as buying up some of the 'rotten boroughs' and giving them to the new industrial cities, the Whig Ministry led by Earl Grey decided to abolish all nomination boroughs without compensating their owners.

Earl Russell, Introduction to *Selections from Speeches of Earl Russell, 1817 to 1841* (1870)

So little were the opposite party prepared for the Bill, that a few days before the first of March, Sir Robert Peel, in a careful speech, derided what had been done on the subjects of peace and retrenchment, and predicted that when the plan of Reform should be developed, it would occasion disappointment by the meagreness of its proportions and the trifling nature of the changes recommended. The effect, therefore, of the revelations of the first of March was astounding. I had purposely omitted, or passed slightly over, those arguments in favour of reform, which in 1822 I had developed at length. Sir Robert Peel observed sarcastically that I had said that many ingenious arguments were urged in favour of the ballot, but that I had not stated any ingenious arguments in favour of my proposition of that night. This was substantially true. It seemed to me that the arguments in favour of reform had made their impression—a very deep impression—upon the country; but that those arguments had become trite and familiar, and that the great novelty of my speech must consist in a clear and intelligible statement of the nature of the proposition I had to make. The extinction of 150 seats in the House of Commons, all taken from the class of boroughs which were either dependent or venal, would amount, if carried, to a revolution.

It was no wonder that this proposition, when placed boldly and baldly before the House of Commons, created feelings of astonishment, mingled with joy or with consternation, according to the temper of the hearers. Mr John Smith, himself a member for a nomination borough, said the proposal took away his breath. Some, perhaps many, thought that the measure was a prelude to civil war, which, in point of fact, it averted. But incredulity was the prevailing feeling, both among the moderate Whigs and the great mass of the Tories. Sir Henry Harding told Sir James Graham that he supposed we should all go out the next morning. Many of the Whigs thought it impossible the Government could succeed, either in the existing House of Commons, or by an appeal to the people.

The Radicals alone were delighted and triumphant. Mr Joseph Hume, when I met him in the streets a day or two afterwards, assured me of his hearty support of the Government. He said on another subject, in a public speech, that he was ready to vote black white in order to carry the measure of Reform. Lord Durham, who was sitting under the gallery on the first of March, told me he was inclined to doubt the reality of what was passing before his eyes. A noble lord who sat opposite to me, and who has long ago succeeded to a seat in the House of Lords, cheered me so vociferously that I was myself inclined to doubt his meaning. I found afterwards that his cheers were meant derisively, to show his thorough conviction of the absurdity and impracticability of my proposals.

John Cam Hobhouse, Lord Broughton, *Recollections of a Long Life* (1911)

Never shall I forget the astonishment of my neighbours as Lord John Russell developed his plan. Indeed, all the House seemed perfectly astounded; and when he read the long list of the boroughs to be either wholly or partially disfranchised, there was a sort of wild ironical laughter. Lord John seemed rather to play with the fears of his audience; and, after detailing some clauses that seemed to complete the scheme, smiled and paused, and said, 'More yet.' When Lord John sat down, we of the Mountain cheered long and loud, although there was hardly one of us that believed such a scheme could, by any possibility, become the law of the land.

The Reform Bill passes its First Reading in the House of Commons

T. B. Macaulay, Letter to Thomas Flower Ellis, March 30, 1831

Such a scene as the division of last Tuesday, I never saw, and never expect to see again. If I should live fifty years, the impression will be as fresh and sharp in my mind as if it had just taken place. It was like seeing Caesar stabbed in the Senate House, or seeing Oliver taking the mace from the table; a sight to be seen only once and never to be forgotten. The crowd overflowed the House in every part. When the strangers were cleared out and the doors were locked, we had 608 members present—more by fifty-five than ever were in a division before. The ayes and the noes were like two volleys of cannon from opposite sides of a field of battle. When the Opposition went out into the Lobby, an operation which took up twenty minutes or more, we spread ourselves over the benches on both sides of the House; for there were many of us who were not able to find a seat during the evening.

When the doors were shut, we began to speculate on our numbers. Everybody was desponding. 'We have lost it. We are only 280 at most. I do not think we are 250. They are 300. Alderman Thompson has counted them. He says they are 299.' This was the talk on our benches ... I had no hope, however, of 300. As the tellers passed along our lowest row on the left-hand side the interest was insupportable—291, 292—we were all standing up and stretching forward, telling with the tellers. At 300 there was a short cry of joy, at 302 another, suppressed, however, in a moment, for we did not know what the hostile force might be. We knew, however, that we could not be severely beaten.

The doors were thrown open, and in they came. Each as he entered brought some different report of their numbers ... We were all breathless when Charles Wood, who stood near the door, jumped on a bench and cried out, 'They are only 301.' We set up a shout that you might have heard to Charing Cross, waving our hats, stamping on the floor, and clapping our hands. The tellers scarcely got through the crowd, for the House was thronged up to the table and all the floor was fluctuating with heads like the pit of a theatre. But you might have heard a pin drop as Duncannon read the numbers. Then again the shouts broke out, and many of us shed tears. I could scarcely refrain. And the jaw of Peel fell; and the face of Twiss was the face of a damned soul; and Herries looked like Judas taking his necktie off for the last operation. We shook hands and clapped each other on the back, and went out laughing, crying, and huzzaing into the Lobby. And no sooner were the doors opened than another shout answered that within the House. All the passages and stairs into the waiting-rooms were thronged with people who had waited till four o'clock in the morning to know the issue. We passed through a narrow lane between two thick masses of them; and all the way down they were shouting and waving their hats, till we got into the open air. I called a cabriolet, and the first thing the driver asked was, 'Is the bill carried?' 'Yes, by one.' 'Thank God for it, sir!' And away I rode to Gray's Inn. And so ended a scene which will probably never be equalled till the reformed Parliament wants reforming; and that I hope will not be till the days of our grand-children,—till that truly orthodox and apostolical person Dr Francis Ellis is an archbishop of eighty.

The Government dissolves Parliament to seek the support of the electorate for its Reform Bill

Following the Government's victory by one vote in the Commons, General Gascoyne proposed an amendment which was carried. The Bill was withdrawn and Parliament was dissolved so that Grey's administration could seek a popular mandate.

Charles Greville (1794–1865) was a grandson, on his mother's side, of the Duke of Portland, and was educated at Eton and at Christ Church, Oxford. His grandfather's influence secured him the sinecure secretaryship of Jamaica (which he never had to visit) and the clerkship to the Privy Council in 1821. Thus he was able to become closely acquainted with leading politicians and observe high politics, while indulging his love of the turf—for several years he was partnered in training racehorses with his cousin, Lord George Bentinck. He kept a political diary for over forty years, from 1817 to 1860, which was published posthumously in eight volumes.

Charles Greville, Diary, April 24, 1831

On Thursday the Ministers were again beaten in the House of Commons on a question of adjournment, and on Friday morning they got the King to go down and prorogue Parliament in person the same day. This *coup d'état* was so sudden that nobody was aware of it till within two or three hours of the time, and many not at all. They told him that the cream-coloured horses could not be got ready, when he said, 'Then I will go with anybody else's horses.' Somebody went off in a carriage to the Tower to fetch the Crown, and they collected such attendants as they could find to go with his Majesty. The Houses met at one or two o'clock. In the House of Commons Sir R. Vyvyan made a furious speech, attacking the Government on every point, and excited as he was, it was very well done. The Ministers made no reply, but Sir Francis Burdett and Tennyson endeavoured to interrupt with calls to order, and when the Speaker decided that Vyvyan was not out of order, Tennyson disputed his ruling, which enraged the Speaker, and soon after called up Peel, for whom he was resolved to procure a hearing. The scene then resembled that which took place on Lord North's resignation in 1782, for Althorp (I think) moved that Burdett should be heard and the Speaker said that 'Peel was in possession of the House to speak on that motion'. He made a very violent speech, attacking the Government for their incompetence, folly, and recklessness, and treated them with the utmost asperity and contempt. In the midst of his speech the guns announced the arrival of the King: and at each explosion the Government gave a loud cheer, and Peel was still speaking in the midst of every sort of noise and confusion when the Usher of the Black Rod knocked at the door to summons the Commons to the House of Peers.

There the proceedings were, if possible, still more violent and outrageous. Those who were present tell me that it resembled nothing but what we read of the '*Serment du Jeu de Paume*', and the whole scene was as much like the preparatory days of a revolution as can well be imagined. Wharncliffe was to have moved an Address to the Crown against dissolving Parliament; and this motion the Ministers were resolved should not come on; but he contrived to bring it on so far as to get it put upon the Journals. The Duke of Richmond endeavoured to prevent any speaking by raising points of order, and moving that the Lords should take their regular places (in separate ranks), which however is impossible at a royal sitting, because the cross benches are removed; this put Lord Londonderry in such a fury that he rose, roared, gesticulated, held up his whip, and four or five lords held him down to prevent his flying on somebody. Lord Lyndhurst was equally furious, and some sharp words passed which were not distinctly heard. In the midst of all the din, Lord Mansfield rose and obtained a hearing. Wharncliffe said to him, 'For God's sake, Mansfield, take care what you are about, and don't disgrace us more in the state we are in.' 'Don't be afraid,' said he; 'I will say nothing that will alarm you.' And accordingly he pronounced a trimming philippic on the Government, which, delivered as it was in an imposing manner, attired in his robes, and with the greatest energy and excitation, was prodigiously effective. While he was still speaking, the King arrived, but he did not desist even while his Majesty was entering the House of Lords, nor till he approached the throne; and while the King was ascending the steps the hoarse voice of Lord Londonderry was heard crying 'Hear, hear, hear!' The King from the robing-room heard the noise, and asked what it all meant. The conduct of the Chancellor was most extraordinary, skipping in and out of the House and making most extraordinary speeches. In the midst of the uproar he went out of the House, when Lord Shaftesbury was moved into the chair. In the middle of the debate Brougham again came in and said, 'it was most extraordinary that the King's undoubted right to dissolve Parliament should be questioned at a moment when the House of Commons had taken the unprecedented course of stopping the supplies', and having so said (which was a lie) he flounced out of the House to receive the King on his arrival. The King ought not properly to have worn the crown, never having been crowned; but when he was in the robing-room he said to Lord Hastings, 'Lord Hastings, I wear the crown; where is it?' It was brought to him, and when Lord Hastings was going to put it on his head he said, 'Nobody shall put the crown on my head but myself.' He put it on, then turned to Lord Grey and said, 'Now, my Lord, the coronation is over.' George Villiers said that in his life he never saw such a scene; and as he looked at the King upon the Throne, with the Crown loose upon his head, and the tall, grim figure of Lord Grey close beside him, with the Sword of State in his hand, it was as if the King had got his executioner by his side, and the whole picture looked strikingly typical of his and our future destinies.

The last night of the Reform Bill in the House of Commons

The debate on the second Reform Bill lasted three nights, and the Second Reading was carried on July 7 by a majority of 136 in a House of 598. The third Reading debate commenced on September 19; and finally, in the early morning of September 22, the Bill passed the House of Commons by a majority of 109.

Sir Edward George Earle Lytton Bulwer-Lytton (1805–73) was the son of a general and was educated at Trinity Hall, Cambridge. A successful novelist and poet in his day, he was a close friend of Disraeli and sat as Conservative MP for St Ives, 1831; for Lincoln, 1832–41; and for Hertfordshire, from 1852 until 1866, when he was given a peerage.

Edward Bulwer, 1st Lord of Lytton, Sketch, 1831

It was not till about ten o'clock on the night of the twenty-first of September that it was generally known in the House that a division was certainly to take place. Before that hour many members of consideration on the Ministerial Benches had professed some intention of speaking,—Sir Francis Burdett and Mr Sheil among the most prominent. But at the conclusion of a very long speech from Mr Grant—a speech extremely beneficial to the cause—there was an impatient cry for Sir Charles Weatherall who, after a few vehement remarks from Lord Valletort, girded up his loins and sprang to his post. Then full well did the hapless aspirants to oratory, who had arisen night after night by sixes and sevens, but had not yet caught the Speaker's eye, feel that for them all hope was over. A two hours' speech from the Ex-Solicitor-General brought the time to midnight—and Lord Althorp to reply. Perhaps that fine-hearted, fine-minded, noble, man never distinguished himself more than by that speech; and it was something like the entrance of a new world into active politics when a Minister condescended to be a Philosopher. The Chancellor of the Exchequer said:—He trusted the time was come when the wisdom of mankind would render them less eager to plunge into war, would force upon Nations the conviction that the phantoms of national glory and national triumph were not worthy the expense of blood and treasure by which they must be purchased.

Compare that sentiment with the memorable warlike bursts of Canning— Yes! we have gained wonderfully upon civilisation in the last ten years.

Sir Robert Peel commenced in a tone of great solemnity, declaring that he was about to put aside all details and embark at once on the grand principle of the Bill. He kept his promise not only by reading thro' every detail in the Reform Bill, but by creeping also into the details of the Beer Bill, and at last settled himself, to the great delight of his supporters, on the Bill for setting Spring Guns. Nevertheless, the speech was the speech of a great Master—it would be unfair to deny it; it showed remarkable ingenuity and address, not without passages of a far higher order of eloquence than many men could arrive at. Lord John Russell's reply, which did not commence till after three o'clock in the morning, was the finest speech he has made since the Bill was first introduced . . .

Amidst great confusion Mr Hunt rose and regaled the House for some ten minutes with assurances that the Bill had ceased to be popular. Unhappily he let fall some remarks about the Livery of London, and up sprang Alderman Wood—we were well off with only one Alderman. At half-past four in the morning the debate closed on the most important Act that for a century and a half had passed the National Assembly. The last words spoken on the subject were an assurance as to the number of Liverymen that had constituted a Common Hall.

The Ayes (the Reformers) went forth, and the Lobby was crowded to excess. When we returned (the writer of this was among the majority) there was a scene somewhat picturesque and imposing in character. The writer was one of the first who re-entered the House, and he seated himself at the back of the Benches under the Reporters' Gallery. From thence was obtained perhaps the best view of the whole tide of members that flowed in till the body of the House was completely covered. The candles, with the exception of the centre lustre, were burnt down to the sockets, and the continued fatigues and the series of late hours we had undergone for so many weeks made themselves strikingly visible at that hour and by that light in the persons of most of the dark mass that filled the chamber ('that old oak chamber' as it is called by one of Horace Walpole's correspondents).

From the place where I sat it was curious to note here and there conspicuous in the crowd the most eminent supporters, the most eminent antagonists of that Great Measure about to pass from our Tribunal. Just to the left of the doors about half way up the House, the first who arrested my eye was the great Irish Agitator—Daniel O'Connell; his broad hat slouched over that remarkable countenance so indicative of strength of will, resolution, and perserverance. Having raised my eyes—I am opposite and standing near the entrance of the House—I saw a face that presented the strongest possible contrast, the calm, serene features of the 'reverent old Man'—the author of the *Vindiciae Gallicae* [Sir James Mackintosh]. Farther on, you might just catch a glimpse of Lord Althorp turning round with that same imperturbable expression of honesty and kindness on his face, which no one can mark without loving the man as well as honouring him. Then Murray's chivalrous head, with its sad, proud look. Peel I could not discover. But just below me (one of the Tellers) was the keen, cunning-like face of Croker—the bald head and working mouth and dark, fine eyes—handsome enough in their way, but I would not trust them. However, Croker is an indisputably unappreciated man; his powers are brilliant. I do not know whether the features of Macaulay, one of the most rising men in the country, are familiar to many—there is something very peculiar about them. At a distance the full forehead, the firm lips, the large, cloven chin, the massive, bald brow that overhangs an eye small but full of deep, quiet light. I scarcely saw a head so expressive of intellectual grandeur. At the moment I saw his face looking up among a press of much taller men, and close to him was old Burdett. It was curious to see in such juxtaposition ambition commencing its career and ambition retiring from it—one who might see in this vast and difficult measure the commencement of a new era, and another who could only see in it the extinction of the old. Everyone knows Burdett's person. Who would have thought that he saw in that tall, patrician figure, with the gentle bearing, the mild eye, the serene bare brow, the restless pupil of John Horne Tooke, the mob's darling—the Gracchus of the hustings.

I could not for a long time see the introducer of the Bill, Lord John Russell. At last he appeared. Just fancy a small, spare man, with delicate, well-cut features, a handsome curved lip, a good forehead, thin, darkish hair—that is Lord John Russell. What a light events may give to that name.

But Wetherall, where's Wetherall? the broad, bluff, humorous, muscular-minded, lame-thinking Ex-Solicitor-General, the most resolute of Anti-reformers, the most long-winded, yet how often the most effective, of orators, now all fury, now all levity, now the brave, now the buffoon, always odd, always great, always Wetherall. There he is. His person sustains his character. You see the humorist, you also see the genius; a deep-lined, sagacious countenance, plenty of courage in the forehead, plenty of honesty in the face, plenty of shirt between the waistcoat and breeches.

I stopped a short time in the lobby, and Peel passed through. One of his supporters came and shook hands with him. Certainly Peel did not look happy, nor pleased, nor triumphant. We went forth into the open air; it was broad daybreak, a grey, chill mist floated round the old Abbey. 'Thank Heaven,' said we all, 'we have done with the Bill at last!' And I believe our Posterity will not be ungrateful either!

Although it passed the Commons, the Bill was thrown out by the Lords. The Bill again passed the Commons between December 12, 1831, and March 23, 1832, and passed Second Reading in the Lords. However, it foundered in Committee in May: this prompted the resignation of Ministers, a rash of popular unrest (the 'days of May'), and finally William IV's threat of a mass creation of peers to ensure the passage of the Bill. The Lords passed the Bill and it received the Royal Assent in early June.

The fall of Lord Melbourne's Administration

On June 4, 1841, Sir Robert Peel moved a resolution of No Confidence in Melbourne's Administration, which had been in power, apart from a short break in 1839, since 1834. Its reforming zeal had been sapped and it had run out of supporters.

W. E. Gladstone in conversation, recalled by Henry W. Lucy,
Strand Magazine, September 1898

'The Whips of those days,' he observed parenthetically, 'somehow or other seemed to know more precisely than they do now how a division would go. It was positively known that there would be a majority of one. On which side it would be was the only doubt. There was a member of the Opposition almost at death's door. He *was* dead,' Mr Gladstone added emphatically, 'except that he had just a little breath left in him. The question was, could he be brought to the House? The Whips said he must come, and so they carried him down. He was wheeled in in a Bath-chair. To this day I have never forgot the look on his face. His glassy eyes were upturned, his jaws were stiff. We, a lot of young Conservatives clustered round the door, seeing the Bath-chair, thought at first they had brought down a corpse. But he voted, and the resolution which turned out Lord Melbourne's Government was carried by a majority of one.

The Repeal of the Corn Laws

The Corn Laws, which had been introduced at the end of the Napoleonic Wars, levied a protective duty on imported corn if the domestic price fell below the level of 80 shillings a quarter. These measures favoured the agricultural interest which formed a powerful bloc among Tory MPs, but were unpopular with the ordinary consumer and the industrial and mercantile interests. Although a sliding scale of duty was introduced in 1828, which made the system more flexible, there was increasing pressure to abandon the Corn Laws from MPs representing the new urban seats created by the 1832 Reform Act. Peel reduced the sliding scale in 1842, but an extra-parliamentary organisation, the Anti-Corn Law League, led by Richard Cobden and John Bright, was set up to campaign for repeal of the Corn Laws in their entirety. The Whigs under Lord John Russell lost their nerve when it came to initiating repeal and it was left to Peel to achieve this with the support of the Duke of Wellington, in the teeth of opposition from his own country members.

Sir John Cam Hobhouse (1786–1869), 1st Baron Broughton, was educated at Trinity College, Cambridge, and became a partner in Whitbread & Co., the brewers. A close friend of Lord Byron's, he later published his *Journey through Albania with Lord Byron*. In 1819 he was sent to prison by the House of Commons for his pro-Reform activities, and he was Whig MP for Westminster from 1820 to 1833, serving as Secretary-at-War in 1832 and briefly as Irish Secretary before resigning in protest over the Government's failure to cut taxes. He resigned from his seat, but was MP for Nottingham from 1834 to 1847, and for Harwich from 1848 until he was created Baron Broughton in 1851. From 1835 to 1841, and again in 1846, he was in the Cabinet as president of the Board of Control (overseeing the affairs of the East India Company).

John Cam Hobhouse, Lord Broughton, *Recollections of a Long Life* (1911) and extracts from his diaries

January 22, 1846. Read Queen's Speech, which some people thought proved sufficiently that Peel resolved to go all lengths in regard to Corn-laws, though it only declared in favour of going further towards Free Trade than he had gone.

I walked about with Ellice, who says we are coming on revolutionary times because there is no party strong enough of itself to govern the country.

House of Commons. Peel made a long speech of near two hours. He confessed his opinions had undergone a change as to Corn-laws, but confined the events which had caused the change to the three last years, and then stated his versions at large and in detail, all of them used by anti-Corn-law leagues.

The latter part of his speech was a personal defence, a proof of his being a true Conservative Minister, by reference to all he had done, from the infusing a new spirit into our Indian army! to the putting down agitation—the one about as true as the other. He concluded by a long peroration about his having served four Sovereigns and having sought for no reward but their approbation of his services, and of his being under no obligations to his or any party, but being free and resolved to act solely upon the strength of his own honest cautions for the benefit of the country. It seemed clear that he was resolved to go all lengths in regard to the Corn-laws.

Lord John Russell then spoke. He made no remark on Peel's conduct, but merely said that he and his party had never had fair play as those formerly in power.

Disraeli made one of his speeches, a great deal of it very true as regarded Peel's character and conduct. He very happily ridiculed Peel's proclaimed love of fame and appeal to posterity, and called his cabinet followers three imps of fame. Peel and Graham, too, looked much distressed.

January 23. House of Commons. Williams of Coventry complimented Peel for some argument which in fact was made by Russell, but when Peel spoke he pocketed the compliment very quietly. Russell said to me, 'That is always the way, our people give Peel the credit for everything, and he never refuses to accept it, though he knows it does not belong to him.'

January 26. Went to the House of Lords to hear the Duke of Wellington's explanation. He excused his coming back to office without any change of opinion upon the ground that the Queen had a right to his services, and that the formation of a Government under the late circumstances was of more importance than his private opinions on Corn-laws or any other law, and that therefore he consented to stand by Sir Robert Peel in his proposed change of the Corn-laws. What that change was to be he did not tell; he said positively it would be satisfactory to their Lordships and the landed interest, and would be accompanied by compensation. If the Duke's excuse is worth anything it would go to the support of any Government or any Ministerial measure, however unconstitutional or unprincipled. Such language would not be borne for an instant except from him; but, coming from him, it serves to protect, not only him, but all his colleagues who are in the same predicament.

January 27. The House of Commons was crowded in all parts, and, for the first time, Prince Albert was under the gallery with the Duke of Cambridge and Lord Jersey. Peel spoke, in all, three hours and twenty minutes. His statement was clear and plain, without any rhetorical flourishes or personal appeals.

Amongst other things, he said the Corn-laws were to be abolished altogether in three years, but in the meantime a small duty adjusted on the sliding-scale principle was to be levied on all foreign grain. The great measure, the total Repeal of the Corn-laws, was secured. We therefore cheered when Peel sat down, but not very heartily.

January 28. I dined at Lord Auckland's. Lord John Russell, Lord Melbourne, Lord de Mauley, and Lady Stanley the party. Poor Lord Melbourne was a melancholy sight, depressed and evidently conscious of some imminent calamity; he spoke but little. I sat next to him. He said Peel's compensation was no compensation at all. Lady Stanley told me she had heard Peel was nervous when speaking, and thought once or twice his own people were laughing at him.

It seems the Protectionists now give out that Peel is a coward. The scheme of last night has, they say, reconciled some of those who had resolved to resign to stay in office, yet why I cannot imagine.

February 8. I read up my news of last week, and looked over some of the things published to show the inconsistency of Peel and Graham, particularly what they said in opposing the motion for a committee on Corn-laws in 1839. Certainly their conversion is more miraculous than any that has happened since the days of St Paul. It must be confessed Peel cannot have had a bad motive for his change. All his interests, all his connections, must have been against it; nothing but sincere conviction could have produced it. The grave charge against him is, I think, that he could not have been sincere when he supported Protection, but did so for mere party purposes and a love of power.

February 16. I went to the House of Commons and heard Sir Robert Peel make his promised speech, It was certainly a great effort, and I went across the House and told Sir George Clerk and others on the Treasury Bench what I thought of it. Clerk said, 'Come and tell him so.' I replied, 'No, do you tell him'; on which Sir George said, 'D——, he would turn [or kick] me away if I dared speak to him.' This, whether said in joke or half earnest, does not speak much in favour of the Premier. A man who will not accept a civil or complimentary truth from a subaltern is but a sulky fellow after all. There is nothing of true dignity or proper pride in such reserve.

February 2. I went to the Speaker's Levee. Went up and shook hands with the Speaker and Sir Robert. They were talking of the prolonged debate, and the Speaker said it degraded the House to a speaking club. Peel said it was to be regretted, but did not know what was to be done. I said that the new Opposition were waiting for fresh members. Peel, at this, drew up as if he had been too familiar, and at once changed the subject to Lord Byron's statue at Cambridge. I took the opportunity of asking after his health, which he said was very good, and again looked reserved.

February 21. Count Pahlen told me that Lord Aberdeen had positively assured him that Peel has no intention of resigning after he has carried the Corn-law repeal. On the contrary, he is determined to persevere to the last, and not quit his post unless compelled by a vote of Parliament.

May 15. House of Commons. Disraeli speaking against the Corn Bill. His arguments were the old ones, well put. His conclusion for a good twenty minutes was a steady philippic against Peel, which was very powerful indeed, and produced a great effect on all parts of the House. Peel looked miserable, and his brother Jonathan more wretched still, and bursting with mortification; even Macaulay told me he thought the effect very powerful, and the speech the best Disraeli ever made. Russell, who followed, was unable to go on for some time on account of the prolonged cheering.

Peel got up after Russell, and talked in terms of ill-affected contempt of Disraeli, more than hinting he had been a candidate for office in 1841, and saying, truly enough, that if Disraeli had thought so badly of all Peel's career, why did he support him up to 1844. However, Peel spoke in a manner not usual with him, and on one occasion was completely put out by a cheer which conveyed no obscure hint of disbelief in his honour both personal and political. He stopped, looked round, and stopped again, then seemed to try to speak, but was choked, and his eyes full of tears. At last he faltered out: 'The honourable gentlemen have succeeded,' and, after a pause resumed with, 'I was going to observe.' I never saw Peel *beat* before, and much as I dislike him and disapprove his conduct, I felt much distressed, and so did others of our front opposite to him. However, he went on tolerably well afterwards, though in a lower tone than usual. He made no allusion to Russell's reproof of his having kept back his opinions too long, nor did he say a single civil thing of our party. On the whole the speech was a failure, though much cheered by our friends when he sat down.

Disraeli got up and explained what had occurred in regard to himself in 1841. He said a friend of Peel's had called on him and asked him if he would take office; but he had never asked for office, nor had any communication with Peel about it. Peel reiterated what he had said, that Disraeli had no objection to office in 1841 under him, who he now said had always been a dishonest politician, and so the matter ended. Disraeli had better not have spoken.

We divided at last. Peel spoke to us in the lobby: 'I take the liberty to remind you that we may have a second division on the passing of the Bill.' Russell was rather the man to take that liberty, for Peel had only about 107 out of 327. It was said our majority was about 100, but it was 98, i.e. 327 to 229. There was great cheering when the numbers were announced, and more when the Bill passed without a division.

The Protection Parliament has voted and passed, by a great majority, the total repeal of the Corn-laws! No living soul could have done this but Peel, and I am not surprised at the increasing rage of the Protectionists. They appear more angry than ever.

June 8. House of Commons. Lord George Bentinck made a furious attack on the Government, saying he was for kicking out the Irish Coercion Bill and the Ministers together, and ending with a deliberate charge against Peel of having confessed that he had changed his opinion on the Catholic question so early as 1825, although he had refused to join Canning in 1827, because Canning was for the Catholics, and afterwards helped to chase and hunt him to death. Bentinck said that Peel had declared he could not conceal his opinions without being base and dishonest, and he asked whether he was not now convicted, out of his own mouth, of having acted basely and dishonestly. These words were repeated two or three times, and John Russell whispered to me, 'Is that parliamentary?'

The effect of the speech, however, was very great and cheering from the Protectionist benches tremendous. I looked at Peel and thought he bore the attack quietly enough, though I heard that when he rose about some trifling matter at the end of the evening he could scarcely speak.

June 9. *The Times* and other papers speak of the Government as at an end, but certain of our people, Radicals and Free Traders, talk of supporting Peel.

June 12. House of Commons. Debate on Irish Coercion Bill continued. Peel spoke, confessing that the Whigs had given his Free Trade measures 'disinterested and active support', and that we were at perfect liberty to oppose his Coercion Bill. He then went into a defence of the measure, and showed that crime still continued to justify it. The latter part of his speech was a defence of himself against Lord George Bentinck's attack, which he prefaced by appealing to his previous career of thirty-five years, and asking whether he had ever treated his antagonists discourteously. There were approving cheers from our benches, except Palmerston, myself, and a few others, who knew the facts: the truth being that, although Peel is not discourteous, he is not fair, and never helps a friend or spares a foe, and, though not daringly rude, is disparaging and sneering, and if he can hurt a man by a hint will not fail to do so.

June 15. Disraeli made a powerful speech today in defence of Lord George Bentinck's attack on Peel's conduct in regard to the Catholic question and Canning. The whole was exceedingly effective for the time, and Peel was completely knocked down by it. He rose, however, and begged permission to say a few words, asking the House to suspend its judgement.

June 16. A great deal of excitement caused by Disraeli's speech, which seemed a complete answer to Peel's defence.

June 18. I heard Peel had given notice that next day he should, on moving the order of the day, give an explanation of his conduct in 1825, 1827, and 1829. The announcement was received with cheers, but what a position for a Prime Minister and a public man of thirty-five years' standing, to be compelled to show, or attempt to show, that he had not told a lie!

June 19. House of Commons. I thought Peel answered the charges against him successfully. That, he dealt with what had been said against him so as to show that it did not furnish ground for the inferences of Lord George Bentinck and Disraeli. I thought he proved there was good reason to believe that the report of the *Mirror of Parliament* and the *Times*, which he showed were identical, was incorrect, and that he did not say *that in 1825 he had told Liverpool the time was come something must be done for the Catholics.*

Lord George Bentinck, nothing daunted, replied, and still persisted in his attack, going again over his proofs, both direct and indirect, and more than hinting that Peel had lied, and that his character was such as to give no weight to his words.

June 20. Bannerman showed me a passage in the *Edinburgh Review* for March 1829, which gives Peel's words just as quoted by Bentinck. The article was written by Jeffery just after Peel had spoken. I mentioned this to Macaulay, who acknowledged it was a striking circumstance, but that, after all, it only showed that Jeffery had read the misreport in the *Times.* Yet it seems strange that Peel did not think it worth while to contradict a report given in such a paper as the *Times* and in such a review as the *Edinburgh.* Lord Carrington told me that he was in the House of Commons in March 1829 when Peel made his speech, and is positive he did make use of the words quoted by Bentinck. I was in the House too, but I do not recollect the fact.

❖

The fall of Sir Robert Peel

On June 25, 1846, in the evening, it was announced to the House of Commons that the Corn and Customs Bill had been passed without amendment by the Upper Chamber.

Following this, the debate on the Irish Coercion Bill reached its conclusion and a division was called.

Benjamin Disraeli, *The Life of Lord George Bentinck* (1852)

At length, about half-past one o'clock, the galleries were cleared, the division called, and the question put. In almost all previous divisions where the fate of a Government had been depending, the vote of every member, with scarcely an exception, had been anticipated; that was not the case in the present instance, and the direction which members took as they left their seats was anxiously watched. More than one hundred Protectionist members followed the Minister; more than eighty avoided the division, a few of these, however, had paired; nearly the same number followed Lord George Bentinck. But it was not merely their numbers that attracted the anxious observation of the Treasury bench, as the Protectionists passed in defile before the Minister to the hostile lobby. It was impossible that he could have marked them without emotion; the flower of that great party which had been so proud to follow one who had been so proud to lead them. They were men to gain whose hearts and the hearts of their fathers had been the aim and exultation of his life. They had extended to him an unlimited confidence and an admiration without stint. They had stood by him in the darkest hour, and had borne him from the depths of political despair to the proudest of living positions. Right or wrong, they were men of honour, breeding, and refinement, high and generous character, great weight and station in the country, which they had ever placed at his disposal. They had been not only his followers but his friends; had joined in the same pastimes, drank from the same cup, and in the pleasantness of private life had forgotten together the cares and strife of politics.

He must have felt something of this, while the Manners, the Somersets, the Bentincks, the Lowthers, and the Lennoxes passed before him. And those country gentlemen, 'those gentlemen of England', of whom, but five years ago, the very same building was ringing with his pride of being their leader—if his heart were hardened to Sir Charles Burrell, Sir William Jolliffe, Sir Charles Knightly, Sir John Trollope, Sir Edward Kerrison, Sir John Tyrell, he surely must have had a pang when his eye rested on Sir John Yarde Buller, his choice and pattern country gentleman, whom he had himself selected and invited, but six years back, to move a vote of want of confidence in the Whig Government, in order, against the feeling of the Court, to install Sir Robert Peel in their stead. They trooped on: all the men of mettle and large-acred squires, whose spirit he had so often quickened, and whose counsel he had so often solicited in his fine Conservative speeches in Whitehall Gardens . . .

When Prince Metternich was informed, at Dresden, with great ostentation, that the Emperor had arrived—'Yes; but without his army,' was the reply. Sir Robert Peel was still First Minister of England, as Napoleon remained Emperor for a while after Moscow. Each, perhaps, for a moment had indulged in hope, it is so difficult for those who are on the pinnacle of life to realise disaster. They sometimes contemplate it in their deep and far-seeing calculations, but it is only to imagine a contingency which their resources must surely baffle; they sometimes talk of it to their friends, and oftener of it to their enemies, but it is only as an insurance of their prosperity and as an offering to propitiate their Nemesis. They never believe in it.

The news that the Government were not only beaten, but by a majority so large as 73, began to circulate. An incredulous murmur passed it along the Treasury bench. 'They say we are beaten by 73!' whispered the most important member of the Cabinet, in a tone of surprise, to Sir Robert Peel. Sir Robert did not reply, or even turn his head. He looked very grave, and extended his chin, as was his habit when he was annoyed and cared not to speak. He began to comprehend his position, and that the Emperor was without his army.

❖

The Canton debate

A Chinese vessel fraudulently flying an English flag was boarded in Canton by the Chinese authorities and twelve of her crew were arrested for piracy. The British Plenipotentiary in Hong Kong demanded that the Chinese Government should surrender the men and apologise, but his demands were not met and he gave orders for the English fleet to bombard Canton. Cobden brought forward a motion censuring the British Government for its violence and obtained cross-party support from Gladstone, Disraeli, Lord John Russell, Lord Robert Cecil and the Radical, J. A. Roebuck.

William White, *Illustrated Times*, March 7, 1857

The great and all-absorbing topic of the week has been the Canton debate. The excitement in the House and the Lobby has been intense—unequalled by anything of the sort that has occurred since the great Corn-Law contest. The Lobby has been so crowded, that it has been only with the greatest exertion that the police could keep a clear passage to the House for the Members; and all the galleries, from four o'clock until the House broke up, have been on every night of the debate filled; and there have been besides hundreds of eager and anxious expectants waiting about the House for admittance; and then, many of them—indeed most of them—did wait all the night, and went home disappointed at last. Members' orders they could get, and seemed astonished that, though they had this talismanic paper, they could not get in, forgetting that though, when there is room, this slip of paper is a veritable 'open-sesame', yet there is one thing that it cannot do—it cannot make space. An order is a good thing to have when there is room, but when there is not it is as useless as a cheque upon a bank at which there are 'no effects'. Poor fellows! We could not help pitying them as we saw them jammed together, knowing, as we did, the utter hopelessness of their case. Many of them had come up from the country on purpose to hear the debate, relying upon the omnipotence of their Members, and some, perhaps, had never been in the House in their lives. 'What, cannot you get me in?' we heard one say to his Member. 'Oh, do try! I never heard a debate, and I have come to town on purpose to hear this.' 'My dear fellow, what can I do?' was the answer, 'every place is full.' 'Can't you ask the Speaker to put me *somewhere?*' 'Impossible; the Speaker himself couldn't put his own brother in where there is no room.'

Nor was the excitement amongst the members less marked, and, *crescit eundo*, it increased as the debate went on. It is true that in the early part of the first evening the members did not seem to be awake to the importance of the crisis. That there was to be a stout fight, everybody knew; but it was generally considered that a majority for Government was secure. But when Mr Cobden had delivered his masterly speech, and in his quiet but telling way had unrolled before the House his terrible indictment, and when it was made known by the cheering which came from all parts of the House what numbers of Members, of all parties, were prepared to support the Hon. Member for the West Riding, then a change came over the spirit of the House, and especially over the Government side. It became apparent that this contest was no child's play, and that if the Government meant to resist successfully this formidable attack, they not only had not a moment to lose, but that every art of manoeuvre which the science and skill of the 'Whips' could bring to bear must be put in requisition. Everybody accustomed to political contests in the House was aware of this change. It might be seen in the looks of the Ministers on the Treasury bench; Hayter's face betrayed it—all calm and imperturbable as it generally is; and the knots of members about the lobbies and in the waiting-rooms—some quietly, and some violently discussing the subject—showed that a crisis of no ordinary importance was at hand.

But the excitement was at its height when Lord John Russell delivered his remarkable speech. During the whole of the evening there had been anxious questionings about the way in which Lord John would vote, and but few seemed to be quite decided upon the point until he arose in the House. His Lordship did not, however, leave the House long in doubt; he very soon showed that he not only meant to support Mr Cobden, but that he intended also to carry all his followers with him; and when he sat down, after having delivered one of the most telling speeches that we have heard for some years past, things looked very gloomy indeed for the Ministry, and many an Under-Secretary and junior Lord began to shake in his shoes. Indeed, there can be no doubt that if the division had come off on that night Government would have been defeated by a large majority. But that was not to be—trust Palmerston and Hayter for that! Nor was it to be on Friday, the next night. Before Friday night many a message had been dispatched by post and by telegraph, and the large increase in the number of members on Friday showed that all this had not been done without effect. But still further time was required to make things at all pleasant, and the long interval between Friday and Monday night would be invaluable to the Government. In the first place, it would give still further time for members to come up from a distance, and then, secondly (and this is even more important), it would afford opportunity for the appliance of those mysterious arts and powerful incantations at which your Ministerial 'Whips' are such adepts. Exactly what these Circean arts are no one knows but the initiated, but that they are of wondrous power is certain and not to be disputed, and many an indignant patriotic feeling have they damped down, but how it is done must ever remain a mystery to all but those who are behind the scenes. And so on Friday the debate was again adjourned.

On Monday—and the change was apparent—the Government had recovered from its panic—and the troublous nervousness observable in Hayter's face had passed away—letters had been received, books examined, and it had become apparent that things were not so bad as they seemed—Mr Hayter was himself again, and the Lords of the Treasury and the Admiralty began to see prospects of salaries beyond the coming quarter-day.

The most extraordinary speech during the debate was unquestionably Mr Whiteside's. We have heard the learned gentleman deliver many wonderful harangues, but this was the most wonderful of all. We don't mean as to matter, but manner. The matter was reported duly in the morning papers; but who can describe the manner? As we witnessed the gesticulations, how we longed for Cruikshank or Leech to be there that the orator might be presented in one, even if only one, of his wonderful positions; but, alas! no artist is allowed in the House, and words are altogether powerless. We remember Edward Irving, and we have seen many an actor 'tearing a passion to tatters', but nothing comes up to Whiteside.

Since the above was written the smash has come. In a House of 510 Members, at half-past two o'clock on the morning of Wednesday, the Government was beaten by a majority of sixteen. Up to the last the event was uncertain; such was the confusion of parties, that no one could calculate accurately who would win. As the moment for dividing came the excitement throughout the House grew more intense than ever, and so crowded were the Peers' Seats and Diplomatic Galleries, that it was with the utmost difficulty they were cleared in time. In fact, the Diplomatic Gallery was not cleared, for one unfortunate foreigner was shut in, and very perplexed he looked when he was made to understand that he was in custody, and not less so when, after due consultation held with the Speaker, the Sergeant opened the door and drove him to the outer Lobby. The Duke of Cambridge and members of the diplomatic corps, the Russian, American, Austrian Ministers, etc., not only sat patiently listening to the debate, but waited outside until the numbers were declared. The great speech of the debate was Gladstone's. Some went so far as to say that it was the greatest harangue that he ever delivered. The cheers whilst he spoke were almost incessant. Palmerston's speech evidently produced but little effect. Poor old man! it was painful to see him hobbling upstairs on two sticks to fight such a battle. It is bad enough at seventy-four years of age to sit from five o'clock till one, and then to rise and reply in a speech of an hour to such opponents as Gladstone and Cobden, Russell and Graham, but to have to contend with the gout as well must be anything but pleasant. Well, we suppose that the Palmerston Ministry is at an end, unless the plucky Premier should dissolve. And now, Mr Cobden, 'What next? and next?'

Cardwell's Motion

Following the defeat and resignation of Palmerston, the Tories under Derby and Disraeli formed a Cabinet despite being outnumbered by almost three to two in the House of Commons. Before long they came close to defeat themselves over a matter of Indian administration. The Governor-General, Lord Canning, had issued a proclamation that the proprietary right in Oudh was transferred to the British Government. The Cabinet Minister responsible for India, Lord Ellenborough, had written a high-handed and critical dispatch to the Governor-General, based on a degree of misunderstanding, and this had found its way into *The Times* with the result that Edward Cardwell, one of the Peelites, put down a motion of censure in the Commons. In the fluid party situation of the time, MPs tended to be more independent-minded, so that John Bright and Sir James Graham, for example, defended the Tory Government because they strongly disapproved of Canning's dictatorial proclamation. Lord Ellenborough meanwhile resigned and during the debate on the affair Cardwell discovered that few MPs were eager for the dissolution which would presumably have ensued. Not wishing to be blamed for such an outcome, he withdrew his motion. The collapse of the Opposition was wondrous to behold. 'It was like a convulsion of nature rather than any ordinary transaction of human life,' explained Disraeli in a speech at Slough soon afterwards. 'I can only liken it to one of those earthquakes which take place in Calabria or Peru. There was a rumbling murmur, a groan, shriek, a sound of distant thunder. No one knew whether it came from the top or the bottom of the house. There was a rent, a fissure in the ground, and then a village disappeared; then a tall tower toppled down; and the whole of the opposition benches became one great dissolving view of anarchy.'

Edward Cardwell (1813–86), later Lord Cardwell, was educated at Balliol College, Oxford, where he scored a double First and became a Fellow. He was MP for Clitheroe, 1842–7; for Liverpool, 1847–52; and for Oxford City from 1853 to April 1857, and from July 1857 until he became a peer in 1874. While president of the Board of Trade he had been responsible for the Merchant Shipping Act of 1854, and he later served as Chief Secretary for Ireland and as Secretary of State for the Colonies. As Secretary of State for War in Gladstone's first administration, he was responsible for reforming the Army.

Sir William Fraser, *Disraeli and his Day* (1891)

Of all the Parliamentary struggles which I have witnessed, none approached that of 1858. The circumstances which led to this brilliant debate were, briefly, these: Lord Derby was in office: at that time the Governor-General of India was subordinate to the authority of the Hon. East India Company. He was appointed by them: and was their servant: but the Government of this vast and important Dependency was checked by 'The Board of Control', representing the Imperial Government. After the confiscation of the Kingdom of Oude, and the nameless horrors which history records of that dreadful period, Lord Canning, Governor-General of India, an amiable and clever Statesman, had issued a Proclamation, addressed to the inhabitants, stating that, as a result of what was called their Rebellion, the whole of the land in the late Kingdom of Oude was confiscated: and would in future be held by British authority. Lord Ellenborough, who had filled the office of Governor-General, and, showing considerable administrative, and military talents, although a civilian, had made himself conspicuous by several brilliant achievements, now occupied the place of President of the Board of Control. On receiving a draft of the proposed dispatch from Lord Canning, he wrote a reply which seemed a most statesman-like, able, and temperate paper. Lord Ellenborough pointed out that, although we had subdued the mutiny, in which murder, and every crime had been committed by the soldiers who were receiving our pay, and who had eaten our salt, yet that Humanity, and Policy, both forbad a vindictive retribution. He pointed out that, whereas we had captured a Kingdom, which only recently had been an independent state, our conduct should be actuated by lenity towards the general inhabitants. Reading the dispatch now, the terms which I presumed to use in the House in relation to it in this debate, represent precisely what still I feel. However, the issue was not joined in this manner. The grievance which was supposed to exist against the Government was that this dispatch, written by Lord Ellenborough, had become known at home; and was considered to blame Lord Canning, for issuing a proclamation of Confiscation, in Oude. Angry discussions took place: and Lord Ellenborough, in the finest speech which I have ever heard, announced that he had resigned his office to the Queen; and that Her Majesty had accepted it. This, however, did not satisfy the Opposition: they believed that the Government was weak; the Government were not in a majority in the House of Commons: and this attack, as they were pleased to call it, upon Lord Canning, was the excuse of the Opposition for a violent assault upon the Ministry: with the avowed object of removing them from Office. A longer debate has hardly taken place in the history of the House of Commons. It spread, with intervals, over ten nights: Ross, who for fifty years was the sagacious and excellent head-reporter of *The Times*, told me that, from beginning to end, there was not, in his judgement, one bad speech delivered. I was astonished to find what brilliant powers of argument, and of elocution, the House then held. The brain of every man of capacity was, of course, stimulated to the highest degree: and the result was a series of scenes that no one who took part in them, or witnessed them, will ever forget. The mover of the hostile resolution was Mr Cardwell, afterwards Viscount Cardwell. He was of the school of Sir Robert Peel: a contemporary of Mr Gladstone: and he, like him, had seceded from the Tory Party at the time of Sir Robert Peel's change. The Government was in a minority in the House. I listened carefully to Mr

Cardwell's speech: and made up my mind that he would not carry his Resolution. I have never seen anything approaching the personal feeling, and resentment, which was shown during this debate; not only in the House, but in Society. Wherever you went, nothing else was spoken of. Language almost transgressing the borders of decency was used: and it seemed at one time as if men would have come to blows. 'The Derby' intervened: this breathing space gave a little time to cool: but the fury was renewed afterwards: nothing like it has occurred since. It must have resembled the state of things at the time of the Reform Bills of 1831, and 1832. No one can form the least idea from looking at *Hansard* of what took place. The cheering, groaning, laughing, were beyond belief. We considered ourselves justified in using inarticulate means of rendering the eloquence of the other side nugatory. Our system was this; there were about twenty-five of us; and I am afraid that I was, to a certain extent, the organiser, and captain of the party. If a speaker on the Opposition side uttered any offensive remark, we greeted him with the most crushing ironical cheers: if he uttered some noble sentiment of Patriotism we affected to be overwhelmed with the grandeur of his ideas; exclaiming as the public do when a rocket goes up: if he became pathetic, we groaned for five minutes: on the other hand, should any member of the Opposition venture upon a joke, we affected convulsive merriment, which lasted until the unfortunate man's voice was completely drowned. When I say that we absolutely demolished a man of such consummate effrontery as Bethell, ex-Attorney-General, and later Lord Chancellor, any reader who remembers him will wonder at our prowess. I have glanced at *Hansard*; I find that Bethell's speech has been toned down, probably by his own alteration, to mildness, and gentleness. I will give the reader a specimen of what he really said: He leant on the table of the House; and, looking steadily at Disraeli, lisped these words in a manner the peculiarity of which it is impossible to describe; but which will not be forgotten by those who heard him speak. 'Since you have been in Office yar whole conduct has been absurd! Yar India Bill was a tissue of nonsense! How did we receive it? We covered you with good-humoured widicule!' When things reached this point, I turned to Vansittart, Member for Windsor, and said, 'This will never do!' From that moment, whatever may be recorded of the future Lord Chancellor in *Hansard*, no word of his could be heard by those in his immediate neighbourhood.

I drew my conclusion that the Resolution would not be carried entirely from a careful and steady observation of the House while Mr Cardwell was speaking. The final night of the Debate was the Friday in the second week. On Thursday, the day previous, I was returning at a little past midnight from a party, at the west end of Piccadilly. By the dead wall between the gates of Devonshire House I met Disraeli, arm-in-arm with Sir William Jolliffe, then Secretary of the Treasury, and Manager for the Party. Disraeli said, 'Where have you been?' I replied, 'To Baron Rothschild's.' The street was empty; and a bright Moon was shining. Disraeli said, 'What does the Baron say about it? He knows most things!' I replied, 'There was a great crowd; and I did not see him. You need have no anxiety; the Motion will not be put from the Chair.' I shall never forget Disraeli's look of blank astonishment: his face was quite clear in the moonlight. He was silent: after half a minute had passed, he said 'Good night!' I answered, 'Good night: *dormez bien!*' I found, some months afterwards, that he had sent his most trusty colleague in the Cabinet at ten the next morning to my mother, in Belgrave Square, to ascertain how I had found this out. She answered that I had not found it out: that it was my opinion: that I had said in the previous week that the Motion would not be carried: and that the day before I had said that it would not be put. I find in the betting-book at 'White's' that I backed my opinion against Lord M's for ten pounds. I went down to the House on that memorable Friday at five. Waiting in the circular Hall outside the door, I saw my friend and school-fellow Lord Dunkellin come up the Members' stairs with Mr Cardwell. Mr Cardwell went into the House: I said to Lord Dunkellin, 'So your cock won't fight after all!' 'What do you mean?' 'I mean what I say: that Cardwell's Motion will be withdrawn.' He answered, 'Withdrawn! impossible!' 'I will bet you five pounds it will be withdrawn tonight.' He said, 'My dear fellow, I can't bet with you, because I know.' 'What do you know?' 'I have walked from the Treasury with Cardwell: he told me that nothing will induce him to withdraw: he feels that he is personally committed: he told me that the thing would decidedly go on: and the Division be taken tonight.' 'Is that what he said?' 'Yes, word for word.' 'Then I will bet you ten pounds he withdraws it.' 'With that knowledge?' 'With that knowledge.' We went into the House. At first everything seemed to go on as before: but at half-past five some Members on the Opposition side began speaking about 'the good of the country': 'the absence of party feeling': 'the wish for the sake of India that things might quiet down'. The moment I heard this I ejaculated, 'The Lord has delivered them into our hand.' The perception rapidly grew among the five-and-twenty whom I have mentioned acting, more or less, under my orders. For an hour and a half speaker after speaker rose on the Opposition side. Obviously the whole scene had been planned. They implored Mr Cardwell to withdraw his resolution. Each time that one of these high-minded patriots rose, we greeted him with shouts of so derisive a character as would have shaken a heart of adamant. The more virtuous their language, the more we laughed at them: finally, when Lord John Russell requested Cardwell to withdraw his Resolution, our merriment reached the skies. At last the Speaker, Denison, who in his heart was a pretty stiff partisan, rose; and with a pale countenance asked, 'Is it your pleasure that this Motion be withdrawn?' Our shout of 'Aye' was deafening: I can still see Palmerston leaning forward in his seat, with a broad grin on his face, evidently appreciating our enthusiasm, and, though its victim, amused at our triumph.

Two crisp five pound notes were in my pocket when I left the House.

One terrible drawback, however, we had. Disraeli intended to wind up the

Debate; to advance with the column of his Imperial Guard; to make a final desperate effort for Victory. He was by this sudden collapse deprived of his opportunity. He delivered the speech, which he had prepared for the House of Commons, a few days later at a meeting at Slough. The leader of the attack on Lord Ellenborough in the House of Lords had been Lord Shaftesbury; a man who had earned universal respect by the sacrifice of his career to charitable and, in the main, wise objects. He had at one time represented Dorsetshire on highly Protectionist opinions. My uncle, Mr Farquharson of Langton, who had the key of the County at that time in his pocket, had removed him from the House of Commons on his change. Under the present circumstances, notwithstanding his high character, no very kindly feeling towards him prevailed on the Tory benches. It was felt that he had taken advantage of his reputation for generosity and high-mindedness to make what was not altogether a worthy attack upon the Government: and that if the Government had erred, it was on the side of Humanity. He had prefaced his speech against the Tory party by saying that no one could impute to him that in acting as he did, he was moved by the Spirit of Party. Disraeli said at Slough, 'In another place' (the House of Lords) 'a higher reputation descended on the scene. Gamaliel himself came down: and bearing the broad phylactery of Faction on his brow, he thanked his God, like the Pharisee of old, that he at least was not as other men: and that he was influenced by no party motive.' These words would, under the circumstances of intense excitement to which the House of Commons had worked itself, if delivered there, have had an unequalled reception.

Many years afterwards, Disraeli said to me, 'I shall never forget that night when I met you in Piccadilly at the time of Cardwell's motion. I believed that we were smashed. At the moment you met us, I was arranging with Jolliffe the details of our going out. I had no more doubt that the Government would be defeated the next day than I had of my own existence. You, in a light and airy manner, said, "Don't be anxious: it is all right: the resolution will never be put from the Chair!" I shall never forget that moment, so long as I live.'

Gladstone introduces his first Home Rule Bill

Gladstone was converted to Home Rule but gradually. In the 1885 General Election campaign Parnell had advised Irish voters in English constituencies to vote Conservative. The result was that Gladstone's majority was reduced by between 25 to 40 seats and Parnell was left holding the balance of power between the parties. For the time being a Tory Ministry under Lord Salisbury was sustained by Irish support, but at the end of 1885 indiscreet statements to the press by his son, Herbert, indicated that Gladstone was coming round to Home Rule. In March 1886, Joseph Chamberlain and Charles Trevelyan resigned from the Cabinet over the Home Rule Bill which Gladstone proposed. Gladstone introduced the Bill, in an atmosphere of intense public anticipation, on April 8.

According to the Irish Nationalist MP Tim Healy, Members had arrived 'to secure seats at 3 a.m., 4 a.m., 5 a.m., and 6 a.m. By 8 a.m. the overhanging galleries of the House were black with silk hats left by their owners to entitle them to places ... A prank of the young member for North Tyrone, Lord Frederick Hamilton, amused many. He deposited in the members' hats tracts against Home Rule. This delighted us, but British Liberals deemed it a trespass ... At 4 p.m. Gladstone, arrayed in furs, drove to Palace Yard with Mrs Gladstone—his noble face reflecting the gravity and dignity of the occasion. Causton, ex-MP (now Lord Southwark), approached his carriage as he alighted and conveyed him to the private stairs used by Ministers.'

After Gladstone had finished and Sir Edward Clark had risen to reply, Healy 'chaffed Biggar with, "Well, Joe, is he still your 'industrious man but dishonest'?" He purred, "Well, he's industrious, anyhow." '

John Edward Ellis (1841–1910) was born in Leicestershire and educated at the Friends' School, Kendal. He was a JP in his native county as well as in the borough of Nottingham and the North Riding of Yorkshire, where he also held the post of Deputy-Lieutenant. He was the Liberal MP for the Rushcliffe division of Nottinghamshire from 1885 until his death, and held office as Under-Secretary of State to the India Office, 1905–6. He was created a Privy Councillor in 1906.

John Edward Ellis, Letter to his wife Maria, April 11, 1886[9]

I have waited for a quiet hour or two before sending my impressions of the wonderful scene in the House of Commons last Thursday. As the hours went by I jotted a few notes down on my 'Orders of the Day', and such as they are will let you have the benefit of them.

The newspapers have only partially conveyed the extraordinary rush to secure seats that day. Rumour does much in such a case to increase the eagerness, and the result was a state of things absolutely unknown within living memory. John Dillon told me the day before that I should find no good seat after 9 o'clock a.m. Entering the House at five minutes before ten, I was delighted to see no hat in the place I usually occupy. I almost ran to it and deposited my pledge of occupation with the requisite card. Turning back down the gangway and out, my passage was blocked by a stream of members who had evidently all aimed for about ten o'clock. Returning to the House thirty minutes after, no seat on the floor remained unsecured.

The beautiful range of libraries overlooking the Thames, the newsroom and all other quarters of our fine pile of buildings were overflowing with Members congratulating or condoling with one another about 'seats', reading, writing, or chatting on the one absorbing topic. I had a Committee at twelve which formed a pleasant interlude. Hastening in to the House about two, during our quarter of an hour's interval for luncheon, my peace of mind was great to find my hat undisturbed (ugly rumours on the point having been afloat). By this time there was not only not a vacant place on either floor or in the galleries, but the gangways and passages everywhere were becoming full of hats with the little cards on them.

By half-past three our Committee began to get fidgety, and the chairman making no sign, two or three of us boldly arose and putting our papers away in our cupboards prepared to leave the room. The Chairman made a virtue of necessity and declared our sitting adjourned.

Pouring downstairs and along the corridors to *our* Lobby, the stream swelling as it progressed by tributaries from each room we passed, we were confronted there by a struggling mass of men whom by shouts and entreaties Inspector Denning and his men were vainly endeavouring to reduce to some sort of order. A new Member said to me in a sort of awestruck manner, 'Why these are the Peers,' and looking at their faces I saw such was the fact.

By dint of one thing or other we secured an entrance to our own Chamber, and amidst a great murmur of excitement went each to his seat. One could not do so without noticing the strange feature of 28 chairs placed on the floor of the House. This is absolutely unprecedented, and Mr Gladstone remains unique as the only man, to hear a speech from whom, it has been needful thus to provide for Members' accommodation.

The newspapers have told how as J. Bright, Goschen, Lord Hartington and J. Morley entered they were received. Mr Parnell's entrance (quiet as it was) was the occasion of a very fine demonstration by his supporters. I sat next but one to Mr Trevelyan, and his comments were interesting. He said it was in every sense an unprecedented scene, but I was glad to hear him say how much (in his opinion) good humour had grown during the last fifteen years. He remarked it would have been almost impossible then for any one dissenting as he did, from the policy of the Government, and having resigned so recently, to come and sit amongst its staunch adherents.

About ten minutes to four the Speaker entered, his Chaplin not (as usual) walking at his right hand, but, owing to the chairs, behind him. As the sonorous voice of the doorkeeper warned us of 'Mr Speaker' and the serried rows of men rose to their feet on right hand and left, above and below, and from every corner and coign of vantage in the building, it was a remarkable sight. It may have been one's attitude of mind, but I thought I could not help detecting a deeper and more emphatic tone in the Chaplain's voice as he read the Psalm and the beautiful prayers under it.

These over, our eyes went towards the Gallery near the clock attracted by an unwonted sound. The Peers rushed in pell mell, struggling, laughing, and behaving in much the same way as people say the Commons do at the opening of Parliament.

We left the House during the half hour of private business. The tea room I found one mass of members struggling with the waitresses, carrying their own trays, etc.

Soon the House fills again, and after Sir M. Hicks-Beach had drawn a hearty burst of cheers from what relatively to those present seems a small party, all eyes on our side turn eagerly to the glass doors behind the Speaker's Chair. A few men (one hardly knows where) give tongue, and in a moment all below the gangway sprang to our feet and were joining in one of the most extraordinary and I suppose unprecedented receptions the House of Commons has ever witnessed.

As the cheers rose and fell (from very lack of breath) the Old Man, pale, but with his wonderful eyes turned over the benches and now and again hidden from us by the inclination of his head, walked to his seat. Still we cheered on. A sort of cowed look began to steal over Lord Randolph Churchill's face, and never again wholly left it till we streamed out to dinner.

At 4.33 the Speaker called for the first 'question' but the reception was not encouraging for the member concerned, and he collapsed. All the others being postponed, precisely at 4.35 Mr Gladstone rose again amid a hurricane of cheers, only less remarkable because of what had gone before.

The almost awful calmness of his opening words and whole manner stilled the surging emotion of the assembly, and after two or three sentences every one settled into an absolute and striking hush. This remained until the words 'we should no longer fence and skirmish with this question', when a burst of sympathy broke from us and the Parnellites, the more impressive for the great silence from which it had emerged.

The expressions 'a man cannot live upon medicine', the vigorous attack upon the policy of vacillating coercion, the mention of the 'alternative' that had never yet been tried, 'the expedient of stripping law of its foreign garb', impressed the House wonderfully, effectually won the Parnellites, and from my reading of faces opposite convinced me that their owners felt that we were again under the wand of the magician. By the time the introduction ended, the great art of the orator had begun to suffuse the mind, and from this point (as I found was the case with other men) I never lost the feeling that we were listening to one of the greatest of historical speeches.

As Mr Gladstone applied his lips to his 'pomatum' bottle, nature asserted herself by a shuffle and change of position through the Chamber. (It was curious to note during the momentary pause that one of the clerks was fast asleep!) With the words, 'I have now to ask attention to the problem before us,' attention became riveted once more.

The light was slowly dying now men's faces became indistinct in the gathering gloom, and a certain sombre feeling crept over one after the tension of the first hour. Cheers came now and again, but their first force had been expended, and the historical disquisition and geographical comparisons were listened to with eager interest but without much perceptible excitement.

The words 'What is the essence of the Union? That is the question,' roused this once more, and the full but mellowed light of the gas on the sea of upturned faces revealed the eager lines on both benches. Parnell's handsome, calm face was a study at the moment. Hitherto he had sat with folded arms, closely attentive, but for the most part impassive, leaving the cheering to his lieutenant and followers. But his attitude now became if possible keener, and his face ever and anon wore a smile.

It was curious to note the effect of Mr Gladstone's beautiful tribute to Lord Spencer. The front opposition bench was sulky and half-ashamed, we (Liberals and Radicals) cheered lustily, the Parnellites looked as if they would have liked to, and I am not certain some few did not. The object of it was visibly moved as we all turned to look up to him near the clock, and directed our voices that way.

After brushing aside with a certain impatience, if not scorn, as entirely inadequate, the alternative proposals of National Councils and other arrangements, Mr Gladstone said, 'We find the settlement in the establishment of a legislative body sitting in Dublin.' The effect on Mr Parnell was very marked. He at once began taking notes, talked to Dillon and Healy, and no longer hesitated to cheer. This had again an influence on his supporters, and I felt, so far as visible signs went, the day was won with them.

The manner of the speaker now grew much more emphatic, he resorted to his second bottle, turned constantly to his supporter, and appeared more or less indifferent to those opposite. The tension of mind growing at times almost painful was relieved just now by one of those incidents people might call ominous. Bringing his hand down twice with rapid gestures Mr Gladstone struck, not the familiar box, but the Mace, which emitted a ringing sound and seemed to totter on its supports. Men whispered to one another 'the bauble', and tittered.

Still the great argument marched on with its wealth of ideas, its felicity of diction, and its unabated impressiveness of manner. As the need for protecting the Protestant minority and the method of doing it were insisted on and elaborated, as the canker of religious ascendancy at the root of the attempted settlement of 1872 was exposed and reprobated, as these and other points were conclusively established beyond cavil or contradiction, the conviction grew and ripened in one's mind that we were listening to something unique, and to be remembered for life.

Two and a half hours had passed without any sign of weariness or even huskiness of voice.

Still every now and then a murmur of sympathy ran down our benches, still now and then cheers arose, still a few hostile cries broke from the opposition back benches. But the wand of the magician was working its spell. The front Tory bench was fairly cowed, and sat with downcast eyes in silence.

Soon the exposition descended to a lower range. From the highest policy our minds were called to ponder currency, bank notes, weights and measures and other such like details verging on the common-place; almost by way of relaxation they provoked a smile, quickly checked, however, by admiration at the dextrous way in which the speech moved through all this complexity and intricacy of matter.

Then came the Constitution of the domestic legislature, its relation to Judges, and, what was in its way as wonderful a part of the speech as any, the calculation of respective burdens for Britain and Ireland, and the Budget of the new legislature. The proportions of one to seven, one to fourteen and the like, each insisted on with emphasis and drawn out with precision and lucidity alike marvellous, carried the mind to the days of 1853, thirty-three years ago, and their great financial triumphs.

By this time almost all cheering had ceased, for clearly men's minds were beginning to think of what had been said rather than what was coming. Mr Parnell was still watching closely, and diligently taking notes with now and then an aside to Dillon or Healy.

But a pause on Mr Gladstone's part, a pushing away of his arithmetic papers, a certain drawing up of his figure and a throwing back of his head told us the end drew nigh. 'The House has heard me with astonishing patience,' called forth a great tempest of cheers by no means confined to the Liberals or Parnellites, and once and for the last time a great silence fell on us, and every man strained his attention so as not to lose a syllable.

The '51 years ago' brought home to us the unrivalled experience of him who was addressing us.

'Our choice has been made' roused once more what seemed an echo of the enthusiastic reception more than three hours ago.

With the last sentence, a fitting conclusion to this marvellous performance, came the chance of giving vent to our pent-up feelings, and once more the shouts broke forth.

Then we streamed forth in a dense mass which thronged doorways and lobby until it impeded its own progress, our faculties, as Mr Trevelyan said soon after, 'fairly benumbed' by what we had witnessed and heard.

But as I sat down at half-past nine in the stillness of the beautiful library at the Reform Club, and closed my eyes the better to allow thought to flow, I found the great panorama of fact and argument as clearly mirrored as the shadow of some great mountain in a still lake at its foot.

The first Home Rule Bill is defeated

George Washburn Smalley (1833–1916) was a graduate of Yale and of Harvard Law School, and he practised law in Boston from 1856 until 1861, when he became a war correspondent covering the Civil War for the *New York Tribune*. He organised that paper's European Bureau in 1866–7 and served as its European correspondent until 1895, when he returned to live in Washington as the American correspondent of *The Times*. He published two collections of his dispatches: *London Letters and Some Others* (1890), which includes this sketch, and *Studies of Men* (1895).

When the Bill was defeated, it is said that Gladstone returned to 10 Downing Street 'entirely immersed in the occupation of counting the passing omnibuses'.[10]

George W. Smalley, *New York Tribune*, June 8, 1886

A stranger arriving yesterday at four o'clock in the afternoon would have thought it a joke had any one told him that the occasion was one of unparalleled excitement and interest. There was the Speaker, robed and wigged as usual, in the chair, the clerks were at the table, business was proceeding, but on the benches of the House not twenty members were to be seen. He might have remarked that the strangers' gallery and the Speaker's gallery were crowded, but that is not uncommon on an ordinary night. If he had known that the House of Commons was to say Aye or No to the most momentous question of the period—to give or to deny Home Rule to Ireland—he would have said that, if the English take their pleasures sadly, they perform grave business in the most light-hearted way. There was, in fact, but a single indication inside the House of the greatness of the occasion, but that one, though easily overlooked, was decisive. In the little frame at the back of each seat was a member's card. The card signified that its owner had come down to the house before prayers, had been present, actually or constructively, at that ceremony, had deposited his hat, and so had secured the seat which the card retained for him. And not one of the little frames was empty, except behind seats reserved for Ministers or great persons. The oblong bits of white card, which gave the green benches the look of a curiously constructed chess-board, signified that presently the House would be thronged to its utmost capacity.

For the moment, it is private bill business that is going on, and the owners of all these cards are in the lobby, the library, the smoking-room, or squiring dames on the terrace. The Speaker transacts this routine business in a business-like way, ready, decisive, unfaltering. But he will be seen at his best later in the evening when, amid the interruptions that beset orator after orator, Mr Speaker Peel enforces order and restores the dignity of debate by what can only be described as the dignity of his own presence. When he has to call an offending member or a riotous party to order, his voice rings out with military sharpness, and the Irishmen themselves are not slow in paying heed to his authority. But for the present he is doing the ordinary duty of the presiding officer of what Englishmen are fond of calling the greatest parliamentary assembly in the world. The word which best describes him is urbanity.

As question time comes on, the House slowly fills. The front Opposition bench has long been crowded before Ministers begin to arrive. The Irish quarter is densely populated while yet the Liberal and Tory domains are like a Western Settlement. It is a belief among the older members that the Parnellites never leave the House; certain it is that they are never absent nor their ranks ever thin when work is to be done. Their discipline is the admiration and the despair of Liberal and Tory Whips alike. If Mr Parnell is not himself very punctual in attendance he is the cause of punctuality in the Parnellite Phalanx. The martinet colonel of a fighting regiment is not stricter at roll-call than the champion of Irish liberty. Familiar faces begin to light up both sides of the House but they are allowed to come without much audible welcome. The Tories have no greeting for their leader, Sir Michael Hicks-Beach, nor for his leader, Lord Randolph Churchill. But it was noticed that Lord Randolph was the bearer of a monster petition. It was assumed that the petition was against Home Rule, and the Tories saluted the great roll of paper with the usual but not always apt cry of 'Hear, hear!' Then came a laugh when Lord Randolph in his best House of Commons manner announced that his petition was from 40,000 of the Lord's Day Rest Association who object to the opening of museums on Sundays.

The first real cheer was at a quarter to five for Mr Goschen, who is to resume the debate. Mr Gladstone's arrival a minute or two later was the signal for an outburst that started from the Parnellite benches, was caught up by the Ministerialists opposite, and presently seemed to kindle even in Tory breasts a spark of enthusiasm for their great adversary. The acoustic properties of the House are peculiar and it is not always easy to say where the cheers come from or where they end. Time was when the matter was simple. Tories on one side, Liberals on the other, and few mistakes made by either. But the House has become a House of groups; on Mr Speaker's left, Tories above the gangway, Parnellites below; while on the right are huddled together Ministerialists, Hartingtonians, Chamberlainites, Radicals, Waverers, in inextricable confusion.

Mr Gladstone has under his arm a red dispatch-box which presently is found to contain the copious notes of his speech, and in his hand that jar of yellow, and no doubt 'judicious', mixture, which is irreverently known in the House as his pomatum pot. A white rose in the button-hole of his black frock-coat looks hardly whiter than his face, on which falls the strange light that enters the chamber from the stained windows close to the carved oaken cornice. The chemical composition of these ghastly rays, whatever it be, produces upon the human countenance an effect like electric illumination. Complexions streaked with sharp gray shadows are to be seen all over the House. By and by a soft yellow radiance streams through the glass panelling of the ceiling, puts out the deepening dusk of the afternoon, and restores to most of these faces a more cheerful look. But nothing from the outside can warm the pallor of Mr Gladstone's countenance, though more than once you will see, as the debate goes on, a flush of angry carmine come into those cheeks

He advances swiftly along the narrow lane between the clerks' table and the bench whence stretch out the innumerable legs of his colleagues, who seem to compose a centipede Cabinet. The Liberal leader's step, if less elastic than of yore, is firm and quick, his air confident if not buoyant. The pose of the head, which has sunk deeper than it once was between the shoulders, is still a pose of beautiful dignity; the head, I almost think, more unapproachably magnificent, the whole bearing more august, than ever. Right or wrong, never was he so great as in his loneliness of today, when friends have fallen off from him, when his political associates are arrayed against him, when he is fighting all but single-handed, when the comrades who once stood by him have set the lance in rest against their old chief, when there is only the single white plume of Navarre to which his hosts can rally. If he wins this battle he may well say 'Alone I did it,'—but he is not to win it, and so one must be content to declare that if unconquerable courage, if conduct and resource, if matchless dexterity and a power of debate to which no rival has attained, could win, Mr Gladstone would indeed have won.

Lord Hartington slips past unnoticed from behind the Speaker's chair, but presently going out is cheered as he returns. He is perhaps the one man who through all this difficult business has earned the respect of all parties and escaped the censure of all. Anybody might do as much by concession, by compliance, by compromise. Lord Hartington has broken with his leader, divided his party, disappointed keen hopes, brought to wreck a great policy, adhered inflexibly to his principles. But he has so borne himself as to extort admiration from those who most deplore his course,—even from Mr Gladstone. No man doubts his sincerity or his simplicity of aim; none ever imputed to him the least indirectness of method or selfishness of motive. He, if anybody, is a representative of class, as Mr Gladstone would say, and if class had no unworthier representative, the spirit of class would be a reproach to no man.

Mr Chamberlain walks in from the opposite door, gets a noisy welcome from the Tories, a quieter one from his friends below the gangway, and nothing but black looks from the Irish. He has done the Irish less harm than Lord Hartington; he takes with him a less numerous following into the lobby, but he is detested by Mr Parnell's company of patriots as no other man is detested. Calumny rains down on him, and not from Irish skies alone. The true Gladstonian—the idolater—who can speak with kindly regret of Lord Hartington, whitens with anger when he names Mr Chamberlain. I think he has had hard usage and I have faith in his sincerity, but I set down the facts as they are. He faces friend and foe with unruffled serenity of mien; a smile just softens the outline of his smooth cheek as the music of the cheers reaches him; and of the black looks he is, or he seems, blissfully unconscious. He would not be Mr Chamberlain without his orchid, any more than Mr Gladstone would be Mr Gladstone without his rose or his shirt collars.

Stranger still is it to mark the welcome of the Tories to Mr Bright, for whom their cheers rise high. Singular days are these upon which we have fallen when Tory applause heralds the approach of every Liberal, save one, whom Liberals have delighted to honour, and when the Liberal party in the House of Commons consists of Mr Gladstone and a certain number of ciphers after his name. Mr Bright has not spoken, will not speak; has no longer, they say, confidence enough in his nerve to address the House in a great debate and in antagonism to the great leader he still dearly loves. He has made his contribution to the cause he believes in by letter—a letter which, as much as any one influence, sent the waverers finally into the No lobby. It is pathetic to see his snow-white head and closed lips. He takes his place next Mr Chamberlain on the second bench below the gangway, above or below which are grouped nearly all the Liberal leaders who have declined Mr Gladstone's Home Rule Shibboleth. Mr Trevelyan is one of them. His deep-set, eager eyes look out from a fringe of white hair that belongs not to his years. We all know what long agony and loyal service it was that gave the look of premature age to a man still in the prime of life and of his fine abilities.

Questions, which are often exciting, are so dull today that the murmur of talk is never stilled on the floor below us, and members come up to the galleries to chat with friends whom they have recognised. There is no such muster of spectators as on the first night of this long debate. No Royalty over the clock; the Royalties are at Ascot, where the sport is more to the mind of the Royal Highness who, were he here, would be seated over the clock. A Peer whom none of us knows sits in his place. The Peers themselves are mostly at Ascot; their benches are pretty full but late-comers still find places. The foremost figure among them is the Red Earl, who owes his picturesque name to a faint hue of flame colour in his yellowish brown beard—Earl Spencer. The stamp of the patrician is on him,—no man so quiet in manner, none of quite the same personal distinction; none, I fancy, who relishes less the adulation now poured on him from the lips that used to reek with calumny and curses. His successor in the Vice-royalty of Ireland, the young, black-bearded, glittering-eyed, popular Earl of Aberdeen, sits not far off. The Earl of Dalhousie is in the row behind them; he, at any rate, a convinced or convincible Home Ruler, so long ago as when he was Lord Ramsay and Liberal member for Liverpool; not so very long ago either, as the fresh youthfulness of his sympathetic and sincere face testifies. At one time or another during the long evening the Duke of Norfolk is visible; visible also is that remarkable person Lord Brabourne, who accepted a peerage from Mr Gladstone only to find his conscience compelling him to vote steadily against his creator, and to wear his coronet, as Lord Rosebery told him in the House of Lords, as a crown of thorns. He has lately taken Mr Chamberlain under his ill-omened patronage, and Mr Sexton, who is capable of epigram, christened this noble author of nursery tales Mr Chamberlain's fairy godmother. If you look at his face you will not think the point of the epigram blunted by the change of sex.

All these and many more are on the left of the clock, which is exactly opposite the Speaker. On the right, in the diplomatic and special galleries, celebrities are select rather than numerous. The tall figure of Count Hatzfeld, the German Ambassador, looks down on Count Corti, his colleague from Italy, whom he completely dwarfs. Into this front row came later, not long before Mr Gladstone rose, a slight, gray-haired, keen-eyed, wrinkled, delightful and admirable little man, about whom whispers began at once to circulate. I suppose there were few men who did not recognise the piquant personality of Dr Oliver Wendell Holmes, for some weeks past the person to be met most frequently in the greatest variety of places in all London. I had noticed in the lobby the genial face of Mr Burnand but saw him in none of the three galleries accessible to the stranger. Nor even on so great a night as this could I discover any one else who could be named as a distinguished stranger.

I can look past Count Hatzfeld's broad shoulders or over Count Corti's head, and over the countless heads of honourable members below, to the gallery where the ladies present ought to be visible but are not. Between them and the House is still the close grating which, for some reason inappreciable by the non-parliamentary mind, the Commons persist in maintaining. I have never heard that the open galleries in the Lords, where the Peeresses gather for a dress debate in dazzling raiment, impaired the political virtue or the business efficiency of the Upper Chamber. Perhaps the Commons are more susceptible or less confident. Behind the bars of the cage one sees dimly certain forms, or certain patches of colour, the flash of a jewel or the gleam of bright eyes; but to recognise the owners of them is impossible. Nor is there much time to mourn over this deprivation. While we have been gazing the House has filled ever fuller, the droning answers to tiresome questions have ceased; a hush has come over the multitude. A clear voice is heard from the far end of the chamber saying, 'Government of Ireland Bill,' and a moment later Mr Goschen is up . . .

. . . The cheers which followed Mr Goschen were echoed in shriller notes when Mr Parnell was seen on his feet. The eighty-five, or perhaps eighty, obedient servants by whom he is surrounded possess collectively—by some caprice of nature, capable no doubt of scientific exposition—a voice set in a singularly high key. It is a convenience to all those who have part in the proceedings of the House, for an Irish cheer is instantly distinguishable from every other cheer. Their greeting to Mr Parnell is taken up on the Ministerial benches, with an effect at least as peculiar as that of Tory salutations to Mr Chamberlain or Mr Bright. Moments elapse before the cries grow still. The greater part of the company are yet under the influence of Mr Goschen's concluding sentences. Members are discussing eagerly, briefly, the effect of his speech; whose votes it will win or shake. The Irish all the while are lifting high their voices—higher and ever higher, and it is not till this din has died away that the Speaker is heard. It may interest you to know that the Speaker calls on the Irish leader as Mr Parnell; accent on the first syllable.

The uncrowned king of Ireland would hardly be described by his warmest admirer as kingly in his appearance and mien. To us who look down on him from the gallery over the clock he seems under medium height; but this may be due to optical laws which the National League has not yet repealed. Nice customs, we know, curtsey to great kings. The Court Circular is witness to the truth of it when a Drawing Room is held, and the Clothes question becomes a question of State. I therefore record the fact that Mr Parnell wore an unusually long black frock-coat, buttoned from waist to the brown beard which has now grown full and bushy and curling. Mr Gladstone's shirt collars are historical; Mr

Punch has made them so. Mr Parnell's collar scarcely rises to historical proportions: it is of the kind known as a turnover and but the faintest rim of linen emerges above the collar of his coat or beyond the sleeves for which his tailor has been something too liberal in cloth. This penury in linen is perhaps a protest against Belfast. He stoops a little, and the stoop enlarges one's view of that anterior portion of the skull which the ravages of time have left unprotected by hair. Not once does he turn his face full to our gallery. It is the Speaker, the Tories on his right, the Ministerialists or Radicals opposite, who have that front view of his visage which we in the other direction vainly desire. At most, it is a profile to us; straight-featured, high-browed, square in the temple; mouth and jaw all buried in beard and moustache. Altogether, a cold, masterful face; colder still, and more masterful still, when more of it was visible and the beard shorn off as formerly.

The slight figure is all but motionless all through the speech. The gestures are few and inexpressive. The voice has hardly a touch of pathos in it, even when its owner means to be pathetic and declares that he and his cannot and will not part with a single Irishman. Its best quality is clearness, which would be more effective if it were less monotonous. Of oratorical quality Mr Parnell is devoid; never did any man deliver to an eager universe so many harangues so totally deficient in passion, in rhetoric, in sympathy, in persuasiveness. It matters little what they are deficient in; they are listened to; studied as the voice of an oracle is studied. Mr Gladstone said of Mr Parnell that he and Palmerston—at another time he added Mr Chamberlain's name also—were the only men he had known in the House of Commons who said precisely what they meant; never more and never less.

This precision in Mr Parnell's case is the easier, today at any rate, since he reads the greater part of his speech from a loosely written manuscript, carefully fastened at the left upper corner that no leaf may be displaced in delivery. The manner in which it is delivered is dry, hard, despotic; the edicts of no crowned king could be more absolute in tone. Here beyond question is a man who knows what he wants, and means to have it. As sentence after sentence falls in measured deliberation from those hidden lips, you cannot but think that this coldness is the coldness of contempt. He is speaking to a body of men whom he has often denounced as an alien legislature; whom he has defied, whose rules he has broken, whose laws he has trodden under foot, whose most cherished traditions he has mocked at, whose dignity he has brought down; and who in return have cast him out from among them, only to let him come back seven times stronger than before. Between him and them is a feud; a race feud if not a blood feud. He faces his foes today in a new attitude. The greatest of them is his foe no longer but his ally. The Liberal party and Liberal leader have capitulated. Parliament itself has silently made terms with an adversary grown too powerful for the nursery discipline it used to apply. Of course he feels the change.

Presently the arctic mood melts a little. Mr Parnell has done with his figures about Ulster and his statistics of the four provinces, and his geographical demonstrations of the impossibility of carving out minorities for protection. He turns upon the right honourable member for West Birmingham with an anger which is certainly human, if not inhuman. He reproaches Mr Chamberlain with a bitterness in which the steadiness of his voice at last shakes. He turns upon the Tories in a temper there is no mistaking; he means mischief to his old—or rather his recent—allies, and he condenses into a couple of sentences a charge of Tory complicity in Home Rule, which sets the roof ringing with Ministerial cheers. Finally, there comes into his voice a note which impresses the House as a note of sincerity, when he proclaims his belief that this settlement would be accepted by Ireland as a final settlement. Nor does any one doubt that the emotion with which the ex-prisoner of Kilmainham recites the catechism of coercion is a genuine emotion. His prediction that Ireland must be left to govern herself or must be governed as a Crown Colony meets with a grim reception from the House in general. Cover it up as he may, John Bull takes it as a threat, and the murmur which greets it deepens into a growl.

Mr Gladstone sat up during Mr Parnell's speech and listened to each word as it dropped ice-cold from Mr Parnell's lips. A masterly exposition he called it later, and Mr Gladstone's judgement in this matter is no more to be impugned than the phrase he selected to express it. With the exception I have noted, it was a speech adapted successfully to a particular purpose; a statement of certain propositions, a proffer of certain assurances, essential in the judgement both of Mr Gladstone and Mr Parnell to the further progress of the Home Rule cause. But there are two men in Mr Parnell—three, no doubt, according to Dr Holmes, but two are enough for the moment. There is an orator and a poor one; a political leader and a very great one. I shall not be thought partial to Mr Parnell, nor am I. My account of him as he stood and spoke in the House on Monday is not partial. It is impartial. But I have this to add. His mediocrity in mere speech-making is the most convincing proof of his genius in council. His leadership rests on something very different from commanding stature or from that copious fluency of rhetoric which is the cheapest of Irish talents.

It is because Mr Parnell has known how to guide a people that the House now listens intently, as Mr Gladstone listens, to these halting sentences. The manner is almost embarrassed. The firmness of purpose so characteristic of Mr Parnell is scarcely indicated. The voice falls at the end of a phrase; the action as a whole is the action of an amateur. As Mr Gladstone has done him the honour to borrow his principles, he borrows in return—it is not much—Mr Gladstone's curious trick of touching a particular spot on his head with his thumb. With every word in writing before him he seems to be feeling his way from one end of a sentence to the other, and looks furtively out on his auditory to see how they take it. For such traits, interesting as they are to the observer, the House cares little or nothing. This proud assembly of Englishmen know well that the Irishman who is struggling with difficult diction to make known his will is, if not their master, a power with whom they must treat as with an equal. If they could forget the past with its conflicts and its tragedies they would, I think, feel that Mr Parnell is speaking his real conviction. But to forget the past is not easy. Mr Parnell himself cannot forget it, and he sits down knowing that other words than those of conciliation abide in the memory of his hearers . . .

. . . Tory cheers rose high and the Tory leader is ready to close the debate for the Opposition. Sir Michael Hicks-Beach is supposed to owe his leadership of the Tories in the House to the nomination of Lord Randolph Churchill, whom men think a more fiery and resolute spirit. He is not an orator whom the House delights in for the sake of his oratory merely; is, nevertheless, a very capable debater and man of business, and tonight is about to prove himself something more. So far as the general debate is concerned he rises to the occasion, and begins a good speech with prepossessing ease of manner and firmness of tone. But what the House is on tiptoe to hear is his answer to Mr Parnell's charge of Tory complicity in Irish Home Rule.

He does not keep us waiting long. A brief review of the relations between Mr Parnell and the Ministerialists is followed by a reference to past insinuations against the Tories, 'which I think,' says Sir Michael, 'have been sufficiently answered by Lord Salisbury'. Is that all he has to say to Mr Parnell? asked members. No, not all. 'Tonight,' continues Sir Michael, 'a more definite statement than I have ever heard before has come from the honourable member for Cork.' The Irish cheer, but the rest of the House is intent on what is coming. The Conservative leader picks up from the table before him a piece of paper and reads from it, very slowly and clearly: 'I think he stated that the demand for power to protect Irish industries was made at a time when he had every reason to suppose that, if the Conservative party had been successful at the polls, they would have offered him a statutory Parliament.' Then he turned round to Mr Parnell, waited, and as Mr Parnell made no sign, asked, 'Is that correct?' Mr Parnell rose, nodded, and added in a tone which signified that Sir Michael had wilfully omitted it: 'With power to protect Irish industries'; whereupon Irish and Ministerial cheers, as if the Tory leader had been caught. Louder Tory cheers followed Sir Michael's still more significant repetition of the words. The House is quick at such moments and everybody saw that the repetition was what Sir Michael wanted to emphasise the point. Then: 'That, I suppose, would be a more agreeable proposition to the honourable member for Cork than the present bill?' An awkward query, but the speaker again turns to the Irish quarter, pauses for his answer, and finally gets a reluctant assent from Mr Parnell; upon which followed the question, 'Why then does he not vote against the measure now before the House?'—a sally greeted by bursts of laughter, derisive and other. Waiting till these had subsided Sir Michael proceeded: 'That is not all. I must for myself and my colleagues state in the plainest and most distinct terms that I utterly and categorically deny that the late Conservative Government had any such intention.'

The uproar was prodigious. Shouts of 'Parnell' from every quarter, ungovernable delight of the Tories at the denial by their leader of a story long current and commonly credited. Mr Parnell hesitated and consulted Mr Sexton who sat next to him. But the shouts continued. Lord Randolph Churchill, without rising, was conspicuous among those who cried 'Parnell', and there by the table stood Sir Michael Hicks-Beach, silent and with an air of having the whole night before him, politely expectant. Mr Parnell struggled to his feet, a round of cheers greeted him. Sir Michael resumed his seat, and amid dead silence the Irish chief launched this question: 'Does the right honourable baronet deny that that intention was communicated to me by one of his own colleagues, a Minister of the Crown?' Cheers of expected triumph saluted this interrogatory; again followed by a hush as Sir Michael once more got to his feet and answered firmly, 'Yes, sir, I do,' to the noise of a still more triumphant roar from the benches behind him. But he presently spoiled the effect by an apologetic 'To the best of my knowledge and belief', which elicited cries of 'Oh, oh!' 'If any such statement,' continued the undaunted Sir Michael, 'was communicated by any one to the honourable member, I am certain he had not the authority of the Cabinet to do so.' Whereupon from every quarter of the House, now thrilling with excitement as thrust and parry followed each other swiftly in this duel, came cries of 'Name, name, name.' Members turned their eyes on Lord Randolph as if it were his name they expected to hear. But Lord Randolph was seen half up from his place beside Sir Michael, vehemently challenging Mr Parnell with voice and gesture to answer. The storm grew wilder, the House echoed with the ever-repeated challenge for a name, and still Mr Parnell remained speechless. At last Sir Michael Hicks-Beach, cool, smiling, facing round full on the surging mass of Irish below him whom the hesitation of their leader puzzled and enraged, took up the appeal. 'Will the honourable member do us the pleasure to name to the House——' The rest of the sentence was lost in a hurricane of hurrahs from the Tory benches. Answer of some sort Mr Parnell saw he must vouchsafe; Mr Healy and Mr O'Brien with hot faces were plainly telling him he must, and Sir Michael blandly sank into his seat as Mr Parnell finally rose. There was a spot of red on the one cheek visible to us in the gallery, and the words came from between the teeth: 'The right honourable baronet has asked me a question which he knows is a very safe one.' ('Oh' and laughter.) 'I shall be very glad to communicate the name of his colleague when I receive his colleague's permission.'

Now there is in such matters a well-understood unwritten law of the House of Commons that accusations like Mr Parnell's are not to be made unless the accuser is prepared to stand by them. On Liberal not less than on Tory benches it was felt that Mr Parnell had failed to comply with this law. The verdict of the whole House, the Irish quarter of course excepted, went instantly and unmistakably against him as he made this reply. Silence—the silence of disappointment and chagrin—fell upon the Liberals. The Tories roared themselves hoarse with delight. The only man who seemed perfectly unmoved was Sir Michael Hicks-Beach, and the smile never departed from his countenance as he replied to Mr Parnell: 'Insinuations are easily made, but proof is a very different thing; and I have observed that the code of honour of honourable members below the gangway stops at the point where proof becomes necessary.' With this stinging epigram the incident ended, leaving Sir Michael Hicks-Beach master of the position. Rightly or wrongly, the House, the whole House, awarded him the victory of the moment. He proceeded with his speech but everything seemed an anti-climax after such a combat. Probably he never spoke so well; certainly never before had he so well satisfied his party.

During the last few sentences of the Tory leader, Mr Gladstone, foreseeing the end near, opened the red dispatch-box, arranged his papers, said a last word to the Chancellor of the Exchequer, and took his first sip from the pomatum pot. He has been restless for some minutes; Old Parliamentary Hand as he is, it is a nervous business to speak to such a House as this, on such an occasion as this. I doubt whether he does not think that the supreme moment of his life has come. He is deadly pale. He cannot satisfy himself about the disposition of his coat sleeves which, like Mr Parnell's, are too long. He has taken a reef in his shirt collar but the most patriotic Ulsterman could not accuse him of showing too little linen. Mr Gladstone is the one Englishman in the House who arrays himself like an American. He is in morning dress while his waistcoat is of the evening and shows three black studs amid the rather troubled expanse of his shirt-front. He wears a black tie very carelessly fastened. It does not matter what he wears. The head is the head of a ruler of men, and his subjects hail his rising with long peals of acclamation of which any ruler might be proud.

We all listen for the first tones of the voice,—half the effect of his speech will depend on whether he is in good voice or not. The first sentences emerge a little huskily, then the throat clears, and thence to the end the changing tones came at will; no key in this organ of many stops failed to respond with the right note to the touch of the master. He began quietly enough but with more solemnity than he is wont. It was plain that he had strung himself to the great performance of a great task. His opponents may say what they like, the House of Commons is a different body when Mr Gladstone is addressing it. To the lofty spirit, the ennobling influence, of the orator many of them are insensible; it none the less exists. The playfulness of fancy in the exordium surprises, but every word goes to the mark; and as the words are numerous that is saying much. Agree with him or not, you feel that he does approach his subject as no other man approaches it; with an elevation of view not attained by his rivals, if rivals he have; in a spirit of seeming disinterestedness even when the contest is a contest of party; with a grandeur that is all his own.

He disclaims all thought of reproach on the conduct of the late Ministry.

His disclaimer provokes laughter which those of us who are not Tories think unmannerly. His face flushes as the jeers reach him across the table, and he answers with a proud gesture: 'If they do not like to do me that justice I shall not ask it.' But again and again he had to endure this laughter; sometimes, I must say, his own audacity encouraged it. He was more than once in that strange mood of mental refinement which the House has come to regard as a proper subject of merriment. He drew perceptible or imperceptible distinctions with equal confidence. When he is not too serious about them it is a delight to watch these intellectual gymnastics. He traversed Sir Michael Hicks-Beach's statement of what he called simple facts. 'I will not say his simple facts are pure fictions because that would hardly, perhaps, be courteous. But they are as devoid of foundation as if they had been pure fiction'—a piece of sportive casuistry which Mr John Morley received with a delighted toss of the head and a broad smile. There are no two minds in the House which have had more training in the use of words for the purpose of delicate discrimination. Mr John Morley is still young and may pause on the perilous path which Mr Gladstone has pursued till it has led him to dizzy heights. I wonder whether he ever read Doudan's remark on another great artist in language, Victor Hugo—*il a tellement joué avec les mots qu'il en est devenu l'esclave.*

It came into my head as I listened to Mr Gladstone expounding to an open-mouthed House the distinction between a person who, having promised that a bill should be reconstructed, is bound to reconstruct it, and a person who has promised that a bill shall be reconstructed, and is free to reconstruct it, but not bound to. The logical validity of the distinction did not protect it from the laugh of a House which remembered perfectly the passionate 'Never, never!' which he was now explaining away.

After a few minutes spent in trying his muscles, in this way, on he went to higher flights and excursions into wider fields. If while under the fascination of the orator's voice and manner you can keep your mind clear, you will admire the structure of the speech as a work of art. He passes easily from the personalities and controversy of the opening to a statement of his position with reference to the bill, and what the House was to vote on. He broadened his previous concessions by not a single inch and won not a single vote from the waverers. Ulster was touched with no better success—hope of success in such matters he had abandoned—but it served as an easy transition to the historical argument which was the burden of the whole discourse, and perhaps, for the immediate purpose of the evening, a little over-burdened it. A reference to the Colonies offered him the opening he wanted for an attack on Mr Chamberlain; one of the sensations of the debate. It took the form of elaborate banter, good-humoured and harmless on the surface, very bitter in substance. Mr Gladstone delivered it with an appearance of affectionate interest in the political ingenuity of his younger friend; with a variety of intonation and feline gesture which amused the House in general and gratified to the core the resentments of the

Parnellites against the Radical leader. His attack on Lord Salisbury as the author of a policy of coercion which compelled Mr Gladstone to admit that his own scheme had a rival in the field, foreshadowed the policy of the coming campaign and exasperated the Tories.

But this and everything else was forgotten in the peroration. With a sustained splendour of diction and dignity of thought and feeling, Mr Gladstone held the House for perhaps a quarter of an hour completely in his grasp. As sentence followed sentence, each in the same lofty key, each seeming to reach the oratorical climax which still receded farther and farther, the hearer thought each sentence must be the last. But on and on went the orator, his voice more melodious, his manner more impressive, his eloquence even more pathetic. He silenced his Tory opponents. Not one of them cared to lose a note of that incomparable voice as it rose and fell in musical cadence amid the deep hush that had come upon the House. The oldest member had heard nothing equal to this; the youngest cannot hope that it will ever be heard again.

Mr Gladstone began his speech at half-past eleven, spoke till four minutes past one, and resumed his seat amid a tumult of cheers which for some minutes prevented the Speaker from putting the question. The House could not regain its composure. The feelings which the great orator had stirred came from the depths of human nature, and the agitation would not be calmed. He had spoken, and he knew it, for a lost cause. He knew the division was going against him; everybody knew it, but the faith in future triumph overmastered the certainty of immediate defeat. Nay, such was the enchantment of that last quarter of an hour that, to many of his followers, defeat no longer seemed possible; they were sure that men who doubted must have been converted. A member of the Government who sat in the next gallery leaned over to me and in the flush of this new-born faith asked, 'Will you have a sovereign even on the division?' I could not well refuse.

If there were one man in the multitude who seemed impervious to all this enthusiasm it was the Speaker, who presently put the question. The Ayes answered with a great shout, prolonged into a cry like nothing the House ever before heard. The Noes responded. 'The Ayes have it,' said the Speaker. There was the usual dissent; the division bells rang; the question was again put, and the House was cleared for the division at ten minutes past one on Tuesday morning, July 8, 1886. The excitement, the anxious strain, the suspense of the next fifteen minutes were to be imagined rather than seen, or to be seen only by reading the faces of the men who had most at stake. The House filled again slowly. When Mr Marjoribanks, the junior teller of the Government, was seen to come in, it was known that the Ayes must be fewer than the Noes, and a murmur ran along the benches. It was only the signal of a result certain beforehand. The murmur grew as the clerk handed the paper with the figures to Mr Brand who, with Mr Caine, told for the Opposition. Mr Brand read out the figures: 'Ayes to the right 311, Noes to the left 341.' The Tories burst into wild cheers. The Liberals answered faintly. A moment later a dense, compact throng of men with angry faces were seen on their feet, fronting the Tories above the gangway, and the Irish were, to use their own language, hurling back defiance upon their foes. Confusion and tumult reigned; the most discordant cries came from all quarters; for some minutes all thought of order or decorum was lost; honourable members had become boys, and behaved like boys, some of them bad boys. Presently Mr T. P. O'Connor called for three cheers for the Grand Old Man, and then three groans for Mr Chamberlain. This last outbreak of anger brought a smile to the heretofore impassive face of the Radical leader; well he knew that such a demonstration could injure nobody but those who took part in it.

The scene lacked no element of excitement, but I imagine most eyes turned to the Treasury Bench where sat Mr Gladstone, visibly affected by the greatness of the majority against him. He had counted on ten, or twenty as a possibility; the majority of thirty was a blow that staggered him. The noble head was brought low by the shock; the face grew ashen white. The formal motion which it was his duty to make had to be written for him and read, and the hand which held the written paper shook, and the voice shook, and the figure was the figure of a man who had suddenly aged. Not even the loyal greetings of loyal friends could bring back into his wearied face the light of delight in the battle, or the joy of the personal triumph he had won and of the political triumph he still expects to achieve.

❖

Grey announces the declaration of war against Germany

Rowland Edmund Prothero (1851–1937), 1st Baron Ernle, was born in Worcestershire, the son of a vicar, and educated at Marlborough and at Balliol College, Oxford. He gained notice as a man of letters and a biographer. He was elected to Parliament in June 1914 as a burgess of Oxford University, holding the seat again in 1918.

Rowland Prothero (Lord Ernle), *Whippingham to Westminster:*
The Reminiscences of Lord Ernle (1938)

Six weeks after I entered the House of Commons, war was declared. It was an impressive scene, on August 3, 1914, when Sir Edward Grey as Foreign Secretary announced the decision of the Government which ranged the British Empire by the side of France, Russia, and Belgium against the Central Powers. It seemed only yesterday when Grey and I—he as an undergraduate of Balliol, I as an idle Fellow of All Souls—spent so many mornings on the tennis court in Merton Street at Oxford, that his tutor protested against my jeopardising his pupil's chance of a degree. Now I sat at his feet at a supreme crisis in the world's history. Grey was marked out among his contemporaries, not so much by his abilities, which were not in any way exceptional, as by his character.

His heart was in country scenes—on the banks of rivers and among the haunts of birds. But his high sense of duty had forced him into public life. For such an occasion as the present, he seemed peculiarly well fitted. His speech had no rhetorical flourishes, no burst of eloquence; it bore no trace of preparation. But it was transparently truthful—a plain unvarnished statement of facts as he knew them. The wisdom of the course taken at this or that crisis may be questioned; it may be thought also that the certainty of our intervention in given circumstances might have been more strongly emphasised. But standing in the position into which we had been forced, the nation, as I thought, could have had no better interpreter of its mood and purpose than this man, whose words drew their force not from oratory but from his own character and convictions. The story, as he told it, illustrated many of the qualities by which Englishmen like to think that they are distinguished—the love of peace and of fair play, the loyalty to friends, the chivalry towards the weak, the slowness to take offence, and, when the time for action had come, the tenacity of purpose, the firm resolution, the deliberate courage. As I remember the scene, the speech was received not, as it has sometimes been described, with noisy demonstrations of enthusiasm, but in almost awed silence.

The fall of the first Labour Government

The fall of the first Labour Government was brought about by the case of Campbell, a crippled ex-serviceman and the editor of the *Worker's Weekly*, who had encouraged soldiers to disobey orders. The Government's law officers at first sought to prosecute Campbell for sedition, but dropped any action at the insistence of their followers. The Liberals demanded an inquiry and the Tories tabled a vote of censure.

Years later when Winterton encountered Sir Patrick Hastings at dinner, he happened to mention the House of Commons. 'Don't talk to me of the place,' said Hastings bitterly; 'it treated me as no honourable man should be treated.' Winterton 'tried in vain to persuade him that, though he had made a good speech, the House was entitled to put its own interpretation upon his actions'.

Earl Winterton, Diary, October 8, 1924

The debate on which so much hangs! I think in 20 years I have never known the issue of a debate so doubtful or where the result was going to be so momentous. Horne was there: had an angry question time, but the actual debate was quiet and dignified, partly owing to the Speaker's intervention. Horne made a completely effective and virile, though un-impassioned, attack on the Government; Patrick Hastings spoke next and was, I must say, very good—so much so that I was shaken in my own conviction as regards his guilt and that of the Government. Simon followed and was also brilliant but, as usual, coldly chiselled. The Prime Minister followed and was poor; up to dinner the issue was still in doubt. After dinner, however, it was clear that we were going to refuse to fall into the trap which the Government were anxious to set and S.B. put our doubts at rest by announcing that we should vote for the inquiry. Douglas Hogg and Thomas followed for their respective sides in a shouting House and the division was taken. The Government were heavily defeated. There were the usual scenes inside and outside the House.

Hannen Swaffer (1879–1962) was born in Sussex, the son of a draper, and was educated at Stroud Grammar School. He was a journalist and in 1924 was briefly editor of the *People*.

Hannen Swaffer, *Hannen Swaffer's Who's Who* (1929)

I first met F.E. [Smith], as he will always be, on Friday, October 3rd, 1924, when Grant Mordern, who owned *The People*, of which I was editor, wanted to pay him £100 a week for a year, to write articles I did not value. As one-tenth of the profits, if any, were to be mine, I disliked paying Lord Birkenhead £10 a week out of my own pocket, for something I did not want.

However, when they proved I should not lose by it, I met the great man, who asked me for his first subject.

'Write about the fall of the Socialist Government,' I said.

'What on earth do you mean?' he asked.

'The Government falls next Wednesday night,' I replied.

'Nonsense,' was his astounded answer.

'I tell you the Government falls next Wednesday night,' I replied. 'At about quarter past eleven, there will be no Government.'

'Why do you say such stupid things to me?' said Birkenhead.

'Ben Spoor, who is the Government Whip, has just told us,' was my insistence.

'But I have just left L.G.,' protested Birkenhead. 'He did not tell me.'

'Lloyd George does not know,' I replied. 'Jim Thomas is going to make a speech that will make the House throw Ramsay out, whether it wants to or not.'

Even then, Birkenhead would not believe me, and he would not write about it. So I did—although no one believed it.

Next Wednesday night, I went down to the House of Commons to see the Government fall. No one believed my story—not even a policeman at the door.

For three hours I was disbelieved. Then Jim Thomas made his speech, and at 11.15 the Socialist Government was no more.

Chamberlain announces war

Harold Nicolson, Diary, September 1, 1939

Go down to the House 5.30. They have already darkened the building and lowered the lights. The lobby is extremely dark, and the Chamber, which generally seems like a dim aquarium, appears quite garish in comparison. The

Speaker arrives punctually at 6 and we all bow to him. Lloyd George and Winston are already in their places facing each other. We have prayers. The Chaplain adds a little special prayer saying, 'Let us this day pray for wisdom and courage to defend the right.' The Prime Minister and Greenwood enter together and are received with a loud cheer. A few enthusiasts try to rise and wave their order papers. They then sit down again rather foolishly. People crowd into the Distinguished Strangers Gallery. The Polish and Russian Ambassadors find themselves next to each other. I grin up at Maisky and he grins back.[11] The Dukes of Kent and Gloucester sit above the clock.

Chamberlain rises immediately. He begins by saying that the time has arrived when action rather than speech is required. He then, with some emotion, reminds the House how he prayed that it would never fall upon him to ask the country to accept the 'awful arbitrament of war'. 'I fear', he continued, 'that I may not be able to avoid that responsibility.' He then goes on to say that we have neglected no means of making it crystal clear to the German Government that if they use force we should reply by force, and he raises his voice and strikes the box with a clenched fist as he says, 'The responsibility for this terrible catastrophe lies on the shoulders of one man, the German Chancellor, who has not hesitated to plunge the world into misery in order to serve his own senseless ambition.' This met with a loud cheer from all benches. He then continues calmly explaining the recent course of negotiations, resting the back of one hand upon the palm of the other, and every now and then taking off his pince-nez between his finger and thumb. When he reveals the fact that the sixteen points which Hitler claims to have been rejected were never even communicated to the Poles, a gasp of astonishment rises and Lady Astor exclaims in ringing tones, 'Well, I never did!' He then reaches the climax of his speech, and after saying that the two Ambassadors have been instructed 'to hand to the German Government the following document', he fiddles with his papers for some time and then produces a document which he reads very slowly. He is evidently in real moral agony and the general feeling of the House is one of deep sympathy for him and of utter misery for ourselves.

I am afraid that the Lobby opinion is rather defeatist and they all realise that we have in front of us a very terrible task. The Prime Minister's speech is generally approved, although the Opposition mind very much his having brought in that friendly reference to Mussolini.

September 2. The House meets at 2.45 and we get through the Conscription and other Bills. They pass with slight discussion. Strange rumours begin as usual to circulate: that a supposed Havas message has gone out saying that Mussolini has announced that he will mediate and that a Conference must be summoned at once; that there is to be a War Cabinet with Winston in it, without the Labour people, who rightly refuse to join; that the Polish Ambassador in Paris had a meeting this morning with Georges Bonnet which was so unsatisfactory that on his return to the Embassy he wrote a record of it and sent it to

Daladier with the words, 'Herewith my record of my interview with your Foreign Secretary.'

At 7.30 we reassemble. The House is packed and tense and we wait there exactly like a court awaiting the verdict of the jury. At 7.35 the Clerks come in and take their places. At 7.37 the Speaker enters from behind the chair and we all rise. There is an unpleasant silence. At 7.42 the Prime Minister enters with Greenwood. He gets up to speak.

He begins with the chronological method: 'On Wednesday night Sir Nevile Henderson, our Ambassador in Berlin, handed to Herr von Ribbentrop . . .'— that sort of thing. His voice betrays some emotion as if he were sickening for a cold. He is a strange man. We expected one of his dramatic surprises. But none came. It was evident when he sat down that no decision had been arrived at. The House gasped for one moment in astonishment. Was there to be another Munich after all? Then Greenwood got up. The disappointment at the PM's statement, the sense that appeasement had come back, vented itself in the reception of Greenwood. His own people cheered, as was natural; but what was so amazing was that their cheer was taken up in a second and greater wave from our benches. Bob Boothby cried out, '*You* speak for Britain.' It was an astonishing demonstration. Greenwood almost staggered with surprise. When it subsided he had to speak and did so better than I had expected. He began to say what an embarrassing task had been imposed on him. He had wanted to support and was obliged to criticise. Why this delay? We had promised to help Poland 'at once'. She was being bombed and attacked. We had vacillated for 34 hours. What did this mean? He was resoundingly cheered. The tension became acute, since here were the PM's most ardent supporters cheering his opponent with all their lungs. The front bench looked as if they had been struck in the face.

The PM makes a conciliatory speech saying that he does not mean to give way but that we must work *pari passu* with the French. He makes the mistake of saying that he does not believe for one moment that the French are weakening, whereas he must know very well that the better-informed among us already know about Georges Bonnet. He is not telling the truth, and we know it.

The House then adjourns. The lobby is so dark that a match struck flames like a beacon. There is great confusion and indignation. We feel that the German ships and submarines will, owing to this inexplicable delay, elude our grasp. The PM must know by now that the whole House is against him. He might (had he been a more imaginative man) have got out of his difficulty. It was not his fault but that of Georges Bonnet. But he is too secretive by nature to be able to create confidence. In those few minutes he flung away his reputation. I feel deeply sorry for him.

(*Sunday*) *September 3.* The papers announce that we are sending an ultimatum which expires at 11 this morning.

To Ronnie Tree's house. The usual members of our group are enlivened by the presence of Bob Boothby and Duncan Sandys of the Churchill group. We discuss first whether Anthony [Eden] is to accept the offer to join the Cabinet, although he is not included in the inner Cabinet. Anthony rather writhes and wriggles, from which I gather that he has already committed himself to join, and does not relish all these suggestions. I watch the minute-hand of my watch creeping towards 11 a.m., when we shall be at war. The Prime Minister is to broadcast at 11.15 and we have no wireless. The housemaid has one and she comes and fixes it up in a fumbling way. We listen to the PM. He is quite good and tells us that war has begun. But he puts in a personal note which shocks us. We feel that after last night's demonstration he cannot possibly lead us into a great war. One of the group who had come back into the Chamber after the adjournment says that Chamberlain remained on the bench with Margesson. The latter was purple in the face, and the former was as white as a sheet. It must be clear to them that if it had come to a vote at the time, he would have been defeated.

At 11.40 we decide to stroll down to the House. I walk ahead with Leo Amery, and Anthony and Duff [Cooper] walk behind. Hardly have we left 28 Queen Anne's Gate when a siren blows. Amery says, 'They ought not to do that after what we have heard on the wireless. People will think it is an air-raid warning.' Hardly has he said these words when another siren takes it up. 'My God!' I say, 'it *is* an air-raid warning!' Anthony, who was walking behind, catches us up. 'We had better make for the House,' he said. 'We still have time.' We walk on trying to make casual conversation. The sirens scream all around us and policemen wave at us. At that moment [Edward] Spears drives up in his car. We tumble in. I sit on Amery's knee and Anthony sits on mine. We reach Parliament Square. As we enter it the crowd, which had massed itself against the railings, breaks up like a flock of pigeons. They run away towards Westminster Hospital. They cut across the grass plot where the statues are. We go on to Palace Yard. We get out of the car and walk quickly but not without dignity into the House. I give my hat up in the ordinary way and mount the stairs to the Members' Lobby. The police there are in steel helmets and tell us to go down to the air-raid refuge. I do so, and find the corridor towards the Harcourt Room blocked by all manner of people from Cabinet Ministers to cooks. It is very hot. People chat to each other with forced geniality. After ten minutes we are released and go on to the terrace. People assert that they heard gunfire and bombs dropping. I suggest that it was merely the carpenters nailing in the asbestos linings to the windows. The terrace is flashed with sunshine, and we watch with disapproval the slow movements of people at Lambeth trying to get a balloon to rise. It has been dampened by last night's rain.

Nobody really knows whether the raid is over, but at noon we return to the Chamber. The Speaker takes his seat with the usual calm procedure. We have prayers. The Prime Minister then makes a speech which is restrained and therefore effective. He looks very ill. Winston intervenes with a speech which misses fire since it is too like one of his articles. The sirens continue during the debate, but we pay no attention to them. They are sounding the all-clear. We learn afterwards that the whole air-raid was a mistake. It was some strayed reveller returning (*male sobrius*) from Le Touquet. But the effect of this alarm was that nobody was really attuned to listen with any real receptiveness to the speeches that were made.

The fall of Chamberlain

Bob Boothby, Journal, May 1940

I was standing beside the Speaker's Chair when the result of the division was announced. It clearly came as a surprise, and a great shock, to the Prime Minister. For a moment he blanched, but quickly recovered himself, and smiled at some of his supporters. Then he rose abruptly, and walked out alone. I watched his solitary figure going down the dark corridor behind the Speaker's Chair until it disappeared from sight. I thought of him standing in Downing Street, barely eighteen months before, with the cheering crowds surging around him. All is vanity, saith the preacher. I felt very sorry for him in the hour of his fall. God knows he had struggled, according to the light that was in him, for peace. But I called to mind a sentence in John Buchan's *History of the Great War*: 'If a man is determined not to fight, and his enemy knows this, it is unlikely that he will escape without finding himself in strangely undignified positions.'

Parliament recognises the plight of the Jews

Harry Boardman (1886–1958) was the son of a Lancashire hand-loom silk weaver. He worked on local newspapers, then served in the Army during World War I before joining the *Manchester Guardian* in 1919. From 1929 to 1945 he was the paper's Westminster Political Correspondent, and from 1945 until his death he was its Parliamentary Correspondent.

Harry Boardman, *Manchester Guardian*, December 18, 1942

It was complained here on Wednesday that the House of Commons was not doing itself justice in the matter of the Jewish massacres and that it was falling behind the House of Lords, which had several times debated the subject, while the Commons had not debated it once. The House of Commons certainly redeemed itself yesterday. Its demeanour when Mr Eden was reading the United Nations' declaration condemning 'the bestial policy of cold-blooded extermination' was worlds removed from the day-to-day bearing of the House. A stranger might have thought he was intruding on a religious service.

The House was hushed. Every syllable of the Foreign Secretary dropped clear and distinct into the silence. A few minutes before there had been some irritable exchanges between Major Lloyd George and several Scottish members. So striking and so unpremeditated a change of mood was sufficient testimony of itself that the Commons are as troubled and appalled as the peers or anybody else.

But there were more proofs. Mr James de Rothschild, pale with the ivory pallor that is said to have belonged to the elder Disraeli, rose to the full height of his tall figure and thanked Mr Eden for 'the eloquent and just denunciation' of the German crimes. He spoke in faltering but admirable phrases. His prayer at the end that some words of the declaration might percolate through to the victims and help them 'still to uphold the dignity of man' was offered with humility and not with any oratorical design, and it was therefore all the more moving.

Of course, Mr de Rothschild was completely out of order. Only questions were in order. It shows how far the House had got from its moorings that this speech—it was nothing else—was made without check or challenge.

There followed a still more impressive manifestation of the deep feelings of the House. When it was about to pass to 'the orders of the day', a Labour member, Mr Cluse, who sits for South Islington, got up from the obscurity of a back bench and, in a mild voice, proposed to the Speaker that members should stand in witness of their detestation of Germany's barbarism. Mr Cluse is an infrequent speaker, but he was inspired yesterday.

In a moment all members were on their feet, and the Lord Chancellor, in the Peers' Gallery, with them. Nothing comparable with this has happened before. The House stood and sang *God Save the King* when war was declared in 1914, and it rather went off its head when Mr Chamberlain announced his journey to Munich, but these were occasions when national feelings were racing at the flood.

Yesterday the Commons rose in calm to perform something like a judicial action to brand Germany for these infamies. This was the House of Commons in one of its great moments. It has a genius for the appropriate on these unrehearsed occasions.

Mr Eden was weak when it came to the possibilities of positive relief action. He sees the difficulties large, and no doubt they are great, but they do not become less by merely calling them 'immense' or 'tremendous'. Limited in scope though each may be, practical suggestions have been made for assisting those Jews who can escape, but Mr Eden did not touch upon them. It would have been no bad addendum to the declaration if Mr Eden could have announced that there would be free asylum in this country for any refugee who can manage to get here.

Sir Henry 'Chips' Channon, Diary, December 17, 1942

An extraordinary assembly today in the august Mother of Parliaments. It was sublime. Anthony [Eden] read out a statement regarding the extermination of Jews in east Europe, whereupon Jimmy de Rothschild rose, and with immense dignity, and his voice vibrating with emotion, spoke for five minutes in moving tones on the plight of these people. There were tears in his eyes, and I feared that he might break down; the House caught his spirit and was deeply moved. Somebody suggested that we stand in silence to pay our respects to those suffering peoples, and the House as a whole rose and stood for a few frozen seconds. It was a fine moment, and my back tingled.

Churchill announces D-Day

William Barkley (1898–1968) was born in Galashiels, Scotland, and educated at Lenzie Academy and at Glasgow University, where he was awarded a First in Greek and Latin. After working for a few years on the *Glasgow Herald*, he took a holiday job as a medical consultant's secretary while teaching himself Gregg's shorthand and wrote a research article for the *Daily Express* which appealed to Lord Beaverbrook. He joined Lord Beaverbrook's staff at the *Daily Express* in 1925. In 1948 Beaverbrook, in introducing a collection of Barkley's columns, *William Barkley's Notebook*, wrote that his 'night-by-night commentary on Parliament is the morning joy of nearly four million British homes'.

William Barkley, *Daily Express*, June 7, 1944

Anybody who thinks the House of Commons tore up its business in a rush of excitement to hear the great news yesterday does not know the first thing about this venerable institution.

MPs had heard the bare outline of the landing in France when they assembled from their Whitsun holiday at 11 o'clock. Groups of them had lively conversation as they moved into the Chamber.

But, once they were there, no one, to look at them or listen, would have known that this morning of 6th June was to be ever memorable.

The Speaker took the chair. The chaplain read the prayer. The announcement of the death of an MP during the recess was made, in accordance with form.

The Speaker then announced: 'I have received a telegram from the Chilean Chamber of Deputies containing a copy of a resolution of friendship towards the British House of Commons.' (Cheers.) 'It will be your desire that I should send a suitable reply.' (More cheers.)

Warm reply, accordingly, sent to Chile. Then came the hour of questions, one MP after another agitating Minister after Minister on topic after topic concerning the people.

Are soldiers securing their voting rights?

Could not cheaper houses be built if interest did not have to be paid on the loans?

Why has a disabled soldier been refused a permit to open a shop in Wimbledon?

Mr Lloyd George, whose arrival is an omen nowadays of a special occasion, smiled and nodded his way to a front Opposition seat while the hours of employment of staff in Service canteens were engrossing attention.

Sir Richard Acland (Common Wealth, Barnstaple) was told that politics did not enter into AMGOT appointments. Mr Evelyn Walkden (Soc., Doncaster) was told that his information on some question to the Treasury was contrary to that of the Treasury.

It was, you might think, a normal day, with Lady Apsley (Cons., Central Bristol) asking Sir James Grigg, the War Minister, to issue berets to the ATS, Sir James replying that this is not time for new hats for ATS and Sir Archibald Southby (Cons., Epsom) gallantly championing the rights of women to new headgear in the springtime.

The House was filling all the time, and some of the galleries, too, with peers, with visitors such as Captain Montgomery, brother to General Montgomery and chaplain to the Forces, who last saw his brother from the water as he landed to begin the drive on Sicily.

Mrs Churchill came in above. It was now ten to 12, but Mr Churchill had not yet entered below.

An unusual pause occurred. Questions were ended. For once the flood of curiosity had abated, with ten minutes still to go.

Mr Attlee and Mr Eden studied the clock. A message was hurriedly sent to the Prime Minister's room. Still no Prime Minister.

The Speaker remarked: 'I think the House would like to hear the Prime Minister.' The House instantly showed its agreement with that view in a loud 'Hear, hear!'

So the unusual scene occurred of the House sitting in full session, with no business except chat and small talk, for ten minutes, until, on the accustomed stroke of midday, Mr Churchill entered.

He strode with a firm, unhurried pace to the dispatch box. Members gave him a great cheer, one or two standing up the better to expand their lungs.

He was in a mood neither solemn nor smiling. A trace of distress might have been noted in his features. It was explained at once when he said:

'I must apologise to the House for having delayed them, but questions went through more rapidly than I anticipated.' On this day of days MPs answered back to him. 'No need to apologise.'

Brisk and businesslike, Mr Churchill took things in their order. He spoke of the fall of Rome before he came to the landing in France. The fall of Rome!— let us see, that was 48 hours ago; we move fast these days.

There was actually some impatience as the Prime Minister, saying: 'The

House should, I think, take formal cognizance of the liberation of Rome,' gave nearly ten minutes to this memorable and glorious event, as he called it.

Loud were the cheers at the mention of General Alexander, at the way he 'broke the teeth' of the German attacks at Anzio before launching a frontal attack all along the front in which, counting from right to left, Polish, British Empire, French and United States forces all broke through the German line.

Then a sigh of anticipation wafted through the audience as Mr Churchill, without variation of voice or manner, proceeded:

'I have also to announce to the House that during the night and the early hours of this morning the first of a series of landings in force on the European Continent has taken place.'

Thereat a burst of cheers stopped him. It was still a composed and almost formal demonstration. Here at last, after all these weary years of waiting, was the beginning of the grand assault.

And as the rapid, steady voice of the Prime Minister piled one piquant detail on another, with admirable selection of red-hot fact and without emotion, rhetoric or frills, the great news began to take shape and to assume reality.

'In this case,' the voice continued, 'the liberating assault fell on the coast of France. An immense armada of upwards of 4,000 ships, together with several thousand smaller craft, crossed the Channel.

'Mass airborne landings have been successfully effected behind the enemy lines.'

Mr Churchill's emphasis on 'successfully' stirred the audience deeply, spreading the impression that we had been able to jump over Hitler's west wall. Yet the next sentence was:

'Landings on the beaches are proceeding at various points at the present time.'

And then the splendid news: 'The fire of the shore batteries has been largely quelled,' and this delicious revelation of mastery of another German secret weapon, as it seemed:

'The obstacles which were constructed in the sea have not proved so difficult as was apprehended.' (Loud cheers.)

Last in this catalogue of favourable items: 'The Anglo-American Allies are sustained by about 11,000 first-line aircraft, which can be drawn on as may be needed for the purpose of the battle.'

Mr Churchill then continued: 'I cannot commit myself to any particular details. Reports are coming in in rapid succession. So far, the commanders who are engaged report that everything is proceeding according to plan.

'And what a plan!' the Premier exclaimed, yielding for one moment to rhetorical impulse. 'This vast operation is undoubtedly the most complicated and difficult which has ever occurred.

'It involves time, tide, winds and visibility both from the air and the sea, and the combined employment of land, sea, and air forces in the highest degree of intimacy.'

He had one more hint of a great achievement: 'There are already hopes that actual tactical surprise has been attained' (cheers), 'and we hope to furnish the enemy with a succession of surprises during the course of the fighting.

'The battle which has now begun,' Mr Churchill concluded, 'will grow constantly in scale and intensity for many weeks to come. I will not attempt to speculate on its course.

'This I may say: Complete unity prevails throughout the Allied Army. There is a brotherhood in arms between us and our friends of the USA. There is complete confidence in the Supreme Commander, General Eisenhower' (loud cheers), 'and also in the Commander of the Expeditionary Force, General Montgomery' (cheers again).

'The ardour and spirit of the troops, as I saw myself, embarking in these last two days was splendid to witness. Nothing that equipment, science and fore-thought can do has been neglected, and the whole process of opening this great new front will be pursued with the utmost resolution both by the commanders and the USA and British Governments whom they serve.'

The statement began with cheers, and with cheers it ended.

Mr Arthur Greenwood, voice of such organised Opposition as there is in this all-party Victory Government, well expressed what all were thinking:

'There is nothing much we can do except pledge ourselves and our physical and spiritual resources to the unstinted aid of the men and women serving overseas, to let them know the pride we shall feel in their victories and the sadness we shall feel about their losses.'

Mr Greenwood asked the Prime Minister to report events to Parliament and the people as frequently as possible—'so that we may share such tribulations as may come to them and take joy in their achievements.'

Mr Churchill promised to do so, at any rate in the early part of the battle.

1. Quoted in Robert Rhodes James, *An Introduction to the House of Commons* (1961), p. 12.
2. Alexander Mackintosh, *Echoes of Big Ben: A Journalist's Parliamentary Diary, 1881–1940* (1945), p. 36.
3. Frank Dilnot, *The Old Order Changeth* (1911), p. 37.
4. Sir Henry Morris-Jones, *Doctor in the Whips' Room* (1955), p. 159.
5. Aneurin Bevan, 'Inside Westminster', *Tribune*, January 1, 1937.
6. T. F. Lindsay, *Parliament from the Press Gallery* (1967), p. 45.
7. S. H. Romilly (ed.), John William Ward, *Letters to 'Ivy' From the First Earl of Dudley* (1902), p. 157.
8. R. C. K. Ensor, *England 1870–1914* (1936), p. 67.
9. Quoted in Arthur Tilney Bassett, *The Life of the Rt Hon. John Edward Ellis MP* (1914), pp. 65–72.
10. L. G. Redmond-Howard, *John Redmond: The Man and the Demand* (1910), p. 229.
11. I. M. Maisky was the Soviet Ambassador.

5 Law and Disorder

The object of Parliament is to substitute argument for
fisticuffs.

Winston S. Churchill, Speech to the House of
Commons, June 6, 1951

Order in the House of Commons is determined by the Speaker and enforced by the Serjeant-at-Arms and his team of door-keepers, who in modern times have often been ex-servicemen or retired policemen. Also in modern times, Metropolitan Police officers have been at the disposal of the Serjeant and have twice been called upon to eject offenders by force: when Bradlaugh attempted to take his seat in 1881, and when certain Irish MPs led by Flavin refused to leave the Chamber during a division in 1901.

The authority of the Speaker, who was originally a royal appointee, was not always recognised. Indeed, in 1610 the Speaker complained that an MP had 'put out his tongue, and popped his mouth with his finger, in scorn' at him.[1] On another occasion, an MP crept up behind Mr Speaker Lenthal, who was about to put a question to the vote, and shouted 'Baugh!' in his ear, 'to his great terror and affrightment'.[2] The first instance of an MP being singled out by name for censure by the Speaker occurred on June 9, 1641, when Mr Speaker Lenthal, finding himself unable to silence 'divers members who were talking at the lower end of the House, in the west corner under the gallery, at last called on Sir W. Carnabie, by name, to desist'.[3]

In November 1641 the Grand Remonstrance, a tally of grievances against the Crown, was passed by the House of Commons. John Hampden proposed that it be printed, but the King's party were against this and the mood of the House was extremely tense. The Remonstrance 'passed so tumultuously two or three nights before the King came to town', recalled Sir Philip Warwick, 'that at three of the clock in the morning, when they voted it, I thought we had all sat in the valley of the shadow of death; for we, like Joab's and Abner's young men, had catched at each other's locks, and sheathed our swords in each other's bowels, had not the sagacity and great calmness of Mr Hampden, by a short speech, prevented it, and led us to defer our angry debate until the next morning'.[4] The tendency of MPs and Peers to appear drunk in their respective Chambers also led to fisticuffs. In 1621, for instance, the Earl of Berkshire set upon Lord Scrope and was duly committed to the Tower. An even worse assault occurred at a conference between the two Houses of Parliament in 1666. The Duke of Buckingham and Lord Dorchester exchanged heated words, then the Duke knocked off the other's hat and pulled him about the Chamber by his periwig until they were separated and both sent to cool off in the Tower.[5]

In order to avoid physical violence, it became the practice that certain provocative epithets would be deemed unparliamentary. In the late eighteenth century abusive language was often used, even by such distinguished performers as Burke, and some bitter exchanges resulted in duels outside the Chamber, a practice which increased to such an extent that one Member anxiously predicted in 1780 that, if it were to continue, 'Parliament would resemble a Polish diet'.[6] The distinction between what is acceptable abuse and what is unparliamentary was succinctly explained by Macaulay in a letter to his sister Fanny: 'The rule of debate is that you must abstain from personalities, but that you may be as severe on opinions, institutions, etc. as you please. You must not say that Mr John O'Connell is a traitor or a knave. But you may say that conventual institutions are seminaries of vice and madness; and, though the expression may be violent and reprehensibly coarse, it is quite within the limits of parliamentary language.'[7] After an exchange of unparliamentary language in 1834, a member of the Cabinet, Lord Althorp, and the Irish Radical Sheil were locked up by the Serjeant-at-Arms at the Speaker's insistence until they were ready to apologise both to each other and to the House.[8] 'The modern House of Commons would seem, to its predecessors of the eighteenth and even of the nineteenth century, absurdly mealy-mouthed,' wrote the *Daily Telegraph* journalist T. F. Lindsay in the mid-1960s. 'The language of our ancestors was considerably more robust. Their skins were thicker, and the Speakers of former days would have allowed many expressions which would be quite inadmissible today.'[9]

In December 1770 Colonel Barré was in the Gallery of the House of Lords listening to a duke speak on the subject of Gibraltar and Minorca when 'suddenly the whole scene became changed. I could not suppose that a single peer remained in the House. It seemed as if the mob had broke in: and they certainly acted in a very extraordinary manner. One of the heads of this mob—for there were two—was a Scotchman. I heard him call out several times, "Clear the Hoose! Clear the Hoose!" . . . It was altogether the most violent mob I ever beheld . . . at the latter end of the day, these two men took their places as door-keepers, and executed the office with as much exactness, as if it had been a well-regulated assembly.'

Sylvester Douglas wrote that his father-in-law Lord North, the former Prime Minister, 'agreed with me that the noise in the corner behind and to the right hand of the chair was under such a regular system of tactics that Pitt by a look could, in most cases, excite or stifle it, and he agreed that it was injustice to suffer it to take place on that occasion when a person who had so recently filled so considerable an office under his own Government rose to contribute to the defence of that administration in Ireland of which he had made a part'.[10]

On the occasion of the State Opening in February 1892, two Ulster men, Colonel Saunderson and Mr Wallace, the Member for Limehouse, had an altercation over a seat in the Chamber. Mr Wallace accused the Colonel of taking his place and, what was more, sitting on his hat. He attempted to pull the Colonel out of the seat. 'The Colonel stands six feet high, is all bone and muscle, and was born fighting,' wrote Henry Lucy. 'He gently but firmly laid Mr Wallace on his back and resumed his seat.' The matter did not come before the House, as the Colonel promised Wallace a new hat.[11]

Incidents like this were as nothing compared with the Free Fight of 1893, as it came to be known, which took place during the final stages of Gladstone's second Home Rule Bill. 'Asquith said to me many years later that we in the Press Gallery, the descriptive writers, had exaggerated the worst features of the scene,' wrote Alexander Mackintosh. 'But Balfour declared in the House that no scene of a similar character had occurred for more than two hundred years, and Morley wrote of it as the most violent since the Civil Wars.'[12]

Later, the vast Liberal majority of 1906 found itself opposed by a disorderly Tory rump which 'made itself conspicuous with cat-calls, cock-crows, hee-haws, and other farmyard noises in order to prevent their opponents' arguments being heard'.[13] In 1914 when yet another Liberal Home Rule Bill was being debated, certain Tories engaged in a demonstration, continually shouting 'Adjourn'. The Speaker asked the Tory Leader, Bonar Law, if these troublemakers had his approval. 'I would not presume to criticise what you consider your duty,' stated Bonar Law, 'but I know mine and that is not to answer any such question.' At the next sitting the Speaker apologised for having used an unfortunate expression and the tension was defused.[14]

John Beckett, a Labour Member who was later to be involved in a notorious incident involving the mace, wrote an article in the *Daily Herald* in 1926 repudiating the Tory claim that it was Labour MPs who were responsible for hooliganism in the Chamber. Indeed, the Tory majority elected in 1924 had been quick to glory in the superiority of its numbers:

> Mr Snowden was moved to vigorous protest; Mr MacDonald, the least provocative of speakers, was constantly subjected to a torrent of heckling and interruption . . . Inoffensive Liberals like Mr Percy Harris have been treated disgustingly, and Captain Garro-Jones has been repeatedly barracked. Even Captain Wedgwood Benn, who is universally popular, has been frequently insulted. It is impossible to acquit the Government Front Bench itself from these charges. Mr Churchill is a constant interrupter. Sir Kingsley Wood maintains an habitually sneering manner, and Mr Amery has resorted to physical violence against Mr Buchanan.
>
> This session has been the worst yet. Even Miss Susan Lawrence has been subjected to a torrent of barracking. On the day Mr Maclaren returned after a serious operation, Sir Frederick Hall, a huge Tory from Dulwich, threatened to give him a 'damned good hiding'. Mr Roy Bird, one of the biggest men in the House, struck Mr Gardner, one of the quietest, and Captain T. J. O'Connor, after privately threatening Mr Neil Maclean, has promised to flog me within an inch of my life![15]

While Labour MPs tended to disrupt the general course of proceedings, Tory MPs were more inclined to choose personal targets for their misdemeanours, though it was not only the Tories who lost their tempers with other MPs. Earl Winterton once saw Josiah Wedgewood 'as he was leaving the Chamber after a debate, kick a Conservative member, Mr Mitchell Banks, on the shin with the remark "Take that, you swine!" The latter said nothing, the Chairman of Committees discreetly averted his eyes, no one raised a point of order, so the incident passed unreported. Mr Banks's sole offence had been to attack Zionism in debate.'[16]

The twentieth century has not witnessed a consistent deterioration in the conduct of Members, as some outsiders might have assumed. The naming and suspension of miscreant MPs is a fallible guide to levels of misconduct, since the disciplinary powers of the Chair are invoked at the discretion of the Speaker, and different Speakers have had different threshholds of intolerance towards incidents of disorder.

Mr Speaker Selwyn Lloyd, for example, adopted a 'softly, softly' approach in dealing with the excesses of Bernadette Devlin. On January 31, 1972, the day after 'Bloody Sunday' in Northern Ireland, she interrupted the Home Secretary, Reginald Maudling, calling him a liar and a 'murdering hypocrite'. The Speaker thought it better 'to invoke my selective deafness to take no notice of her allegations and to steer the House into quieter waters' rather than to name and suspend her. She then assaulted Maudling physically and a Unionist MP rushed to Maudling's aid, while Miss Devlin was removed from the Chamber by a couple of Whips—Tory and Labour. Selwyn Lloyd was criticised for not having acted more swiftly. The next day he issued an edict to say that any future unparliamentary language or acts would meet with the severest sanctions. He had deliberately showed restraint, he later wrote, because if Miss Devlin had been removed by force she would have become a martyr. Similarly, on a later occasion, Selwyn Lloyd heard that Miss Devlin, by then heavily pregnant, was intending to provoke trouble by asking a question. When she made some offensive remarks in her supplementary question, he ignored them and then disallowed supplementary questions from Labour MPs. When they later complained to him privately, he asked them how they would have dealt with the situation if it had resulted in her being named, suspended and forcibly ejected from the Chamber, with all the appalling consequences in giving publicity to her cause.[17]

Selwyn Lloyd used the weapons of forbearance wisely on another occasion during the 1972 miners' strike. He had called a female Labour MP who asked an extraordinarily long supplementary question. By allowing her to spin out the full 435 words he defused the situation: 'At the beginning of her question, the atmosphere was tense and trouble was brewing, by the end both friends and foes were laughing. The temperature had dropped perceptibly.'

On other awkward occasions Selwyn Lloyd invoked temporary suspensions of the House to calm the atmosphere.[18] This is the Chair's ultimate weapon against collective disorder and it has been applied sparingly. The number of times when a sitting has been suspended for reasons of grave disorder has followed a similar pattern to that of namings and suspensions. The House was adjourned or suspended five times in the 1920s, once during the 1950s, twice during the 1960s, four times during the 1970s and five times during the 1980s.[19] However, the unreliability of such statistics as indicators of a trend is demonstrated by the fact that while the Clerk of the House in 1988, C. J. Boulton, recalled that 'at the time of the Suez problem the House was in a very tense and difficult mood and I do not know that one has seen quite that atmosphere since', yet during that period not a single MP was named and there was only one suspension of a sitting.

Another Speaker who faced a dangerous situation was George Thomas. In May 1976 a debate on the Aircraft and Shipbuilding Bill resulted in a tied vote. Thomas had already made it clear he would follow the precedent of Speaker Denison in the 1860s and would give his casting vote on an Opposition amendment in favour of the Government and on a Government Bill in favour of the Opposition. In the event, the Government won the vote on its Bill by a single vote and as a result Labour MPs began singing the Red Flag, Tories gave Hitler salutes, and Michael Heseltine, the Opposition spokesman for Industry, took hold of the mace and held it aloft. 'Heseltine told me later he was going to give it to Labour, but just how was never made clear,' Thomas wrote in his memoirs. 'It looked to me as if he was going to crash it down on top of them. That was the moment I suspended the sitting for twenty minutes.'[20]

A disorderly scene which was reckoned by the *Daily Telegraph*'s Charles Bateman to be 'one of the worst I have witnessed in a quarter of a century's service in the Parliamentary Press Gallery' did not result in the naming or suspension of a single Member, let alone an adjournment or suspension of the sitting.[21] When Bills are due to receive the Royal assent, Black Rod is dispatched to summon the Commons to the Upper House in order that the titles of the Bills may be read in their presence, while the Clerk of the House of Lords utters the Norman French words '*La Reine le veult*'. The doors of the Commons Chamber are shut in the face of Black Rod, who strikes them three times with his staff, a ritual that symbolises the independence of the Lower House. On 13 April, 1960, the House of Commons was in the middle of a debate about the Conservative Government's policy on guided missiles, and the bulk of Labour MPs resented Black Rod's interruption, which came at 4 p.m. They demanded that the doors of the House be closed, shouted as Black Rod proceeded into the Chamber, and barely allowed him to be heard. Speaker Mowbray King felt it best to proceed as usual and led the exodus of MPs to the Lords, but later discovered that all but three Labour MPs (Hugh Gaitskell, George Brown and Herbert Bowden) had petulantly declined to follow him.

The Speaker asserts his authority

William Cavendish (1641–1707), Lord Cavendish, was an enthusiastic member of the Opposition. He wanted British troops in French service against the Dutch to be recalled and when this motion was lost in grand committee on the chairman's casting vote, he spluttered his objection in anger, thus provoking Sir John Hanmer to spit back. The Speaker, Edward Seymour, eventually resumed the Chair and took Cavendish and Hanmer off in his coach for a conciliatory dinner.

Anchitell Grey, *Debates of the House of Commons, 1667–94* (1769),
May 10, 1675

The question being put, whether a further address should be made to the King for recall of his subjects now in the service of the French king, the grand committee divided, and the tellers, Trevor Williams and Sir John Hanmer, differing in their account of the yeas and noes, some called 'Tell again', others 'Report'; on which great disorder began, gentlemen rising from their places and mingling in the pit: hot and provoking discourses and gestures passed on both sides, especially betwixt Lord Cavendish and Sir John Hanmer. Some said that Lord Cavendish's sword was half drawn out, but prevented by Mr Russell, who kept close to him; others said that Lord Cavendish spat in Sir John Hanmer's face, but that was only eagerness of speech; but it was visible to all that Sir James Smith, setting his arms on his side, did in a rude manner make through the crowd, and jostled several, and came to the table, where yet more hot discourses passed between him and Lord Cavendish, Mr Sacheverell, and several others; Mr Stockdale and some others setting their feet upon the mace, which lay below the table, in the usual place at grand committees. The disorder continuing near half an hour, the standers-by on the upper benches expected very fatal consequences might have followed, especially when the young gallants as Mr Thynne, Mr Newport, and several others leaped over the seats to join Lord Cavendish. But the Speaker [Sir Edward Seymour] very opportunely and prudently rising for his seat near the bar, in a resolute and slow pace, made his three respects through the crowd, and took the chair. The mace was still retained by the said gentlemen; but at last being forcibly laid upon the table, all the disorder ceased, and the gentlemen went to their places. The Speaker said that, to bring the House into order again, he took the chair, though not according to order. His act was generally approved. Sir Thomas Lee moved that there might be an engagement passed, on the honour of every member, standing up high in his place, to proceed no further in anything that had happened.

Marvell's ear-boxing incident

Andrew Marvell (1621–78), the metaphysical poet, was born in Hull, the son of a clergyman, and was educated at Trinity College, Cambridge. He defeated the republican Sir Henry Vane as MP for Hull at the general election of 1659 and held the seat until his death. Although he did not speak much in the House, he often acted as a teller and sat on committees.

Back in 1662 he was found to have provoked a fellow MP, Thomas Clifford, into striking him, and was obliged to apologise. As we know from his *Flagellum Parliamentarium*, he was scornful of most of the MPs whom he sat alongside, knowing them to be 'court cullies' and corrupt place-men.

William Cobbett, *Parliamentary History of England from the Norman Conquest in 1066 to 1803* (1806–12)

Debate on Mr Andrew Marvell's striking Sir Philip Harcourt, March 29, 1677.

Mr Marvell, coming up the House to his place, stumbling at Sir Philip Harcourt's foot, in recovering himself, seemed to give Sir Philip a box on the ear. The Speaker acquainting the House, 'That he saw a box on the ear given, and it was his duty to inform the House of it', this debate ensued.

Mr Marvell. What passed was through great acquaintance and familiarity betwixt us. He never gave him an affront, nor intended him any. But the Speaker cast a severe reflection upon him yesterday, when he was out of the House, and he hopes that, as the Speaker keep us in order, he will keep himself in order for the future.

Sir John Ernley. What the Speaker said yesterday was in Marvell's vindication. If these two gentlemen are friends already, he would not make them friends, and would let the matter go no farther.

Sir Job. Charlton is sorry a thing of this nature has happened, and no more sense of it. You in the Chair, and a stroke struck! Marvell deserves for his reflection on you, Mr Speaker, to be called into question. You cannot do right to the House, unless you question it; and moves to have Marvell sent to the Tower.

The Speaker. I saw a blow on one side, and a stroke on the other.

Sir Philip Harcourt. Marvell had some kind of stumble, and mine was only a thrust; and the thing was accidental.

Sir H. Goodrick. The persons have declared the thing to be accidental, but if done in jest, not fit to have been done here. He believes it to be an accident, and hopes that the House believes so too.

Mr Sec. Williamson. This does not appear, that the action for that time was in some heat. He cannot excuse Marvell who made a very severe reflection on the Speaker, and since it is so required, whether you have done your duty, he would have Marvell withdraw, that you may consider of it.

Col. Sandys. Marvell has given you trouble, and instead of excusing himself, reflects upon the Speaker: a strange confidence, if not an impudence!

Mr Marvell. Has so great a respect to the privilege, order and decency, of the House, that he is content to be a sacrifice for it. As to the casualty that happened, he saw a seat, empty, and going to sit in it, his friend put him by, in a jocular manner, and what he did was of the same nature. So much familiarity has ever been between them, that there was no heat in the thing. He is sorry to give an offence to the House. He seldom spoke to the House, and if he commit an error, in the manner of his speech, being not so well tuned, he hopes it is not an offence. Whether out, or in the House, he has a respect to the Speaker. But he has been informed, that the Speaker resumed something he had said, with reflection. He did not think it fit to complain of Mr Seymour to Mr Speaker. He believes, that is not reflective. He desires to comport himself with all respect to the House. This passage with Harcourt was a perfect casualty, and if you think fit, he will withdraw, and sacrifice himself to the censure of the House.

Sir Henry Capel. The blow given Harcourt was with his hat; the Speaker cast his eye upon both of them, and both respected him. He would not aggravate the thing. Marvell submits, and he would have you leave the thing as it is.

Sir Robert Holmes saw the whole action. Marvell flung about three or four times with his hat, and then gave Harcourt a box on the ear.

Sir Henry Capel desires, now that his honour is concerned, that Holmes may explain, whether he saw not Marvell with his hat only give Harcourt the stroke 'at that time'. Possibly, 'at another time' it might be.

The Speaker. Both Holmes and Capel are in the right. But Marvel struck Harcourt so home, that his fist, as well as his hat, hit him.

Sir R. Howard hopes that the House will not have Harcourt say, he received a blow, when he has not. He thinks what has been said by them both sufficient.

Mr Garroway hopes, that, by the debate, we shall not make the thing greater than it is. Would have them both reprimanded for it.

Mr Sec. Williamson submits the honour of the House to the House. Would have them make friends, and give that necessary assurance to the House, and he, for his part, remains satisfied.

Sir Thoe. Meres. By our long sitting together, we lose, by our familiarity and acquaintance, the decencies of the House. He had seen 500 in the House, and people very orderly; not so much as to read a letter, or set up a foot. One could scarce know any body in the House, but him that spoke. He would have the Speaker declare that order ought to be kept; but as to that gentleman (Marvell) to rest satisfied.

Fuller's fulmination

John Fuller (c. 1756–1834), the son of a clergyman, was educated at Eton. He was MP for Southampton from 1780 to 1784 and a supporter of Pitt. He was a magistrate in Sussex, where he was active in the militia, and he was Sheriff of Sussex, 1796–7. He returned as MP for Sussex, 1801–12, during which time he gained a reputation as a vulgar troublemaker in the House, provoking much laughter at his expense which he mistakenly supposed to be a response to his wit. A self-important buffoon, he was often shouted down. Following the incident described below, Fuller apologised to the House, was reprimanded and discharged, after which he made himself scarce for a month or so.

Lord Palmerston, Letter to a relative, February 27, 1810

We had last night a most extraordinary display of folly, coarseness, and vulgarity from Fuller, who, because Sir John Anstruther, Chairman of the Committee, would not take notice of him, when he several times attempted to rise, in order to put some very gross and absurd questions to Lord Chatham, flew out into such a passion, and swore, and abused the Chairman of the House to such a degree that it became at last necessary to commit him to custody. As he went out he shook his fist at the Speaker, and said he was a d—— insignificant little puppy, and, snapping his fingers at him, said he did not care *that* for him or the House either. He is now amusing himself with the Serjeant-at-Arms, and I think was very lucky in not being sent to Newgate or the Tower.

Coughing down Mr Hunt

Henry Hunt (1773–1835) was known as 'Orator' Hunt for exhorting the crowd at 'Peterloo', the demonstration at St Peter's Fields, Manchester, which ended in a massacre. Born in Wiltshire, he was a successful farmer and later a blacking-manufacturer. He was imprisoned for six weeks in 1800 and for three years (1820–3) after his speech at Peterloo, which was held to be an incitement to riot. A relentless advocate of parliamentary reform and the repeal of the Corn Laws, he was Radical MP for Preston from 1831 to 1833.

James Grant, *Random Recollections of the House of Commons* (1836)

All parties in the house, not even excepting the most ultra-radicals themselves, laboured hard to cough him down whenever he attempted to speak. It was on these occasions that he generally gave the most striking proofs of his wit. Nothing could discomfort him: the greater the uproar his rising to speak caused in the house, the more did he enjoy it. That was to him a luxury of the most exquisite kind. The fact was, he had been formed for scenes of confusion, and had all his life long been accustomed to them at the meetings of his Radical disciples; hence they came to him quite naturally. In many of his repartees there was great point. One honourable member, on one occasion when Mr Hunt was speaking, was unusually persevering in his efforts to cough him down.

Mr Hunt cured the honourable gentleman of his cough by one short sentence, which, delivered as it was with infinite dramatic effect, created universal laughter. Mr Hunt put his hand into his pantaloons' pocket, and after fumbling about for a few seconds, said with the utmost imaginable coolness, that he was extremely sorry to find that he had not a few lozenges in his pocket for the benefit of the honourable member, who seemed to be so distressed with the cough, but he could assure him that he would provide some for him by next night. Never did doctor prescribe more effectually: not only did Mr Hunt's tormentor from that moment get rid of his cough, but it never returned, at least while Mr Hunt was speaking.

❖

Animal noises

James Grant, *Random Recollections of the House of Commons* (1836)

'Mr G. W. Wood rose to reply. (The laughing, jeering, shouting, and coughing, were such as we never before witnessed.) The hon. gentleman said, it had been declared that the Bill, in its present stage, was essentially different from what it was when he had the honour to introduce it to the house. (At this moment two hon. members, "o'er all the ills of life victorious", suddenly entered from the smoking-room into the opposition gallery, and stretching themselves at full-length on the seats, secure from the observation of the Speaker, commenced a row of the most discreditable character.) This he denied ("I say, can't you crow?" Laughter and uproar)—the provisions had not been altered ("Hear him, how he reads!")—the enactments were in every respect unaltered (Loud cheering, followed by bursts of laughter). The question was ("Read it—read it!" and great uproar)—the question was ("Just so, read it")—the question was (great cheering and laughter) whether the universities should be open to all, or be for ever under the control of mere monopolists. ("Where's the man what crows?" Laughter and cries of "Order!" from the Speaker.) Public opinion— ("Order!" and great uproar, during which the Speaker, evidently excited, was loudly calling for order.) The scene here was indescribable.'

The preceding quotation [from the *Morning Chronicle*, June 1834] will give some idea of the scenes occasionally to be witnessed in the House of Commons. The general scenes have usually their origin in the impatience of honourable members to get away for the night, but who dare not venture to leave before the division, lest the non-appearance of their names in the lists of the majority and minority the following morning should lead to some unpleasant questions from their respective constituents, if not to a requisition to resign their seats.

I shall allude to only one more scene of this kind. It occurred towards the close of last Session. An honourable member, whose name I suppress, rose, amidst the most tremendous uproar, to address the House. He spoke, and was received, as nearly as the confusion enabled me to judge, as follows:—'I rise,

Sir (Ironical cheers, mingled with all sorts of zoological sounds), I rise, Sir, for the purpose of stating that I have ("Oh! oh!" "Bah!" and sounds resembling the bleating of a sheep, mingled with loud laughter). Hon. gentlemen may endeavour to put me down by their unmannerly interruptions, but I have a duty to perform to my con——(Ironical cheers, loud coughing, sneezing, and yawning extended to an incredible length, followed by bursts of laughter). I say, Sir, I have constituents who on this occasion expect that I——(Cries of "Should sit down," and shouts of laughter). They expect, Sir, that on a question of such importance ("O-o-a-u-" and loud laughter, followed by cries of "Order! order!" from the Speaker). I tell honourable gentlemen who choose to conduct themselves in such a way, that I am not to be put down by——(Groans, coughs, sneezings, hems, and various animal sounds, some of which closely imitated the yelping of a dog, and the squeaking of a pig, interspersed with peals of laughter). I appeal——("Cock-e-leeri-o-co!" The imitation, in this case, of the crowing of a cock was so remarkably good, that not even the most staid and orderly members in the house could preserve their gravity. The laughter which followed drowned the Speaker's cries of "Order! order!") I say, Sir, this is most unbecoming conduct on the part of an assembly calling itself de——("Bow-wow-wow," and bursts of laughter). Sir, may I ask, have honourable gentlemen who can——("Mew-mew," and renewed laughter). Sir, I claim the protection of the Chair. (The Speaker here again rose and called out "Order! order!" in a loud and angry tone, on which the uproar in some measure subsided.) If honourable gentlemen will only allow me to make one further observation, I will not trespass further on their attention, but sit down at once. (This was followed by the most tremendous cheering in earnest.) I only beg to say, Sir, that I think this a most dangerous and unconstitutional measure, and will therefore vote against it.' The honourable gentleman then resumed his seat amidst deafening applause.

The House in implacable mood

William Jeans (c. 1823–1916) was born in Edinburgh and educated at Edinburgh University. He entered the Reporters' Gallery in 1863 and was the London editor and parliamentary correspondent of the *Dundee Advertiser* for forty years. He also wrote for the *Liverpool Daily Post*, the *Leeds Mercury* and the *Yorkshire Observer*.

William Jeans, *Parliamentary Reminiscences* (1912)

Even in this peaceful Palmerstonian Parliament there were occasional outbreaks. One of the most exciting scenes that I ever witnessed in the House of Commons occurred on July 2, 1863. I heard Sir S. Northcote, Mr Lowe, Mr Disraeli and Mr Gladstone successively silenced by an angry and determined House. The question which aroused so much feeling was a comparatively small one. It was only the vote for the purchase of the Exhibition building of 1861. Somehow the idea had got abroad that the proposal partook of the character of what was then called a Court job; but the opposition to the vote was based chiefly on the ground that the building itself was hideously ugly. Mr Gladstone—then Chancellor of the Exchequer—explained and defended the vote in a speech of considerable length. He was obliged to admit that the Exhibition building as it stood was not very good, but he gave the opinion that it was capable of being so embellished on the exterior surface as to make it very handsome. This statement was received with laughter and incredulity. The opposition to the vote was led by Lord Elcho—the present Earl of Wemyss—who then as now was a very independent politician and sometimes attacked one party and sometimes the other. He quoted the opinion of Prosper Mérimée that the Exhibition structure had the pretensions of a monumental building without even the merit of being a commodious shed. It soon became evident that whatever the two front benches might say or do the opinion of the great majority of the House was against the vote. Sir S. Northcote endeavoured by a friendly manoeuvre to extricate the Government from their difficulties. He had recourse to the usual resource of politicians in distress, and suggested that the matter might be the subject of inquiry by a Committee. This idea roused the furious hostility of members, and they expressed their opinion on it by refusing to hear Sir S. Northcote. He was assailed with cries of 'Divide' from all parts of the House, and finding it impossible to proceed he endeavoured to checkmate his assailants by threatening to move to report progress. Then Mr Lowe, who as Vice-President of the Council was officially responsible for affairs at South Kensington, rose with the object of making a statement in defence of the vote. His appearance was the signal for an outbreak almost as stormy as I have seen or heard in the House of Commons. He was met by loud and determined cries of 'Divide' from the benches on both sides. The clamour was worse than when Mr Asquith attempted to explain and defend the advice which he had given to the sovereign with regard to the use of the prerogative for carrying the Parliament Bill. The cries which greeted the Liberal leader came from a small group of members; but in the case of Mr Lowe the shouts of 'Divide' rose from the large body of gentlemen on both sides. They were not acting under the influence of passion. They were simply determined not to hear another word in defence of the vote. Mr Lowe had finally to retire before the storm, but as the *Times* reporter wrote at the time the scene of uproar and confusion was almost unexampled in parliamentary experience. Mr Disraeli rose under the belief that he would be able to calm the excited and stormy assembly. He endeavoured to play the part of Pacificator, but he encountered the same sort of reception as Mr Lowe. Loud cries of 'Divide' arose, and the remarkable thing was that they came from his own supporters quite as much as from the occupants of the ministerial benches. After vainly struggling with the House for a minute or two he gave up the effort. Lord Robert Cecil, afterwards the Marquis of

Salisbury, appealed to the House to behave in a more orderly manner, and Mr Disraeli again rising attempted to address the House. He was allowed to utter a few sentences, and then the storm broke out again. He was heard to give an approval to the suggestion of a Select Committee, but this mode of shelving the question seemed to deepen and intensify the opposition to the vote, and amidst the incessant cries of 'Divide' Mr Disraeli resumed his seat. Mr Henley, one of the most respected and independent of the Conservative leaders, was a man of shrewd judgement and racy tongue, and as he spoke in opposition to the vote he at once obtained the attention of the House. He denounced the proposal in unmeasured terms. He compared the attempt to beautify the Exhibition building to the showman who was going about the country exhibiting a black woman. 'I can make her red,' said the showman, 'I can make her white, but do what I will I cannot make a handsome woman of her.' This story exactly hit off the situation, and it was received by the crowded House with uproarious delight. Mr Gladstone made a last effort to save the position. The House, however, had made up its mind. He was allowed to explain one or two points, but he could not proceed with the defence of the vote, and he sat down in the midst of an unfinished sentence. The vote was rejected by 287 to 121—an enormous majority in view of the fact that it was supported by both front benches.

A violent threat

Sir Alfred Edward Pease (1857–1939) was the eldest son of Sir Joseph Pease, Bt., himself a Liberal MP in Durham. He was educated at Trinity College, Cambridge, and became a director of his family coal-mining firm. A Liberal who supported Home Rule and temperance reform, he sat as MP for York, 1885–92, and for the Cleveland division of the North Riding of Yorkshire, 1897–1902.

Sir Alfred E. Pease, Diary, February 28, 1889

O'Hanlon (P.), who was sitting on a back bench, made some remark to T. W. Russell (L.U.), who was sitting in front of him, which I did not catch. Russell turned round and said, 'I have nothing to do with Piggott!' whereupon Sir Henry Havelock-Allan (L.U.), who was wandering about the back benches on our side on the war-path, deliberately barged into O'Hanlon and threw himself on top of him. O'Hanlon appealed to the Speaker, and H. J. Wilson (L.) corroborated O'Hanlon's statement. Sir Henry said he noticed O'Hanlon's irregular remark, but had 'not the slightest intention of touching him'!! The Speaker ordered him to apologise. Sir Henry is clever enough to make even an apology offensive, and did so on this occasion. Later he selected me for some blasphemous and obscene insults, and dogged me to the Library and back again; amongst his petty threats was one 'to do me in on my doorstep, where he would be at 2 a.m., when he would cut my —— liver out'. I told him I should report him to the Speaker for a nuisance, and I did, but asked him to speak to Sir Henry privately; he did this at the Chair, and Sir Henry returned to me and with profuse apologies begged my forgiveness and added, 'You see, Pease, it was because I was in great pain from pinching my finger in shutting a window yesterday!' I will say this for him, that he was almost as much tickled as I was with his excuse (and we laughed together, sitting side by side not far from the Speaker, who seemed puzzled by the reconciliation).

Mr Speaker Peel's admonition of the Directors of the Cambrian Railway

Austen Chamberlain, *Down the Years* (1935)

A Select Committee of the House had been inquiring into the hours of work of Railway Servants, and among the witnesses who had given evidence before it was the stationmaster of some small station on the Cambrian Railway. He had subsequently been called before three of the Directors and the General Manager of the Company and dismissed, nominally for some irregularities in his accounts but really, as was obvious from the questions put to him by the Directors, on account of the evidence which he had given before the Select Committee. The Committee, of which Sir Michael Hicks Beach was chairman, took evidence as to what had passed and made a special Report to the House on the case as a breach of Privilege. Of the three Directors involved one, Sir John Maclure, was an old and much-liked member of the House. A day was fixed for the discussion and an order was made by the House that the honourable member for Stratford should attend in his place and that his co-Directors and the General Manager should appear at the Bar. They were asked if they had anything to say and Sir John Maclure offered an apology with which the others associated themselves. They were then ordered to withdraw while their case was considered, and Hicks Beach moved: 'That this House while recognising that they had expressed their unqualified regret for having unintentionally infringed any of its Rules and Privileges is of opinion that they have committed a breach of Privilege . . . and that they be called in and admonished by Mr Speaker.'

This seemed a rather lame conclusion and there was a good deal of sympathy with the proposal made by T. P. O'Connor to add that the House would not consider that they had purged their contempt till they had reinstated the discharged man. Efforts were made privately to get them to do this, or at least to compensate him, but they remained obdurate. Hicks Beach's resolution was supported by Mr Gladstone, but his advice was rejected by the great majority of his followers whose zeal for the injured man was perhaps stimulated by the value of the railway vote at the general election which was known to be imminent. A long, wrangling discussion followed and it was not till midnight that a division was taken and Hicks Beach's resolution carried.

Then the Directors were once more called in. Sir John Maclure evidently felt his position acutely, but the other three appeared at the Bar defiantly and almost jauntily. They had successfully resisted the desire of many members, not confined to one side of the House, that they should compensate the man, and now they were to have what schoolboys call a 'pi-jaw' from the Speaker—that was all the House of Commons could do to them.

Mr Speaker Peel spoke for less than ten minutes. 'I would have you to know—each and all of you gentlemen—that though the Privileges of this House are not to be put into operation on any light or trivial occasion . . . yet a Privilege of this House is no unreal, shadowy or unsubstantial thing; it is what the House clings to and what it is determined to maintain.' And then after expatiating on the enormity of their particular offence, he declared, 'The House in its judgement and, I should add, in its mercy has decided that I should admonish you,' and he proceeded to administer the admonition.

The bald words of what he said, recorded in *Hansard*, convey no idea of the devastating effect of that short allocution. The men who had come to the Bar so defiantly a few minutes earlier wilted under his admonition; beads of perspiration stood out on their foreheads and, when he dismissed them, they crept away like whipped hounds, while the rest of us shook ourselves like dogs coming out of the water and thanked heaven we had not been in the position of poor Maclure.

❖

The Free Fight of 1893

The worst scene of disorder in parliamentary history took place on July 27, 1893, at the end of the Committee Stage of Gladstone's second Home Rule Bill. In the first of two extracts given below, J. L. Garvin, Joseph Chamberlain's biographer, describes the duel between Chamberlain and Gladstone that gave rise to the 'parliamentary tempest'.[22] The journalist Alexander Mackintosh later remembered how the incident had affected him: 'I trembled for the fame and fate of Parliament as I witnessed the extremely violent, disgraceful scene, in July, 1893, and saw members hitting each other . . . The Speaker hoped the House would let the incident pass into oblivion. It has never been forgotten by anyone who witnessed it.'[23] A Conservative MP, Arthur Griffith-Boscawen, described it in his memoirs, published in 1907, as 'the most disgraceful [scene] I ever witnessed in the House'.[24]

Who was to blame? T. P. O'Connor, the Irish Nationalist MP, sparked off the explosion by shouting an unparliamentary expression—'Judas!'—at Joseph Chamberlain. It was not the first time that Chamberlain had been so insulted. Only a few weeks before, the same nickname had been hurled at Chamberlain from across the chamber; and as far back as July 1888, O'Connor had shouted 'Judas Chamberlain' at the Liberal Unionist leader: Chamberlain had complained to the Speaker and O'Connor had withdrawn the remark. O'Connor's biographer, Hamilton Fyfe, revealed forty years later that O'Connor had been tipsy on that occasion: 'He used to say later in life that he had dined out on this evening and had had a glass more than usual of champagne!'[25] O'Connor, though, was not involved in the ensuing fracas. Anyway, as the Radical MP Henry Labouchere pointed out, O'Connor's shout came in response to Chamberlain's comparison of Gladstone to Herod, which was arguably worse.

During the mayhem that followed O'Connor's taunt, Sir Ellis Ashmead-Bartlett, a Conservative MP, blamed Gladstone for laying the explosive charge that detonated the violence. On reflection, Griffith-Boscawen also felt that Gladstone should have taken much of the blame: 'It was the result of pent-up feelings produced by Mr Gladstone's attempt to force so great a revolutionary change as Home Rule through the House by means of a gag [i.e. the guillotine].' But Griffith-Boscawen also blamed the Chairman of Committees, J. W. Mellor, who presided over the debate in the absence of the Speaker: 'It was rendered possible, moreover, by the complete laxity of debate allowed by the Chairman, and his want of proper control over members, which had emboldened the Irish members to continually interrupt proceedings, and to shout opprobrious nicknames at their opponents, in which they were followed by those of the Liberal Party whose manners had been corrupted by association with them.'[26]

Yet, as can be seen from the second extract, written by the sketch-writer Henry Lucy, the episode degenerated into a brawl more out of confusion and misinterpretation of the motives of individual MPs by other MPs than from any wilful desire to assault and batter adversaries. This is endorsed by Garvin as well as another lobby correspondent, Michael MacDonagh: 'Most of the struggling Members, Nationalist and Unionist, were really peacemakers endeavouring to restrain and calm their more pugnacious colleagues.'[27] The Irish Nationalist MP Tim Healy pointed out that a procedural innovation had caused Logan to sit provocatively on the Unionist benches: 'A device of ex-Chancellor Ritchie's had been adopted to save a few seconds in the lobbies. Each party then, instead of leaving by opposite doors, passed out beyond the Speaker's Chair in commingled streams. Sir J. W. Logan, a Liberal, blocked by the throng, seated himself on the front Opposition Bench to allow the block to clear.'[28] Healy moved across the floor to bring Logan (whom Garvin describes as 'a muscular Christian among the Gladstonians') back to his own side of the House. The fight ensued.

Charles Darling, the Conservative Member for Deptford, happened to be entering the Ladies' Gallery at the moment when the affray began. According to one witness, the lobby journalist Lincoln Springfield: 'Several ladies, in evident alarm, cried out "Oh, they are fighting! How dreadful! What is it?" "It is," declared Mr Darling, "the beginning of the Irish Parliament. Every night in Dublin will be like this one . . ."'—a forecast which ultimately proved to be incorrect and was anyway based on the false assumption that the Nationalist MPs had been responsible for starting the fight.'[29] Another view from the Gallery was given by Sir Algernon West, Mr Gladstone's private secretary, in his diary: 'I sat next to [Michael] Davitt in the Gallery, who was much pained at the scene, so new to the English House of Commons, but we are learning much at the hands of the party of law and order. "Very sad!" Davitt said, "T. P. O'Connor ought to have known better." Mellor's conduct was feeble, and we agreed he was a failure . . . Home, very sick and grieved, and thinking how cruel it was that a Deputy Speaker should not be clothed with some symbols of authority to help him to assert his position.'[30]

The press talked up the affair, though Garvin believed it had been 'preposterously though honestly exaggerated' for the simple reason that 'from all the galleries it looked worse than it was'. Garvin also offered two further factors in explanation of the event. The physical as well as the emotional temperature had been high ('Members had been fanning themselves with their order-papers . . .') and Mellor, the Chairman, had just recovered from a punishing bout of influenza, which had left him generally weak, and he had therefore been taking quinine, which had impaired his hearing.[31]

J. L. Garvin, *The Life of Joseph Chamberlain*, Vol. II (1933)

The long-brooding storm muttered before raging. Strained by a thousand troubles, the Prime Minister himself made the atmosphere more combustible. His intimates doubted whether he could go on for many weeks. Yet in the Cabinet Morley and Harcourt, both differing deeply from Rosebery, were no longer on speaking terms with each other.

On July 25 Gladstone fell upon Chamberlain. The Liberal Unionist leader, declared the Prime Minister, used 'language of habitual, gross and enormous exaggeration'; he 'constantly and deliberately, and with the utmost confidence and infallibility, ascribes to men who have a right to stand on a level with him, and who were at one time his colleagues and supposed to be his friends, motives for their acts the direct contrary of that which they state themselves, and motives which they indignantly disclaim'. The Prime Minister described the Radical Unionist as playing generally in this trial the part of 'Devil's Advocate'. Next day Chamberlain replied to this impassioned outbreak: Gladstone, he said, had made a 'ferocious speech', and as to the ecclesiastical allusion, he had this unfailing repartee. 'My right hon. friend, in a passage which was extremely humorous and which no one enjoyed more than myself, compared me to the Devil's Advocate . . . The function of the Devil's Advocate is often one which has been most usefully fulfilled . . . It has been his privilege to expose many doubtful virtues and to destroy on more than one occasion the angelic theory. Sir, I modestly hope I may enjoy a similar privilege.'

Reporting with studied brevity, he had got a good deal into a very few adept words. He intended on the following night to speak for a quarter of an hour, reviewing the Bill and depicting the political position with clinching terseness.

That intention was cut short by a parliamentary tempest.

July 27 was to be the last of forty-seven sittings in Committee. At ten o'clock the beheading-machine was to begin its final exercises. At a quarter to ten Chamberlain rose from his coign of vantage on the third bench below the gangway. His accents had his peculiarly ominous intonation—the under-swell of anger made more contagious by sardonic modulation of voice. Real and pent-up were the passions of that night. Though the guillotine was about to descend on masses of undiscussed clauses, the dense tiers of Unionist benches believed to a man that the country was with them. This view Chamberlain meant to drive home with blistering mockery. His opponents felt that his sentences sprayed vitriol.

We may follow him as far as he got. He gibed—that the Government by the guillotine procedure had reduced to a discreditable farce the forms of the Mother of Parliaments. He jeered—that they regarded their Bill as perfect and unimprovable.

At this, Roby, an excellent Gladstonian, was misled to throw in the banal phrase, 'under the circumstances'. It was notoriously unsafe to interrupt

Chamberlain. No one approached him in seizing an interjection to improvise a satire. Quick as a flash he caught up the word and sported with it:

They think that—'under the circumstances'—the proposals cannot be improved. Yes, but they thought the last scheme was perfect and could not be improved. They think every scheme as it successively proceeds from the fertile brain of the Prime Minister is perfect and cannot be improved—'under the circumstances'. That has been their attitude with regard to the whole, notwithstanding the fact that the measure has been changed again and again in the course of the last few weeks . . .

I say this Bill has been changed in its most vital features and yet it has always been found perfect by the hon. members behind the Treasury Bench.

The Prime Minister calls 'black' and they say 'it is good'; the Prime Minister calls 'white' and they say 'it is better'. It is always the voice of a god. Never since the time of Herod . . .

It is admitted that his tone and air, as he watched the clock so as to be sure of putting in as much as possible in a quarter of an hour, were quizzical, not savage; but at the last word—'Herod'—a furious cry broke, not for the first time that summer, from the Irish camp—'Judas!' One more audible sentence, and only one, Chamberlain got in—'Never since the time of Herod has there been such slavish adulation.' Whether he tried to add another syllable never can be known. Typhoon swooped on the House.

Henry W. Lucy, *A Diary of the Home Rule Parliament, 1892–1895* (1896)

29 July, 1893. Nothing has been told in connection with the riot in the House of Commons on Thursday night equal in heartrending effect to the simple story of Colonel Gunter. Unlike twenty-one colleagues seated in various parts of the House, who have been induced by an enterprising evening paper to record their impressions of the scene and their personal experience of its episodes, the gallant Colonel reserves his epic for the ear of his friends. Like the annals of the poor, it is short and simple. Ten o'clock having struck, the fatal hour for the condemned amendments, the Colonel heard Mr Mellor put the question from the Chair and subsequently order the House to be cleared preparatory to a division. Thereupon the member for Barkston-Ash, trained in the tented field to habits of obedience, rose from his accustomed corner on the fourth seat above the gangway behind ex-Ministers, squared his shoulders, and began to march down the gangway steps.

Before he had advanced two paces he received an Irish member full in the pit of the stomach. During twelve years' active service, much of it spent in the Crimea, the Colonel has grown used to alarums and excursions, but candidly confesses that he was never so much surprised in his life. The inconvenience was not to be slighted, the Irish member arriving head first—and so soon after a hasty dinner, too! The situation is complicated by the fact that to this hour the Colonel does not know who the projectile was. He suspects Mr Crean, but that may be an after-thought consequent on subsequent observation of that hon. member's active and eccentric proceedings. Apart from the immediate consequences of the ramming process, the attention of the Colonel was distracted by the circumstances that the unceremonious visitor, whoever he might be, commenced vaguely but vigorously to thump him with his fists. Thereafter, in the tempest that suddenly surged down the gangway and over the benches adjoining, he disappeared in the throng.

This uncertainty of the identity of persons more or less prominently engaged is one of the notable peculiarities of this amazing outbreak. There is, for example, the mystery which surrounds Colonel Saunderson's participation in the proceedings. His earliest conviction that something was wrong was borne in upon him by discovering an hon. member tumbling over the back of the bench on which he was seated and, to a certain extent, dispersing himself over him. There is no standing order or written injunction against that method of moving about the House. But it is unusual and inconvenient. Taken in conjunction with what Colonel Saunderson saw going on two benches below, where Mr Hayes Fisher had hold of Mr Logan by the back of the neck, and Sir Ellis Ashmead-Bartlett was apparently pummelling him in the region of the shirt-front, it conveyed the impression that things were in an abnormal state.

Colonel Saunderson, though constitutionally prone to the pathways of peace, could not but regard this almost burglarious procedure as an act of war. Accordingly, having assisted the intruder to his feet and recognising in him Mr Crean, the Colonel aimed a blow at him straight out from the shoulder and hit Mr Austin on the left jaw. It is a question which was the more surprised at this, Colonel Saunderson or Mr Austin. With opportunity for calmer consideration it would have been recognised as fresh evidence of the general topsy-turvyism prevalent. But opportunity for calm reflection was limited. Before Colonel Saunderson could explain the little mistake that had occurred Mr Crean, whose activity was *catapulti*, gave Colonel Saunderson what Dick Swiveller's friend, the Marchioness, was accustomed to describe as a 'wonner' on the right temple.

This made discrimination impracticable, and the Colonel hit out right and left, a lurid light seeming to flash up and down his waistcoat as glimpses were occasionally caught of it, through the surging mass. It was merely the reflection of the gaslit roof. To the overwrought mind of on-lookers it lent a new terror to the scene.

This battle royal by the gangway was the Waterloo of the campaign. Quatre-Bras had immediately preceded it. That engagement took place on the Front Opposition Bench, and was the precursor of all that followed. It is strange to reflect upon the triviality of circumstances that sometimes lead to momentous issues. Had Mr Logan chanced to be voting in the other lobby, he would have passed out by the doorway under the clock. Not skirting the Front Opposition Bench, Mr Carson would not have called out 'Yah!' to him, nor would Mr Hayes Fisher have observed 'Bah!' That being so, Mr Logan would not have loftily remarked—

'Mr Carson, I did not speak to you, and you have no business to address such an impertinent remark to me.'

Mr Carson, in the circumstances alluded to, would not, however appositely, have responded, 'Get away; you are a gang of gaggers.'

Mr Logan would not thereupon have sat partially upon Mr Carson and, to some extent, upon the Front Opposition Bench. Mr Hayes Fisher would not have clutched him by the back of the neck whilst Sir Ellis Ashmead-Bartlett ministered to him in front. The Irish members below the gangway would not have rushed forward in a body with intent, as Mr Harrington later explained, to assist the Sergeant-at-Arms in keeping order. That being so, Mr Crean would not have rested under strong suspicion of being the projectile that momentarily took away Colonel Gunter's breath. Nor would he thereafter have rolled over the back of the bench upon the knees of Colonel Saunderson. Colonel Saunderson, hitting out at Mr Crean, would not have struck Mr Austin, and the general scrimmage which followed might have been avoided.

All this shows how careful we ought to be in considering and ordering the most trivial actions of our daily life.

Amongst the prominent martyrs of the misunderstanding that prevailed were the Irish members. Even Dr Tanner did not escape the prevalent influence. When at the height of the scrimmage he was observed advancing rapidly in the direction of the Front Opposition Bench it did not occur to anyone that he was bent on pacific errand. Several of his own compatriots even intercepted him, gently, but firmly, turning his steps aside. It was the same with Mr Tim Healy. Observing the incident on the Front Opposition Bench, he has told the world how 'I went towards Mr Fisher, having my hat in my hand'. That is a piece of evidence introduced with the skill of a trained advocate. If Mr Healy had had a shillelagh in his hand, it would be easy to understand what followed. 'Some of the Tories objected to my passing down their bench,' Mr Healy writes, 'and one of them, Mr Harry Foster, rushed at me.' Finding his signal of peace not understood, Mr Healy placed it on his head, and, as he gently puts it, 'was borne from the gangway', and looking back saw 'a tangle of men on the gangway striking at each other. I saw no one hit.'

That is still another peculiarity of the great fight. The spectacle of Mr Healy looked upon from his position of retreat must, it seemed, inevitably lead to the serious disabling of at least a score of legislators. One could see the teeth set, the eyes flashing, faces aflame with wrath, and a thicket of closed fists beating about in wild confusion. Yet, including Colonel Gunter's misfortune, there were not more than four men who bore about them marks of the fight. When it was over, Colonel Saunderson, an old campaigner, walked out with a bunch of keys held to his bruised cheek—a simple remedy so efficacious that when he appeared on the scene next day only a slight scratch showed what might have been. The appearance amid the throng of the Sergeant-at-Arms was portentous, and seemed to show that things were desperate indeed. But Mr Erskine's sternest remonstrance was addressed to a member standing up below the gangway, watching the fight.

'I beg your pardon,' said the Sergeant-at-Arms gently, 'but you're standing up with your hat on, which you know is a breach of order.'

The conscience-stricken member dropped down on the seat, and the Sergeant-at-Arms passed up the House on his message of peace.

As Dr Tanner rushed into the House ready to do battle, J. A. Pease jumped on to his back 'and in an old Rugby Union style I collared and held him back on the floor of the House to keep him out of the scrimmage, much to his annoyance . . . Two incidents then are still vivid in my memory—the Serjeant-at-Arms to my amusement addressing me and protesting my unseemly conduct while himself helplessly standing by, and the sight of John Burns in the gangway separating the combatants and hurling them back on to their seats, exhibiting astonishing muscular power which in a few seconds produced a sudden and unexpected stoppage of the fight.'[32]

The arrival of Mr Speaker Peel had what Garvin called a 'magical' effect. 'I shall never forget', wrote a later Speaker, James Lowther, 'the stern and reproachful manner in which Mr Speaker Peel rebuked the offending Members, who seemed cowed by his dignified appearance and commanding tones.'[33] In Austen Chamberlain's opinion, Peel's character shone through on occasions like this. Other Speakers, he wrote, have served the House of Commons 'faithfully and many of them with great distinction, but Speaker Peel dominated it'.[34]

According to Lucy, when Peel received a summons to the House from his train-bearer at ten o'clock, he only knew that there had been a row of some kind, not a full-blown fight. 'When he took the chair he was in absolute ignorance of what had passed . . .'[35] Not only did Peel restore the House to its senses, but the incident apparently helped restore him to good health. He had previously been prescribed a tonic for his nerves by his doctor. 'When his doctor called early next morning, without having opened his daily paper, he found his patient's condition much improved. "I am glad to find you so much better this morning," he said. "That new tonic has given you a fillip." Only later did he discover that it was not his tonic but the row in the House which had restored the Speaker's nerves.'[36]

And what of Gladstone, whose decision to use the guillotine on this legislative measure had undoubtedly formed the background to the incident? 'I noticed', wrote Michael MacDonagh, 'that Gladstone not only averted his gaze, but with a perturbed expression of face reclined on his side along the Treasury bench, so that the Table might the more effectively hide the horrid business from his view.'[37] Alexander Mackintosh concurred: 'Gladstone, with the nightly letter to the Queen in his hand, looked extremely pained. A loud-voiced, bellicose, junior ex-Minister stood at the table and shouted across to him—"This is your doing." '[38] Griffith-Boscawen observed that 'the most pitiable sight was Mr Gladstone . . . as pale as a sheet . . .'[39] Austen Chamberlain, too, noticed Gladstone's reaction, in this case once order had been restored and the division recommenced: 'I shall never forget the spectacle of Mr Gladstone sitting with bowed head and face half hidden by his hands as we once again moved into the division lobbies.'[40] In his diary entry for the following day, July 28, Sir Algernon West wrote that: 'Mr Gladstone had borne it well. He read me his sad description of it all to the Queen. I differed on one point, when he said T. P.'s apology was not ample, and I told him so; but he said it was prefaced by "If I have offended"—as people generally do. Mr Gladstone thought it all very sad, and had never heard of such a case since the one in Pitt's time, the details of which he had, however, forgotten. He asked me if I thought the Speaker was right in passing over the blows. I thought in the circumstances he was, as the evidence with regard to them was so contradictory.'[41]

The public spectators had evidently been disgusted by the episode. 'The dread rebuke of hissing from the gallery', wrote Garvin, 'helped to recall the House to its senses.'[42] And Tim Healy wrote that this hissing was the only admonition by 'strangers' ever known to affect the House.[43] One anecdote, however, suggests that this might have been an expression, at least in part, of an altogether different form of disapproval. Austen Chamberlain compared his experience of that evening with the Conservative Member for Deptford, Charles Darling, QC (later Lord Darling): ' "Did you hear the hissing in the gallery?" I asked him. "Yes," he said. "It's rather curious. I had two constituents up there. I went up afterwards and asked them what they thought of it all. They happened to be two prize-fighters. 'We was fair disgusted,' they said. 'When we saw that fellow let out right and left and no one went down, we was that disgusted that we hissed, we did.' " . . .'[44] Once peace reigned again, business went on as usual until the end of the sitting and there was an amusing coda to the episode, remembered by James Lowther: 'A ludicrous incident brought the evening to a close, for, on the next order being called, Sir Reginald Palgrave, the Clerk of the House, read it out in such a whimsical tone of voice and with so much emphasis, that the whole House burst into a shout of laughter. The next order happened to be "Pistols Bill—Second Reading"— *Solvuntur Tabulae risu.*'[45]

Another comic consequence of the event involved Tim Healy, the Irish Nationalist MP who had crossed the floor and braved the Unionist benches in order to restrain his Liberal colleague Logan. In his memoirs, Healy wrote the following: 'I must have been depicted by the American Press as a prominent combatant, for next day I got a cablegram from the Mayor and Corporation of Alexandria, La. (Louisiana), declaring that the city had voted me a silk hat to replace one battered by my prowess against the Tories. The message asked for the measurement of my head by return cable. My headgear, however, was unharmed, but at the cost of several silk hats I cabled thanks, and received an elegant "topper" (alas! too small) in a handsome case. In gratitude to the Mayor and Corporation of Alexandria, La., I crushed it onto my head, and for the next twenty years wore it until my resignation from the House in October, 1918.'[46]

Some years later, in February 1902, memories of this controversial incident were revived when the Welsh Liberal MP David Lloyd George accused Chamberlain, by then Colonial Secretary, of having led the riot. By reference to *Hansard* Chamberlain was able to demonstrate that he had left the chamber before the fight began. In an entry for February 11, 1902, Henry Lucy reported the account of the 1893 incident given to him by Arthur Balfour, now Prime Minister, shortly after it had occurred: 'When at ten o'clock the guillotine descended and the Chairman of Committees rose amid deafening shouts to put the question, Mr Balfour strolled forth into the division lobby, where he found himself in company with Mr Chamberlain. Only a few members were in the lobby. Hearing prolonged uproar, they went back to the House, and tried to return. But the door was locked, and the attendant had no authority to open it until the division was over. It was only after considerable interval that they managed to get back and receive hurried accounts of what happened.'[47]

For Tories it was difficult to decide which was more shameful: the appalling fisticuffs of July 27, 1893, or Gladstone's determination to drive his Home Rule Bill through the

House in the teeth of legitimate efforts to scrutinise the measure in detail. Garvin reminded his readers that *The Times* had published a full-page report giving the text of the Bill as it had been amended when it emerged from the Committee stage—'out of thirty-seven clauses only ten had been discussed at all, four of those only in part. Twenty-eight clauses and all the schedules had been put through without debate.'[48] The Home Rule Bill of 1893 eventually foundered in the House of Lords. The verdict of Queen Victoria, as reported by Sir Algernon West in his diary, was politically naive: 'I gave him [i.e. Gladstone] a letter from the Queen, attributing the row to the Home Rule Bill, which had been introduced into the House, as she thought Mr Gladstone must see, contrary to the wishes of the large majority of the people, as against a small minority of Irish!'[49] Of course, the electorate had elected Gladstone on a platform that included Home Rule, and his Bill had been allocated 82 days for discussion, during which time the Tories and Liberal Unionists had spent 152¾ hours speaking against the Bill in Committee, whereas its supporters had confined themselves to speeches lasting 57¼ hours.

Don Roberto is asked to withdraw from the House

A. F. Tschiffely, *Don Roberto: Being the Account of the Life and Works of R. B. Cunninghame Graham, 1852–1936* (1937)

Conditions among the nail- and chain-makers of Cradley Heath ('Hell Hole', as Disraeli called it) were appalling; in fact, for 150 years the condition of the nailers—who were 'sweated'—had been wretched in the extreme. The average earnings, for twelve to fifteen hours' hard work per day, were six shillings per week, and women, most of who worked naked down to the waist, earned less than half that amount.

Don Roberto had paid several visits to Cradley Heath, and when he pressed the House for an inquiry into conditions among nail- and chain-makers, a Conservative Member put down what is called a 'blocking motion', in order to prevent a debate on the subject.

Don Roberto then asked the First Lord of the Treasury if, before the end of the session, he would give a day to discuss the motion.

The First Lord of the Treasury answered that the subject to which Don Roberto had drawn attention was receiving the earnest attention of the Government, but that, owing to the pressure of Public Business, he could not make any further disposition of the public time.

Leaping to his feet, Don Roberto flashed back: 'May I remind the Right Honourable Gentleman that he has not in the least degree answered my question. I asked a definite question: Whether he would afford facilities for the discussion of a Motion of one of his own supporters? If he does not do so, I characterise that Motion as a dishonourable trick to avoid discussion.'

Mr Speaker: 'Order! Order! The Honourable Member is conducting himself in a most unusual and un-Parliamentary manner in making use of language of that kind. I must request him to withdraw the expression he has made use of.'

Don Roberto: '*I never withdraw!* I simply said what I mean.'

Mr Speaker: 'I must ask the Honourable Member to withdraw the expression "dishonourable trick", which is a strictly improper and un-Parliamentary expression.'

Don Roberto: 'Mr Speaker, I wish, as on former occasions, to acquit myself of an intentional discourtesy to you; but I am compelled again to characterise the action taken with regard to this Motion by the Honourable Member for Dudley as a dishonourable trick.'

Mr Speaker: 'I must again ask the Honourable Member to withdraw so improper and un-Parliamentary an expression.'

Don Roberto: 'I refuse, Sir, to withdraw it.'

Mr Speaker: 'Then I must ask the Honourable Member to withdraw from the House.'

Don Roberto: 'Certainly, Sir. I will go to Cradley Heath.'

And so he did, taking the midnight train. This naturally annoyed the Member for Dudley, in whose constituency Cradley Heath was situated. The displeasure at Don Roberto's intrusion into his constituency he aired in a later Session in the House, to the great joy of Don Roberto.

Don Roberto is suspended

A. F. Tschiffely, *Don Roberto* (1937)

On one occasion, interrupting his old friend (although political opponent) Mr Asquith, who spoke on a Local Authorities Purchase of Land Bill, he shouted: 'Perhaps the Honourable Member will explain how the shareholders in swindling companies——'

(Cries of 'Order! Order!')

Don Roberto: 'Oh, I am not going to be put down!'

(Cries of 'Order!' and 'Name!')

Don Roberto: 'It is a matter of no importance to me whether I am named or not.'

Mr Speaker: 'Order! Order!'

Don Roberto: 'What I want to know is, how do swindling shareholders in a company derive their funds?'

(Shouts of: 'Order! Name!')

Mr Speaker: 'Order! Order!—The conduct of the Honourable Gentleman is such that I must name him to the House. I name you, Mr Cunninghame Graham.'

Don Roberto: 'All right! I am simply named for standing up for Socialism in this House in the face of a swindling speech endeavouring to draw ridiculous distinctions. That is why I am named.'

The Secretary of State for the Home Department: I beg to move, in the terms of the Standing Order, that the Honourable Member be suspended from the service of the House.'

Don Roberto: 'Suspend away! . . . I do not care a damn!'

(Shouts of: 'Order! Order!' as Don Roberto strides out of the House.)

A Tory scene

Philip Snowden, *An Autobiography*, Vol. I (1934)

On a Monday afternoon, when members are late in turning up, the Tories organised an unexpected division. They had arranged for a full attendance for their supporters to be within call at four o'clock. Sir Frederick Banbury produced a manuscript amendment to the Financial Resolution of the Home Rule Bill. The division on it was taken at once. The Liberal Whips were unprepared, and the Government were defeated by twenty-one votes. The amendment was a vital one, and unless it were reversed it would be impossible to proceed with the Home Rule Bill.

Two days later Mr Asquith produced a resolution to rescind the Banbury amendment. The debate on this motion proceeded quietly for two hours. There were no indications of the coming storm. A Tory member was speaking, and when making some references to Mr Asquith there broke out from the Tory benches cries of 'Traitor'. The 'traitor', of course, was the Prime Minister. The Speaker intervened and said that if he knew who had used the expression he should call upon him to withdraw it. A candidate for martyrdom was there. The redoubtable Sir William Bull announced that he was the man, and to support his claim he again shouted 'Traitor'. He was ordered to leave the House. He received his crown of glory the next evening at a great Unionist demonstration in the Albert Hall, where he was uproariously received as a hero who had said 'Traitor'.

After Sir William Bull's expulsion from the House the Tories evidently got together and decided they would have a row. About half-past seven Sir Rufus Isaacs, the Attorney-General, rose to speak. There was no obvious reason why he should be attacked. But immediately he rose the whole Tory Party burst into a chorus: 'Adjourn! Adjourn!' The Speaker appealed in vain for order. The chorus gained strength. It was clearly evident that there was a determined conspiracy to prevent any discussion. Front-bench Tories openly defied the Speaker. The uproar was terrific. Liberals were on their feet shouting and shaking their fists at the Opposition. It was useless to go on, so the Speaker rose and said: 'In my opinion grave disorder has arisen.' 'I think so, too,' interjected Jerry MacVeagh. So the Speaker suspended the sitting for an hour.

It was thought that an interval would allow passions to cool. But the Tories employed the hour to revive their strength from the resources of the dining-room. When the House resumed the rowdyism was renewed with greater violence than before. Sir Rufus Isaacs was permitted to say 'Mr Speaker,' and no more. A Tory member, Lord Helmsley, rose, but his Tory colleagues howled him down. The Speaker pleaded with the Tory front bench to give a hearing to him. It was all in vain. It was quite obvious that there would be no speaking that evening, so the Speaker adjourned the House till next day. The Tories acclaimed their victory by jumping up, shouting and waving handkerchiefs and papers for several minutes. The Labour members had been silent and disgusted spectators of this scandalous exhibition. It was a revelation to them of the breeding and culture of the 'gentlemanly' Party. The Liberals and Nationalists behaved with great restraint throughout the whole proceedings. It was a scene to cause feelings of contempt rather than of anger. As members were walking out of the House, the sight of Mr Churchill and Colonel Seely together—two former Tories—exasperated the Tories, who assailed them with cries of 'Rats! Rats!' Mr Ronald M'Neill, the seven-foot Ulster Unionist, seized a book from the table and hurled it at Mr Churchill, who was struck on the side of the face and bruised.[50] The House met the next day in a subdued mood.

Asquith is accused of murder

George Lansbury (1859–1940) was the son of a car contractor. He was educated at an elementary day school and was a Liberal agent until he joined the Social Democratic Federation in 1892. He made several unsuccessful attempts to enter Parliament from 1895 onwards until he was elected as Labour MP for the Bow and Bromley division of Tower Hamlets in December 1910. He resigned over the women's suffrage issue in 1912 and lost the by-election. He later sat as MP for the constituency from 1922 until his death. He was a councillor for Poplar, 1903–40, and twice served as Mayor (1919–20 and 1936–7). He was editor of the *Daily Herald* from 1913 to 1922 and was Leader of the Labour Party from 1931 to 1935.

An older, Liberal MP advised Lansbury to apologise to the Speaker, to Mr Asquith and to the House the next day, assuring him that he would thereby make himself 'a name in this place forever', but Lansbury was adamant in his attitude. 'There was no apology or explanation forthcoming from me,' he later wrote. 'I think I would have preferred to have my tongue cut out rather than do any such thing. I had said what I thought, and that was all there was to it.'[51]

Philip Snowden, *An Autobiography*, Vol. I (1934)

I remember another instance of disorderly conduct which was not the outcome of premeditation, but of 'spontaneous combustion'. Mr George Lansbury had been returned to Parliament at the second General Election of 1910. He soon made himself conspicuous by asking innumerable questions on every possible subject, and by impulsive interventions in debate. At this time the militant suffragist agitation led by Mrs Pankhurst and her daughter Christabel was attracting a good deal of public notice. Their activities had not yet assumed the violent form they did later. A number of women had been arrested for small offences and had gone to prison as the alternative to promising to be of good behaviour. Mr Lansbury, always the champion of people in distress, put questions to the Home Secretary about the alleged harsh treatment of these women, for Mr Keir Hardie and myself were quite as active on their behalf, until their activities became criminal and alienated all sympathy. In reply to a question which Mr Hardie had put about one of these prisoners, the Prime Minister made the remark that 'these women could walk out of prison this afternoon if they gave the undertaking asked for'. For some reason this remark put Mr Lansbury into a state of uncontrolled passion. He was sitting beside me, and he hurled this remark at Mr Asquith: 'It is perfectly disgraceful that the Prime Minister of England should make such a remark!' This caused an uproar. Mr Lansbury left his seat below the gangway and walked up to the Ministerial Bench, shook his fist in Mr Asquith's face, and hurled at him a volume of abuse the like of which I have hardly ever heard. 'You are murdering, torturing and driving women mad, and tell them they can walk out! It is the most disgraceful thing in the history of England. You will go down to history as the man who tortured innocent women. It is disgraceful to tell women who are in prison on principle that "they can walk out".' And so he went on for several minutes. The Speaker was very lenient with him. He called him to order several times, but Mr Lansbury was too excited to realise what was being said. Finally he cooled down and turned to the Speaker and said, like a man recovering his senses: 'What do you want me to do, Mr Speaker?' The Speaker replied that he had told him three times to leave the House for grossly disorderly conduct. Mr Lansbury withdrew. This was one of those scenes which do not arouse the indignation of the House. Members realised the deep sincerity of Mr Lansbury, and that he had been carried away by his emotions and probably did not know what he was saying.

❖

The shouting down of Mr Asquith

July 24, 1911, was the only occasion when a British prime minister has been unable to make himself heard before the House for any appreciable time, and the ordeal suffered by Herbert Henry Asquith endured for almost an hour. The occasion of this shameful scene was a statement by the Liberal Prime Minister as to why his Government had rejected their Lordships' amendments to the Parliament Bill, a measure of reform disqualifying the House of Lords from voting on a money bill which had been provoked by the rejection of Lloyd George's 1909 Budget. Asquith cannot have been expecting quite so hostile a reception as he got. His daughter Lady Violet Bonham-Carter, in her memoir of Winston Churchill, recalls the day: 'I had never looked forward to a debate with more tense excitement. Although I knew from intimate experience my father's powers of concentration and detachment, he surprised even me by deciding to keep an

227

old engagement with Winston to meet the King of Portugal at luncheon a bare hour or two before this most crucial Parliamentary occasion. At 3.15 p.m. Downing Street was thronged with waiting crowds, the Master of Elibank was champing and chafing with us in the hall, secretaries were telephoning frantically right and left, when at last he and Winston arrived together. We drove to the House of Commons in an open car and were cheered all the way down Whitehall and in Parliament Square.' This can hardly have prepared Asquith for what subsequently happened in the Chamber. Lady Violet and her mother, Margot Asquith, made their way to the Speaker's Gallery, which 'was packed to suffocation with female friends and foes, those in the back standing upon their chairs'.[52]

Herbert Henry Asquith (1852–1928), 1st Earl of Oxford and Asquith, was educated at the City of London School and at Balliol College, Oxford, where he later became a Fellow. He was called to the bar in 1876 and became a QC in 1890. He sat as a Liberal MP for East Fife from 1886 to 1918 and for Paisley from 1920 to 1924. He held office as Home Secretary, 1892–5; Chancellor of the Exchequer, 1905–8; and as Prime Minister, from 1908 until he resigned in 1916. He later led a splinter group of Asquithian Liberals.

Frank Dilnot (1875–1946) was educated privately and worked as a special correspondent for the *Daily Mail* from 1902 to 1912, which included a stint as a parliamentary correspondent. In 1912 he became editor of the *Daily Citizen*, a Manchester-based paper backed by the Labour Party. It closed within two years. He went to the United States and became president of the Foreign Correspondents' Association. He came back in 1919 and edited the *Globe* until 1921 when it was merged with the *Pall Mall Gazette*. He also wrote *The Adventures of a Newspaperman* (1913).

Frank Dilnot, *The Old Order Changeth* (1911)

Members of the House of Commons knew that it was to be a thrilling day. The Benches were filled immediately after the Speaker had taken the chair, notwithstanding the fact that there were eighty questions to be put to Ministers before the principal business of the day was reached. The House was a-quiver with excitement from the moment business began, and questions were answered in a turmoil which made most of the replies inaudible a dozen feet from the Minister who was speaking. At the start there were two absentees from the Front Bench—Mr Asquith and Mr Balfour not coming in till questions were well on the way, but the fighting forwards were in their places, keen and eager for battle. In the corner seat below the gangway to the left of the Speaker was Lord Hugh Cecil, a lean, nervous figure, with face aflame, whose lively eyes and continual conversation with those near him told that he anticipated a field day. Above the gangway immediately behind the Front Bench were enthusiasts of lesser calibre—Mr Goulding and Mr Remnant catching the eye by reason of their surface eagerness and animated talk. In the same seat near them was F. E. Smith, one of the arch movers, prepared for all contingencies, but quite cool. Ministers were packed tightly on the Treasury Bench, and the Conservative leaders were crowded side by side facing them. Up in the gallery, over the clock, a score or more of Peers were crushed into the scanty accommodation, each of them too interested in the scene below to give any attention to physical inconvenience. Over all the gathering ran waves of emotion, rising and falling, but ever present, and filling the building with that rhythmic hum, deep and sinister and regular, which presages a rending storm. No good humour was in the noise. Spluttering epithets were tossed across the floor amid the surges. No student of humanity was required to see that elements of passion were near being unloosed, and that some little incident might send these men at each other's throats.

Midway through question-time Mr John Redmond entered and took his place with the Nationalists, and at the sight of him, there leapt forth ironic shouts of welcome. Here was the real hero of the day; here was the man who had dictated the terms; here was the man who had coerced the Prime Minister, and through him, had brought the Lords to their knees![53] Why should he not be honoured? To the victor, the spoils! That was the bitter meaning of the cheers. There was not a long interval before feelings found another outlet. On the order paper appeared the usual sundry questions to the Prime Minister, and the fact that he had not come in when they were reached would not on an ordinary day have called for remark. But this afternoon, when his first question was reached, and it was found that he was not on the Treasury Bench, unofficial Conservatives demanded the reason. 'Where is he?' they shouted challengingly, 'Where is he?' Liberals affected to laugh. 'Where is he?' retorted the Conservatives rancorously, insistently.

As if in answer to the cries, Mr Asquith within a minute or two came into the House. He entered from behind the Speaker's chair. He was wearing a frock coat; an indication, as a rule, that he had been to see the King. In his hand he had a sheaf of typewritten notes, his shoulders were squared, his head strongly set. He walked slowly and composedly as usual. Withal, his face showed traces of the strain he was undergoing, for it was hard as marble, and his eyes seemed strangely bright, without any expression in them. As he came into view, the New Liberal Army, Liberals, Labour men, and Nationalists, broke into loud cheering. As an honourable tribute the long line of Ministers on the Treasury Bench rose as he began to pass in front of them to his place. The cheering rank and file rose up also, and, shouting enthusiastically, waved their order papers as a demonstration of joy at the arrival of their chieftain. It must have been one of the great rewards of life. Mr Asquith would have been no man if his heart had not swelled under the music of those rushing cheers. The 'no surrender' party on the Conservative Benches were hurling ugly words in the effort to drown or at least to modify the acclamations. A channel of vengeful passion was suddenly opened up. 'Traitor' was the word united on. 'Traitor!' thundered a score or more. 'Traitor, traitor, traitor!'

The New Liberals took a deep breath. The outrage was so profound that it was at first hard to realise it. 'Traitor, traitor!' rose the malignant chorus. Not often has the House rung with that word applied deliberately and of set purpose to a Prime Minister. I think some of the leading Conservatives were shocked— certainly the Liberals were. But the Labour men and the Radicals below the gangway promptly pulled themselves together and began shouting back across the floor with no less temper. That was the beginning of the greatest parliamentary scene I have witnessed.

A lull occurred a few minutes later, when Mr Balfour entered. All the Conservatives rose to their feet and cheered as the Liberals had done at the incoming of Mr Asquith, a little while before, and much warmth was displayed, though, of course, there was not the same reason for the wild welcome given to the Prime Minister. Indeed, in the circumstances, the 'no surrender' party, though they loyally cheered their chief, were a trifle doubtful of him, and whether he would show the fighting spirit which was thought to be essential.

At twenty-five minutes to four, Mr Asquith rose to the Table to make his statement with regard to the Lords' amendments. He had had only time to smooth his typewritten notes on the dispatch box, and to say, 'Mr Speaker, in offering the advice—' when a hurricane swept the words from his mouth. He stood firm, eyeing his attackers, apparently thinking that a momentary outburst stood between him and his speech, and after a few seconds he turned once more to the Speaker in order to begin again. The motion was enough. The storm rose to its most tremendous fury, and not a word could he utter. Dozens of different phrases were mingled in the assailing chorus. Some members shouted ''Vide, 'vide, 'vide, 'vide.' Others again, 'Where is Redmond?' But, vibrating through all the babel was that one deep all-pervading unchanging call of 'Traitor!' The Speaker rose and, almost against their will, members hushed while he appealed to them to conform to the courtesies of debate. 'Traitor, traitor!' volleyed back members. 'He has degraded Parliament! This is no ordinary occasion.' I could see Lord Hugh Cecil leaning forward from his corner seat as though he desired to jump bodily on the members of the Government. Near him was Mr Remnant, rocking himself to and fro and roaring at the top of his voice. All that was said it was impossible to hear, but now and again phrases jumped into notice from the din like the spray whipped from the waves in some frightening storm at sea.

Liberals were retorting in kind. Members on each side were flinging out their arms at individuals opposite as they shot wrathful words at them. The state of the House may be imagined when I say that the great resonant cockney voice of Mr Will Crooks was immediately drowned when he got up to put a point of order to the Speaker. Again and again Mr Lowther, bringing into effect all his tact and persuasiveness, tried to secure quiet. High as was the respect in which he was held, he had to speak through a motley of protests and murmurings. He knew there was a great deal of excitement on both sides, he said, but he asked members very earnestly to give a courteous hearing to the Prime Minister. 'I would ask them, as this is a serious occasion, to treat the occasion seriously, and to let the conduct of the House be worthy of its traditions.' Lord Hugh Cecil was up in a moment, but the Ministerialists, recognising him as the ringleader, howled him into silence. He continued standing, waiting the arrival of the periodical interval of seconds when a voice might be heard, in order to throw in a poignant phrase. 'I rise to respond to your appeal, Sir——' Bursts of mocking laughter prevented another syllable. 'The best way to respond to my appeal would be to listen in silence,' exclaimed the Speaker.

The clamour fluctuated, but never ceased. Sometimes it developed into pandemonium, at other times it sank to a pitch which would allow a strong voice to make itself audible for a word or two. Every few minutes the Speaker was on his feet trying to produce quiet, but without avail. At these times Mr Asquith would drop to his seat, and rise again immediately the Speaker's appeal was over, to resume that silent listening vigil at the Table, to face the stream of personal insults. Sometimes he managed to make a half-sentence heard, but his voice grew harsh with the effort. Like bullets the abusive words descended on him. 'Trickster, Constitution-breaker, traitor!' With whitening face, but with perfectly steady mien, he gazed first at one portion and then at another of the turbulent, swaying mob opposite to him.

For the discerning he was a picture of the emotions—this denounced Prime Minister. He had come to the House of Commons to state in carefully chosen words that the moment for making a change in our ancient constitution had arrived, and that he intended to make it. He must have known that his announcement would be recorded in history. The King had approved of his statement; his followers in the Commons, whom he had knit into a devoted force, had assembled with high hearts to listen to these final clinching words. Once in a hundred years, perhaps, a British Prime Minister is the central figure in such a situation. Rising to his feet, Mr Asquith found that not only would his opponents give him no hearing but were yelling at him offensive ejaculations which are ruled out of common converse. The shock was the greater because Mr Asquith was always a stickler for courtesy, was always in Parliament an essentially dignified man, and never failed to mould his conduct and deportment on the great exemplars. He must have looked forward to this sitting of Parliament as one which would afford the supreme hour of his career. He had risen to the Table with his speech in his hand, uplifted by the consciousness he had now to take his part in the making of the nation's story. And with these things singing through nerves and brain, he was confronted with irresponsible screaming hostility. I shall always remember him as he stood, rigid and contemptuous, and how, as the minutes went on, icy anger transformed him. At the beginning he had flattened out his manuscript on the dispatch-box, as was his usual custom, but when the systematic disorder made itself apparent, he took it up and held it in his hand, and stood away from the Table a little, in order that he might swing the easier to see all his revilers. For five years in Parliament I had had the opportunity of watching Mr Asquith closely, and his self-control, his extraordinary command over himself had become increasingly evident to me, and this afternoon, though his heart may have been a volcano of anger, he showed to the casual observer but little trace of feeling. Those of us, however, who knew him better could see signs which were not to be misunderstood. He held himself very stiff, almost like a man in a trance, and his eyes seemed to sink in and become brighter, until they were but sparkling points in a face of pallor. As he stood there, silenced and helpless, the sympathy of all his army went out to him, and they launched great heartening shouts. For the first time it came upon many that Mr Asquith was an old man. The ruddiness of strong manhood had left him, his hair was snow-white, his delicate white hand holding the unspoken speech was trembling. Only the stiff back, the reared head, the thin line of his lips, told of the virile spirit within him. With their champion thus before them, there were periods when the Ministerialists were more genuinely frenzied than the far noisier men on the other side. The picture of their one man beaten down by a hundred was almost too much for them. A Labour member in the corner seat below the gangway screamed with hoarse abandon at the taunts of Lord Hugh Cecil opposite; Mr M'Callum Scott, a Scottish Radical, jumped up with face transfigured, his fist extended towards the Conservatives. Friends near flung their arms around him and pulled him down.

Once, early in the scene, I noticed Mr Balfour turn to the Conservatives behind him and say, 'Order, order.' He might as well have addressed quieting words to a sea gale. He gave up all attempts to interfere, and sat with bowed head, waiting for the storm to wear itself out. Possibly he recognised that any further effort on his part would have been resented by the 'no surrender' group, and that he himself might have shared the same fate as the Prime Minister. The disturbance among the Conservatives was not below the gangway only; it reached above the gangway, and through the seats immediately behind the leader; indeed, except for the Front Bench, it was difficult to find a section of the Opposition who were not joining more or less in the outcry. Of course, there were individuals here and there who sat silent—and regretful—and to their honour some of them later made clear their detestation of the rowdyism they had witnessed. Moments came when the more violent seemed to lose all measure of their speech. Lord Hugh Cecil was livid with excitement, carried away by the consuming realisation that he was leading a righteous demonstration against black Asquithian iniquity. A score of times he darted to his feet with phrases. The Liberals raved at him. Overjoyed was he. He writhed in his seat with delight at the din. Once or twice, when there was a lull in the uproar, and a chance that by shouting the Prime Minister might make a sentence or so heard, Lord Hugh, crouching low, with bent head kept up the loud unbroken monotone of "Vide, 'vide, 'vide, 'vide,' and set the storm going again. 'Hold up your head, skulker,' was one of the remarks addressed to him by a Labour member. He paid not the slightest attention. "Vide, 'vide, 'vide, 'vide,' he called. Not through any lack on his part should the Prime Minister be allowed to say a word. He was like a thing possessed with electrical energy. Once Mr Asquith turned to Mr Churchill and indicated Lord Hugh at work, with a wondering gesture, as though the member for Oxford University were a creature devoid of reason.

At four o'clock, Mr Asquith, by straining his voice, managed to get in a few consecutive sentences in which he made a reference to the death of King Edward. 'Who killed the King?' roared the revolters. 'Who killed the King?' At this fresh outrage, Mr Burns, who was seated near the Prime Minister, appeared to be begging his chief to sit down and give up his obnoxious task. Mr Churchill apparently joined in the supplication. For some time Mr Asquith would not yield. The uproar seemed, however, to increase instead of decrease as time went on, and at a quarter-past four, Mr Asquith showed that he despaired of making himself heard by quickly turning over his manuscript to the last page. His exasperated supporters were jubilant at the action. 'I will not degrade myself further——' 'You could not,' came the hot exclamation, 'you are a disgrace!' 'I will not degrade myself further by endeavouring to press my arguments upon the attention of honourable gentlemen opposite, who are obviously resolved not to listen to me.' Then, in two or three sentences he explained, by straining his voice, that the Government intended to invoke the exercise of the prerogative of the Crown, if the Lords were obstinate. He sat down amid rolling shouts of encouragement from Ministerialists, and a chorus of 'Traitor' from the Opposition.

What followed Mr Asquith's speech was the most dramatic feature of a dramatic day. In the course of his attempts to ameliorate the savage hubbub, the Speaker had suggested to the shouters that it was not likely when Mr Balfour got up to speak the incensed Liberals would allow him to say anything. Revenge, he pointed out, was almost inevitable. Fiercely the Conservatives had shouted on. The Liberals, Labour men, and Nationalists were, it must be remembered, in a white heat of temper at the treatment given to Mr Asquith. Their feelings, as I have indicated, were such that an outbreak of physical violence was among the possibilities of the half-hour. Among the men so heated and enraged hurried the Liberal whips, explaining the possibilities of a stabbing revenge. That was how it came about the House had such a surprise when Mr Balfour rose to speak. The whole of the army of New Liberals dropped to the politest silence. Bravado was in that silence, but it was a very fine bravado. Stirred to the depths, these politicians, including a generous sprinkling of Labour men who had worked with their hands, had set themselves with clenched teeth to give a lesson in courtesy to the noisiest spirits of the party which claimed to represent the gentlemen of England. There was tenseness in the silence, but the silence was nevertheless very real. Lord Hugh Cecil put on an air of completest indifference, and some of those who had been most turbulent with him accepted with certain assured complacency the tribute of respect which it was fitting and right that the army opposite should pay to the leader of the Conservative party. As for Mr Balfour, a man of very chivalrous nature, I think he found that courteous hearing a little trying. He began by expressing regret that Mr Asquith had not been heard—though he sought to avoid offence to the 'no surrender' group by remarking that the proceedings of the Government must necessarily excite deep and passionate feelings.

Mr Balfour's subsequent arguments could not possibly have their due weight having regard to the electric atmosphere of the House. Members were more interested in two brief interruptions from the Prime Minister. In his indictment of Ministers, Mr Balfour used the following words:—

'For the Government to come down in the middle of a crisis, and in order to bring a crisis to an end to ask for these unconstitutional powers, I think that is beyond pardon. But that they should do so in cold blood, months before the crisis arose, before they knew how it would be used, and, above all, before the King could have known how it would be used, surely that will mark this administration in the history of all administrations as the one least sedulous to keep intact the treasure committed to them and the most utterly regardless of all the duties which devolve upon the advisers of a constitutional monarch. It was an amazing and a most unqualifiable proceeding. What was the reason for it? The only reason——'

Mr Asquith rose to the Table: 'The right honourable gentleman has not heard the reason because I was not allowed to state it.'

A minute later Mr Balfour expressed his doubt as to whether the Prime Minister would have dealt with a certain point even if he had been heard. Mr Asquith, his eyes blazing with anger, rose again. He spoke very deliberately, but a glance was sufficient to know that to his finger-tips he was tingling. 'I was going, had I been permitted the courtesy never before refused to a leader of this House, to give a detailed and reasoned argument of the grounds for the advice which His Majesty's Government have tendered to the Sovereign.'

'When?' called out some of the Conservatives. The Prime Minister turned on them. 'I decline absolutely to answer any questions now. I was not allowed to do so.' He thrust a lurid face across the Table towards Mr Balfour. 'I was prevented by the right honourable gentleman's friends from doing so. He has had an advantage of a courtesy which has been denied to me.'

When Mr Balfour had finished his speech, Sir Edward Grey, the Foreign Secretary, got up from the side of the Prime Minister to address the House. Aloofness of manner and calm independence of thought had helped to secure for Sir Edward Grey a remarkable position in the House of Commons. His conduct of foreign affairs was endorsed by both sides, his dignity and reserve gave all men a strange respect for him. He was not an extreme politician, but was quite fearless. His appearance fitted in to help the general impression. With the touch of youth still on him, he was tall and serious-looking, with classic features and raven hair, such a man as one reads of in the great romances. A tragic domestic bereavement, just at the time when he was promoted to high office, robbed life of much for him, and black was always in his dress from that time onward. No statesman was there for whom the House of Commons had a more lofty regard. His very coldness and disdain of popular words endeared him the more. This was the man who now rose to hold aloft the banner of his chief, and to utter a warning to his opponents. His words, delivered with unusual feeling, stirred great gusts of enthusiasm on the Ministerial Benches at every few sentences.

'Never did any leader of a party of a majority in the House of Commons have behind him a more chivalrous personal loyalty, a more united political support than my right honourable friend the Prime Minister has at this moment. The feelings of the majority as well as those of the minority are deep and strong. Members opposite may easily imagine whether those feelings are less strong after the scene we have just witnessed. In so far as it was a personal discourtesy to the Prime Minister, every one of us resents it. The Prime Minister has announced the course of the Government. If arguments are to be used in support of that course they are arguments to be used by the Prime Minister as representing all of us. If those arguments are not to be listened to from him there is not one of us who will attempt to take his place.' Ministers on the Treasury Bench led the loud cheer which followed this announcement, and the warmth of the demonstration brought a touch of pink to the Prime Minister's pale cheeks. Sir Edward Grey finished his speech by moving the adjournment of the debate. Mr F. E. Smith got up to speak. The Ministerialists were in no mood to extend any patience to one who had helped to lead the earlier disorder, and they howled at him unceasingly. At last the Speaker took action.

'I remind the House,' he said, 'of Standing Order No. 21, which says, "In the case of grave disorder arising in the House the Speaker may, if he thinks it necessary to do so, adjourn the House without question put or suspend any sitting for a time to be named by him." In my opinion a case of grave disorder has arisen, and, acting under the authority of the rule, I now adjourn the House.'

Cheering from the Ministerialists was met by retaliating cries from the Conservatives, and as the Speaker left the chair, members began to converge from the benches into an excited crowd on the floor of the House. Provocative cries still rang from side to side of the chamber, but the confused mass of members, talking, arguing, denouncing, slowly gravitated to the lobbies. The excitement of the day had been crammed into a short sitting. The House which met at a quarter to three had separated at eight minutes past five.

The day after Asquith was shouted down, the *Standard* reported that he had been derided, scorned and insulted. Midway through the episode, Margot Asquith scribbled a note and had it sent down to Sir Edward Grey, imploring him to intercede on her husband's behalf. 'They will listen to you, so for God's sake defend him from the cats and the cads.'[54]

Many MPs on both sides of the House were as appalled as she at what had happened, and as the historian George Dangerfield has commented: 'One thing was certain. The Tory rebels had done no good either to themselves or the cause they were promoting.

If the champions of hereditary government were a learned upstart and a noble hooligan . . .'[55] By this, of course, Dangerfield meant F. E. Smith and Lord Hugh Cecil. (Indeed, the incident soon became known as 'The Cecil Scene'.)

However, the hooligan element in the Conservative Party was not a minority that could be easily scorned. The Conservative MP Leo Amery attended a meeting in one of the Commons committee rooms the next day which had been intended by its convenors to vent indignation against the rebels, but it transpired that opinion, including Amery's, was firmly on their side. Instead, it was what they saw as the pusillanimity of their leader Balfour that was criticised: 'There was a general consensus on the subject of loyalty to Mr Balfour which resembled the warm loyalty to King George shown by the American rebels both before and after the actual outbreak of the revolution.'[56] As a protest against Balfour's leadership, F. E. Smith thereafter vacated his accustomed position behind the Front Bench and went to sit alongside Lord Hugh Cecil below the gangway.[57]

Apart from shouting down Asquith, the Tory hooligans had further aggravated an already fractious situation when one of their number had shouted the name 'McNally' at the Irish Nationalist contingent. 'McNally' was the name of a notorious Irish informer to the authorities in the early nineteenth century and thus a stinging insult to a Nationalist. No sooner was this name uttered than William O'Brien was on his feet. As Dangerfield puts it, O'Brien 'looked and behaved like a slightly demented minor prophet, and . . . now enlivened the proceedings with an eldritch scream of, "What ruffian said 'McNally'?" '[58]

Three weeks later, Asquith responded to a Unionist motion of censure with a cogently argued defence of his policy. According to his wife, Margot: 'It was a speech that will live in history, as he built up his case in orderly sequence the ranks of the Conservatives looked shattered and broken.'[59] Indeed, they were. Threatened with a mass creation of Liberal peers, the Tories had no choice but to accede to Asquith's terms. On August 10 the House of Lords passed the Bill with a majority of seventeen, there having been a large number of abstentions. Margot Asquith was in no doubt as to the significance of her husband's ultimate victory. On the day the Bill received the Royal Assent she wrote in her diary: 'Thus was accomplished the greatest constitutional reform since 1688, a success due to the patience, ability and foresight of one man and that the Prime Minister.'[60]

♣

A *sit-down protest*

Edward Hugh John Neale Dalton (1887–1962) was the son of the Canon of St George's, Windsor, and was educated at Eton; at King's College, Cambridge; and at the LSE. He became a barrister in 1914 and, after serving in the Army in World War I, he was Reader in Economics at the University of London from 1920 to 1935. He sat as a Labour MP for the Peckham division of Camberwell from October 1924 to 1929; for the Bishop Auckland division of Durham from 1929 until he was defeated in 1931; and for the same seat from 1935 until he retired in 1959. He was president of the Board of Trade during most of World War II and Chancellor of the Exchequer from July 1945 until November 1947, when he had to resign after inadvertently leaking budget details to a journalist. He was made a life peer in 1960.

Hugh Dalton, *Call Back Yesterday: Memoirs 1887–1931* (1953)

This success meant that I now had to sit on the Front Bench.[61] And there, through subsequent sessions and Parliaments, I stuck. This cramped my style and limited my opportunities. I am sorry I didn't have a longer back-bench life. It would have been more fun.

But I reacted against respectability by getting myself suspended on April 15th, 1926. Neville Chamberlain had introduced an Economy Bill, penalising ex-Servicemen and a number of those entitled to benefits under National Insurance. It was a mean little Bill and, admirably led by Jimmy Thomas, we fought it obstructively. We kept the House up all night and divided whenever we could. Then, in the small hours, we started to go slow in the division lobbies. We dragged our feet and took our time. Then thirteen of us, having passed the clerks, who marked our names on the register as having voted, sat down in a circle on the floor, and refused to pass the tellers, who counted the number of those voting at the exit of the lobby. The division, therefore, could not be completed. The tellers continued standing at the door, and we continued sitting on the floor. This impasse lasted for three-quarters of an hour. Various members looked in on us through the glass door of the lobby. We exchanged pleasantries, and sang, to the tune of 'John Brown's Body', 'The Clerk will now proceed to read the Orders of the Day'. Jimmy Thomas urged us, vainly, not to be such bloody fools. The Sergeant-at-Arms took a note of our names.

The next thing we knew was a rush of Tories coming through our recumbent and obstructive forms. 'What are you doing?' we asked. 'Voting for your suspension,' they replied. Mr Speaker Whitley had been roused from his sleep, since the House, being in Committee, was presided over by the Chairman or Deputy Chairman of Committees, but a suspension can only be moved with the Speaker in the Chair. The Chairman having reported our names to the Speaker, Mr Chamberlain now moved that we all be suspended for six days from the service of the House. But now the impasse was repeated. A number of our friends, voting in the other lobby against our suspension, passed the clerks, but then sat down upon the floor, refusing to pass the tellers. The Speaker, however, after waiting another fifteen minutes, ruled that a reasonable time had now elapsed since the division was called, and summoned the tellers to the Table to announce the numbers of those who had actually passed through. The Division which we obstructed was called just after 5.30 a.m. The Division suspending us was concluded just after 7 a.m.

Thus did we draw attention, through the Press, to the injustices of the Economy Bill and to our own fighting spirit. The morning placards and the headlines blared: 'Thirteen Socialists suspended. Amazing scenes.'

My twelve associates in this demonstration included George Lansbury, John Wheatley, Jack Lawson and Joe Compton. I am the only one of the thirteen who is still alive and in the House of Commons.

The 'rape of the Mace'

Towards the end of the summer session of 1930, Fenner Brockway, on behalf of the Independent Labour Party, asked the Prime Minister for an opportunity to discuss the plight of political prisoners in India. Baldwin refused and Brockway persisted. This led to his colleague John Beckett making off with the mace.

'When Beckett seized the mace,' wrote the Labour MP Frederick Jowett, 'his action immediately was given the importance of a first-class outrage. But, indeed, it was a trivial thing to do. Why there should be this indignant demand for penalties I cannot understand. He only took from its place an ornament of some historic importance, and then, a few seconds later, handed it back to its official custodian. For this he was suspended for five days.' In his biography of Jowett, Brockway suggested that while Jowett's account of the incident 'showed a healthy disregard for totems and ritual' it nonetheless understated one aspect: 'Beckett surrendered the mace to the Serjeant at Arms without a struggle, but he hardly "handed it back".'[62] The Tory MP Harold Balfour recalled that the Serjeant-at-Arms, Sir Colin Keppel, 'caught hold of Beckett. As Beckett reached the Bar I could see the Mace being tossed about over the heads of those standing there. With the aid of the "Chains" [the attendants—so called because they wear chains and badges of office around their necks] the Mace was recovered and Sir Colin Keppel marched up the Chamber to replace it on the table. Afterwards someone asked Beckett what he had intended to do with it. "Oh! Put it in the cloakroom," said Beckett.'[63]

John Beckett (1894–1964) was educated at council schools and at the Polytechnic. After working in advertising and journalism and serving as a councillor in Hackney, he sat as Labour MP for Gateshead from 1924 to 1929 and for the Peckham division of Camberwell from 1929 to 1931. He joined the ILP in 1931 and was opposed by an official Labour candidate, thereby losing his seat. He followed Sir Oswald Mosley into the British Union of Fascists, left with the renegade William Joyce to form the National Socialist Party, and later co-founded with the Duke of Bedford another fascist organisation, the British People's Party, before being interned from 1940 to 1943. After the war he was involved in organising the National Union of Ex-Servicemen. He took no part in politics thereafter and eked out a living as a journalist, producing a fortnightly stock market letter and acting as London correspondent for an American intelligence service.

(Archibald) Fenner Brockway (1888–1988) was the son of a missionary clergyman in Calcutta and was educated at Eltham College. He became a journalist and was a conscientious objector during World War I. He was editor of *Labour Leader*, 1912–17; and of *New Leader*, 1926–9 and 1931–46. He was a senior official in the Independent Labour Party and was Labour MP for East Leyton from 1929 until 1931, when he left the Labour Party. After rejoining the party in 1946, he sat as Labour MP for Eton and Slough from 1950 to 1964. That same year he was awarded a life peerage by Harold Wilson.

Fenner Brockway, *Inside the Left* (1942)

The session was nearing its end. Mr Baldwin asked the Prime Minister what would be the business for the remaining period. Mr MacDonald read out a string of Bills and Orders. I rose and asked quietly whether an opportunity would be allowed to discuss the imprisonments in India. 'No, Sir,' came the reply. I rose in my place again. 'Is the right honourable gentleman aware that sixty-thousand Indians are in prison for demanding the freedom which he himself has claimed for them?' The Prime Minister did not answer. I addressed the Speaker. 'I wish to protest, Sir, against the adjournment of this House whilst this injustice is being done in India.' The Speaker rose. I remained standing. 'I mean no disrespect to you, Sir, but I cannot be silent whilst this injustice persists,' I said. The Tories began to shout 'Order, Order.' I remained standing. The Speaker rose again. 'I must name the honourable Member if he continues to disobey the Chair,' he said. I remained standing.

My further words were drowned by the angry cries from the Tories. The Speaker warned me a third time. I continued my protest. The Speaker rose and 'named' me. The Prime Minister moved my suspension from the House. I sat down. I had deliberately challenged this. I wanted India to know that she had friends in the British Parliament.

The ILP Group demanded a division on the motion for my suspension. I sat quietly whilst it proceeded. John Beckett was one of the tellers. With his three colleagues he advanced up the House, bowing three times as required and standing in front of the Mace on the Clerks' Table before reporting the figures. Suddenly his hands plunged forward, he gripped the Mace and lifted it to his shoulder; then he turned and strode as rapidly as its heavy weight would allow towards the door of the House.

The Members were scandalised. First, there was a gasp of astonishment, then a storm of angry cries of 'shame', 'scandalous', and even 'you swine'. The Labour MPs were as shocked as any, a revelation of how deeply they had fallen in idolatry of the capitalist State. They regarded Beckett's action as sacrilege. I was surprised, then amused. I was also a little irritated that Beckett's sensational *coup* would get the Press and that my protest about the Indian prisoners would be smothered. Before Beckett reached the door, the Sergeant of Arms, a weedy man in a black-beetle suit, with a sword dangling at his side, stepped out of his pew-like box and barred John's way, and two of the magnificent messengers clutched him and, after a brief struggle, regained the Mace. The Speaker solemnly named Beckett, the Prime Minister moved his suspension in a tone of disgust, and the MPs angrily shouted 'Aye'. Some of our group courageously challenged a division, but the vote for Beckett was small compared with mine. The Speaker requested us to withdraw. I bowed to him as I crossed the bar of the House. Beckett went out with head held defiantly. We were accompanied across Old Palace Yard by a Police Superintendent and Inspector and then given our freedom.

'What in the world was the idea, John?' I asked Beckett. He laughed. 'It came to me suddenly—the House is in session only when the Mace is on the table. If I could get away with it, they couldn't suspend you.'

Shinwell strikes another Member

Emanuel Shinwell (1884–1986) was born in London. He sat as a Labour MP for Linlithgow from 1919 to 1924 and again from April 1928 to 1931; for the Seaham division of Durham from 1935 to 1950, and for the Easington division of Durham from 1950 to 1970, when he was made a life peer. He first held office in 1929 and later sat in Cabinet as, successively, Minister of Fuel and Power, Secretary of State for War and Minister of Defence.

Emanuel Shinwell, *Conflict Without Malice* (1955)

The growing tension in the world and the obvious mismanagement of Britain's affairs both at home and abroad were reflected in the growing acerbity in the House. Lord Winterton once said that in the heyday of the Baldwin regime the House was like a tea-party with the 'dear vicar' in the chair. That atmosphere rapidly disappeared in the last months of his premiership before Chamberlain took over. And it was in the following year—1938—that I was guilty of un-parliamentary behaviour though I felt it justified from the standpoint of personal honour.

On the whole, debates in the House of Commons are free from personalities. There is plenty of hard-hitting and occasionally MPs make use of invective. References of an offensive nature to the personal character of a colleague are frowned on though sometimes tolerated when the heat of the moment and the anger of the speaker makes it a human and understandable error. But this abuse is not permitted to go beyond the limits: every speaker is normally careful to avoid reference to an opponent's personal affairs or his origin.

The Mother of Parliaments is very rarely shocked by any worse examples of bad behaviour than these verbal infringements. Physical measures are so occasional that they become historic. I was not present when Ronald McNeill, one of the Ulster MPs, threw a book at Churchill, but I was there when Leopold Amery, one of the most brilliant and sincere Tory leaders, crossed the floor of the House to slap George Buchanan, and I remember Neil McLean engaging in a bout of fisticuffs with a Tory MP. In 1938 I was involved in a physical clash myself.

The occasion was question time, and from the Opposition Front Bench I was asking about the privileges and facilities accorded by the Government to General Franco's agent in London. Commander Bower, then MP for Cleveland, shouted out: 'Go back to Poland'; the relevance of this comment on my question escaped me, but I thought that his intention was to be offensive. I have never been to Poland, but presumably my Polish ancestry was suggested as a reason for my returning there. It should be remembered that this was 1938; a short time later the world knew that to have Polish blood in one's veins was something to be proud of; at the time of Commander Bower's interjection Poland was to many unthinking people just another country in Eastern Europe.

John McGovern drew the attention of the Speaker to what seemed to be an intentional insult. I felt that my fellow members would regard my acquiescence to be a sign of cowardice. I was not aware that Bower had been a boxer in the Navy, but in my frame of mind this would not have intimidated me. I crossed the floor and struck him on the face. Immediately the House was in confusion, and I walked to the Bar of the House, realising that what I had done was a serious infringement of the House's code of behaviour, whatever extenuating circumstances there might be. Friends on the Opposition benches, however, called me back. I returned and apologised to the House. Bower also rose and made an apology, which was taken badly by members on our side of the House. Officially the matter had ended.

To my great regret I learned a little later that Commander Bower had suffered damage to the ear drum and he had to stay away for some time. It was a worrying period, and some of my Front Bench colleagues gave me the cold shoulder. On his return I felt quite certain that he would have the matter out, and in view of his fighting ability and the injury he had suffered I thought there might be trouble. But nothing happened until one day, after I had delivered a speech which had been well received in the House, he approached me in the Lobby. I braced myself up and really thought that the show-down had come at last; instead he warmly congratulated me on my speech, and so the dispute between us ended—though the incident disturbs me even now.

♣

The suspension of Mrs Braddock

Elizabeth Margaret Braddock (1899–1970) was educated at Liverpool elementary schools and sat as Labour MP for the Exchange division of Liverpool from 1945 until her retirement, a few months before her death. She had been a member of the Communist Party until 1924 and was a Liverpool councillor from 1930 to 1961 and an Alderman from 1955 to 1961.

Jack and Bessie Braddock, *The Braddocks* (1963)

At 3.23 p.m. on March 26, 1952, the House of Commons began to debate the textile industry. About midnight I made a short interjection and at 1.30 a.m. on March 27 I made another. By 9.15 a.m. I had begun to get restless. I stood up and asked the Deputy-Speaker why I was the only Member on our side who had failed to catch his eye, for I had been jumping up at every opportunity for hours, and I still hadn't been called to speak.

The big thing in this debate was whether the Tories were to hand back the Cotton Exchange to private enterprise. The Exchange was in my own constituency and it dealt with cotton imports and exports. The cotton did not necessarily come to Liverpool, but was sampled on the quay-side at any port in Britain, then sold over the floor of the Exchange.

I did not think the very large profits of the Exchange should once again be distributed among a small number of merchants in most unsatisfactory capitalist manner. I failed to see why the cotton industry should be an unrestricted benefit for these people. I had previously made bitter attacks on the merchants, and they knew my views well. So well, that I believe they were behind a scheme to keep me from repeating in the House damaging remarks about their disproportionate profits.

I was going to make sure that plenty of attention was drawn to this manoeuvre, so I pressed the point with the Deputy-Speaker, who eventually told me: 'If the Parliamentary Secretary (Mr Strauss) does not rise now I will call Sir Leslie Plummer and then, on that side of the House, I will call the Hon. Lady next.'

That was fair enough, and I sat down.

Sir Leslie Plummer was called at 9.33 a.m., but when he had finished Mr Strauss rose to wind up the debate. I jumped up and said: 'On a point of order, Mr Deputy-Speaker. I was promised that before the Parliamentary Secretary replied to the debate, you would call an Hon. Gentleman and then myself.'

The Deputy-Speaker replied: 'I said that I would call the Hon. Lady next on that side of the House, but that if an Hon. Member got up on the Government side I would call that Hon. Member in preference to her.'

I was amazed at this.

'I am making a definite protest,' I said levelly. 'What is more, under the circumstances I refuse to sit down. I refuse to sit down, in view of what has happened.'

That stopped the racket. There was shocked silence as the Deputy-Speaker said: 'If the Hon. Lady would sit down . . .'

'No,' I chipped in. 'I will not sit down.'

'She will be well advised to do so,' he warned.

'No, no,' I repeated, 'I am just not going to sit down.'

He tried again. 'If the Hon. Lady——'

'I am very sorry, Mr Deputy-Speaker,' I cut in again.

'If she will not sit down I must ask her to withdraw from the House.'

This was the point of no return. We had long since passed the stage at which I had to decide whether to make my protest from inside the rule of the assembly, or whether to focus attention by shattering that rule. Although I was angry because of what had happened, my judgement was unaffected. I am too used to facing situations of this sort not to know instinctively what to do. I knew that it was no use making a formal protest and then sitting down and submitting to this demonstration of Tory control in the Chamber. It was essential to bring the proceedings into disrepute and, by so doing, expose their inadequacies. I was now sure that I had so much support from the Labour benches that my own political reputation would certainly not be diminished by the firm stand that I was now compelled to make, and which I knew could have only one procedural ending.

I told the Deputy-Speaker that I was afraid he would have to ask me to withdraw from the House.

'Under the circumstances,' I said, 'representing the constituency I do and considering the debate which has been going on, my constituents and the country as a whole will take strong exception to this.'

The duel between us went on for some time, with the Deputy-Speaker continuing to try to get Mr Strauss going, and me refusing to let him. Eventually, the Deputy-Speaker sent for the Speaker, as I knew he would, and the Speaker had to 'name' me for disregarding the authority of the Chair. This meant that I was to be ejected.

I had hoped that because he had received only a second-hand report of proceedings—which, naturally, did not put my point of view—the Speaker would allow me to make a statement to him. But this he refused to allow.

So the Leader of the House, Mr Harry Crookshank, moved my suspension amid cries of 'Shame,' and this was carried by the Tory majority. Sydney Silverman came to me and suggested that I leave the House quietly, because the Sergeant on duty was old and not very strong. So I went out of my own accord, the first woman to be suspended from the House of Commons in history.

After I had gone, Sydney tried to have the session adjourned 'in view of the serious limitation upon the debate which has just occurred'. But the motion was defeated.

I confess I was disappointed at the publicity given in the national Press to my suspension. The Tory papers naturally tended to report the fact that I had been suspended, but avoided saying why. However, my own constituents received a more full account, and so did the rest of the cotton area. So the business proved worth while. People were aware that I had not let them down, as I should have done if I had been unable to speak and had made no protest.

It was far from the only row I have had in the House. There was one minor spot of bother with Arthur Colegate, the Tory from Burton-on-Trent, who punched me as I was on my way to a division lobby in November, 1951. The incident occurred when I tried to break up a heated argument between him and another Member.

I was forced to bring it to the notice of the Speaker during the division, and so I had to comply with the rule that I must be seated and 'covered', instead of standing. I must have looked rather odd wearing the silk topper which is kept handy for 'covering' oneself and—perhaps just as well—the business caused some mirth; even more when I told the Speaker that if Colegate had done it outside the House, I would have flattened him. He apologised afterwards.

But much more serious matters sometimes arise. I have even been forced to go to law for satisfaction. This is something I detest because, as I have said

243

earlier, you never know whether or not you will get justice when politics are involved. The most celebrated of my cases resulted from a leading article in a newspaper which commented unfavourably on a report that I had danced a jig on the floor of the House of Commons. This was supposed to be my way of celebrating the passing, under the Labour Party's administration, of the Transport Bill. I thought the words used by the newspaper meant that I had behaved in a ridiculous way, and I considered that this inference was politically damaging. I didn't win the action, but the plain fact was that I didn't dance a jig, or anything else.

This, however, is not to say that I won't go in for light entertainment in the Chamber if I think there is some political benefit to be obtained. When I was asked to do something about air pistols—nasty, easily obtained things which had caused a spate of serious eye injuries—I took a couple into the House, seriously infringing the rules, and laid them down in front of the Home Secretary. This caused quite a stir. It startled the Right Hon. Gentleman, disturbed the Speaker, and, as there was no machinery for getting these forbidden objects out of the Chamber again, it caused one of those minor procedural crises we are always having. For the red tape and the dependence upon precedent in the House of Commons is truly amazing.

1. Journals of the House of Commons, July 16, 1610.
2. Sir Reginald Palgrave, *The House of Commons* (1878), p. 51.
3. ibid., p. 109.
4. Sir Philip Warwick, *Memoirs of the Reign of King Charles I with a Continuation to the Happy Restoration of King Charles II* (1701), pp. 201–2.
5. Harry Graham, *The Mother of Parliaments* (1911), pp. 191–2.
6. The diet was the Polish legislative assembly; quoted in Patrick Howarth, *Questions in the House: The History of a Unique British Institution* (1956), p. 33.
7. T. B. Macaulay, Letter to Frances Macaulay, March 24, 1851.
8. Graham, op. cit., p. 188 n.
9. T. F. Lindsay, *Parliament from the Press Gallery* (1967), p. 55.
10. Lord Glenbervie, *Diaries*, September 7, 1802, Vol I, p. 336.
11. Henry W. Lucy, *A Diary of the Home Rule Parliament, 1892–1895* (1896), p. 47.
12. Alexander Mackintosh, *Echoes of Big Ben: A Journalist's Parliamentary Diary, 1881–1940* (1945), p. 32.
13. John Beckett, 'Who Are the Rowdies?', *Daily Herald*, July 22, 1926.
14. Mackintosh, op. cit., p. 67.
15. Beckett, op. cit.
16. Earl Winterton, *Orders of the Day* (1953), p. 97.
17. Selwyn Lloyd, *Mr Speaker, Sir* (1976), pp. 71–2.
18. ibid., pp. 72–3.
19. These figures come from the First Report from the Select Committee on Procedure, Session 1988–9, *Conduct of Members in the Chamber and the Alleged Abuse of Parliamentary Privilege*, March 23, 1989, p. viii. I am not including the two occasions in the 1970s when the House was suspended after missiles had been thrown from the Strangers' Gallery.
20. George Thomas, *George Thomas, Mr Speaker: The Memoirs of Viscount Tonypandy* (1985), p. 152.
21. *Daily Telegraph*, April 14, 1960.
22. J. L. Garvin, *The Life of Joseph Chamberlain*, Vol II (1933), p. 571.
23. Mackintosh, op. cit., pp. 31–2.
24. A. S. T. Griffith-Boscawen, *Fourteen Years in Parliament* (1907), pp. 33–4.

25. Hamilton Fyfe, *T. P. O'Connor* (1934), p. 165.
26. Griffith-Boscawen, op. cit., p. 34.
27. Michael MacDonagh, *The Speaker of the House* (1914), p. 351
28. T. M. Healy, *Letters and Leaders of My Day* (1928), p. 397.
29. Lincoln Springfield, *Some Piquant People* (1924), p. 110.
30. Horace G. Hutchinson (ed.), *Private Diaries of the Rt Hon. Sir Algernon West, GCB* (1922), p. 183.
31. Garvin, op. cit., Vol. II, p. 574.
32. J. A. Pease (later Lord Gainford), quoted in William Kent, *John Burns: Labour's Lost Leader* (1950), p. 367.
33. Viscount Ullswater (James Lowther), *A Speaker's Commentaries* (1925), Vol. I, p. 235.
34. Austen Chamberlain, *Down the Years* (1935), p. 70.
35. Henry W. Lucy, *The Balfourian Parliament, 1901–1905* (1906), p. 131.
36. Chamberlain, op. cit., p. 88.
37. MacDonagh, op. cit., p. 351.
38. Mackintosh, op. cit., p. 32.
39. Griffith-Boscawen, op. cit., p. 33.
40. Chamberlain, op. cit., p. 88.
41. Hutchinson, op. cit., p. 184.
42. Garvin, op. cit., Vol. II, p. 574.
43. Healy, op. cit., p. 397.
44. Chamberlain, op. cit., pp. 88–9.
45. Ullswater, op. cit., Vol. I, p. 235
46. Healy, op. cit., pp. 397–8.
47. Lucy, *The Balfourian Parliament*, p. 130.
48. Garvin, op. cit., Vol. II, p. 575.
49. Hutchinson, op. cit., p. 184.
50. According to the lobby journalist Alexander Mackintosh, the book which Ronald McNeill flung at Churchill was a leather-bound volume of the Standing Orders that he had picked up from the Chair, not the table; the missile, he says, cut its target on the forehead. However, McNeill and Churchill later served in office together: Mackintosh, op. cit., p. 66.
51. George Lansbury, *My Life* (1931), pp. 118–19.
52. Lady Violet Bonham-Carter, *Winston Churchill as I Knew Him* (1965), p. 216.
53. After the general election of 1910, which had been called to obtain a mandate for the Government's bill to abolish the Lords' power of veto over legislation (including Home Rule), the Irish Nationalists, led by Redmond, held the balance of power.
54. Mark Bonham-Carter (ed.), *The Autobiography of Margot Asquith* (1962), p. 276.
55. George Dangerfield, *The Strange Death of Liberal England* (1935), p. 58.
56. Leo Amery, Diary, July 25, 1911.
57. Dangerfield, op. cit., p. 58.
58. ibid.
59. Mark Bonham-Carter, op. cit., p. 278.
60. Margot Asquith, *Autobiography* (1920–2), Vol. I, p. 116.
61. Dalton had been elected to the Executive of the Parliamentary Labour Party shortly before Christmas 1925.
62. Fenner Brockway, *Socialism over Sixty Years* (1946), pp. 274–5.
63. Harold Balfour (Lord Balfour of Inchrye), *Wings over Westminster* (1973), p. 93.

6 'The Blasted Irish'

> The Irish members, brought as they are to this house, are
> a foreign element in this house . . . a body to whom the
> ancient glories and the great traditions of this house have
> no meaning. So long as we are forced to come to this
> house to endeavour, in the midst of a foreign majority,
> to transact our Irish business, we will use every form of this
> house, every right, every privilege, every power which
> membership of this house gives us—we will use these
> things just as it seems to be best for Ireland, quite
> regardless of the opinion and so-called dignity of British
> members, and absolutely careless of the penalties you may
> devise for our punishment.
>
> John Redmond, Speech to the House of Commons[1]

Once, during the session of 1876, when Sir George Campbell was speaking, Major O'Gorman rose to order and demanded of the Speaker 'whether the hon. member is justified in stigmatising my beloved country-people as "the blasted Irish"?' After a few tense moments, with the Speaker stating that he had not caught the expression but that such an expression, if used, would be 'certainly unparliamentary and most improper', it emerged that the Major had misheard Sir George's remarks. 'What I said,' Sir George explained 'was "Glasgow Irish", and not "blasted Irish" '—a reply which, according to *Hansard*, drew 'much laughter and cheering'.[2]

There is no doubt that the phrase 'blasted Irish' summed up what many English MPs felt about the Irish who were sent to Westminster during the period from 1801 to 1921. Henry Grattan, lamenting the demise of the Irish Parliament that was abolished with the Act of Union in 1801, was said to have made an ominous prediction to some English gentlemen: 'You have swept away our constitution, you have destroyed our Parliament, but we shall have our revenge. We will send into the ranks of *your* Parliament, and into the very heart of *your* constitution, a hundred of the greatest scoundrels in the kingdom.'[3] In the early 1880s Lord Granville, a member of Gladstone's Cabinet, advocated Home Rule because it would banish the disruptive Irish Members whom he castigated as 'the dry rot in the . . . commons', and he believed that this very banishment of the Irish from Westminster would be enough to render Home Rule popular.

The Irish arrived at Westminster in 1801, supplying 100 Members at first. William Pitt had envisaged that the Parliamentary union would be accompanied by concessions to the largely Catholic population of Ireland in the form of the right of Catholics to sit in Parliament (Catholic Emancipation), their right not to pay tithes to the established

Protestant Church, and the payment by the state of Catholic priests; what he achieved was the destruction of the Irish Parliament. In the early years of the nineteenth century, the foremost cause of the Irish MPs was Catholic Emancipation, with the economic conditions engendered by the land tenure system a close second, and Repeal of the Act of Union third. But Irish MPs did not confine their exertions to the interests of their poor Catholic constituents. Gladstone recalled how O'Connell 'poured out his wit, his pathos, and his earnestness in the cause of negro emancipation'. According to a leading abolitionist Member, Sir Thomas Fowell Buxton, O'Connell was approached by a representative of the twenty-seven MPs who were also West India merchants and whose commercial interests were threatened by abolition. The representative proposed a pact with the Irish Members. If they would withdraw their support for abolition, then the plantation grouplet would follow their lead in voting on Irish measures. O'Connell replied: 'God knows I speak for the saddest people the sun sees; but may my right hand forget its cunning, and my tongue cleave to the roof of my mouth if to help Ireland—even Ireland—I forget the negro one single hour!'[4]

O'Connell decided to postpone his campaign for Repeal and in 1835 forged the 'Lichfield House Compact' with the Whigs. At the 1841 general election his band of Repealers was reduced to eighteen, but he stepped up his campaign in Ireland. However, there emerged a division between the Protestant nationalists of Young Ireland, such as Charles Gavan Duffy, who wanted a complete break with England, and the Catholic Repealers like O'Connell who were ready to settle for a form of devolution under the Crown.

After O'Connell's death in 1847, the Irish Nationalists as a group lacked focus. A mini-party led by James Sadleir and William Keogh emerged, but Sadleir committed suicide on Hampstead Heath, and Keogh accepted office as Irish Solicitor-General under Aberdeen in 1853, and as Irish Attorney-General under Palmerston in 1855. Charles Gavan Duffy, then in his late thirties, sat in Parliament from 1852 to 1855, but the Irish MPs then were a motley collection of Conservative Catholics, anti-Repeal Protestant Liberals, Repealers and plain seekers of patronage. It was not until Isaac Butt, a former Irish Conservative MP, founded the Home Rule Association in 1870 and was elected as a Home Ruler MP the following year, that the modern Irish Nationalist Party was born. At the 1874 General Election fifty-nine Home Rulers were returned, whom Butt led until shortly before his death, although he resolutely stuck to constitutional methods. At the outset of the session of 1874, Butt gingerly proposed an amendment to the Queen's Speech expressing the view that there was widespread dissatisfaction in Ireland with the existing system. Naturally, this was defeated.

Charles Stewart Parnell abandoned this supplicatory approach for a more effective policy: obstruction. First elected as a Home Rule MP in 1875, he soon joined Joseph Biggar in cultivating this tactic. On the night Parnell took his seat, Biggar spoke for four hours in Committee on the renewal of the Irish Peace Preservation Bill. Five nights later Biggar adopted the old rule of 'espying strangers', so obliging the galleries to be cleared while a division was called. To add insult to injury, he had adopted this ploy because he had noticed the Prince of Wales in the Peers' Gallery. Not every Home Ruler agreed with these methods. 'I have not yet been able to see', stated the Fenian journalist John O'Leary, 'how Ireland is to be freed by keeping the Speaker of the English House of Commons out of bed.' In July 1877 an MP asked a question of Parnell in the House about a speech he had allegedly made in London claiming that obstruction was having the desired effect and that if only he and Biggar had another ten obstructionists they could bring the business of Parliament to a halt. In 1877 the minorities in 69 divisions consisted of no more than eleven MPs, and in 100 divisions they consisted of no more than twenty-two.[5] That same year Parnell and Biggar were criticised by Butt for obstructing the Mutiny Bill; they also protracted the debate on the Transvaal Annexation Bill to twenty-six hours.[6] When Butt discovered that these tactics met with widespread support back home in Ireland, he resigned. Parnell took command of the Irish Nationalist Members in 1878 and thereafter they sat below the gangway on the left of the Speaker: regardless of which party was in power they remained on the Opposition side of the House. True, obstruction was not invented by Parnell. As one political journalist of the period has pointed out, it 'had been practised occasionally in the 'seventies, notably by the "Colonels" in opposing the abolition of Purchase in the Army';[7] but it did not emerge as a regular and familiar Irish tactic until the debates on the Army Regulation Bill in 1879. Parnell and Biggar opposed the Bill, as did the Radicals, wishing to abolish flogging. They were defeated by the Tory majority and the Tory leader in the Commons, Stafford Northcote, tried to alter the procedural rules slightly so as to conquer the Irish 'hold-up'.

However, the watershed was the General Election of 1880, at which ten or so landowners were replaced by members of the lower professions. 'Gone were all the colleagues who symbolised the union of Ireland under Isaac Butt,' wrote F. H. O'Donnell, 'gone Lord Francis Conyngham . . . gone O'Conor Don . . . gone Hon. Charles ffrench and Hon. Wilfred O'Callaghan . . . Penny-a-liners from New York and Lambeth, from Mallow and Drumcondra; out-of-works from half a dozen modest professions had come in their place to earn the wages of Mr Patrick Egan and Mr Patrick Ford [the treasurer of the Land League and the proprietor and editor of the New York *Irish World*].'[8]

Obstruction had an immediate effect. Queen Victoria wrote to Disraeli in February 1880 to ask: 'Ought you not to come to some agreement with some of the sensible, and reasonable and not violent men on the other side, to put a stop to what clearly is a determination to force the disruption of the British Empire?' Disraeli wrote back that there 'are no "sensible and reasonable, and really not violent men" in the ranks of the Opposition on whom your Majesty might now act'.

Another Irish Member, William O'Brien, recalled that a callow recruit once asked Parnell 'How is a man to learn the rules of the House of Commons?', to which Parnell replied, 'By breaking them.'[9] Actually, what the Irish Nationalists did was 'to try to wreck the whole business of government by impeding the work of the House *within its rules*'. 'The Parnellites made use not only of Irish questions but of every question,' Herbert Gladstone, Mr G.'s son, later recalled. 'They came into the House loaded with blue-books from which they made interminable quotations . . . Members in these days had to read their questions to the House though they were printed in the Order paper. The Irishmen wrote immensely long questions and read them slowly to the House. During the first two years [1880–2] what we hoped would be the Government express lumbered along like a blocked, half-empty goods train.'[10]

In the session of 1881, which lasted for 154 days, fourteen Irish Members between them delivered 3,828 speeches—a daily average of almost twenty-five speeches from that group alone. In the same session, questions were multiplied several times over, so that *Hansard* required nine volumes for the complete debates of the year, compared with four or five in former years.'[11] The result was that Mr Speaker Brand, with the co-operation of Mr Gladstone, the Prime Minister, introduced the *clôture*, or closure. This meant that the Speaker could put the question to the House even though the Irish Members wished to continue speaking. The Irish had forced a change in the rules. In the middle of a sitting that continued for forty-one-and-a-half hours, Disraeli wrote to Lady Bradford: 'The H. of C. is still sitting, having had a whole night of it, and, as yet, half of this day I don't see the end of it. We are the laughing-stock of Europe.'[12]

As Arthur Balfour explained in a letter to Lady Randolph Churchill in 1883, 'the Irish have a talent for turning everything into an Irish debate . . .'[13] Even more so than the Parliament of the early 1880s, the Parliament of 1892–5 was dominated by the Irish question. 'All Parliamentary roads lead to Ireland,' wrote the descriptive writer Henry Lucy. 'With whatever object or prospect a sitting may commence, some Irish question is safe to interpose. Publicists are used to speak of "the" Irish Question as if it existed in the singular number. There is, truly, only one Irish Question, as the earth has only one atmosphere. But it is everywhere, varying as the atmosphere varies, yet ever present.'[14]

The heyday of the Irish Nationalists was in the mid-1880s, when Parnell was at the height of his powers, with his parliamentary troops holding the balance in a hung parliament. Indeed, his followers were known as the Parnellites until their leader's fall from grace in November 1890, which resulted in a split: nor was the split overcome by Parnell's death a couple of years later. But obstruction, the tactic which Parnell had unleashed on the House of Commons, ended up cutting both ways. Following the defeat of Mr Gladstone's first Home Rule Bill in 1886, the seceding Liberals, or Liberal Unionists as they called themselves, supported a Conservative Government. In the Parliament of 1892 to 1895, it was the Liberal Unionists and Tories who employed obstructionist tactics against a Liberal Home Rule Government and became victims of the closure. Whereas in the early 1880s, before Gladstone had been converted to Home Rule, the obstructionists numbered a mere 37 and the closure was invoked to protect the ability of MPs, Liberal and Tory, to do business, the General Election of 1892 produced a Home Rule majority of 355 as against 315 anti-Home Rulers—in effect, 315 obstructionists. 'We are having a trying time of it here—fighting against Tory obstruction,' wrote Justin McCarthy to Mrs Campbell Praed in March 1893. 'Only think how times have changed. They are determined to wreck the Home Rule Bill if they can by the force of their obstruction, and we had one or two very bad divisions—the government majority shrinking down to 21 or 23. Many of our Irishmen were absent, not expecting this serious work.'[15] As Gladstone explained to the House, the amount of time given over to his second Home Rule Bill—82 days—was generous indeed. The Reform Bill of 1831 had taken up 47 days; the Irish Land Bill of 1881, 46; the 1887 Coercion Bill, only 42. Moreover, the Government side had made 459 speeches in Committee on behalf of the Home Rule Bill, whereas Tories and Liberal Unionists had made 913 speeches against; in actual time, it was $57\frac{1}{4}$ hours for Government speeches and $152\frac{3}{4}$ hours for Opposition speeches.

In the early part of the Parliament of 1892–5 the Irish were keen to support the Liberal administration of Mr Gladstone, since it was engaged in introducing a Home Rule measure in the teeth of Unionist resistance. Roles were reversed so that Tories and Liberal Unionists became obstructionists while the Irish had to keep quiet. 'Time has therefore been an object of the first importance,' wrote Sir Richard Temple, a staunch Tory, 'and their policy has been to keep silence as much as possible and to economise the precious hours, for fear lest their opponents should talk the Bill to death . . . Their Leaders have, of course, orated *more Hibernico*, in every full-dress debate regarding Irish measures; but the rank and file of the Party, having no amendments to move against the Gladstonian side in the Committee stages, have confined their activity mainly to the process of interpellating Ministers at question time every afternoon.'[16]

However, according to Temple, it went against their nature for the Irish to muzzle themselves:

This enforced inactivity . . . was bound to have its revenge and their fondness for clamour found vent in another direction. They assumed to themselves the function of bothering and disconcerting every English member who might be engaged in interpellating or arguing with the Ministers on purely English questions. Claiming and exacting for themselves the fullest right to question and dispute, they used to set themselves to prevent Englishmen from doing so, and in this way they thought to help the Gladstonian Government. Themselves disposed more than any other class of members to a certain kind of noisy disorder, they would now interrupt the English members with meaningless cries of 'Order, Order,' merely to cause interruption. Some of them have been observed to do this quite systematically, as if they had been told off by Party arrangement for this peculiar duty.[17]

The cause of their undoing, in Temple's opinion, was their tendency to fight among themselves:

It appears that, though in some respects the Nationalists have an aptitude for Party discipline with all its bonds, which is wonderful—indeed, they have quite a genius in that particular respect, at least within Parliament—yet they have another, incompatible with it and equally wonderful, for quarrelling among themselves. The other Parties do not actually see the ebullition of these disagreements within the House or its precincts; but they cannot but notice its effect in the bearing and demeanour of the Party towards each other. The particulars of the disputes, such as they are, may be read in the newspapers. Nobody in Parliament studies the controversies, but everybody gathers the outcome—the Irish politicians, engaged in a common cause to which they have pledged themselves and declare to be sacred, disagree about it in an acrimonious and violent manner, with a carnival of disputation, as it were. This weakens the moral influence of the Irish in the House and retards indefinitely any chance of realisation that Home Rule can have as a principle. Even Members of Parliament say to each other: Are these Home Rulers who thus quarrel fit to conduct a Government of their own? If this is said in the House, their constituents will be saying the same thing in still stronger terms outside it.[18]

Even a Radical Liberal troublemaker like Henry Labouchere found the antics of some of the Irish members tiresome. William O'Brien remembers a young Irish MP who prophesied wildly that 'the Cossacks of Russia would yet stable their horses in the House of Commons', while the Tories and Unionists, 'most of whom had profusely dined, were expressing their alarm at the prospect with yells of laughter'. Labouchere, wrote O'Brien, 'sidled up to me with the pained remark: "What sort of young man is this now Mr—— you've sent over to us? It isn't that he's against law and order—we're all against law and order—but, you know, he's such a blawsted ass!" . . .'[19]

In Anthony Trollope's novel *The Land Leaguers* (1884), Mr O'Mahony, an Irish-American, is elected to the House and quickly reveals himself as an over-eager, tiresome laughing-stock. He makes the mistake of using unparliamentary language, having described a Government minister responsible for incarcerating 'suspects' as a 'disreputable jailer'. A colleague suggests he withdraw the phrase and substitute 'distasteful warder'. He does so, then loses his self-respect: 'It isn't so very easy for a man not to make a goose of himself in that place. You've got to sit by and do nothing for a year or two. It is very difficult. A man cannot afford to waste his time in that manner. There is all Ireland to be regenerated, and I have to learn the exact words which the prudery of the House of Commons will admit . . . Of course I was a goose, but I was only a goose according to the practices of that special duck-pond.'

It is not hard to explain why the Irish Members were treated as gargoyles or figures of fun. When he first saw J. G. Biggar, one of the ugliest men ever to sit in Parliament, Disraeli 'exclaimed, "What is that?" adding after a closer examination, "He seems to be what in Ireland you call a Leprechaun." ' An Irish businessman speaking as an MP for the first time caused Disraeli to turn to David Plunket and say: 'My dear David, you usually send us here from Ireland either gentlemen or blackguards; but this is neither.'[20]

One of the signal failings of the progressive Irish MPs was their failure to enlist the two giants of nineteenth-century English radicalism to their cause, namely Richard Cobden and John Bright. An exasperated Cobden wrote to his friend George Combe in 1848:

> Why do your friends amuse one another with such bubble-blowing? The real difficulty in Ireland is the character and condition socially and morally of the people, from the peer to the Connaught peasant. It is not by forms of legislation or the locality of parliaments, but by a change and improvement of the population, that Ireland is to have a start in the career of civilisation and self-government. Now instead of phantom-hunting, why don't your friends (if they are worthy of being your friends) tell the truth to their countrymen, and teach them their duties as well as their rights? And let them begin by showing that they understand their own duties and act up to them. The most discouraging thing to an English Member of Parliament who wishes to do well to Ireland is the quality of the men sent to represent it in the House of Commons. Hardly a man of business amongst them; and not three who are prepared cordially to co-operate together for any one common object. How would it mend matters if such men were sitting in Dublin instead of London.[21]

In a second letter to Combe, Cobden explained that despite his having thought much about Ireland and having been there frequently owing to a family connection, he had not spoken on Irish issues during his seven years as an MP:

> I will tell you the reason. I found the populace of Ireland represented in the House by a body of men, with O'Connell at their head, with whom I could feel no more sympathy or identity than with people whose language I did not understand. In fact, *morally* I felt a complete antagonism and repulsion towards them. O'Connell always treated me with friendly attention, but I never shook hands with him or faced his smile without a feeling of insecurity; and as far as trusting him on any public question where his vanity or passions might interpose, I should as soon thought of an alliance with an Ashantee chief.[22]

As John Morley, Cobden's biographer, noted, this was a little unfair, since O'Connell had actually been a firm and consistent opponent of protectionist legislation. Nonetheless, unfair or not, Cobden's sympathies were not engaged by O'Connell and his followers.

Cobden died in 1865, some thirteen years before the Irish MPs, led by Charles Stewart Parnell, began to employ obstructionist tactics on a systematic basis. One can only imagine that his scorn for such antics would have matched that of John Bright, who, although a champion of Irish grievances throughout his career, remained hostile to Home Rule from the 1840s to the 1880s. Bright represented a constituency in Lancashire—a county which he described as 'periodically overrun by the pauperism of Ireland'—and in 1849 he undertook a fact-finding visit to Ireland in the wake of the Famine and the 1848 Rebellion. He had voted for coercion in 1847 as a temporary expedient, but argued that the long-term remedy for Irish grievances lay in land and ecclesiastical reform— the termination of the Protestant ascendancy and the granting of tenant right. Bright could never be accused of lacking sympathy for the plight of the Irish peasantry, but the obsession of Irish MPs with a constitutional solution to the country's problems struck him as absurd. 'To have two Legislative Assemblies in the United Kingdom would, in my opinion, be an intolerable mischief,' he wrote to O'Donoghue during the Kerry election of 1872, after he had heard that he, Bright, had been represented as a Home Ruler.[23]

From 1878 onwards he was appalled and further alienated by the policy of obstruction adopted by the Parnellites. His diaries are full of angry references to the 'Irish insurrectionary party' or 'Irish rebel party', whose members are characterised as 'noisy and interrupting', 'unruly and almost beyond control', and 'violent and their conduct disgraceful'. On May 6, 1880, Bright spoke in a debate on the condition of Irish labourers, provoking the 'Irishmen of the rebel party' to anger: 'Simulated anger, I suspect, my advice being too honest and wise for their ruffianly objects and conduct.' By the mid-1880s, when it was apparent that Gladstone was embracing Home Rule, Bright discovered that Gladstone was in favour of excluding all Irish representation from Westminster. 'I told him I thought to get rid of the Irishmen from Westminster, such as we have known it for 5 or 6 years past, would do something to make his propositions less offensive and distasteful in Gt. Britain, tho' it tends to more complete separation.' Much though he would have liked to see them vanish from Westminster, he nonetheless rejected Home Rule on its own demerits.[24] His brother Jacob, a Manchester MP, supported Gladstone over Home Rule, although John Bright's sons took opposite sides, John Albert becoming a Liberal Unionist MP (1889–95) and William Leatham, a Liberal MP and an ardent Home Ruler.

Other attempts by Irish Nationalists to broaden the agenda of their party came to nought. F. H. O'Donnell claimed to have been approached in 1874 by Indian nationalist leaders seeking a reciprocal arrangement with the Irish parliamentary party offering 'political and pecuniary support of a great Indian movement, on condition that Ireland should elect some representatives of India to speak for India in the House and that India in her turn was to endorse the Irish demand for self-government'.[25] Butt approved of the idea but was anxious not to provoke English opinion, whereas Parnell could not see the relevance to Irish voters. When Michael Davitt revived the idea in 1883, proposing to allocate an Irish seat to Dadabhai Naoroje, Parnell feared this would be misunderstood.[26]

After the reconciliation of the Parnellites and Redmondites in 1900, the band of Nationalist MPs continued to treat with the Liberals, not only securing once again, at the general election of 1910, the balance of power between the two main parties, but also savouring, at the same election, the defeat of the Lords' veto, thereby paving the way for the successful passage through Parliament of a Liberal Home Rule Bill. Nevertheless, the rise of militant Ulster and the radicalisation of the Nationalist movement in Ireland served to marginalise their role. The Home Rule movement played safe. 'For four years in the House of Commons, 1906–10,' wrote the Irish-born MP C. J. O'Donnell, 'I watched, as a London member, its quiet disintegration and its impotent old age before its death in the short Easter Rebellion of 1916 . . . Except for occasional outbursts from John Dillon and Joe Devlin, no National movement in any assembly was ever supported by such meek and mild representatives. They had their field days and much eloquence was wasted on empty benches, but the Liberal Whip could usually rely on Irish subservience on other occasions.'[27]

In 1914, when Asquith's Home Rule Bill received Royal Assent, the House of Lords found itself temporarily invaded by cheering Home Rulers who had crossed from the Commons. 'Never before in my time was there such a breach of etiquette,' reflected the journalist Alexander Mackintosh in his memoirs. At the announcement of the prorogation in the House of Commons, the reaction of those in the Chamber was unrestrained: 'Patriotic emotion broke conventional bound when the House, led by Will Crooks, the popular Labour member, sang the National Anthem. Not only the members, but also officials, journalists and strangers rose and joined in the demonstration. "God save Ireland," cried a Liberal who had heard the royal assent to Home Rule. "And God save England, too," John Redmond fervently exclaimed.'[28] However, it was Redmond's mistaken decision to commit Irish Volunteers to fight the imperial cause in foreign theatres of war rather than simply defend Ireland itself which destroyed his credibility with the Nationalist movement and precipitated Ireland towards civil war.[29]

Even after the Irish achieved their independence with the partition of Ireland in 1921, the Irish question has haunted the British Parliament. In the 1920s, according to C. J. O'Donnell, it was deracinated Catholic Ulstermen who, 'especially in Glasgow, form a most subversive population, sending able Communists to the Westminster Parliament'.[30] In later times, it has been the militant Republican Bernadette Devlin and the extreme Unionists led by the Revd Ian Paisley who have harked back to the disruptive role of Irish MPs in the past.

All in all, Earl Winterton's judgement of the role of the Irish at Westminster was severe though fair. 'The Irish Nationalists, unlike any other party within my long recollection of the House of Commons, with the exception of the members representing the Clyde for a short period after the 1922 election (they soon adopted a more reasonable attitude), have been the only party or group who deliberately attempted to injure the House as an institution by uproar, insults and obstructions; they atoned for this, to some extent, by their wit and the remarkable standard of parliamentary eloquence among them.'[31]

❖

Six members of the O'Connell family take their seats

Daniel O'Connell (1775–1847), 'The Liberator', was a landowner and an Irish QC, and the pre-eminent advocate of both Catholic Relief and the Repeal of the Union. He was MP for Clare, for Waterford County in 1830, for Kerry in 1831. He sat for Dublin from 1832 to 1836, for Kilkenny from 1836 to 1837, for Dublin from 1837 to 1841, and for County Cork until his death.

John O'Connell (d. 1858) was a barrister like his father and also the author of the *Life and Speeches of Daniel O'Connell, Esq.* He sat as MP for Youghal from 1832 to 1837, for Athlone from 1837 to 1841, for Kilkenny City from 1841 to 1847, thereafter for Limerick until 1851, and finally for Clonmell from December 1853 until he retired in 1857.

John O'Connell, *Recollections and Experiences during a Parliamentary Career from 1833 to 1848* (1849)

Early in the forenoon of Tuesday, the 5th of February, 1833, my father led what might have been called his *household brigade*—viz. his three sons, and two sons-in-law, down to the House of Commons, to be present at the opening of the first Reform Parliament, of which all six had just been elected members.

In the passages we met, and were introduced to, Cobbett, who, like some of ourselves, was then for the first time in Parliament, having been just returned for the newly enfranchised borough of Oldham. Some—at least I may speak for *one*—of our party felt no little interest at seeing and speaking to that singular man, whom, hitherto, we had only known by his powerful, but coarse and unscrupulous writings. He was habited, as I recollect, in a kind of pepper-and-salt-coloured garb, in fashion something between that of a Quaker and of a comfortable farmer; and wore rather a broad-brimmed white hat, a little on one side, and thrown back, so as to give the fullest view of his shrewd though bluff countenance, and his keen, cold-looking eye.

We also fell in with Thomas Attwood, of Birmingham, the Lafayette of the Birmingham movement party; quite as respectable and as politically imbecile as his French prototype. With him and two or three more of the English Reformers, who had been recently conspicuous in agitation, we had an inter-change of congratulations on the *actual assemblage* of a Reformed Parliament, and of some large anticipations as to further victories—congratulations and anticipations speedily to be put an end to by disgust and disappointment.

As the hour drew near when the business of electing a Speaker was to be proceeded with, we went into the House of Commons, which was then, as formerly, the old Chapel of St Stephen's; the destructive fire that has given such scope to Mr Barry's great, although somewhat elaborate and decidedly expensive, architectural genius not having occurred for a year and a half later.

No man, whether young or old, ever entered the House of Commons for the first time without some degree of emotion. The same may doubtless be said of the novice in other public assemblies, but the emotion is peculiar on entering the House of Commons of England; or, at any rate, such *was* the case, while it met in the scene of its ancient labours and struggles.

To call it the oldest deliberative assembly in the world is a mere phrase at best; and particularly so considering the *nonage* of the representative bodies existing in other countries. But turning from phrases to facts, it *is* (at least I so felt it) an exciting thing to enter an assembly replete with such historic recollections, and where the democratic principle has maintained so hard and stout a fight during centuries.

As usual, at the assembling of a new Parliament, before what the Americans style the 'calling to order of the meeting', the floor of the House was covered with members, either exchanging greetings, intelligence, etc. with old parlia-mentary acquaintances, or wandering from group to group in quest of such, and in curious examination of the *Reform* recruits.

I could discern that our 'household brigade' were the objects of rather par-ticular scrutiny and criticism, and in especial were favoured with rather a long quizzing from Lord Stanley's eye-glass,—an ordeal to which a hot spirit of our party manifested a good deal of disrelish, that he could hardly be restrained from making an active demonstration on the spot. In our turn, such of us as were new to Parliament were not idle, but took ample revenge in commenting upon the strange herd amongst which we found ourselves, and on the discrep-ancies between our preconceived notions of the more remarkable persons and the reality.

At length the hubbub began to cease, and the chaos resolved itself into some order. Mr Ley took his seat at the table of the House in his usual place as first Clerk, but acting for the nonce as Chairman. A very pardonable feeling in my father induced him to range his three sons in a line on the bench where he sat himself, the second bench on the opposition side. Before us, ranged upon the front bench of the same side, were Attwood, Duncombe, Fielden, and, most conspicuous of all, William Cobbett. Around and below us were others of the Radical Reform party. In front, filling all the seats on the Treasury side, the benches at and below the bar; and even outflanking us, spread the motley and multitudinous gathering of the more Whiggish Reformers and ministerial followers, while in a narrow segment of the benches, at the upper end of the House (on our side), frowned the small but compact and well-ordered array of the so recently discomfited Tories.

'Few and faint—but fearless still!'

While occupied in scanning all these dispositions, and noting the aspects of the various leaders, our attention was suddenly called to the business of the hour, by Joe Hume opening fire just over our heads. He spoke from what was, in the old House, his accustomed and recognised place, close by one of the pillars of the gallery, and near the end of the third opposition bench.

Mr Hume rose to propose that Mr Littleton, then MP for Staffordshire (the present Lord Hatherton), should take the chair. The Whig ministry proposed the former speaker, Mr Manners Sutton, the late Lord Canterbury; and, on a division, carried it by a majority of eight or nine to one, but not till after a very animated debate, very exciting to us novices.

Manners Sutton *acted* speaker very well—perhaps a little *overacted* it; but certainly looked and filled the part well. His chief faults were an imperiousness and hastiness of temper, and a not entire forgetfulness of the partisan in the discharge of his duties as arbiter and president of a political assembly: occasionally allowing too much of the intolerant arrogance which his party affected towards the Radicals to peep out, when he had to do with members belonging to the latter political denomination.

My father used to say that for the first two years of his parliamentary life, he repeatedly remarked a deliberate neglect of him by the Speaker, when endeavouring to catch the latter's eye. But he always added that during the subsequent years, until Lord Canterbury's removal to the Upper House, matters were entirely changed in this respect, and there almost seemed, as it were, an anxiety to make a kind of *reparation*.

Among the various little things which showed his lordship's fondness for the externals of his dignity while Speaker was the manner in which he used to keep in submissive attendance, at either side of his chair, the members who wanted to get his signature to the tickets of admission for strangers. This custom, fruitful in annoyance to members, and eminently so in disturbance to the business of the House, was done away with two years later, during the short speakership of Mr Abercrombie, the present Lord Dunfermline.

As I shall have afterwards to speak of a much more interesting debate on a Speaker's election, that of the last-named noble lord, when the contest was between him and Lord Canterbury, in 1835, I pass from that of 1833, to the opening of the *real* business of the session in that year.

The newly elected Speaker having then duly gone through the chrysalis stage of the bobwig (which is *de rigueur* before he is presented to the sovereign), and thence emerged into the full-winged or full-wigged splendour of his confirmation in office, and the bulk of the members having dawdled through five or six days of oath-taking and roll-signing, we met at last as a duly constituted House of Commons, upon the 9th or 10th of February, about half an hour before his Majesty was expected down to Westminster to deliver the royal speech—opening the session in form.

Presently we heard at our door the customary three knocks, solemn and awful, which announce a special summons; and Sir Augustus Clifford stalked in, stately and stiff, and delivered his message, calling on us to attend his Majesty at the bar of the House of Lords. On all such occasions a pause ensues, evidently mercifully intended to give Sir Augustus Clifford time to save himself, ere the House break from their seats and rush, push, and scramble like a parcel of schoolboys through the passages and even up to the very bar of the Lords; hurrying the unhappy Speaker before them like the sacrificial ox; urged along reluctant to the horns of the altar!

Even at this early stage of the session there was earnest given of the hostile spirit towards Ireland that was to mark its course. The only part of the speech of William IV which his infirmities or his inclinations allowed him to deliver with any distinctness was that in which he threatened Ireland: and even this agreeable topic did not give more dignity to his demeanour than that of a *good scold!*

We listened to the speech, and returned from the hearing with hearts full of bitterness; mitigated only by a feeling of pity for the statesmen who were thus so evidently bent upon throwing away the opportunities for fame that their somewhat unexpected success on one great question had opened to them with regard to others; above all, with regard to the yet unachieved object worthy of *real* statesmen—the pacific, equitable, and therefore mutually beneficial, settlement of the long-distracted international relations between Great Britain and Ireland.

In England there has been much outcry against Irish Repealers, for what is called their unwarrantable attacks on the Imperial Parliament, on the score of negligence or of hostility towards Ireland. Whether those attacks be justifiable or not is a question with regard to which some materials for coming to a judgement may be supplied ere the closing of this record. The writer of it readily pleads guilty to the charge of being one of those who have made the attacks in question; but he does not so plead as having lightly come to the convictions which impelled them, or having entered Parliament with any predisposing prejudices. On the contrary, up to, and for some little while after, the time when Irishmen of the popular party got admission to the British

Parliament, there was, among the greater number of them in fact, a *credulity*, of which they have been long since painfully disabused, with regard to the dispositions of that Parliament. 'Englishmen are just, Englishmen are fair-minded,' was the cry; 'they have done us wrong because they have not known us. Hitherto the representation of Ireland has been all in the hands of that faction in our country whose interest it ever has been to misrepresent and to mislead the English with regard to the real state of things in Ireland. But now that the Irish people are, to some extent at least, directly represented—now that their state, wants, sufferings, and claims, will fairly and fully be exposed, Englishmen will see and acknowledge their error, and be prompt to do us justice.'

I do not mean to say that a soliloquy in the exact terms and to the exact effect of the foregoing was delivered by the new Irish MPs on their first appearance on the parliamentary stage, but most certainly there were expectations and convictions to that effect; and most certainly and most utterly have those expectations been disappointed.

An Irish Member tries to speak twice

James Grant, *Random Recollections of the Lords and Commons* (1838)

An Irish member, whose name I will not mention, having risen, he was assailed by loud cries of 'Spoke! spoke!' meaning, that having spoken once already, he had no right to do it a second time. He had evidently a second speech struggling in his breast for an introduction into the world, when seeing, after remaining for some time on his legs, that there was not the slightest chance of being suffered to deliver a sentence of it, he observed with imperturbable gravity, and in a rich Tipperary brogue—'If honourable gintlemin suppose that I was going to spake again, they are quite mistaken. I merely rose for the purpose of saying that I had nothing more to say on the subject.'

The House was convulsed with laughter, for a few seconds afterwards, at the exceedingly ready wit of the Hibernian MP.

❖

O'Connell complains about the misreporting of one of his speeches

John O'Connell, *Recollections and Experiences during a Parliamentary Career from 1833 to 1848* (1849)

In the session of 1833 a speech of Mr Daniel O'Connell's, upon an Irish question of considerable interest and importance, was not only grievously abbreviated (by the reporter), but the sense of it entirely perverted in several passages. As I recollect, it was a speech on the then very exciting and difficult subject of the tithes of the Protestant Church in Ireland; and Mr O'Connell, among other things, was made to say that he would vote in a certain way on the immediate point under consideration, 'although it was directly in the teeth of all his former opinions on the subject!' On his bringing the matter before the House under the usual form of a 'Breach of Privilege', and making complaint of being thus treated, the defence set up by the reporter was that, during his walk from the House to the newspaper office, the rain, which was falling heavily at the time, had most unfortunately streamed into his pocket and washed out the notes he had made of Mr O'Connell's speech. Upon which the latter remarked that it was the most extraordinary shower of rain he had ever heard of, inasmuch as it had not only *washed out* the speech he did make, but had *washed in* another, and an entirely different one.

O'Connell accuses the House of 'beastly bellowings'

T. B. Macaulay, Journal, June 11, 1840

The House was engaged upon Stanley's Irish Registration Bill. The night was very stormy. I have never seen such unseemly demeanour, or heard such scurrilous language in Parliament. Lord Norreys was whistling, and making all sort of noises. Lord Maidstone was so ill-mannered that I hope he was drunk. At last, after much grossly indecent conduct, a furious outbreak took place. O'Connell was so rudely interrupted that he used the expression 'beastly bellowings'. Then rose such an uproar as no OP mob at Covent Garden Theatre, no crowd of Chartists in front of a hustings, ever equalled. Men on both sides stood up, shook their fists, and bawled at the top of their voices. Freshfield, who was in the chair, was quite unable to keep the smallest order. O'Connell raged like a mad bull; and our people—I for one—while regretting and condemning his violence, thought it was much extenuated by the provocation . . . A short and most amusing scene passed between O'Connell and Lord Maidstone, which in the tumult escaped the observation of many, but which I watched carefully. 'If,' said Lord Maidstone, 'the word beastly is retracted, I shall be satisfied. If not, I shall not be satisfied.' 'I do not care whether the noble lord be satisfied or not.' 'I wish you would give me satisfaction.' 'I advise the noble lord to carry his liquor meekly.' At last the tumult ended from absolute physical weariness. It was past one, and the steady bellowers of the Opposition had been howling from six o'clock with little interruption.

What would Parliament do without the disruptive Irish Members?

E. M. Whitty, *History of the Session 1852–3, A Parliamentary Retrospect* (1853), May 14, 1853

What should we do without the Irish members? The monotony of Budget debates would be intolerable without the Irish members. English members can misconduct themselves, on proper provocation; but we should have no provocations were there no Irish members. Could Pitt have thought of this when he was petting Castlereagh into passing the Union? At any rate the reflection is universal at present; and though we affect indignation at the recurring rows—as if we were devoted to public business, and never thought of the House of Commons as our principal public amusement—we have all of us, during the week, been exceedingly obliged to those Celtic gentlemen who have made 'a holy show' of themselves, after the manner of their race, in the Imperial Senate.

There were some fears at the general election, that a grave, sedate, business-like, and honourable set of men were about to be presented to Parliament as the 'Irish party'; but the experience of the fortnight has manifested the groundlessness of those apprehensions. It is gratifying to discover, taking the public amusement view of public affairs, that the Irish members are as silly, as broguey, as useless, as quarrelsome, and as contemptible as ever they were. That is, in the mass; the exceptions are conspicuous, and need no particularisation: they are to be found in the little confederation for pure but perhaps *too* national purposes—the 'Irish party'—a party, despite all desertions, still left. And as this is the exact character of the general Irish representation, is it not most insane to entertain any hopes of them, as a manageable confederation, for combination purposes, or of the country which selects them? They know each other best; and what can England do but take their accounts of one another? There is one very remarkable circumstance in these Milesian brawls,[32] as in all Milesian brawls, whether in back streets or senates, and it is a circumstance which should operate to the destruction of the theory that the Irish is a witty or a humorous race, which it certainly is not—that there is never any 'fun' in the rows. A jest, a *mot*, a smart saying, never comes from Irish senatorial lips—they deliver only vulgar, brainless abuse, in heavy, foolish fashion. Gaiety itself is graceful; but your Irish orators, in these days, attempted the inflated, solemn style of talk—every one of them stands upright, looks austere, and delivers himself like Norval when Norval was in the act of giving his name and address. What amusement the House does get is consequently at the expense both of the fame for brains and the reputation for respectability of gentlemen from Ireland, who are set down not only as being injudicious and somewhat loosely moral, but as dull dogs who are only useful for worrying one another. If they had that sense of humour which is supposed to be a national trait, they would have with it a sense of the ridiculous, and so would avoid these sinister 'scrimmages'. They make fools of themselves; and in a sober, advertising way. Captain Magan, the teterrimous [*sic*] occasion of the wars of the week, enters battle in a red shirt! You find it difficult to realise the picture of Captain Magan, who, you know, has suspicious-looking moustaches and *prononcé* eyes, wearing a red shirt; but it is a fact; and what are you to think of the party who let loose a leader in an *oriflamme*!—'this style, 5s.?' The idea of a man talking of public honour in a red shirt! What treasury whip would keep a compact about income tax with a man in tittlebat moustaches and a red shirt? And that is from the deficiency in the party of a sense of the ridiculous—a sense which keeps parties, like individuals, out of many improprieties. Take another Irish incident of the week. At the Thursday sitting—at about one in the morning—when all the business was over; when Secretary Wilson had his hand on the peak of his hat, about to take it off, and wink at the Speaker—which is motion of adjournment—when only about seven members were left; and when even Mr Brotherton looked as if he could go home, a gentleman rushed in, lurched about, and took his stand near the middle of the floor. 'Misther Spaiker, Surr.' All eyes were on the voice and the reeling figure; and dead amazement crept over the faces of the seven members, and Secretary Wilson removed his hand and shut his eyes. The voice was undoubtedly in the possession of the floor—it was a matter of calculation when it would take possession, horizontally, of the said floor. 'Surr,' said it again: and the Speaker said, 'Order, order,' in faint and appalled terms; and the eyes of the seven members and the thin galleries were on the gentleman in the staggering voice who could not get beyond the exordium of his oration. What was it?—has anything serious happened?—for one did not know at first whether it was drink or agitation which affected the orator. Something came at last. 'Surr, the bill [stagger]—inspection of nuns—honourable gentleman—in his place—bill—on nuns [stagger],—I'm a Catholic—want time—when will it come on?—consider' (stagger and sits down). It was only a 'question': the drunken gentleman wanted Mr T. Chambers to say when he would face the Government with his Bill for the Inspection of Conventual Establishments: and Mr T. Chambers answered with crushing politeness. Then the voice staggered up again 'in reply'. 'Surr— [stagger]—holy Roman religion—[stagger]—inshult to Ireland': and the voice and the man dropped again; and Mr Wilson opened his eyes, took off his hat, winked, and the House adjourned; the theory in the gallery being, that the drunken gentleman would be taken home in a cab by Lord Charles Russell, as Serjeant-at-Arms,—rather a fine, chivalric nobleman—who goes through that sort of inconvenience for the sake of his salary. The drunken gentleman was an Irish gentleman, of the essentially 'religious' section of the Irish representation; and rather venerated by the priests, and accordingly permitted to assist in the Government of the British Empire. Well, that is not an uncommon scene—uncommon neither of the man nor of his party; and, of course, the English House does not excuse it; because, however merciful it would be to the gentlemen who come in 'gay', and happy, and graceful, and laughing—as several very notorious and estimable gentlemen, English and Irish, punctually do at eleven o'clock p.m.,—it can only feel disgust for those who are offensive, because they are stupid, and who never get drunk but they insist upon the wrongs of Ireland and the rights of Popery. So that, on the whole, the Irish memberdom is not advancing in the British Parliament. Mr Duffy and Mr

Moore, and their little party, have two Irish reforms to effect:—first, to make Irish 'Liberal' members honest; next, to make them respectable.

Mr Delahunty and other oddities

James Delahunty (1808–85) was the son of a Waterford merchant and was educated at a local school before himself becoming a merchant and an Alderman of the city (1842–5). He was Coroner for the County of Waterford from 1850 to 1867. A Liberal in favour of Home Rule, he sat for Waterford City, 1868–74; and for the County of Waterford from 1877 until his retirement in 1880.

Henry W. Lucy, *Memories of Eight Parliaments* (1908)

The dull respectability of the present House of Commons is a condition of things largely due to the change in the *personnel* of the Irish members. After the election of 1874 they flooded Westminster with rich and rare individuality of the kind hitherto familiar to the Saxon chiefly in the novels of Lever and Lover. This type has disappeared from the present House. Perhaps the only Irish Member who today habitually rises into flights of humour is Tim Healy.

Among those who delighted the Parliament of 1874–80 was Mr Delahunty, Member for Waterford City. His panacea for all the woes of Ireland had something to do with one-pound notes. I am ashamed to say, though I have often heard him discourse on the topic, there does not dwell in my mind a clear impression as to whether he desired to have one-pound notes authorised or whether he would have had them abolished. However that be, the peace and prosperity of Ireland were, according to his view, wrapped up in the one-pound note.

One Wednesday afternoon, in the Session of 1878, the fortune of the ballot gave Mr Delahunty an opportunity of dealing with this burning question. He had brought with him a small black bag, in which, according to the testimony of his compatriots, he had been accustomed to store the depositions taken before him as Coroner of the City and County of Waterford. Now, it was primarily requisitioned for holding the convincing notes of his oration. It is presumable that he had promised himself when his task was completed, a few hours' relaxation in one of the inner circles of London Society. In view of this arrangement of his evening he had, after filling his bag up to the top with manuscript notes, found just room enough to put in a comb, brush, and a few other toilet necessaries. Hauling out a handful of papers from the bag, and finding them not exactly what he wanted, he turned around and, amid an awful silence, deliberately resumed the search. Of course, the first things that came to hand were the comb and brush.

Hastily thrusting them back among the documents he made another start with his speech. The fresh batch of papers also led to nowhere in particular.

Coming to a break in his argument he turned once more to the bag, fearfully conscious of the presence of the comb and brush. With increased deliberation he rooted round, and finally, under the impression that he had at last seized the papers he sought, he produced a pair of grey worsted stockings. These approached the Irish question from a quite unexpected avenue. The House roared with laughter. Mr Delahunty, still failing in his endeavour to come across the missing note, took the miscellaneous articles out of the bag, spread them on the bench, and with his back turned to the Speaker, prosecuted his search. When at last he found the desired sheet of paper he went on as if nothing had happened, the House listening with high good humour to a story that had neither beginning, middle, nor end, through which the comb and brush came and went, as Harlequin and Columbine purposely flit across the stage in the intervals of pantomime business.

Among other oddities who occur to the memory, emerging out of the now distant past, was Mr Tom Connelly, who sat on the Conservative Benches and stirred up his compatriots on the opposite side with the long pole of scornful insinuation or vitriolic vituperation. There was Mr McCarthy Downing, faithful to the last to his old leader, Isaac Butt, growing nearer and nearer in facial resemblance to a plucked jackdaw, as Butt's fortunes faded and he found himself thrust aside by the more strenuous Parnell. There was Mr Ronayne, one of the wittiest of Irishmen. There was Frank Hugh O'Donnell, with his pleasing habit of presenting himself after a big debate had been closed by the leaders on both sides, and insisting on continuing it indefinitely. There was Dr O'Leary, a magniloquent monocule. There was Captain Stackpool, with his hands in his pockets and his reminiscences of Lord Palmerston. 'Ah,' he was accustomed to say sadly, shaking his head at recurrent difficulties, 'things wouldn't be like this if old Pam were here!'

Another type of the now extinct Irish Member was The O'Gorman Mahon. He was, when he came back to the House, returned for County Clare in 1879, one of the few living Members who had sat in the unreformed Parliament. He was Member from 1847 to 1852, returning to the old scene after an interval of twenty-seven years. Meanwhile he had seen fighting both by land and sea. On one occasion, offended by a Conservative Member opposite whom he suspected of 'sniggering' at an Irish Nationalist Member on his feet at the moment, The O'Gorman Mahon crossed the floor, handed his 'cyard' to the offender, and went into the Lobby ready to complete the preliminaries of a challenge.

So recently as 1884 Sir Patrick O'Brien, another richly endowed Irish Member, went even further than that in the arrangements for a duel. In debate on a local Dublin Bill Sir Pat, it being two o'clock in the morning, got a little mixed as to whether it was Mr Wm. O'Brien or Mr Harrington who had interrupted his observations with what he described as 'a guffaw'. At first he leaned towards conviction that it was Mr Harrington, of whom he incidentally remarked that 'the honourable Member was carrying parcels for a wage of three-and-sixpence a week when I represented King's County in Parliament'.

After staring with blood-shot eyes for some time at the little band of Parnellites opposite, Sir Pat accidentally got Mr William O'Brien in focus, and convinced himself that it was he who was the offender. Several times, leaning forward, putting his hand to his mouth, he enquired across the House, in a stage whisper, whether Mr O'Brien was 'afraid'? No notice being taken, Sir Pat hurriedly left the House, looked up The O'Gorman Mahon, engaged him as a second, and, returning, informed Mr O'Brien that everything was settled. All he had to do was to put his man in communication with the ancient warrior. Sir Pat waited in the Lobby for an hour. Mr O'Brien made no sign, and in the cooler atmosphere of the following day the blood-thirsty enterprise was abandoned.

The Government ambushed

Joseph Philip Ronayne (1822–76) was educated in Cork and was a civil engineer by profession. A Liberal in favour of Irish self-government, he was MP for Cork from 1872 until his death.

Tim Healy, *Letters and Leaders of My Day* (1928)

W. H. Smith was a likeable man. When moving the 'closure' he used to repeat a settled formula without dreaming it could grow stale. He declared it was essential to 'promote the business of the House and the interest of the country'.

Of his early days as Minister it is recorded that, being reproached by Disraeli for his absence from a division in 1874, when the Government was beaten on a question about herring-branding in Ireland, Smith replied, 'This is a neglect that shall not occur again.' If he had told Disraeli that he was dining at the St Stephen's Club, opposite Palace Yard, and that members deemed this 'safe', relying on being warned by the electric bells, it would have been the fact. The electric bells were a new installation, and were intended to clang in the Club when a division was called, but J. P. Ronayne, Member for Cork, a wag and an engineer, severed the wires with a pliers, and the Government was defeated.

John Doherty's maiden speech

Michael MacDonagh, *Irish Life and Character* (1898)

The Right Hon. John Doherty, who was Chief Justice of the Common Pleas in Ireland from 1830 until his death in 1850, was elected member for Kilkenny in 1826; and appointed Solicitor-General for Ireland by George Canning. 'When I first addressed the House of Commons,' Doherty said in after life, 'I was really in a great fit of nervousness, and would have given much to be back again at the Four Courts. It was a trying thing to wish to speak well in the presence of Canning, and Brougham, and Peel, and Plunket, and Tierney. When I sat down, Canning turned round and said to me: 'Well done, Doherty; very good indeed. You only made one mistake. Like every Irishman, you said "Sir" to the Speaker too much. You should say "Sir" only at the beginning and end.' 'Well,' I answered, 'I really don't care how I called him since I did not say "Ma'am" to him.'

♣

Major O'Gorman's playfulness with Disraeli

Major Purcell O'Gorman (d. 1888) was a Liberal Home Ruler who sat for the city of Waterford from 1874 to 1880, when he was defeated. During those six years he gained a reputation as a parliamentary star.

Henry W. Lucy, *Memories of Eight Parliaments* (1908)

One night, rising to wind up debate on a Coercion Bill, Disraeli opened his speech with the characteristic remark, 'This is a measure of necessity, passed in the spirit of conciliation.' The Major had just come in refreshed from dinner. Taking his usual seat below the Gangway he folded his hands over his capacious stomach, closed his eyes, and prepared for a snooze in anticipation of an all-night sitting. The voice of the Premier daintily propounding his paradox roused the Major.

'No,' he roared in thunderous voice.

'If that is to be taken for a reply,' Disraeli wittily said, 'I must observe that in accordance with the rules of debate that forbid a Member to speak twice on the subject before the House, the gallant gentleman is precluded from taking further part in these proceedings.'

The Major rose with such alacrity as was possible to his weight and shaking his hat threateningly at the Premier roared, 'I have not spoken one word.'

The Ministerialists almost drowned his voice in cries of 'Order, Order!' But he stood there, symbol of sound and fury, what time the Premier, silent at the table, waited till cessation of the uproar should give him opportunity to proceed. At length the Speaker interposing, and several compatriots hauling on to his coat tails, the Major sunk back to his seat and Disraeli recommenced his speech.

The truce did not last long. The Major, who had been undergoing a series of internal convulsions that shook with earthquake force his capacious frame, rose, stepped down the Gangway behind the chair of the Serjeant-at-Arms. This was a short cut to the doorway, and it was too lightly assumed that the gallant Member was temporarily retiring for further refreshment. To the horror and apprehension of the crowded House, he was observed to turn to the right, and with slow pace, like an East Indiaman with sails bellied with the summer breeze, to make straight down for the table at which the Premier stood.

What did he mean to do? Would he take up the frail figure standing by the Mace, tuck it under his arm, and walk out with his prize into the Lobby? It would have needed slight effort on the part of the herculean Major, even after dinner, to accomplish this feat. A later Parliament has seen history repeat itself in a similar impulse of an Irish Member to correct by physical assault alleged political shortcomings on the part of a Prime Minister. A newly arrived Irish Member, differing from Mr Arthur Balfour on a controversial point, suddenly descended from a back bench below the Gangway, dashed across the floor and making for the Premier danced round him with clenched fists after the manner of street *gamins* wanting another boy to 'come on'.

Happily it turned out to be only the Major's fun. Having thoroughly alarmed the House he, when he arrived almost within grip of the Premier, again turned sharp to the right, and, walking up the centre Gangway, seated himself on the fourth bench behind the Leader of the Opposition. This bringing him directly opposite to the Premier enabled him with more point and precision to punctuate his speech by an occasional roar.

Sir William Fraser, *Disraeli and his Day* (1891)

I never saw Disraeli unnerved but once. It was by a curious character who sat in the Parliament of 1874–80, Major O'Gorman. Major O'Gorman had been not only a distinguished officer, but a handsome man. He was, however, at this time remarkable for a most extensive 'bow-window', which was conspicuous in the pale blue trousers which he usually wore to the House.

He had a peculiar physical ailment, the exact character of which I do not know; the effect was about every third or fourth minute, a visible spasm of the abdomen, for which Members opposite used to watch with something of the same anxiety as one watches the discharge of a big cannon. You heard Members say, particularly when the Debate was dull, 'There it is again': and many took a morbid interest in counting the number of spasms in an hour: the less educated MPs held that 'the Major' had a weasel in his inside. However, once on his legs, Major O'Gorman was a very good speaker. He knew well how to get and keep the ear of the House: and frequently told amusing Irish stories, briefly and with great judgement . . .

On one night Major O'Gorman seemed to have taken an extra glass of Usquebaugh. He left his usual place, the third bench along the gangway on the Opposition side, and walking up the centre of the House, took post on the second bench opposite Disraeli, who was speaking on some very serious subject. Major O'Gorman uttered, at intervals, inarticulate sounds of a baffling description. These seemed to upset Disraeli completely: after a while he said, 'This House admits every peculiarity of human nature, from Pitt to Rory

265

O'More.' He intended to fix on the Major a nickname. It fell perfectly flat: it was not accepted by the House.[33]

Joseph Gillis Biggar

Joseph Gillis Biggar (1828–90), the son of a merchant who was also a chairman of the Ulster Bank, was educated in Belfast and became a merchant there himself. He was Chairman of the Belfast Water Commissioners (1869–72) and was MP successively for the County of Cavan (1874–85) and the West division of County Cavan, from 1885 until his death. He was one of the ugliest men in the House and the father of obstruction, although he was also immensely respectful towards the forms of the House once the guillotine had been introduced. Born a Presbyterian, it is said that he converted to the Catholic faith in 1877 with the specific intent of irking his sister. His *Dictionary of National Biography* entry accorded him a dubious distinction: 'Probably no member with less qualifications for public speaking ever occupied so much of the time of the House of Commons.'[34]

Michael MacDonagh, *Irish Life and Character* (1898)

Once in a way, Biggar showed some trace of the pawky humour of the Scoto-Irish race from which he sprang. After he had made himself hoarse with three hours' speaking, consisting chiefly of readings from Blue Books, the Speaker, hoping to bring him to a close, intimated that he really could not hear what the hon. member was saying. 'Quite right, Mr Speaker,' was the bland response; 'the acoustic properties of this House are something shocking. I will come nearer.' And, gathering up his Blue Books and documents, Biggar cheerfully trotted off to the front Opposition Bench, and, to oblige Mr Speaker, began his oration all over again *da capo*.

He was, without exception, the most fearless man I ever met. Others, greatly fearing, might defy their fears; to him there was no merit in fearlessness, inasmuch as the sensation of fear was simply inconceivable, like a missing sense of smell. When he 'espied strangers' on an historic occasion, for the purpose of having the Prince of Wales turned out of the Gallery, he enjoyed the looks of rage and hate darted at him from the eyes of five hundred horrified colleagues, as another man would enjoy a fine wine. It was business, and not in the least a mere elfish delight in worrying the Prince, as slow-witted Englishmen supposed. In later and happier years, when it was equally good business for Ireland, he walked into the Lobby with a beaming face to vote an addition of £30,000 a year to the Prince's income.

A far more severe trial of his patriotism was to relinquish obstruction when obstruction had done its work. The old Adam so far survived that when he himself subsided into one of the most decorous and unobtrusive supporters of the Home Rule Government, he would instruct the young men of the Party, by the half-dozen, how to block the Bills of obnoxious private members, and sit quietly chuckling, like a hen-mother over her chicks, when after midnight his catechumens, one after one, raised their hats with the fatal 'I object.'

Major O'Gorman and Joseph Gillis Biggar

Henry W. Lucy, *Memories of Eight Parliaments* (1908)

Recalling some of the figures in the motley following of Mr Butt, I find no parallel in the *personnel* of the House today.

There was Major O'Gorman, for example, a personage who seems impossible in the present prosaic Parliament. The mere appearance of the major was exceedingly striking, lending indescribable comicality to the part he played. Considerably over six feet high, stout to boot, he was more like a mountain than a man.

All sorts of stories were told about him. One was to the effect that the moment he emerged on Palace Yard, just before the House rose, there was a wild stampede of the four-wheeled cabs. The hansoms were safe, for the major could not with whatsoever manoeuvring screw himself into one. He could just manage to get into a four-wheeler. It was a serious undertaking for a one-horsed shay to get him up the hill as far as the Hotel Metropole, where he sojourned. So cabby fled lest he should be called upon.

Among the legends lingering around his name was one setting forth how, on the door of the cab being one night opened on arrival by the hotel porter, the major was found standing upright, breathless. The bottom of the conveyance had fallen through under his weight, and in order to save his life, he had to trot along at the same pace or rate of progress as the horse, fortunately not too rapid.

Another story is quite true, as I can personally testify. When Doctor Kenealy, being returned to Parliament by the electors of Stoke, took an early opportunity of moving a vote of censure on the judges, he found a teller in Mr Whalley. On the House dividing, it was found that four hundred and thirty-three men of all parties voted in the negative, Doctor Kenealy's proposition being supported by a single member. The major was the minority. Asked afterward why he had gone against his own party, for once merged in the majority, the major, mopping his massive brow, answered, 'Bedad, it's a hot night, and I knew there would be more room in the "Aye" Lobby.'

It would be difficult to quote from any of the major's speeches in the hope that the passages would account to the cold-blooded reader for the uncontrollable mirth into which he threw the House whenever, under whatever circumstances, he addressed it. I have seen Gladstone rolling about on his seat with laughter when the major was holding forth; Disraeli sitting opposite with the painfully puckered face that in latter days served him as a smile.

It was only Ireland that, in one Session of Parliament, could contribute to the same assembly Mr Joseph Gillis Biggar and the major. In later years Mr Biggar began to assume a grave, statesmanlike air, to abjure his imitation sealskin waistcoat, and to regard the Speaker with deference. On his first appearance in the House he and the major were inseparable, allies drawn together by allurement of the common instinct of 'goin' agin the Government'.

Sometimes in the obstructive divisions, the Speaker permitted himself the joke of naming the Major and Mr Biggar as tellers. Mr Biggar was a little humpbacked man, and to see him skipping up the House with the gigantic major rolling astern, like a line-of-battle ship in the trough of the Atlantic, was a delight that never palled on the appetite of the House.

Mr Biggar's waistcoat was a prominent feature in a night's proceedings. Whips and Ministers in charge of Bills, anxious for the progress of business, carefully studied the attire of the Member for Cavan, when with curious outspread gesture of his hand, as if he were hailing a bus, he tried to catch the Speaker's eye.

If his coat were allowed to fall in ordinary fashion over the waistcoat, things were moderately well. If it were thrown back and a wide expanse of yellow stuff visible, things were queer. The equivalent to hoisting the South Cone was found when Mr Biggar addressed the House with his coat recklessly thrown back, a thumb in each armhole, exposing the whole breadth of the waistcoat.

❖

The suspension of 37 Members

Henry W. Lucy, A *Diary of Two Parliaments* (1886)

February 3, 1885. That the Government were aware that something remarkable would happen in the House of Commons tonight is certain. Arrangements of an unprecedented character had been made with the object of keeping order. Large bodies of police were distributed throughout the building. Half a hundred stood at ease in the Court Yard, and at a signal through the telegraph wires an additional hundred would have marched down from Scotland Yard. What was less explicable was the extraordinary gathering of strangers, 'distinguished' and otherwise. The galleries over the clock are now always filled. Time was when to see this part of the House crowded from front bench to ceiling was a subject of comment. Now it is a matter of every-day occurrence, and it is easier for a rich man to get into the kingdom of heaven than for any one less than an Ambassador to gain entrance into the Speaker's gallery. Tonight the seats, to which admission is gained by ticket, were crammed. The peers' gallery, which sometimes presents vacancies striking amid the throng, was also full, so full that Royalty, in the person of the Duke of Cambridge, stood forlornly in the doorway. The Royal Princesses who came down at half-past five to see the commencement of the comedy were more fortunate. The ladies' gallery is divided into two sections, one open to the orders of members, and the other the private domain of the Speaker. The Duchess of Connaught and the Duchess of Edinburgh found no difficulty in securing places on the front bench, the only part of the ladies' gallery from which the House can be viewed. They found on their arrival Mrs Gladstone already seated; and presently Lady Granville arriving completed the distinguished party of four.

The questions on the paper passed over without incident. When they were concluded, Mr Parnell, rising without notice, abruptly asked the Home Secretary whether it was true that at one o'clock today Mr Davitt had been arrested. This question, conveying to many members the first intimation of the fact, was received with some cheers, which were repeated and prolonged when the Home Secretary answered, 'Yes, sir!' When silence was restored, Sir W. Harcourt went on to state that he and the Irish Chief Secretary had come to the conclusion that Mr Davitt's conduct had been incompatible with the ticket-of-leave by which, as a convict, he was permitted to be at large. Renewed cheers broke forth from the general body of the House, through which cries of 'Shame!' came from the Irish quarter. Mr Parnell asked which condition of his ticket-of-leave Mr Davitt had violated. This request for further information was met by cries of 'No!' from the Ministerialists, and Sir W. Harcourt sat unresponsive. Mr Parnell jumping up again excitedly, the Speaker, half rising from his chair, motioned to Mr Gladstone, who advanced to the table and commenced to move the Resolutions amending the Standing Orders of which he had given notice.

He had not advanced many sentences when Mr Dillon rose, and was greeted with loud cries of 'Order!' The Speaker said Mr Gladstone was in possession of the House, and called upon him to proceed, he having, in accordance with the custom of the House, resumed his seat when Mr Dillon rose, presumably on a point of order. Mr Dillon, who also resumed his seat when the Speaker rose, now again stood up. Three members thus simultaneously presented themselves to the notice of the House—the Premier at the table, Mr Dillon in his place, and the Speaker before the chair. Mr Gladstone, paying deference to the Speaker, again resumed his seat, leaving Mr Dillon confronting the right hon. gentleman. Loud cries of 'Chair!' 'Order!' broke forth from all parts of the House, while Mr Dillon stood with folded arms silent amongst the clamour.

The House presently grew very quiet, waiting for what might follow on this strange and unprecedented scene. The Speaker was still on his feet, and Mr Dillon still stood with folded arms below the gangway. Some members cried 'Name! Name!' whilst from the Irish members there came a low, persistent chorus of 'Point of order! Point of order!' The Speaker named Mr Dillon as being guilty of wilful and persistent obstruction, and a piece of paper which Ministers now find necessary to have in readiness was passed along the Treasury bench till it reached the hand of Mr Gladstone. The Premier rising, and reciting from the manuscript before him, moved in due course that Mr Dillon be suspended. The Speaker put the question to the House, and it was answered by a loud cry of 'Aye!' followed by some shouts of 'No!' from the Irish members. All this time Mr Dillon was standing with folded arms gazing upon the House, the only silent man in the assembly. Mr Cowen, crossing over to him, appeared to offer some counsel, which was supported by Mr Labouchere, the result of which apparently followed when Mr Dillon sat down. Mr Sullivan remaining seated, and, taking off his hat, called out at the top of his voice, 'Mr Dillon rose to a point of order. I object to the division.'

The Speaker issued the customary order to clear the House for the division. For some moments the Irish members remained seated, but after consultation rose and left the House.

Owing to the numbers being so greatly in excess on one side, the division took a long time. When the tellers came to the table it was announced that 395 had voted 'Aye!' and 33 'No!' The Speaker having recited the figures called upon Mr Dillon to withdraw. Mr Dillon replied that he respectfully declined to withdraw. This defiance being repeated, the Speaker called upon the Sergeant-at-Arms to advance. A scene of extraordinary excitement now followed. The Sergeant-at-Arms stood at the corner of the gangway waiting for Mr Dillon to surrender himself. Mr Sullivan was shouting out from his place, 'On a point of order,' an exclamation met by angry cries that he also should be 'named'. Mr Dillon still declining to withdraw except force were used, the Sergeant-at-Arms beckoned in a number of attendants, at sight of whom Mr Dillon rising, consented to go, and walked out amid some cheering from the Ministerialists, and cries of 'Shame!' and 'Cowards!' from the Irish members. As soon as he was gone Mr Sullivan, rising, 'respectfully submitted' that in the case of Mr Bradlaugh debate had been permitted on the question that he be suspended. But the Speaker explained that in that case there had been no order of the House such as he now acted upon. Mr Dillon had defied the authority of the Chair, and in accordance with a standing order had been suspended. Mr Sullivan attempting to continue the contest, the Speaker quietly said, 'The point of order is disposed of; I now call upon Mr Gladstone to proceed.' Mr Gladstone approached the table, The O'Donoghue jumping up to move the adjournment of the debate.

The Speaker ruled Mr Gladstone was in possession of the House, whereupon Mr Parnell, rising amid cheers from the Irish members, moved that Mr Gladstone be not heard. The Speaker again calling upon Mr Gladstone, Mr Parnell shouted out, 'I insist upon my motion being put.' The Speaker having warned Mr Parnell that his conduct was wilfully obstructive, again called on Mr Gladstone, who had not proceeded beyond his first sentence when Mr Parnell, rising again, excitedly insisted upon his right to be heard.

'I name Mr Parnell as disregarding the authority of the Chair,' said the Speaker, and Mr Gladstone moved his suspension.

The House was again cleared for the division, Liberals and Conservatives walking out in the usual manner; but the Irish members remained seated, Mr

R. Power, the whip, walking round and round as a shepherd's dog guards a flock of sheep. The majority were a long time clearing out, members lingering in the passages to watch the result of this new proceeding. Having communicated with the Irish members, Lord Richard Grosvenor, approaching the table, reported to the Speaker that certain members declined to leave the House. Mr Sullivan shouted out, 'We contest the legality of the proceeding.' The Speaker quietly answered that if members did not go into the division lobby their votes could not be counted. After a brief pause the Sergeant-at-Arms was directed to open the door of the 'Aye' lobby, and the majority came pouring in. In this division 405 voted for the suspension of Mr Parnell and 7 against. The figures being announced, the Speaker reported to the House that certain members having challenged the division, declined to leave and that their votes had not been recorded. He then called upon Mr Parnell to withdraw, an invitation which that gentleman, always 'respectfully' declined. The Sergeant-at-Arms was then ordered to remove him. Mr Parnell declining to retire except by superior force, four assistants were called in, at the sight of whom his scruples vanished, and he at once rose and left the House amid cheers from the Irish party.

Once more Mr Gladstone approached the table. His voice betrayed traces of the physical exhaustion from which he was suffering, and it was with some difficulty he was heard. His purpose now was to take note of the fact reported by the Speaker, as to the refusal of certain members to leave the chamber when the division was called, and to assure him of the support of the House in preserving its order. He then reverted to his speech, and had got through a few words when Mr Finigan rose and moved that he be not heard. The Speaker, proceeding more quickly now as he grew accustomed to the work, promptly 'named' Mr Finigan, and Mr Gladstone with equal celerity moved that he be suspended.

The House dividing, the Irish members kept their seats as before, the circumstance being reported in the same way to the Speaker by Lord Richard Grosvenor. The Speaker informed the recalcitrant members that they were disregarding the authority of the Chair, and directed the Assistant Clerk to take their names. This Mr Milman did amid profound silence, just broken by the sound of the distant murmur of the majority penned up in the Aye Lobby. In this division 405 voted for the suspension, and two against. Lord Richard Grosvenor reported the names of the members who had remained seated in defiance of the Speaker's order. But before this was dealt with Mr Finigan had to be disposed of, and the Sergeant-at-Arms went through the same process as in the case of Mr Parnell. The Speaker then reverted to the case of the Irish members, 37 in all, who had refused to leave the House.

Mr Balfour and Mr Gorst, eager in the cause of order, wanted to know whether these gentlemen could be dealt with *en bloc*, or whether it would be necessary to divide on each expulsion. From this prospect the House shrank with undisguised apprehension, and the Speaker proceeded to put the question, being interrupted by a cry from one Irish member of 'No Law!' and the despairing answer from another, 'No; it's all over.' The House dividing, 410 voted for the suspension of the members named and 6 against. The Speaker then called upon Mr Barry, whose name was first on the list, to retire. Mr Barry, echoing the formula used by Mr Parnell, declined to go except upon compulsion, which was supplied in due form.

What was to be done with Mr Leahy, puffing like a porpoise? This was the question which next presented itself. Mr Leahy is a gentleman upon whom Nature, feeling the kind necessity of making up the average in some way, has bestowed much adipose matter. He is a heavy man, not in the same sense as Mr McCoan, Dr Commins, or Mr Dawson, for he rarely speaks. But now his opportunity has come, and Ireland, proud of her patriots, might the next morning be thrilled with admiration of the great deeds done by this, one amongst the most silent of her sons. Captain Gosset,[35] already a little 'blown' with manifold marching and counter-marching, resulting in the arrest of twenty of the Parnellites, looked with critical eye upon the twenty-first. In the last few years the Sergeant-at-Arms has had his experience of humanity considerably enlarged. He has brought up to the Bar a railway contractor, two printers, and one attorney, severally charged with offences against the high privileges of Parliament. He has arrested Mr Plimsoll's saltatory movements, and conducted him, still waltzing, beyond the Bar. He has brought up Mr Bradlaugh, and more than once has had occasion to sally forth from his chair, and by strategic movements interrupt that gentleman's unauthorised advance towards the table. But he never had anything to do with a person so large as Mr Leahy. Would he go? and if not, could he be carried?

Mr Leahy himself had evidently made up his mind to make the most of his natural advantages. A fine expression of scorn mantled his massive features as he looked towards the Sergeant-at-Arms and the posse of attendants, some grown grey in the State service, others evidently out of condition with sitting up all night. Ireland should know that there were other patriots in the party besides Mr Parnell, other defiers of the decencies of debate in addition to Mr Dillon, other breakers of Parliamentary law beyond Mr Biggar. Mr Leahy had been weighed in the balance, and he knew he should not be found wanting. If they had a crane handy nothing would be left for him but submission. But as yet a crane has not been introduced into the machinery of Parliamentary procedure, and in its absence Mr Leahy felt he could safely defy any of the 'superior force' which his colleagues in more or less elegant phrase had severally declared was the only thing that, on their conscience, they could yield to.

In an unfortunate moment for his possible fame Mr Leahy began to con a little speech, so that nothing should be lacking to his triumph in this new Parliamentary warfare. If he had been content to rise and say, 'Mr Speaker, Sir: I respectfully beg to inform this hon. House that the last time I was weighed the beam kicked at nineteen stone,' he would have carried dismay into the cohorts of Ministerialists and Opposition, now combined in hateful conspiracy against unhappy Ireland. But that was not the sort of thing his colleagues were saying. It is true they all began 'respectfully', but thereafter branched off into some lines of blank verse, in which Liberty, Freedom, Tyranny, and things of that sort figured in large capitals. Mr Leahy felt he must do something in the same way, and the effort was fatal. The unwonted movement in his mind paralysed his control over his body, and having struggled through a sentence, faithfully modelled on Mr Parnell's, he, to his infinite surprise and profound disgust, found himself standing in the Lobby, whither he had unconsciously walked at the mere invitation of the Sergeant-at-Arms. Opportunity comes to a man but once in his life. Mr Leahy had had his, and it was gone.

After this the House saw with a smile the Rev. Mr Nelson clinging to the post at the cross benches. No one quite knows what Mr Nelson does in this *galère*. But since his congregation have spared him from the pulpit the House would gladly welcome him in the forum. He is evidently an honest man, though politics are not precisely his *forte*. He does not speak nearly so often as he would be gladly heard, the loquacity of his colleagues in the representation of Ireland leaving no opening for him, nor indeed for any one else. But when he has found his opportunity, the House has witnessed with amazement his tendency towards gymnastics. He literally dances round his subject, as wrestlers walk round each other, seeking for advantage in the grip. His favourite bench is the front one below the gangway, whence he rose tonight, and whence, when he does succeed in catching the Speaker's eye, members flee in trepidation. It is said that Mr Nelson is the only man in the House of whom Mr Gorst is afraid, or at sight of whom pirouetting in the convulsions of oratory the cheek of Lord Randolph Churchill grows pale. The House has seen Mr Nelson performing a speech, and when it beheld him throw his arm round the post, lean his head back, and look defiantly in the face of Captain Gosset, nothing less was expected than that in the course of the next few moments a portion of the cross benches, with Mr Nelson attached, would be carried out of the House. But it was only the rev. gentleman's playfulness. No sooner, at signal from the Sergeant, had there arrived the four attendants ('whose united ages', as paragraphs in the *Times* occasionally put it, would have 'amounted to 260 years'), than Nelson shirked this new Trafalgar, hauled down his flag, and went out.

It was from this very place that Mr Biggar had been taken early in the proceedings, which, in accordance with precedent, had been carried on in alphabetical order. It was Mr Biggar who insisted upon that show of force which thereafter accompanied the Sergeant-at-Arms. Mr Biggar had declared that nothing but superior force would justify to himself his leaving the House. He did not recognise it in the presence of the Sergeant-at-Arms. If he must needs go, he would have the full paraphernalia of force; and to observe him carefully counting the number of men at the Sergeant's command was one of the finest episodes in the long drama. Mr Metge, a gentleman of whom no one has heard of before, now distinguished himself by the length of his valedictory address, and the determination with which he sat back in his seat and threatened active resistance. But he went without being carried, and so did Mr Redmond, on whom the fates were a little hard. Never before has it happened to a duly-elected member of Parliament that he should take the oath and his seat at a quarter to six on Wednesday evening and be expelled at eight o'clock on the following Thursday.

Had The O'Gorman Mahon turned recalcitrant the executive power would have had a tough job, seeing that, though he lacks the flesh of Mr Leahy, he is large in bone and long in limb. Moreover, his experience in warfare is so varied and extensive that he would have been able to meet whatever form of attack had been decided upon. A man who has not only been general of an army but admiral of a fleet is not so easy to be taken either at point of the bayonet or by an attack of boarders. Moreover, The Mahon has in his day pinked his man, nay many men. He has been 'out' oftener than any of his contemporaries, except, perhaps, M. Paul de Cassagnac. No one could say that when the Sergeant-at-Arms approached him he might not pull out of his coat-tail pocket a case of pistols, and drawing out of one of his boots a pair of jewel-hilted daggers, offer Captain Gosset his choice of weapons. But The O'Gorman Mahon had had a surfeit of glory of that kind. Now what he hankered after was oratorical fame. He has been in the House more Sessions than one, and as yet had not made his mark as an orator. Like a modest gentleman, he had been content to devote the earliest years of his return to Parliament to studying the manners of the new generation. Few men are alive now of those with whom he sat in Parliaments of yore. New men, new manners, oratorical and otherwise, and The O'Gorman Mahon has been content to cruise about, dropping anywhere where anchorage was possible, and where there was opportunity of studying some new orator. Sometimes he is to be found on the front Opposition bench, sometimes on that behind, occasionally below the gangway amongst his colleagues, still more often on the bench opposite.

It was here he had his famous conflict with a gentleman who objected to the redundancy of his cheering. The O'Gorman Mahon, fixing his interlocutor with a stately stare, rose, walked across the House to the bench opposite, and having vainly endeavoured to induce some of his friends to convey his 'cyard' to the gentleman, he himself returned and handed it. This incident, and the fact that nothing came of the cartel, did not discourage The O'Gorman Mahon in his search after knowledge. Now his opportunity was come, and he felt glad that he had spent all this time in study. Rising to his full height, which is over six feet, and stretching out his hand, he began with leisurely intonation,

'Tis fifty years ago—'

This, considering the hour of the evening, was a promising exordium, though it smacked a little of paraphrase from *Waverley*. An autobiography of the gallant Colonel commencing at the date named would have been interesting; but the

Speaker thought the time inopportune, and at a signal from him the Sergeant-at-Arms advanced, and the amazed Mahon, who had revived on the seaboard of South America the traditions of that Elizabethan era which Lord Salisbury recently mourned, walked out by the side of the Sergeant-at-Arms as a sheep goes to the slaughter.

But all was not over yet, though eight o'clock had struck and the scene had been prolonged over three hours. Mr Molloy, having escaped inclusion in the general indictment, had an expulsion all to himself. This done, Mr Gladstone again attempted to make his speech, when Mr O'Kelly rose and moved that he be no longer heard. Mr O'Kelly was dispatched with a celerity possible only after extended experience. He was named by the Speaker, and the motion of suspension put from the Chair. Mr R. Power challenged a division, but, being unable to tame tellers, the resolution was declared carried, and Mr O'Kelly was conducted to the door. Again Mr Gladstone rose; and now Mr O'Donnell, unfortunately absent when the performance began, hastened to associate himself with the expelled members by moving that Mr Gladstone be not heard. Mr O'Donnell was distinguished by having a division taken in his case, when one vote (Major Nolan's) was lodged in protest against the resolution, 311 voting for it. Two more 'lives' remained in this curious Parliamentary game—Mr R. Power and Mr O'Shaughnessy, who succeeded in obtaining their expulsion by the less discourteous method of remaining seated whilst the division was taken in Mr O'Donnell's case, and, being named as disorderly, were suspended.

All this had taken three hours and a half, and it was in an almost empty and altogether weary House that the Premier, himself scarcely able to stand, at length commenced to make his speech, with some apparent prospect of being able to finish it. All traces of weariness passed away as he continued, and before he had finished he had added another to the long list of his triumphs of oratory. The peroration in which he appealed to the House to uphold its dignity and traditions was exceedingly fine, and drew forth enthusiastic cheers, not only from Liberals, but from Tories who perhaps never cheered Mr Gladstone before.

❖

Balfour beards an Irish Member

Sir Alfred E. Pease, Diary, August 8, 1889

I led off in an hour's speech on the vote for Resident Magistrates (Irish Estimates). My attack was directed against the 'Coercion RMs', generally known as Balfour's 'Removables', being specially appointed to carry out Coercion, and who held their posts at Balfour's pleasure. They were in a different category to other RMs, who were permanent. The contrast between the sentences given by one class and those of the other was very great. I singled out one 'Removable' as an example for outrageous conduct in a judicial capacity. He had been a paid lecturer of the party previous to this job. I reviewed the genesis of the enmity to our rule and laws, and cited terrible instances in connection with the clearance of estates. Balfour listened to me attentively throughout, and then proceeded to lecture me, after telling me that for a speech of such violence he had never known such mildness of tone and absence of action. After spending an hour shouting and gesticulating at me, and denouncing my conduct in collecting facts, I thought on the whole he had treated me more fairly than he usually does his opponents, and he at any rate paid me the compliment of saying later that mine was 'the only important contribution to the debate'.

In the course of his speech Balfour charged Edward Harrington with having called the police 'uniformed bloodhounds'. Harrington jumped up, pale with rage, and demanded Balfour's authority for this. Balfour declined to give it, and shook his fist as Harrington. At this Harrington went into a tearing rage, flung his hat on the floor, and was actually 'going for' Balfour had not his Irish friends forcibly held him back. It is one of Balfour's amusements to tell a thumping lie about an Irish MP, pay no heed whatever to any contradiction, and when pressed for authority to just smile and wave a hand about, and when the Irish blood is up he is satisfied. In the papers will be 'Another Irish Row'. 'Disgraceful conduct of Irish MPs.' It is very curious why they allow themselves to be drawn like this, but even our Old Hand Gladstone is easily drawn by Churchill, who only does it to amuse himself.

'T.P.' prevents an anti-Catholic speech

John Pius Boland (1870–1958) was the son of a Dublin banker and miller. He was educated at the Oratory School in Birmingham, at London University, and at Christ Church, Oxford. He was called to the bar in 1897 and sat as Nationalist MP for Kerry from 1900 to 1918 (he was a Whip from 1906). He was later General-Secretary of the Catholic Truth Society (1926–47).

John Boland, *Irishman's Day* (1944)

The right to pillory the Tory government for its actions on Dursey island, off the coast of County Cork, had been gained earlier in the day. Now that the time had arrived, the drama of the situation lay in the undisclosed background of the picture. As in all dramatic situations, there was a central figure. This was 'X', a North of Ireland Unionist member. After years of balloting he had won the privilege of speaking on a subject of his own choice. He had days, if not weeks, to prepare his speech, nurse it, coddle it, chuckle in advance over his most telling points. He could see his supporters in his own constituency reading greedily every word of his attack on monastic and conventual institutions. Nay, more. Everyone in England or Scotland who had been brought up on the so-called revelations of Maria Monk, and on tales of walled-up nuns, would lap up every word that fell from his lips. What matter that seventy years ago, and in every year that had passed since then, Maria Monk's inventions had been thoroughly discredited and exploded, that the myth of the walled-up nun had been conclusively shattered! The anti-Catholic prejudice which had always been sedulously fostered as one of the political weapons against Home Rule was there. It formed a hard core of the population which refused to listen to, or even read, refutations of the slanders. To such he was to have spoken.

It was the chance of a lifetime. Two hours of Parliamentary time absolutely at his disposal. Weekly papers of his own way of thinking holding columns of space for his words of denunciation. But it was not to happen. His own hours of glory were snatched from him, and he was left with just a despairing hope that some few precious minutes might be spared to him. Relentlessly, right up to the stroke of the clock which marked the end of the evening sitting, Dursey island held the field, and not a word could be said about Catholic convents. Not till he succeeded again, after years of waiting for success in another ballot, could he hope to fight in the House of Commons against Home Rule for Ireland with such despicable weapons.

And to make matters worse for 'X' (I suppress his name, but it may be found in *Hansard*, 4th Series, Vol. 145, col. 871), the debate which now took the place of his was not on a great imperial subject. If it were, that might have tempered to some extent his sense of defeat. And all this strictly in accord with the rules of his own House of Commons, just because 'a definite matter of urgent public importance' took precedence of any matter already set down for debate on that particular evening sitting. It was a triumph for the leaders of the Irish party because of their unrivalled knowledge of Parliamentary procedure, and that his defeat should have come from us filled the cup of bitterness for 'X' to the full.

T.P. O'Connor, member for the Scotland Division of Liverpool, was known to all as 'T.P.' (You would be sure to raise a titter if you referred to him in debate, by an intentional mistake, as the honourable member for 'Scotland Yard'.) He was in his best form this evening. He had an established position as one of the best journalists of his generation. The London evening paper, *The Star*, which he had founded, held a commanding position. As an orator, he had a splendid delivery, knew how to mingle grave with gay, and, whilst keeping within the rules of order, could talk on any political topic for any required length of time. (Later he was to become 'Father' of the House, i.e., the member who held the same constituency longer than any member then in the Commons.) At this time he shared with John Redmond and John Dillon a commanding position in our party deliberations, gained not only by his long service (he had been in the House since the late 'seventies) but because of his intimate knowledge of all English political parties. Kindly by nature, and open-hearted, he was the spokesman, above all, for the Irish in England, Scotland, and Wales. This Dursey island episode appealed to every instinct in his nature.

But let T.P. himself speak: 'The island consisted largely of rock. There was not a single rood of land cultivated upon it that had not been laboriously won from rocky stone. There were practically no roads on the island, there was not a farmer's cart... The loads had to be carried on the backs of donkeys or mules, or on baskets on either side of the animal, and when the people had to convey their cows to the fairs or markets on the adjoining mainland they did not employ cattle vessels or boats, but the animals had to swim across.

'There were twenty-five families on the island... What they really lived on was fishing, and if he wanted to appeal to the emotions of the House and to the feeling of humanity which he believed pervaded it, he would ask them to have some sympathy for this little cluster of islanders who earned every penny with which they purchased tea and bread for the maintenance of their children at the risk of their lives on one of the most tempestuous parts of the coast...

'On a day in April an astonishing spectacle was seen. There were off the coast two ships of the British Navy, carrying over 200 police... They effected a landing. It was the first time in history the British Fleet had made a successful landing on the island of Dursey. Other explorers had tried, many admirals had risked their reputations in the great enterprise, but the fact that this was the first time a landing had been made would always mark the present Chief Secretary's administration...

'He came now to the case of Daniel Healy. This Daniel Healy had the large fortune of four cows and a farm the extent of which was forty or fifty acres and its valuation £12 per annum... It used to be rented at £13, but a previous agent reduced it to £9 15s. Daniel Healy owed four years' rent, or £39 in all, and that was the argument for this great expedition...

'There was an English point of view. This invasion of the island of Dursey would cost a considerable amount of money. To enforce a debt of about £39 not less than £700 had been expended... He would like to know who sanctioned the employment of the ships of the nation for this purpose. Were they to understand that the landlords and the police of Ireland were so omnipotent that they were able to employ the ships of the State without consulting the Admiralty?'

Half an hour, three-quarters of an hour, and still T.P. was going strong. 'X', with his eyes on the clock, saw his chances of talking about the horrors of monastic and conventual institutions ebbing away. At last T.P. sat down, to be followed by another of our men. And by another. And by another. Then Walter Long, the Irish Chief Secretary, who had succeeded George Wyndham, made the best defence he could of the aid given for the eviction of Daniel Healy. A division. And time was up.

Healy lambasts the Tory Government

Tim Healy was the Independent Nationalist MP for Louth-North: he stood as an anti-Parnellite at the general elections of 1892 and 1895. A barrister, he was a master of the minutiae of Irish land legislation.

David Lloyd George, Letter to his family, August 12, 1890

We were at it until 3 o'clock this morning. Healy spoke about twenty times. On one occasion he held the House for a hour and ³/₄s but he delivered such a sparkling, savage speech that scarcely one man dropped out of his place. It was a very brilliant affair. He attacked the Government for sending some General Lintorn Simmons to Rome to negotiate some mysterious business with the Pope. He was sent there presumably to settle some difficulty about Maltese marriages but Healy would have it that he was dispatched there to induce the Pope to use his influence with the Irish Catholics to abandon the Nationalist leaders. He was frightfully biting. Lintorn Simmons he called all sorts of hideous names, 'this ecclesiastical horse soldier' was one of the mildest of them. 'This clumsy diplomatist' was another. He broke the rules of propriety which are so stringent in the House but it was very amusing. There is a psalm-singing Wesleyan on the Tory side—the only Wesleyan on that side—a fellow who is always at Church and missionary meetings. Healy called him the 'honourable and *pious* member for Boston'. The Chairman very angrily pulled him up but the House roared with delight at this impudent sally. He referred to the Under-Secretary, a sanctimonious-looking Scotch Protestant, as 'sleeping with Foxe's *Book of Martyrs* under his pillow'. A more impudent, audacious speech has hardly been delivered ever with impunity within these walls. The Celts are having their revenge upon the brutal Saxon.

Dr Tanner plays a trick on a troublesome English Member

Dr Charles Tanner (1849–1901) was born in Cork, the son of a captain in the Dragoons. He was educated at Paris; at Winchester; at Queen's College, Cork; and at the University of Leipzig and Berlin. He was a physician to various hospitals in his home town and was elected Mayor of Cork in 1890. He became MP for Cork Mid in 1885 and kept the seat until his death. He later joined the anti-Parnellite wing of the Irish Nationalist Party.

Arthur Brookfield (1853–1940), the victim of this practical joke, was educated at Rugby, and at Jesus College, Cambridge. He was a lieutenant in the Hussars from 1873 to 1880 and sat as a Conservative from 1885 until, owing to financial difficulties, he took the Chiltern Hundreds in 1903, thereafter joining the consular service. He went back to fight in the Boer War and was British Consul for Danzig (1903–10) and Savannah (1910–23).

Tim Healy, *Letters and Leaders of My Day* (1928)

During the debates of 1893, Michael Davitt, then a new Member of the House, met with an interruption from Mr Brookfield (brother of the actor), who objected to his speaking from notes. Davitt's loss of an arm caused an awkward manipulation of his notes, and this doubtless led to the charge that he was reading his speech—contrary to the practice of Parliament. Mr Speaker was reluctant to interfere with a maiden speech, delivered under difficulties, yet he had to rule in Brookfield's favour, but his manner was kindly and his judgement suave. On subsequent days Brookfield rose several times, but did not 'catch his eye'. Irish Members were much gratified, and Dr Tanner determined to take further vengeance on him.

One night, when Brookfield had risen frequently, but in vain, Tanner sent him an imaginary letter from Mr Speaker in terms such as these:

9 p.m.

Dear Mr Brookfield,—

I regret very much that in spite of the number of times you have risen, you have failed to catch my eye. I write this to assure you that when next you get up I shall certainly call you.

Sincerely yours,
Arthur Peel.

Tanner got this delivered by one of the Speaker's attendants, and Brookfield swelled importantly. He went to his place at once, and when the previous orator finished, rose confident that he would be 'taken'. The Speaker, however, called on quite a different person, and Brookfield remained on his legs challenging possession. Sternly Mr Speaker called him to order, and bade him resume his seat. The jeers of the Irish Members, who had mustered for the comedy, were galling. He muttered an indignant protest, and sat down. Then he went round to the Chair to complain. 'You promised, sir, to call on me,' he protested.

'What!' quoth Mr Peel. 'The Chair does not bargain with Members.'

'But I have it from you in writing.'

'Never, sir.'

'But here's your letter.'

'My letter!' replied the Speaker. 'I wrote no letter.'

'Look at that,' said Brookfield, producing the document.

'A forgery, sir!' was the reply. 'I care not who is involved in it. Retire to your place!'

The Irish Members could hardly retain their convulsions. That day they talked no more.

❖

Redmond vows that Ireland will defend itself against Germany

Stephen Lucius Gwynn (1864–1950), the son of a professor of Divinity at Trinity College, Dublin, and a grandson on his mother's side of William Smith O'Brien (one of the rebels of 1848), was educated in Ireland and at Brasenose College, Oxford. Starting out as a teacher of literature, he became a journalist and a prolific author of books. He sat as Nationalist MP for Galway from 1906 to 1918.

Only a week and a day earlier, Redmond had moved an adjournment to protest at Government troops disarming the Irish Volunteers and shooting without permission upon a Dublin crowd. Memorial masses and demonstrations had followed and Ireland was a in a state of extreme tension when Redmond assured the House that his MPs would sink their differences with the Government and that Ireland would undertake to defend herself, thus enabling imperial troops to be withdrawn. If only he had left it at that, but he subsequently offered the Irish Volunteers to fight in the trenches of Flanders and France—fomenting revolt in Ireland.

Stephen Gwynn, *John Redmond's Last Years* (1919)

Then Redmond rose, and a hush of expectation went over the house. I can see it now, the crowded benches and the erect, solid figure with the massive hawk-visaged head thrown back, standing squarely at the top of the gangway. While he spoke, as during Sir Edward Grey's speech, the cheering broke out first intermittently and scattered over the House, then grew gradually universal. Sitting about me were Tory Members whom I did not know; I heard their ejaculations of bewilderment, approval and delight. But in the main body of the Unionists behind the front Opposition bench papers were being waved, and when Redmond sat down many of these men stood up to cheer him.

1. *Hansard*, 4th series, xc. 862.
2. Michael MacDonagh, *Irish Life and Character* (1898), pp. 280–1.
3. W. E. H. Lecky, *Leaders of Public Opinion in Ireland* (1903), Vol. I, p. 276.
4. Quoted in Michael MacDonagh, *Daniel O'Connell and the Story of Catholic Emancipation* (1929), p. xx.
5. Harry Graham, *The Mother of Parliaments* (1911), p. 170.
6. Patrick Howarth, *Questions in the House: The History of a Unique British Institution* (1956), pp. 181–4; *Dictionary of National Biography*, Supplement I (1901), pp. 195–6.
7. Alexander Mackintosh, *Echoes of Big Ben: A Journalist's Parliamentary Diary, 1881–1940* (1945), p. 15.
8. F. H. O'Donnell, *History of the Irish Parliamentary Party* (1910), Vol. I, p. 467.
9. William O'Brien, *Evening Memories* (1920), p. 72.
10. Herbert Gladstone, *After Thirty Years* (1928), pp. 184–5.
11. Strathearn Gordon, *Our Parliament* (1952), p. 101.
12. Benjamin Disraeli, Letter to Lady Bradford, February 1, 1881; quoted in W. F. Monypenny and G. E. Buckle, *The Life of Benjamin Disraeli, Earl of Beaconsfield* (1910–12), Vol. II, p. 1473.
13. Arthur Balfour, Letter to Lady Randolph Churchill, 1883; quoted in Lady Randolph Churchill, *Reminiscences* (1908), pp 92–3.
14. Henry W. Lucy, *A Diary of the Home Rule Parliament, 1892–1895* (1896), p. 38.
15. Justin McCarthy, Letter to Mrs Campbell Praed, March 11, 1893.
16. Sir Richard Temple, Bt., *Letters and Character Sketches from the House of Commons* (1912), edited by his son, Sir Richard Carnac Temple, Bt., pp. xv–xvi.
17. ibid., p. xvi.

18. ibid., pp. xvi–xvii.
19. O'Brien, op. cit., pp. 7–8.
20. Both anecdotes from Monypenny and Buckle, op. cit., Vol. II, p. 841.
21. Richard Cobden, Letter to George Combe, August 28, 1848.
22. Richard Cobden, Letter to George Combe, October 4, 1848.
23. John Bright, Letter to O'Donoghue, January 20, 1872; quoted in R. A. J. Walling (ed.), *The Diaries of John Bright* (1930), p. 96.
24. He would no doubt have been scandalised by the tribute paid to him in the House of Commons after his death by Justin McCarthy who, on behalf of the Irish Members, claimed 'the right to lay an Irish wreath on this great Englishman's grave'.
25. O'Donnell, op. cit., Vol. II, p. 428.
26. Michael Davitt, *The Fall of Feudalism in Ireland* (1912), p. 447.
27. C. J. O'Donnell, *Outraged Ulster* (1932), p. 49.
28. Mackintosh, op. cit., p. 70.
29. R. F. Foster, *Modern Ireland 1600–1972* (1988), p. 472.
30. C. J. O'Donnell, op. cit., p. 22.
31. Earl Winterton, *Orders of the Day* (1953), p. 11.
32. Milesian: after Milo, the ancient Roman mob leader.
33. Sir William Fraser, *Disraeli and his Day* (1891), pp. 425–7.
34. *Dictionary of National Biography*, Supplement I (1901), pp. 195–6.
35. Captain Gosset was the Serjeant-at-Arms.

7 Fear and Failure

> To this Bill Mr Zacharias Locke began to speak, but for
> very fear shook, so that he could not proceed, but stood
> still a while, and at length sat down.
>
> Heywood Townshend, *Historical Collections, or an*
> *exact account of the Proceedings of the last four*
> *Parliaments of Queen Elizabeth* (1682),
> December 2, 1601

> Sir John Guise spoke also in this debate, in which he
> was not very short neither, but it was difficult to
> perceive, whether he was for, or against, the Bill.
>
> Anchitell Grey, *Debates of the House of Commons,*
> *1667–94* (1769), February 10, 1693

Macaulay wrote of the House of Commons that there 'is not a more terrible audience in the world' and Disraeli called it 'the most chilling and nerve-destroying audience in the world'.[1] Part of the reason for this, according to such witnesses as H. G. Wells and A. P. Herbert, is the peculiar arrangement of the Chamber and the freedom of other MPs to come and go as they please.

Returned for Liskeard in 1774, Edward Gibbon sat for eight sessions without uttering a word. 'Timidity was fortified by pride,' he later explained in his *Autobiography*, 'and even the success of my pen discouraged the trial of my voice.' In a letter to a friend, he wrote: 'I am still a mute: it is more tremendous than I imagined; the great speakers fill me with despair, the bad ones with terror.'[2] Another man of accomplishments, Francis Horner, confessed to having a 'dread of finding it an effort above me, to discuss a large subject in public after many speakers, and with numerous details and arguments to manage'.[3] He put down his failure to speak often to 'an idle history of indolence, fastidiousness, dread of failure, etc.'.

Sir Egerton Brydges, who entered the House 'on the verge of fifty years', felt it was too late in life for him to take to oratory: 'My natural shyness and timidity were overcome with so much difficulty that I seldom spoke, but hundreds of times sat with a palpitating heart till I lost my turn, and let others in succession rise before me till it was too late.'[4] William Lambton explained in a speech that when he addressed the House 'he found himself in a state of trepidation, somewhat like a man half seas over';[5] while Sir John Pakington once told Sir William Fraser: 'Whatever a man may go through in life, he will tell you that he has never had such a trial of his nerves as the second time he rises to speak in the House of Commons. The first time he does not know what is coming: the second is awful!'[6]

Mark Boyd relates an anecdote about Richard Jones, the comedian, who was paid three hundred guineas by a peer to tutor his son in the art of addressing Parliament. Jones rehearsed the peer's son several times in his studio, sitting in a pulpit and pretending to be the Speaker. The peer's son conquered his fears and 'within a few years became a Cabinet Minister and one of our ablest debaters'.[7]

Gladstone, in his early years in Parliament, sought inspiration from his Creator in overcoming his fear and was a stern self-critic: 'Spoke on the Irish church—under forty minutes. I cannot help here recording that this matter of speaking is really my strongest religious exercise. On all occasions, and today especially, was forced upon me the humiliating sense of my inability to exercise my reason in the face of the H. of C., and of the necessity of my utterly failing, unless God gave me the strength and language. It was after all a poor performance, but would have been poorer had He never been in my thoughts as a present and powerful aid . . . to hold in serene contemplative action the mental faculties in the turbid excitement of debate, so as to see truth clearly and set it forth such as it is, this I cannot attain to.'[8]

Although he had a reputation as a demagogue, John Bright was another nervous speaker. 'I suppose I ought to be ashamed of myself,' he remarked, 'but the fact is I never rise in the House without a trembling at the knees and a secret wish that somebody else would catch the Speaker's eye and enable me to sit down again.'[9] Lord Randolph Churchill, 'unsuspected as the fact may be, never, even in his most audacious days, got over that feeling of House of Commons fright which to the last possessed Mr Bright'.[10]

Fear does not necessarily depart once an MP attains high office. Lloyd George always found addressing the House of Commons unnerving, though he was able to conquer his fear and achieve many triumphs. Ramsay MacDonald—never a scintillating speaker—expressed anxiety in diary entries about his performances at the dispatch box. 'Fit but with feeling of coming flop . . . would I were a Winston Churchill so that I might express adequately my disgust with myself.' And on another occasion: 'Trying to get something clear into my head for the H. of C. tomorrow. Cannot be done. Like man flying in mist: can fly all right but cannot see the course . . . Tomorrow there will be another "vague" speech impossible to follow and as usual with these attacks of head and eyes no sleep tonight.' Indeed, the prospect was matched by the performance: 'Thoroughly bad speech. Could not get my way at all. The Creator might have devised more humane means for punishing me for overdrive and reckless use of body.'[11] Macmillan, though a more successful House of Commons performer than MacDonald, was no happier: 'Repeatedly he confessed that, on a question day, or before a major speech, he would feel physically sick and seldom eat anything,' his biographer Alistair Horne has written.[12] Consequently, he never lunched out on question day. The secret of his parliamentary skill was 'never to give in, never to show how nervous and awful the whole business is . . . I think I did seem to have what was called unflappability—if only they knew how one's inside was flapping all the time, they wouldn't have said that . . .'[13]

There have been other causes of failure than fear, of course. In Anthony Trollope's novel *The Way We Live Now* (1875), the financial speculator Augustus Melmotte makes a fool of himself when he rises to speak for the first time. He is ignorant of the rules of procedure, calls another Member by his surname, forgets to remove his hat, and makes a speech of only a couple of sentences before finding himself at a loss for words. His performance produces 'a violent ebullition of laughter from both sides of the House'. Ignorance of parliamentary ritual was the reason for the failure of Sir Wilfrid Lawson's début in 1860, because he attempted to deliver his maiden speech at around the start of the dinner hour and the House decided to shout him down. 'When he spoke his words were drowned in the storm,' wrote William White, 'and bursts of laughter met his patient and imploring looks.'[14]

Describing a debate in a letter to his brother, Lloyd George wrote that an MP called Richmond 'mixed up his notes and evidently had lost a few sheets. This so distracted him that he floundered and had to sit down without delivering a third of his speech. He repeated himself, made many efforts to recover himself—at last he came to his peroration and sat down.'[15]

Otherwise, over-eagerness combined with self-regard can be a fatal combination. Sir Robert Wilson, a former soldier and the MP for Southwark from 1818 to 1831, failed because he 'would speak for the mere sake of speaking. He introduced every species of topics. The consequence was that he set the House against him, and I very much feared a general coughing would ensue. It was solely his want of judgement in timing ill his speech, for his manner and voice were good, and if the occasion had called for his saying anything, I am sure he would have succeeded; but it was so evident that he got up to make *a* speech, that it failed entirely.'[16]

Some fail through misapplication, because they do not render unto the House that portion of their souls which it feels it deserves. This was Harold Nicolson's self-estimation of failure: 'A Scottish debate in the House. I like these family affairs. What a good Parliamentarian was lost in me! I am too busy with other interests to give to the House that passion for trivialities, that constant assertion of an individual point of view, which leads to power. I feel sometimes that my failure is due entirely to myself. I have had every opportunity and have missed them.'[17]

Bores are failures, yet inevitably they are fearless. The parliamentary correspondent Henry Lucy noted that former Indian statesmen tended to fail, citing the examples of Sir George Balfour, Sir George Campbell and Sir Richard Temple.[18] Balfour's rising was greeted with 'the roar of " 'Vide! 'Vide! 'Vide!" ', Campbell combined a surfeit of information with a comical, rasping voice, and Temple arrived in the House aged fifty-nine, too old for the House to learn to appreciate him. 'Those who have entered after forty, and gained renown,' another MP has reflected, 'can be counted on the fingers of one hand.'[19] Lawyers, also, have tended to be failures. Again, Lucy cites Sir Horace Davey, Sir Charles Russell, Sir Richard Webster and Sir John Rigby. A Chancery barrister who heard the mocking cry of 'Rigby! Rigby!' towards the end of the debate on the Home Rule Bill one night in 1893 commented on the oddity of that fact that 'a man who can any day earn a hundred guineas by fees at the Bar should be a laughing-stock in the House of Commons'.[20]

Brilliance in other fields was no guarantee of success in an MP. According to the sketch-writer E. M. Whitty, the two principal failures in the 1852–3 session were also the 'two most brilliant Irishmen of the day': Whiteside and George Henry Moore. Whiteside was a brilliant advocate at the Irish bar who 'imported his polemical zeal into the Senate' and 'made one-third of the House of Commons his enemies for life'; Moore was 'so full of talent that he has no room for tact' and 'repudiates the knack of the House of Commons, and is elaborate, ornate, polished, brilliant—and is not listened to'.[21]

Even politicians marked out for leadership, who were generally liked, have sometimes failed to inspire. In December 1943 'Chips' Channon wrote how 'Anthony Eden, smartly dressed, delivered a pretty travelogue which interested nobody particularly. He has not got the gift of holding the House, and there was little wit, humour or eloquence in his tedious description of the momentous meetings in Teheran and Cairo. After twenty minutes Members got up, and began to trickle out.'[22]

Joseph Addison

Joseph Addison (1672–1719) was educated at Amesbury, Salisbury and Lichfield grammar schools, and at Charterhouse, before going up to Queen's College, Oxford. He gained fame as a Whig poet and essayist, writing for the *Tatler* and *Spectator*. He was MP for Lostwithiel (1708–9), and for Malmesbury from 1710 to 1719, but never spoke in the House after his first attempt when he was so frightened by the cries of 'Hear him! Hear him!' that he collapsed back on to the bench. This did not prevent him from reaching high office, as Macaulay explains.

Thomas Babington Macaulay, *Edinburgh Review*, July 1843

Addison sat for Malmesbury in the House of Commons which was elected in 1708. But the House of Commons was not the field for him; the bashfulness of his nature made his wit and eloquence useless in debate. He once rose, but could not overcome his diffidence, and ever after remained silent. Nobody can think it strange that a great writer should fail as a speaker; but many, probably, will think it strange that Addison's failure as a speaker should have had no unfavourable effect on his success as a politician. In our time a man of high rank and great fortune might, though speaking very little and very ill, hold a considerable post; but it would now be inconceivable that he should in a few years become successively Under-Secretary of State, Chief Secretary for Ireland, and Secretary of State, without some oratorical talent. Addison, without high birth, and with little property, rose to a post which dukes—the heads of the great houses of Talbot, Russell, and Bentinck—have thought it an honour to fill. Without opening his lips in debate, he rose to a post the highest that Chatham or Fox ever reached; and this he did before he had been nine years in Parliament.

A prime minister's son

Frederick North (1766–1827) was the third son of Lord North, 2nd Earl of Guilford. He was educated at Eton and at Christ Church, Oxford, where he became a passionate philhellene. He travelled to the Greek islands and was received into the Orthodox Church. His father died in his absence and he inherited the family borough seat of Banbury from his eldest brother, George, who became the 3rd Earl. He was in the House for about sixteen months and left to become a diplomat, first in Corsica, and later as the first Governor of Ceylon. He eventually succeeded as 5th Earl, though he spent the last years of his life as Chancellor of the University of the Ionian Islands, in Corfu.

Frederick North, quoted in J. S. Harford, *Recollections of William Wilberforce* (1864)

I once attempted to speak in Parliament, and it was not unnatural when I rose that my family name should at once fix every eye upon me. I brought out two or three sentences, when a mist seemed to rise before my eyes. I then lost my recollection, and could see nothing but the Speaker's wig, which swelled and swelled and swelled till it covered the whole House. I then sank back on my seat and never attempted another speech, but quickly accepted the Chiltern Hundreds, assured that Parliament was not my vocation.

Sylvester Douglas

Sylvester Douglas (1743–1823), Baron Glenbervie, was born in Aberdeen, and educated at the Universities of Aberdeen and Edinburgh, and at Leyden, before embarking on a continental tour. He was called to the bar in 1776 and specialised in controverted election cases. In 1789 he married Lord North's ugly though witty daughter, Katherine, and in 1793 he became a KC. He was MP for four seats between 1795 and 1806 and, though originally a Whig, held various minor ministerial posts under Pitt, culminating in the governorship of the Cape of Good Hope—he was sworn in, and given an Irish peerage to enhance his status, but Pitt fell before he had left and so he sought and obtained the post of joint Paymaster-General instead, while retaining his title. In 1802 he secured the lucrative post of Surveyor-General of Woods and Forests.

Sylvester Douglas, Journal, December 26, 1794

I have of late got rid of a great weight which had remained on my mind, by the very ill success of a speech I made in Parliament soon after I had taken my seat. I had not before spoken in the House of Commons unless once or twice when Thomas Grenville brought in his Bill to amend certain parts of the election judicature. When Mr Jekyll made his motion concerning the recall of Lord Fitzwilliam, I thought it my duty to repel as well as I could the censure, which Jekyll, Fox and others had for the sake of their argument bestowed on Lord Westmorland's Government. I was, I own, glad too of such a very fair opportunity of making an experiment of myself in the English House of Commons.

I was in a manner a new speaker, who is always treated with indulgence. I was from a laudable sentiment undertaking the defence of an administration and of measures which belonged to a period prior to my Secretaryship, so that I had no personal motive. Yet I was heard with decisive marks of disapprobation and impatience. My voice was drowned very early by the cry of 'Question— Question,' repeated with unusual vociferation; and with a great deal of abridgement and all the confusion of mind arising from strong mortification, I found it very difficult to give anything like an appearance of method and regular argument and conclusion to my speech. Not a friend or acquaintance came near me after this circumstance had happened and men whose good nature or habits lead them to be very fertile in topics of consolation on such occasions did not make any attempt to comfort me.

I believe, indeed, the House as well as the public had become heartily tired of the subject, the Opposition hardly knowing how to treat it. They wished to regain Lord Fitzwilliam, but he was not yet ripe to conviction by them on the heads of the war, French principles, and parliamentary reform, and his conduct had been too manifestly rash and weak to furnish them with plausible grounds for his defence on his proceedings either in Ireland or towards his colleagues in England, or for any very successful attack on the unavoidable measure of his recall. The line, too, which I had thought fit for me to pursue, namely, an enumeration of advantages which Ireland had reaped under the administration of Lord Westmorland, was naturally uninteresting to the great majority of the English House of Commons. All these things are true, but still I am persuaded that if my task was not such as I could expect would in its performance secure much attention or applause, it failed in securing any degree either of the one or the other, and chiefly, I believe, from the awkward and inefficient manner in which I performed it.

This failure left a very strong and very disagreeable impression on my mind, which certainly tended much to unfit me by some more successful effort to recover the ground which I was so conscious I had lost, and which, however, I was determined to attempt.

❖

Sir Samuel Romilly

Sir Samuel Romilly (1757–1818) was the son of a Soho jeweller and was educated at Mr Flack's, London. He was articled in 1773 and called to the bar in 1783, developing a strong Chancery practice and becoming a KC in 1800. In 1806 he entered Parliament as a Whig MP and was immediately made Solicitor-General and knighted, though he was never a Minister again after the Whigs lost office in April 1807. During his career he sat for six different boroughs, and was a consistent advocate of reform of the criminal code. Within a few days of his wife's death in 1818, he cut his own throat.

Diary of Parliamentary Life, April 9, 1807
Memoirs of the Life of Sir Samuel Romilly (1840)

My speech upon the whole was a very bad one, and was by no means favourably received by the House. I felt mortified and chagrined to the utmost degree. I have this Session, upon some occasions, particularly on the Slave Trade, and in my reply to the Master of the Rolls on the Assets Bill, spoken with very great success, and met with very great applause. I have received compliments without number, and some very extravagant ones; but all the gratification which my vanity may have had upon these occasions would be much more than compensated for by one tenth part of the mortification which the coldness and the appearance which I thought I plainly discovered of the House beginning to be tired of me, have given me. One or two expressions in my speech, which I think were very foolish, have haunted my memory ever since I sat down. It will be long, I think, before I shall venture to speak again.

Lord Byron

Journal, November 1813

I have declined presenting the Debtors' Petition, being sick of parliamentary mummeries. I have spoken thrice; but I doubt my ever becoming an orator. My first was liked; the second and third—I don't know whether they succeeded or not. I have never yet set to it *con amore*;—one must have some excuse to one's self for laziness, or inability, or both, and this is mine. 'Company, villainous company, hath been the spoil of me';—and then, I have drunk medicines, not to make me love others, but certainly enough to hate myself.

Sir William Maxwell

Sir William Maxwell (1771–1838) sat as MP for the Scottish county seat of Wigtownshire from 1805 to 1812, and later, from 1822 to 1830. An army officer by profession, he was a supporter of Pitt and subsequently of Ministers in general. Although adept at addressing a county meeting, the audience of the House of Commons apparently filled him with dread.

Mark Boyd, *Social Gleanings* (1875)

When I was a youth, I recollect Sir William dining at our home . . . and my father took the opportunity of expressing the disappointment felt throughout the county that their Member had not come out on three occasions on certain Scottish questions, in which he was so much at home.

Sir William confessed that no one felt it more than himself, as he was quite prepared each time to have addressed the House. 'Then,' said my father, 'may I ask you to account for your silence?' 'Very easily . . . it being a much lighter affair to address the lairds of the county of Wigton, in their town hall, than the commoners of the United Kingdom in St Stephen's; for I had actually caught the Speaker's eye on each occasion, but my tongue all at once seemed to cleave to the roof of my mouth, and as for rising I felt pinned to my seat as if by cobbler's wax. If, however, you and my friends here suppose it was from any neglect on *my* part, or that I was not prepared to speak, you shall, if you choose, have one or all of my non-delivered speeches forthwith.'

The offer was at once accepted, and the honourable baronet, now rising, without the embarrassment of the Speaker's wig before his eyes, delivered a most able and effective speech to the great amusement and delight of the party.

James Johnston

Michael MacDonagh, *Parliament: Its Romance; Its Comedy; Its Pathos* (1902)

In the early years of the nineteenth century a Mr James Johnston was member for Sandwich. He carefully prepared his maiden speech, and committed it to memory; but when he rose to address the House his utterance failed him completely. Again and again he essayed to speak, but in vain, for the words would not come, and he resumed his seat without having uttered a single syllable. An Irishman named Mark Supple, a celebrated Parliamentary reporter of the time, and a practical joker, had a squib in the form of a broad-sheet issued, and, as then was the fashion in London, cried through the streets of Westminster and the City. On the top of the broad-sheet appeared in large type the words: 'The maiden speech of James Johnston, Esq, MP for Sandwich, as delivered yesterday in Parliament'. The rest of the paper was blank!

Althorp and Stanley confess their fear

T. B. Macaulay, Letter to his sister Hannah, August 29, 1831

We talked about timidity in speaking. Lord Althorp said he had only just got over his apprehensions. 'I was as much afraid,' he said, 'last year as when I came into Parliament. But now I am forced to speak so often that I am quite hardened. Last Thursday I was up forty times.' I was not much surprised at this in Lord Althorp, as he is certainly one of the most modest men in existence. But I was surprised to hear Stanley say that he never rose without great uneasiness. 'My throat and lips,' he said, 'when I am going to speak, are as dry as those of a man who is going to be hanged.' Nothing can be more composed and cool than Stanley's manner. His fault is on that side. A little hesitation at the beginning of a speech is graceful, and many eminent speakers have practised it, merely in order to give the appearance of unpremeditated reply to prepared speeches; but Stanley speaks like a man who never knew what fear, or even modesty, was. Tierney, it is remarkable, who was the most ready and fluent speaker almost ever known, made a confession similar to Stanley's. He never spoke, he said, without feeling his knees knock together when he rose.

Gibson Craig

Sir William Gibson Craig, Bt. (1797–1878), was born in Scotland and became an Advocate at the Scottish bar. He was Liberal MP for the county of Edinburgh, 1837–41; and for the city of Edinburgh from 1841 until his retirement in 1852. He later served as Lord Clerk Register, 1862–78, and Keeper of the Signet for Scotland.

Benjamin Disraeli, Letter to his wife Sarah, November 21, 1837

The address was moved by Lord Leveson, a child apparently, in a rich diplomatic uniform, and seconded by Gibson Craig, a new member in a court dress. Leveson made a crammed speech like a schoolboy; Gibson Craig, of whom the Whigs had hopes, rose, stared like a stuck pig and said nothing. His friends cheered: he stammered; all cheered; then there was a dead and awful pause, and then he sat down, and that was his performance. The address was then read, and Wakley made a most Radical speech and amendment, determined to bring affairs to a crisis. He was fluent, flippant, and vulgar; a second-rate hustings orator. He was seconded by Molesworth, a most odious speaker, who wearied the House . . .

❖

A dying bird to kill

Thomas Gisborne (d. 1852) was born in Derbyshire, the son of a priest. He sat as a Reformer for Stafford in the Parliaments of 1830 and 1831, and for Derbyshire, 1832–7. He was also MP, briefly, for Carlow, 1839–40; and for Nottingham, 1843–7.

Benjamin Disraeli, Letter to his wife Sarah, January 31, 1840

Sir George Grey made a dashing House of Commons speech which I should have liked to have answered, but as he concluded about 8, and I had not dined, it was impossible. I had no intention of speaking the first night, and am very sorry I did, for, although I said some good things and was very well received, I was debarred by circumstances from making the speech I had intended. The fact is the Government put up Gisborne, who is sometimes a most rakehelly rhetorician, and produces great effects in a crowded house, but uncertain. There was and had been for some time a general rumour that he was to make a great display, and when he got up Fremantle came to me and asked me to reply to him. He began very well, but after some little time regularly broke down, was silent for some moments, sent for oranges, coughed, stuck again and again and again, and finally, pleading 'some physical inability' which had suddenly deprived him of his voice, sunk overwhelmed with his own exposure. We thought he was drunk, but the Whigs say the fault was he was not, and that when he is tipsy and is not prepared he is very good. I found, however, I had a lame bird to kill, or rather a dying one: and though I made a somewhat brilliant guerilla operation, there was not that solid tactical movement that I had originally contemplated.

The next night we had it all our own way. Howick making the most extra-ordinary announcement which you have read and alone justifies the debate. Graham very rigorous and malignant, and Macaulay plunging into the most irretrievable slough of failure you can possibly conceive; nothing could be worse—manner, matter, and spirit, ludicrously elaborate and perfectly inappro-priate. The Speaker with difficulty preserved order, and it was clear to everyone that in future Macaulay will no longer command the House, on such an occasion, and to such a personage, of course, always lenient.

Edwin James

Edwin James (d. 1882) was the son of a solicitor. He was called to the bar in 1835, made a QC in 1852, and appointed Recorder of Brighton in 1855. He obtained a seat for the borough of Marylebone in 1859, as a Reformer, but in 1861, after running up debts of £100,000, was disbarred and forced to retire from the House. Thereafter, he lived in New York for ten years.

Sir William Fraser, *Disraeli and his Day* (1891)

He was a *farceur* of the most unequivocal description. At that time Lord John Russell, who had seceded from the Whig Party, invariably sat on the end seat of the lower bench next to and below the gangway on the Opposition side. Edwin James's face, being the most blustering and brow-beating of advocates when in Court, was ghastly in the extreme: a very florid man, his countenance usually flushed, on this occasion was deadly pale: and his nervousness painful to see even by an enemy. He had arranged a carefully prepared maiden speech: a more complete fiasco the House never beheld. He began in highly declamatory style; threw his arms about with great vehemence; and went so near to striking Lord John Russell's hat, that that nobleman, obviously, to our extreme merriment, became much alarmed. Leaving his seat would indicate desertion of his supporter. Repeatedly Edwin James's right hand went close to Lord John's head, who was affecting to listen to him with great interest; his dodgings to avoid the fist were exquisite; but he was unprepared for the crushing blow that fell, not on his hat, but on Edwin James's Parliamentary prospects. As everyone knows, you address the Speaker, not the Members. In a very unconstitutional apostrophe Edwin James shouted to Lord John the words, 'No, My Lord! I tell you—' What he was about to tell Lord John we shall never know. The House had been laughing during this speech: it now burst into a roar; in the midst of which the bully collapsed.

Dr Kenealy

Edward Vaughan Hyde Kenealy (d. 1880) was educated at Trinity College, Dublin. He was called to the Irish bar in 1840, and the English bar in 1847, and was elected as MP for Stoke-on-Trent on 'Independent principles' in 1875. Because of disapproval of his methods of defence at the trial of the Tichborne claimant (Arthur Tichborne was supposedly an impostor who attempted to claim the inheritance of an aristocrat believed to have been lost at sea), no Members were prepared to introduce Kenealy to the House. The convention was that two MPs would escort him to the Table where he would bow to the Speaker, but this was waived and Kenealy approached the Table by himself. He was defeated in 1880 and died soon afterwards.

Henry W. Lucy, *Strand Magazine*, June 1899

When, in 1875, Dr Kenealy entered the House, triumphantly returned by the men of Stoke, he was an undoubted power in the land. I remember Mr Adam, then Opposition Whip, showing me an appalling list of constituencies, some held by Liberals, some held by Conservatives, common in the peculiarity that if a vacancy occurred the next day Kenealy could return his nominee. He was conscious of his power, and meant to make the House of Commons feel its influence. The crowded benches that attended his utterances furnished flattering testimony to his power and the interest excited by his personality.

On the occasion of his first appearance, the House was filled as it had not been since critical divisions on the Irish Land Bill, or the Irish Church Bill, of the preceding Parliament. Amongst the spectators from the galleries over the clock were the Prince of Wales, Prince Christian, and the ex-King of Naples, at the time a visitor to London. Mr Evelyn Ashley, at the safe distance of the Isle of Wight, had been saying something about Kenealy, who made it a question of privilege. In this speech was set that gem of oratory remembered long after the rest is forgotten.

'Of one thing I am certain,' said Kenealy, in deep chest-notes, wagging his hands and his fore-finger, as through many days of the Tichborne trial they had wagged at hostile witnesses and an unsympathetic judge, 'that the calumnious reflections thrown on my character will recoil on their authors. As for me, I shake them off as the lion shakes the dewdrops from his mane.'

Before his first Session closed, Kenealy flickered out like a damp torch. He tried again and again to obtain a footing in the House. Without being rudely repelled he was set back, and long before the Parliament ran its course he became a non-entity.

❖

Asquith in decline

Winston Churchill, Letter to his wife Clementine, April 22, 1911

On Thursday night the PM was very bad: and I squirmed with embarrassment. He could hardly speak: and many people noticed his condition. He continues most friendly and benevolent, and entrusts me with everything after dinner. Up till that, he is at his best—but thereafter! It is an awful pity, and only the persistent freemasonry of the House of Commons prevents a scandal. I like the old boy and admire both his intellect and his character. But what risks to run. We only got him away the other night just before Balfour began the negotiations which I conducted but which otherwise would have fallen to him—with disastrous consequences. The next day he was serene, efficient, undisturbed . . .[23]

Sir Austen Chamberlain

A. P. Herbert, *Independent Member* (1950)

Not long before he died, Sir Austen Chamberlain, to whom the whole House listened with respect, said to me: 'I never rise in the House without a sinking feeling in the pit of my stomach.' He showed the single sheet of notepaper on which were the 'notes' for a delightful speech he had just delivered. Something, I forget what, was written in large capitals across the middle. I said, 'But you didn't say anything about that, Sir?' 'No,' said the Elder Statesman, sadly, 'it was the one thing I wanted to say. So I wrote it large like that. But you know how it is. I forgot.'

Tony Crosland

Charles Anthony Raven Crosland (1918–77) was educated at Highgate School and at Trinity College, Oxford. After serving in the Royal Welch Fusiliers and the Parachute Regiment during World War II, he returned to his old college as a Fellow and as a University Lecturer in Economics. He was Labour MP for Gloucestershire South from 1950 to 1955; and for Grimsby from 1959 until his death. He entered the Cabinet as Education Secretary in 1965 and held various Cabinet posts throughout the Wilson premierships. In 1976 he succeeded James Callaghan (who had become Prime Minister) as Foreign Secretary. He was the chief intellectual proponent of democratic socialism from the mid-1950s onwards. This extract is from the biography by his second wife, the American-born journalist Susan Barnes.

Susan Crosland, *Tony Crosland* (1982)

Near the end of July, the Tories used their three Supply Days to put down their censure motions. One was that in the Labour Government's nine months of office it had failed to carry out its election pledges for a five-year programme. The Prime Minister opened the debate. Tony wound up for the Government. He was concentrating on the economic policy argument dominating Cabinet and grudged spending time on what he saw as a ritual; remembering how easy his previous winding-up speech had been, he assumed a grasp of subject was sufficient. He put aside twenty minutes to prepare the speech.

I had rarely been to the House but decided to drop in that evening, mounting the stairs to the gallery to an increasing din. This baying—it really does sound like hounds—came from the chamber, where Iain Macleod was well into the Opposition's winding-up speech, returned to his old form, waspish, savaging. Tony never got his speech off the ground. From the moment he took his place at the dispatch box the Tories jeered and shouted, stamped their feet, slapped their thighs, rocked back and forth in a manner alarming to one unfamiliar with the House of Commons. The Labour benches sat packed and silent. When the hand of the clock over the Speaker's chair somehow, eventually, reached 10, I went down to Tony's room to wait for him. Bill Rodgers came in.

'Tell Tony that nobody could have done any better in the situation. It is everyone's nightmare that they'll be caught in just such circumstances. Harold opened the debate in his most brilliant form, and he had lifted our backbenches into euphoria. The Tories were sunk in depression until Macleod fired them. After that they had no intention of letting Tony get the House under his control.'

Dick Crossman stopped in to send much the same message. So did Douglas Jay, who hadn't spoken to me for two years: adversity can effect reconciliation. They'd left when Tony appeared, poured a drink for each of us and began the post-mortem:

'The thing could be controlled at least 20 per cent by turning it into a shouting match. It's sheer technique: learning to switch from one gear to another.' The more the technique became clear to him the more regret he felt.

'Why didn't anyone on your side make some noise and try to help? Do they sit there like lumps out of a mixture of schadenfreude and genuine curiosity about how their comrade will extricate himself?'

'I didn't deserve support, the speech was so abysmal.'

Over breakfast the next morning he glanced at the papers. 'That's a good knock-on-the-head to begin the day.' He tossed me the *Daily Telegraph*; he was outclassed and there was no room at that level for an elegant lightweight, it said.

The next day, Saturday, Evelyn and Alan Taylor came for a drink. How would Alan have avoided the débâcle?

'Why do you call it a débâcle,' I asked, 'when on Thursday night it seemed to me a distressing incident?'

'It *was* a débâcle,' he replied. His self-confidence was badly shaken. Alan said that even when he was speaking five times a week and on top of his form, he still found it hard to change gear. Tony found this interesting but remained subdued when we were alone.

He discussed it with Roy Jenkins who was now becoming a master of the art of addressing the House of Commons, bringing it under his control however adverse the circumstances.

'I think of it rather as if I were in a bullfight,' Roy said. 'I try to feel the House, to play the House, like a matador playing a bull, for if you slip, it's very difficult to get up again. On a major speech to a full House I like to go on the 20:1 ratio—allow twenty times as long for the preparation of the speech as the speech itself will be.'

1. A. P. Herbert, *Independent Member* (1950), p. 34.
2. George Henry Jennings, *An Anecdotal History of the British Parliament from the Earliest Periods to the Present Time* (1880), p. 165.
3. Quoted in R. G. Thorne (ed.), *The History of Parliament: The House of Commons 1790–1820* (1986), Vol. IV, p. 240.
4. Sir Egerton Brydges, *The Autobiography of Sir Egerton Brydges, Bt.* (1834), Vol. I, pp. 252–3.
5. William Lambton, Speech, February 12, 1793; quoted in Thorne, op. cit., p. 372.
6. Sir William Fraser, *Disraeli and his Day* (1891), pp. 492–3.
7. Mark Boyd, *Reminiscences of Fifty Years* (1871), pp. 255–8.
8. John Morley, *The Life of William Ewart Gladstone* (1903), Vol. I, p. 126.
9. Herbert, op. cit., p. 45.
10. Henry W. Lucy, *A Diary of the Home Rule Parliament, 1892–1895* (1896), pp. 60–1.
11. David Marquand, *Ramsay MacDonald* (1977), pp. 698–9.
12. Alistair Horne, *Macmillan 1957–1986* (Vol II. of the Official Biography) (1989), p. 154.
13. Quoted in ibid., p. 154.
14. William White, *Illustrated Times*, March 31, 1860.
15. David Lloyd George, Letter to his brother William, February 20, 1905.
16. William Lambton, Letter to Charles Grey, January 27, 1819; quoted in Thorne, op. cit., Vol. V, p. 605.
17. Harold Nicolson, Diary, July 8, 1942.
18. *Strand Magazine*, January 1897.
19. Sir Henry Morris-Jones, *Doctor in the Whips' Room* (1955), p. 165.
20. Lucy, op. cit., p. 263.
21. E. M. Whitty, *St Stephen's in the Fifties: The Session 1852–3, A Parliamentary Retrospect* (1906), pp. 43–4.
22. Nicolson, op. cit., December 14, 1943.
23. Asquith had developed a drink problem.

8 The Bubble Reputation

We have had a most noble debate on Ireland. Burdett's
and Canning's speeches were superlative. As an object
of ambition, there is nothing to compare with such
exertions; and there was a time when my bosom burned
to achieve them; but that folly is defunct. After all they
are but an object of ambition; they convey no reality
of honour or of happiness. Falstaff and I are exactly of
the same opinion on the subject of reputation. I shall
speak as well as I can for usefulness, but not for fame;
my serious opinion being, that good woodcock shooting
is a preferable thing to glory.

Sir Thomas Fowell Buxton, Bt., Letter to a friend,
February 24, 1825

'Be in your place when O'Gorman speaks,' Disraeli once advised an MP seeking a cure
for his low spirits; 'that will enliven you—if anything can.'[1] When 'the word, "O'Gorman
is up", flew through the Palace, the diner dropped his knife and fork, the smoker his
cigar, the reader his book or newspaper, and from dining-room, smoking-room, and
library the crowd came rushing into the Chamber to catch the mellow thunder of the
brogue and the random pearls of speech from the lips of the Major'.[2] Lord Willoughby
de Broke considered 'the filling of an empty House at the beginning of his speech' to
be the mark of a parliamentary celebrity. 'The name of the speaker is posted in the
other rooms in the building, and if members, directly they see his name on the tape,
leave their game of chess, throw away their cigars and rush into the House to listen to
him, you may be sure that he is not far from achieving a first-class Parliamentary
reputation.'[3]

The ability to enthral, enlighten or entertain the House, whether by a leading light
or a lesser light, is a certain guarantee of a parliamentary reputation. Justin McCarthy,
for example, remembered the impression made by the Radical backbencher Joseph
Cowen: 'No one who heard him deliver his first great speech in the House of Commons—
it was during the debate on the Empress of India Bill—is ever likely to forget the
sensation it created.'[4] And of another Radical maverick, John Arthur Roebuck, he
wrote: 'No man was listened to with more attention in the House of Commons, for,
although he had no claim to the higher qualities of oratory, he always spoke in a clear,
cutting style, that chipped its way into the attention of the listener, and kept him
constantly on the watch, as one might watch the movement of a sculptor's chisel . . . it
always seemed to me that Roebuck's consciousness of his own ability was enough for

him, and that he needed no other satisfaction . . . To make a clever speech was its own reward for him.'[5]

Brilliance is not an essential prerequisite for a parliamentary celebrity if other qualities are present: for example, honesty, moral authority, or courage. Special physical attributes have also been helpful. Pitt the Elder, Sheridan and Gladstone were all said to have terrible eyes, which could reduce some Members to quivering wrecks; while Palmerston's 'dexterous hemming and hawing . . . made his audience sympathetically anxious to help the struggle of the honest advocate of a sound cause against the disadvantage of his own oratorical defects'.[6] Disraeli is customarily renowned for his oratorical brilliance, but it was his commonsense and psychological shrewdness which impressed Sir William Fraser: 'So far from there being any assumption of superiority, or of surpassing virtue, he appeared to wish to make the House believe that he was not in any way, morally, nor intellectually better than any one of them; that the comments which he was making were those of an astute advocate: and that he neither more nor less pretended to be right, than a lawyer who is pleading upon the facts which he brings before you.'[7]

Sir Robert Peel noted that his rival Canning 'would often, before rising in his place, make a sort of lounging tour of the House, listening to the tone of the observations which the previous debate had excited, so that at last, when he himself spoke, he seemed to a large part of his audience to be merely giving a striking form to their own thoughts'.[8] Peel himself must have taken this observation to heart, for he was not a natural performer in any other context than the Commons, as Disraeli pointed out: 'This remarkable man, who in private life was constrained, and often awkward, who could never address a public meeting or make an after-dinner speech without being ill at ease, and generally saying something stilted, or even a little ridiculous, in the senate was the readiest, easiest, most flexible and adroit of men. He played upon the House of Commons, as on an old fiddle.'[9]

Another seemingly aloof figure, Lord John Russell, nonetheless gained an impressive reputation. 'The frigid voice, the didactic tone, the reserved gesture—consisting of catlike and cautiously placing his hand on the table, and slowly withdrawing it—are very repulsive to a stranger, who cannot understand how that cold nature got a leadership,' wrote the sketch-writer E. M. Whitty. 'But Lord John Russell is essentially a House of Commons hero: deeply imbued with the tone of the place, bred up in all its knacks and mannerisms, and as an orator, in the House of Commons sense, keeping parties together—he still holds the first place.'[10]

Two parliamentary celebrities of quite different character who have mastered the House in the twentieth century were David Lloyd George and Stanley Baldwin. Lloyd George was a chancer whose silver tongue, cunning and mental acuity enabled him to survive many a travail, while Baldwin's instinctive feel for the popular mind meant that he could often pre-empt parliamentary opinion. 'He is a difficult man to corner,' wrote Sir Almeric Fitzroy of Lloyd George in November 1917, 'especially in the House of Commons, which he knows with the instinct of an old virtuoso for his favourite instrument. Last night he reaped the reward of sheer parliamentary talent.'[11] When Lloyd George managed to get himself out of a scrape in 1917, Asquith described his speech as 'part whitewash, part balderdash', but, as one observer recalled, 'the tremendous cheering at the end showed that he had won another round in the Parliamentary ring'.[12] Baldwin had an uncanny aptitude for divining how MPs would think after returning from a weekend in their constituencies. His biographer G. M. Young once said to him, 'I believe you were the only man on Friday who knew what the House of Commons would be thinking on Monday.' Baldwin had replied, 'I have always believed in the weekend. But how they do it I don't know. I suppose they talk to the stationmaster.'[13]

Oliver Cromwell

Oliver Cromwell (1599–1658) was the son of a Huntingdonshire landowner and MP, and the cousin of John Hampden, the great parliamentarian. He sat as MP for Huntingdon in the parliament of 1628–9 as well as in both the Short Parliament of 1640 and the Long Parliament. During the Civil War he distinguished himself as a military commander, leading the New Model Army to victory. He brought Charles I to trial and obtained the signatures for his death warrant. He then subdued the Irish and Scots and later dissolved the Rump of the Long Parliament in 1653, establishing himself as Protector. He was convicted posthumously of high treason and his body was disinterred and hung from the gallows at Tyburn.

Sir Philip Warwick (1609–83) was the oldest son of the organist of Westminster Abbey and the Chapel Royal, and was educated at Eton. He entered the service of courtiers such as Lord Goring and Bishop Juxon (Lord Treasurer from 1636 to 1641) and sat in the Long Parliament, voting against the Bill of Attainder which led to Strafford's execution. During the Civil War, he fought in the royal cause at Edgehill, sat in the Oxford Parliament, and later served as Charles I's secretary. Throughout the Protectorate he hoped for a reconciliation between the Presbyterians and the royalists, and in December 1659 he negotiated on the King's behalf. After the Restoration he became MP for Westminster and served for over twenty years, holding various minor offices.

Sir Philip Warwick, *Memoirs of the Reign of Charles I* (1701)

The first time that ever I took notice of him was in the very beginning of the Parliament held in November, 1640, when I vainly thought myself a courtly young gentleman, for we courtiers valued ourselves much upon our good clothes. I came one morning into the House well clad, and perceived a gentleman speaking, whom I knew not, very ordinarily apparelled, for it was a plain cloth suit, which seemed to have been made by an ill country tailor. His linen was plain, and not very clean; and I remember a speck or two of blood upon his little band, which was not much larger than his collar. His hat was without a hat-band; his stature was of a good size; his sword stuck close to his side, his countenance swollen and reddish, his voice sharp and untunable, and his eloquence full of fervour. For the subject-matter would not bear much of reason, it being on behalf of a servant of Mr Prynne's who had dispersed libels against the Queen for dancing, and suchlike innocent and courtly sports; and he aggravated the imprisonment of this man by the Council-table unto that height that one would have believed the very Government itself had been in great danger by it.

William Pitt, Earl of Chatham

Joseph Cradock (1742–1826) was born at Leicester, but moved to London as a young man where he became a man of letters and a friend of the actor-manager David Garrick.

Joseph Cradock, *Literary and Miscellaneous Memoirs* (1826)

I once was very near to his Lordship when he was in the utmost danger of his life; it was on the opening of Parliament, about the time that Wilkes was so popular, and number Forty-five was displayed in every street; a long debate was expected, after his Majesty's Speech had been delivered, in consequence of the Middlesex Election having been set aside. Confusion might then be said to be at its height, for the mob had broke into the passage that leads to the Throne; his Majesty was just robed, and was proceeding from the closet, when many of us were pressed directly forwards; and with our clothes torn were absolutely thrown into the House. Lord Carlisle, seeing my distress, most kindly recognised me, and made room for me between himself and another nobleman; but no more could be made out concerning Lord Mansfield, till we heard that he had safely escaped at the opposite entrance. After his Majesty had finished his most gracious Speech, he retired, and intruders made every effort to follow, but found it impossible, and as candles were then lighted, I became less alarmed, and was assured I might remain quiet till the commencement of the debates; however, through favour or necessity, I staid in the House to hear the whole of them. I felt myself but little interested till the nobleman that sat next me got up to speak, and then I perceived that it was the great Lord Chatham, whom I had never seen but as Mr Pitt, and was not in the least aware to whom I was indebted for much civility and condescension. He arose, and spoke; but I by no means recognised the complete orator I had formerly so greatly admired, and indeed was never much more disappointed; he spoke only for a short time, was confused, and seemed greatly disconcerted, and then suddenly turning to me, asked, whether I had ever heard him speak before? 'Not in this House, my lord,' was my direct reply. 'In no House, Sir,' says he, 'I hope, have I ever been so disgraced myself; I feel quite ill, and have been alarmed and annoyed this morning before I arrived; I scarce know what I have been talking about.' I could only bow and look civil; for, to say the truth, I could not sincerely declare that I was of an opposite opinion. I still wished only to get away; but as the debates grew more interesting, I became more reconciled to my intrusive situation, and I was confidently assured that no notice would then be taken.

One nobleman was uncommonly keen and sarcastic, and directed some invective with great warmth personally against Lord Chatham; when, feeling himself stung to the quick, he suddenly arose, and poured forth a torrent of eloquence that utterly astonished; the change was inconceivable, the fire had kindled, and we were all electrified with his energy and excellence. At length he seemed quite exhausted, and as he sat down, with great frankness shook me by the hand, and seemed personally to recollect me, and I then ventured to say, 'I hope now your Lordship is fully satisfied?' 'Yes, Sir,' replied he, with a smile, 'I think I have now redeemed my credit.'

T. B. Macaulay, 'William Pitt, Earl of Chatham', *Edinburgh Review*, January 1834

He was no speaker of set speeches. His few prepared discourses were complete failures. The elaborate panegyric which he pronounced on General Wolfe was considered as the very worst of all his performances. 'No man,' says a critic who had often heard him, 'ever knew so little what he was going to say.' Indeed his facility amounted almost to a vice. He was not the master, but the slave of his own speech. So little self-command had he when once he felt the impulse, that he did not like to take part in a debate when his mind was full of an important secret of state. 'I must sit still,' he once said to Lord Shelburne on such an occasion; 'for when once I am up, every thing that is in my mind comes out.'

Yet he was not a great debater. That he should not have been so when first he entered the House of Commons is not strange. Scarcely any person has ever become so without long practice, and many failures. It was by slow degrees, as Burke said, that the late Mr Fox became the most brilliant and powerful debater that ever lived. Mr Fox himself attributed his own success to the resolution which he formed when very young, of speaking, well or ill, at least once every night. 'During five whole sessions,' he used to say, 'I spoke every night but one; and I regret only that I did not speak on that night too.' Indeed, with the exception of Mr Stanley, whose knowledge of the science of parliamentary defence resembles an instinct, it would be difficult to name any eminent debater who has not made himself a master of his art at the expense of his audience.

But as long as this art is one which even the ablest men have seldom acquired without long practice, so it is one which men of respectable abilities, with assiduous and intrepid practice, seldom fail to acquire. It is singular that in such an art, Pitt, a man of splendid talents, of great fluency, of great boldness, a man whose whole life was passed in parliamentary conflict, a man who, during several years, was the leading minister of the Crown in the House of Commons, should never have attained to high excellence. He spoke without premeditation; but his speech followed the course of his own thoughts and not the course of the previous discussion. He could, indeed, treasure up in his memory some detached expression of a hostile orator, and make it the text for lively ridicule or solemn reprehension. Some of the most celebrated bursts of his eloquence were called forth by an unguarded word, a laugh, or a cheer. But this was the only sort of reply in which he appears to have excelled. He was perhaps the only great English orator who did not think it any advantage to have the last word, and who generally spoke by choice before his most formidable opponents. His merit was almost entirely rhetorical. He did not succeed either in exposition or in refutation; but his speeches abounded with lively illustrations, striking apothegms, well-told anecdotes, happy allusions, passionate appeals. His invective and sarcasm were terrific. Perhaps no English orator was ever so much feared.

But that which gave most effect to his declamation was the air of sincerity, of vehement feeling, of moral elevation, which belonged to all that he said. His style was not always in the purest taste. Several contemporary judges pronounced it too florid. Walpole, in the midst of the rapturous eulogy which he pronounces on one of Pitt's greatest orations, owns that some of the metaphors were too forced. Some of Pitt's quotations and classical stories are too trite for a clever schoolboy. But these were niceties for which the audience cared little. The enthusiasm of the orator infected all who heard him; his ardour and his noble bearing put fire into the most frigid conceit, and gave dignity to the most puerile allusion.

The antagonist whom William Pitt first encountered, on his entering into public life (after having served in the Blues), was the veteran Walpole, who instinctively dreaded him the moment he heard his voice, and exclaimed, 'We must muzzle that terrible cornet of horse!'[14]

Henry Brougham, *Historical Sketches of Statesmen Who Flourished in the Time of George III* (1839)

In his earlier time, his whole manner is represented as having been beyond conception animated and imposing. Indeed, the things which he effected principally by means of it, or at least which nothing but a most striking and commanding tone could have made it possible to attempt, almost exceed belief. Some of these sallies are, indeed, examples of that approach made ludicrous by the sublime which has been charged upon him as a prevailing fault. It is related that once, in the House of Commons, he began a speech with the words, 'Sugar, Mr Speaker,'—and then, observing a smile to pervade the audience, he paused, looked fiercely around, and with a loud voice, rising in its notes and welling into vehement anger, he is said to have pronounced again the word 'Sugar!' three times; and having thus quelled the House, and extinguished every appearance of levity or laughter, turned round and disdainfully asked, 'Who will laugh at sugar now?'

Colonel Barré

Colonel Isaac Barré (1726–1802) was the son of a Huguenot merchant who had emigrated to Dublin. He was educated at Trinity College, Dublin, and joined the British Army, serving with General Wolfe in Canada, losing an eye at the Battle of Quebec, and returning to England with endorsements from Wolfe which gained him the rank of lieutenant-colonel. Under the patronage of the Earl of Shelburne, he was returned in the Whig interest for Chipping Wycombe in 1761, where he sat until 1764, thereafter sitting for Calne from 1774 to 1790. Although upon his début, described below by Walpole, he excoriated Pitt the Elder, he later joined administrations headed by Pitt (as the Earl of Chatham). He wished to regulate the East India Company and was opposed to the taxation policies which drove the American colonies to rebellion. His style was theatrical. 'In his younger days,' wrote Horace Walpole, 'he had acted plays with so much applause that it was said Garrick had offered him a thousand pounds a year to come upon the stage.'[15]

Horace Walpole, *Memoirs of the Reign of King George III* (1845)

My ear was struck with sounds I had little been accustomed to of late, virulent abuse on the last reign and from a voice unknown to me. I turned, and saw a face equally new; a black, robust man, of a military figure, rather hard-favoured than not young, with a peculiar distortion on one side of his face, which it seems was owing to a bullet lodged loosely in his cheek, and which gave a savage glare to one eye. What I less expected from his appearance was very classic and eloquent diction, and as determined boldness as if accustomed to harangue in that place. He told the House that in the late King's reign we had been governed solely by Hanoverian measures and councils; and . . . he proceeded with the same vociferous spirit to censure all ministers but Lord Bute; and for Mr Pitt, who was not present, he reserved the appellation of a profligate minister, who had thrust himself into power on the shoulders of the mob.

Robert Symmers, Letter to Andrew Mitchell, May 14, 1762

Colonel Barré set out in a flaming, scurrilous speech as usual, but was discountenanced by the House. Many gentlemen as soon as he rose went out of the House; many of those who stayed shuffled about from their places, talked with one another, coughed, and would not hear him. And as he proceeded to talk in an unbecoming manner of the late King, abusing him for his German measures, Lord Barrington rose up and called him to order.

Charles Townshend

Charles Townshend (1725–67) was the grandson of Charles, 2nd Viscount Townshend. He became an MP in 1747 and later served as a Lord of the Admiralty and, under Chatham, as Chancellor of the Exchequer, in which capacity he introduced the taxes that drove the American colonies to seek independence. His 'champagne speech', as it became known, was his greatest moment in Parliament.

Horace Walpole, Memorandum, May 8, 1767

Charles Townshend had come to the House with a black silk hanging over his wounded eye, which in the warmth of the debate he turned aside, and discovered two very small slips of sticking-plaster over and below his eye, not amounting to more than scratches. In the beginning of the day he made a fine speech, in which he said he hoped his behaviour in the conduct of the transaction with the East India Company had wiped out the levities and imperfections of his former life; and he magnified his own firmness in having borne and overborne much reproach and contradiction, which he insinuated to have received from Lord Chatham, whom he had not seen during the winter. At four o'clock he left the House, though the management of the day depended on him; and taking one or two members with him, he went to dinner. His presence growing absolutely necessary, Mr Conway sent for him. He returned about eight, as Mr Grenville was speaking; after whom Townshend rose, half drunk, and made the most extravagantly fine speech that ever was heard. It lasted an hour, with torrents of wit, ridicule, vanity, lies, and beautiful language. Not a word was premeditated, yet every sentence teemed with various allusions and metaphors, and every period was complete, correct, and harmonious. His variety of tones and gesticulation surpassed the best actor in comedy, yet the faltering of his pronunciation from liquor, and the buffoonery of his humour and mimicry, would not have been suffered in high comedy. Nothing had given occasion to his speech, and there was no occasion on which it would not have been as proper, or, to say truth, as improper; for if anything could exceed his parts, it was his indiscretion. He meant to please everybody and exalt himself; but lest he should not enough distinguish the latter, he took care to overturn all he had done to effect the former. The whole of his speech was diverting to every man that hated any set of men; it was impertinent and offensive to all it described or seemed to compliment; and was most painful to those who had any love for him. The purport seemed to be an intention of recommending Lord Rockingham's party for ministers, with himself at the head of them; complimenting but sneering at Grenville, and slightly noticing Conway. But lest the great families whom he adopted should assume too much, he ridiculed the incompetence of birth and high blood, cried up the sole advantage of abilities and experience, and informed those he protected that rank was not talents, and that they must wait till ripened, and not come to government as if forced in a hot-bed. The most injurious part fell on the crown, he stating the mischiefs of the late so frequent changes, calling for restitution of the first post in administration to the House of Commons, and treating the actual ministry as no longer existent. Government, he said, must not continue to be what he himself was always called, a weathercock.

Nobody but he could have made that speech; and nobody but he would have made [it], if they could. It was at once a proof that his abilities were superior to those of all men, and his judgement below that of any man. It showed him capable of being, and unfit to be, First Minister. Yet though it was rather the tittle-tattle of a coffee-house, and the flower of table eloquence, still was it the confusion of affected and laboured oratory. Nature in him made sport with rules and meditation; and half a bottle of champagne, poured on genuine genius, had kindled this wonderful blaze.

The House was in a roar of rapture, and some clapped their hands with ecstasy, like audience in a theatre. Nor was it the least striking circumstance of this speech, that, laying his hand on his heart, he called God to witness that he had not been made privy to the business of the day. Fourteen of the ministerial managers, who then were actually sitting round him, had concerted with him at the motion at Townshend's own house that very morning, and were thunderstruck at his madness and effrontery; and when Conway, the moment he concluded, asked him how he could utter such a falsehood, he thought it the most favourable way of recommending the business to the House.

In this speech, he beat the Lord Chatham in language, Burke in metaphors, Grenville in presumption, Rigby in impudence, himself in folly, and everybody in good humour; for he pleased while he provoked at random; was malicious to nobody, cheerful to all; and if his speech was received with delight, it was only remembered with pity.

Charles James Fox

Charles James Fox (1749–1806) was third son of the 1st Lord Holland and was educated at Wandsworth School, at Eton, and at Hertford College, Oxford. He became an MP at the age of nineteen, sitting for Midhurst. Within two years of entering Parliament he was given office as a junior lord of the Admiralty. He supported Lord North's administration, but resigned over North's policy towards the American colonies. He held the post of Secretary of State for Foreign Affairs three times: once in 1782, then in 1783 when he formed a coalition with North, and again, following the death of Pitt, in 1806, though he himself died within a few months. A champion of liberal causes, he supported the French Revolution and opposed the war with France.

Lord Erskine, Letter to J. Wright,[16] May 1, 1815

This extraordinary person, then, in rising generally to speak, had evidently no more premeditated the particular language he should employ, nor frequently the illustrations and images by which he should discuss and enforce his subject, than he had contemplated the hour he was to die; and his exalted merit as a debater in parliament did not therefore consist in the length, variety, or roundness of his periods, but in the truth and vigour of his conceptions; in the depth and extent of his information; in the retentive powers of his memory, which enabled him to keep in constant view not only all he had formerly read and reflected on, but every thing said at the moment, and even at other times, by the various persons whose arguments he was to answer; in the faculty of spreading out his matter so clearly to the grasp of his own mind, as to render it impossible he should ever fail in the utmost clearness and distinctness to others;—in the exuberant fertility of his invention; which spontaneously brought forth his ideas at the moment, in every possible shape by which the understanding might sit in the most accurate judgement upon them; whilst, instead of seeking afterwards to enforce them by cold, premeditated illustrations or by episodes, which, however beautiful, only distract attention, he was accustomed to repass his subject, not *methodically*, but in the most *unforeseen* and fascinating review, enlightening every part of it, and binding even his adversaries in a kind of spell for the moment, of involuntary assent.

The reader must certainly not expect to be so carried away by the sketches now before me. Short hand alone, secured too at the moment, against the numerous imperfections inseparable from following the career of so rapid and vehement an elocution, could have perpetuated their lustre and effect; but, still the correct, and often the animated substance remains, which preserves from oblivion more that is worthy of preservation, than by such means would apply to almost any other speaker in the world. Eloquence, which consists more in the dexterous structure of periods, and in the powers and harmony of delivery, than in the extraordinary vigour of the understanding, may be compared to a human body, not so much surpassing the dimensions of ordinary nature, as remarkable for the symmetry and beauty of its parts:—if the short hand writer, like the statuary or painter, has made no memorial of such an orator, little is left to distinguish him, but, in the most imperfect reliques of Fox's speeches, THE BONES OF A GIANT ARE TO BE DISCOVERED.

Edmund Burke

Edmund Burke (1729–97), the son of a Dublin attorney, was educated at Trinity College, Dublin, and at Middle Temple. He was Private Secretary to the Marquis of Rockingham, a Whig grandee, who helped secure him his first seat in the Commons, Wendover, from 1765 to 1774. He subsequently sat for Bristol, 1774–80; and Malton, 1780–90. He was a staunch opponent of Lord North's administration (1770–82) and held office under Shelburne and the Fox–North coalition.

Horace Walpole, Letter to the Revd William Mason, February 12, 1778

Apropos, his last Friday's parody of Burgoyne's talk with the Indians was the *chef d'oeuvre* of wit, humour, and just satire, and almost suffocated Lord North

himself with laughter; as his pathetic description of the barbarities of the Cis-
atlantic army

Drew iron tears down Barré's cheek

I wish I could give you an idea of that superlative oration. He was pressed to
print it, but says he has not time during the session. How cold, how inadequate
will be my fragment of a sketch from second, third, and thousandth hands; yet
I must send you a bit of a daub with probably even the epithets wrong or
misplaced, though each was picturesque. Well, though I can neither draw nor
colour, *invenies etiam disjecta membra*. Hurlothrumbo exhorted seventeen Indian
nations, who so far from understanding the Hurlothrumbic dialect, are probably
almost as ignorant of English; he exhorted them by the dictates of *our* holy
religion, and by their reverence for *our* constitution, to repair to his Majesty's
standard. 'Where was that?' said Burke: 'on board Lord Dunmore's ship;—and
he exhorted them (I suppose by the same divine and human laws) not to touch
the hair of the head of man, woman, or child, while living, though he was
willing to deal with them for scalps of the dead, being a nice and distinguished
judge between the scalp taken from a dead person and the head of a person
that dies of being scalped. 'Let us state this Christian exhortation and Christian
injunction,' said Burke, 'by a more family picture. Suppose there was a riot on
Tower Hill, what would the keeper of his Majesty's lions do? would he not fling
open the dens of the wild beasts, and then address them thus? 'My gentle lions,
my humane bears, my sentimental wolves, my tender-hearted hyenas, go forth;
but I exhort ye, as ye are Christians and members of a civilised society, to take
care not to hurt man, women, or child, etc., etc.' Barré's codicil was to threaten
to paste on churches this memorable talk under the injunctions of the bishops
for a fast. Governor Johnstone said he rejoiced there were no strangers in the
gallery, as Burke's speech would have excited them to tear the ministers to
pieces as they went out of the House; the ministers are much afraid of losing
their places. Eloquence, like music, is too much improved in our days to have
any of their old effects on the passions of a large audience.

James Prior, *Life of Burke* (1826)

In a new Parliament which met in May, 1784, Burke was not viewed with
much favour by many of the members. A prejudice or combination, chiefly of
the younger members of the House, was formed so strong against him, that the
moment of his rising became the signal for coughing or other symptoms of
pointed dislike, by men who had no chance of success against him in any other
manner. On one occasion, instead of threatening, like Mr Tierney when similarly assailed, to 'speak for three hours longer', he stopped short in his argument
to remark that 'he could teach a pack of hounds to yelp with more melody and

equal comprehension'. At another time, having occasion to rise with papers in his hands, a rough country gentleman, who had more ear, perhaps, for this melody of the hounds than for political discussion, exclaimed, with something of a look of despair, 'I hope the honourable gentleman does not mean to read that large bundle of papers and bore us with a long speech into the bargain.' Burke is said to have felt so much irritation that, incapable of utterance for some minutes, he ran out of the house. 'Never before,' said the facetious George Selwyn, who told the story with great effect, 'did I see the fable realised—a lion put to flight by the braying of an ass.'

William Pitt the Younger

Pitt had just concluded a treaty with the French, but his government had been replaced by a coalition between Fox and his former adversary Lord North. Despite an attack of vomiting, arising from an excessive intake of port, Pitt gave an effective performances.

William Wilberforce, quoted in George Henry Jennings, *An Anecdotal History of the British Parliament from the Earliest Periods to the Present Time* (1880)

When Pitt undertook, on February 21st, 1783, the difficult task of defending the recent peace, I well remember that he was so oppressed by a severe sick headache as to be scarcely able to hold up his head. Fox assailed him in a very able speech, in the midst of which Pitt was obliged, from actual sickness, to retire to the entry door called Solomon's Porch, behind the Speaker's chair. I seem to see him holding the door in one hand, while he yielded to his malady, and turning his ear towards the House, that, if possible, he might not lose a single sentence that Fox uttered. Never do I recollect to have witnessed such a triumph of mind over physical depression. When Fox sat down he replied to him with great ability, though with less brilliancy than usual; but on a renewal of the same discussion, a few days after, in a different form, he made one of the finest speeches ever delivered in Parliament.

Sir Nathaniel Wraxall, Bt., *Historical Memoirs of My Own Time* (1815)

Those who heard Mr Pitt . . . cannot easily forget the impression made upon his audience by a speech which might be said to unite all the powers of argument, eloquence, and impassioned declamation. He seemed to fight, indeed, as the first Caesar did at Munda, not merely for empire or for power, but for life. After defending, article by article, the treaties concluded, he finished by deprecating 'the ill-omened and baneful alliance' which had just taken place between Lord North and Fox, as teeming with pernicious effects of every kind to the country. Then reverting to the consequences which it might produce personally to himself, he professed his readiness to retire to a private station without regret. Alluding to so material an impending change in his own condition, he exclaimed—

> 'Fortuna saevo laeta negotio, et
> Ludum insolentem ludere pertinax,
> Transmutat incertos honores, Nunc mihi, nunc alii benigna.
> Laudo manentem: si celeres quatit
> Pennas, resigno quae dedit.' . . .

With a presence of mind which never forsook him, he here paused, and, conscious that the words of the Roman poet immediately following, '*Et mea virtute me involvo*', might seem to imply a higher idea of his own merit or disinterestedness than it would become him to avow, he cast his eyes on the floor. A moment or two of silence elapsed, while all attention was directed towards him from every quarter of the House. During this interval, he slowly drew his handkerchief from his pocket, passed it once or twice across his lips, and then recovering as it were from his temporary embarrassment, he added with emphasis, striking his hand on the table—

> '—probamque
> Pauperiem sine dote quaero.'

Perhaps a more masterly and beautiful piece of oratorical acting is not to be found in antiquity. Even if we suppose the whole passage to have been studied and prepared, yet the delicacy of the omission is not less admirable. I believe, however, that the lines which he cited and the one which he suppressed were all equally suggested to him by his feelings and judgement at the time. Its effect on that part of the House which perfectly understood it corresponded to its merit. But Pitt, who well knew how large a part of his audience, especially among the country gentlemen, were little conversant in the writings of the Augustan age or familiar with Horace, always displayed great caution in borrowing from these classic sources. In the lapse of nearly fourteen years that I have heard him almost daily address the House of Commons, I question if he made in all more than eight or ten citations. Fox and Sheridan, though not equally severe in that respect, yet never abused or injudiciously expossessed. Burke's enthusiasm, his exhaustless memory, and luxuriant imagination, more frequently carried him away into the times of Virgil and Cicero, while Barré usually condescended, whenever he quoted Latin, to translate for the benefit of the county members.

James Edward Harris (1778–1841), Lord FitzHarris, was the eldest son of the 1st Earl of Malmesbury, diplomat, MP and friend of Pitt's. The occasion was a debate about whether to impeach Lord Melville (who, as Harry Dundas, had formerly been Pitt's closest ally in the Commons). In his capacity as Treasurer of the Navy under Pitt's administration, Melville was unable to account for some £10,000 of public money. William Wilberforce, Pitt's great friend, excoriated Melville's conduct and the House divided with 216 for and 216 against, and Mr Speaker Abbot gave his casting vote in favour of the motion to impeach. Melville was subsequently tried by the Peers in Westminster Hall and acquitted on all ten counts of the impeachment. The result of the debate was said by some contemporaries to have hastened Pitt's demise.

Lord FitzHarris, *Lord FitzHarris's Note Book*, 1806

I have ever thought that an aiding cause of Pitt's death, certainly one that tended to shorten his existence, was the result of the proceedings against his old friend and colleague, Lord Melville. I sat wedged close to Pitt himself the night we were 216 to 216; a casting vote against us. Pitt immediately put on the little cocked hat that he was in the habit of wearing when dressed for the evening, and jammed it deeply over his forehead, and I distinctly saw the tears trickling down his cheeks. We had overheard one or two such as Colonel Wardle say they would see 'how Billy looked after it'. A few young ardent followers of Pitt, with myself, locked their arms together, and formed a circle in which he moved, I believe unconsciously, out of the House; and neither the Colonel nor his friends could approach him.

The fourth man

Sir Thomas Fowell Buxton, Bt., Letter to his father-in-law, Mr Gurney, November 1819

We have had a wonderful debate; really it has raised my idea of the capacity and ingenuity of the human mind. All the leaders spoke, and almost all outdid themselves. But Burdett stands first; his speech was absolutely the finest, and the clearest and the fairest display of masterly understanding, that ever I heard; and, with shame I ought to confess it, he did not utter a sentence to which I could not agree. Canning was second; if there be any difference between eloquence and sense, this was the difference between him and Burdett. He was exquisitely elegant, and kept the tide of reason and argument, irony, joke, invective, and declamation, flowing for nearly three hours. Plunket was third; he took hold of poor Mackintosh's argument, and griped it to death; ingenious, subtle, yet clear and bold, and putting with the most logical directness to the House the errors of his antagonist. Next came Brougham—and what do you think of a debate in which the fourth man could keep alive the attention of the House from three to five in the morning, after a twelve hours' debate.

Lord Castlereagh

Robert Stewart (1769–1822), Viscount Castlereagh, was the son of the 1st Marquis of Londonderry, and was educated at the Royal School, Armagh; then privately by a cleric; and finally at St John's College, Cambridge. He went on the Grand Tour and returned to enter Parliament for the first time in 1794. He sat as a Tory for several seats between 1794 and his death, being out of the House for only a few years. He first held office in 1797 and went on to become Leader of the House of Commons and Foreign Secretary (1812–22). The diarist Greville thought him 'one of the best managers of the House of Commons who ever sat in it' and 'eminently possessed of the good taste, good humour, and agreeable manners which are more requisite to make a good leader than eloquence, however brilliant'.[17] However, the strain of office and party conflict ground him down and he committed suicide by cutting his throat.

Henry Brougham, *Historical Sketches of Statesmen Who Flourished in the Time of George III* (1839)

No man ever attained the station of a regular debater in our Parliament with such an entire want of all classical accomplishment, and indeed of all literary provision whatsoever. While he never showed the least symptom of any information extending beyond the more recent volumes of the *Parliamentary Debates*, or possibly the files of the newspapers only, his diction set all imitation, perhaps all description, at defiance. It was with some an amusement to beguile the tedious hours of their unavoidable attendance upon the poor, tawdry ravelled thread of his sorry discourse to collect a kind of *ana* from the fragments of mixed, uncongruous, and disjointed images that frequently appeared in it. 'The features of the clause'; 'the ignorant impatience of taxation'; 'sets of circumstances coming up and circumstances going down'; 'men turning their backs upon themselves'; 'the honourable and learned gentleman's wedge getting into the loyal feelings of the manufacturing classes'; 'the constitutional principle wound up in the bowels of the monarchical principle'; 'the Herculean labour of the honourable and learned member, who will find himself quite disappointed when he has at last brought forth his Hercules' (by a slight confounding of his mother's labour, which produced that hero, with his own exploits which gained him immortality)—these are but a few, and not the richest samples, by any means, of a rhetoric which often baffled alike the gravity of the Treasury Bench and the art of the reporter, and left the wondering audience at a loss to conjecture how anyone could ever exist, endowed with humbler pretensions to the name of orator . . .

When the Tory party, 'having a devil', preferred Lord Castlereagh to Mr Canning for their leader, all men naturally expected that he would entirely fail to command even the attendance of the house while he addressed it, and that the benches, empty during his time, would only be replenished when his highly gifted competitor rose. They were greatly deceived; they under-rated the effect of place and power; they forgot that the representative of a Government speaks 'as one having authority, and not as the scribes'; but they also forgot that Lord Castlereagh had some qualities well fitted to conciliate favour, and even to provoke admiration, in the absence of everything like eloquence, and without ever having written a line in the *Anti-Jacobin*. He was a bold and fearless man:

the very courage with which he exposed himself unabashed to the most critical audience in the world, while incapable of uttering two sentences of anything but the meanest matter, in the most wretched language; the gallantry with which he faced the greatest difficulties of a question; the unflinching perseverance with which he went through a whole subject, leaving untouched not one of its points, whether he could grapple with it or no, and not one of the adverse arguments, however forcibly and felicitously they had been urged—neither daunted by recollecting the impression just made by his antagonist's display, nor damped by consciousness of the very rags in which he now presented himself—all this made him, upon the whole, rather a favourite with the audience whose patience he was taxing mercilessly, and whose gravity he ever and anon put to a very severe trial. Nor can anyone have forgotten the kind of pride that mantled on the fronts of the Tory phalanx, when after being overwhelmed with the powerful fire of the Whig Opposition, or galled by the fierce denunciations of the 'Mountain', or harassed by the brilliant though often tinsel displays of Mr Canning, their chosen leader stood forth, and presenting the graces of his eminently patrician figure, flung open his coat, displayed an azure ribbon traversing a snow-white chest, and declared 'his high satisfaction that he could now meet the charges against him face to face, and repel with indignation all that his adversaries were bold and rash enough to advance'.[18]

Charles Wetherell

Sir Charles Wetherell (1770–1846) was a son of the Dean of Hereford and Master of University College, Oxford. He was educated at St Paul's School and at his father's college, and called to the bar in 1794. He established a practice in equity, which brought him before the House of Lords and parliamentary committees as well as the courts. In 1816 he was made a KC and, although a Tory, successfully acted for one of those involved in the Spa Field riots against a high treason indictment brought by the Tory Government. He was MP for Rye, 1812–13; for Shaftesbury from 1813 to 1820; for the city of Oxford from 1820 to 1826; for Hastings, from June to December 1826; for Plympton Earl, in Devonshire, from then until 1830; and for Boroughbridge, in Yorkshire, from 1830 to 1832. He was vehemently opposed to Catholic emancipation and parliamentary reform; indeed, he twice left office as Attorney-General (resigning the first time, dismissed the second) because of his views on Catholic emancipation. After losing his seat in 1832, he returned to his legal practice (which included a post as Standing Counsel to Oxford University), serving as Recorder of Bristol until his death following a riding accident.

Charles Greville, Journal, March 21, 1829

The anti-Catholic papers and men lavish the most extravagant encomiums on Wetherell's speech, and call it 'the finest oration ever delivered in the House of Commons', 'the best since the second Phillipic'. He was drunk, they say. The Speaker said 'the only lucid interval he had was that between his waistcoat and his breeches'. When he speaks he unbuttons his braces, and in his vehement action his breeches fall down and his waistcoat runs up, so that there is a great *interregnum*.

James Grant, *Random Recollections of the House of Commons* (1836)

He never opened his mouth, but the House was sure to be convulsed with laughter. When he rose all eyes were invariably turned towards him: honourable members expected a profusion of jokes, and they were never disappointed. Sir Charles's personal appearance strikingly contrasted with his matter. Lavater would have pronounced him one of the dullest and most morose of human beings: a person meeting him in the streets would at once infer, if any faith is to be put in physiognomy, that he was some Friar just escaped from a twenty or thirty years' seclusion in a convent. He usually looks sulky: his appearance is to a stranger's mind the *beau ideal* of a cynical philosopher. When lashing the Liberals, and denouncing what he terms revolutionary doctrines, his countenance darkens with an expression of extreme scorn. His face is deeply furrowed with wrinkles, though apparently not more than from fifty-five to sixty years of age. In person he is tall and athletic. His complexion is dark, and his features are large. Nothing can daunt him or put him out of countenance. He is impervious alike to the coarsest and most refined sarcasms which may be levelled at him,—and few men within the walls of Parliament have been the butts of so much ridicule; certainly none on account of their personal appearance. He was a target for every Liberal to shoot at. His clothes are always threadbare. I never yet saw a suit on him for which a Jew old-clothes man would give ten shillings. How or where he gets his wardrobe nobody knows, but every one has remarked that a new suit, or even a new hat, coat, waistcoat, or trousers singly, was never yet seen to grace his person. I cannot think he has a tailor, or if he have, it is impossible Snip can ever take his measure. His clothes always look as if made by accident; they never fit him. They literally hang loosely about him. As for braces, he has an unconquerable aversion to them. Whether, like the elder Hannibal towards the Romans, he has sworn eternal hostility to what he calls 'suspenders' is not known; but no one can doubt he would as soon that his neck were encircled in a halter, as that his breeches should be adjusted by means of braces.

Though the cause of so much laughter in others, I scarcely ever yet knew a smile play on Sir Charles's own countenance. I doubt much if he himself sees the wit and humour with which his speeches sparkle; certainly there is not the least appearance of an effort to be witty or humorous.

He is capable of undergoing great fatigue. His physical as well as mental exertions during the time the Reform Bill was in Committee were extraordinary. Night after night—and this, too, after being busily and laboriously engaged all day in the discharge of his professional duties—did he oppose every successive clause of that measure. It was in a great degree owing to his pertinacious opposition and 'much speaking', that the debate immediately before the memorable division was only one of several which had taken place in the course of the previous night. Sir Charles, on leaving the house at a quarter past seven, finding that it rained heavily, raised his eyes towards the clouds, as a wild duck, to use the phraseology of an Irish peasant, would do in a thunderstorm, and exclaimed, 'By G— if I had known this, we should have had a few more divisions.'

Henry Brougham

Henry Peter Brougham (1778–1868), Baron Brougham and Vaux, the son of a Perth clergyman, was educated at Edinburgh High School and Edinburgh University. He was interested in mathematics and natural sciences and was made a Fellow of the Royal Society at the age of twenty-five. Called to the bar in 1808, he had already acquired a journalistic reputation as a regular contributor to the *Edinburgh Review*. He was Whig MP for Camelford (without visiting the seat) from 1810 to 1812; for Winchelsea from 1815 to 1830; and briefly for Knaresborough before he was raised to the peerage, as Lord Chancellor, in 1830. He was a supporter of the anti-slavery movement and of Parliamentary Reform. In 1831 he spoke for six hours on Law Reform.

Charles Western, Letter to Thomas Creevey, February 1816

I have often marvelled at the want of sense, discretion, judgement and common sense that we see so frequently accompany the most brilliant talents, but damn me if I ever saw such an instance as that I have just witnessed in your friend Brougham. By heaven! he has uttered a speech which, for power of *speaking*, surpassed anything you ever heard, and by which he has damned himself past redemption. You know what my opinion of him has always been: I have always thought he had not much sound sense nor too much political integrity, but he has outstripped any notion I could form of indiscretion; and as to his politics, they are, in my humble opinion, of no sterling substance (but that between ourselves). He has been damaging himself daily, but tonight there is not a single fellow that is not saying what a damn'd impudent speech that of Brougham's— four or five driven away—even Burdett says it was too much, He could not have roared louder if a file of soldiers had come in and pushed the Speaker out of his chair. Where the devil a fellow could get such things and such a flow of jaw upon such an occasion as this surpass my imagination.

I was sitting in the gallery by myself, and he made my head spin in such a style I thought I should tumble over. He quite overcame one's understanding for a time, but when I recovered, I began to think—this will never do— impossible—I will go down and see what other lads think of it: perhaps my nerves are a little too sensitive. I soon found, however, that everybody was struck in the same way, and even more. Now, when I say that he has damaged himself past redemption, I mean as a man aspiring to be leader, for to that his ambition aspired, and for that he is DONE now . . . Brougham has put them [the ministry] up 20 per cent; that is to say by inducing people more to support them to keep opposition out.

Lord Campbell, *The Lives of the Chancellors and Keepers of the Great Seal of England* (1845–7)

It certainly was a wonderful performance to witness. He showed a most stupendous memory, and extraordinary dexterity in handling the weapons both of ridicule and reason. Without a note to refer to, he went through all the speeches of his opponents delivered during the five nights' debate, analysing them successively, and, with a little aid from perversion, giving them all a seemingly triumphant answer. The peroration was partly inspired by draughts of mulled port, imbibed by him very copiously towards the conclusion of the four hours during which he was on his legs or his knees . . . 'I pray and exhort you not to reject this measure. By all you hold most dear; by all the ties that bind every one of us to our common order and our common country, I solemnly adjure you—I warn you—I implore you—yea, on my bended knees [he kneels] I supplicate you—reject not this bill!' He continued for some time as if in prayer; but his friends, alarmed for him lest he should be suffering from the effects of the mulled port, picked him up and placed him safely on the Woolsack. Like Burke's famous dagger scene in the House of Commons, the prostration was a failure; so unsuited was it to the spectators and to the actor that it produced a sensation of ridicule, and considerably impaired the effect of a speech displaying wonderful powers of memory and of intellect.

Edward John Littleton (1791–1863), 1st Baron Hatterton, was educated at Rugby and at Christ Church, Oxford, and sat as Whig MP for Worcestershire from 1806 to 1820.

Lord Hatherton, Diary

August 17, 1835. Sharp debating between Lyndhurst and Brougham . . . Lord Lyndhurst's manner admirable for a Committee—slow, considerate, perspicuous, and decided. Nobody more briefly makes his view comprehensible to others— the statement always sufficiently eloquent—without any attempt at figurative eloquence. In short, his manner is judicial . . . Brougham on the contrary is distinguished by acuteness, and what is called debating power—finding weak places, enforcing strong points, gathered accidentally while speaking, the whole uttered with the eagerness of a mind exuberant in matter, agitated by extraordinary fervency of feeling, his language always strong and highly eloquent— impatient under reply from unceasing irritability of temperament, and always rising five or six times in the discussion of one point—besides divers audible interruptions by remark while his opponent is speaking. I was amused with watching him all night—while seated he scratched the top of his head with his fingers or picked his nose continually. His brain works so actively, he can never allow himself time to attend to his person, and is accordingly not cleanly. While Chancellor he seemed to pride himself a little on attention to his dress. He rendered himself singular by wearing a broad green and red Scotch-plaid pair of trousers and a round hat—for the latter, Lyndhurst had set him the fashion— and the judges generally are now growing less quizzical in dress.

February 13, 1844. I sat close to the Woolsack, where Lyndhurst was continually talking to Brougham, who was sitting as usual on the Woolsack by his side. They were continually making interlocutory observations aloud on the speeches, in a coarse and disgusting manner, Brougham frequently spitting between his legs on the fine carpet of the House, and rubbing it with his feet—his common practice—imitated, however, by nobody else.

❖

Viscount Althorp

John Charles Spencer (1782–1845), Viscount Althorp and 3rd Earl Spencer, was a Whig MP from 1804 to 1834. He was made Chancellor of the Exchequer by Earl Grey in 1830 and as Whig leader in the Commons was credited with smoothing the passage of the Great Reform Bill. He was not known for his oratorical skills—indeed, he was frequently inaudible, hence Praed's poem below—but was nonetheless much admired: 'It was Althorp carried the Bill; his fine temper did it.'[19] He retired in 1834.

T. B. Macaulay, Letter to his sister Hannah, August 29, 1831

My opinion of Lord Althorp is extremely high. In fact his character is the only stay of the ministry. I doubt whether any person has ever lived in England who, with no eloquence, no brilliant talents, no profound information—with nothing in short but plain good sense and an excellent heart—possessed so much influence both in and out of Parliament. His temper is an absolute miracle. He has been worse used than any minister ever was in debate; and he has never said one thing inconsistent, I do not say with gentlemanlike courtesy, but with real benevolence. His candour is absolutely a vice in debate. He is perpetually shewing excuse and ways of escape to his adversaries which they would never find of themselves. Lord North perhaps was his equal in suavity and good nature. But Lord North was not a man of strict principles. His administration was not only an administration hostile to liberty; but it was supported by vile and corrupt means—by direct bribery, I fear, in many cases. Lord Althorp has the temper of Lord North with the principles of Romilly. If he had the oratorical powers of either of these men, he might do any thing. But his understanding, though just, is slow; and his elocution painfully defective. It is however only justice to him to say that he has done more service to the Reform Bill even as a debater than all the other ministers together, Stanley excepted.

Winthrop Mackworth Praed, 'A Member's Musings', March 14, 1834

> 'Order, order!'—'Bar, bar!—'Door, door!'
> Such are the cries as he stands on the floor,
> Waving his hand for a little while,
> And wreathing his lip in a gentle smile:
> We stoop our head, we strain our ear;
> Nobody hears him;—'Hear, hear, hear!'
>
> What is he talking of?—figures or facts?
> Liberal principles?—Algerine acts?
> The rise of the unions, or of stocks?
> The weight of the debt, or the last prize ox?
> Crops or cholera?—Jews or beer?
> All of them!—none of them?—'Hear, hear, hear!'
>
> Quick is O'Connell in debate;
> Cunning is Hume to calculate;
> But Hume and O'Connell their way will miss,
> 'When it's a proper time to cheer,
> Wake me, dear Ellice!'—'Hear, hear, hear!'
>
> There is a lady in a play,
> Who speaks, though she does nothing say;
> Fortune has brought us a lord in her freaks,
> Who just says nothing, though he speaks.
> What in the papers will appear?
> Only 'Lord Althorp', and 'Hear, hear, hear!'

Sir Denis Le Marchant, *Memoir of John Charles Viscount Althorp, third Earl Spencer* (1876)

Once, in answer to a most able and argumentative speech of Croker, he arose and merely observed 'that he had made some calculations which he considered as entirely conclusive in refutation of the right honourable gentleman's arguments, but unfortunately he had mislaid them, so that he could only say that if the House would be guided by his advice they would reject the amendment'—which they did accordingly. There was no standing against such influence as this.

William Cobbett

William Cobbett (1763–1835) was a journalist and author for many years before he entered the House as independent MP for Oldham in 1832, after the Reform Act of that year, and was equally scathing of Radicals and Tories. He published *Cobbett's Weekly Register* from 1802 to 1835.

Sir Henry Lytton Bulwer (Baron Dalling of Bulwer), *Historical Characters* (1868)

No other instance exists, and perhaps no other instance will ever exist, of a man entering the House of Commons at seventy-six years of age, and immediately taking his place as one of the best debaters in it. He who could do this was of a giant race. With his usual self-confidence he spoke on the first occasion that presented itself, proposing an amendment to the Address; but this was not his happiest effort, and consequently created disappointment. He soon, however, obliterated the failure, and became rather a favourite with an audience which is only unforgiving when bored.

It was still seen, moreover, that nothing daunted him; the murmurs, the 'Oh!' or more serious reprehension and censure, found him shaking his head with his hands in his pockets, as cool and as sarcastic as when he first stuck up a picture of King George in his shop-window at Philadelphia. He exhibited in Parliament, too, the same want of tact, prudence, and truth; the same egotism, the same combativeness, and the same reckless desire to struggle with received opinions, that had marked him previously through life, and shattered his career into glittering fragments, from which the world could never collect the image, nor the practical utility of the whole.

A foolish and out-of-the-way motion, praying his Majesty to strike Sir Robert Peel's name out of the Privy Council, for the change which he had proposed in the currency in 1819, was his wildest effort and most signal defeat, the House receiving Sir Robert, when he stood up in his defence, with a loud burst of cheers, and voting in a majority of 298 to 4 in his favour.

Cobbett, however, was nothing abashed; for this motion was rather a piece of fun, in his own way, than anything serious; and he was really angry with Sir Robert Peel, not because he had altered the currency in 1819, but because he was the most able speaker in Parliament in 1833.

♣

Mr Secretary Stanley

Edward Geoffrey (1800–69), Lord Stanley, was the eldest son of the 3rd Earl of Derby. He was elected first as a Whig in 1820 and served in Whig administrations as Irish Secretary (1830–3) and Secretary of State for the Colonies (1833–4). He resigned from the Cabinet over Church Reform. He was given office under Peel in 1841 and later served as a Tory Prime Minister in 1852–3, 1858 and from 1866 to 1868. He went to the Lords in his father's barony in 1844 and succeeded to the earldom in 1851. In his early days Edward Bulwer Lytton bestowed on him the nickname 'the Rupert of debate', after Prince Rupert, the bold, royalist cavalry leader of the English Civil War.

Earl Russell, *Recollections and Suggestions 1813–1873* (1875)

A measure of coercion containing very strong provisions was sent over by the Government of Ireland. Lord Grey accepted it, because, in his opinion, the protection of life and property was a duty incumbent upon every Government. Lord Althorp accepted it also, because, in his opinion, the stronger the measure the more likely was it to be temporary, and to give way after a short time to the restoration of the ordinary law. But while Lord Althorp was as fully persuaded as any member of the Cabinet of the necessity for this bill, he was little fitted to persuade a Liberal House of Commons to acquiesce in a proposal repugnant to their dispositions, and at variance with their settled opinions. It was thought right, however, that he, as the leader of the Government in the House of Commons, should introduce the Coercion Bill. He did so in a manner tame and ineffective. His detail of the outrages committed in Ireland was like reading a few of the blackest pages of the Newgate Calendar. The Liberal majority were disappointed, sullen, and ready to break out into mutiny against their chief. Mr Stanley, who was sitting next to me, greatly annoyed at the aspect of the House, said to me, 'I meant not to have spoken till tomorrow night, but I find I must speak tonight.' He took Lord Althorp's box of official papers, and went upstairs to a room where he could look over them quietly. After the debate had proceeded for two or three hours longer, with no change of temper in the House, Stanley rose. He explained with admirable clearness the insecure and alarming state of Ireland. He then went over, case by case, the more dreadful of the outrages which had been committed. He detailed, with striking effect, the circumstances attending the murder of a clergyman, and the agony of his widow, who, after seeing her husband murdered, had to bear the terror of running knocks at the door, kept on all night by the miscreants who had committed the murder. The House became appalled and agitated at the dreadful picture which he placed before their eyes; they felt for the sorrows of the innocent; they were shocked at the dominion of assassins and robbers. When he had produced a thrilling effect by these descriptions, he turned upon O'Connell, who led the opposition to the measure, and who seemed a short time before about to achieve a triumph in favour of sedition and anarchy. He recalled to the recollection of the House of Commons, that at a recent public meeting, O'Connell had spoken of the House of Commons as 658 scoundrels. In a tempest of scorn and indignation, he excited the anger of the men thus designated against the author of the calumny. The House, which two hours before seemed about to yield to the great agitator, was now almost ready to tear him to pieces. In the midst of the storm which his eloquence had raised, Stanley sat down, having achieved one of the greatest triumphs ever won in a popular assembly by the powers of oratory.

Benjamin Disraeli

Sir William Fraser, *Disraeli and his Day* (1891)

Very few persons have had an opportunity of hearing Disraeli speak. The Members of the House, as we know, number about 650: a space is allotted to the public in the Speaker's and Upper Gallery: a very small space is allowed to ladies. Besides these, and the three clerks, the Serjeant-at-Arms, and the door-keepers, no one under any circumstances has an opportunity of hearing the speaking in the House of Commons. When any matter of great importance is discussed, when the fate of a Government is to be decided, or a measure of vast influence accepted or rejected, every place is filled long before the Debate. I have known many who have taken the keenest interest in politics, and who were well able to appreciate eloquence, not one of whom has ever had an opportunity of hearing Disraeli speak.

No one who has not done so can form any idea of his powers. His speeches when read give no adequate idea of their effect. The impression made on an emotional Assembly like the House of Commons can never be put in print. The varying sensations, fluctuating like the breast of the ocean; the minute rhetorical effects, which moved his audience so powerfully; the alterations of voice; the pauses; the grand gestures, which he occasionally, but not frequently, used: all these are utterly lost upon the reader of a debate. Disraeli had a perfectly melodious voice; and what is rare, a voice increasing in beauty of tone the more loudly that he spoke: he had the proud consciousness of having a mastermind; and a masterly power of influencing men. He wrote to his sister early in life, 'I have listened to the great speakers in the House of Commons: I can surpass them all!' His judgement was right: and he lived to give his prophecy a splendid fulfilment. To the reader who has read and admired his speeches I say, '*Quid si tonantem ipsum audivisses!*'

Disraeli's behaviour in the House of Commons was always studied; even when not addressing the House. When about to speak on an important topic, he always sat with his hat off: he invariably sat with one knee over the other; his arms folded across his breast; leaning against the back of his seat; his hat slightly over his brows: the more vehement the attack of his adversary became, the more he affected somnolence: when it waxed very hot indeed, he, without removing the pendent leg, brought his body round towards the west; placing his eyeglass, with the forefinger of his right hand curved over it, to his right eye, he glanced for about three seconds at the clock over the entrance door; replacing the glass in the breast of his coat, he again relapsed into simulated sleep.

In the first Parliament in which I sat, Disraeli wore his frock-coat open, displaying his plush waistcoat; he had a nervous trick difficult to describe. It was this. He raised both forearms from the elbow as if struck with a sudden idea of throwing the lapels of his coat wide open; but invariably failed to accomplish his object; he touched each lapel with the points of his finger and thumb; producing no effect upon the coat. He entirely gave up this practice: in later years he rose with his coat buttoned across his breast: he usually moved his open hands downwards above his hips; he then pulled his coat down in front, and threw his shoulders back. He began slowly, and very deliberately. Whenever he was about to produce a good thing, and his good things were very good, any one in the habit of watching him knew precisely when they were coming. Before producing the point, he would always pause, and give a nervous cough: the action of his hands was remarkable. He carried a cambric handkerchief, of spotless whiteness, in his left skirt pocket. He would place both hands in both pockets behind him; then bring out the white handkerchief, and hold it in his left hand before him for a few seconds; pass it to his right hand: then with his right hand pass the handkerchief lightly under his nose, hardly touching it; and then with his left hand replace the handkerchief in his pocket; still holding his hand, with the handkerchief in it, in his pocket, until a fresh topic.

I was fortunately in the House of Lords, shortly before his departure with Lord Salisbury for the Berlin Conference. Lord Granville had spoken, and had expressed real or affected regret that Lord Beaconsfield and Lord Salisbury should both be absent at the same time from the Councils of the Queen. Disraeli replied, 'The Noble Earl has expressed his regret that my noble friend sitting on my right and myself should be abroad at the same time: he has been pleased to add that he considers that the absence of the Noble Marquess and of myself from the Cabinet will diminish the personal importance of those that remain. My Lords'; here out came the handkerchief; 'I can conceive no circumstance, ahem! more calculated to add to it!'

Richard Cobden

William White, *Illustrated Times*, June 4, 1864

We have had, if we remember rightly, three set debates on China this Session. Yes, reader, and possibly we may have three more. For, though China lies at the distance of half the circumference of the globe from our shores, we have vast interests there. Witness the fact that we have lying in Chinese waters some forty-six ships of war, besides some other ten vessels belonging to the English Government. The first two debates on China did not attract much notice, having been rather dull affairs. On Tuesday last, however, we had really an important, if not a lively, debate upon China. And the reason was this. A master came upon the scene—a performer who always attracts a crowd of members, and stamps with importance everything which he touches. Mr Cobden began his speech about five o'clock, and from the time he rose until the last sentence fell from his lips the House was unusually full; every eye was upon the speaker, and the attention which the honourable member secured and held was worth noting. The power with which Mr Cobden holds the House of Commons is very remarkable. He is not an orator. He is not what some critics would call eloquent; his manner is not specially attractive, nor is his voice particularly musical; and we have known more than one man, after listening to him for a time, turn away disappointed. But whenever it is known that he is about to speak, all the wandering members rush into the House to hear him. He seizes their minds at once, and can hold their attention as long as he continues upon his legs. Now, how is this? Well, to answer this question fully would demand more space than we have to spare. Suffice it to say that, in our opinion, Cobden's power lies in his knowledge of his subject, his ability to impart that knowledge intelligibly to his hearers; his clear, acute, logical, comprehensive mind; and last, though not least, in his thorough honesty and sincerity of purpose. Cobden, to us, dwells in light. He honestly wishes all to be brought within the circle of his own radiance; and he can and does, whenever he speaks, succeed in doing what he sincerely intends.

Cobden and Bright

John Bright (1811–89) was a Rochdale cotton-spinner and manufacturer and was prominent in the Anti-Corn Law League. He was a Liberal MP for Durham City from 1843 to 1847; for Manchester from 1847 to 1857; for Birmingham from 1857 to 1885; and for Central Birmingham from 1885 until his death. He held office as president of the Board of Trade (1868–70) and Chancellor of the Duchy of Lancaster (from 1873 to 1874, and, again, from 1880 to 1882).

Sir William Fraser, *Disraeli and his Day* (1891)

The characters of Cobden and Bright were nearly so different as those of Don Quixote and Sancho Panza. I believed in Cobden: I utterly disbelieved in Bright. Cobden was a well-intentioned man, with a conviction of the truth of his ideas on the particular subjects in which he worked; he was, so far as a man can be, devoid of personal ambition, and vanity; he felt, as he frequently said, acutely the disadvantages arising from a want of breadth of mind; for he was narrow-minded; in accomplishing what he did, he thoroughly believed that he was benefiting his countrymen. I liked his style of speaking: there was no apparent pretension: very quiet, very distinct; the words uttered slowly, and most carefully: he paid his audience the compliment of convincing them that whatever he uttered in the House of Commons was the result of long, deep, and minute thought: he was a born logician. Like all masters of that great art, he scorned to be base: a man who will, knowingly, use false arguments is quite capable of stealing, if he thought he would not be detected. I never heard Cobden sophisticate: though I not unfrequently disagreed with his views, I do not believe that he would have intentionally argued falsely: this is saying much for a man who was very much in earnest in his cause. Nothing could be more delicate than his manner of conducting an argument. He convinced you that he believed what he was saying: without which few arguments really avail. His style was this; I am not of course quoting words that he ever uttered, 'I look round me, and I see three or four hundred Members of the House of Commons, all of whom have the belief that at this moment they are wearing black coats. Now I know the disadvantage under which I labour: I have not been half so well educated as most of you: but if you will listen to me for a few minutes I shall endeavour, so far as my humble capacity goes, to convert you to my own belief that your coats are not black.' He would then use the most deep and subtle arguments: and at the end of a quarter of an hour, if you had reasoning power in your mind, you would begin to doubt whether he was not right. I have never heard a more finished reasoner: his premises were not unfrequently wrong.

A greater contrast could hardly have been seen to him than Bright. Bright was believed by some to be honest, because he was fat and rude. A plain-spoken man, that is to say one who has that name, is, in nine cases out of ten, utterly insincere: his roughness is a brutal attempt to cover his deceit. There can be no greater mistake than to suppose that Bright was, as Cobden was, a power in the House of Commons: he was nothing of the sort; I speak of course of his best days: once in Office, he sank into obscurity. Sitting, as he did, on the flank of the Whig Government, and frequently attacking them, it was not the game of the Tory Party to disconcert him. We, of course, enjoyed the sarcasms with which he pelted his friends above the gangway: and on no occasion was an attack made upon him personally from the front bench on the Tory side.

One of the things, to which I look forward with hope, was a distinct attack on Bright by Disraeli. Occasionally sarcasms of a very disagreeable sort passed between them, but a hand-to-hand engagement never took place. Bright's style in the House of Commons was that of a man who tells his audience that they are all fools, and most of them rogues; whereas he is about to express the views of the only sensible and honest man in the place. Speaking very slowly, and very distinctly, a carefully prepared speech, with one or two bright points, but very little effective argument. The sophisms, and false arguments, with which Bright indulged the inhabitants of populous cities, were not used in the House of Commons. He knew well that there they would be detected and exposed. Whatever power Bright had in Parliament was due to the influence which he had obtained out of doors by addressing an audience that could not detect, nor refute, his sophistry. He never lost an opportunity of pouring his venom, nine-tenths of which was utterly unmerited, upon what he was pleased to call the 'upper classes'.

On one occasion Disraeli fired a shot at him which caused us keen delight. Bright had been away from the House for upwards of two years. On coming back he looked particularly neat, and smart, as a man does who has not had on his best clothes for some time: his hair was very carefully brushed. On that evening a debate took place on the genial subject of turnpikes: a Baronet from the west of England, a County Member, gave us his views at some length. Turnpikes, I suspect, were a subject in which Disraeli was not deeply versed. Anticipating this, Bright rose: and in a most offensive manner recommended Disraeli to listen to the sage counsel of the Baronet who had just sat down. Disraeli followed: alluded to the arguments of the Baronet, and then said, 'I now come to the Member for Birmingham.' Bright immediately 'pavonered' himself, threw his shoulders back; and obviously anticipated that Disraeli would say in the conventional manner, 'Whom we are all glad to see back again.' Disraeli had no intention of the sort. He placed his glass in his right eye: looked at Bright: and calmly said, in a tone of depreciation which cannot be described, 'Of whom we have not seen much of late.' Bright turned livid: I never saw a human countenance express passion so deeply. We of course laughed. Disraeli then quietly added, 'The Hon. Gentleman has indulged us once more this evening with that self-complacent catalogue of his own achievements with which in former years the House was familiar. I fail to find anything novel in his remarks, and I pass on at once to the Member for ——' For Comedy I never saw anything finer. One rudeness for which Bright was constantly guilty was this; when Disraeli in the course of a great speech was approaching a point of exceptional brilliance Bright would rise from his place, and walk slowly out of the House: immediately returning behind the Speaker's chair; I have known him do this over and over again, for the sole purpose of insulting Disraeli . . .

Lord John Manners gave an admirable reply to Bright. Bright had quoted some boyish lines from a Poem of Lord John: the latter replied, 'I would far sooner be the foolish young man who wrote the lines; than the malignant old man who quoted them.'

Lord Palmerston

Henry John Temple (1784–1865), Viscount Palmerston, was the son of the 1st Viscount Melbourne, an Irish peer, and was educated at Harrow, at the University of Edinburgh, and at St John's College, Cambridge. He was a Whig MP for Newport, Isle of Wight (1807–11); for the University of Cambridge (1811–31); for Bletchingly (1831–2); for South Hampshire (1832–4); and for Tiverton from 1835 until his death. He held office from early in his parliamentary career, as Secretary at War (1809–28). He was three times Foreign Secretary (1830–4; 1835–41; and 1846–51) and was twice Prime Minister (1855–8 and 1859–65).

Sir William Fraser, *Disraeli and his Day* (1891)

Lord Palmerston presided at an annual dinner of the 'Royal Literary Fund'. I asked Monckton Milnes, afterwards Lord Houghton, how Palmerston got on at the dinner: he answered, 'For a man who never read a book in his life, I think he did very well.' Lord Palmerston might have led the House of Commons at thirty-five; but declined: giving as his reason that 'his life would be a perpetual canvass', and that he could not endure it. Whether this were the real cause or not I do not know; the reason of his ultimately achieving his position in Parliament was that he was twenty years older than any other leading man: that he knew the Country well: and that on one subject he knew a great deal, and no one else knew anything: Foreign Affairs.

Lord Palmerston never was a good speaker: he had a hesitation which came in at the most inappropriate times: a good voice; but no art: in speaking he would constantly use an anti-climax: he would say, for instance, 'The language of the honourable gentleman is unusual, unparliamentary, violent, discreditable, and ahem!'—a pause—'to be deprecated.' I never knew him rise to real eloquence: and on one occasion only did I hear him speak with great ability: this was on the Danish question. Everybody who attended to such matters had been completely puzzled by the complicated affairs of Schleswig-Holstein. The clearest heads could make nothing of it: and the vast majority of the House of Commons did not attempt it. Lord Palmerston made a speech admirable in its clearness. I could not have believed it possible that he could make such a speech. Solving the difficulties, and presenting the essential points of the question, to the appreciation and comprehension of the House. Disraeli, seeing the effect that had been produced, in his reply characterised the speech as 'perspicuous; but not satisfactory'. It was splendidly perspicuous.

I was not in Parliament at the time of the celebrated 'Pacifico Speech': nor up to this time have I been able to understand by reading it the effect which it produced: but I may say that except on these two occasions Lord Palmerston never made a great speech . . .

Even the Garter Ribbon did not give him an aristocratic look. One of Lord Palmerston's aphorisms was that 'the best thing for the inside of a man is the outside of a horse': he rode every day, unless prevented by press of business: and invariably took a long ride on Sunday . . .

On the last occasion on which I saw him I was passing through Westminster Hall from the House of Commons; he had just dismounted from his horse. Thinking it would save the old boy trouble, I said, 'The House is up, my Lord.' He replied, 'Thank you! I am very much obleeged to you: how about Ayrton, and the Balance of Power?' I told him gently that nothing had been said on the subject.

Lord Palmerston had a peculiarly flattering manner of leaning forward when you were addressing the House, standing opposite to him of course. As he did this to me on several occasions, I assume that he did the same to others. Once, however, he did his best to snub me: without ultimate effect.

It was the first time that I heard Lord Palmerston speak: Admitting a certain prejudice in his favour, I thought it was a good speech. He was an adroit speaker; never a great one: even the tone of generosity which pervaded that speech did not give me an impression of its depth nor sincerity. It was the speech of a man of the world, who felt what I have expressed, that the vindictive character of Mr Villier's motion was not desirable; nor would it tend to the ultimate benefit of the Whig party . . .

Lord Palmerston was not only incapable of a fine style: he never attempted it. He never sacrificed his speech to himself. He said what he had to say in seemingly careless, and absolutely inartistic, language: it gave no pleasure to his hearers; but at the end of a speech you always knew what he meant.

❖

Thomas Babington Macaulay

As a speaker, Macaulay received mixed reviews. His friend Dean Milman characterised his delivery as 'far too rapid to be impressive; it wanted also variety and flexibility of intonation. Even the most practised reporters panted after him in vain; how much more the slower intellects of country gentlemen and the mass of the House!' Nonetheless, Milman conceded that 'on two occasions a speech of Macaulay's actually turned the vote of the House, and carried the question (a very rare event) in his own way— the debate on the Copyright Act, and the question of judges holding seats in the House of Commons'. Although he took his seat there, Macaulay never got round to speaking in the House of Lords, 'which would have been so congenial a field for his studied and matured eloquence'.[20] Others were dismissive of Macaulay's oratory. 'I heard Macaulay speak once in Parliament,' wrote Sir William Fraser. 'His manner and style were very heavy: and his appearance equally so: his features and expression meaningless. My first remark on seeing him was, "He is like Palmerston with a cold in his head." '[21]

E. M. Whitty, *History of the Session 1852–3, A Parliamentary Retrospect* (1853), June 4, 1853

It was pleasanter talking on Wednesday, when the position of Mr Macaulay in Great Britain was measured in a great way. On a Wednesday the House and the committees are sitting at once, and the building is filled with scattered MPs—some at work, many looking at those who are at work, but more loitering about the lobbies and corridors, picking up old or new acquaintance and feeling for public opinion. About three, on Wednesday, one was loitering about, too; for the talk in the House was not interesting—on a Wednesday it seldom is—and one could pick up members' opinion, which is as important as public opinion.[22] You were walking along the committee lobby, wondering which 'room' you would take next, when, as you paused uncertain, you were bumped against by somebody. He begged your pardon, and rushed on, and you looked to see who it was: a member—a stout member: a man you couldn't conceive in a run: and yet he's running 'like mad'. You are still staring at him when two more men trot past you, one on each side; and they are members, too. You are very puzzled, and see the door close to you—'Members' Entrance' above it—dashed open, five members dash from it, and plunge furiously down the lobby. Why, what can be the matter? More doors open; more members rush out; members are tearing past you from all points, in one direction—towards the House. Then wigs and gowns appear; they tell you, with happy faces, their committees have adjourned; and then come a third class—the gentlemen of the press, hilarious. Why, what's the matter? Matter! Macaulay is up; and all the members are off to hear him. You join the runners in a moment, and are in the gallery to see the senators who had the start of you perspiring into their places. It was an announcement one hadn't heard for years; and passing the word, 'Macaulay's up,' emptied committee rooms now, as of old it emptied clubs. It was true; he was up, and in for a long speech; not a mere 'spurt', but an oration. He was in a new place, standing in the second row (above the Treasury bench) from the table, and looking and sounding all the better for the elevation and the clearer atmosphere for orators which must be found in that little remove from the green boxes. The old voice, the old manners, and the old style—glorious speaking. Well prepared, carefully elaborated, confessedly essayish; but spoken with perfect art and consummate management; not up and down, see-saw, talking off a speech, but the grand conversation of a man of the world, confiding his learning and his recollections, and his logic to a party of gentlemen, and just raising his voice enough to be heard through the room. That is as you heard him when you got in; but then he was only opening and waiting for his audience. As the House filled, which it did with marvellous rapidity, he got prouder and more oratorical; and then he poured out his speech with rapidity, increasing after every sentence, till it became a torrent of the richest words, carrying his hearers with him into enthusiasm (yes, for dry as was the subject he gave it grandeur by looking at it from the grand and historical point of view), and yet not leaving them time to cheer. A torrent of words— that is the only description of Macaulay's style when he has warmed into speed: and such words!—why it wasn't four o'clock in the afternoon, lunch hardly digested, and yet the quiet reserved English gentlemen collected there to hear the celebrated orator were as wild with delight as an Opera house after Grisi at ten. You doubt it? See the division; and before Mr Macaulay had spoken you might have safely bet fifty to one that Lord Hotham would have carried his bill. After that speech the bill was not thrown, but pitched, out. Speeches seldom do affect measures; and yet this speech will have altered British policy, on a great question, and—don't forget that—on a Wednesday, in a day sitting! People said, when it was over, that it was superb, and so on, and one began to have a higher opinion of the House of Commons, though it is queerly 'led', seeing that if the Macaulay class of minds would bid for leadership, they would

327

get it, and that, perhaps, the Lord Johns only get it, at present, by a sort of moral justice, because they work for it. But it wasn't all congratulation. Mr Macaulay had rushed through his oration of forty minutes with masterly vigour; and, looking at his massive chest and enormous head, you couldn't be surprised. That is the sort of man who would go through whatever he undertook. Yet the doubts about his health, which arise when we meet him in the street (he never meets anybody)—when you take advantage of his sphinx-like reverie, 'Staring right on, with calm, eternal eyes', to study the sickly face—would be confirmed, by a close inspection, on Wednesday. The great orator was trembling, when he sat down: the excitement of a triumph—the massive head, notwithstanding— overcame him, and he had scarcely the self-possession to acknowledge the eager praises which were offered by the Ministers and others, in his neighbourhood. Evidently he had reasons for being as quiet as Gibbon was, in the House; and in this case, too, no doubt, we must think enough will have been done for fame and for our pleasure, if the *History* is finished.

G. F. Francis, *Orators of the Age* (1847)

In the House of Commons, abstraction is his chief characteristic. He enters the House with a certain pole-star to guide him—his seat; how he reaches it seems as if it were a process unknown to him. Seated, he fold his arms and sits in silence, seldom speaking to his colleagues, or appearing to notice what is going forward. An opening is made in the discussion, and he rises, or rather darts up from his seat, plunging at once into the very heart of his subject, without exordium or apologetic preface. In fact, you have for a few seconds heard a voice, pitched in alto, monotonous, and rather shrill, pouring forth words with inconceivable velocity, ere you have become aware that a new speaker, and of no common order, has broken in upon the debate. A few seconds more, and cheers—perhaps from all parts of the House—rouse you from your apathy, compelling you to follow that extremely voluble, and not very enticing voice, in its rapid course through the subject on which the speaker is entering, with a resolute determination, as it seems, never to pause. You think of an express train, which does not stop even at the chief stations. On, on he speeds, in full reliance on his own momentum, never stopping for words, never stopping for thoughts, never halting for an instant, even to take breath—his intellect gathering new vigour as he proceeds, hauling the subject after him, and all its possible attributes and illustrations, with the strength of a giant, leaving a line of light on the pathway his mind has trod, till, unexhausted and apparently inexhaustible, he brings this remarkable effort to a close by a peroration, so highly sustained in its declamatory power, so abounding in illustration, so admirably framed to crown and clench the whole oration, that surprise, if it has even begun to wear off, kindles anew, and the hearer is left utterly prostrate and powerless by the whirlwind of ideas and emotions that has swept over him.

John Stuart Mill

John Stuart Mill (1806–73), the Liberal philosopher and essayist, was educated by his own extensive reading and by his historian-father John Mill, and worked briefly as an Indian civil servant before devoting himself to scholarship and writing. He was an 'advanced Liberal' who favoured universal suffrage, for women as well as for men, and he sat as MP for Westminster from 1865 until 1868, when he was defeated.

W. McCullagh Torrens, *Twenty Years at Westminster* (1893)

Westminster had returned John Stuart Mill, from whom much was expected, not only on account of his varied and elaborate speculative writings, but because he was known to have taken an active and influential part for many years in the home administration of the East India Company. His appearance and bearing tended rather to chill such anticipations. His finely chiselled features and expansive brow seemed ill-supported by his feeble frame, and his gait, abstracted look, and somewhat feminine voice suggested involuntarily the impression of premature old age. Still, when he rose for the first time to address the House, there was intense anxiety to catch every word; and, irrespective of party distinctions, the demonstration of personal respect was manifest.

The subject he had chosen for his notable speech was retrenchment, coupled with the policy and duty of paying off the National Debt while prosperity lasted, lest the time should come when the cost of existence would render it practically impossible. The source of danger on which he chiefly dwelt was that of the approaching exhaustion of the coal supply, which, according to Professor Jevons, was already within measurable distance; and upon the statistics collected by him, the great logician had built up an argument he declared to be irrefutable, and which the most incredulous and reluctant of his hearers felt himself unable offhand to refute.

Before passing to other topics Mr Mill paused, as though he had forgotten what was to come next. The House cheered as it always does to help a stranger over his embarrassment; but it would not do, and the painful pause continued for some minutes. He appeared to have notes of some sort in his hand, but he did not refer to them; and at length a fickle memory resumed her office, and jilted him no more. It is impossible to describe the contending impressions of the hour.

Roebuck and Cornewall Lewis had been class-fellows with him in Bentham's school, but Lewis was there no more to hear his first essay. Roebuck awaited with interest an appearance in Parliamentary life so long deferred, and characteristically said afterwards, 'I always said he would never do here.' But the lecture—for it was more of a lecture than a speech—produced an effect nobody dreamed of.

Mr Gladstone, in the course of a highly complimentary speech, welcomed his accession to the intellectual and political strength of the Legislature, and seemed to be so sympathetically impressed with the impending possibilities of fuel-dearth that many were led to apprehend some modification might be attempted of financial policy. Men like Thomas Baring and Edward Bouverie amused themselves and their friends with the grounds of their scepticism; and misgivings spread lest what soon came to be caricatured as the Jevons crotchet might mislead worthier if not wiser men than the member for Westminster.

The Cabinet decided to grant a Royal Commission to inquire into the national resources underground, who after two years' elaborate research and computation pronounced Mr Mill's dream to be no better than a nightmare, and we heard of the matter no more.

William White, *Illustrated Times*, February 24, 1866

Mr John Stuart Mill has spoken in the House four times, and 'is a failure'. This big giant, whom we were all so much afraid of, is, after all, no giant at all, but a mere pigmy. This is the decision; but then, please to remember, readers, that it was the pigmies of the House that delivered the verdict, and pigmies—at least intellectual pigmies—are no fit judges of a giant. They cannot with their pigmy eyes take in his vast proportions, any more than a fly settling on the cornice of a cathedral can comprehend its magnitude. Speaking in fable, one can imagine a couple of bluebottles settling upon a string-course of Westminster Abbey, and thus discoursing: 'Well, brother, what do you think of this famous abbey, so much thought of by mortals?' 'A decided failure, I should say'; and straightaway the verdict would be made known through all Flydom. And so we may imagine Squirt saying to Squilibet, as they sipped their wine at Lucas's, or smoked their havannah below: 'Did you hear this great Mill, about whom there has been so much talk?' 'Yes.' 'What did you think of him?' 'Well, I should say he was a failure. I could see nothing in him.' 'Nor I. By the way, what has he done that so much noise was made about him?' 'Oh! written some books.' 'Ah! these writing fellows never show well in the House.' Then Mr Mill is not a failure? we think we hear some reader say; to whom we answer, No; Mr John Stuart Mill has not failed, nor can he fail. To ascertain whether a man is a failure we must ascertain what he aims at. Mr Mill never thought to startle and dazzle the House by his oratory, as Disraeli did when he first rose to speak. Mr Mill has no oratorical gifts, and he knows it. Nor can he be called a rhetorician. He is a close reasoner, and addresses himself directly to our reasoning powers; and though he has great command of language, as all his hearers know, he never condescends to deck out his arguments in rhetorical finery to catch applause. His object is to convey his thoughts directly to the hearer's mind, and to do this he uses the clearest medium—not coloured glass, but the best polished plate, because through that objects may be best seen. Mr Mill did not succeed as an orator; but then he did not attempt oratory. He did not excite a furore of cheering; but then he neither expected nor wished for applause. Mr Mill, we should say, cares very little for applause. Rapturous cheering, such as that which Mr Horsman and Mr Lowe can evoke, would, we venture to think, be an offence to Mr Mill. He would, perhaps, ask, with the old Roman orator, 'What foolish thing have I said that these people applaud?' And, indeed, we ourselves have, after long experience, come to think that applause in the House of Commons is often uproarious in proportion to the foolishness of the sentiment that calls it forth. Deep attention, broken only by significant murmurs, is, to our mind, far more complimentary to a speaker than fierce and uproarious applause. What Mr Mill intended to do was to reason calmly with his opponents, and this he succeeded in doing. True, his first speech was scarcely in any way a success, for few could hear it. Mr Mill was in an entirely new position, and what wonder if he was nervous? Moreover, not having tested the acoustic properties of the House, he could not tell what exertion was necessary to make himself heard; and here we may remark that, so close is Mr Mill's reasoning and so concise his sentences, that if you cannot hear all that he says you might as well hear nothing. There are speakers in the House out of whose speeches every third word might be taken, and the speeches would be all the better for the operation; but Mr Mill uses no superfluous words—every word is necessary to make his meaning clear, and to this special end is chosen. Mr Mill's subsequent speeches were heard in all parts of the House and commanded silent attention. He has not a powerful voice, but then it is highly pitched and very clear; and this class of voice goes much further than one of lower tone—as the ear-piercing fife is heard at a greater distance than the blatant trombone. The giant, then, is not a failure; no, except in the eyes of the pigmies.

Sir Robert Harry Inglis

Sir Robert Harry Inglis (1786–1855), the son of a clergyman, was educated at Christ Church, Oxford, and called to the bar in 1818. He was a Tory (and later a Protectionist) and sat as MP for Dundalk from 1824 to 1826; for Ripon from 1826 to 1828; and for Oxford University from 1829 until he accepted the Chiltern Hundreds in 1854.

The Times, May 7, 1855

Sir R. H. Inglis has been for a whole generation one of the most conspicuous and honourable personages in the great council of the nation. Much more than any other living man, he illustrates the force of what English people are proud to call 'character'. People may or may not have valued his opinions, or respected his reasoning powers; they may or may not have followed the lead of one who scarcely ever assumed to guide; but all respected, admired, and even loved the honest, hearty, genial, courteous gentleman, who spoke the whole truth, as he held it, from his whole soul, with no respect either of persons or of circumstances, and apparently with no other object than to record a clear testimony and quiet his own conscience. Hence, while it would be difficult to say what Sir R. H. Inglis has done, what vote he has carried, what measure he has forwarded or delayed, he has undoubtedly possessed a great, though indefinite, weight in the Legislature. No one who ever heard him speak could fail to understand how it was that he won the respect and affections of men who, nevertheless, declined to acquiesce in his conclusions.

Harty Tarty

Spencer Compton Cavendish (1833–1908), Marquis of Hartington and later 8th Duke of Devonshire, was educated at Trinity College, Cambridge. He was a Liberal MP for North Lancashire (1857–68); for Radnor district (1869–80); for Lancashire North-East (1880–5); and for the Rossendale division of Lancashire (from 1885 until he succeeded to the dukedom in 1891). He entered the Cabinet as Secretary of War in 1866, and was first Postmaster-General and then Chief Secretary for Ireland during Gladstone's first administration. When Gladstone retired in 1875, he assumed the Liberal leadership in the Commons, but on Gladstone's return to office in 1880 he served under him as Secretary of State for India and subsequently as Secretary for War again. In 1886 he led the Whig anti-Home Rulers into a loose coalition with Chamberlain's Radical followers. These Liberal Unionists were eventually subsumed within the Conservative Party and the Duke held Cabinet office under later Tory administrations as Lord President of the Council (1895–1903), president of the Board of Education (1900–2), and Leader of the House of Lords (1902–3). He resigned from Balfour's Cabinet when the administration split over Free Trade.

Herbert Gladstone, *After Thirty Years* (1928)

On great occasions Hartington could speak with a force given to few. Usually he sat silent, almost somnolent, imperturbable. Once Tim Healy was flashing out a bitter attack. Hartington was on the front Opposition Bench with his hat over his eyes, apparently asleep. Healy turned on him suddenly: 'There is the noble Marquis. Like a pike at the bottom of a pool.' Hartington's hat never stirred, but I saw his whole body shake with laughter. When moved by a great subject and the sense of his own responsibility, no man that I have known in the House of Commons, apart from Mr Gladstone, and in later days Asquith, could speak with such telling power. His views were never distributed to the lobby and the press. His great honesty, reticence, cool impassive judgement, his stately figure and solid ability fascinated an audience usually intolerant of slow and somewhat ponderous speech. His failure to form any progressive or even helpful views on the Irish troubles, which eventually submerged the Whig party, was to many of us who had to part company with him little less than a tragedy.

Lord Randolph Churchill

Lord Randolph Churchill (1849–95) was the third son of the 7th Duke of Marlborough, and was educated at Eton and at Merton College, Oxford. He was Conservative MP for Woodstock from 1874 to 1885; and for Paddington South from 1885 until his death. He held office as Secretary of State for India (1885–6) and as Chancellor of the Exchequer and Leader of the House of Commons (July–December 1886). He died of a wasting disease, sometimes, though not conclusively, claimed to be syphilis.

As Lord Hartington told Frank Harris, Churchill 'knew the House of Commons better than the House of Commons knew itself. He led it with such genius as it has never been led in my time. Such a Leader does not come once in a century. Every hour he was in the House strengthened his hold upon it, his control of it.'[23]

Sir Richard Temple, Letter to his wife, March 5, 1886

Towards ten o'clock the House filled again, and Churchill rose and baited Gladstone quite superbly. It really was a wonderful performance; and Gladstone no doubt was furious. Besides this, Churchill made a strong, frank, and effective defence of himself and his friends respecting their alleged understanding with Parnell in the autumn. His challenges to the Treasury Bench were famously delivered. All this time the benches, the galleries, and all the standing places were crowded, and it was an affair at which I was very glad to be present. We, of course, cheered Churchill at every suitable point; and when the other side made any demonstration, we made counter-demonstrations; and so the evening went on in a very cheerful way. At last we divided, not on the main question, but on the adjournment, losing by 160. Against us we found arrayed, not only the Irish, but the whole Liberal party, and that looks ominous.

John Redmond, 'Fifteen Years in the House of Commons', Lecture in New York, November 29, 1896

Lord Randolph had many great qualities, but he had an ungovernable temper and an overweening opinion of his own power. In a moment of temper, caused by a temporary difference with his Party, and thinking it was impossible for them to do without him, he resigned office. His resignation was accepted, and from that day his career may be said to have closed. He absented himself from Parliament for a considerable time, and when he returned it was evident some fell disease had laid its paralysing grasp upon him. He was still quite a young man, but he came back strangely aged and bent and broken. I have never witnessed a more pathetic scene. All his old friends assembled to welcome him. It had been arranged he was to commence the debate for the evening, and the knowledge that he was to make his *re-entrée* on the stage upon which he had played so brilliant a part brought together a remarkable assemblage. The Prince of Wales sat in the Peers' Gallery, which was crowded to overflowing. There was but one feeling amongst men of all parties—a desire to give a kindly welcome to the man who had been when in his prime a general favourite. In appearance he was strangely altered. It has recently been stated, and I believe it was true, that he had taken some drug to help him through the ordeal he had to face. Owing to a strange piece of ill-luck, an unexpected discussion which occupied an hour or more, intervened between him and his speech. During this time he sat the very picture of nervousness and misery. The effect of the drug had time to wear away, and when he finally rose to address the House, members were shocked to see his physical weakness, and to mark the sad havoc made on him by his fell disease. His nervousness was painful. In vain he sought to rouse himself and collect his thoughts. He was inaudible, almost inarticulate. No one could follow his speech. In silence the tortured House, tortured by the spectacle of his evident suffering, sat patiently until at last he abruptly ceased and fell back in his seat. It was pitiful. He was so young. His prospects had but yesterday seemed so bright. He was so brilliant, so full of life and vigour, so masterful, and now he was so utterly crushed and broken. From that day he never recovered. Again and again he strove with pathetic persistence to re-gain his lost position. It was of no avail. He became worse and worse, and finally sank into his grave. All during my experience of Parliament, I know of nothing more pitiful than this story of sudden dazzling success, followed by swift and utter disaster and destruction.

Charles Stewart Parnell

Charles Stewart Parnell (1846–91) was the son of a Protestant Irish landowner, a former High Sheriff of County Wicklow, and was educated privately and at Magdalene College, Cambridge. He was Home Rule MP for Meath (1875–80) and for Cork City (from 1880 until his death). He was Leader of the Irish Nationalist Party from 1879 to 1890, when the scandal surrounding the O'Shea divorce case (in which he had been cited as co-respondent) led to his being deposed. Twenty-six MPs remained loyal to him and separate from the other Irish Nationalists until 1900.

John Redmond, 'Fifteen Years in the House of Commons', Lecture in New York, November 29, 1896

The truth is, the English never understood Parnell. They never could fathom his aim and his policies. Though a man of strong passion, his outward demeanour was invariably cold and impassive. He seldom spoke once he had risen to a commanding position in Parliament. When he did speak the silence which crept over the House was absolutely painful in its intensity. He had something of that quality which Coleridge attributed to the Ancient Mariner. 'He held them with a glittering eye, they could not choose but hear.' He was no orator in the ordinary acceptation of the phrase. Indeed he commenced his Parliamentary career as a halting speaker, with almost an impediment in his speech. As time went on it is true he spoke with ease and fluency, but the great quality of his oratory was its clearness, directness, and terseness. 'No man,' said Mr Gladstone of him, 'is more successful in doing that which in my opinion few really do—namely, in saying what he means.'

At one time Parnell was the most hated man in the House of Commons. At another he was probably the most powerful and respected . . . You have already seen him as an obstructionist, detested, absolutely loathed, by Englishmen, fighting almost single-handed against all parties in the House of Commons, certainly the most unpopular men in Britain.

A few years later his position had somewhat changed. He was now more feared than hated, and when in the spring of 1882 he was released from prison, and the policy of Coercion was abandoned by Mr Gladstone, it seemed as if a reaction was about to set in in England with regard to Ireland, and to Mr Parnell personally. Suddenly the Phoenix Park murder took place, and the fury and hatred of England burst out afresh with a hundred-fold greater intensity than before. A blind unreasoning fury took possession of the public, and there was but one thought in every English mind, Parnell was the man responsible. Imagine yourselves in the House of Commons at its first meeting forty-eight hours after the murder. All London surged down towards Westminster. The police with difficulty cleared a passage for Members to enter the building through the crowds in the street outside. Such one or two of the Irish Members as were recognised were greeted with howls of execration. Inside the House there was the stillness of the tomb. By a strange and mysterious instinct every Member had come down dressed in black as to a funeral. Every available inch of room on the floor and in the galleries was occupied, and when Mr Gladstone, looking strangely old and haggard, rose to move the adjournment of the House in consequence of the crime, a sort of shiver seemed to run through the entire assembly. Mr Gladstone himself broke down. He had loved Lord Frederick Cavendish, and he could barely articulate his words in expressing his horror at the deed. When he resumed his seat Mr Parnell rose, pale and worn after his six months' imprisonment, but calm, erect, and defiant. A strange, fierce murmur ran round the House, the like of which I had never heard. It could not be described as a growl, though it had in it a note of savage hatred. We looked up startled, and knew not what was about to happen, but it suddenly died away into a silence so intense we could almost feel it. What had this man to say? This man, the indirect if not the actual cause of the murder? What right had he to speak—What right had he to be there at all? His very presence was an outrage! Never, as long as I shall live, shall I forget the looks of fierce detestation turned upon Mr Parnell at that moment. We, his friends, tried to counteract all this by a cheer, but so chilled were we by the scene that it died away unuttered on our lips. Mr Parnell, however, did not falter. In a few simple words, expressed without any outward sign of the influence of the scene upon him, he expressed his horror at the crime and sat down the most hated, distrusted, and feared man in England.

A. J. Balfour

Sir Arthur James Balfour (1848–1930) was educated at Eton and at Trinity College, Cambridge. He was a Conservative MP for Hertford, 1874–85; for Manchester East, 1885–1906; and for the City of London from February 1906 until he was created Earl of Balfour in 1922. He was Private Secretary to his uncle the Marquis of Salisbury as Foreign Secretary, 1874–80; Chief Secretary for Ireland, 1887–91; Leader of the House of Commons, 1891–2; and Prime Minister, July 1902–5. He later served as Foreign Secretary in the Lloyd George Coalition, from December 1916 to October 1919. He also wrote some books on philosophy.

Austen Chamberlain, *Down the Years* (1935)

He was in fact always strongest in attack and weakest in exposition, much better in the House of Commons, which had learned to know him, than in a mass meeting which was puzzled by his ways and often found it difficult to follow his argument and extract its meaning.

His power over the House was never more amazingly shown than in the months which followed his return to it as member for the City of London after his defeat at Manchester in the disastrous rout of the party in 1906. A mere remnant of his followers in the preceding Parliament had survived the débâcle. The House was full of strange faces. The majority, flushed with victory after ten years of defeat, was intolerant and rude to him. It was not so much that they disliked him as that they despised him, and contempt is less easy to conquer than hatred. They openly jeered at him and constantly interrupted him when speaking. In the midst of it all he remained unmoved even when his friends were provoked to fierce indignation and remonstrance, and before the year was out, he had won the respect of every one of his opponents. However much they disagreed with him or smarted under his rapier thrusts, they felt that he gave distinction to the House and brought qualities to its service which no other of its members possessed in a like degree.

David Lloyd George

David Lloyd George, Letters to his brother William George

August 2, 1904. I had an exceptional time last night. The House was packed. The *Manchester Guardian* 'Descriptive Sketch' which speaks highly of it is not in the Welsh Edition. It had not arrived in time and the Bank Holiday disarranged things. *Daily Telegraph* says in its leading article that if they were Radicals they would put their money on Mr Lloyd George becoming the leader of the Party! I said a word or two today with unction. Healey warned me today as a friend not to take any office which the Liberals wish to give me but to stand out for the post I wanted. He said, 'You are the only man amongst them who is worth a damn—stand out for your own terms.' He said that he had a talk with Carson about me and he said Carson told him I was the only man who was any real good on the Licensing Bill. Asquith too wooden, he said.

April 19, 1905. Made a severe attack on Balfour and Chamberlain. The former there but not the latter. B. delighted when I attacked Joe—wretched when I came to him. T.P. in his speech following referred to the eloquent peroration in the very fine speech delivered by the Member for Caernarvon.

Austen Chamberlain, Letters to his family circle

April 30, 1909. It is certainly a 'great' budget and affords infinite matter for discussion and amendment, if we are allowed time. It will touch up a great number of people and make the Government many enemies, but I should think will be popular with their party gatherings and afford many good texts for their tub-thumpers. But I do not profess to have got its cumulative effect or even its separate provisions clearly in my mind as yet, for it is enormously complicated and was not well explained by Lloyd George. He was fagged before he began. Halfway through he was dead beat and had to ask for a half-hour adjournment. He recovered somewhat after this, but much of the speech was read and badly read. He stumbled over the sentences, rushed past full stops, paused at the commas, and altogether gave the impression that at these points he did not himself understand what he was saying. The speech lasted from three to eight including the half-hour interval. The best part of it was the exposition of the large programme with which he began—a regular electoral manifesto, having little or no connection with the Budget.

'Did you notice,' said A.J.B., 'how I, I, I, recurred in that portion? I can't help thinking that he meant it as a bid for position against Asquith.'

Alec Hood told me afterwards that he had been watching the faces of Lloyd George's supporters and colleagues while he spoke. He thought them very unsympathetic and contrasted them, and Asquith's in particular, with the sympathetic and eager faces that surrounded me in my first and most difficult Budget.

May 1. I find from Lobby gossip and the Press that Lloyd George's statement is universally considered a failure as a statement—tedious, diffuse and confused. 'A pitiful exhibition,' Burns called it in speaking to Balcarres. 'What do you think of it?' asked Douglas of Nicholson, the second clerk at the Table. 'Why, I think he reads even worse than Palgrave!' Father will recall Palgrave's reading of documents which had to be 'read at the table' and will appreciate the bitterness of the criticism.

May 9. 'It seems to me,' said Leverton Harris to Haldane in the smoking-room on Budget night, 'that he read that speech like a man who does not understand what he is reading.' 'Of course he doesn't,' replied Haldane. 'Why we have been trying for weeks to make him understand clause —— of the Bill and he *can't*!'

H. H. Munro ('Saki'), *Outlook*, February 21, 1914

Tuesday, February 17—House of Commons engaged on seemingly humdrum topic of rural housing, which afforded one of the most entertaining discussions that the debate on the Address has given rise to. Royds, who is gifted with an excellent manner in Parliamentary aggression, all bite and no snarl, made effective attack on the Chancellor's Budget legislation, as exemplified by its result on the building trade. The Chancellor defended himself noisily, helped, rather than disconcerted, by the guerilla attacks made on him by Lord Robert Cecil and one or two others. With crowded benches of supporters behind him, ready to cheer his wildest assertion, and to giggle at his most trumpery flippancies, Lloyd George was quite capable of putting up a good fight. His half-truths and his jerry-built statistics would not bear cold inspection, but they would suffice for the exigencies of the moment. Then the House thinned out during the dinner-hour and the most interesting period of the discussion arrived. Pretyman was on his feet, with only a small knot of keen determined Unionists behind him; the noisy skirmishers had gone. Even more deserted were the Ministerial benches: Lloyd George had the merest handful of supporters at his back, and with the noisy giggling crowd had gone the Chancellor's inspiration; the fighting power had trickled out of him. Pretyman exposed the hollowness of his assertions, held up the working of his legislation to ridicule, demolished his figures, confronted his claptrap statements with the diametrically opposed statements of his brother Ministers, dominated him as the man who knows can always dominate the demagogue in a face-to-face encounter. The Chancellor rose again and again, but collapsed each time, worsted. Pretyman was dealing with indisputable fact and relentless logic, and those were not the weapons that the Chancellor fights with. Then the attack took a more personal turn. The misrepresentations and perversions of fact with which Lloyd George had assailed the Dukes of Sutherland and Montrose were suddenly flung back at him across the table. He was taunted with his meanness and his inaccuracy, the one as glaring as the other. There, in the cold dispassionate arena of the almost empty House, he was challenged to make good the statements that had bubbled up from him on the platforms of crowded meetings. But the fight was not in him. He had spoken already, he protested; his chance of defending himself was gone. The House was ready to accord him the privilege of a personal explanation there and then. But no! there were other people waiting to speak; he would be silent; he would be Saint Sebastian, quivering under yet another arrow of undeserved censure.

'It's not Saint Sebastian, you know,' said Clode to me afterwards; 'on these occasions he reminds me of the line: "Oh, a pitiful man was Saint Aloys." But he will have his revenge. He will discover that Pretyman's grandmother sold a piece of waste land to a needy community for some preposterous figure. Of course it will turn out that the figure was one-sixth, that it wasn't waste land, and that it wasn't Pretyman's grandmother. But Saint Aloys will have had his little moment of revenge; only a little moment, certainly, but then, you must remember, he is only a little man.'

In the evening the House settled down to the futile occupation of bringing Lloyd George to book for his numerous inaccuracies and offensive attacks on individuals. One might as well lecture a mole on colour-blindness. The Chancellor of the Exchequer is one of those very vain men to whom all opposition is a personal offence calling for reciprocal outbursts of offensiveness. He has no animus against wealthy titled owners of land as long as they are not opposed to him in politics—witness how gentle he can be with Baron de Forest. But a duke who does not agree with his land policy; a duchess who condemns his Insurance legislation; a marquess who does not preside at luncheon in his honour at Liberal clubs; a member who interrupts him at a meeting—these are more than Celtic flesh and blood can stand. There is no offensiveness, to Mr Lloyd George's mind, in calling a land agent a flunkey, likening a trustee to Ananias, telling a member of the House that he is skulking, or charging an unknown individual with having come into a meeting with a forged ticket. The charges may be grotesquely untrue, but these people have put themselves outside the pale of decent controversy by being opposed to Mr Lloyd George, and no language used in regard to them can be considered offensive. They may extract apologies from him by means of a lawyer's letter, but that is the only form of reparation that he will ever be persuaded to make.

A section of the Liberal members cheered and jeered themselves hoarse while the Chancellor triumphantly extolled his inaccuracies and repudiated the idea that he had ever been guilty of offensive personalities, but the majority recorded in his favour could not be whipped up to more than sixty-four.

Earl Winterton, Diary, August 18, 1919

L.G.'s speech on the adjournment. He started by a long and rather platitudinous discourse that was a mixture of Philip Kerr and Callisthenes[24] on our national outlook and the need for increased production . . . The interesting thing about the speech was that while it contained some good matter it utterly failed to thrill or even hold the House, and for the first time in my recollection L.G. didn't produce his own special H. of C. atmosphere; and he knew it! Was it because we are all tired? Or is it because L.G.'s stock is really down with the clay feet of the Idol peeping out?

Albert James Sylvester (1889–1989) was educated at Guild Street School, Burton-on-Trent. He became a civil servant and was private secretary of the Committee of Imperial Defence, 1914–21, and secretary of the War Cabinet, 1916–21, during which time he established a close relationship with Lloyd George. He later left the civil service to work as private secretary to Lloyd George until the latter's death in 1945.

A. J. Sylvester, Diary, June 7, 1932

L.G. comes to the House so seldom these days that a number of new MPs have not even seen him, let alone heard him speak. Today was an occasion. He went to the ladies' gallery entrance and waited behind the Speaker's chair until prayers were over. Then, on the call 'Speaker in the chair', he entered. I was in my front seat under the gallery. When he walked to the corner seat of the front opposition-bench, members leaned forward, nudged one another and pointed, and this process went on as more members entered the chamber. The sun streamed in through the stained-glass windows and fell on L.G. He looked a fine picture, dressed in a blue suit, with his white hair and russet-coloured face. Professor Morgan Jones was the first speaker, and he greeted L.G., and the House applauded that welcome. When he came to his room, Megan said that one felt one would like to wet one's finger and rub it on his face to see it was not painted, he looked so well.

Frances Stevenson (d. 1972), later Countess Lloyd George of Dwyfor, was educated at Clapham High School and Royal Holloway College, obtaining a degree in classics from London University. After teaching for a while in a girls' boarding school, she became tutor to Lloyd George's daughter Megan. She became Lloyd George's secretary at the Treasury and his mistress over Christmas 1912 and eventually married him in 1943, after he became a widower. She became a countess when he was created an earl in 1945.

Frances Stevenson, Diary

November 30, 1934. Went up on Wednesday [28 November] with D. for the Defence Debate in the House. D. looking a little cheap and under the weather, but decided nevertheless to make his speech, for which I was glad, for it was an excellent one. He spoke I thought very slowly, even for him, and his voice rather lower than usual. But the speech has been much praised since especially by Tories. Simon too sent him a congratulatory note (D. says he was so pleased that he had not been attacked in D.'s speech, for D. has on occasions handed him some stingers). Today Gwilym telephones that the Tories are talking of nothing else, and that some say an entirely new political situation has been brought about. They speak of a possible combination of S.B., Winston, and D. Winston, by the way, had almost an ovation when he sat down after his speech, at which I was somewhat surprised, for I did not consider that he spoke as well as usual. But I suppose it was the *matter* of the speech that was more important than the delivery, and there is no doubt that Winston's line greatly pleased the

Tory party, as did D.'s speech, than which he has never delivered a wiser, or, I think, more statesmanlike. There was imagination in it, too, coupled with a patriotism that was almost imperialistic. I was unable to stay to hear the end of a speech as we were all turned out of the Ladies' Gallery at 7.30 in accordance with an absurd rule to that effect. The Sergeant at Arms found difficulty in getting us out, and he said to me as I went: 'I wish you would get your man to sit down before 7.30. I always have the greatest difficulty in getting the ladies out of the Gallery if he is speaking!'

June 20, 1936. D. had smashing success in House on Thursday, a real resurrection of his old fighting days. The House almost hysterical and so was I. The Front Bench literally cowed before his onslaught, and Baldwin's reply was pitiable. There was consternation on the faces of the Tory back benchers. After the speech a young Tory Member went up to Winston and said he had never heard anything like it in the House. 'Young man,' replied W., 'you have been listening to one of the greatest Parliamentary performances of all time.'

Bob Boothby, *Recollections of a Rebel* (1978)

I sat in the House of Commons with Lloyd George for twenty years, and our friendship, which steadily grew, is one of the things I have valued most in life. As the saviour of this country in 1940, Churchill goes into a category of his own; but Lloyd George was, without doubt, the greatest man I have ever known. In the House itself, by the time I got there, he was nothing more or less than a great artist expressing himself through the medium of politics. It was pure theatre. But the theatre and the capacity audiences he attracted were both too small. The back benches on both sides applauded, while the front benches sat in glum and sometimes miserable silence. Almost always he scored a century. Only once did I see him bowled out for a duck. That was by Aneurin Bevan in a debate about the miners, and he was visibly disconcerted. But the nation saw and knew nothing of all this.

In Parliament he was rather a lonely figure. He abhorred—and who can blame him?—the company of his Liberal colleagues, whose primary objective was to get rid of him. Except for one memorable occasion, which I have already mentioned, he lost touch with Churchill. He made no effort to talk to, still less to get to know, the Labour Party. He befriended only two of the younger Conservative members, Harold Macmillan and myself. He never came to the Smoking-Room. He preferred to remain in his dressing-room until it was time to go on stage. But if you ever got him alone, or with a few friends with whom he was at ease, he was the best company in the world. And he could never keep away from the House of Commons. I once met him behind the Speaker's chair on a Friday afternoon when it was empty. I asked him what on earth he was doing, and he replied: 'To anyone with politics in his blood, this place is like a pub to a drunkard.'

341

Stanley Baldwin

Stanley Baldwin (1867–1947), 1st Earl Baldwin of Bewdley, was the son of an iron and steel manufacturer and was educated at Harrow and at Trinity College, Cambridge. He was elected as Conservative MP for the Bewdley division of Worcestershire in 1906, but did not make his maiden speech for a couple of years. He emerged as Leader of the Conservative Party and Prime Minister in 1923, and served two subsequent terms as Prime Minister, from 1924 to 1929 and from 1935 to 1937 (as head of the National Government). He was created an earl when he retired in 1937.

G. M. Young, *Stanley Baldwin* (1952)

I asked him once how he prepared his speeches. He said, 'There is a cloud round my mind, it takes shape, and then I know what to say.' Sometimes, when he was tired, or the material too bulky to absorb, it would not take shape, and then the speech would be toneless and lifeless. But when the mood and the occasion met, few speakers have ever had the Commons so completely in hand.

His deliberate, patient courtesy—deliberate, because he chafed under bores, and most members of Parliament can be bores sometimes and some of them bores all the time—is only part of the secret. It was said, 'When you listen to Churchill you think of the speaker; when you listen to Baldwin you think of the speech.' Of all the great orators in our history, it is to Baldwin that a Greek would have awarded the palm of *charis*—grace, ease, charm: alluring listeners to agree with him if they could, and, if they could not, at least to listen. Very rarely did he have to encounter an unfriendly reception, and if there was some noise or disturbance when he rose, he would drop his voice—never try to outshout an interruptor, was another of his rules—so that members hushed themselves, and one another, to hear. To this add—a steady irradiation of humour, never unkindly, sometimes flippant, and flippant perhaps more often than a fastidious taste would approve or an impatient judgement endure; and a modest bearing which saved his earnestness from the least shadow of the homiletic, and which was in truth the outward expression of what at all times he felt most deeply, the immense significance of statesmanship and the immense insignificance of politics and politicians.

Harold Balfour, *Wings over Westminster* (1973)

The House of Commons may be the kindest and most sentimental body of men when its heart has been touched, but it is also the most critical assembly. It contains all sorts and conditions but all have one common factor. They must have done something to have been elected by tens of thousands of their fellow citizens. Some may have got there by loyalty or integrity or oratory, others by having the sense to keep quiet and let their friends speak and work for them. Anyhow, it is a remarkable cross-section of human character and quality. To hold the House is no mean achievement for anyone. I heard Baldwin hold the House in the palm of his hand, silent and enthralled, for forty-five minutes and with scarcely a note. It was in the early thirties, when the Tory Party was split from end to end on India. Churchill was leading the Indian Defence League in opposition to the Government's liberal reform proposals. Finally a full-dress debate on India was arranged. It was announced that the Prime Minister would speak.

Baldwin rose to a packed House. He had his notes written on the back of an envelope which he held up to his nose and sniffed at every few minutes— a very odd trick. He started his speech with a wide philosophical sweep of the tendencies and changes in distant lands. He gave us a few minutes of his favourite Mary Webb.[25] There was never an interruption. It was a superb achievement. He sat down to general cheers including my own. I went out to the lobby saying to a friend that I had not heard such a moving speech. Suddenly it hit me. What had he said about India? Absolutely nothing. That was oratory—that was.

❖

James Maxton

James Maxton (1885–1946) was the son of a Glasgow schoolmaster. He was educated at Glasgow University and worked as a teacher. He was an Independent Labour Party MP for the Bridgeton division of Glasgow from 1922 until his death, and was Chairman of the ILP from 1933 to 1939.

James Johnston wrote a weekly portrait of an MP for the *Yorkshire Post* over a period of two years. He also wrote a book about styles of oratory in Parliament, *Westminster Voices* (1928).

James Johnston, A *Hundred Commoners* (1931)

So far the picture is one of a fiery, impetuous nature. But the portrait is still far from complete. Traits have to be filled in which few people would expect to find in a revolutionary of Mr Maxton's type. He is, reasonably, expected to be brusque, angular, domineering, so possessed by his ideas as to have no room for the genialities of life. That such a man should sweep over the House with tornado-like speech, that he should cry aloud like a voice in the wilderness, and that his cry should be at times poignant, is perfectly natural; but that he should play with the House, that he should be one of its few sprightly jesters, that he should charm it by a kind of fanciful wit, that he should entertain it and should receive from it in return the tribute of rippling laughter, are quite unexpected things in a character so permeated by a revolutionary idea. Yet such is the part he often plays. He is one of the wittiest speakers in the House; he has a wayward, freakish humour, a touch of fantasy which is slightly reminiscent of Barrie.[26] He knows this gift of his, and he does not scruple to use it and so please the Philistines, the capitalist ranks opposite him.

It is due to his softening qualities of wit and humour that he is the popular, one might say the unusually well-liked, figure that he is in the House. Though he is ever ready to purvey laughter to the capitalists, he never compromises his sincerity by so doing. Without an effort, without a suggestion of having derogated from his mission or of simulating a passion which he does not feel, he passes from gay banter to fiery denunciation or fervid pleading. His humour extends to himself and takes note of his own peculiarities. He can laugh at himself as well as at others, a faculty which saves him from the devastating habit of revolutionaries to take themselves too seriously.

He has been called by one critic of Parliamentary speech the only natural orator in the House, but the description is misleading and suggests a style of speech which is not his. If the critic meant by it that Mr Maxton has the most spontaneous, the most natural and the most easily flowing speech in the House, the description would not be very wide of the mark; but if he meant to place him in the highest circle of the speaking hierarchy and to attribute to him the uplifting, exalting power which proceeds from what is quite properly called inspiration, he was wrong. Mr Maxton is not an orator, nor has he the finish, much less the majesty, which we naturally associate with the orator. He has the rougher eloquence which comes from a strong and sincere nature; he begins somewhat haltingly, but quickly he gathers momentum, and his words rush out precipitately and headlong.

Less sympathetic critics might describe his speech as glorified street-corner oratory. Although good speeches may be delivered at the street corner, the general idea is that the street-corner speech is a rather debased style of address, and the soap-box has become a subject of scoffing. The considerate and appreciative critic, therefore, would reject this description of Mr Maxton's speaking, and would prefer to describe it in its fervid aspect as akin to field preaching, the kind of impassioned utterance which one associates with a preacher in goatskins speaking in a lonely place amid the silence of Nature. There is something in him which links him with some of the prophetic figures in the Old Testament. He has a good deal of their ascetic ruggedness. Underlying this ruggedness, however, there is a flow of charm which causes the rocklike elements in his speech to be overgrown with a pleasant verdure.

He is happy in the voice which he possesses, a voice which harmonises with his nature and is indicative of his mixed qualities. It is a rugged voice, loud and strong, one might say rough, but it is musically rough. Its music is like the bustling rush of a mountain stream in spate, hurrying over a stony bed. I think one would be comforted and reassured by it if one heard it near by in a desolate place when fear or a sense of loneliness was creeping over one. It is a Scottish voice, free, however, from any marked local peculiarities, and it pleases Southern ears.

Bob Boothby

Sir Robert John Graham Boothby, KBE (1900–86), was the son of Sir Robert Boothby, KBE (who was Manager throughout most of his career of the Scottish Provident insurance company), and was educated at Eton and at Magdalen College, Oxford. He was Conservative MP for the East Aberdeenshire division of Aberdeen and Kincardine from 1924 to 1950; and for Aberdeenshire East from 1950 until he was made a life peer in 1958. He was Churchill's PPS, 1926–9, and Parliamentary Secretary, Ministry of Food, from May 1940 until his resignation the following year over the matter of failing to declare an interest in the freeing of Czech assets, which he had advocated in the House and in submissions to the Treasury. Churchill suspended him from his ministerial duties and instructed a Select Committee to investigate. Unfortunately, the maverick Boothby found that several of his enemies were appointed to this Committee, which eventually concluded that his conduct had been 'contrary to the image and derogatory of the dignity of the House and inconsistent with the standards which Parliament is entitled to expect from its Members'.

Boothby defended his honour in a remarkable speech which won the favour of the House and prevented his resignation as an MP. 'The House of Commons listened in absolute silence—in fact, when someone sneezed there was a murmur of "Order, Order",' wrote one witness; while Boothby recalled that on leaving the Chamber at the end of the speech 'there was a subdued but sustained cheer from both sides; and Maxton gave one of his unforgettable smiles'.[27] Churchill remained fond of Boothby, but never brought him back into government. Boothby gained popularity as an outspoken broadcaster in the 1950s, and he held various extra-parliamentary posts, such as rector of St Andrew's University, chairman of the Royal Philharmonic, and president of the Anglo-Israel Association. The writer of the following letter to Boothby's mother, the publisher Roger Senhouse, had been a contemporary of Boothby's at Eton.

Roger Senhouse, Letter to Mabel, Lady Boothby, January 28, 1941

Bob was as calm as I have ever known him when I called at 11 a.m. There were a few pieces of crumpled paper on the floor scrunched up and some thrown in the fire. I at once asked him whether he was going to read his speech. 'I now know every word by heart,' Bob said, 'but I shall of course take the speech with me.' . . .

Bob had arranged for a ticket for me, and St John Hutchinson and I were in the gallery some minutes before he was called. He had come in and sat next to Walter Elliot some five minutes before speaking. He started with a full audience, never faltered once, and carried through the full thirty-five minutes without a break in his voice or a hesitation of any kind. As a rhetorical feat it was, in its complete execution, an unqualified success, as an exposition of his case I found it utterly convincing, dramatic, but with the proper humility, and varied according to the content. It was heard throughout in pin-dropping silence—not a cough, not an interruption of any sort.

I am not myself sufficiently conversant with the attitude of assembled MPs in listening to Bob—or indeed to any other Member—to say or give any critical opinion of the true effect of the speech; but he did with them whatever he wanted, there can be no doubt of that. I could not help comparing this 'set piece', given in such awe-inspiring circumstances, with some stage piece given in a theatre where the actor can gauge at any moment the exact reaction he may expect from his audience and play upon the mass emotion, as he alone has learnt how after many rehearsals and many other performances in the same theatre of the same words arranged in the same order.

Bob knew his limits, it is certain, and was familiar with his surroundings and was therefore able to control the periods of his speech, but he could never give full bent to his true feelings: such action would have been fatal; he could not even be judge of the temper of his audience, or test it. Comparatively, it must be mere child's play for an accomplished actor to be certain of his house on any given night and give them emotionally as much as they will appreciate, but in the House of Commons today Bob could rely only on that really very chilling cliché 'a sympathetic hearing'. It was clear to me after a very short wince that the assembly was giving him that and very much more. But he was perfectly correct in giving himself no extra rein. He was at all times interesting and therefore held their attention and the well-trained range of his voice carried him along as so many of his listeners would have failed miserably. His voice rang out and by its quality alone compelled attention. Hutchinson was riveted throughout, I was always sure of that. My observation hardly extended across the floor as I did not wish to miss a word. Nor did I. Yet I found I could not always remain with my eyes fixed on the orator, for there were at least two reasons when I was not certain of my own emotional state or imminent reaction to whatever might come next.

There were, it seemed to me, two perorations, and the second was taken at a faster pace and therefore in a major key. The effect was terrific. He could not have given a better account of himself—or a truer. All must have been aware of his intention and on this speech history must judge him. The fourfold repetition of 'it is not true' was the highest point in the peroration to my mind, as no doubt it was intended by its author.

He carried himself so well throughout, his right hand sometimes in his jacket pocket, his papers usually in his left, and an occasional short dramatic gesture throwing sometimes into a wider sweep. There was a quiet and proper dignity in delivery and his departure and general bearing were really superb. Yet at no time could he be accused of acting—that is the very last impression I wish to convey—it was the very accomplished control and individual aplomb that gave him the great advantage of making this nightmarish ordeal appear so easy, when the whole House must have been keenly aware of the bleak and lonely apprehension with which such a cruelly shattering experience had to be tackled.

The whole tenor of his speech had been delivered with great confidence and, I would add for myself, consummate understatement. He had once mentioned his chief antagonist by name and left his listeners to draw their own conclusions.

He accepted in principle the findings of the Committee but clearly stated his guilt lay in the folly of omission and nothing else. Those are the words by which history—and not only his fellow Members—will judge his conduct, and every one of them rang out in the clearest tones.

Winston rose to his hateful task with every outward sign of constrained emotion and distaste. He began with short, staccato, hesitating utterances—shifting his position continuously in the limited space at his disposal, in his curious, delicate, almost pirouetting movement of first one foot, and then the other, such small feet so easily controlled under the rotund tummy—all eloquent of his unease at this 'heart-breaking business'. I found this unutterably moving. The impression given was one of grave doubt in the face of inexorable duty, and the expression of a sincere and lasting friendship to which he was determined to give full weight. 'It is at least the interruption of a career of high parliamentary promise' are words of high praise and encouragement. To follow these in almost the next sentence with references to the present personal friendship 'often a supporter in lonely and difficult moments' was a glowing tribute and his final words I take to be of high encouragement for the future. From any other man they would have rung quite differently—the mention of 'honour' even without 'glory' is dangerously close to claptrap and I felt certain that it was not the PM's intention . . . I do trust that all will now be well for you, for here was the great vindication of the victim of a vicious attack.

Aneurin Bevan

James Johnston, *A Hundred Commoners* (1931)

He has a keen debating faculty. That is one of the first things which one notes in him, and it is in these days a faculty which is too scarce. Good, however, as his debating powers are, he would not by means of them alone have made the impression which he has made. What has conquered the House is his vitality, his enlistment of all his bodily as well as mental powers in the expression of his argument. He thinks quickly, and he does not think quietly. His thought seems to take possession of him. Some speakers are gestureless, others make use of gestures, but he seems to be all gesture, involuntarily turning his whole muscular machinery into a means of expression. His gestures are both profuse and vivid. They combine vigour with picturesqueness and significance. He is the most vitalised speaker in the House.

Yet there is nothing thunderous or overwhelming about him. He is swift and tumultuous, he has the speed, the impetuosity, even the force of the wind, but whatever metaphor of storm may be suitable to him, those of a thunderstorm are entirely inadmissible. The reason is that he has the Welshman's lightness of voice. The overpowering, the majestic, are beyond the usual compass of the Welsh voice, perhaps beyond the usual compass of the Welsh temperament. Mr

Bevan has the voice of his country—not the most pleasant or melodious type of Welsh voice, but one that is pleasanter than the majority of voices in the House. It sometimes rises rather high. As he becomes excited, it becomes higher. He would do well to keep to the low, soft tones which are habitual with Mr Lloyd George.

He has one conspicuous quality which has already invested his speeches with distinction—he has courage. He is bold in attack, and he is ready to tilt against anyone, however formidable. Young Members are generally chary of provoking the prominent veterans, and if they do attack them they are inexpert and feeble. Mr Bevan fears no one, shrinks before no one. In recent years there has been no finer display of Parliamentary courage than his attack upon Mr Lloyd George during the Committee stage of the Coal Bill. So well was it carried out that for the moment no one thought of its audacity. He spoke to him and against him as equals in experience and power are in the habit of doing. He faced him, separated from him only by the breadth of the unbenched part of the floor. Excitedly and angrily, with a flood of words and a profusion of gestures, yet without any loss in coherence or incisiveness, he upbraided him for his treatment of the Bill, and roundly charged him with mere demagogy. So daring, so precipitate was the assault, that it left its victim astonished and slightly breathless. Veterans are not accustomed to such attacks from youths, and when youth does assail age and experience, it does not usually do so with such weakening, even paralysing, effect and with such an absence of braggart insolence. Mr Aneurin Bevan is clearly a man with a distinguished future.

Hugh Gaitskell, Diary, February 16, 1951

Last night in the Defence debate, where I had been the first speaker with a long, serious, read speech—suitable for the press and country rather than the House—Nye gave one of the most brilliant performances I have ever heard him give. It was also in good taste, good humoured, interesting and glittering with striking phraseology.

It is an extraordinary thing—the contrast between this and the previous incident of which I have spoken. What a tragedy that a man with such wonderful talent as an orator and such an interesting mind and fertile imagination should be such a difficult team worker, and some would say even worse—a thoroughly unreliable and disloyal colleague. Will he grow out of this? Will he take on the true qualities that are necessary for leadership? Who can say. Time alone will show.

Sir Henry 'Chips' Channon, Diary, April 23, 1951

Bevan has resigned [over the Budget]. This means a serious split in the Socialist Party and possibly the fall of the Government.

He made the traditional explanation to the House after Questions: but it was not a success and pleased nobody, for he was savage, vindictive, dramatic and too long-winded. He in turn assailed Gaitskell, insulted the Tories and railed against the Government and Attlee. Twice during his harangue the Speaker half rose to silence him, but lacked the guts. At the end of 32 minutes he sat down exhausted and defeated—temporarily. It may be that his bubble was burst, but I think it is more likely that he has run away, to fight another day. Much whispering in groups and rumours of an Election, etc. On the whole the Labour people are furious at his 'betrayal'. Harold Wilson has also resigned as President of the Board of Trade ... John Freeman also. In fact there is practically no Government since the Prime Minister is in hospital, and all his henchmen are deserting him. I watched Winston while Bevan was speaking. He sat grinning and dangling his watch chain. He looked like a plump naughty little boy dressed as a grown-up.

Tony Benn, Diary, April 23, 1951

The resignation of Nye was announced this morning. Harold Wilson's position was uncertain though it was announced later today that he too intended to go. I arrived at the Commons at two and went up into the Members' Gallery. With the sunlight pouring through the windows opposite, the Chamber was suffused in a warm glow of light. Jennie Lee came in at about ten past three and sat, flushed and nervous, on the very back bench, below the gangway. At twenty past three Nye walked in briskly and jauntily and went straight to his seat three rows back. He looked pale and kept shifting his position and rubbing his hands. The Front Benches on both sides were very full—Churchill, Eden and the Tories sat quietly.

Morrison, Chuter Ede, Noel-Baker, Dalton, Gaitskell and the others sat unhappily together. Then the Speaker called Nye Bevan to make his resignation statement.

His rising was greeted by a few 'hear hears'. Not many. The Government Front Bench looked sicker and sicker as the speech went on and the violence of the attack intensified. Jennie Lee behind him sat forward and became more and more flushed. Every now and again he pushed back the lock of his iron-grey hair. He swung on his feet, facing this way and that and his outstretched arm sawed the air. He abused the Government, he threw in a few anti-American remarks for good measure. He attacked the Treasury, economists, and the unhappy combination of an economist at the Treasury. Gaitskell showed clearly the contempt he felt. Dalton looked like death once warmed up and now cooled down.

The fact is that though there was substance in what he said Nye overplayed his hand. His jokes were in bad taste. I felt slightly sick.

He sat down, the hum of conversation started and the exodus began. Nye stayed put for a few moments. He rose to go, and Emrys Hughes shook his hand as he passed the Front Bench.

1. Michael MacDonagh, *Irish Life and Character* (1898), p. 263.
2. ibid., p. 268.
3. Lord Willoughby de Broke, *The Passing Years* (1924), p. 184.
4. Justin McCarthy, *Reminiscences* (1899), p. 173.
5. ibid., pp. 184 and 186.
6. Robert Cecil, 3rd Marquis of Salisbury, *Saturday Review*, May 4, 1861.
7. Sir William Fraser, *Disraeli and his Day* (1891), p. 284.
8. Sir Henry Lytton Bulwer (Baron Dalling of Bulwer), *Historical Characters* (1868), Vol. II, p. 428.
9. Quoted in Charles Whibley, Introduction to Benjamin Disraeli, *Lord George Bentinck: A Political Biography* (1905), p. xiv.
10. E. M. Whitty, *St Stephen's in the Fifties: The Session 1852-3, A Parliamentary Retrospect* (1906), p. 40.
11. Sir Almeric Fitzroy, *Memoirs* (1929), Vol. II, pp. 664-5.
12. Alexander Mackintosh, *Echoes of Big Ben: A Journalist's Parliamentary Diary, 1881-1940* (1945), p. 83.
13. G. M. Young, *Stanley Baldwin* (1952), p. 242.
14. Pitt had been a cornet in the Blues regiment.
15. Horace Walpole, *Memories of the Reign of King George III* (1845), Vol. II, p. 87.
16. Wright was editor of *The Speeches of the Right Honourable Charles James Fox in the House of Commons* (1815).
17. Lytton Strachey and Roger Fulford (eds.), *The Greville Memoirs 1814-1860* (1938), Vol. I, pp. 127-8.
18. The azure ribbon was the Order of the Garter.
19. *Dictionary of National Biography*, Vol. LIII, p. 364.
20. Quoted in George Henry Jennings, *An Anecdotal History of the British Parliament from the Earliest Periods to the Present Time* (1880), p. 280.
21. Fraser, op. cit., p. 450.
22. The subject was Lord Hotham's Judge Exclusion Bill.
23. Frank Harris, *Latest Contemporary Portraits* (1927), p. 244.
24. Philip Kerr was one of Lloyd George's principal private secretaries, later created Lord Lothian; and Callisthenes was the pseudonym of the man who wrote newspaper advertisements for Selfridge Stores.
25. Mary Webb, Baldwin's favourite novelist, wrote about country life.
26. J. M. Barrie, the creator of *Peter Pan*.
27. Quoted in Robert Rhodes James, *Bob Boothby: A Portrait* (1991), pp. 290-3.

9 Bores and Curiosities

Disraeli once said to a colleague on the front bench about
an MP who was speaking, 'For twelve years this man
was a bore: he has suddenly become an institution.'[1]

> Hesketh Pearson, *Dizzy* (1951)

Went to H of C. Told whips I had paired and should be
away for 3rd Reading of Home Rule Bill but would stay
and vote against Home Rule, if they would let me make
a speech in favour of it. Left them annoyed . . .

> Aubrey Herbert, Diary, May 15, 1914[2]

The dividing line between the bore and the curiosity is a fine one, which is why I have
combined them in this chapter. Whereas the one is abhorred for his obsession and his
capacity to induce tedium, the other is welcomed for producing 'chaff', or light relief
from weighty though tedious business. Some bores are nonetheless admired for their
tenacity, integrity, ingenuity, or ability to undermine Ministers, but the degree of tolerance for them always depends on the circumstances. Some are thought to be detaining
or amusing precisely because they have no conception of their comic personae. Some
bores just talk endlessly. Both bores and curiosities tend to be blind to the impression
that they make on others.

In the seventeenth century, the Revd G. Garrard, in a letter to Sir Thomas Wentworth
(afterwards the Earl of Strafford), wrote: 'I'll end, fearing I have now, at the month's
end, run into the same error which I condemned in old Sir George Moore in time of
Parliament, who, as your lordship may remember, would about eleven of the clock rise
up, and make repetition of all that had been spoken that day.'[3] Sergeant Hewitt, the
MP for Coventry in 1761, was widely regarded as a bore. 'Is the House up?' asked a
friend of Charles Townshend seeing him leave St Stephen's Chapel. 'No, but Hewitt
is!' was Townshend's reply.[4] One long-winded MP, in the midst of vigorously addressing
a House that was virtually empty, whispered to a friend, 'I am speaking to posterity.' 'If
you go on at this rate,' his friend replied, 'you will see your audience before you.'[5]

One evening Richard Sheridan asked Pearson, the doorkeeper, what was on and who
was speaking, to which Pearson replied: 'Indian affairs—the Major's up—the House is
asleep; why, Sir, haven't you brought your night-cap?', adding to Colonel Fitzpatrick
who was standing beside Sheridan, 'If the House, Colonel, are too sleepy to *cough* him
down, by G— they'll soon *snore* him down!'[6] Another MP, General Grant, once asked
Pearson how long Sir George Younge would continue to harangue. 'As long, General,
if he was allowed,' Pearson answered, 'as you would be in marching thro' and conquering

351

America.' Apparently, the General was amused at this joshing reference to a long and self-congratulatory speech he had made.[7]

Sir John Mowbray recalled that a Right Honourable friend of his, who liked the sound of his own voice more than his audience did, described the Parliament of 1860 to 1865 'as a "damnable dining Parliament"; and so it was. Bores were not encouraged; count-outs were frequent.'[8] Counting out the House was one way of stopping a bore in his tracks, but another means of achieving the same end, as John Bright said, was for the House as a whole to deploy noise 'as a remedy'.[9] For, as the sketch-writer E. M. Whitty wisely observed, the House of Commons 'is a body without any principles or prejudices, except against bores'.[10]

❖

Serjeant Wylde

Thomas Burton, Diary, March 18, 1659

Serjeant Wylde stood up to speak. Some moved that he had spoken, but leave was asked for him to speak, till the House was full.

He mumbled on, and cited a great many cases.

It seems, in the time of the Long Parliament, he was always left speaking, and members went to dinner, and found him speaking when they came in again.

❖

Like a dinner bell

John Timbs, A Century of Anecdote from 1760 to 1860 (1864)

There sat in the Parliament of 1783, David Hartley, member for Hull, the intolerable length and dullness of whose speeches rendered him a nuisance even to his own friends. His rising operated like a dinner bell. One day, when he had thus wearied out the patience of his audience, having reduced the House from 300 to about 80 persons, half asleep, just at a time when he was expected to close, he unexpectedly moved that the Riot Act should be read, as a document, to prove some assertion he had made. Burke, who sat close by him, and who had been for more than an hour and a half bursting with impatience to speak upon the question, finding himself so cruelly disappointed, bounced up, exclaiming, 'The Riot Act, my dear friend, the Riot Act! to what purpose? don't you see that the mob is already quietly dispersed?' This sarcastic wit, increased in effect by the despairing tone of Burke, convulsed every person present except Hartley, who never changed countenance, and insisted on the Riot Act being read by one of the clerks.

Mr Jenkinson, afterwards Earl of Liverpool, used to relate that Hartley, having risen to speak, at about five o'clock, in the Session of 1779, and it being summer, and generally understood that he would continue a long time on his legs, Mr Jenkinson profited by the occasion to breathe some country air. He walked, therefore, from the House to his residence in Parliament-street; from whence, mounting his horse, he rode to a place that he rented some miles out of town. There he dined, strolled about, and returned to London. As it was then near nine, he sent his servant to the House, to enquire who had spoken in the course of the debate, and when a division might be expected. The footman brought back for answer, that Mr Hartley continued still speaking, but was expected to close soon, and that no other person had yet risen. In fact, when Mr Jenkinson entered the House, Hartley remained exactly in the same place and attitude as he was near five hours before, regardless of the general impatience, or of the profound repose into which the majority of his hearers were sunk. However incredible this story appears, Wraxall declares that he has related it without exaggeration.[11]

Major Scott

Major John Scott (1747–1819) sat as MP for West Looe from 1784 to 1790 and for Stockbridge from 1790 to 1793. Virtually his only role in Parliament was as the champion of Warren Hastings, by whom he was handsomely remunerated.

T. B. Macaulay, 'Warren Hastings', *Edinburgh Review*, October 1841

Hastings intrusted his interests to . . . a major in the Bengal army, named Scott. This gentleman had been sent over from India some time before as the agent of the Governor-General. It was rumoured that his services were rewarded with Oriental munificence; and we believe that he received much more than Hastings could conveniently spare. The major obtained a seat in Parliament, and was there regarded as the organ of his employer. It was evidently impossible that a gentleman so situated could speak with the authority which belongs to an independent position. Nor had the agent of Hastings the talents necessary for obtaining the ear of an assembly which, accustomed to listen to great orators, had naturally become fastidious. He was always on his legs; he was very tedious; and he had only one topic, the merits and wrongs of Hastings. Every body who knows the House of Commons will easily guess what followed. The Major was soon considered as the greatest bore of his time. His exertions were not confined to Parliament. There was hardly a day on which the newspapers did not contain some puff upon Hastings signed *Asiaticus* or *Bengalensis*, but known to be written by the indefatigable Scott; and hardly a month in which some bulky pamphlet on the same subject, and from the same pen, did not pass to the trunk-makers and the pastry-cooks.

Pearson's aversion to bores

Joseph Pearson, *Pearson's Political Dictionary* (1793)

FINANCE—Sheridan makes even this dry subject *pleasant* as well as *instructive*. But how the devil can the House keep awake, when *David Hartley*, or his brother the *Major*, get hold of it? There is *Lord Newhaven*, too, a terrible bore this way. I don't pretend to be a *Poet*, but, as Pye would say—

Whole hours he talks of arithmetic
And makes things clear as any *candlestick*!

GALLERY—A place up stairs where strangers are admitted to hear the debates, and take a *nap* when tired out with dull speakers.—N.B. Can always tell when Sir Henry Houghton is up.

LOWERING THE BRANCH—The House is lighted by a large chandelier, called a Branch, and, whenever Lord Beauchamp, Conway, Luttrel, or David Hartley, get up to speak, an order immediately comes out of the House for *lowering the branch*, that the candles may be lighted, all likelihood of the House being soon up being entirely at an end.—N.B. When any of the long-rob'd Gentlemen get up, I always call out to the messengers to have fresh candles ready.[12]

RUBBING OUT—A cursed hawking, and spitting, and shuffling of the feet, at any Member the House does not like to hear speak. *Sir Joseph Mawbey* was rubbed out the last Parliament.—*Mem.* I am always in fear about my friend Hartley. Major Scott is no friend of mine.

Colonel Barré gives a tedious speech

J. S. Harford, *Recollections of William Wilberforce* (1864)

On an occasion when Colonel Barré brought forward a motion on the British navy, Lord North said to a friend of his who was sitting next him in the House, 'We shall have a tedious speech from Barré tonight. I dare say he'll give us our naval history from the beginning, not forgetting Sir Francis Drake and the Armada. All this is nothing to me, so let me sleep on, and wake me when we come near our own times.' His friend at length roused him, when Lord North exclaimed, 'Where are we?' 'At the battle of La Hogue, my lord.' 'Oh, my dear friend,' he replied, 'you have woke me a century too soon!'

Dr Laurence

Dr French Laurence (1757–1809), the son of a Bath watchmaker, was educated at Winchester and at Corpus Christi College, Oxford. He was called to the bar in 1785 and acted as chamber counsel for the prosecution in the trial of Warren Hastings. He was a Whig and a protégé of Burke. In 1796 he became Regius Professor of Civil Law at Oxford and also MP for Peterborough, which he represented until 1809. He had a curious appearance and style of speaking, and in spite of obvious gifts veered towards boorishness. Lord Glenbervie said he was 'a sort of dinner bell to the great majority of the House, even of those of his own party';[13] Francis Horner wrote of 'the darkness and turbidness of Dr Laurence, who would fairly have talked his audience to death, if they had not coughed him to silence; his expectoration ... was dreadful to the hearer, but seemed to be full of knowledge and sense and acuteness, as I have always found him whenever I have had the self-command to listen';[14] while Sir Gilbert Elliot remarked that 'though a very clever man, with more information than anybody, he is not a famous articulator, and it is difficult to catch all he says. His conversation is like a learned manuscript written in a bad hand'.[15]

George Henry Jennings, *An Anecdotal History of the British Parliament from the Earliest Periods to the Present Time* (1880)

Dr Laurence's outward aspect was unwieldy, and almost grotesque. His mouth especially excited observation; and being fancied to resemble a shark's, the House of Commons jest ran that Alderman Brook Watson, who had lost his leg by that animal's bite, avoided the side where the doctor sat or lay.

James Hare, quoted by the Duchess of Devonshire, Journal, November 5, 1801

November 5. Dr Laurence to the great and natural terror of all present rose to speak at 3 o'clock and upon not being listened to said that 'nothing earthly nor scarcely anything heavenly should'—upon which a general laugh—he then said 'scarcely a divine revelation', upon which so much noise that he gave up the point.

Henry Brougham, *Historical Sketches of Statesmen Who Flourished in the Time of George III* (1839)

[He had] the very worst delivery ever witnessed—a delivery calculated to alienate the mind of the hearer, to beguile him of his attention, but by stealing it away from the speaker, and almost to prevent him from comprehending what was so uncouthly spoken. It was in reference to this unvarying effect of Dr Laurence's delivery that Mr Fox once said, a man should attend, if possible, to a speech of his, and then speak it over again himself: it must, he conceived, succeed infallibly, for it was sure to be admirable in itself, and as certain of being new to the audience. But in this saying there was considerably more wit than truth. The doctor's speech was sure to contain materials not for one, but for half-a-dozen speeches; and a person might with great advantage listen to it, in order to use those materials, in part, afterwards; as indeed many did, both in Parliament and at the Bar where he practised, make an effort to attend to him, how difficult soever in order to hear all that could be said upon every part of the question.

A *windy bishop*

Charles Greville, Diary, October 8, 1820

A certain bishop in the House of Lords rose to speak, and announced that he should divide what he had to say into twelve parts, when the Duke of Wharton interrupted him, and begged he might be indulged for a few minutes, as he had a story to tell which he could only introduce at that moment. A drunken fellow was passing by St Paul's at night, and heard the clock slowly chiming twelve. He counted the strokes, and when it had finished looked towards the clock, and said, 'D—— you, why couldn't you give us all that at once?' There was an end to the bishop's story.

Colonel Sibthorpe

Colonel Charles Delaet Waldo Sibthorp[e] (d. 1855) sat as Conservative MP for Lincoln from 1826 to 1832, and again from 1835 until his death. He was a vehement Protectionist and much loved for his eccentric resistance to progress of any sort. *Punch* dubbed him 'Mother Goose of Lincoln', while it has been said that Dostoyevsky, who read English parliamentary reports, used Sibthorp as the model for the railway-hating Lebedev in *The Idiot*. His son, Gervaise, sat as Conservative MP for Lincoln—though as a progressive Conservative—from 1856 until he died in 1861.

James Grant, *Random Recollections of the House of Commons* (1836)

I now come to decidedly the most curious personage, all things considered, in the House—whether on the Tory, Neutral, Whig, or Radical side. Honourable members will guess who I mean. I think I hear them with one accord pronouncing the name of Colonel Sibthorpe, the member for Lincoln. There is not a greater Tory than the gallant Colonel in the house; but the notoriety he possesses could never have been acquired by that circumstance alone; for though there are none greater, there are several as great. His eccentric manners have done a great deal to bring him into notice. He has all the singularity, all the horror of Liberal principles, none of the attachment to Toryism, and a great deal of the humour, of Sir Charles Wetherell, though without a particle of his talent. Even all this, however, would never have secured to him his surpassing notoriety. It is his physiognomy, embellished as it is by his whiskers and moustachios, that has clearly made him what he is. Denude him of these,— apply a razor or a pair of scissors to his face, commencing the operation at one ear and ending with the other,—and the gallant Colonel would be nothing— not even a personage at whose expense a joke might be innocently enjoyed. He would in that case be like Sampson [*sic*] shorn of his strength, when cropped by the Philistines.

Colonel Sibthorpe's countenance is altogether unique. It stands out in broad relief from the countenances of all the other members. Two or three other senators rejoice in tufts, and a few more in whiskers of decent proportions; but compared with the moustachios and whiskers of the gallant Colonel, one feels indignant that they should be dignified by the name. The lower section of his face, drawing a straight line from ear to ear, immediately under his nose, is one dense forest of hair. Had Dominic Sampson been fated to witness the whiskers and moustachios of the gallant Colonel, he would have exclaimed 'Prodigious!' for hours together. You hardly know whether he has a mouth or not—it is so completely buried amidst the surrounding crop of hair—until he begins to speak. He is extremely proud of his whiskers and moustachios. He would do and suffer a great deal for his party and principles; but rather than submit to be shaved, he would see Tories, Toryism, Constitution and all, scattered to the four winds. As already hinted, the gallant Colonel's countenance is not of the most prepossessing kind, and yet, in defiance of the maxim that 'they who live in houses should take care not to throw stones', he has a sort of *penchant* for finding fault with the countenances of others. Immediately after the dissolution of Sir Robert Peel's Ministry, he let loose on the Ministerial side of the House in the following strain:—

'Those honourable gentleman opposite (the new Ministry) will require at least three months before they are what is called comfortable in their offices—(Cheers and laughter)—and before they could enter and sit upon their new and, as he trusted they would always be to them, thorny seats—(Renewed cheers and laughter). When he saw those twenty-three gentlemen now going to enter the lists like racing horses, but not like horses of true mettle, but like splintered, spavined, broken-winded racers—(great laughter), with not a single sound one amongst them—(Renewed laughter); when he saw such a state of things, and the country in such a condition, he must protest against a motion in every respect so unjustifiable. He was no party man—he had never acted from party feelings; but he must say he did not like the countenances of honourable gentlemen opposite—(Loud laughter)—for he believed them to be the index to their minds—(Continued laughter). He would only say in conclusion, that he earnestly hoped that God would grant the country a speedy deliverance from such a band—(Shouts of laughter).'

Mr O'Connell, in reply, said: 'He would not quarrel with the observations of the gallant Colonel; they were delivered with so much good humour, and were like every thing that fell from him, couched in language of gentlemanly politeness—(Laughter). But on one point at least he must differ from the gallant Colonel. They who sat on that (the Ministerial side of the House) certainly had not such remarkable countenances as that of the gallant Colonel—(Peals of laughter). He would not abate the gallant Colonel a single hair (Renewed laughter) in point of good humour on that or any other occasion.'

Considered as a speaker, it is no easy matter to describe the gallant Colonel.

Sometimes he delivers himself in so low and indistinct a tone as to be inaudible to all but those immediately around him; at others, he makes himself heard in the remotest part of the house. Sometimes he is full of fun, calling into full play the risible faculties of his auditors; at others he has all the solemnity of a Daniel come to judgement. When in the former mood, he is remarkably well pleased with himself and his jokes; when in the latter, you would take it for granted that he fancies the world is come to an end. When in a funny humour his right arm is put into great requisition; he beats the air with it in all directions, but chiefly above his head. In his left hand there is always a roll of papers confusedly put together, just as if he had caught them floating in the water, when he was in the act of drowning. In his more pathetic moments he looks the very incarnation of seriousness, and puts himself into every conceivable variety of attitude. He turned his face from one part of the house to another, as if the body sat on a pivot, and were whirled round, not by a mere act of mental volition, but by some external application of force. A better specimen of the mock heroic you could not wish to see than that afforded by the gallant Colonel when in his graver moods. He is woefully deficient in judgement; if there be a right and wrong side of any subject, he is sure to adopt the wrong one. Indeed there are some honourable members who seek no better proof of the right side of a question, than to know that the gallant Colonel is on its opposite. He has, as already hinted, little intellect. If he does stumble by accident on a tolerable idea, it is like an oasis in a desert of nonsense. His voice has a sort of unearthly shrillness about it which cannot be described by words. He scarcely ever opens his mouth without exciting the laughter of the House. Honourable members generally attempt to put him down when they expect from him a speech of any length, but seldom with effect. On such occasions he stands quite cool and collected, looking at the papers in his hand until the vociferations of hon. gentlemen opposite, as he always calls them, begin to die away from sheer exhaustion on the part of the performers. In his serious moods he is a bore to his own party, as well as an infliction on the House generally. They would give any price to purchase his silence, but it is not to be purchased. He will speak. He never makes a very long speech, because he cannot; a quarter of an hour is the utmost length of time I ever knew him occupy the Speaker's attention on any occasion; but then the mischief is, he speaks on every subject, and when the rules of the House allow it,—in other words, when the House is in Committee,—it is no unusual thing for him to make fifteen or twenty speeches on one night.

It is but justice to the gallant Colonel to add, that he is good-tempered. He seems to have no personal resentments—no vindictive feeings towards any honourable member. His hostility is towards the principle, not towards the person holding it. Hence, he does not offend by any personalities, those on the opposite side of the house. I am sure the feeling in the house generally would be one of regret, were he to share the fate of his friend and prototype, Sir Charles Wetherell—that is, be excluded from it.

The bores of Supply

Robert Cecil, 3rd Marquis of Salisbury, *Saturday Review*, June 27, 1857

Mangnall teaches us all, at an early age, to recognise and admire the excellences of Parliamentary rule, and to understand that our paternal Government, like other paternal governments in private life, exists entirely by the power of stopping the supplies.[16] It has always been the object of unbounded reverence to theoretical writers on the Constitution, and to the select circle who believe in them. And yet, 'tis distance lends enchantment to the view. Their admiration would undergo a melancholy chill, if they could see how the Committee of Supply has degenerated, since the days of the Long Parliament, into an exercise-ground for convicted bores. Control over the public purse there is none—save when some Irish jealousy combines with a factious frolic of the Opposition to pare down one of the scanty doles which Science or Art, unrepresented in the House of Commons, has, by force of public opinion, painfully wrung from the Exchequer. Except for these fitful exercises of power, which are not of a nature to make us lament their rarity, the House has little left of its old prerogative, save the Saturnalia of dunces who practise their English in badgering the Government during some score of nights in June. We should be sorry to shock the nerves of any eulogist of the Constitution, by introducing him to one of these exhibitions.

The Ministry begin by trying to look cool and good-humoured, with as much success as a landsman generally achieves when he is going to be playfully shaved with an iron hoop and a bucket of tar-water on 'crossing the Line'. But, as the evening wears on, they give up the attempt. The bland smile fades from the features of Wood, Mr Lowe perspires freely, and even the gentle Ramsden is betrayed into a retort. All feel the effect, except Mr Wilson, who takes matters arithmetically, looks upon his supporters only as inconstant units of a constant quantity, and so contrives to keep his temperature and his temper. Except the all-suffering Government, all the talent has fled from the House— all, that is to say, that the electors of England, in their late mania for blood without the brains, have mercifully spared to us. You will in vain look for Graham or Russell, for Gladstone or Pakington, on a supply night. It is the day of small things—Sir Henry Willoughby is listened to as a financier, and Mr Bentinck as the leader of a party. The Bores of Supply reign supreme, and the graces of metropolitan diction are the order of the day—the letter 'h' is put under the table with the mace—most people sleep, some snore, a few talk, nobody listens—and the reporters sharpen their pencils with supreme indifference, contemptuously regardless of the piteous glances of some young half-fledged bore, not yet quite hardened, whom an exacting constituency or a vaulting ambition have plunged into a shoreless sea of bad grammar, and whose entreating eyes say, as plainly as eyes can speak, 'Do, do mend my sentences for me.' A Tenant League meeting in Ireland, convoked for the purpose of adjusting the claims of rival editors, a Knightsbridge vestry, entranced by the eloquence of Mr Westerton, are dignified and august bodies compared to the House of Commons in Supply.

First in fame among the creatures who reign in this misrule, and *facile princeps* in the terror which his uprising excites, is Mr Williams, by some irreverently termed 'the Wiscount'. There have been those who have affected to doubt the touching tale of Ministerial corruption and Roman virtue from which this historical sobriquet has arisen. To us it seems to bear the strongest internal evidence of truth. Mr Williams sits exactly over Mr Hayter. Night after night through a sultry summer, those dulcet tones, strained into more than their natural melody by a really honest zeal which makes the torture all the worse because the more hopeless, issue within a few inches of Mr Hayter's ear. We can well believe, that in some passing frenzy of unutterable bore, the temptation may have shot through his brain to transfer that nightly torment to a venerable assembly, where one proser the more would be scarcely noticed.

It would be invidious to attempt to decide between the claims of the rival candidates for a second place on this honourable list. Who shall determine the precedence of Mr G. Alcock or of Sir G. Pechell—two grey-haired sinners in this line? Who shall decide between the merits of the dinner-bell or the lullaby? How gaily the members crush away to their dinners through the half-opened door when the one begins to hammer! How sweetly they slumber while the other drones! Some of the new hands, too, show the greatest promise, but we will not blight their unfolding beauty by premature publicity. To change the metaphor, the diagnosis of the disease of boredom is strongly marked, and its victims may be easily recognised. It principally consists in a morbid and insatiable craving for divisions. The true Supply-bore is never known to listen to a compromise, even though he can only get two brother-sufferers to support him. When the voices are taken, he always says 'the Ayes have it', though his own solitary squeak has been heard alone above a chorus of Noes; and then, when he sees 150 men forced to spend a quarter of an hour in recording their opinion upon his microscopic crotchet, he feels that he is an important man, and has advanced a step on the pedestal of fame. It is needless to say that he stands high in the estimation of the Administrative Reform Association, and of all others who measure legislative excellence by attendance at divisions. It was because Sir W. Clay was a man of too good sense and taste to stoop to such a part that he was ejected by the sagacious electors of Tower Hamlets. The member is generally a fair specimen of the constituency; and the glory of the Supply-bore reflects a full halo on the sages whom he represents. And instead of an exception, he will be a sample of the House of Commons, if the new Reform Bill is merely to run in the groove of the old, and can devise no more statesmanlike improvement of our representation than by confining it to mere dense aggregates of numbers.

Whalley

George Hampden Whalley (1813–78), the son of a Gloucester merchant and banker, was educated at University College, London, where he gained a First in Rhetoric and Metaphysics. He was called to the bar, spent nine years as an assistant tithe commissioner, and served as a magistrate for Denbighshire and Montgomeryshire. He was High Sheriff of Caernarvonshire in 1852. He sat briefly for Peterborough (1852–3) and again for the same constituency from 1859 until his death.

Sir William Fraser, *Disraeli and his Day* (1891)

Whalley, Member for Peterborough, annually plagued the House on the subject of 'Maynooth'; he bored the House extremely. There was, however, some lingering good in Whalley. In the second year of the Parliament of 1874, at about half past eleven at night, he crossed the floor, and seating himself by me, said, 'Sir William, will you allow me to address you?' 'Certainly, Mr Whalley; what is it about?' 'You have taken an interest, Sir William, in the "Metropolitan Commons Enclosure Bill". Will you allow me to ask you to do me a great favour?' 'That entirely depends upon what it is.' 'You must have observed the impatience with which the House usually listens to my remarks.' 'I have.' 'I have sent to the Peterborough papers two columns of a speech, which I intended to deliver on the subject. The Business of the House is late: and they will not endure me after twelve o'clock, of that I am sure.' 'They will not.' 'Sir William, there is only one thing that will enable me to speak: and unless I do so, you will understand I shall be in a dilemma at Peterborough; for my speech will appear tomorrow.' 'How can I help you, Mr Whalley?' 'In one way: I can only speak in reply to a strong personal attack. Am I trespassing too far upon your good nature if I ask you to make it?' 'I assure you, Mr Whalley, that, though exceptionally kind-hearted, I can say very disagreeable things if I choose.' 'Of that I feel confident, Sir William. I hope I am not taking too great a liberty.' 'In short, you wish me to pitch into you thoroughly: to give it you hotly.' 'I should consider it extremely kind if you would.' 'Well, Mr Whalley, when is it to be done?' 'You know when the "Hocus Pocus" begins at the table: when the Clerk reads out the day for the second, and third reading of Bills, etc, etc. If you will get up when he reads out "Metropolitan Commons Enclosure Bill": and go on so long as you feel inclined, I can then reply to you; and shall feel everlastingly obliged.'

Whalley retired to his place: and affected to go to sleep. Accordingly having gone out, and got a copy of the Bill, in order that I might know something about it, I observed on the back of it, as the parents of the Bill, the names of

Mr Whalley and Sir George Bowyer. This was quite enough for my text. Sir George Bowyer being a Roman Catholic, and representing the Pope in the House; Whalley, on the contrary, being, or professing to be, the most rabid of Protestants. Accordingly when Sir Erskine May stood up, at the termination of business, and read the long list of Bills to be postponed on various days, on his arriving at this particular Bill, I rose: I will not trouble the reader with my speech: I gave it Mr Whalley so hotly, and so strongly as I possibly could; accusing him of the most horrible forms of Jesuitry; that while affecting to champion the Protestantism of England, he was really a secret agent of the Pope: that his demonstrations against Maynooth had always been a sham: that in this, as in other things, a secret, but perfectly cordial, understanding existed between him and Sir George Bowyer; that no one could put the slightest confidence in him hereafter: that as for his unfortunate constituents, pity for them must, in every honest breast, be mingled with contempt, etc, etc.

Had Sir George Bowyer been present, not being in the secret, his writhing would have diverted me.

Whalley, who had affected to sleep during the beginning of my harangue, opened his eyes suddenly; seized the paper of the proceedings of the day: glanced at it hurriedly; asked his neighbour what it was all about; gazed at me with horror; and when I sat down, rose and delivered a speech of half an hour, to the utter bewilderment of the few Members left in the House, of the Speaker, the clerks, and the door-keepers.

The House adjourned: walking down the centre of the House I said, without turning towards him, 'Mr Whalley, I hope I played my part well.' In a voice, hoarse with emotion, gratitude, and lack of breath, he replied, 'Admirably! Sir William; Admirably! the best done thing I have ever known: I thank you heartily: I wish you a very good night.' We parted.

To the uninitiated reader I may explain that these little comedies, occasionally played, are perfectly consistent with absolute sincerity, and straightforwardness of principle in serious matters.

Lord Raynham

John Villers Stuart (1831–99), Viscount Raynham, 5th Marquis Townshend, was educated at Eton and worked as a clerk in the Foreign Office from 1850 to 1854. He sat as Liberal MP for Tamworth from 1856 until he succeeded to his father's title in 1863.

Robert Cecil, 3rd Marquis of Salisbury, *Saturday Review*, May 8, 1858

Lord Raynham is the well-meaning man of the House of Commons. The locality is one in which the species is not encouraged; but the House has no right to be ungrateful to him, for he has more than once furnished it with a good laugh.

Last year, he produced a Bill which, among other wise provisions, made it a penal offence, punishable with fine and imprisonment, 'to give any unnecessary pain to any animal whatever'. Great was the triumph among the lower creation at the news of their proposed emancipation. The eels wriggled with joy at the prospect of being no longer skinned. The lobsters' eyes gleamed with delight at the vista of an unboiled millennium. The fleas and bugs forgot their ancient rivalry, and joined in a deputation to the noble Lord to press upon him a distinct provision for the immediate abolition of cracking. But, in spite of this support from his clients, the House of Commons only received his Bill with inextinguishable mirth. In the present year, in imitation of more ambitious emancipators, he has abandoned his larger measure, and tried the policy of 'bit-by-bit Reform'. This time, the canine creation is the object of his care. Though sinful man be still condemned to the ravages of frequent war, on man's faithful companion at least Lord Raynham will cause to shine the halcyon days of universal peace. But we must say that his mode of making peace consists, like that of the old Roman tyrant, in a preliminary devastation. 'If any person'—so, in effect, runs the Bill—'shall cause any dog to fight with any other dog, the dog shall be killed, and the owner shall be fined.' We have here an admirable illustration of the principle of vicarious responsibility. The dog is to be killed, and the owner fined, for an offence committed by a third person who has no sort of interest in the wretched dog's life or in the owner's purse. We need hardly say that this peculiar scheme of canine relief was received by the House of Commons with an equally mirthful negative.

Nothing daunted, however, Lord Raynham made another attempt, on Tuesday night, at philanthropic legislation. The hour was late, the House was full, the excitement of a sharp debate on the Danubian Principalities had not yet evaporated. It had been an evening of no small interest, not only from the momentous import of a question on which hinged for ages the destinies of five millions of men, but also from the features of the debate. All the chief actors had played their parts with various but characteristic success. Mr Gladstone had delivered a stirring oration, worthy of his fame, but in a fence of repartee had been foiled by Mr Disraeli's lighter weapon. Lord Palmerston had appeared in his habitual part—Mr Disraeli had eaten his accustomed leek—and Lord John Russell had defended the cause of the Principalities with a skill which would have been effective if, unfortunately, he had not written in exactly an opposite sense three years before. The division was over—men were discussing in twos and threes the features it disclosed, the majority which Government always had at its command on the numerous occasions when it agreed with its opponents, and the test which it afforded of the relative forces of Lord Palmerston and Lord John—when the Speaker, in a voice scarcely audible through the hum, called on Viscount Raynham. The evocation produced a small, meek-looking personage at the end of the House, who rose and looked despairingly first at the clock and then at the throng, then shuffled his papers and looked again. His lips were seen to move, and some few members fancied, but were not quite certain, that another murmur was added to the noise. A few more pantomimic appeals, and another display of formidable papers—a sight which at midnight rouses the House as red cloth rouses a bull—and suddenly members turned from their chatting, and set to work to bait the unfortunate philanthropist into silence. 'Move, move,' 'divide, divide,' 'agreed, agreed,' incessantly vociferated by three hundred indignant voices, is an ordeal before which everybody but an Irishman soon gives way. Lord Raynham sat down; and, amid roars of laughter, the President of the Poor Law Board said that he could not assent to the motion—which was about Metropolitan Workhouses—because the mover had given no reasons in its favour, to which cruel mockery the mover only rejoined by a mute look of helpless despair. But the crushed worm will turn, and revenge is sweet even to a philanthropist. By the forms of the House, which jealously protect the minority, it is always in the power of any two members, by the simple process of calling for a division, to delay proceedings for half-an-hour, and to punish the majority by cramming them during that time into a narrow lobby, compared to which the Black Hole of Calcutta was a paragon of ventilation. Supported by Mr O'Brien—who forms the most prominent part of the decaying rump of the brass band, and is therefore *ex officio* factious—Lord Raynham insisted on inflicting this punishment on the audience that had refused to listen to him. But happily the tears of his friends appeased his wrath. During the two minutes which always elapse while the bells are being rung for the division, it was amusing to watch the towering presence of Mr Bentinck, the soft insinuating grace of Mr Williams, and the official eagerness of the Clerk of the House, all crowding at the feet of the obdurate lord to implore him to yield, while the House, mad with the anticipated punishment, positively screamed 'agreed'. Better counsels prevailed, and the negative was passed without a division.

Charles Newdegate

Charles Newdegate (1816–87) was educated at Eton and at Christ Church, Oxford. He sat as Conservative MP for North Warwickshire from 1843 until his retirement in 1885.

Justin McCarthy, *Reminiscences* (1899)

There was a time when the figure of Charles Newdegate was familiar to everyone who visited the Lobby. Newdegate was the type of a class of men that has now faded almost altogether from public life. I do not know how I could better describe him than by saying that he represented the No Popery theory. With Newdegate the duty of the true Englishman was beyond everything else to resist the encroachments, and to detect and to defy the emissaries of the Church of Rome. He was a steady Conservative in politics, and he followed his leaders loyally when they would lead; but there were fields of enterprise into which they would not always lead, and then Newdegate had to become a leader for himself, and it not uncommonly happened that when he rose to lead the way, nobody followed, and he went along undismayed. He was often a solitary watcher on the tower straining his eyes to discover some new and treacherous advance of Popery, and it happened, only too often, that when he gave warning to the defenders of the tower the warning was given in vain. Even those who had command of the garrison would not listen, or did not believe, or did not care; and the one man who saw the danger might as well have shut his eyes for all the good that was done by his keenness of vision. Poor Newdegate had fallen upon an age that was at once too practical, too busy, and too sceptical, to believe in prophetic vision. His Conservative colleagues had their minds occupied, for the most part with things that seemed to them of more immediate concern than the doings of the Church of Rome. Their minds were taken up with the consideration of the best methods for resisting Gladstone's new-fangled financial projects; for preventing Cobden from entering into commercial alliances with the Emperor of the French; for preventing Bright from bringing about a reduction of the Franchise. They could not be got to interest themselves in the machinations of the Jesuits and the projects of the Pope. As to Mr Disraeli, Newdegate soon found that he could not place any possible reliance on such a leader. Why, during the troubles of 1860, Disraeli had positively stood up for the security of the Pope's temporal throne, as a guarantee against Italian revolution, when Newdegate was made aware, on the most trustworthy information, that the Pope and the Italian Revolution were secretly working hand in hand for the upset of the Protestant Church, and the establishment of Popery as the State religion in England. When the Tories were in office there was not—will it be believed?—one single man on the Treasury Bench who gave his full sympathy to the great purpose of Newdegate's political life! When the Tories were out of office Newdegate found just the same want of sympathy among the occupants of the Front Opposition Bench! There was, therefore, nothing left for him to do but to stick to his annual motion for a periodical inspection, under State authority, of all the Nunneries and Convents in Great Britain and Ireland. Even this annual motion found but a feeble and half-hearted support from Newdegate's Conservative colleagues.

The more responsible members of the party intimated plainly enough that they considered the annual motion a bore, and some of the younger Tories sneered at it and made jokes about it. Newdegate was in many ways a fine type of the English country gentleman. He had a stately presence, he was a splendid rider; his horsemanship won the admiration of no less competent an authority than Rarey, the famous American horse-tamer, who once paid a brief visit to England. Newdegate was a man of education, according to the old-fashioned system of the Universities of his younger days; he had courteous manners, and was on friendly terms with all those around him, no matter what their opinions might be on the great No Popery question.

The House extinguishes a bore

The bore on this occasion was Augustus Smith (1804–72). Educated at Harrow and at Christ Church, Oxford, he was a Deputy-Lieutenant of Cornwall and was Liberal MP for Truro from 1857 until his retirement in 1865.

Robert Cecil, 3rd Marquis of Salisbury, *Saturday Review*, March 24, 1860

The adjourned debate on the Reform Bill was on the orders of the day; and some members of weak mind imagined it would come on. But its prospects were intercepted by the peculiar constitutional implement with which the House of Commons, without infringing on freedom of speech, extinguishes a bore. The process is not uncourteous, but thoroughly effectual. Tuesday night was a happy instance of its beneficent operation. A few minutes after the Ballot division, an Irishman got up with a grievance concerning some Irish harbour, unpronounceable to Saxon lips. His appearance produced a marked anxiety for their dinner on the part of the few members who lingered still. But something far more terrible remained behind. There was a notice that the Fore-shores of Cornwall were to be discussed by Mr Augustus Smith, the distinguished pro-prietor of the Scilly Islands. Now, enthusiasm on the subject of Fore-shores is confined to a very limited circle. In fact, we shrewdly suspect that the only account most MPs would be able, if catechised, to give of it would be a modest hypothesis that fore-shores were the reverse of back-shores. It was soon easy to see that the distant prospect of a Reform debate had not fascination enough to reconcile those who were to be reformed to a preliminary study of harbours and fore-shores. Almost all that remained of the House of Commons was the dirty benches glistening with greasiness under the glare of the Bude lights. A few resigned members dotted them here and there; the Speaker, embowered in an arbour of green silk, might have slept or watched for all that human eye could tell; the orator himself could scarcely help yawning between his own sentences; and the only sign of life was a crowd of eager, grinning faces, spying through the glass door of the House opposite to the Reporters' Gallery. Presently, the fruit of their consultations began to appear. Two or three unknown, and therefore irresponsible, members—none but the most insignificant venture to meddle in such work—lounge in, listlessly, at various doors, and each sits himself down demurely by the side of one of the resigned, and hitherto immov-able, listeners. After a few minutes of exhortation, each man succeeds in luring off his prey. The poor mover of the unpopular motion knows too well what those manoeuvres mean, and nervously tries to get on faster with his case. Presently he sits down as if he were shot, as he sees a figure run up and whisper something in the Speaker's ear. The count-out has been moved, the glass is turned, the bells are rung, and the Speaker waits for the result, probably in sanguine hopes of a joyful release, while the luckless mover, who has been for weeks past preparing for this speech, looks the picture of despair. Meanwhile, a much livelier scene is being enacted in the lobby. The whole enterprise is a *coup manqué* if a sufficient number of men come in from library or dinner; so the managers of the count-out throng the door-way, crushing, arguing, shouting, and trying by imprecations, entreaties, actual force, and piteous tales of the Speaker's illness, to deter men from coming in. At last the allotted two minutes are over—the tale of members present falls short of forty—and the exulting officials and the disgusted orator bestow themselves for the rest of the evening on whatever amusements they can improvise.

The Speaker grows impatient

Lord Palmerston, Letter to Queen Victoria, August 13, 1860

Members are leaving town; but the tiresome ones, who have no occupation of their own, and no chance of seeing their names in the newspapers when Parliament is up, remain to obstruct and delay by talking. The Speaker, who has not been quite well, grows as impatient as any official who has hired a grousing moor and cannot get to it; and a few nights ago, when a tiresome orator got up to speak just as the end of the debate had been expected, the Speaker cried out, 'Oh, oh!' in chorus with the rest of the House.

The Scotch MP with his companion, McCulloch's Commercial Dictionary

Mark Boyd, *Reminiscences of Fifty Years* (1871)

A member who had sat in Parliament for many years, and was held in high respect on the Treasury as well as the Opposition bench, described to me a class of men who came into Parliament, but who neither from education nor from experience of the world and society were qualified to do anything beyond voting, but who nevertheless fancied themselves statesmen, and occupied the time of the country in hearing themselves talk, so that they might next morning see the report of a speech infinitely better than any they had delivered paraded to the country. He often told me that in his opinion the gentlemen in the Reporters' Gallery were far too indulgent to these parliamentary bores. He described to me such a member, whose only qualification, it was alleged, was giving good dinners. This man fancied himself the successor of Adam Smith and David Ricardo; for if a financial or politico-economical question was to be discussed, the honourable member for —— took his place early in the evening, passing to it along the floor of the House with slow step and grave countenance,

367

looking patronisingly on the Treasury as well as the Opposition bench, so as to convey the impression to the minds of the Commons of the United Kingdom that for this evening 'I am Sir Oracle'. His companion-in-arms on such occasions was that most valuable of all commercial volumes, *McCulloch's Commercial Dictionary*. One memorable evening, when seated with his 'trusty and well-beloved' mercantile lexicon at his side ready for instant reference, he found that the debate which he was to illuminate would not come on for another hour, giving him time for dinner. He left his McCulloch behind him on his seat, and a well-known and facetious member, one of the wags of the House, having ascertained that he was snugly seated at dinner, took the *great* absentee's place to the infinite amusement of his fellow MPs. The wag carefully inspected the marked passages of the volume, and looking up at his friends, who were enjoying the scene, exclaimed, 'Why, good gracious, if he gives us all McCulloch says on the subject, he must speak for hours. This won't do, I must stop it; the interests of Parliament as well as our own domestic comforts demand it. We shall be regularly bombarded, therefore, in nautical phraseology, I must close the channels by lifting the buoys.' He at once proceeded to give an advanced or retrograde position to all the slips of paper which the coming orator had so carefully arranged to lead him unerringly to those lengthened quotations which were to constitute the main staple of his intended speech.

Dinner over, the honourable member returned to his place, where the great fear was that before he commenced his speech he might detect the displacements of his marks; but this event did not occur. A very few introductory remarks sufficed, when his hands were forthwith on his bulky tome; on went the spectacles, up went the volume. 'I shall now read to the *Hoose* what Mr McCulloch says.' But, alas! the eminent political economist's authority was not forthcoming. Up and down and across did his eyes flit and wander, but as nothing would avail, he made the important announcement that he would save the time of the *Hoose* (hear, hear) and proceed to another branch of the subject. And on this head he would refer also to Mr McCulloch, but with like success. After floundering and floundering, to the vast relief of the *Hoose* he resumed his seat.

All the consolation and the sympathy he got was from his next neighbour, an old and experienced member, who asked him why he always borrowed or attempted to borrow Mr McCulloch's brains instead of applying to his own; for that he, like many others in that House, had a copy of the work, which he infinitely preferred reading at home, and for the future would advise him to do the same, otherwise another such exhibition in the House of Commons might render the volume unpopular, and make its distinguished author very angry.

One of London's city celebrities, an alderman and ex-lord mayor, who disliked this MP very much, was highly pleased at what had occurred the previous night in St Stephen's, and for two or three days occupied himself chiefly in asking his friends if they had read the account of the absurd exhibition of Mr —— in the House of Commons. 'I always was prepared,' said the alderman, 'for what happened: for I knew him to be a most pretentious individual. He never,' continued the alderman, 'rose to any eminence as a tradesman, and because he had some 60,000*l*. left him by a relation, he imagines he is shortly to become Chancellor of the Exchequer.' The alderman usually wound up his criticism— 'Well, as long as he continues in Parliament he must be a distinguished member, as he is considered the ugliest man in it.'

Prithee cut it short

Peter Rylands (1820–87) was educated at Boteler's Grammar School, Warrington, and became an ironmaster. He was a magistrate for Lancashire, Cheshire and for Warrington, where he was Mayor, 1853–4, and a director of the Manchester and Liverpool District Bank. He sat as Liberal MP for Warrington from 1868 until he was defeated in 1874; and for Burnley from 1876 until his death.

Henry St John Raikes, *The Life and Letters of Henry Cecil Raikes* (1898)

Mr Rylands had many solid qualities, but he was not an inspiring speaker, and on one occasion in the House, when he was on his legs and appeared likely to remain there for some time, this was brought home to him in a somewhat unkind manner.

As he proceeded with his indictment of the Government a slip of paper began to travel along the benches, and in its course aroused a good deal of merriment. At length it reached the orator, and on looking at it he was confronted with the following doggerel:—

> 'Preposterous Peter, prithee cut it short;
> That Dizzy doeth what he didn't ought
> We know. Yet life were sweeter,
> Which gave ten Dizzys and dispensed with Peter.'

The cruel part of it was that the effusion emanated from his own side of the House.

Hartington's yawn

Alexander Mackintosh, *Echoes of Big Ben: A Journalist's Parliamentary Diary, 1881–1940* (1945)

The story of his yawn has come down from one generation to another. I witnessed the incident. Hartington, making his Indian Budget statement, put his hand over his mouth, gave a huge yawn, and turning to Porter, the Irish Attorney-General, who was the only occupant of his bench, muttered 'this is damned dull'. When I told the story in a little book it was challenged by a reviewer, who had read elsewhere that the yawn was invented, but Sir John Horsburgh-Porter, to whom I wrote, assured me that his father often recalled the incident and was greatly amused by 'the humanity of the aside'.

King Edward told von Bulow about it, as is recorded in the German's Memoirs. Hartington 'yawned over his own tediousness', King Edward said, 'but after he had had a huge yawn he went ahead with his speech, without turning a hair'.

James Caldwell

James Caldwell (1839–1925) was educated at the Universities of Glasgow and Edinburgh and practised as a procurator in Glasgow, where he also lectured on law. He retired from the law to run the family calico-printing business. He was a Liberal Unionist MP for the St Rollox division of Glasgow (1886–92), then stood unsuccessfully as a Liberal Home Ruler elsewhere in the city. However, he was Liberal MP for Mid-Lanarkshire from 1894 until his retirement from the House in 1910. From 1906 to 1910 he was deputy-chairman of Ways and Means.

Henry W. Lucy, *Strand Magazine*, August 1897

Students of the Parliamentary reports have no opportunity of realising the individuality of Mr Caldwell. He has a rich gift of what an eminent American at present on visit to this country calls 'platitudinising'. The word will not be found in the *New Oxford Dictionary*. But it is most effective as indicating a constant, ever-fed supply of pointless words, wrapped up in cotton-wooly sentences. Amongst other attractions, he has a loud, level voice, a rapid intonation, and an almost inhuman staying power. He can go on talking for two hours just as conveniently as he can gabble through one, and probably will say less to the point than he might by accident have compressed in a spin of sixty minutes.

One day a suffering colleague on the Select Committee on the Scotch Public Health Bill cut a notch on a stick every time Mr Caldwell rose to make a speech. When the Committee adjourned the stick was found to contain forty-one notches. Of course, the member for Mid-Lanarkshire is never reported, for the managers of newspapers have to consider their interests with the public. That reflection does not lessen the anguish of those who, whether in Select Committee or the House, have to suffer Mr Caldwell at length.

It was late at night, in debate on a Superannuation Bill, that the Lord Advocate quietly scored off this contribution from Scotland to the business resources of the House. The proposal of the Bill was that superannuation should take place at the age of sixty. Mr Caldwell, anxious for economy, moved an amendment extending the period for five years. No man, he argued, ought on the ground of incapacity to be laid on the shelf before he reached the age of sixty-five.

'Oh yes,' said the Lord Advocate [Graham Murray] sternly regarding Mr Caldwell; 'some persons become incapable long before they are sixty-five.'

Members roaring with laughter turned up *Dod*, and found that Mr Caldwell is only fifty-eight.

A 'Bores Eleven'

Harold Balfour, *Wings over Westminster* (1973)

Every Parliament has its own particular 'Bores Eleven' and the 1931 Parliament was no exception. I expect the younger members were just as annoying to the old hands as some of them were wearisome to our back-benchers. Captain of the 'Bores Eleven' was dear old Sir Edward Campbell, who sat for Bromley. He was Parliamentary Private Secretary to Kingsley Wood. Invariably loquacious, with eyes that gleamed until, by popular acclaim, he was superseded by the Liberal, Sir Percy Harris. Harris carried the distinction of being known throughout the Commons as 'the Housemaid' because whenever he spoke he emptied the Chamber. First wicket down and second bat was Loftus, who sat for Lowestoft. He was a currency expert and used to stop you in the Lobby, breathe in your face and push a currency pamphlet in your hands. Another fine player was Sir Waldron Smithers, MP for Orpington, round-faced, bald and friendly, and who played the organ every Sunday in his local church. His main claim to fame is as author of the song rendered at many a Tory supper of those days, 'Stanley boy, You're the boy for me'.

1. Hesketh Pearson, *Dizzy* (1951), p. 208.
2. Aubrey Herbert (1880–1923) was a son of the 4th Earl of Caernarvon. Something of a maverick, he sat as a Conservative MP from 1911 until his death, though he spent World War I in military service in the Middle East and the Balkans.
3. Quoted in George Henry Jennings, *An Anecdotal History of the British Parliament from the Earliest Periods to the Present Time* (1880), p. 484.
4. J. Roderick O'Flanagan, *Lives of the Irish Chancellors* (1870), Vol. II, p. 128.
5. W. Charles Townsend, *History of the House of Commons, 1688–1832* (1844), Vol. I, p. 143.
6. Anon., Preface to Joseph Pearson, *Pearson's Political Dictionary* (1793), p. 10.
7. ibid., pp. 10–11.
8. Sir John Mowbray (ed. by his daughter Edith M. Mowbray), *Seventy Years at Westminster* (1900), p. 173.
9. Harry Graham, *The Mother of Parliaments* (1911), p. 167.
10. E. M. Whitty, *St Stephen's in the Fifties: The Session 1852–3, A Parliamentary Retrospect* (1906), p. 10.
11. The same story is related by Professor Pryme in his memoirs, but there it is mistakenly told about Hartley and Sir Robert Walpole (who had died in 1745), Alicia Bayne (ed.), *Autobiographic Recollections of George Pryme Esq., MA* (1870), p. 218 n.
12. 'Long-rob'd Gentlemen' were barristers.
13. Francis Bickley (ed.), *The Diaries of Sylvester Doublas [Lord Glenbervie]* (1928), Vol. II, p. 170.
14. L. Horner (ed.), *Memoirs and Correspondence of Francis Horner* (1843), Vol. I, p. 285.
15. Countess of Minto (ed.), *Life and Letters of Sir Gilbert Elliot, First Earl of Minto, from 1751 to 1806* (1874), Vol. I, p. 139.
16. Richmal Mangnall (1769–1820) was a schoolmistress in Yorkshire who wrote *Historical and Miscellaneous Questions for the Use of Young People* (1800). This became a standard textbook and was published in various revised editions throughout the nineteenth century.

10 Mr G.

Occupied 18,000 columns of Hansard in his life, and
appears in 366 volumes.

Geoffrey Madan[1]

In the 1890s William Ewart Gladstone was able to look back with a sense of pride and nostalgia on his unique parliamentary career—it spanned sixty-two-and-a-half years with a break of twenty months in the mid-1840s. 'I am the only commoner now living who sat in the old burned House of Commons,' he wrote. 'I also dined with the Speaker (Manners-Sutton—first of the seven whose subject I have been) in Saint Stephen's Chapel then his dressing-room. I look back upon it with a warm interest and resource on account of its grand oratorical traditions in particular.'[2] When he arrived in the House, he encountered MPs whose experience stretched back into the eighteenth century: 'On the opposite benches he saw George Byng, who had been first returned for Middlesex in 1780 as the colleague of Wilkes; on his own was Sir Charles Burrell whose earliest colleague for Shoreham had been the father of Shelley.'[3]

Gladstone described himself as 'a steady and close attendant' in his first year, but he 'made only twice what could be called speeches': his maiden speech on the Slavery Abolition Bill on June 3, 1833, and another in 1834 against the proposal for the admission of Nonconformists to the universities. He was eager to serve Sir Robert Peel, the Tory leader, and when Peel asked him to be ready to attack one of the Opposition, the Irish Radical MP Richard Lalor Sheil, he was obedient though reluctant, preferring to develop his own argument rather than attack the argument of another. 'A mean man may fire at a tiger,' he wrote in his journal, 'but it requires a strong and bold one to stand his charge: and the longer I live the more I feel my own (intrinsically) utter powerlessness in the H. of C. But my principle is this: not to shrink from any such responsibility when laid upon me by a competent person—Sheil, however, did not speak, so I am reserved and may fulfil my own idea, please God, tonight.'[4]

In 1834, during Peel's brief administration of that year, Gladstone was appointed Under-Secretary of State for War and the Colonies and because his department's chief was Lord Aberdeen found himself its leading spokesman in the Commons. A few years later, in 1841, he was disappointed to be given only the vice-presidency of the Board of Trade. He entered the Cabinet for the first time in 1843, as president of the Board of Trade, but resigned the following year over Peel's decision to increase the government grant to the Roman Catholic seminary at Maynooth. Although he was protesting against this decision (which contradicted the argument of a book he had written about the relations between Church and State), he ended up, for complicated reasons, both voting and speaking in favour of the Maynooth Bill, much to the bewilderment of his fellow

372

MPs of all colours. In December 1845 Peel brought him back into the Cabinet as Secretary for War and Colonies, but he was without a parliamentary seat throughout his seven-month tenure of this office.

Yet by the 1850s Gladstone had become a parliamentary force. The sketch-writer E. M. Whitty noted his 'capacity for exposition and debate, which has been improving yearly (one sure sign of genius), and which, when he gets rid of some lingering defects, such as a too rotund up-and-downish management of the voice, will constitute him the first House of Commons speaker—which is not being an orator—of his time, Disraeli not excepted'.[5] Gladstone himself was most proud of his 1853 Budget, which one economist has called 'perhaps the most brilliant of his achievements in the House of Commons'. Yet it was his 1860 Budget which was undoubtedly his greatest parliamentary triumph in this field, all the more so because it was achieved in a period of his career when he was not the leader of a large, whipped majority in the Commons. George Saintsbury, biographer of the Earl of Derby, the Tory leader, judged that 'few greater feats have ever been performed than the mustering, chiefly by mere force of individual advocacy, of a majority of 116 in favour of a Budget which revolutionised English commercial policy, which affected all manner of interests, and which was not very warmly beloved, even by all the Chancellor's own colleagues, in a House where the normal Government majority was not much more than the odd sixteen'.[6] Hugh Childers, later to become Chancellor of the Exchequer under a Gladstone premiership, recorded in his diary: 'Gladstone's wonderful Budget speech for just four hours. Sat close behind him.'[7]

Gladstone's parliamentary duels with Disraeli started in the 1850s, when Gladstone crushed Disraeli's 1852 Budget, but reached their apogee in the 1870s. Balfour, according to Margot Asquith, said that 'when roused, Mr Gladstone without any preparation could pulverise all his opponents, as his moral indignation was always more formidable than Disraeli's facile ridicule. He added: "Mr Gladstone's flexible rhetoric was a dangerous instrument in debate." '[8] Yet there were times when Disraeli had the upper hand. During the latter's tergiversation over parliamentary reform in 1866, Gladstone 'was not nimble enough to deal with Disraeli's opportunistic turn of speed'—according to Gladstone's most recent biographer, Roy Jenkins. 'As a result the good humour of his speeches, on which Dean Stanley had so strikingly commented in 1854, temporarily deserted him and he was judged by many to be blundering and blustering.'[9]

He was a stickler for attendance in the House of Commons and for many years, whether as Leader of the House or as Prime Minister, wrote his nightly report of parliamentary proceedings to Queen Victoria from his seat on the Treasury bench. 'As Prime Minister, Gladstone regularly sat on the Treasury bench in the Commons for seven hours a day, and often for over nine hours,' one Gladstone expert has pointed out. He 'usually began sitting in the Commons about 2.15 p.m. and often sat, with an hour off for dinner, until after midnight.' The mornings he devoted to his correspondence, which was prodigious even by the standards of the day. 'My brain assumes in the evening a feminine susceptibility,' Gladstone once noted in his diary, 'and resents any unusual strain: tho' strange to say, it will stand a debate in the House of Commons.'[10] Despite his demanding attendance during the Session, he managed to keep up his reading in many subjects for purely intellectual edification, such as literature, history, biography or religion. This shone through in his parliamentary speeches, showing 'a mind hardly ever at a loss for a fact or a reference'.[11]

His administration in the early 1880s was precariously dependent on the coalition of different interest groups that comprised the Liberal Party, but he steeled himself against blows that would have felled a lesser parliamentarian. One commentator noted that 'his eloquence does not always carry by his force the bills that he presents, and when he is not followed in a question his adversaries, and even his friends show him no pity; an adverse vote scarcely seems to touch him. In the sittings of the 26th and 27th of April, 1883, he was beaten over and over again by a powerful majority; but this did not disturb him at all. On the 12th of May, 1882, he even sustained a total defeat, after having threatened to dissolve the House; but when beaten and driven into a corner about the dissolution, he put it off and resigned himself to the facts.'[12]

The same commentator wrote that Gladstone owed his success to 'his eloquence, his dexterity in Parliamentary conflict, and his sympathetic manners'.[13] A Tory newcomer in 1885, Lord Ernest Hamilton, was another who was impressed by both Gladstone's rhetorical skills and his courtesy: 'Mr Gladstone was a source of ceaseless delight. His splendid presence, his arresting voice with the curious burr in it, his magnificent Homeric periods, which sounded so superb and which meant so little, fascinated me from first to last. His courtliness to foe no less than friend was even more captivating than his oratory. While I was stumbling and halting through my absurd maiden speech, Mr Gladstone sat throughout with his hand to his ear in an attitude of reverent attention. My own front bench talked loudly among themselves the whole while—a direct snub which quickly reduced me to imbecile incoherence . . . Gladstone was magnificent and sonorous, but his utterances were cryptic and left no sense of completeness.'[14] Although he was noted for his civility and manners towards MPs of all parties, Gladstone was forceful in his antagonism towards opponents within the parliamentary arena, but as Balfour put it: 'We may be sure that outside of the House of Commons Mr Gladstone never made a butt of any man.'[15]

In the 1892–5 Parliament, Gladstone's performances were still remarkable. 'Mr Gladstone rose amid cheers—the whole of his supporters rising—at 3.45,' recorded his private secretary Sir Algernon West in February 1893. 'A quarter of an hour very fine, in an impressive, but not loud voice. Two hours' explanation nearly, and a quarter of an hour's peroration—fine, and his voice good, though low throughout. What an effort for a man of 88!!!'[16] Henry W. Lucy felt there was 'no falling away in mental power or in oratorical effect',[17] though he noted that Gladstone could not resist the opportunity to give the House the benefit of his views on almost any subject. The principal plank of the legislative programme, his second Home Rule Bill, was held up not only by Tory obstruction, but also by Gladstone's compulsion to speak and to speak at length. The Irish MPs had reached a covenant of silence in order to expedite proceedings. But, as Lucy asked: 'What is the use of a policy of silence, if the Minister it is designed to support speaks on every amendment submitted in Committee, rarely takes less than half-an-hour to do it in, and sometimes approaches three-quarters of an hour?'[18] On one occasion he upstaged his own Under-Secretary of State for India. He stood up to suggest a procedural compromise, but 'having stood for a moment on his feet at the table, said a few words and listened to the welcoming cheer with which he was received, was irresistibly drawn into the vortex of debate'. By the time he had sat down he had spoken for three-quarters of an hour, thereby taking up one quarter of the time allotted to the debate and leaving no time for his Under-Secretary of State to speak.[19] Later in the Parliament he was confining himself to shorter speeches in general. 'He was on his legs only five minutes over the hour,' Lucy noted, 'and he seemed to have left nothing unsaid.'[20]

Throughout most of his career Gladstone spoke with the comforting knowledge that his devoted wife, Catherine, was gazing down in wonderment at his performances to the exclusion of those of others. 'Mrs Chamberlain met Mr Gladstone coming out of the little buffet behind the ladies' gallery,' one historian has recorded. 'She bowed to Mrs Chamberlain and whispered with reverent joy, "I believe *he* is going to speak." She felt there was only one *he* for all of them.'[21]

Gladstone takes his seat

W. E. Gladstone, quoted by John Morley, *The Life of William Ewart Gladstone*
(1903)

I took my seat at the opening of 1833, provided unquestionably with a large
stock of schoolboy bashfulness. The first time that business required me to go
to the arm of the chair to say something to the Speaker, Manners Sutton—the
first of seven whose subject I have been—who was something of a Keate, I
remember the revival in me bodily of the frame of mind in which a schoolboy
stands before his master. But apart from an incidental recollection of this kind,
I found it most difficult to believe with any reality of belief, that such a poor
and insignificant creature as I could really belong to, really form a *part* of, an
assembly which, notwithstanding the prosaic character of its entire visible
equipment, I felt to be so august. What I may term its corporeal conveniences
were, I may observe in passing, marvellously small. I do not think that in any
part of the building it afforded the means of so much as washing the hands.
The residences of members were at that time less distant: but they were
principally reached on foot. When a large House broke up after a considerable
division, a copious dark stream found its way up Parliament Street, Whitehall
and Charing Cross.

I remember that there occurred some case in which a constituent (probably
a maltster) at Newark sent me a communication which made oral communication with the treasury, or with the chancellor of the exchequer (then Lord
Althorp), convenient. As to the means of bringing this about, I was puzzled
and abashed. Some experienced friend on the opposition bench, probably Mr
Goulburn, said to me, 'There is Lord Althorp sitting alone on the treasury
bench, go to him and tell him your business'. With such encouragement I did
it. Lord Althorp received me in the kindest manner possible, alike to my
pleasure and my surprise.

Gladstone's maiden speech

W. E. Gladstone, Diary, June 3, 1833

Began *le miei Prigoni*. West India meeting of members at one at Lord Sandon's.
Resolutions discussed and agreed upon; Rode. House 5 to 1. Spoke my first
time, for 50 minutes. My leading desire was to benefit the cause of those who
are now so sorely beset. The House heard me very kindly, and my friends were
satisfied. Tea afterwards at the Carlton.

Lord Albemarle, quoted by Henry W. Lucy, *Strand Magazine*, March 1899

One evening, on taking my place, I found on his legs a beardless youth, with whose appearance and manner I was greatly struck. He had an earnest, intelligent countenance, and large, expressive, black eyes. Young as he was he had evidently what is called 'the ear of the House', and yet the cause he advocated was not one likely to interest a popular assembly—that of the Planter *versus* the Slave. I had placed myself behind the Treasury Bench. 'Who is he?' I asked one of the Ministers. I was answered, 'He is the member for Newark—a young fellow who will some day make a great figure in Parliament.' My informant was Edward Geoffrey Stanley, then Whig Secretary for the Colonies, and in charge of the Negro Emancipation Bill, afterwards Earl of Derby. The young Conservative orator was William Ewart Gladstone—two statesmen who each subsequently became Prime Minister and Leader of the Party to which he was at this time diametrically opposed.

The 1852 Budget

The Tories had been out of office since the split over the Corn Laws, and the defection of the Peelites had left them with a distinct shortage of ministerial talent, especially of the financial kind.

Sir William Fraser 'noticed that Sir George Grey, and Sir Charles Wood, nearly related, facing Disraeli, the latter having been Chancellor of the Exchequer, kept interchanging signs, and nudging one another, laughing occasionally, while Disraeli was speaking; in fact turning him into ridicule, in a manner which was not only unfair, but ungentlemanlike; considering their social position compared to Disraeli's, their life-long experience of the House, and his extreme difficulties: difficulties which he had encountered in a manly, and well-bred manner'.[22]

The occasion had other peculiar aspects, as Fraser records. 'During the invective of Disraeli's speech, the Opposition presented a most remarkable appearance; not speaking to each other, pale in the gas-light. It reminded one of the scenes in the National Convention of the French Revolution. To complete the effect, although in Mid-winter, a loud thunderstorm raged: the peals were heard and the flashes of lightning could be seen in the Chamber itself.'[23]

W. E. Gladstone, Letter to his wife Catherine, December 15, 1852

I have been down at the House almost all day trying to unravel a dodge of Disraeli's about the manner in which the question is to be put by which he means to catch votes: and I think after full consultation with the Speaker and Wilson Patten that this will be accomplished. The debate may close tomorrow night. I am sorry to say that I have a long speech fermenting in me and I feel as a loaf might in the oven. The Govt. it is thought are likely to be beaten.

Lord Stanley, Diary, December 16, 1852

... The debate languished until Disraeli rose, at about 10.30 p.m., and delivered I think the most remarkable speech I remember to have heard in the Commons. He took little notice of other critics but applied himself seriously to answer Graham and Wood. The latter he attacked again and again, demolishing him at each onset, and closing with a personal invective which maddened the House with excitement. Never did one parliamentary speaker receive a severer infliction at the hands of another. Gladstone replied at past one in the morning: he rose choked with passion, for which he could find no vent in words, and his first utterances were the signal for fresh explosions from each side of the House alternately ... Gladstone's look when he rose to reply will never be forgotten by me: his usually calm features were livid and distorted with passion, his voice shook, and those who watched him feared an outbreak incompatible with parliamentary rules. So stormy a scene I have never witnessed. I went to the Carlton after the division: those who had voted with Gladstone prudently kept away: they could not have escaped insult.

W. E. Gladstone, Letters to his wife Catherine

December 16, 1852. I have been engaged in the House till close on post time, Disraeli trying to wriggle out of the question and get it put upon words without meaning to enable men to vote as they please, i.e. his men or those favourably inclined to him. But he is beaten on this point and we have now the right question before us. It is not now quite certain whether we shall divide tonight: I hope we may for it is heavy work waiting with a speech fermenting inside one.

December 17. We had an evening of the most intense interest. It began with a struggle of two hours on the point what question should be put; our purpose being to screw Disraeli up to the mark and oblige him to vote on an intelligible issue instead of a vague one. At length this was accomplished. The general debate then went on. He rose at 10.30 and spoke till one. His speech on the whole was grand: I think the most powerful I ever heard from him. At the same time it was disgraced by shameless personalities and otherwise. I had therefore to begin by attacking him for these. I see my speech is scarcely reported in the *Times*: i.e. about half may be given. My great object was to show the Conservative party how their leader was hoodwinking and bewildering them—and this I have the happiness of believing that in some degree I effected, for while among some there was great heat and a disposition to interrupt me when they could I could *see* in the faces and demeanour of others quite other feelings expressed. But it was a most difficult operation and altogether it might have been much better effected.

Well you see the Govt. is beaten—immense cheering followed the announcement and indeed the House was for the last five or six hours in a state of towering excitement. Today there has been a Cabinet and at three o'clock Lord Derby went down to Osborne with a view as is supposed to resignation—indeed it can hardly be anything else . . . My nervous excitement has not yet thoroughly subsided: but I *hope* to sleep tonight, please God, like a stone.

December 18. I have never gone through so exciting a passage of parliamentary life. The intense efforts which we made to obtain, and the Govt. to escape, a definite issue and which you might notice in the bye discussions, were like a fox-chase and prepared us all for excitement. I came home at 7, dined, read for a quarter of an hour, wetted my head, and actually contrived (only think) to sleep in the fur cloak for another quarter of an hour: got back to the House at nine. Disraeli rose at 10.20 and from that moment I was of course on tenterhooks, except when his superlative acting and brilliant oratory from time to time absorbed and made me quite *forget* that I had to follow him. There was a question whether it would not be too late but when I heard his personalities I felt there was no choice but to go on. The House I think has not been so excited for years. The power of his speech and the importance of the issue, combined with the lateness of the hour which always operates, were the causes. My poor brain was strung very high and has not yet quite got back to calm but I slept well last night. On Thursday night after two hours of sleep I awoke and remembered a gross omission I had made which worked upon me so that I could not rest any more. And still of course the time is an anxious one, and I wake with the consciousness of it, but I am very well and really not unquiet. When I came home from the House I thought it would be good for me to be mortified. Next morning I opened the *Times*, which I thought you would buy, and was mortified when I saw it did not contain my speech but a mangled abbreviation. Such is human nature at least mine. But in the *Times* of today you will see a very curious article descriptive of the last scene of the debate. It was evidently written by a man who must have seen what occurred or been informed by those who did so. He by no means says too much in praise of Disraeli's speech. I am told *he* is much stung by what I said. I am very sorry it fell to me to say it: God knows I had no wish to give him pain, and really with my deep sense of his gifts I would only pray they might be well used.

The 1853 Budget

Lord Stanley, Diary, April 18, 1853

Gladstone's budget, which occupied five hours, an extraordinary effort of rhetorical skill: no fault could be found except too great length, and a hackneyed quotation from Virgil spoiling a fine peroration: it was said that for three nights before this display he was unable to sleep from excitement, but the success was worth the suffering.

❖

The 1854 and 1856 Budgets

Justin McCarthy, *Reminiscences* (1899)

The telegraph system was then coming into operation for the reporting of the great parliamentary speeches in the interest of provincial newspapers. I had meanwhile obtained an engagement in Liverpool, and the newspaper to which I was attached tried to distinguish itself in that way. The attention of the whole country turned towards the Budget Speech of Mr Gladstone in the spring of 1854.

The Crimean war was on the verge of breaking out, and it was felt that Mr Gladstone's financial scheme could not but be affected by the impending crisis. In any case, Mr Gladstone's fame was lighting up splendidly, and when he spoke, all England listened. It was therefore resolved that we should have a telegraphed report of the Budget speech. Three reporters were to go up to town, of whom I was one. The question arose—how were we to get into the House? We could not get places in the Reporters' Gallery—at that time there was no idea of finding seats there for representatives of the provincial press. Mr Cardwell, the late Lord Cardwell, was applied to. He was then one of the members for Liverpool. It was pointed out to him that it was of the utmost importance that the merchants and traders of Liverpool should have the earliest and fullest report possible of such a speech on such an occasion. Mr Cardwell undertook to work the negotiation for us, and he was successful. The three reporters went up to London; and in the House of Commons were shown the arrangement that had been made. We were aghast when we saw the places set apart for us. In a little corridor behind the last row of the Strangers' Gallery, walled off from the ultimate limit of the House itself by the partition of the Strangers' Gallery; set thus far behind the worst placed visitor to the remotest gallery, and with the partition, made to some extent of glass, further shutting us off—thus we were to take our notes of Mr Gladstone's speech. A little table was set out for us with a lamp upon it, and that was all. We were accompanied by the then First Commissioner of Works, who was very courteous and good-natured. We expressed to him our disappointment and alarm. He only smiled and said, 'You need not be afraid; you will hear every word Mr Gladstone says.' So he went his way and left us to our fate.

Never have I felt more nervous. Every second that passed made me feel more and more alarmed, more and more despondent. There was a rather long list of questions to be got through before the Chancellor of the Exchequer could begin his speech, and we found, to our horror, that we could hardly hear a word of either question or answer. Each question was then read out in its fullness. Each questioner did not then merely get up and say, after our present fashion, 'Mr Speaker, I beg to ask the Right Honourable Gentleman the Secretary of State question number ——'; whatever the number might happen to be. As each member read out his questions, and each reply was given, our hearts kept sinking. We did not then know that questions are nearly always asked and answered in mumbling tones by members of the House of Commons. Even men who have clear and powerful voices get into the way of talking to their beards, as the Eastern phrase would put it. One little gleam of encouragement shone upon us. A question which we could not hear was answered by a Minister who spoke with the utmost apparent ease, but who, nevertheless, was perfectly audible to us far remote listeners. An attendant who was near told us that was the Chancellor of the Exchequer, Mr Gladstone. Our spirits rose; a load was lifted from our breasts.

Soon the last lingering doubt was dispelled, for Mr Gladstone began his great Budget speech. Not one single word of that speech was lost on us. The orator did not seem to be making the slightest effort, and yet his voice came soaring up to our far-off eyrie, not a half-note failing to reach our ears. Nor did he seem to be speaking deliberately for the sake of making himself heard. Sometimes the words came pouring out like a torrent, but never was any word inaudible; never did any word get mixed up with or run into another word. Oh! how unspeakably grateful we felt to Mr Gladstone; how we gladdened doubly in his eloquence because of his voice and his elocution; how happy we felt, now that we could accomplish our mission with perfect success and return home in triumph! Mr Gladstone had a houseful of admirers that night, but he had, I am well satisfied, no such devoted admirers among them all as the three Liverpool reporters behind the Strangers' Gallery. Other men were delighted with his eloquence; we regarded ourselves as rescued by it.

Two years after, we three were to go up to London for the Budget. We went up this time under what seemed to be happier auspices. We had succeeded in obtaining tickets of admission for that one night to the back of the Reporters' Gallery. We were to be admitted one at a time. We felt a little nervous, but, naturally, much happier than the former year in our far-off seats; but our hopes were soon sadly dashed. The Chancellor of the Exchequer this year was not Mr Gladstone, but Sir George Cornewall Lewis. I sat in the outer room waiting and watching the clock. At a certain moment I was to go into the gallery and take the place of one of my comrades, who was at once to come out. The moment arrived, and I went in. I had never been in the Reporters' Gallery before, and felt confused and dazed by the novelty of the situation. My comrade had instantly to give his place to me and leave the gallery; but as he passed he had time to turn on me a countenance of despair. What had gone wrong? At first I was too anxious about settling into my place to think of what was going on; but when I did settle down I began to ask myself what had become of the Chancellor of the Exchequer and the Budget speech. Then I saw that all the reporters in the front seats, the men trained to the ways and the voices and the acoustics of the House, were craning and straining forward in their places, and holding their hands to their ears, and now and then dashing down a hasty word or two in their notebooks; and then I was aware, as the old writers put it, of a kind of muttering or whispering that was going on in the region of the Treasury Bench. I listened, and I found that now and then—at rare intervals—the full formation of a whole word reached my anxious ears. Now and then, too, some fragments of figures and arithmetical calculations seemed to be flung upwards in our direction; and at length my mind had to settle down to the conclusion that this was the Chancellor of the Exchequer's Budget speech, and that, to use a homely phrase, 'I could not make head or tail of it.'

Here again Mr Gladstone came to the help of his three unknown admirers from Liverpool; for he did us the unspeakable favour of rising to criticise the propositions of the Budget, and he spoke at considerable length, and in short he let us know what the Budget was all about.

The 1860 Budget

William White, *Illustrated Times*, February 18, 1860

When the House opened on Thursday night it was still somewhat doubtful whether Mr Gladstone would be strong enough for his work on Friday. Late in the evening, however, a letter was received by Lord Palmerston from Mrs Gladstone, informing his Lordship that her husband had received Dr Ferguson's full permission to return to the House on the following day. Thus the question was set at rest. On Friday we need hardly say that the anxiety to get into the House was general and intense. [It had become well known that the Budget was to be emphatically a Free Trade scheme, and to be founded, in great measure, on the Commercial Treaty with France.] There were 'strangers' in attendance with orders as early as eleven o'clock, and long before the House opened the waiting-room was filled, and some forty or fifty people were ranged in St Stephen's Hall. Many of these, of course, did not get in. They had members' orders; but orders, when there is no room, are as useless as a cheque upon a bank when there are 'no effects'. The Speaker's gallery was crammed as soon as it was opened; and as to the Peers, they came down in such numbers that, after the seats which are set apart for them were filled, they besieged the Ambassadors' gallery and filled up every available seat there, and even then many of them were obliged to stand in the passage at the back of the benches. Amongst the peers that were present we noticed particularly the venerable Lord Chancellor, Lord Stratford de Redcliffe; his Royal Highness the Duke of Cambridge, who commands our Forces; the First Lord of the Admiralty, the Duke of Somerset; his grace the Duke of Argyll, who presides over our Post Office; Earl Granville, the Lord President of the Council; Earl Stanhope, Lord Stanley of Alderley, Earl de Grey and Ripon, Lord Chelmsford, Lord Wensleydale; the Earl of Derby, who for a time was obliged to stand; and last, though not least by a long way, Lord Brougham. The Foreign Ambassadors were not there in large numbers. Mr Dallas was present, and two or three more, including Count Persigny; but the diplomatic body was not represented in such strength as it usually is on great occasions. Touching Lord Brougham we have to record a curious fact. The noble Lord left the Lower for the Upper House in 1832, twenty-eight years ago, and until that night he never honoured the scene of his former triumphs with his presence. Until Friday night he had never even seen the new House. Surely this is a strange fact. It would be interesting to know the reason why the noble Lord has never availed himself of his privilege of listening to the debates of that assembly in which he won his fame and honours. Lord Brougham sat in front of the Peers' gallery below, where a seat was courteously reserved for him by his brother peers, and for nearly four hours he listened attentively, and apparently with deep interest, to Mr Gladstone's speech.

It was about 4.25 when Mr Gladstone entered the House. At that time it was very full—indeed, such was the anxiety to secure comfortable places that many of the members were down as early as three o'clock. The lobby was also full of strangers; but the right honourable gentleman glided by the expectant crowd almost unnoticed. He was there and gone before the few strangers who knew him could recognise him. 'That's Gladstone!' some one or two exclaimed, and every eye was turned to see him; but in a moment the right honourable gentleman vanished behind the doors. He did not walk up the floor of the House, but entered behind the Speaker's chair, and proceeded quietly to take his seat; but he was soon recognised, and then a hearty cheer burst from the Ministerial side. The Opposition, we need hardly say, did not cheer heartily. We cannot say that they offered no greetings, for there certainly was a faint cheer, which, being interpreted, seemed to say, 'We are glad to see you are recovered from your illness, but what have you got in that red box of yours? We should like to know that before we accord you a hearty greeting.'

This was Friday night; and on Friday night, when the adjournment of the House till Monday is moved, there is usually a host of questions to be discussed. On this occasion there were some upon the paper, and among them one standing against the name of Mr Bernal Osborne; and at the proper time Mr Bernal Osborne arose to introduce it. Mr Bernal Osborne is, as we all know, a very acceptable speaker in the House; not that the honourable member has anything very valuable to communicate, for he has not; nor that he ever succeeds in throwing much light upon the subjects on which he speaks. He is rather the rollicking merryman of the House than its teacher; and his speeches are looked upon as comic interludes, pleasant as varieties to relieve the dull tedium of prolonged business, but otherwise of not much value. But on this occasion the House had met for a serious and an important purpose, and was in no humour for fun. Later in the evening, when the real business of the night was over, Mr Osborne might have been received with the usual cheers, and a speech from him, as a relief after four hours' tension of the mind, would probably have been hailed as a pleasant relaxation; but just then, when every member was all eye, all ear, all expectation, when the Peers and Commons of England—all the people of England, and, indeed, all Europe—were waiting to know what was to be our future fiscal policy, Mr Osborne was unanimously voted a bore, as great a bore as an acrobat, Punch or Judy, or an organ-grinder would be opposite the window of the Bank parlour when a financial and commercial crisis is on, and the governors are anxiously debating the propriety of raising the discount another one per cent. And so, when Mr Osborne rose, instead of being received with the usual cheers and laughter, he met with a storm of 'Oh! oh! oh!' so loud and resolute that it cowed even him. 'There is a time to be serious and a time to laugh, Mr Osborne; this is our serious time.' And so Mr Osborne sat down, not a little chagrined, we may be sure; but, if so, he owed his mortification to himself. How could he dream that the House would hear him, or anybody, when the great Chancellor was there with that ominous box of his before him—that box which by many was expected to prove a horn of plenty, and by others a very Pandora's box, without even hope at the bottom?

Mr Gladstone rose at about ten minutes to five. By his own side he was again greeted with loud and hearty cheers, while again on the Opposition there only arose here and there a faint and spiritless 'Hear, hear!' The right hon. gentleman looked pale and haggard; appeared, moreover, not to be very firm upon his legs, and altogether seemed but little competent to perform the great task that was before him. Dr Ferguson was under the gallery, and had his eye upon him, and no doubt must have been anxious for his patient as hour after hour he heard his voice and saw him upon his legs, and must have felt relieved when he saw him at last drop into his seat. But there was one present who would be more anxious than Dr Ferguson, for in the ladies' gallery, peering through the brass screen, sat Mrs Gladstone; and one can easily imagine how her anxiety would prevail over every other feeling as she watched, and watched, and carefully noted every apparent failure of her husband's voice, and every time that his eloquence was interrupted by his hollow cough.

And now let us notice for a few minutes the appearance of the House as the Chancellor settles himself to his work and unfolds his scheme. He himself, the great orator of the night, stands upright, with his papers before him in the official box, pale and wan, but calm and collected. 'What nerves the man must have!' said a friend to us. And the duty of Mr Gladstone that night was indeed one that must have taxed his nerves severely; for it was not merely the House of Commons that was listening, but all Europe; and, indeed, if we reflect but a moment, we shall see that even future generations were to be addressed that night; for the words of Mr Gladstone will not, like most of the words which are uttered here, pass into oblivion as soon as spoken, but will become an historic record, and be read with interest and delight, and quoted as authorities, by ages yet unborn. When the cheering had subsided there was a slight coughing, as if the members were clearing their throats at the beginning that they might offer any interruption thereafter; and then there was a rustling, which showed that every man was settling himself down into his easiest position. When the tones of Mr Gladstone's voice were first heard there were cries of 'Order, order!' to repress the rustling; and then followed profound silence. And now let us survey the House. Lord Palmerston, you see, settles himself down into an attitude of the closest attention. He does not lean back as often as he does, but sits sideways, with his face turned to the Chancellor, and very happy he looks, as if he were conscious that his Chancellor is about to unfold a scheme of finance that will do credit to his Government. Lord John Russell leans backwards, as usual, with his hat over his eyes and his arms folded across his breast. Sir Charles Wood stares at the ceiling, and now and then shows signs of approbation by jerking his head, as is his wont. Mr Sidney Herbert, as you see, stretches his long legs out before him and throws his head back upon the edge of his seat, looking as if he were lying upon an inclined plane, and has an air of supreme satisfaction. Gladstone and Sidney Herbert are both disciples of Sir Robert Peel; and, as the Chancellor further develops the political economy of their great master, it is not surprising that the Secretary for War should look pleased. Mr Milner Gibson is not very demonstrative at any time; but, as Mr Gladstone unfolds roll after roll of his vast scheme—and especially when he comes to the paper duties—are we wrong in interpreting that look of his as indicating a quiet inward chuckle? It seems to us as if he were saying to himself, '*Quorum pars magna fui*'. The gentleman who sits sideways, with his face towards the Speaker, at the further end of the Treasury bench, is Mr Villiers. We can hardly see his countenance here; but when we remember how, year after year, before the League was formed, he attempted to plant the tree of Free trade in an uncongenial soil, we can easily imagine his satisfaction at seeing, at last, these magnificent results of his patience and toil. Bright, on the first seat of the second bench below the gangway, is leaning back and looking upwards, evidently drinking in with quiet enjoyment every word that is said. He will himself have something to say on this subject before it is done with. Sir James Graham, who has lately shifted from No. 1 below to No. 1 above the gangway, reclines backward and stares into vacancy—very attentive, though, no doubt. Mr Hadfield is right behind Sir James, on the top bench but one. His face is turned towards Gladstone, and he is unquestionably pleased that his sentiments are making such progress; for he, too, is an old Free trader—so free, indeed, that he wishes to carry out his principles in matters ecclesiastical as well as fiscal; and sometimes, when the eloquent Chancellor hits more exactly, in his opinion, the nail upon the head, he utters a peculiar and expressive cheer . . .

We venture to express the hope that every Englishman will read Mr Gladstone's speech. Every Englishman ought to read it; for it is not only the greatest that Gladstone has delivered, but it is the greatest that has been delivered by any one in the House or out of it for many years. In whatever light we look upon it, it is a great speech. The scheme which is unfolded is one of the boldest, most comprehensive measures which have ever been propounded to the English Parliament, and is fraught with consequences which can never die except with the nation itself. We do not often offer a political opinion in these columns, but we cannot help saying that we look upon this Budget of Gladstone as a magnificent argosy freighted with untold wealth, which is freely offered to the people. The manner in which Gladstone unrolled his prophetic scroll was something wonderful. Let our readers note the marvellous skill that was shown in the gradual evolving and grouping of his facts—the artistic way in which he made every statement seem naturally to lead to what was to follow—and everything that followed to be the natural consequence of that which had gone before. Remark, further, those little picturesque touches of anecdote which he every now and then gave us; and, finally, by all means, let all give themselves up to that magnificent peroration with which he closed. The effect of this speech upon the House was remarkable. There was but little cheering. The House was too deeply absorbed to cheer—too anxious to catch every word. For four hours did the great master hold the House as with a spell. During that time the dinner hour and the postal hour came and went, but no one moved; and through all those hours the House was silent as a desert. Not a whisper nor a rustle was heard—nothing but the clear, musical voice of the speaker. Of course, at the close of the speech there was cheering, hearty, loud, and long-continued, and no wonder; for cold must have been the nature of the man who could listen to that marvellous peroration, delivered, as it was, with almost unequalled power and earnestness, without being moved.

Cobden admires Mr Gladstone's talent

Richard Cobden, Letter to W. E. Forster, January 19, 1865

Gladstone's speeches have the effect on my mind of a beautiful strain of music. I can rarely remember any clear unqualified expression of opinion on any subject outside his political, economical, and financial statements. I remember on the occasion when he left Sir Robert Peel's Government on account of the Maynooth grants, and when the House met in unusual numbers to hear his explanation, I sat beside Villiers and Ricardo for an hour, listening with real pleasure to his beautiful rhetorical involutions and evolutions, and at the close turning to one of my neighbours and exclaiming, 'What a marvellous talent is this! Here have I been listening with pleasure for an hour to this explanation, and I know no more why he left the Government than before he commenced.' It is, however, a talent of questionable value for public leadership.

His temper

Lord Stanley, Diary, July 16, 1869

Gladstone's own temper is visible and audible whenever he rises to speak . . . the mixture of anger and contempt in his voice is almost painful to witness. With all his splendid talent, and his great position, few men suffer more from the constitutional infirmity of an irritable nature: and this is a disease which hard mental work, anxiety and the exercise of power all tend to exacerbate. Disraeli is quite aware of the advantage which he possesses in his natural calmness: and takes every opportunity to make the contrast noticeable.

On the 'qui vive'

Sir James T. Agg-Gardner, *Some Parliamentary Recollections* (1927)

Both when Prime Minister and as leader of the Opposition, Mr Gladstone was constantly in attendance at the House. Unlike his great rival, who assumed an air of solemn repose, Mr Gladstone was very much on the *qui vive*.[24] As an instance, I recall how on a dull evening while the Navy Estimates were being considered, a distinguished Admiral, finding plenty of room on the bench on which he was sitting, put up his leg thereon. Mr Gladstone, catching sight of the Admiral's attitude and being a great stickler for the forms and cere-monies of the House, disapproved of it and made various gestures and beckonings to that effect. But the Admiral, either dozing or short-sighted, remained unobservant. Mr Gladstone thereupon rose and enquired with some heat from the Chairman of Committees if it was in order for an hon. Member to recline on the benches. Before the Chairman could reply, the Admiral had hastily withdrawn his leg and, apologising for his mistake, explained that he was merely resting a wounded leg which was sometimes painful and was quite unconscious of the breach of order. Mr Gladstone at once withdrew his objection and overwhelmed the Admiral with generous apologies and compliments on the heroism which had occasioned the injured limb.

Another instance of Mr Gladstone's versatility I may mention which is perhaps more amusing. A young Cavalry officer, newly elected, was delivering himself in a thin House, mainly composed of friends, of his maiden speech. Encouraged by their applause, and seeing Mr Gladstone sitting in the Front Opposition bench, he heedlessly shaking a warning finger in his direction, said, 'And now let me give the Right Honourable gentleman a word or two of advice.' Mr Gladstone at once crossed over to the bench below the youthful speaker, and sat there with bowed head and his hand to his ear as if not to lose a single syllable that might fall from his self-constituted mentor. The comedy of the situation sent the House into a fit of laughter, in the midst of which the audacious young instructor subsided into his seat . . .

One of the conspicuous gifts of Mr Gladstone was his extraordinary grasp of knowledge. There seemed to be hardly any subject within the limits of human learning with which he was not conversant, or on which he could not express a learned opinion. An instance of this is supplied by an occurrence which took place one evening in the House of Commons. The occasion was a debate on Canals. A dull and tedious discussion had been in progress for some time and the supporters of the Government had dwindled to an extent that alarmed the Government Whips. It was necessary to keep the debate going, and to bring from the Reform Club, or other rendezvous of the Liberal Party, a sufficient number to ensure a majority on a vote that was to follow the Canal debate. As it was before the days of taxis and telephones, to send for supporters was a work which would take time. The Government Whip in scouring the purlieus of the House in search of someone to carry on the debate encountered Mr Gladstone in the library, snatching a few moments of well-earned repose by the perusal of some recondite work on a theological dispute which was at that time absorbing the interest of the 'Intelligentsia'. The Whip exposed to him the exigencies of the situation, the importance of keeping the debate going for at least another half an hour and the difficulty of obtaining anyone to do so. With a sigh Mr Gladstone closed his book, enquired as to the subject of the debate and entered the Chamber. Within a few moments he was on his feet delighting those present with an interesting and elaborate history of canals, their origin, their uses, their present conditions, their past mismanagement, and prospects of future development. By the time he had concluded this interesting and impromptu discourse, the absentees had been recovered and the situation saved. His perorations were always on the highest plane of eloquence.

Back from Cannes

T. P. O'Connor, *Gladstone's House of Commons* (1885)

March 10, 1883. There were various opinions about Mr Gladstone's reappearance in the House of Commons. The Administration organs insisted that he was received with tumultuous cheering. I was present when he was first caught sight of, and also when he first rose to speak, and my estimate was that the reception was remarkably cool, and profoundly below the level of expectation. An accident brought this matter into bolder relief. Mr Fawcett, the Postmaster-General, made his reappearance, for the first time after a severe and dangerous illness, on the same night as Mr Gladstone. Mr Fawcett, as many of your readers well know, is blind, and the splendid energy and will power by which he has overcome this terrible obstacle to success as a politician, together with a singularly pleasant combination in character of manliness and amiability, have made him one of the greatest favourites of the Assembly. When he rose, there burst forth a tumultuous cheer, and the Tory squires joined as heartily in swelling the cry as the most rabid Radical. The reception of Mr Gladstone came shortly afterward, and it was then easy to observe that the cheers to him came almost exclusively from the advanced Liberals. The Tories were dumb; the Parnellites rigidly impassive; the Whig-Liberals but faintly murmured an applause that only seemed to hint dislike. Let me make just a few comments on this incident in so far as it illustrates the present position of the Premier.

He is not loved by the Whigs; he is loathed by many of the Tories. The infinite subtleties of his extraordinary mind, the infinite resources of his boundless rhetoric, appear to many of them only the mean devices of a tricky and unscrupulous gambler with truth, and the fervid passion which he throws into his speeches—which, rightly regarded, are the expression either of the fervour of a vehement nature, or the superficial emphasis of an emotional actor—excites in his opponents anger as hot as his own appears to be. The Tories distrust and fear Mr Gladstone, and Mr Gladstone lashes and envenoms the Tories. The Whigs, on the other hand—modest, contented landowners, who favour progress on the essential condition that the car of progress shall be drawn by slow-footed steeds—dread Mr Gladstone's impulsiveness, changeableness, and dangerous tendency to be heated by the popular fire which he himself is so well able to kindle. All these enmities to Mr Gladstone are, of course, submerged when the tide of his popularity and strength runs high, and bitter enemies join with devoted friends in slavish lip-service. If, then, the reception of Mr Gladstone on his return to the House of Commons was cool, it must be because his position is not considered to be as strong as it was. And in this respect the thermometer of the keen watchers of the political and parliamentary atmosphere was correct. I believe I wrote rather slightingly of the illness of the Premier, in a communication I addressed to you shortly after his retreat to Cannes. From what I have heard from private sources and since seen myself, I believe this view was not altogether correct. His state before he left Hawarden was physically bad, but mentally worse. His nature, as a rule, is bright and sunny; but he had for some weeks, during this last spell of illness, a fit of profound depression, such as, I believe, is quite a new thing in his experience. He began to think that his powers were going, if not gone; that his brain was losing all its creative energy, and that constructive statesmanship had passed away from his gifts. It was, then, to minister to a mind deceased, rather than to a body, that he had to fly to the south of France.

I was very much struck with the expression his face wore on the first night of his return. I could see no trace whatever of that ruddiness with which a southern sun was said to have coloured his cheeks. They appear to me on the contrary, ghastly pale and very much sunken, and the flesh in the space immediately above the jaw-bone was pursy and flabby. More curious than this was his general air. As a rule, the spectator can find in Mr Gladstone's face the House in microcosm, so completely does its expression reflect every passing mood. But on this evening, he appeared to take not the slightest interest in what was going on. His eyes were bent on the ground, and his thoughts were either far away, or consisted of brooding and unhappy fancies. He looked as if he were taking a prolonged retrospect of the long years of past achievements and glories to the accompaniment of a song with the sad refrain, 'My sun is set'. And what Mr Gladstone had to come back to was certainly not enlivening. I have written to you already of the complete breakdown, up to the present, of all the Ministerial plans for a busy session of useful English legislation. The Premier had a couple of days ago to confess that there was no chance of their making any further progress with any of their bills until after Easter, and it is doubtful if it will then be able to make anything like rapid progress. Meantime, while the Premier sat in moody reverie, the small group around Mr Parnell—despite the new rules of procedure, despite the distinct and emphatic exclusion of Irish questions from the Queen's Speech, despite the oft and loudly repeated announcement that this was not to be an Irish session—the group around Mr Parnell was hammering away at the eternal Irish question as though nothing had happened in the interval. The Carnival must have been a deal more amusing than this. On the whole, the impression one got from Mr Gladstone's first night in the House of Commons this year was that the Irishmen would break the session, and the session would break Mr Gladstone. In connection with this prophecy, it will not be unamusing to repeat a *mot* of Sir William Harcourt, the Home Secretary. He has been, of all the Ministers, with scarcely the exception even of Mr Forster, the bitterest and most rancorous enemy of Mr Parnell and his followers. Dogged, as he believes, everywhere by assassins; attended by a small bodyguard of detectives even in the corridors of the House of Commons; and of a temperament at once fierce and timid, he has been driven well-nigh crazy by the events of the last two years. He has shrieked for coercion, and foamed at the mouth in his speeches. The poor man all the time has not, I believe and hope, been in the least danger. Yet there he is. He knew before Carey the informer was produced in court the kind of evidence he was going to give, and, seeing in what good spirits the Irish party were one evening, he dropped the remark, 'The starch will be all out of the boys by next Monday.' Carey has given his evidence; Mr Forster has made his attack; the Irish party, having lived down the fierce hurricane against them, are more active and successful than ever; and the people in whom there does not appear to be one bit of starch left are Sir William Harcourt and his colleagues.

Rough work for 73!

W. E. Gladstone, Letter to his wife Catherine, August 22, 1883

Yesterday at 4½ I entered the House hoping to get out soon and write you a letter when the Speaker told me Northcote was going to raise a debate on the Appropriation Bill and I had to wait, listen and then speak for more than an hour, which tired me a good deal finding me weak after a sitting till 2.30 the night before and a long Cabinet in the interval. Rough work for 73!

Mr G. with a stick

T. P. O'Connor, *Gladstone's House of Commons* (1885)

March 8, 1885. The Prime Minister is a great master of stage effect. There was no special reason why he should come down this evening to the House, and yet there he was some time after questions had been on. He entered rather pale, and he carried a stick on which he leaned—even when he rose to speak. It was the first time I ever saw anything about him that brought home to the mind the undeniable, but usually forgotten fact that he is a very old man. The effect was excellent. When he entered, the cheer was not very keen, but when, towards the close of question time, he did rise—still with the ominous stick supporting him—there was a really strong and sympathetic cheer. The old man could not conceal his delight; he paused for several minutes, gave a profound bow after the manner of a prima donna, and paused again until the applause had died away with the same—shall I say—simper on his face, as if he were a member of a great operatic or theatrical corps.

His first Home Rule Bill

Mary Drew (Gladstone's daughter), Diary, April 8, 1886

Breakfast as usual . . . to Downing St. at 3.30. Excitement rather its highest pitch as we threaded the waiting crowds, and I found Helen, Agnes and Mama all more or less quaking. Edward L [Lyttelton] was in the little blue room, such a break, and we all went together to Palace Yard to see the reception outside the House. The rain came down in torrents, but above the storm and above the roar of London thrilled the cheers, all the way fr. D. St. we heard them, and we stared and stared as if we had never seen him before, or as if he wd. look quite different, and then we flew up the 200 steps to the gallery and saw the splendid reception there. The starting to their feet of the MPs, the wonderful cheers. Every spot was covered. The floor had seats up to the table like the free seats in a church—the air tingled with excitement and emotion, and when he began his speech we wondered to see that it was really the same familiar face— familiar voice. For 3 hours and ½ he spoke—the most quiet earnest pleading, explaining, analysing, showing a mastery of detail and a grip and a grasp such as has never been surpassed. Not a sound was heard, not a cough even, only cheers breaking out here and there—a tremendous feat at his age. His voice never failed—we cd. not judge of the effect yet, only that deep and anxious attention and interest were shown throughout and the end was grandly cheered. I think really the scheme goes further than people thought. It is astonishing its faith and courage ... The PM had dinner quietly so as not to talk, but was none the worse. Lucy was present, the first time since '82 ... .[25]

Mr Gladstone as seen by a Tory diehard

Sir Richard Temple, Bt., Letters to his wife

April 17, 1886. Then Gladstone rose to introduce his Irish Land Purchase Scheme. His speech was, for him, halting, lame, prolix. For once in a way he fairly wearied the House. Conversation began, and more than once the Speaker had to call 'Order'. The House was at first crammed, but after the first hour members began to drop off, and at last gasps began to be visible in the benches behind the Treasury Bench. Most of the Conservatives sat the speech out, two-and-a-half hours, but several of them in my neighbourhood were asleep half the time. I kept watchful, however, being anxious to hear what he would say. And a mighty poor performance he made of it! The verbose and laboured speech consisted of two parts; first historical, second expository as regards the Bill. The history was more than half irrelevant, but delivered in what would be called a vicious manner; that is to say, it was calculated to arouse angry feelings against England (as distinct from Scotland) in the minds of the Irish, as was shown by their frequent cheers. The Act of Union he vilified in the strongest terms. What on earth was the use of raking up those old, old stories, except to make mischief in the present? No real Englishman would have made that speech. I had no idea that he had been nursing in his breast all these hostile feelings against the position and conduct of the English in Ireland. However, he brought it all out now. The burden of his song was that no wonder the Irish were naughty when they remember all that happened last century and the century before that. The real point is, of course, whether they are suffering anything in these days, and he did not venture to allege that they were.

After an hour-and-a-half of this sort of talk, he came to this Bill. Here his exposition was the reverse of lucid. He could not apparently get his mind clear to the points. It seemed as if he was not so well as usual, or something of that kind. He did not get his points out at all, and in a few minutes he began to refer us to the Bill, saying that when that was printed and in our hands, we should see for ourselves. Whereat we began to laugh. But soon we saw a little artful method in all this. He was really a little foggy, no doubt; but besides that, he wanted to keep dark a part of his proposal, and to lead our wits away from the point, which was this. He proposed that the plan should cost fifty millions only, whereas it is likely to cost double or even treble that. Of course, we saw through it and let him perceive that we did. All this second part of his speech was received in ominous silence by the Irish members.

May 11. I had to go to the House as early as 1 p.m. yesterday in order to secure a place. When the real business began, Gladstone came in and was cheered vociferously by the Irish section alone. Presently Hartington entered, and passed right in front of his former colleagues on the Treasury Bench. Whereupon a heart-ringing cheer burst forth from the Conservative Benches, and was well sustained in the most significant manner.

Gladstone rose in poor form, husky in voice, laboured in diction, rambling in argument; but the old histrionic power was as good as ever: apparently the only power that is left. He can no longer move this House of Commons with his eloquence. They jeer and chaff him from the Opposition, and his own friends are mute. The Irish alone cheer him. He occupied one whole hour in a discourse of questionable history, without touching at all on the second reading of the Home Rule Bill, which was what the House wanted to hear. This excessive preface gave us the impression that he had nothing businesslike to say. When we got to the second hour of the speech, he came at last to the Bill, having already half-exhausted himself by a needless and academic essay, and produced an unfavourable impression on the House. Then he began to say what he would or would not concede to the Liberal malcontents, and in effect he said he would concede nothing before the second reading. He used, for him and his side, the ominous words, 'I will not have committee before second reading,' which must have the effect of widening, instead of bridging over, the gulf between him and the malcontent Liberals. Then he alluded pointedly to Lord Hartington, lecturing him in the most paternal and impressive manner, to the great amusement of the Conservatives. He concluded in eloquent tones. Still, as we thought, he spoke as a beaten and sinking man, with something of the defiance of despair. All this time both Liberals and Radicals looked silent and depressed, almost aghast.

Unable to resist

Henry W. Lucy, *A Diary of the Salisbury Parliament, 1886–1892* (1892)

July 5, 1888. In one respect Mr Gladstone is, in fullest measure, the representative Parliament man. Several members can be as serious as he when weighty questions are to the fore, but none can equal him in the intensity of unfeigned interest in the purest trifling with forms of debate. Watching him tonight, literally bounding about on the front Opposition bench whilst the question of payment of members was under discussion, a deaf mute in the Strangers' Gallery might have been forgiven if he concluded that news had just come (as it did on a memorable night in Mr Forster's time) that the Russians were at the gates of Constantinople. At least it might reasonably be supposed that the short, sharp fight, with its varying phases, was over, and that Home Rule, which once seemed to have finally wrecked his position, was actually within reach of his nervously extended right hand.

There are some people accustomed to find deep design in Mr Gladstone's most ordinary action, and certainly his presence through the long hours of the debate on Mr Fenwick's motion seems to suggest necessity for research. To ordinary men, as yet far off their seventy-ninth year, the opportunity seemed specially made for quietly going home to bed. It is true the business for which the House was summoned to meet at nine o'clock was Committee of Supply, in which a few hours might well be spent to the advantage of the public service. But there was no chance of getting into Committee. Mr Fenwick had had the personal good fortune to bar the way with a motion, cautiously suggesting the expediency of 'reverting to the ancient custom of paying members for their services in Parliament'. The topic was not without interest, and was precisely suited to that admirable institution the Kensington Parliament. But for the House of Commons, with the Speaker in the Chair, the mace on the table, Supply in arrear, and the Local Government Bill advanced only as far as its 21st Clause, it would seem criminal, if it were not ridiculous, to devote a night to the subject.

Yet here was Mr Gladstone, not a passive listener, looking in late on his way home from dinner, content to take a preliminary doze in the House of Commons, but in a positively electric condition from head to heel. Whoever the speaker might be, whether it was Admiral Field below the gangway, forging ahead under heavy press of canvas, or Sir John Gorst immediately facing him, humorously posing as an old Tory, Mr Gladstone turned in the direction of the voices, with hand to ear, sitting on the very verge of the bench, so as not to lose a word of the precious utterance. It was all, at best, the merest academic trifling, the veriest indulgence in debating society dialectics; and here was the veteran statesman of worldwide fame, with the weight of fifty years' public service on his shoulders, drinking it all in with contagious avidity.

The fact that the discussion was raised on an abstract motion did not check his enthusiasm. The House has often, when convenience has called for protest, heard him declaim in ardent speech against the practice of putting forth abstract resolutions, and the unfairness of asking the House to vote upon them. He might have found in that fact alone adequate reason for stopping away, or, being present, of showing some signs of impatience. Or, taking up other and quite familiar grounds he might have resented the whole business as undignified trifling with precious time. The aspect of the House could scarcely have been congenial to a work-worn statesman. Nearly everyone was in dinner dress. Laughter, hilarious cheering, and more or less humorous interjections prevailed. If one of the gods in the gallery had put a bent finger in his mouth and shrilly whistled, it would have seemed all in keeping. Absence of sound of the popping of the corks of ginger-beer bottles and of smell of orange-peel struck the senses. The broad expanse of white shirt-front on the Conservative benches recalled the 'chappies' in another place. It was like a big night at Evans's in old times, with Admiral Field as Paddy Green to say 'Dear boy!' and affectionately smite newcomers on the shoulder.

It all proved irresistible for Mr Gladstone. When he had, with boyish delight, watched Admiral Field stumbling through his speech, rolling head over heels through mingled metaphors, like an elderly porpoise tumbling in the sea, he showed a disposition to jump in himself. But Sir John Gorst was before him, and with undiminished interest Mr Gladstone followed the Under-Secretary's ordered speech. Then he could wait no longer, and springing up, plunged into the controversy. As he stood at the table, his tall, lithe figure drawn to its fullest height, turning right and left as the ripple of laughter and the roar of cheers followed his sentences, he conveyed to the House a sense of absolute youth alike of mind and body, of undiminished strength and unsapped vitality, that could not fail to make an impression even on those most familiar with his recent appearances.

Peradventure, since the reason is hard to find in ordinary grooves, this was the explanation of his unexpected interposition. There has been talk about pitting the maximum life of a Parliament in its third Session against the accumulating years of 'an old man'. If any were reckoning on Parliament winning, let them look at the Old Man, springing up at midnight on the last day of a laborious week's sitting, delivering an oration of consummate skill, practically about nothing, talking for the simple pleasure of making a speech and working off some surplus energy. As Mr Matthews pointed out in a speech which came nearer to House of Commons style than any he has delivered since a freak of fortune made him Home Secretary, Mr Gladstone 'delivered himself of a charming speech, which contained an abundance of statements, but was absolutely colourless and meaningless so far as regarded expression of opinion'.

That was exactly it. Mr Gladstone is too old a Parliamentary hand to commit himself, even in the maddest exuberance of verbosity, on a matter of comparative unimportance. He made his speech (possibly with the underlying purpose suggested) on the principle avowed by Mr Wemmick when he led Miss Skiffins to the altar. 'Hallo!' said Mr Wemmick, passing down a street with his affianced on his arm, 'here's a church; let's go in and get married.' 'Hallo!' said

Mr Gladstone, looking in at the House of Commons at half-past nine last night, 'here's a debate; let's go in and make a speech.'

Gladstone the actor

Frank Harrison Hill (1830–1910) was editor of the *Daily News* from 1869 to 1886 and a formidable political journalist, though not popular with senior Liberal politicians. A member of the Reform Club, he and his wife gave celebrated dinner parties in a flat in the Victoria Street quarter. He wrote a series of 'Political Portraits' which were published anonymously in the *Daily News* and Justin McCarthy recalls being present at a London evening party when a mutual friend, the editor of a weekly, bluntly asked Hill who was responsible for these sketches. With 'that peculiar look of gravity which those who knew him knew always covered some humorous meaning, [he] answered that the author was an obscure young man from the country, whose name was believed to be Smith. Thus the incident passed off for a moment, but some of us were greatly amused, and the public in general greatly amazed when it was announced in the next number of the weekly paper that the "Political Portraits" of the *Daily News* were the first literary production of a young man from the provinces who bore the name of Smith.'[26]

Frank Harrison Hill, *Political Portraits* (1873)

It is a little before question time. A perceptible stir, a turning of the heads of his colleagues towards the space behind the Speaker's chair, a slight shifting of their seats by Sir William Harcourt and Mr John Morley, so as to leave a gap between them, and opposite the Ministerial box on the table; and Mr Gladstone enters, with rapid step, erect, and looking round him as in invitation of the 'reception' which is as dear to actors in St Stephen's as to actors on any other stage, and which seldom fails him. The massive head, with its eager eyes, and prominent features, and deep lines of labour and passion, seems almost to dwarf the spare and shrunken form which supports it. Mr Gladstone is too much of a dramatic artist to have Mr Disraeli's somewhat theatrical weakness for walking solemnly on great occasions along the whole length of the floor from under the Strangers' Gallery in a stately 'procession of one'. He is not restrained by the curious shamefacedness which clung to Sir Robert Peel to the last day of his Parliamentary life, and which gave a sort of maidenly coyness to his demeanour which did not quit him till he was fairly settled in his seat.

Mr Gladstone has the faculty noticeable in most great actors, though they may come on the scenes from some obscure and distant point, of filling the stage, as the phrase runs, and catching the eye of the spectators. An unobtrusive entrance is dramatically the most effective. That the great man should be discovered by the eyes that are watching for him is far more telling than an ostentatious obtrusion of himself. The manner in which Mr Gladstone drops into his seat, adjusts his paper, and turns to converse with his colleagues on either hand, is so very natural as to seem almost unnatural. It suggests stage business, and Mr Gladstone at once both to be himself and to be acting himself.

This is not strange. For more than sixty years, Mr Gladstone has spent the greatest part of his waking hours in the view and hearing of the world. He lives in the presence of the public as under the eye of his Great Taskmaster, which never slumbers nor sleeps. His demeanour in the House of Commons, his gestures and changes of his posture, and play of countenance, though not addressed to the lookers-on—that would be a blunder like that of a mugging actor—are yet shaped, and informed and controlled by the consciousness of hundreds of watchful eyes and commenting tongues. Mr Gladstone's by-play, when he has no direct part in the speech or business of the scene, is the result of careful study, and it is worth studying.

The same mastery of the business of the Parliamentary stage is shown when Mr Gladstone rises to answer questions. The courteous leaning over the table, the deprecatory or explanatory gestures, the easily and nervously inflected tones, the occasional pleasantry, rather good-humoured and jocose than humorous or witty, are models of the conversational manner in Parliament. A great actor can do not only the highest but the lowest work of his art better than others. If he had simply to deliver a message or hand in a letter, he would do it as if it had not been done before.

Garrick, as the messenger bringing the news of the advance of Birnham Wood, would draw attention from most Macbeths. Something like that is literally true of Mr Gladstone. As he stands below the bar, with a Bill, or the counterfeit presentment of a Bill, which the House has just ordered to be brought in, or with a message from Her Majesty, and in reply to the Speaker's summons advances with it to the chair, the purely formal business is done with a grace and propriety which is not in everybody's reach, as is conspicuous when other Ministers hurry or stumble along like schoolboys advancing to their headmaster's desk to receive the reward of merit on prize-day . . .

Mr Gladstone is a consummate master of the art of listening. It is as good as a play to observe him. He has his various manners. To a Parliamentary beginner, he good-naturedly turns with an air of curiosity and of what must often prove embarrassing attentiveness, with hand to the side of his head, forming an improvised ear-trumpet, and his whole attitude exhibiting a pleased receptiveness. The same posture is assumed on the occasional intrusion into the debate of an habitually silent supporter, who is to be encouraged into the belief that he is making a valuable contribution to the discussion, and who is afterwards to receive the assurance of Mr Gladstone's regret, shared, he is confident, by the whole House, that he does not more frequently give him and it the benefit of his opinions. But the real debates are, of course, with the Front Bench opposite, or with those scattered fragments of his own former Front Bench which are collected together, under Mr Chamberlain, in the back seats below the gangway.

Mr Gladstone's first attitude as Mr Balfour, let us say, rises is different. He seems to sink into himself, in an unnatural quietude, more threatening to those who know him than his habitual restlessness. He is all eye and ear and concentrated attention, as hushed in grim repose, behind his shirt collar, which seems touched up to listen, instinct with life, he waits his evening prey. Signs of uneasiness are exhibited. Mr Gladstone begins to move restlessly. The lounging attitude in which he seems to recline unequally poised on his cervical vertebrae is exchanged for a bolt upright position, which would seem preparatory, as it was sometimes, to Mr Gladstone's getting to his feet to administer the retort which is pressing for escape from behind the bulwark of his teeth. Usually he is content, however, to whisper it into the ears of some deferential colleague. But the period of restraint is now over, and the speech of the adversary has to be delivered to an accompaniment of *sotto voce* reply occasionally propelled like a missile across the table, to his direct address, after the fashion of a shot across a ship's bows, intended to bring him to, or constraining him to change his course and go upon another tack. Ordinarily, however, Mr Gladstone is content to carry on a private debate of his own before his colleagues in contemplation of the time when he will have the whole House for his audience. The conversation, or rather monologue, sometimes becomes so animated and contumacious, that the orator in possession stops as Pitt did, when on a now historic occasion, which shows that Front benches succeeded and resemble each other, and were a hundred years ago pretty much what they are now, he paused until Nestor should have adjusted the dispute between Agamemnon and Achilles. For the moment the 'appeal to the right honourable gentleman to give me his attention' is successful. But the whispered comments begin again, and are accompanied and illustrated by movements of impatience or incredulity, gestures of surprise or indignation. Often a true description would be the speech by Mr Balfour, the gesticulation by Mr Gladstone. It is the triumph of political pantomime . . .

. . . His whole body debates in every part of it, from head to foot, his mobile features, vibrating and pointing finger, threatening arm, restless figure, turning now this way, now that, now erect at the table, now prone over it. To Mr Gladstone, as he himself has said, debating is a wrestle with a single antagonist, or with a succession of antagonists, one up and down, and usually in the issue more of them down than up. His attitude, as the speech to which he is to reply draws to a close, is often that of a *couchant* animal, drawn together for a spring, and he leaps from his lair in a manner which enables the spectator to understand Mr Disraeli's expression of thankfulness for the solid piece of furniture which separated them, and which was destined to receive the resounding blows that seemed in Mr Gladstone's intention to be aimed at the person of his antagonist. Sometimes, however, the mere fact of getting upon his legs has a chastening effect upon the orator. The nervous excitement, which while silence, a relative silence, was imposed upon him, worked itself out in gestures and shrugs and facial play, in the muscles of countenance and limb, and in half-audible comments, like the mutterings which prelude a storm that is about to break, flows in a calmer course when it finds a vent in the natural channel of continuous speech.

Mr Gladstone rises, straightens himself, puts his hands behind his back, and folds them together, as if each were in the custody of the other, as a security against outbreak. He takes a sobering glance at the Speaker, the visible and outward sign of the inward spiritual grace of self-restraint and reciprocal courtesy, to whom by Parliamentary form the opening words of his speech are addressed, as indeed by a fiction never translated into fact the whole of every speech is supposed to be. He begins in easy and natural conversational tones, animated but not turbulent or violent, increasing in vivacity as he goes on: the erect figure becomes mobile, swaying now this way, now that, something after the manner of a preacher essaying to bring the whole of his congregation under the influence of his looks and voice. Gradually one hand escapes from the keeping of its guardian hand, and begins to play with expressive and illustrative gestures. As it returns to its old position, or rests on the table or droops by the speaker's side, the other comes forward *le même jeu*, as the French stage direction has it. On rare occasions, when business is non-contentious, and Mr Gladstone has only to give shape and reason to the acquiescent opinions and foregone conclusion of the whole House, or the great majority of it, the stream of his speech does not burst its banks. It flows well between them, strong without rage. Usually, however, this prelusive calm is short-lived. Ordinarily his business is not to keep the House of one mind, but to excite one side of the House against the other. Then Mr Gladstone lets himself loose. His voice becomes loud and denunciatory. He bends across the table, thrusting his face as nearly as the space between the two Front Benches allows into the face of his antagonist, too much after the manner of a provocative street scold. His blows are literally delivered from the shoulder, not at it but in the direction of his adversaries. If the opponent of the moment is in a remoter part of the House, he turns to him with gestures of distant defiance which seem to challenge him to come down and have it out, or to warn him of what would be his fate if he did. Mr Gladstone's tone and demeanour are those of a man in a sort of frenzy, and it is impossible to witness them without pain at a certain unseemliness in the spectacle.

❖

Mr G. on parliamentary manners

Henry Chaplin (1840–1923), Viscount Chaplin, was the son of a vicar and was educated at Harrow and at Christ Church, Oxford. He was Conservative MP for Mid-Lincolnshire, 1868–85; for the Sleaford division of Lincolnshire from 1885 to 1906, when he was defeated; and for the Wimbledon division of Surrey from May 1907 to 1916, when he went to the Lords. He held office under Lord Salisbury as president of the Board of Agriculture (1889–92) and president of the Local Government Board (1895–1900).

When, in April 1869, Chaplin had delivered his maiden speech against Gladstone's administration, the premier had paid him a generous compliment. 'The honourable member who has just sat down has admonished us, and myself in particular, that the sense of justice is apt to grow dull under the influence of a long parliamentary experience. But there is one sentiment which I can assure him does not grow dull under the influence of a long parliamentary experience, and that is the sense of pleasure when I hear— whether upon these benches or upon those opposite to me—an able, and at the same time frank, ingenuous, and manly statement of opinion, and one of such a character as to show me that the man who makes it is a real addition to the intellectual and moral worth and strength of Parliament.' Years later, he had cause to change his mind about Chaplin.

Thomas Burt (1837–1922), who wrote this next passage, followed his father into the coal-pits at an early age. He was chairman of the Northumberland Miners' Mutual Confident Association, a trades union, from 1865 until 1913, when he became adviser to the same body. From 1874 to 1918 he sat as Radical MP for Morpeth and for the last eight years of his parliamentary career he was Father of the House.

Thomas Burt, An Autobiography (1924)

Mr Gladstone remarked that the manners of Parliament had improved as compared with his youth, instancing O'Connell's reference to Disraeli as 'a direct descendant of the impenitent thief', and Lord Brougham's attack on a statesman, in the course of which he called his opponent a liar, and declared that, but for his cowardice, he would have been an assassin. 'We hear nothing so atrocious nowadays,' said Mr Gladstone. Lord Rosebery said quietly to me that, considering the foul and vulgar attacks upon Mr Gladstone himself, it was very generous of him to say that our Parliamentary manners were improving. Then aloud he said, addressing Mr Gladstone: 'And you really think that House of Commons manners are improving?' 'Undoubtedly,' replied Mr Gladstone, 'I have no objection to such attacks as the member for Sleaford indulges in.' 'No, indeed, you have no need to care, for you scored heavily against the hon. member,' responded Lord Rosebery. 'Besides,' said Mr Gladstone, 'you do not know the provocation I gave. I complimented Mr Chaplin on his maiden speech, now many years ago, and I think he has never forgiven me.'

In explanation of the foregoing, it is necessary to mention an incident that had occurred in the House of Commons a few days before. Mr Chaplin, member for Sleaford, had made a violent attack on Mr Gladstone. He alleged certain gross inconsistencies of statement, sarcastically excusing these on the ground of failing memory from advancing age. In spite of the height to which party feeling runs, the Tories themselves were, most of them, disgusted with the bad taste and vulgarity of the reference. It was well known that Mr Gladstone was to follow Mr Chaplin in the debate, and it was feared that he might gratify the boundless vanity of the member for Sleaford by devoting too much attention to him. But Mr Gladstone tumbled him over in a few sentences. He began: 'I do not feel my temper to be severely tried by the rather violent attacks of the right hon. gentleman who has just sat down. If I were inclined to be angry with him at all it would be with that large infusion of charity which induced him, after attempting to show that I had made inconsistent accusations, to excuse them by a reference to the accruing infirmities of age. I shall not pretend to determine to what extent I am suffering from those infirmities; but I may venture to say that, while sensible that the lapse of time is extremely formidable, and affects me in more than one particular, yet I hope for a little while longer I may remain not wholly unable to cope with antagonists of the calibre of the right honourable gentleman.' This effective hit was received with ringing and long-continued cheers.

Nearing 83

Henry W. Lucy, A *Diary of the Salisbury Parliament, 1886–1892* (1892)

March 3, 1892. There is a temptation to say of succeeding speeches by Mr Gladstone that the one just delivered is equal to any in the long series. This tendency is justifiable on the ground that when a man has passed the age of eighty any successful oratorical effort is a marvel. That consideration apart, it must be admitted that his speech of Thursday night on the vote for the Mombasa Nyanza Railway was an effort which, had it stood alone, would have established a Parliamentary reputation. It was a *tour de force* both intellectually and physically. Those who must widely differ from Mr Gladstone in the view he takes of the question at issue may well be the loudest in their praises, since to them comes the added marvel that having so little to work upon he made it appear so much.

The night's oration, with its thrilling energy, lightning-like brilliancy, and thunderous force, had the advantage of contrast with an afternoon's speech of widely distinct character. The earlier effort was made upon the proposal submitted by Mr Balfour to take morning sittings on Tuesdays and Fridays throughout the remainder of a Session just entered upon. Private members (who so recently as Tuesday had testified to the high value they place upon their possession by allowing the House to be counted out at eight o'clock) were properly aghast at the First Lord's audacity. Had Sir William Harcourt still been in the place of the Leader of the Opposition he would have seized with alacrity upon this opportunity of illustrating the fact that the first duty of that personage is to oppose. Champions of the privileges of private members would have risen in all parts of the House to protest against this new and unprecedented invasion of their rights. Angry passions would have been aroused, half the sitting wasted, a division taken, and morning sittings for the remainder of the Session would have been decreed. The accident of Mr Gladstone's presence entirely changed the scene, and gave an important turn to the issue.

When he presented himself at the table he was welcomed with an enthusiastic and prolonged cheer, which testified to his final and absolute ascendancy in the House of Commons, achieved after many vicissitudes. It was some moments before he found opportunity to speak. After the thunder-clap of applause that had welcomed him his voice sounded singularly musical. It is one of the signs of the marvellous resuscitation of health completed during his sojourn by the Mediterranean that his voice has regained all its rich organ-like tone.

Occasionally, when Mr Gladstone assumes this attitude of benignancy, and his voice in the opening sentences is sweet and low, somebody chiefly concerned in what he has to say begins to feel particularly uncomfortable. Often this attitude is the prelude to a more than usually bitter attack. Mr Balfour, whose acquaintance with the Old Parliamentary Hand is intimate and peculiar, looked uneasily across the table at the stately supple figure, with head slightly inclined in courteous reference to him in his new position as Leader of the House. This was all very well to begin with. But how would it end?

It ended very much as it had commenced, except perhaps with growing graciousness of manner and with notes of kindlier courtesy in the voice. It was, truly, Mr Gladstone admitted—a large order to come forward at the close of the third week of a Session and ask for morning sittings on Tuesdays and Fridays through all that was left of it. If the right hon. gentleman had asked for the concession up to Easter it would be a different thing. Mr Gladstone, in this melting mood, would not do anything to embarrass gentlemen opposite, would not even move the amendment he had written out and deprecatingly held in his hand. He did not give utterance to the delicate thought everyone saw in the benevolent visage bent upon Mr Balfour, that if he formally moved the amendment and the Government accepted it, it would be equivalent to something like a defeat. That he would not bring about by any means. Rather he would build a golden bridge for the adversary to retreat over, a convenience Mr Balfour promptly accepted. And so, almost before the amazed Ministerialists and the still petrified Opposition had quite mastered the situation, it was amicably adjusted, and morning sittings up to Easter were placed at the disposal of the Government.

This was in the afternoon. Ere midnight struck 'Linden saw another sight'. When Mr Gladstone was an older man, say last Session, he was ever careful to arrange matters so that when he took part in debate his speech should be delivered before the dinner-hour, he being thereafter free from the necessity of reappearing. Now that he is younger by the lapse of a year—for in his case the order of nature seems reversed—he is able to discard these precautions against fatigue, and rises to speak on the approach of midnight, as was his wont about the epoch of the Great Exhibition. It was ten minutes past eleven when he interposed in the debate on the vote to cover the cost of survey for the proposed Mombasa railway. What he had to say must needs be compressed within fifty minutes, since in these degenerate days debate automatically closes at midnight. He pathetically alluded to this condition at the outset of his remarks. 'A predicament' he called it. But it was one that happily contributed to the success of his speech. There was no time for diffusiveness or any beating about the bush. If it was to be brought down within the allotted space of time the axe must be driven at the root with every blow, and Mr Gladstone set himself the task with an energy that thrilled the crowded House.

Hitherto, almost without exception since the Session opened, the pulse of life has beat languidly at Westminster. Now it throbbed through every artery. The cry 'Gladstone's up!' echoed through the lobbies and ran along the corridors. At sound of it smoking-room, reading-room, all were deserted. Within a few minutes every bench on the floor of the house had its occupant, and a throng stood at the Bar, all eyes fixed upon the lithe figure at the table carrying its burden of fourscore years as if it were a featherweight. It is a long time since even Mr Gladstone held an audience so completely enthralled as he did through this vigorous speech. The Opposition cheered incessantly, whilst the Ministerialists, unconvinced, paid manifest tribute to the masterful orator.

In the papers laid on the table relating to the proposed survey was a letter from Sir Guilford Molesworth, in which he makes reference to 'the accompanying map'. 'There is no accompanying map!' Mr Gladstone cried, taking up the unoffending Blue Book, seeming to scorch its cover with the flash of indignation that blazed from his eyes. 'Why is there no accompanying map?' he thundered, bending over the trembling table towards the shrinking forms of Mr Balfour and Mr Goschen. That is an interrogation by which some speakers would naturally sink to the level of bathos, inevitably eliciting a shout of laughter. As Mr Gladstone declaimed the inquiry the effect upon the audience was even more striking than when Mrs Siddons in deepest tragedy tone once at a dinner-table asked, 'Where is the salt?' It is probable that if at the moment he spoke there had been spread on the wall behind him, as appears in committee rooms upstairs during inquiries into railway projects, the very map he was asking for, no one would have dared by calling his attention to the circumstance to break the spell that bound the House.

❖

Lloyd George expresses his admiration

David Lloyd George, Letter to his family, February 4, 1891

... The Grand Old Man has just delivered one of the finest orations he ever uttered on his Roman Catholic Disabilities Bill. Give the Old Chap an ecclesiastical topic and he is happy. He bounced, he whirled around, he flung his arms, he banged the brass box, he shouted until the corridors rang. Wonderful old boy. He was as agile as a child. Never heard his like.

Letter to his family, May 24, 1892

... Gladstone has just delivered a superb speech on the Irish Bill. He really is a marvellous old man.

A journalist recalls Mr Gladstone

Sir Alexander Mackintosh (1858–1948) was in the Press Gallery of the Commons for fifty-seven years. He was the representative of the *Aberdeen Free Press* from 1881 to 1921, of the *Aberdeen Press and Journal* for a year, and thereafter of the *Liverpool Daily Post*. For forty years without a break he wrote the 'Parliamentary Letter' for the *British Weekly*. He was chairman of both the Parliamentary Lobby Journalists and the Press Gallery, and he helped the Earl of Oxford and Asquith to prepare his books.

Alexander Mackintosh, *Echoes of Big Ben: A Journalist's Parliamentary Diary, 1881–1940* (1945)

I heard all Gladstone's speeches in the House of Commons for thirteen crowded years.

Gladstone was not merely the greatest Parliamentarian but the greatest man I have known. When his long life ended Lord Salisbury, his principal opponent since Disraeli's death, bore testimony to his transcendent intellect and his great ideals and moral aspirations. Scarcely any political leader aroused such passionate enthusiasm and adoration. No leader excited greater animosity and yet in hot controversy opponents paid him personal respect.

It was an honour for any member to have a word with Gladstone. I do not recollect to have seen him, except on one occasion, chatting in the Lobby. He took scarcely any share in the social life of the House; I have been told that he never dined there until he was over eighty. Members were thrilled when the great man entered the smoking room, on his only visit there, to test thought readings by Stuart Cumberland. Tim Healy, the scathing assailant of the Liberal Government's old-time Irish policy, jumped up and gave him a chair.

In the double role of orator and debater Gladstone was unique. John Bright equalled him—perhaps surpassed him—in oratory; Joseph Chamberlain was his equal in the cut and thrust of debate. But no one combined these qualities so effectively or possessed in such a pre-eminent degree all the arts and artifices of Parliament.

From the reports of his speeches you can have no idea of their effect on his audience. This was due to his personality as well as to his words and their delivery. He mesmerised the House to such an extent that on notable occasions opponents of his policy who had prepared an attack allowed the opportunity for it to slip.

Men quailed before his terrible eye. I remember two occasions when a speaker confronted by it sat down suddenly in silence. One was the case of an indiscreet friend in the House; the other was the case of a Free Church minister on his platform in Scotland who inadvisedly introduced the subject of disestablishment.

Intense earnestness, moral fervour, conviction of the justice of his cause gave fire and force to his speeches. His rich, resonant voice was aided by animated gesture. It is true that he was often prolix. Opponents delighted to quote Disraeli's description of Gladstone as 'a sophisticated rhetorician, inebriated by the exuberance of his own verbosity'. Sometimes his sentences were capable of different interpretations; sometimes he was accused of hair-splitting. Yet he was as effective in the exposition of his policy as he was bold in its conception.

I heard his Budgets in 1881 and 1882 and even when he wandered into by-paths he carried his audience with him. Sustenance in a long effort was provided for him by Mrs Gladstone, who saw from her corner in the Ladies' Gallery that he had his 'pomatum' pot of egg and sherry. Rarely did a member leave the House while he was on his feet, however long he might speak.

He lacked Disraeli's gift of phrase-making. Phrases from his lips became current, but, apart from their context, they were commonplace. Among them I remember 'within measurable distance', 'hold the field', 'the dim and distant future', 'the flowing tide is with us'. There was one phrase for which generations of politicians on crossing from the Opposition to the Treasury bench have been indebted to Gladstone. When he took office in 1880 he apologised for an expression that he used about Austria, when in 'a position of greater freedom and less responsibility'.

I see him on the Treasury bench, in an old-fashioned frock coat, with wide shirt front and a broad, black tie, fastened in a bow under a high collar, wide open at the throat. When baited by an opponent he crouches like a tiger and at the earliest moment jumps up, with eyes blazing and looking as if he might spring across the table. I see him with arms uplifted or sweeping wide, or with finger stretched forth in derision. I see him thumping the brass-bound box on which a later generation has detected the mark of his blows, while his collar mounts to his ears in the manner pictured by the cartoonist. Again I see him at the end of the day dutifully writing his letter to the Queen on a pad on his knee, and occasionally adjusting the stall on the stump of the finger which had been destroyed by a gun accident, or scratching the top of his head with his thumb.

A terrible eye

William Edward Hartpole Lecky (1838–1903) was born in Dublin, the son of a JP of Queen's County. He was educated at Cheltenham College and at Trinity College, Dublin. By profession an academic historian, he sat as the Unionist MP for Dublin University from 1895 until 1903, when he retired shortly before his death.

W. E. H. Lecky, Preface to *Democracy and Liberty* (1896)

He had a wonderful eye—a bird-of-prey eye—fierce, luminous, and restless. 'When he differed from you,' a great friend and admirer of his once said to me, 'there were moments when he would give you a glance as if he would stab you to the heart.' There was something indeed in his eye in which more than one experienced judge saw dangerous symptoms of possible insanity. Its piercing glance added greatly to his strong personal magnetism which he undoubtedly possessed. Its power was, I believe, partly due to a rare physical peculiarity. Boehm, the sculptor, who was one of the best observers of the human face I have ever known, who saw much of Gladstone and carefully studied him for a bust, was convinced of this. He told me that he was once present when an altercation between him and a Scotch professor took place and that the latter started up from the table to make an angry reply, when he suddenly stopped as if paralysed or fascinated by the glance of Gladstone; and Boehm noticed that the pupil of Gladstone's eye was visibly dilating, and the eyelid round the whole circle of the eye drawing back, as may be seen in a bird of prey.

Mr Gladstone takes his leave

George William Erskine Russell (1853–1919), son of the 6th Duke of Bedford (a former MP), was educated at Harrow and at University College, Oxford, where he took an MA. He sat as a Liberal MP for Aylesbury from 1880 to 1885, when he retired. However, he returned to the House in 1892 as MP for Bedfordshire North, holding office as Under-Secretary of State for India (1892–4) and at the Home Department (1894–5).

G. W. E. Russell, *One Look Back* (1912)

On the 1st of March, 1894, Gladstone made his last speech in the House of Commons. In that speech he bequeathed to his party the legacy of a nobly worded protest against the irresponsible power of the 'Nominated Chamber'; and then, having accomplished sixty-one years of Parliamentary service, he simply disappeared, without ceremony or farewell. In my mind's eye I see him now, upright as ever, and walking fast, with his dispatch-box dangling from his right hand, as he passed the Speaker's Chair, and quitted the scene of his life's work for ever.

In spite of warnings and anticipations, the end had, after all, come suddenly; and, with a sharp pang of regretful surprise, we woke to the fact that 'our master was taken away from our head today'. Strong men were shaken with emotion and hard men were moved to unaccustomed tears, as we passed out of the emptied House in the dusk of that gloomy afternoon.

Lord Frederick Spencer Hamilton (1856–1928) was the fifth son of the 1st Duke of Abercorn and married one of G. W. E. Russell's sisters. Educated at Harrow, he became a diplomat. He sat as a Conservative MP for South-West Manchester (1885–6) and for Tyrone North (1892–5). He also edited the *Pall Mall Magazine* and wrote several novels.

Lord Frederic Hamilton, *The Days Before Yesterday* (1920)

I heard Mr Gladstone's last speech in Parliament, on March 1, 1894. It was frankly a great disappointment. I sat then on the Opposition side, but we Unionists had all assembled to cheer the old man who was to make his farewell speech to the Assembly in which he had sat for sixty years, and of which he had been so dominating and so unique a personality, although we were bitterly opposed to him politically. The tone of his speech made this difficult for us. Instead of being a dignified farewell to the House, as we had anticipated, it was querulous and personal, with a peevish and minatory note in it that made anything but perfunctory applause from the Opposition side very hard to produce. Two days afterwards, on March 3, 1894, Mr Gladstone resigned.

Mr G.'s funeral

Of the many MPs who declared their intention to attend the occasion, 166 were Liberals, 50 were Irish Nationalists and 241 were Unionists. The political correspondent Alexander Mackintosh recalled that he 'never saw the House of Commons so mournful in aspect as on the day of Gladstone's death. Members assembled silently and solemnly, each looking as if he felt a sense of personal bereavement. The House adjourned at once—a rare mark of respect for one who was not at the time a member . . . A quarter of a million people, of every class, filed reverently past the bier enclosing the body of the man, whose memory they cherished, as it lay in State, watched by relays of friends, in Westminster Hall. The march past of the Liberal delegates was extraordinarily impressive.'[27]

Sir Algernon West, Mr G.'s private secretary, remembered the circumstances surrounding the funeral. The Prince of Wales, he recalls, had wanted the Bishop of London to speak after the funeral, but the Dean had refused, saying that no bishop had jurisdiction over Westminster Abbey. Sir Algernon recalled the day itself as follows: 'May 28 was the day fixed for the funeral—a magnificent sight, as we walked bare-headed in the procession from Westminster Hall to the Abbey. The solemn music and beautiful service were very impressive, and we left all that was mortal of the great man, lying at the feet of Peel, his old master.' John Burns, also, praised the service, but scorned the presence of 'too many police, too much officialism, too much "Society" everywhere'.[28]

John Burns, Diary, May 26, 1898

I went to Wetsminster Hall and took Herbert and Henry Gladstone to balcony under large window and looked at the double stream of people swarming past like two columns of ants by the body of their dead father. On and on the endless current of human beings came, weirdly fascinating in the shadows of the great Hall, dramatic in the quiet devotion they all displayed. On they poured through the Hall and up the steps mounting on his dead self to what I hope were higher things for themselves and the race of which he was so great and fine a type. All were profoundly affected at the sight below and ere they left the building visited the House itself and stood at the box he dented with his ring and whose chamber he filled with his voice.

Henry W. Lucy, A *Diary of the Unionist Parliament, 1895–1900* (1901)

May 28, 1898. One hundred and twenty years ago, at Whitsuntide, Lords and Commons assembled at Westminster to do honour to a great statesman. It was on May 11th, 1778, Chatham died, having never recovered from the illness that attacked him in the historic scene in the House of Lords. Once more Whitsuntide is with us, and again Lords and Commons foregather to do reverence to the mighty dead. The difference is marked in many ways. Chatham lay in state in what was known as the Painted Chamber of the old Houses of Parliament. It was destroyed with them, and, as nearly as can be ascertained, on its site is erected the dining-room of the modern House. In the June number of the *London Magazine,* 1778, will be found what is doubtless a faithful representation of the scene, where all that was left of Chatham awaited removal to Westminster Abbey. It is rather a gruesome sight. The walls are hung with black. The coffin, draped in black, lies high on a sort of altar. On either side lines of mutes holding torches aloft stand in rigid attitude. The severe simplicity of Westminster Hall—where through two days the body of Mr Gladstone lay in state, a living stream of humanity passing incessantly hour after hour from sunrise to sunset—has been made familiar to the public beyond the limits of those who looked on. This morning there was no alteration. Four candles in big silver candlesticks still burnt dimly in the morning light. Electric light has not yet invaded Westminster Hall, and gas served in the bright brass candelabra that flank the wall by the Members' entrance to the Lobby of the House of Commons. At the head of the coffin stood a brass cross. At its feet the ivory-white pall, sanctified by the memory of Archbishop Benson.

It was ordained that members of both Houses should assemble in their respective chambers before half-past nine. Many, anticipating the hour, were on the spot soon after nine. The Lobby gradually grew crowded, and members showed a disposition to spend the time anywhere but in the House itself. At a quarter-past ten, when the Speaker seated himself in the Chair by the clerks' table (not in his canopied seat, for the House was not formally in Session), the benches, save that allotted to ex-Ministers, were full. A private intimation from the Speaker that it was desirable members should seat themselves and fall into procession within the House, instead of intercepting it on its passage outside, brought in an appreciable addition to the throng. After sitting a few minutes amid silence broken only by an occasional whisper, the Speaker rose and passed out, members falling in four deep.

Westminster Hall was not open to the general public, but, in accordance with the simple and friendly rules that have guided the dignified last scenes in a great career, room was made for a deputation who travelled from Hawarden to take a last farewell of Mr Gladstone. The deputation consisted chiefly of the tenants, colliery managers, and workmen on the Hawarden estate, together with a few friends and neighbours. On the stroke of half-past ten there was a movement at the top of the broad flight of steps that leads out of Westminster Hall to the lobbies of the Houses of Parliament. A glint of sunlight fell on the mace carried by the Serjeant-at-Arms in front of the Speaker. It was the Commons, leading the procession of the two Houses, coming to escort the dead statesman to Westminster Abbey.

The Speaker was dressed in the richly gold-laced gown he wore in Jubilee time. His train was carried by his train-bearer. Behind him came the Commons, walking four abreast. The first four were the Chancellor of the Exchequer, the Home Secretary, Mr Chamberlain, and Sir John Mowbray, thus officially recognised as Father of the House of Commons. Other Ministers followed; then a big muster of the Commons. Not a word was spoken. Nothing was heard but the heavy tread of the procession as it slowly wended its way down the broad flight of steps, along the floor, passing the coffin set in the middle. Often and often had Mr Gladstone, seated on the Treasury Bench, utilised a few spare minutes to go on writing his letter to the Queen whilst the Commons trooped past him into the division lobby. They passed now, as then, much in the same way, save that they were all dressed in deep mourning, and were apparently going into the same lobby. But the eager figure, bending over the paper spread on the blotting pad on his knee, going on writing as he did on that night in June, 1885, when a combination of Parnellites and Tories turned out his Government, was now at ever-lasting peace. Only a coffin to show where he had been. After a pause another procession appeared at the top of the flight of steps. These were the Peers, headed by the Lord Chancellor in wig and gown, accompanied by his Purse-bearer and Black Rod. Leading the thin black line of Peers were the Duke of Devonshire, Lord Cross, Lord Ashbourne, and Lord Carrington. The muster was not nearly so great as it is when a question relating either to land or the Church comes before the House. But there were ten Bishops, fully arrayed. The Peers walked to the right of the coffin, the Duke of Devonshire turning round to look upon it as he went by. Their lordships had, when they started, been ranged in marching order of fours. They broke into much more open order as they passed through the Hall and in the wake of the Commons disappeared through the door opening on Palace Yard.

Another long pause, broken by a sudden incursion from Palace Yard. These were neither Peers nor members of the House of Commons. They were the undertaker's men. Directed by a sign, the advance file seized two of the silver candlesticks, deposited them on one side and pulled away the pedestals on which they had stood. Then the coffin was drawn forward on to the shoulders of twenty men, over whose bare heads and shoulders the pall presently fell.

As they moved forward a step or two the pallbearers silently advanced and took their places on either side of the coffin, now raised shoulder high. In front, on the right-hand side, was Lord Rendel, Mr Gladstone's frequent host on the Riviera. Next came his old Newark colleague, the Duke of Rutland, then Mr Arthur Balfour, Lord Salisbury (wearing a black velvet skull-cap), and the Prince of Wales. On the other side, in like order, stood Mr Armitstead, Lord Rosebery, Sir Wm. Harcourt, Lord Kimberley, and the Duke of York. The Bishop of London read a short prayer, and at a signal from Norroy King of Arms, representing Garter King of Arms, the bearers moved forward, with slow half-step, as if loth to finally bear away the great Parliament Man from neighbourhood of the scene of his many triumphs.

Members of Mr Gladstone's family who had come to Town for the funeral assembled in the new Committee Room, where they remained till signal was given that the Commons were approaching. They then grouped themselves in the space at the foot of the staircase leading to the Committee Room. In the front stood the Rev. Stephen Gladstone; beside him the young heir, Mr Gladstone's eldest grandson, son of the late W. H. Gladstone. Of the family party were Henry and Herbert Gladstone, Dean Wickham, the Rev. Mr Drew, Mr Spencer Lyttelton, Mr Alfred Lyttelton, and three little boys, sons of Mr Stephen Gladstone. As the coffin passed on, following the Earl Marshal, the Duke of Norfolk, and the Earl of Pembroke (representing the Queen), the chief mourner and his kinsmen closed up behind it. In order walked Sir E. W. Hamilton, Sir Algernon West, Sir James Carmichael, and others who have served as Private Secretaries to Mr Gladstone during his tenure of office as Prime Minister. Next came the doctors in attendance through the last illness, the Hawarden Castle servants, and the deputation of neighbours, tenants, and workmen.

> And now, with all your armour laid aside,
> Swift eloquence your sword, and for your shield
> The indomitable courage that defied
> The fortunes of the field,
>
> As in the noontide of your high command,
> So in the final hour when darkness fell,
> Submissive still to that untiring Hand
> That orders all things well—
>
> We bear you to your resting-place apart,
> Between the ranks where ancient foe and friend,
> Kin by a common sorrow at the heart,
> Silent together bend.

As the white-palled coffin emerged from the arched doorway of Westminster Hall, Big Ben began, opportunely it seemed, to toll. It was striking eleven o'clock.

1. J. A. Gere and John Sparrow (eds.), *Geoffrey Madan's Notebooks* (1981), p. 55.
2. Anon., *The Gladstone Papers* (1930), pp. 19–20.
3. Alfred E. Robbins, *The Early Public Life of William Ewart Gladstone* (1894), p. 141.
4. W. E. Gladstone, Journal, April 19, 1840.
5. E. M. Whitty, *Leader*, January 1, 1853.
6. George Saintsbury, *Life of Lord Derby* (1892), pp. 127–8.
7. Hugh Childers, Diary, February 10, 1860.
8. Margot Asquith, *More Memories* (1933), p. 151.
9. Roy Jenkins, *Gladstone* (1995), p. 261.
10. H. C. G. Matthew, *Gladstone: 1809–1874* (1988), p. 233.
11. ibid., p. 236.
12. Count Paul Vasili (pseud.), *The World of London* (*La Société de Londres*) (1885), p. 94.
13. ibid., p. 56.
14. Lord Ernest Hamilton, *Forty Years On* (1922), pp. 223–4.
15. A. J. Balfour, *Chapters of Autobiography* (1930), p. 73.
16. Sir Algernon West, Diary, February 13, 1893.
17. Henry W. Lucy, *A Diary of the Home Rule Parliament, 1892–1895* (1896), p. 55.
18. ibid., pp. 146–7.
19. ibid., pp. 169–70.
20. ibid., pp. 226–7.
21. Elizabeth Longford, *Jameson's Raid* (1960), p. 138 n.
22. Sir William Fraser, *Disraeli and his Day* (1891), pp. 166–7.
23. ibid., p. 172.
24. A French sentry's challenge: translated as 'on the alert'.
25. Lucy Lyttelton was the widow of Lord Frederick Cavendish, who had been murdered in Phoenix Park, Dublin, in 1882.
26. Justin McCarthy, *Reminiscences* (1899), pp. 201–2.
27. Alexander Mackintosh, *Echoes of Big Ben: A Journalist's Parliamentary Diary, 1881–1940* (1945), p. 37.
28. John Burns, Diary, May 28, 1898.

11 Winny

The applause of the House is the breath of his nostrils.
He is just like an actor. He likes the limelight and the
approbation of the pit.

David Lloyd George, quoted in William George,
My Brother and I (1958)

Applause is essential to him; the approbation of his
audience must be sought, if not by force of argument,
then by resort to any other device, however unfair.

Emanuel Shinwell, 'Churchill as a Political Opponent',
Churchill: By His Contemporaries (1953)

When Winston Spencer Churchill took his seat in the House of Commons for the first time, he immediately assumed the demeanour of an old hand. 'Ten minutes after he had been sworn,' recorded the *Daily Mail*, 'he was leaning back comfortably on the bench, silk hat well down over his forehead, figure crouched in the doubled-up attitude assumed by the Ministers, both hands deep in his pockets, eyeing the place and its inmates critically as if they were all Parliamentary novices.'[1]

What for some must have seemed an admirable self-assurance must for others have seemed an intolerable arrogance. Indeed, the ambivalence of MPs and parliamentary observers towards 'Winny' was a constant theme throughout his career. 'No statesman in our history has felt a deeper reverence for the House of Commons,' wrote Lady Violet Bonham-Carter in her memoir of Churchill.[2] He 'is steeped in its atmosphere and traditions', wrote Earl Winterton, ' . . . he has an instinctive understanding of what it will accept and what it will not accept . . .'[3] 'He usurps a position in the House,' said the Labour MP George Lansbury, 'as if he had a right to walk in, make his speech, walk out, and leave the whole place as if God Almighty had spoken . . . He never listens to any other man's speech but his own.'[4] (A distinct contrast in this respect from Gladstone.) J. P. W. Mallalieu echoed this sentiment, criticising Churchill as 'no longer capable of listening' and deploring his desire, as late as 1950, to hold debates in Secret Session and his tendency to deliver full-dress orations rather than respond to earlier speakers. And what of Clement Attlee's terse assessment? 'Curiously, he has never mastered the procedure of the House. He gives the impression that anyway the rules don't apply to him.'[5]

Undoubtedly, Churchill was a formidable politician, a remarkable war leader, and an

411

extraordinary character, but was he, in truth, a great parliamentarian? Woodrow Wyatt has perceived the problem:

Occasionally Churchill has had periods of indifference or even arrogance towards the House which it has resented. Surprisingly these cleavages have at times gone deep. Sir Stafford Cripps told me of a time during the war when, in his view, such a divergence had occurred and he said so to Churchill.

'Two things I put above everything in my life,' said the Prime Minister, 'God and the House of Commons.'

'Well,' said Sir Stafford, 'I hope you treat God better than you do the House of Commons.'

But these were only temporary patches of misunderstanding. Usually the touch was sure and with time it so matured that it is hard to believe that there has ever been anything better in Parliamentary artistry than the handling of the House of Commons by Churchill in his seventies.

Yet underneath it all, there lay a hint of arrogance, of contempt for those who disagreed. There was something in the criticism that Churchill did not often take the opinion of the House into consideration when executing policy. He paid the House of Commons elaborate respect but little attention. His aim was usually either to control the House for his purposes or to use it as a vehicle for appealing to the nation and the world.[6]

Winston Churchill entered the arena in which his father had proved a mere shooting star, determined to win back the fame that had ultimately eluded Lord Randolph Churchill. For almost the next sixty years, apart from two years when he was without a parliamentary seat in the early 1920s, Winston Churchill's ambitions and sentiments were bound up with the House of Commons. This is perhaps more the case with him than with any other figure in parliamentary history. For while Gladstone's attachment to the House may have lasted a little longer, he consistently enjoyed the comforts of a front-bench position from 1839 onwards and even held office when he was without a seat in the mid-1840s. He never suffered, as Churchill did for some eleven years, a prolonged period of being cast out into the wilderness of the back benches.[7]

When Churchill entered the House in 1900 he suffered from a minor speech defect which consisted in a slurring of the letter 's'. Earl Winterton remembered 'one or two occasions in the 1900 Parliament when some ill-mannered Members on the Conservative Benches mocked this defect when Churchill was speaking. They did it in a *sotto voce* manner which made it impossible for the Speaker to detect and rebuke the offenders, but the incidents plainly disconcerted Churchill.'[8] His first speech as a Liberal Minister in 1906 was considered a failure. He was 'torn to pieces by Balfour, who followed him', and was left 'subdued and crestfallen'.[9]

His principal weakness as a parliamentarian was his reliance on prepared speeches. This sometimes left him unable to respond to an unexpected turn of debate—Balfour once mockingly referred to his 'powerful but not very mobile artillery'—but he gradually cultivated a talent for playing off the mood of his audience. 'Although I think that Sir Winston Churchill prefers making set speeches after careful preparation,' wrote Clement Attlee, 'he is a master at improvisation. I recall one occasion when he was defeated. He had to reply to a debate and we knew that he had nothing to say, but we also knew that if he could provoke interventions from our side, he would get away with it. Mr Shinwell and I managed to persuade all our Members to remain silent. In vain he trailed his coat. There was no response and he ran out of matter.'[10] Another weakness was his sentimentality and need for affection even when abasing himself. Lady Violet Bonham-Carter was scornful of his appeal to MPs when he departed office in 1915 after the

Dardanelles fiasco: 'Winston Churchill's plea to the House of Commons like saying "Do you love me?"—quite useless.'[11] Later, during World War II, she was to revise slightly her opinion of this aspect of his character: 'There is nothing more popular in the House of Commons than to blame yourself. "I have killed my mother. I will never do it again," is certain to raise a cheer. Mr Churchill has never been afraid of taking blame upon himself. A sort of genial self-censure is a characteristic and lovable quality. There is a danger, however, that this may not come from humility, nor does self-confident blame always commend itself. I may be wrong, as it is more than possible that it is this confidence in himself which will help us win the war.'[12]

His five Budgets as Chancellor of the Exchequer (1925–9) were regarded as splendid parliamentary performances, although they have been much criticised for their technical inferiority. 'No one', Harold Macmillan later stated, 'could withhold admiration for the wit, humour, ingenuity and rhetorical skill which he displayed.'[13] In Winterton's judgement, his period as Chancellor 'completely re-established his parliamentary position'.[14] 'Like most great speakers, Winston was an actor,' wrote the Earl of Swinton in his memoirs. 'The one occasion in the House, when a speaker is by tradition allowed more than a glass of water to revive him, is the Budget speech. Winston had by the Box a large glass of brandy and soda. "I must now proceed to fortify the revenue"—a pause, during which Winston took a long drink.'[15] But acting it was. Finance was never Churchill's *métier*. 'Listened to Winston's Budget, a brilliant piece of exposition and chaff,' wrote Leo Amery in his diary in April 1929. 'But at heart very sick about the dropping of the preference with the tea duty and the whole of his finance of the last four years when summed up has been entirely mark time and unconstruction.'[16]

In 1931, when he gave evidence before the Select Committee on Procedure, which was inquiring into how the House of Commons should be reformed and modernised, Churchill advocated devolution to large local bodies and the creation of an Economic Sub-Parliament to 'guide and aid Parliament in all commercial business and financial questions'. Committees scrutinising expenditure and legislation to a greater extent than already pertained would free the floor of the House for more general debates. He pointed out that 'the House of Commons, a hundred years ago, debated whatever it wanted to debate and whatever the country wanted it to debate pretty well when it liked'. The solution to the problem, he felt, was 'to lighten the routine work' and 'restore some of the old flexibility which has disappeared . . .' Although he wanted more debating on general topics, he abhorred the idea of a rostrum for speakers and was 'entirely opposed to any alteration in the architectural lay-out of the Chamber or of the arrangement'. He wanted Parliament to meet for no more than five or six months a year except in times of war or other national crises. He thought that devolution for Scotland and Wales would lead to a shortening of the session. 'I think we kill Parliament by going on practically without permission,' he said, 'I think we kill it.'[17]

After the Tories left office in 1929, Churchill's career suffered significant setbacks. His leadership of those Tory backwoodsmen opposed to the Government's reformist policy over India from 1929 to 1935 (Sam Hoare dubbed it 'Winston's Seven Years War') proved to be a forlorn effort. 'When he made his final attack in the House of Commons and took his seat after a tremendous peroration, Leo Amery, his Harrow school-mate, spoiled the effect by rising and saying in solemn tones: "Here endeth the last chapter of the Book of the Prophet Jeremiah." The House roared with laughter. Members had ceased to take Winston seriously on the subject of India.'[18] During the Abdication crisis, Harold Nicolson recorded, Churchill 'collapsed utterly in the House' and undid 'in five minutes the patient reconstruction work of two years'. Bob Boothby told Nicolson that he had been staying the weekend with Churchill, who had been 'silent and restless and glancing into corners. Now when a dog does that, you know that

413

he is about to be sick on the carpet. It is the same with Winston. He managed to hold it for three days, and then comes up to the House and is sick right across the floor.'[19] By the late 1930s the House of Commons was also beginning to find his jeremiads on foreign policy dull and repetitive: on one occasion when he rose to speak, the Chamber half emptied.[20] 'For five years,' he admitted in 1938, 'I have talked to this House on these matters—not with very great success.'[21] Churchill's overwrought and apocalyptic rhetoric alienated MPs. 'When the Rt Hon. Gentleman speaks,' explained one MP in 1935, ' . . . the House always crowds in to hear him. It listens and admires. It laughs when he would have it laugh, and it trembles when he would have it tremble . . . but it remains unconvinced, and in the end it votes against him.'[22]

All changed when war finally came. In January 1940 Harold Nicolson described Churchill's rhetoric as being 'too belligerent for this pacifist age'.[23] Later, he changed his mind, explaining that 'one of the reasons why one is stirred by his Elizabethan phrases is that one feels the whole massive backing of power and resolve behind them, like a great fortress: they are never words for words' sake'.[24] A. P. Herbert compared Neville Chamberlain's voice unfavourably to Churchill's—'when he said the fine true thing it was like a faint air played on a pipe and lost on the wind at once. When Mr Churchill said it, it was like an organ filling the church, and we all went out refreshed and resolute to do or die.'[25] Herbert thought Lloyd George 'gave a better "performance", in the theatrical sense—richer in histrionic gesture, sudden whispers, and changes of key'; and Attlee thought Churchill 'was not the equal of Lloyd George in attack, though excelling him in speeches where a wide sweep over great issues is needed'.[26] Also, Herbert pointed out that Churchill was a master of words, but of the one-syllable word in particular (for example, 'blood, toil, tears and sweat'). He recalled the moment in Churchill's speech in the Vote of Confidence debate when he was asked about the problems of developing the Churchill tank. This tank, Winny replied, 'had many defects and teething troubles, and when these became apparent it was appropriately rechristened the "Churchill" '. The chuckle that this elicited was worked up into laughter by Churchill's next remarks: 'These defects have now been largely overcome. I am sure that this tank will prove, in the end, a powerful, massive, and serviceable weapon of war.' This self-deprecating joke came about halfway through his speech and transformed the mood of the House. It 'gave us all a lesson in how to "mix the bowling" ', said Herbert. 'Nearly always, in the most solemn speeches, there was some sudden quip that made the whole House happy.'[27]

Churchill's speeches during World War II were 'essentially parliamentary news bulletins'[28] and it is noticeable when reading through diaries of the period, such as those of Channon, Nicolson and Winterton, how Churchill's mood on these occasions was a barometer of parliamentary weather, though not infallibly so. 'This was the day of the Greek debate,' wrote Nicolson in a letter to his sons. 'Winston was in one of his boyish moods, and allowed himself to be interrupted all the time. In fact, he seemed to me to be in rather higher spirits than the occasion warranted. I don't think he quite caught the mood of the House, which at its best was one of distressed perplexity, and at its worst one of sheer red fury.'[29]

During World War I Churchill had advocated Secret Sessions of the House of Commons so that ministers could explain their policies to MPs and MPs discuss them freely. Now, in World War II, he introduced the Secret Session for precisely this purpose. He also used the House of Commons as a pulpit for exhorting the nation. 'The fact that the House of Commons in the Second World War was far more helpful to the national war effort than its predecessor of the 1914–18 war', Earl Winterton has written, 'was due to a happy combination of circumstances in which Churchill's personality played a great part.'[30]

Even more remarkable, perhaps, were Churchill's parliamentary performances after World War II. Despite being Leader of the Opposition from 1945 to 1951, he nevertheless 'persuaded the House of Commons as a whole that his views on external affairs were right, despite the furious resentment with which they were met at first by the Labour Party . . . He did this when well over seventy and after having undergone a period of tremendous strain and terrific responsibility as Prime Minister in the previous five years . . . Never has Churchill's skill as a parliamentarian been used to more beneficial effect than when he was Leader of the Opposition and since he has been Prime Minister for the second time.'[31] The speeches since 1945, Wyatt has stated, had to give the House of Commons first place because they were, unlike his wartime speeches, 'delivered among the unrepressed and bubbling informalities of party discord . . . In his last speaking years all his Parliamentary experience and wiliness were blended with his great gifts of meticulously contrived expression.'[32]

In the early 1950s he turned Prime Minister's Question Time into a regular turn. Attlee had learned 'in the Parliament of 1924 what a master he was in the art of answering Parliamentary Questions. He could deliver a knock-out blow or give the retort courteous with equal facility. I recall a reply from those days. Jack Jones, who often scored bull's-eyes at Question Time, for once made a bad shot. Came the retort, "I have often heard the Honourable Member do much better than that." One never can anticipate just what line he will take.'[33]

His approach to Question Time as Prime Minister was characterised by 'his refusal to seek refuge behind the time-honoured, platitudinous phrases which Ministers are apt to use on these awkward occasions. His shield and his lance in these exchanges has been his wit.' Only Churchill could get away with a lackadaisical answer such as this one to a question from the Tory diehard Sir Waldron Smithers:

Sir Waldron Smithers: Would not the Prime Minister agree that the only way to improve the standards of living of backward races and to avert economic disaster is to allow all peoples to buy in the cheapest and sell in the dearest markets, because if goods cannot cross frontiers, armies will? Will he set the people free?

The Prime Minister: Those seem to me, on the whole, unobjectionable sentiments.[34]

Colin Coote, a former parliamentary correspondent and MP who became the editor of *The Times*, has described 'Sir Winston's technique at Question Time—the sighting of the victim—the twinkle—the pounce—the manifest enjoyment (sometimes shared by the victim himself)'.[35]

An ability to put down interruptions with a scathing or witty retort was another of Churchill's gifts. Sydney Silverman, the diminutive Labour MP who sat in a corner seat in the front row below the Gangway, with his legs dangling an inch off the ground, was a frequent victim. 'The hon. Gentleman is always intervening,' Churchill observed. 'On this occasion he did not even hop off his perch.'[36] It was during this period, perhaps, that Churchill achieved a persona which most closely approximated what he himself regarded as the quintessence of the House of Commons: 'the conversational style, the facility for quick informal interruptions and interchanges'.[37]

There were still, however, moments of failure. David Cannadine, who has edited a recent collection of Churchill's speeches, says that 'he made one speech, in April 1954, so ill judged yet so unalterable that he was virtually howled down in the Commons'.[38] Yet although Churchill's career was drawing to its close, he was still able to overawe the House with set-pieces. On March 1, 1955, he spoke with passion about the hydrogen bomb and the future of mankind. His performance contained a typical theatrical touch: he explained that only a small amount of plutonium was needed to produce weapons of mass destruction, 'probably less than would fill this box here on the table', at which point he banged the box.[39]

Elsewhere in this volume we will see that Churchill set great store by the maintenance of friendly relations with MPs of all parties—men such as Philip Snowden, James Maxton, Fenner Brockway. 'His own laugh, and the gusto with which he provokes laughter in others, are among his chief assets,' wrote the Labour MP David Grenfell. 'He encourages the Labour back-benchers to laugh with him, rather than howl at him.'[40] Almost a decade later, this policy of eschewing personal antagonism towards political opponents was rewarded when Labour MPs supported his rebellious stand on rearmament. 'At the end of this debate,' wrote Hugh Dalton in his memoirs, 'Churchill, in a speech lasting three minutes, declared that this was a mournful occasion and that we had encountered a great disaster. He attacked Baldwin for not having spoken. The Prime Minister, he said, had all the power and, therefore, great responsibility. He should not have sat silent. Churchill was cheered from our side, but angrily shouted down from the other.'[41] Manny Shinwell noted that during the 1930s Churchill was treated as a pariah by his fellow Tories: 'I have watched him, accompanied by a sole companion, walking broodingly through the corridors of the House, or conversing in the smoke-room with a few admirers like Brendan Bracken and Robert Boothby. But generally, Tory members gave him a wide berth.'[42]

Churchill's famously mercurial temper, so often regarded as a flaw in earlier days, eventually came to be seen as a loveable attribute. Shinwell described him as 'one moment bristling with anger, real or simulated, the next passing the incident off with a boyish grin, hugely delighted at being able to share in the fun . . .';[43] Winterton said that 'his outbursts of scowling rage' were 'so soon followed by amiability and a cheerful grin', and believed the House of Commons had an 'affection for the generosity of his character'.[44] Woodrow Wyatt met Churchill after attacking him in the Chamber one day and expressed the hope that he had not been too rude. 'I ask for no quarter,' Churchill had replied, 'and I bear no malice.'[45]

After the House of Commons had been bombed in 1941, Churchill insisted that it should be rebuilt in much the same way as before. 'I am a child of the House of Commons,' he said on the day that the Commons entered their new Chamber in October 1950. 'I was much upset when I was violently thrown out of my collective cradle. I certainly wanted to get back to it as soon as possible.' The fact that the rebuilt Chamber could still only seat two-thirds of Members was an advantage because 'the intensity, passion, intimacy, informality and spontaneity of our debates constitutes the personality of the House of Commons and endows it at once with its focus and its strength'.[46]

November 30, 1954, was Churchill's eightieth birthday. No MP before or since has ever been paid the tribute that Churchill received on that day when both the Lords and Commons met in Westminster Hall to present him with a special bound volume containing the inscriptions of his fellow MPs, and the controversial portrait of him by Graham Sutherland which he so detested. Yet while Woodrow Wyatt believed that Churchill was 'the only man of our epoch to be declared an ancient monument in his own lifetime'[47] and Earl Winterton unhesitatingly pronounced him 'our greatest living parliamentarian',[48] the journalist Malcolm Muggeridge was repelled by what he called Churchill's 'totemisation'.

Churchill would appear in the House 'suddenly from behind the Speaker's chair', recalled Wyatt. 'He did not seem to have legs like other human beings: his face and body looked all of a piece like some fabulous Humpty Dumpty. The moment this miraculous creature was noticed coming into sight the atmosphere changed tangibly.' All attention was directed towards him. 'He might not utter a word,' Wyatt continued, 'yet as long as he sat on the bench, the great head moving round, the face animated or so lifeless that it had the quality of a bust worn by time, the changed temper of the atmosphere was sustained.'[49] Norman Shrapnel, the sketch-writer for the *Manchester Guardian*, has written how Churchill's 'appearance in the House of Commons became in itself a performance of great complexity and the most painful drama. Day after day, often several days in a parliamentary week, we watched with agonised fascination— failing to hear a word from whoever it was who nominally had the ear of the House during this massive upstaging act—as the pallid, ancient hulk steered itself towards the front-bench seat below the Opposition gangway. It moved in pitiable slow motion, like a giant refusing to accept that it was extinct, and the end was painfully protracted.' As he sat on the bench for a couple of hours, he appeared to Shrapnel 'like a premature statue of himself'.[50]

There was even the notorious occasion when a speech by Hugh Gaitskell on the economy was overshadowed by Churchill's fumbling search through his pockets for a cough sweet. One journalist headed his report of the debate 'The Fall of the Pastille', while another recalled its effect: ' "I was only looking for my jujube," Churchill said innocently, after he had utterly distracted the House and disrupted Gaitskell's speech beyond repair.'[51]

Until the very last, Churchill was determined to remain upon the stage and savour the applause, immersed in the idiosyncratic forms of parliamentary life: 'It is reported that when Sir Winston Churchill became the Father of the House a member asked the Clerk what his duties were in that capacity. On being told that there were none the member remarked: "That answer won't satisfy the Member for Woodford. If there are no duties he will proceed to invent some!" '[52]

Churchill's maiden speech

Churchill delivered his maiden speech on February 18, 1901. Fortunately for him, he was preceded in the debate by Lloyd George whose attack on the Conservative Government's conduct of the Boer War had, as the *Punch* correspondent put it, elicited the 'frantic cheers of Irish sympathisers' and had lured into the Chamber 'loungers from the lobby, students from the library, philosophers from the smoking-room. A constant stream of diners-out flowed in. When young Winston rose from the corner seat of the bench behind Ministers ... he faced, and was surrounded by an audience that filled the Chamber.'[53]

Winston Churchill, My Early Life (1930)

Parliament reassembled late in February and plunged immediately into fierce debates. In those days the proceedings in the House of Commons were fully reported in the Press and closely followed by the electors. Crucial questions were often argued with sustained animation in three-day debates. During their course all the principal orators contended, and at their close the parties took decisive trials of strength. The House used to sit till midnight, and from 9.30 onwards was nearly always crowded. It was Mr Balfour's practice as Leader to wind up almost every important debate, and the chiefs of the Opposition, having summed up in massive form their case from ten to eleven, heard a comprehensive reply from eleven to twelve. Anyone who tried to speak after the leaders had finished was invariably silenced by clamour.

It was an honour to take part in the deliberations of this famous assembly which for centuries had guided England through numberless perils forward on the path of empire. Though I had done nothing else for many months but address large audiences, it was with awe as well as eagerness that I braced myself for what I regarded as the supreme ordeal. As I had not been present at the short winter session, I had only taken my seat for four days before I rose to address the House. I need not recount the pains I had taken to prepare, nor the efforts I had made to hide, the work of preparation. The question in debate, which raised the main issue of the war, was one upon which I felt myself competent to argue or advise. I listened to counsel from many friendly quarters. Some said 'It is too soon; wait for a few months till you know the House.' Others said 'It is your subject: do not miss the chance.' I was warned against offending the House by being too controversial on an occasion when everyone wished to show goodwill. I was warned against mere colourless platitude. But the best advice I got was from Mr Henry Chaplin, who said to me in his rotund manner, 'Don't be hurried; unfold your case. If you have anything to say, the House will listen.'

I learned that a rising young Welshman, a pro-Boer, and one of our most important bugbears, named Lloyd George, who from below the gangway was making things very difficult for the leaders of the Liberal party, would probably be called about nine o'clock. He had a moderately phrased amendment on the paper, but whether he would move it was not certain. I gathered that I could, if I wished, have the opportunity of following him. In those days, and indeed for many years, I was unable to say anything (except a sentence in rejoinder), that I had not written out and committed to memory beforehand. I had never had the practice which comes to young men at the University of speaking in small debating societies impromptu upon all sorts of subjects. I had to try to foresee the situation and to have a number of variants ready to meet its possibilities. I therefore came with a quiverful of arrows of different patterns and sizes, some of which I hoped would hit the target. My concern was increased by the uncertainty about what Mr Lloyd George would do. I hoped that the lines I had prepared would follow fairly well from what he would probably say.

The hour arrived. I sat in the corner seat above the gangway, immediately behind the Ministers, the same seat from which my father had made his speech of resignation and his terrible Piggott attack. On my left, a friendly counsellor, sat the long-experienced Parliamentarian Mr Thomas Gibson Bowles. Towards nine o'clock the House began to fill. Mr Lloyd George spoke from the third bench below the gangway on the Opposition side, surrounded by a handful of Welshmen and Radicals, and backed by the Irish Nationalist party. He announced forthwith that he did not intend to move his amendment, but would instead speak on the main question. Encouraged by the cheers of the

'Celtic fringes' he soon became animated and even violent. I constructed in succession sentence after sentence to hook on with after he should sit down. Each of these poor couplings became in turn obsolete. A sense of alarm and despair crept across me. I repressed it with an inward gasp. Then Mr Bowles whispered 'You might say "instead of making his violent speech without moving his moderate amendment, he had better have moved his moderate amendment without making his violent speech".' Manna in the wilderness was not more welcome! It fell only just in time. To my surprise I heard my opponent saying that he would curtail his remarks as he was sure the House wished to hear a new member, and with this graceful gesture he suddenly resumed his seat.

I was up before I knew it, and reciting Tommy Bowles's rescuing sentence. It won a general cheer. Courage returned. I got through all right. The Irish—whom I had been taught to detest—were a wonderful audience. They gave just the opposition which would help, and said nothing they thought would disturb. They did not seem the least offended when I made a joke at their expense. But presently when I said 'the Boers who are fighting in the field—*and if I were a Boer, I hope I should be fighting in the field*— . . .' I saw a ruffle upon the Treasury bench below me. Mr Chamberlain said something to his neighbour which I could not hear. Afterwards George Wyndham told me it was 'That's the way to throw away seats!' But I could already see the shore at no great distance, and swam on vigorously till I could scramble up the beach, breathless physically, dripping metaphorically, but safe. Everyone was very kind. The usual restoratives were applied, and I sat in a comfortable coma till I was strong enough to go home. The general verdict was not unfavourable. Although many guessed I had learnt it all by heart, this was pardoned because of the pains I had taken. The House of Commons, though gravely changed, is still an august collective personality. It is always indulgent to those who are proud to be its servants.

After this debate I first made the acquaintance of Mr Lloyd George. We were introduced at the Bar of the House of Commons. After compliments, he said 'Judging from your sentiments, you are standing against the Light'. I replied 'You take a singularly detached view of the British Empire'. Thus began an association which has persisted through many vicissitudes.

Henry William Massingham (1860–1924) was educated at King Edward VI's School, Norwich, and became a reporter with the *Eastern Daily Press* at the age of seventeen. He went to London and after working for the National Press Agency, he joined T. P. O'Connor's new paper, the *Star*, where he succeeded O'Connor as Editor in 1890, leaving after six months. From 1892 to 1899 he worked on the *Daily Chronicle* as, successively, Literary Editor, Special Parliamentary Correspondent, Assistant Editor, and Editor. He resigned because his proprietor wanted him to suppress his opinions about the South African War, to which he was opposed. He succeeded Henry Lucy as the author of 'Pictures in Parliament' in the *Daily News*. He later edited the *Nation* from 1907 to 1922, thereafter writing his 'Wayfarer Diary' for the *New Statesman and Nation*.

Massingham was much impressed by Churchill's speech. Indeed, he compared it favourably to that of Joseph Chamberlain, the Colonial Secretary, which was 'an able piece of debating—clear, rasping, coarse in tone, full of points aimed—and successfully aimed—at the average party spirit of his following . . . But the speech was utterly without elevation—and in insight and breadth of treatment it was far inferior to Mr Churchill's.'

H. W. Massingham, *Daily News*, February 19, 1901

The tragedy of the war was destined to furnish the final interest of the evening. That interest took the shape of a kind of duel between two young members in whose careers the House takes an interest—Mr Lloyd George and Mr Winston Churchill. Mr George never speaks now without drawing a house—a sure sign of mastery of his audience and his subject . . . All these powers Mr George displayed in his speech last night . . . For the most part it was a continuous story of what might be called the true horrors of war—the cruelties of farm-burning, the sufferings of the women and children, and all the train of miserable consequences that follow the path of an invading army . . . It ended on the note that the war was not only cruel but wrong.

Mr Winston Churchill's reply was in very striking contrast to the speech to which it was indeed only nominally an answer. The personal contest was as strong as that of treatment and method. Mr George has many advantages; Mr Churchill does not inherit his father's voice—save for the slight lisp—or his father's manner. Address, accent, appearance do not help him. But he has one quality—intellect. He has an eye—and he can judge and think for himself. Parts of the speech were faulty enough—there was claptrap with the wisdom and insight. But such remarks as the impossibility of the country returning to prosperity under a military government, the picture of the old Boers—more squires than peasants—ordered about by young subalterns, the appeals for easy and honourable terms of surrender, showed that the young man has kept his critical faculty through the glamour of association with our arms. The tone was on the whole quiet and restrained; and through the speech ran, as I have said, the subdued but obvious plea for moderation and sympathy towards the foe.

The 'bonnet' of the Government

H. W. Massingham, *Daily News*, March 13, 1901

To their rescue came Mr Winston Churchill in what was certainly the ablest speech he has made since his entry into the House. I say 'ablest' because it was a pure debating speech conceived on lines of singular breadth, argued with great acuteness and closeness, and now and then with little gestures and tricks of manner—such as bent shoulders and eager, nervous action of the hands—which at moments made one catch one's breath with the thought of how his father looked and spoke. I do not yet find in this young man the depth of character, the great political force that lay behind all his most fantastic adventures. But nothing could be more remarkable than the way in which this youth has slipped into the Parliamentary manner and has flung himself as it were straight into the mid-current of the thoughts and prejudices of the House of Commons. He chose on this occasion to act as the 'bonnet' of the Government, the man who should lead them out of a dangerous pass. And he did it to perfection. Mr Balfour showed his gratitude by vehement and repeated cheering, and there were points in his speech in which he had the applause of Sir Henry Campbell-Bannerman and Sir Charles Dilke . . . The speech was a happy stroke for his own Parliamentary reputation and for the Government which he has placed under so deep an obligation. It is not exactly pleasing to hear this young man for there are defects of manner, thought and speech which do not commend themselves to the fastidious taste. But it is clear he is going to arrive as his father arrived before him.

Churchill attacks his own side

Henry W. Lucy, *The Balfourian Parliament, 1901–1905* (1906)

May 14, 1901. In modest fashion wherein a note of heredity is struck, the new member had proposed to himself to open and lead off the debate with an amendment condemning the scheme. The leader of the Opposition interposing, he necessarily gave way. Having prepared his speech, he delivered it, and has the satisfaction of reflecting that it totally eclipsed Sir Henry Campbell-Bannerman's effort.

It was, indeed, excellent alike in matter and in form, and has established the position of the young member for Oldham as a debater who will have to be reckoned with whatever Government is in office. Probably a Ministry composed of his own political friends have most to apprehend. No case is known in modern history or, indeed, in earlier Parliamentary records, where a striking personality is revived in the person of his offspring. We have to go back to the time of Pitt to find an instance where a great political personage was eclipsed by his son. Winston Churchill is not likely to eclipse the fame of Randolph, who was a statesman as well as a consummate debater. Certainly, as far as he has gone, he recalls with singular fidelity the manner and method of his distinguished father.

One priceless equipment for a Parliamentary career possessed by him is a phenomenal memory. In delivering his speech tonight he was evidently fully supplied with notes, but he did not use his manuscript for the purpose of reading a single sentence. I happened to sit next to him at dinner after his triumph in the House, and mentioned an incident observed in delivery of a speech of nearly an hour's duration. Quoting from the letter his father wrote to Lord Salisbury on the eve of Christmas, 1886, resigning the Chancellorship of the Exchequer, I noticed that when only half-way through reading he closed the book and recited the closing passages.

421

'Yes,' he said, 'I felt it would be easier to recite the letter than to read it from a book held in my hand, so I learned it off.'

He added that his speech, which, fully reported, filled three columns of close print, had all been written out. He then learnt it off by heart, and delivered it as if it were an extemporaneous effort, a delusion artfully assisted by occasional interpolation of sparkling sentences referring to points made by speakers preceding him through the evening.

'If,' he said, 'I read a column of print four times over I commit it so perfectly to memory that I could forthwith recite it without an omission or error.'

Churchill breaks down

Daily Mail, April 23, 1904

He had been speaking with all his wonted force and vigour, brightness of idea and freshness of expression and that courage which leads him to make side thrusts at the Government and Mr Chamberlain ... Mr Chamberlain was sitting watching him through half-closed eyelids, measuring as it seemed the force of this persistent, able young man ... 'It lies with the Government to satisfy the working classes that there is no justification ...' he said with accustomed fire and appropriate action and was on the point of clinching his argument with his right fist smacking left palm. But the words would not come. He hesitated and began again. 'It lies with them to satisfy the electors ... It lies with them ... What?' he ejaculated as someone suggested a word which was not the right word. He lifted a slip of paper from the bench but the cue was not there. He searched the deep pockets of his coat and found no help. Major Seely picked torn scraps from the floor and the words were not there. Plucky and determined Mr Churchill went at the fence again. 'It lies with them to satisfy the electors ...' was all he could say ... Liberals, Nationalists and Unionist Free Traders cheered in warm sympathy as he gave up. He sat down murmuring thanks to the House for its kindness. The Conservative Party looked silently on wondering what had overtaken him so suddenly and dramatically.

Churchill crosses the floor of the House

Increasingly out of step with the Conservative Party, Churchill was critical of Balfour for failing to make clear his position on Tariff Reform, and in his final speech from the Conservative benches Churchill had attacked what he called Joseph Chamberlain's 'bastard Imperialism which was ground out by a party machine and was convenient for placing a particular set of gentlemen in power'.[54]

Manchester Guardian, June 1, 1904

Most of the benches were empty from end to end and on this scene of desolation rested the twilight of a rainy afternoon. Presently Mr Churchill put in an appearance. Standing at the bar he glanced at his accustomed place below the Ministerial gangway, made a rapid survey of the corresponding bench on the Opposition side, marched a few paces up the floor, bowed to the Chair, swerved suddenly to the right and took his place among the Liberals. This might have been a casual choice, but as if to emphasise its significance Mr Churchill in the course of the evening returned again and yet again to the same place. At length some of his new neighbours began to suspect that an event of some importance had occurred.

Howled down by his former friends

Peter de Mendelssohn, *The Age of Churchill* (1961)

When, after the Whitsun recess of 1904, Churchill rose for his first speech from the Opposition benches, he was greeted with a volley of angry taunts from the younger Conservatives seated around Joseph Chamberlain, and was howled down before he had completed his first sentence. He could get no hearing. This upset Mr David Shackleton, a recently elected Labour Member who in the following year became Chairman of the Labour Party and found himself honoured with a knighthood in 1917. Having started life as a half-time weaver in a Lancashire cotton-mill, he was not used to this way of arguing. 'Mr Speaker', he appealed, 'for the last ten minutes I have been endeavouring to listen to the speech of the hon. Member and have been unable to follow him. I think it is one of the privileges every hon. Member is entitled to that he should be heard.' The Speaker agreed in principle but could do nothing. When Churchill made another attempt, the uproar from the Government benches was resumed.

Churchill appealed to the 'good sense of the House' to say whether he was receiving fair treatment. Must it be assumed that the Prime Minister, Mr Balfour, who was in his seat, was a consenting party? Churchill had no sooner suggested this than 'Great Joe' rose on a point of order. 'I merely wish to know,' he said amid shouts, this time from the Opposition benches, 'whether it is in order for the junior Member for Oldham to say that there is a conspiracy against him in which I am an accomplice—a statement which is absolutely untrue!' The Speaker ruled that the Member for Oldham should not make such charges. Churchill withdrew his remark.

Churchill and the Parliament Bill

Churchill was by now Home Secretary, at the age of thirty-seven, and he took charge of the Committee stage of the Parliament Bill during the absence of both the pilot of the measure, the Prime Minister, Mr Asquith, and the absence through illness of Lloyd George. This gave his former Tory colleagues the opportunity to harry him.

Frank Dilnot, *The Old Order Changeth* (1911)

The Home Secretary was a perpetual study for those who have an interest in men. He was an infant prodigy among statesmen, and he somehow looked the part. His clean-shaven face was round like that of a schoolboy, his nose seemed slightly tip-tilted, and in his merry moments a dimple appeared in each of his cheeks. At such times he was the mischievous boy—and that in spite of his frock-coat. But from this mischievous boy there would suddenly spring the hard man of affairs, obstinate, domineering, offensive, and highly capable. Again there would be a transformation, and the young statesman would become an old man bowed down with responsibility, who, seated with hunched shoulders on the Treasury Bench, and poring over documents with the aid of a pair of spectacles, showed to those in the gallery above a head as bald as that of a man of sixty.

The back-bench Conservatives frequently laid themselves out to attack Mr Churchill in order to show him that they still considered him a rather ill-mannered youth of no particular ability, who had left his own party for the sake of what he might get in the other party. None of his opponents were a match for him, but they were able to give him some very unpleasant periods, and it was plain to see that Mr Churchill, notwithstanding much strength of will, was sometimes hard put to it to preserve that Parliamentary balance of manner which is essential in a highly-placed statesman. As a rule, however, he got through all right. I remember one sitting when there was very much turmoil. The Conservatives adopted as an article of faith the supposition that Mr Churchill was fundamentally unfit to take command of the House of Commons. They strove to make it appear that he was unfit. Lively incidents of course resulted. On this particular occasion, the younger Conservatives on the one side and the Nationalists and some of the Liberals below the gangway on the other had worked themselves up to a state of great anger. The Chairman of Ways and Means, Mr Emmott (one of the most amiable of men), was driven to a kind of petulant desperation by the disorder. Mr Churchill, striving hard to maintain the dignity of a Minister in charge, with difficulty restrained himself from a joyous entry into the thick of the fray. He looked the embodiment of Puck as he wriggled about on the Treasury Bench, thrusting here and there a word into the general din. Young Lord Winterton was one of the enthusiasts on the Conservative side, and after a period of rival shouts, he burst out, 'Send for the Speaker; send for someone will keep order.' Mr Emmott rose with a very severe aspect. 'If the noble Lord does not cease those cries, I shall have to deal with him.' Quite unrepentant was Lord Winterton. 'I rise to a point of order,' he said; 'I desire to call your attention to the fact that there are continuous disorderly interruptions from honourable gentlemen below the gangway, and by the Home Secretary, who is in charge of the House, and I am compelled to call for the Speaker from the fact that they have not been once called to order from the Chair.' 'That is not a point of order,' said Mr Emmott severely. 'Then,' cried Lord Winterton, 'I shall continue to call for the Speaker.' Uproar ruled for a few moments, and, in the midst of it, Mr Churchill rose. His tone was that of one of the mildest-mannered men who ever prosed before the House of Commons. 'I am sure I made no disorderly interruptions.' Lord Winteron was up with fierce words at once. 'I must distinctly accuse the right honourable gentleman of making the most disorderly interruptions.' All this while there were eddying cheers and ejaculations from various sections of the House. Many personal charges were flung across the floor. Mr Churchill tried to get in an explanation; but Mr Peel, who was technically in possession of the House, would not give way to him, and the Chairman had to rule that the Home Secretary was not in order. He sat down and waited his time. The circumstances connected with the commencement of Mr Peel's speech (interrupted by the foregoing passages) led to further trouble when the speech was over. Mr Peel had risen with other Conservatives, including Lord Winterton, and Liberals, Labour Members and Nationalists had shouted jubilantly, 'Winterton, Winterton, Winterton,' the suggestion being that the Chairman should call on the young Lord, more fun being anticipated from him than from Mr Peel. Mr Churchill, forgetting that he was a Cabinet Minister, leading the House, could not repress his boyish impulses, and, leaning back in his place, anxious to quiet the debate and not to stir up further strife, called the name of Mr Peel, a fluent but not very stimulating speaker. When he sat down, Mr Churchill had his chance. 'What I wish to say is that I never used a word, nor am I conscious myself of having made any interruption that was discourteous or disorderly in regard to the speech of Lord Winterton. If I have done so I wish to express my regret for it. I do not believe there is the slightest foundation for the suggestion. He may have thrown that taunt across the floor to cover himself in regard to something he said in reference to you, Mr Emmott.'

Lord Winterton, enjoying himself very much, proceeded amid loud Conservative cheers to make things as disagreeable as possible for the Home Secretary. 'My protest,' he said, 'was directed partly against the right honourable gentleman, and his friends behind him, and more distinctly against himself. My accusation was that the right honourable gentleman indulged in discourteous, and as I think, disorderly interruption. When I rose to address the House, some of the right honourable gentleman's friends barracked me. They called out the name of an honourable member—myself—instead of the constituency he represents. Those cries were led by the right honourable gentleman himself, the present leader of the House of Commons, as I understand. If I was mistaken in supposing that the right honourable gentleman did call out my name, I unreservedly withdraw.'

'Perfectly true,' replied Mr Churchill. 'Three honourable members rose from those benches, and several honourable members expressed a preference to hear the noble Lord. I frankly admit that I called out the noble lord's name. That is not a disorderly interruption. Whatever he says, it is not a discourtesy.' Lord Winterton protested that Mr Churchill had 'bawled out' his name in a way intended to be discourteous. Then there was comparative quiet for a few minutes. But the spirit of the occasion was manifested a little later; when Mr Claude Lowther, in a brief contribution to the debate, made the comment that one of the Nationalist members had 'merged his delightful personality into that of a laughing hyena'.

Balfour delivers a put-down

Oliver Lyttelton (Viscount Chandos), *The Memoirs of Lord Chandos* (1962)

Before he was quite so famous, the highly prepared nature of his speeches sometimes came under fire.

One day Arthur Balfour, who had come late into the House, and who was to reply for the Government, asked my father, then Colonial Secretary, what Winston had been saying. My father told him that the line of argument developed by the Government, which was unexpected, had somewhat thrown Winston's speech out of gear and that it had not gone well. Uncoiling himself at the box, A.J.B. began in something of this style: 'We have all listened'— which he had not done—'to the speech of the Rt. Hon. Gentleman who has just resumed his seat, we have all listened with interest, and I might say even with admiration. Unfortunately he has trained his guns up a road along which the enemy has—er—along which the enemy has *not* come. Might I suggest that in future he makes his heavy pieces a little more mobile?'

This inflicted a wound which I have been told took a little time to heal.

This little place

Alexander MacCallum Scott (1874–1928), the son of a rector, was educated at Polmont Public School, Falkirk High School and Glasgow University. He was called to the bar and practised on the Western Circuit. He served on Lewisham Borough Council (1903–6). He became Private Secretary to Lord Pentland, the Secretary of State for Scotland, in 1909 and sat as a Liberal MP for the Bridgeton division of Glasgow from December 1910 until 1922, when he was defeated. From 1917 to 1919 he served as PPS to Churchill, who was Minister for Munitions and Secretary for War. He was briefly a

Coalition Liberal Whip in 1922. Later, he joined the Labour Party and was a prospective Labour candidate at the time he was killed in an air crash.

Alexander MacCallum Scott, Diary, March 5, 1917

As we were leaving the House late tonight, he called me into the Chamber to take a last look round. All was darkness except a ring of faint light all around under the gallery. We could dimly see the table, but the walls and roof were invisible.

'Look at it,' he said. 'This little place is what makes the difference between us and Germany. It is in virtue of this that we shall muddle through to success and for lack of this Germany's brilliant efficiency leads her to final disaster. This little room is the shrine of the world's liberties.'

The Dyer Debate

Philip Cunliffe-Lister (1884–1972), 1st Earl of Swinton, was the son of a colonel and was educated at Winchester and at University College, Oxford. He was called to the bar in 1908 and served in the Army during World War I, winning an MC. From 1918 to 1935, when he was created Viscount Swinton, he was Conservative MP for the Hendon division of Middlesex. He held office as president of the Board of Trade (1922–4), Colonial Secretary (1931–5), Secretary of State for Air (1935–8), Minister resident in West Africa (1942–4), and Minister of Civil Aviation (1944–5). After serving as Secretary of State for Commonwealth Relations and Tory Deputy Leader in the Lords from 1951 to 1955, he was bumped up to an earldom by Churchill.

Another observer of this debate, Colin Coote, was equally impressed with Churchill's ingenious performance. 'On the angriest House I have ever seen,' he later attested, 'Churchill inflicted a thirty-minute disquisition on military law. It was as dull as a poultice, and as a poultice it drew out the inflammation. Then, to an audience bored into quiescence, he gently administered the Government's case.'[55]

The Earl of Swinton, *Sixty Years of Power* (1966)

There had been rioting in Amritsar. General Dyer, an old and experienced soldier, had ordered his troops to fire on a mob in a narrow street and there were frightful casualties. It may well have been that some firing was justified; but there was no doubt that the use of force was excessive and that the firing should have been disciplined and restrained. The War Office relieved General Dyer of his command.

The General had many friends at home who felt that he had been badly treated, and in particular he had the strong support of Sir Edward Carson, the greatest advocate of his day.

The whole matter was debated in a tense House of Commons. Edwin Montagu, the Secretary of State for India, opened with a most infelicitous speech. He was followed by Carson who roused the House to fever heat. Carson was followed by Churchill, who had a prepared speech. But such was the feeling of the House that if Winston had plunged straight into his speech he would have been hardly heard. He realised that he must reduce the temperature of the House. So he embarked on a long, involved and rather dull disquisition on the legal rights and liabilities of the soldiers called in in aid of the civil power, and the responsibility of the Army Council towards a serving officer. As he meandered on, the House simmered down. Members began to talk to one another. One or two, bored by the anticlimax, got up and walked out. Then, having reduced the temperature of the House to zero, Winston launched into his speech. It was a great speech. Towards the end he drew a contrasting picture of a young subaltern waiting, stopwatch in hand, with a barrage raging around him, to lead his platoon over the top at the exact moment, compared with an experienced General, exposed to no risk, in command of his troops. The House was deeply moved. The balance of the debate was restored, events were seen in their true perspective and the Government won a comfortable victory.

A Churchill Budget

Churchill is generally considered to have been a disappointing Chancellor of the Exchequer. However, Clement Attlee recalled enjoying 'his contests with his opposite number, Philip Snowden, whose acidity was an admirable foil to Churchill's more boisterous methods. Each Budget provided the opportunity for a full-dress fight between them. Churchill's Budget speeches were always interesting. It was exciting to speculate which hen roost he would rob next and how ingeniously he would do it.'[56] By 1929 it was still a formidable performance, though even admirers could see the flaws. 'None of us had heard anything of the kind,' Harold Macmillan later wrote in his memoirs, '... such mastery of language, such careful deployment of the arguments, such dexterous covering of any weak point.'[57]

'Essence of Parliament', *Punch*, May 6, 1925

Tuesday, April 8. Mr Churchill had a splendid audience for his first Budget. The Peers' Gallery was so congested that Lord Balfour (now again Lord President of the Council) could find no room there. The Distinguished Strangers included Sir Edward Clarke, the Governor of The Bank of England, Mr Harold Cox and other financial authorities. By Mr Churchill's side on the Front Bench sat three ex-Chancellors, Mr Baldwin and the Brothers Chamberlain; on his flank was another, Sir Robert Horne; and opposite two more, Mr Lloyd George and Mr Snowden. On none of these distinguished predecessors however did his first glance rest when he entered the House, but on a small boy who sat in the Public Gallery with his mother and sister—Master Randolph Churchill.

The Chancellor wasted little time in discussing the details of the past year's finance. He mentioned, however, that the revenue from beer had increased by a million—one proof, at any rate, that 'the consuming power of our people is maintained'.

Having set forth his two objectives—'(i) The security of the home of the wage-earner against exceptional misfortune, and (ii) The encouragement of enterprise through a relief of the burdens resting upon industry'—he explained that a prospective surplus of twenty-six millions was not enough. 'It is imperative,' he said, 'that I should fortify the revenue,' and, suiting action to word, he took a drink—to the huge delight of Randolph junior.

The remainder of the speech rather resembled a cross-word puzzle, 'Across' being represented by proposed increases in taxation, and 'Down' by remissions and other boons. But the whole was skilfully interwoven, and it was easy to follow the clues. Thus the increase in death-duties was balanced by a reduction in super-tax, and the new impost on luxuries (ranging, appropriately, from silk stockings to hops) by concessions to the possessors of 'earned' income.

Twenty years ago the Unionists talked about Old Age Pensions, but funked the cost and left the Liberals to earn credit with the electorate by introducing them. Mr Churchill evidently does not mean to let his old (and new) party make the same mistake again. His scheme for widows' and other pensions is of the most far-reaching character. 'Ninepence for fourpence' has been completely outdone. A man of sixty who begins to pay his fourpence a week now will get something like sixteen shillings and eightpence a week in return. 'Such are the miracles of nation-wide insurance,' said Mr Churchill, with a special tribute to Mr Lloyd George, its originator.

As time sped on and Mr Churchill said nothing about the standard rate of income-tax, some Members must have feared that the expected sixpence was not to be forthcoming and that they were to be treated as the Friend of Humanity treated the Needy Knife-Grinder. But at last came the announcement, and so ended one of the clearest, best-delivered and most interesting Budget-speeches of modern times.

It elicited charming compliments from Mr Snowden, who was sure that, if the spirits of the departed visited their old haunts, Lord Randolph's must be rejoicing over his son's success; and from Mr Lloyd George, who saw in the Budget the working of 'an ingenious, resourceful and exceedingly audacious mind'. Both took exception to the Protectionist flavour of some of the new taxes and both approved (with reserve) the insurance proposals. Mr Jack Jones, however, would have nothing to do with a contributory scheme. With his usual engaging frankness he announced that he drank beer and therefore already paid more than his share of national taxation.

Spain

Sir Henry 'Chips' Channon, Diary, April 15, 1937

Yesterday they discussed Spain again. Why will the Opposition always prefer talking of every country save their own? Winston Churchill made a terrific speech, brilliant, convincing, unanswerable and his 'stock' has soared, and today people are buying 'Churchills', and saying once more that he ought to be in the government, and that it is too bad to keep so brilliant a man out of office; but were he to be given office, what would it mean? An explosion of foolishness after a short time? War with Germany? a seat for Randolph? Of course he gets on better with Neville Chamberlain than he ever did with Baldwin: at least there is no active dislike between the two great men.

Churchillian filibuster

Virginia Cowles (1910–83) was born in New York and was only twenty-six when she went to cover the Spanish Civil War as a correspondent for the North American Newspaper Alliance; she was the only foreign correspondent to visit both the Republican and Francoist forces. In July 1945 she married Aidan Crawley, the newly elected Labour MP for Buckingham. Crawley was defeated in 1951 and later resigned from the Labour Party. Later still, he became a Conservative MP.

Virginia Cowles, *Churchill: The Era and the Man* (1953)

The date was 24 March, 1938, two weeks after the German invasion of Austria. As I looked down from the gallery on the sea of black coats and white faces, he seemed only one man of many; but when he spoke his words rang through the House with terrible finality. He stood addressing the Speaker, his shoulders hunched, his head thrust forward, his hands in his waistcoat pockets. 'For five years I have talked to this House on these matters—not with very great success. I have watched this famous island descending incontinently, fecklessly, the stairway which leads to a dark gulf. It is a fine broad stairway at the beginning, but after a bit the carpet ends. A little farther on there are only flagstones, and a little farther on still these break beneath your feet. Look back over the last five years—since, that is to say, Germany began to rearm in earnest and openly to seek revenge. If we study the history of Rome and Carthage we can understand what happened and why. It is not difficult to form an intelligent view about the three Punic Wars; but if mortal catastrophe should overtake the British Nation and the British Empire, historians a thousand years hence will still be baffled by the mystery of our affairs. They will never understand how it was that a victorious nation, with everything in hand, suffered themselves to be brought low, and to cast away all that they had gained by measureless sacrifice and absolute victory—gone with the wind!

'Now the victors are vanquished, and those who threw down their arms in the field and sued for an armistice are striding on to world mastery. That is the position—that is the terrible transformation that has taken place bit by bit. I rejoice to hear from the Prime Minister that a further supreme effort is to be made to place us in a position of security. Now is the time at last to rouse the nation. Perhaps it is the last time it can be roused with a chance of preventing war, or with a chance of coming through to victory should our efforts to prevent war fail. We should lay aside every hindrance and endeavour by uniting the whole force and spirit of our people to raise again a great British nation standing up before all the world; for such a nation, rising in its ancient vigour, can even at this hour save civilisation.'

When Mr Churchill sat down there was a deep silence for a moment: then the show was over. The House broke into a hubbub of noise; Members rattled their papers and shuffled their way to the lobby. A prominent Conservative came up to the gallery to take me to tea. I was talking to a friend, and when we asked him what he thought of the speech, he replied lightly: 'Oh, the usual Churchillian filibuster; he likes to rattle the sabre and he does it jolly well, but you always have to take it with a grain of salt.' This was the general attitude of the House of Commons in those days. Many years later Churchill wrote: 'I had to be very careful not to lose my poise in the great discussions and debates which crowded upon us ... I had to control my feelings and appear serene, indifferent, detached.' In view of the circumstances, this was no small feat in itself.

❖

The Prince of Peace

Malcolm John MacDonald (1901–81), the son of Ramsay MacDonald, was educated at Bedales and at Queen's College, Oxford. He was a member of the London County Council from 1928 to 1931 and was Labour MP for the Bassetlaw division of Nottinghamshire, 1929–31, and National Labour MP for the same seat, 1931–5. From 1936 to 1945 he was a National Government MP for Ross and Cromarty. He held office as Secretary of State for Dominion Affairs (1935–9), Colonial Secretary (1935 and 1938–40), and Minister of Health (1940–1). Churchill then sent him to Canada for the remainder of World War II as High Commissioner.

Malcolm MacDonald, *Titans and Others* (1972)

During one of my earlier statements in a House of Commons debate he interrupted my peroration with a mischievous interjection which convulsed our fellow Members with laughter—and ruined the peroration.

The date was November, 1938. A few weeks earlier the famous meeting between Neville Chamberlain and Adolph Hitler at Munich had taken place. On his return to London the Prime Minister made his imprudent remark prophesying that the agreement he had reached with the Fuhrer could mean 'Peace in our time', and a false glow of optimism about the possibility of curbing Nazi Germany's European ambitions without resort to war inspired many Members on both the Government and the Opposition sides. Churchill was not of their number.

I had become Secretary of State for the Colonies a few days earlier. My speech was largely analytical of the grim, confused Palestinian problem. In it I

431

sketched first the Jewish and then the Arab case, described the great difficulty of reconciling the two, and declared that nevertheless the Government would devote all its resources and energy towards this reconciliation. Then, as a peroration, I indulged in a flight of somewhat religious appeal. Reminding my fellow Members that Palestine was a Holy Land, I urged that our responsibility for its fate had an especially sacred quality. Working up towards a climax of reverent reflection, I said to a hushed House, 'I cannot remember a time when I was not told stories about Nazareth and Galilee, about Jerusalem and Bethlehem, where the Prince of Peace was born.'

I hesitated a moment for effect before pronouncing a final eloquent sentence of Christian pleading. But the silence was promptly punctuated by Churchill's voice muttering in a stage whisper which all could hear, 'Good Heavens! I never knew Neville was born in Bethlehem.'

The crowded House roared with laughter, and my closing sentence was an anti-climax. Unfortunately the official *Hansard* report of the debate primly ignored that classic interjection.

❖

Churchill unimpressive

Harold Nicolson, Diary, April 11, 1940

To the House. It is packed. Winston comes in. He is not looking well and sits there hunched as usual with his papers in his hand. When he rises to speak it is obvious that he is very tired. He starts off by giving an imitation of himself making a speech, and he indulges in vague oratory coupled with tired gibes. I have seldom seen him to less advantage. The majority of the House were expecting tales of victory and triumph, and when he tells them that the news of our reoccupation of Bergen, Trondheim and Oslo is untrue, a cold wave of disappointment passes through the House. He hesitates, gets his notes in the wrong order, puts on the wrong pair of spectacles, fumbles for the right pair, keeps on saying 'Sweden' when he means 'Denmark', and one way and another makes a lamentable performance. He gives no real explanation of how the Germans managed to slip through to Narvik. We have sunk some eight German transports and two cruisers have been damaged. He claims that this has 'crippled' the German Navy. He says that the Faroe Islands have been seized and that Iceland will be protected. His references to the Norwegian Army and Navy are vague in the extreme. One has the impression that he is playing for time and expects that at any moment some dramatic news will be brought to him. It is a feeble, tired speech and it leaves the House in a mood of grave anxiety.

Prime Minister at last

Harold Nicolson, Diary, May 13, 1940

When Chamberlain enters the House, he gets a terrific reception, and when Churchill comes in the applause is less. Winston sits there between Chamberlain and Attlee, and it is odd to see the Labour Ministers sitting on the Government Bench. Winston makes a very short statement, but to the point. Percy Harris replies for the Liberals and makes an absurd anti-climax. 'The Lord President of the Council', he says, referring to Chamberlain, 'has set a great example . . .' At this there are cheers from every quarter of the House ' . . . for constant attendance on the front bench.' Everybody laughs a great deal. Then Lloyd George gets up and makes a moving speech telling Winston how fond he is of him. Winston cries slightly and mops his eyes.

'Blood, Toil, Tears and Sweat'

Harry Boardman, *Manchester Guardian*, May 14, 1940

The new Government met the House of Commons today and received a vote of confidence that was unanimous except for the opposition of Mr Maxton and Mr Campbell Stephen. These two parachutists, dropping from cloud-cuckoo-land, insisted on dividing the House. The division thus resulted in 381 votes being cast for the Government and none against because, of course, Mr Maxton and Mr Campbell Stephen had to act as 'tellers' for the cloud-cuckoo-land party, and the other member of it, Mr McGovern, was last heard of setting out for a holiday in Holland, last week.

When the division was called it was queer to see Conservatives, Labour men, Liberals, Simonites, National Labour, all massing at the entrances to the 'Aye' Division Lobby. As a too-eloquent Welsh member said, trying to express everybody's puzzlement, 'It is very difficult to re-orientate oneself to what has happened.' Corinthian and true.

There was Mr Churchill sitting opposite the Treasury Box, hands on knee. Mr Chamberlain was on his right, Mr Attlee and Mr Alexander on his left. Sir Archibald Sinclair was further down the bench, while behind the Speaker's chair, peering into the chamber like lost angels outside paradise, were some of the ministers who have gone. Mr Herbert Morrison took the corner seat above the gangway, while below the gangway, three seats up, was Sir Samuel Hoare, in the very place from which he made his speech of resignation as Foreign Secretary.

A solid phalanx of Labour second strings confronted the Government on the Opposition front bench. Very obviously they, like their Welsh colleague, were struggling to 're-orientate' themselves to a world in which Mr Attlee, Mr Alexander and Mr Herbert Morrison sat opposite them.

Mr Churchill had an inspiring cheer when he entered the Chamber, but Mr Chamberlain, when he came in a moment later, was cheered even more loudly by the Conservatives, some of whom stood up to greet the late Prime Minister.

The House was grave, graver than on the September Sunday morning when war was declared. But that does not mean it was depressed. Far from it. It was exalted as well as grave. At last it has seen the peril that impends over us in all its fearful menace, and the vision has raised it to an invincible temper. Now has it become a Grand Committee of National Safety, willing to back Mr Churchill and his colleagues to the utmost limit.

Mr Churchill was the calmest man in the Chamber. Calm in crisis was his great ancestor's quality. He himself has described the mode of address in the House of Commons as 'formal conversation'. That exactly describes his words today. He even had his hands in his pockets at times. And yet there was solemnity enough in his words.

To his new colleagues he could offer nothing but 'blood, toil, tears and sweat'. This echo of Garibaldi prepared the way for the further warning that the country has before it a most grievous ordeal and many long months of struggle and suffering. To those who asked for the Government's policy he answered: 'It is to wage war by sea, land, and air, war with all our minds and with all the strength that God gives us; to wage war against a monstrous tyranny never surpassed in the dark and lamentable catalogue of human crimes.'

As the cheers were echoing round the Chamber Mr Churchill put the second question, 'What is our aim?' To which he replied, 'Victory at all costs and in spite of all terrors; victory, however long and hard the road may be, for without victory there is no survival.' There were again resounding cheers for this pithy yet eloquent definition of the new Government's purposes. Then we heard Mr Churchill concluding on a note of buoyancy and hope, because 'our cause cannot be suffered to fail among men'.

Of the speeches that followed one rose most surely to the height of this moment of destiny. It was Mr Lloyd George's. He called it 'a critical and terrible moment—a graver moment of jeopardy than has confronted a British Minister for all time'. This from the man who saw us so near defeat in 1917. 'We all, from the bottom of our hearts, wish him well. The friends of freedom and of human right throughout the world will wish him Godspeed.' Lincoln could not have bettered this brief speech.

Roaring spirits

Sir Henry 'Chips' Channon, Diary, July 23, 1940

Winston was in roaring spirits today, and gave slashing answers, which he had himself drafted, to foolish Questions, and generally convulsed the House. He is at the very top of his form now and the House is completely with him, as is the country, but he knows very little about foreign affairs. I sat behind him today and he was smiling and friendly, but I am always shy with him, and never get it quite right: I do not know why.

An oratorical masterpiece

John Colville, Diary, October 8, 1940

The PM made a long speech in the House to which I listened. He discussed the bombing of London, our attitude to Japan and the position of Spain (a fine passage which the FO did their best to make him omit). I heard the PM tell Halifax on the telephone that he set great store on speaking of Spain as 'a leading and famous member of the family of Europe and of Christendom'.

He was skilful in dealing with Dakar and insisted that 'this series of accidents and some errors' should be regarded in its true perspective. His peroration with its reminder that 'long dark months of trial and tribulation lie before us', with misfortunes, shortcomings, mistakes and disappointments, was eloquently spoken and enthusiastically received. 'Death and sorrow,' he said, 'will be the companions of our journey, hardship our garment; constancy and valour are our only shield. We must be united; we must be undaunted; we must be inflexible. Our qualities and our deeds must burn and glow through the gloom of Europe till they become the veritable beacon of our salvation.' I followed the speech from a flimsy of the PM's notes, which are typed in a way which Halifax says is like the printing of the psalms. Afterwards John Peck and I corrected the official report and altered the text in many places to improve the style and the grammar; for the PM's speeches are essentially oratorical masterpieces and in speaking he inserts much that sounds well and reads badly.

Before the speech Randolph, recently elected MP for Preston, was introduced, amidst applause, by Winston and David Margesson (a fact which, said R., made him shiver).[58] The applause, needless to say, was for Winston whose popularity in the House, as in the country, remains untarnished.

A *delightful feint*

Oliver Lyttelton (1893–1972) was educated at Eton and at Trinity College, Cambridge. He served as a captain in the Grenadier Guards during World War I, winning a DSO and MC and the rank of Brigade Major. He became a successful businessman and was Conservative MP for Aldershot from 1940 to 1954, having been elected after Churchill had appointed him to a front-bench post as president of the Board of Trade. He sat in the War Cabinet from 1941 to 1945, and was principally involved with war production. He later served as Colonial Secretary from 1951 to 1954, before returning to the electrical industry as Viscount Chandos.

Oliver Lyttelton (Viscount Chandos), *The Memoirs of Lord Chandos* (1962)

At one moment, an old brother officer of mine in the Brigade of Guards, who was commanding an Officers' Training Unit, wrote an ill-judged letter to *The Times* saying that entries from the public schools made far the best officers. This of course gave offence to the Labour Party. About this time the Prime Minister was announcing to the House of Commons the formation of two bodies, one to be called the Production Executive, and the other the Import Executive. These were the first gropings towards a Ministry of Production, and I have reason to remember them because, as President of the Board of Trade, I was a member of both. The announcement was not going well and the House was a trifle restive, because they thought, and as it turned out rightly, that the instruments were unequal to the task. Referring to the Chairman of one of these bodies, the Prime Minister, apparently rather searching for words, said, 'As to the Chairman of this Committee, he is not *facile princeps*, but *primus inter pares*, which for the benefit of any'—he paused almost imperceptibly and several members of the Labour Party seemed about to rise from their seats and protest about the insult on their lack of a classical education that was about to follow. However, he completed the sentence, 'for the benefit of any Old Etonians present, I should, if very severely pressed, venture to translate.' This delighted everyone, and was more than ever felicitous coming from an Old Harrovian, whose knowledge of Latin was of the slightest. The roof nearly came off, and in the few minutes of hilarity he put the most contentious points and rode off with them in his saddle-bags without as much as an interruption.

Confidence Debate

Harold Nicolson, Diary

January 27, 1942. Down to the House. Winston speaks for an hour and a half and justifies his demand for a vote of confidence. One can actually feel the wind of opposition dropping sentence by sentence, and by the time he finishes it is clear that there is really no opposition at all—only a certain uneasiness.

He says that we shall have even worse news to face in the Far East and that the Libyan battle is going none too well. When he feels that he has the whole House with him, he finds it difficult to conceal his enjoyment of his speech, and that, in fact, is part of his amazing charm. He thrusts both his hands deep into his trouser pockets, and turns his tummy now to the right, now to the left, in evident enjoyment of his mastery of the position.

Herbert Williams and Henderson Stewart attack the Government. But the House is not with them. Winston has won in the very first round, and the future rounds will be dull and sad. My God, my love and admiration of Winston surge round me like a tide!

January 28. Wardlaw-Milne makes an impressive speech attacking the Government over Malaya.[59] But the whole thing seems to me unreal since our misfortune is due entirely to the collapse of the American Navy. It is difficult for Winston to say this, and indeed he slid over the point neatly in his speech yesterday. But it is really absurd to expect our people at Singapore to have taken measures of defence on the assumption that the command of the sea would pass suddenly to the Japanese. And even if they had, we could not have provided sufficient to meet such a disaster.

Shinwell makes a vicious speech. Randolph Churchill intervenes to defend his father. He attacks most cruelly those who had abused him, and says that 'Winterton clowned himself out of office within a few days'. He is amusing and brave. Bob Boothby says to me, 'I am enjoying this very much, but I hope it does not go on for long.' I have a dreadful feeling that Randolph may go too far. I see his little wife squirming in the Gallery, and Winston himself looks embarrassed and shy. But I am not so sure that it has done Randolph harm.

January 29. Third day of the Vote of Confidence debate. Winston winds up. He is very genial and self-confident. He does not gird at his critics. He compliments them on the excellence of their speeches. When he reaches his peroration he ceases to be genial and becomes emphatic. He crouches over the box and strikes it. 'It only remains for us to act. I offer no apologies. I offer no excuses. I make no promises. In no way have I mitigated the sense of danger and impending misfortunes that hang over us. But at the same time I avow my confidence, never stronger than at this moment, that we shall bring this conflict to an end in a manner agreeable to the interests of our country and the future of the world. I have finished.' (Then that downward sweep of the two arms, with the palms open to receive the stigmata.) 'Let every man act now in accordance with what he thinks is his duty in harmony with his heart and conscience.' Loud cheers, and we all file out into the thin and stifling lobby.

It takes a long time to count the votes, and finally they are recorded as 464 to 1. Huge cheers. Winston gets up and we rise and cheer him. He turns round and bows a little shyly. Then he joins Mrs Winston, and arm-in-arm and beaming, they push through the crowds in Central Lobby.

There was a scene earlier in the day between Winston and Southby. Yesterday,

437

during Randolph's rather unfortunate speech, Southby had interrupted and hinted that Randolph was not a fighting soldier. ('The Honourable and Gallant Member—I call him that because of the uniform he wears.') The Speaker shut him up, and in the corridor afterwards he went up to Winston and said that had he been allowed to finish, he would have congratulated Randolph on his rapid promotion. Winston shook his fist in his face. 'Do not speak to me,' he shouted. 'You called my son a coward. You are my enemy. Do not speak to me.'

❖

Churchill's mastery of the House

Harold Nicolson, Letter to his sons Ben and Nigel, September 21, 1943

The House met again today. The Speaker startled us by announcing the death of Kingsley Wood.[60] On getting out of bed this morning, he fell down stone dead. After the first moment of surprise, the House buzzed with prognostications regarding his successor. It was still buzzing slightly when Winston came in, beaming genially with a 'Here I am again' look, and was loudly cheered. A few minutes later he rose to make his speech on the progress of the war. The speech was divided into two parts and lasted two hours, broken by a luncheon interval. He began, as always, in a dull, stuffy manner, reciting dates and chronology, reading slowly from the typescript on the box. But as he progressed, he began to enliven his discourse with the familiar quips and gestures. His most characteristic gesture is strange indeed. You know the movement that a man makes when he taps his trouser pockets to see whether he has got his latch-key? Well, Winston pats both his trouser pockets and then passes his hands up and down from groin to tummy. It is very strange. You will have read or heard the main lines of the speech, and I shall comment only on those aspects of it which cannot be conveyed by the wireless or the printed word. It was obvious that he was in some logical difficulty over the implicit anomaly that we had asked for 'unconditional surrender' whereas the Italians had asked in effect to be allowed in on our side. He dealt with this sturdily and stubbornly but in a somewhat laboured way. And when he got through the argument, he leant across to the Opposition and said in a conversational tone, 'That all right?' They grinned back affectionately. When he came to discussing the escape of Mussolini, he took off his glasses, stepped back from the box, and put on an expression of rather perplexed amusement. By his manner, rather than by what he said, he was able to convey to the House that this escape was no more than an irritating and (if one looked at it the right way) an entertaining episode.

At the end of the first act, and before we adjourned for luncheon, he did an amusing thing. He referred to Italy and expressed pleasure that the Italian people, 'rescued from their state of servitude', could now take 'their rightful place among the democracies of the world'.

'The satellite States,' he continued, 'suborned and overawed . . .' and then he raised his arm as if about to deliver the most terrific thunderbolt from his rich armoury of rhetoric, but he dropped his arm suddenly and took off his spectacles, '... may perhaps be allowed to work their passage home', he concluded, grinning. It is in this that one finds his mastery of the House. It is the combination of great flights of oratory with sudden swoops into the intimate and conversational. Of all his devices it is the one that never fails.

A *surprise visit*

Harold Nicolson, Letter to his sons Ben and Nigel, January 18, 1944

This was an exciting day. The House met again after the Christmas Recess and I went down there early. I happened to have been told that Winston had arrived home that morning, but the rest of the House were wholly unaware of that fact. We were dawdling through Questions and I was idly glancing at my Order Paper when I saw (*saw* is the word) a gasp of astonishment pass over the faces of the Labour Party opposite. Suddenly they jumped to their feet and started shouting, waving their papers in the air. We also jumped up and the whole House broke into cheer after cheer while Winston, very pink, rather shy, beaming with mischief, crept along the front bench and flung himself into his accustomed seat. He was flushed with pleasure and emotion, and hardly had he sat down when two large tears began to trickle down his cheeks. He mopped at them clumsily with a huge white handkerchief.

A few minutes later he got up to answer questions. Most men would have been unable, on such an occasion, not to throw a flash of drama into their replies. But Winston answered them as if he were the youngest Under-Secretary, putting on his glasses, turning over his papers, responding tactfully to supplementaries, and taking the whole thing as consciously as could be. I should like to say that he seemed completely restored to health. But he looked pale when the first flush of pleasure had subsided, and his voice was not quite so vigorous as it had been.

Churchill on VE Day

Harold Nicolson, Diary, May 8, 1945

VE day. Lunch at the Beefsteak. Up till then everything had been normal, but I then find the streets crowded and people wearing all manner of foolish paper caps and cheering slightly. When I leave the club at 2.15, I find the roads packed. Trafalgar Square is a seething mass of people with figures draped all over the lions. Whitehall is overflowing, but a few buses try to push their way through. After the Cenotaph it is just a jam. I squeeze in behind a car and manage to reach the House about five to three. I pause to recover myself in

Palace Yard and regret to observe that I have torn a hole in my new suit. The crowds are packed against the railing and the mounted police have difficulty in clearing a path for the Government cars. Then came the great strokes of Big Ben and thereafter an immense hush. From the loudspeakers in Parliament Square Winston's voice booms out to all those thousands. It echoes on the Palace behind me so that I hear it doubly. He tells of the signature of surrender and its impending ratification in Berlin. He is short and effective. The crowd cheer and when he finishes and when God Save the King has been broadcast. But it is not frantic cheering.

I then enter the House. The place is packed and I sit on the step below the cross bench. I see a stir at the door and Winston comes in—a little shy—a little flushed—but smiling boyishly. The House jumps to its feet, and there is one long roar of applause. He bows and smiles in acknowledgement. I glance up at the Gallery where Clemmy (Churchill) should be. There is Mrs Neville Chamberlain there instead. And thereupon Winston begins. He repeats the short statement he had just made on the wireless ending up with 'Advance Britannia' and then he lays his manuscript aside and with more gesture and emphasis than is customary to him, he thanks the House for its support throughout these years. He then proposes that we adjourn to the Church of St Margaret's Westminster. The Speaker then leaves his seat and his mace is fetched before him. He is in Court Robes with gold facings to his gown and his Chaplain and the Sergeant-at-Arms are also in full dress.

We file out by the St Stephen's entrance and the police have kept a lane through the crowd. The crowd are friendly, recognising some of the Members. I am with Nancy Astor, who is, I feel, a trifle hurt that she does not get more cheering. We then have a service—and very memorable it is. The supreme moment is when the chaplain reads out the names of those Members of Parliament who have lost their lives. It is a sad thing to hear. My eyes fill with tears. I hope that Nancy does not notice. 'Men are so emotional,' she says.

We all go to the smoking-room. Winston comes with us. Passing through Central Hall he is given an ovation by the crowd. They clap their hands. A tiny little boy, greatly daring, dashes up to him and asks for his autograph. Winston solemnly takes out his glasses and signs. He then pats the delighted little boy on the head and grins his grin.

An obsession with secrecy

J. P. W. Mallalieu, *Tribune*, August 4, 1950

Although the main subject for debate last week was, literally, vital to each one of us, our immediate interest was caught by a technical point—would the second day's debate be held in secret?

Churchill wanted it secret, was determined to have it secret, but few people could say for certain why. In a secret session, of course, the Government can give more detailed information about defence than it can give in public. But all the information that the Government possesses is already given freely to Mr Churchill, Mr Eden and other Opposition leaders in the joint consultations which take place from time to time.

So Churchill, if he was following this line of thought at all, could only be considering the back-benchers—that they too should share, and have a chance to discuss, this confidential information.

There is, obviously, an arguable point here. But in a one and a half day's debate he chose to make two speeches himself. One of them said nothing and merely took time from the back-benchers. So I doubt whether Churchill was really much worried about bringing back-benchers into the picture.

Another possible reason for a secret session is to give the Opposition a chance to make criticisms of or suggestions to the Government which, at a critical time, the Opposition would not wish, in the national interest, to have published.

But in the joint consultation already referred to, the Opposition has all the chance it needs to put its criticisms and suggestions. Indeed, months ago, the Government asked Churchill and his colleagues to send in a memorandum of suggestion and criticism. But, so far, no such memorandum has been received. So I doubt whether this was the idea behind Churchill's plea for a secret session.

This throws us back on another explanation. It is that Churchill thrives on the dramatic stimulus of war tension, that this is his element, that through it, too, is the one chance he has of returning to power and that, as a secret session heightens this tension, let us have a secret session. Indeed, let us go about disguised and make secret signs to each other.

Such explanation, however, is unlikely. It suggests too high a degree of irresponsibility. Churchill may promise a detailed memorandum on defence and then fail to provide it. He may call for national unity in a time of national crisis and contribute to that unity by splintering the Chamber with party gibes. But I do not really think that he would try to set the House on fire merely in the hope of being called to put the fire out.

Anyway we did not get a secret session.

Shinwell opened on the first day with a long and expertly delivered statement of the Government's views and proposals.

Like Nye Bevan, Shinwell is at his best when he is answering a debate without notes and here he was opening a debate from a carefully prepared brief. Yet he made this brief seem alive and almost unrehearsed.

Those boxer-like movements of his—the hands weaving in front of him as if to parry a blow or probing for an opening through which to strike, his whole body poised with its full weight on the ball of the foot ready in a split second to sidestep or roll with the punch—they were all there. And as Shinwell shares with Churchill the ability to read a prepared speech as though he is making it extempore, the result was vigorous and effective.

441

During this speech, Churchill seemed restive and undecided. I suspect that he had come to the House with a full dress oration inside his breast pocket and that Shinwell's speech was making it obsolete even before Churchill had had time to arrange it in little piles beside the Dispatch Box.

The fact that the immediately preceding speaker has just robbed his prepared oration of any point does not always stop Churchill from delivering it anyway. But this afternoon he appeared in two minds. The stage had been carefully set for him. He was billed to appear in one of the two leading parts. But would it not seem rather silly to deliver a speech which had now lost its point? On the other hand, would it not be rash to scrap the speech and try to answer Shinwell—when debating is not one of Churchill's strong points?

In the end, Churchill stood up and waffled for some thirty minutes. The gist was that he could not answer Shinwell right away, that the performance would be put off until tomorrow and that the curtain had better be down when he played it. The House rambled off for tea and, by and by, Eden was put up in the middle of the debate to make some sort of show for the Opposition Front Bench. He did it very well.

Next came the real show. At the end of questions, Churchill rose with a broad grin on his face and looked towards the public galleries behind the Speaker's chair. Then, still grinning, he looked along the narrow galleries which flank the Chamber. Then, grinning more widely still, he said: 'Mishter Speaker, I spy Strangers.'

It was a perfect little act, delighting everyone. But when Mr Speaker, pursuant to Standing Order No. 105 (Withdrawal of Strangers from the House), put the Question 'that Strangers do withdraw' and we had voted on it, the secret session was defeated by 1 vote.

Thereat Mr Churchill pulled a prepared oration from his breast pocket, arranged it in neat piles beside the Dispatch Box and proceeded to read it energetically and effectively to the House. My bet is that he would have read precisely the same speech even if the vote had gone the other way.

Crossman, who followed, suggested that the finest contribution Churchill could make towards national unity would be to retire from public life. Reggie Paget described Churchill's speech as a 'masterly exposition of the dangers with which we are faced'. Earl Winterton described me as 'a third-rate jackal'.

There the matter rests at present.

A *voluntary sleeper*

Dennis Bardens, *Churchill in Parliament* (1967)

Sometimes his hearing was a trifle defective, yet he never needed to hear anything twice. If he appeared inattentive, it was not necessarily fatigue. The speech of one MP seemed interminable and Churchill slumped low in his seat, eyes closed. 'Must you fall asleep when I am speaking?' cried the angry MP. Dreamily, but in a perfectly clear voice, and without opening his eyes, Churchill answered, 'No, it is purely voluntary.'

A *well-timed entrance*

Oliver Lyttelton (Viscount Chandos), *The Memoirs of Lord Chandos* (1962)

After the war the Prime Minister answered Parliamentary questions three or four times a week. The questions were not usually intended to be helpful. Sometimes I had luncheon with him on a day when they would have been a strain upon the nerves or the digestion of any ordinary man. Yet he was completely relaxed. The Prime Minister's number on the Order Paper was usually in the early 40's, and he knew with uncanny precision when he would be reached. Sometimes a bottle of champagne stood on the table, and he and I drank a glass or two of it. Once or twice during luncheon he would ring the bell for a private secretary, add to an answer or polish a phrase with a relish only equal to that which he attacked the luncheon. At about ten minutes to three the private secretary would come in and say, 'They have reached 23.' 'Good, there's plenty of time,' and he would pour out a small noggin of old brandy. At this moment I would become rather restive and anxious lest he should be late. A quarter of an hour later 'Number 36' would be announced. 'We must go at once,' he said and, with that, shot out of the room into his car and was in his place about two or three questions before his own were reached.

One of his greatest Parliamentary gifts was his skill in answering questions. He revelled in them, and his relish communicated itself to the House. I give an example. It was after the war, in 1952. Mr Callaghan, who was seldom conciliatory and who had a manner which the House thought was a little more assured than was warranted, was pressing the Prime Minister one day upon the subject of the Allied Naval Commander in the Mediterranean. The Prime Minister appeared to have inclined slightly in one direction when Leader of the Opposition and in another direction in office. Things were getting somewhat uncomfortable as the crake-like voice pressed the point: didn't the right honourable gentleman say this in June and now this in October? At last with a beaming smile the Prime Minister replied: 'My views are a harmonious process which keeps them in relation to the current movement of events.' Callaghan shrugged his shoulders and sat down, as if to say it's no use bowling googlies to W. G. Grace.

An ugly scene

Dennis Bardens, *Churchill in Parliament* (1967)

The year closed with an ugly scene in the House—and one for which Churchill himself was to blame. Pressed by Mr Shinwell on information about the projected appointment of a Supreme Commander for the Mediterranean, Churchill lost his temper and wagging a finger at Mr Shinwell said, 'I would warn Mr Shinwell not to be too prophetic about the way in which things are going. They may not be as unfortunate for this country as he would no doubt wish.' The Opposition took this to imply a reflection on the former Minister of Defence's patriotism, and uproar at once ensued, with cries of 'Withdraw', 'Shame' and 'You wicked old man!' On an appeal from Mr Michison the Speaker ruled that to accuse a Member of unavowed motives was out of order, but, pressed to demand that Mr Churchill withdraw his remarks, he said, 'What I heard did not in my judgement amount to that.' Amidst cat-calls, hisses, taunts and cries Mr Churchill tried to speak over the din. Reminded of previous tributes he had made to Mr Shinwell ('I have always felt and always testified, even in moments of party strife, to the right hon. gentleman's sterling patriotism and the fact that his heart is in the right place where the life and strength of our country is concerned') he admitted that, but added that his appreciation had been 'inroaded' in recent months. This caused a tremendous outburst of booing—ugly enough anywhere but especially in the House of Commons. Churchill asked the Chair to rule whether booing was in order; the Speaker pronounced it 'grossly out of order'. 'What else can you say to a goose?' snapped Mr Ross, to be ordered by the Speaker at once to withdraw his remark. Herbert Morrison rose to argue with the Speaker on why 'goose' should be so offensive while an imputation of lack of patriotism be deemed harmless. Eventually Mr Churchill indicated that the word 'goose' did not worry him in the slightest, and tempers at last subsided.

Socialist jeers

Sir Henry 'Chips' Channon, Diary, April 9, 1952

Could there be any more nauseating performance than that of half a hundred hale young Socialists howling at Mr Churchill, jeering at his pronouncements and even at his entrances and exits into the House, taunting him with his advanced age and growing deafness? The man who may be the wrecker of the Tory Party, but was certainly Saviour of the civilised world? It happened again today. However in the 1922 secret Committee he had a rapturous reception, and stood the strain of speaking and answering questions for well over an hour.

A pretty good pub

Geoffrey Williams and Charles Roether, *The Wit and Wisdom of Winston Churchill* (1954)

There had been much talk in the newspapers of his retirement: much pressure had been expended in an effort to make him resign. In the summer of 1954, however, he had a drink at the House of Commons with an old journalist friend.

'What are they saying about me these days?' asked Churchill.

'Well, quite frankly, quite a few of your Conservative friends are saying that it would be a good thing for the party if you were to resign some time fairly soon.'

Churchill glared at him.

'You know, as I look at this room and think back over my long association with this House, I think this is a pretty good pub.'

And he added: 'And as I look at the faces in the House, I wonder why I should leave this pub until someone says, "Time, please!"—in somewhat stronger accents than those of my friends to whom you have been speaking.'

Churchill returns to the House on St George's Day, 1958

Harry Boardman, *Manchester Guardian*, April 24, 1958

It was St George's Day, and the sun was celebrating it in an expansive way. The authorities of the House of Commons had churlishly drawn the curtains along the south side of the Chamber to keep him out, but he beat them. His beams were victoriously streaming towards the Opposition benches. In this, Phoebus was showing no political partiality but merely humbling the said authorities.

There is one glory of the sun and another of the moon, as we know, but there is also a glory of Parliament; and it was manifested yesterday to the equal delight and surprise of numbers of members. While Mr Selwyn Lloyd was answering a question about the Summit conference, a fringe of members at the Bar parted to reveal Sir Winston Churchill. When the House—and it was full—was sure it was not 'seeing visions' it let itself go in a great and joyful cheer.

Sir Winston, valiantly struggling with the infirmity of his legs, made his way to his corner seat below the Treasury bench. Gone is that old, vigorous, cavalryman's stride that we knew of old. All eyes were on him as he settled down, and they were eyes bright with happy recognition. The sunshine and this uncovenanted event lifted everybody's spirits.

Mr Lloyd had been stopped in his tracks by the cheers, and he turned towards Sir Winston to say how glad members on both sides of the House were to see him back in his place. Again there was a surge of cheers. Mr Bevan, generous where he bestows his admiration, flourished a welcoming hand towards Sir Winston, and other Labour members sitting more nearly opposite him were also making welcoming gestures.

Sir Winston smiled acknowledgements. He was pale and had lost weight, but his mind was clearly fully alert. He talked first to his neighbour, Lord Hinchinbrooke, and then with Mr Heath, the Government Chief Whip, whom he had questioned across the gangway and who moved to sit beside Sir Winston on his haunches in the gangway. Now Sir Winston would scan the Order Paper. Next he would spread his fine hands on his knees—hands which used to be employed in handsome inflections when he was speaking. Sometimes a hand would find its way inside his waistcoat, where once—a lively memory—the jujube fell, only to be recovered after an appreciable pause in an important speech and amid shock after shock of laughter.

A division was called. Mr Gaitskell, on his way to the Opposition Lobby, stepped across the floor and bowing over the seated Sir Winston shook him by the hand. Sir Winston smiled his thanks. Would he vote? He did. That calls for a march, and Sir Winston marched, if a little shakily. He pressed Mr Butler's hand as he passed him. He dropped a word in the ear of the Chancellor of the Exchequer; and then he took on the Speaker in conversation, and it was not about Orders of the Day, judging by their mutual amusement.

He made the circuit through the division lobby and returned to his seat. But he was soon off again, for there was another division, this time against the Budget resolution on the Profits Tax. On this occasion he returned to the Chamber with Mr Macmillan at his side. He remained in his seat long enough for the House to close with the Slaughterhouses Bill. As he departed he turned to the Bar to make a solemn obeisance to the Chair.

An eerie presence

Malcolm Muggeridge, 'The Totemisation of Winston Churchill', *Esquire*, June 1961

Thus, from time to time, Churchill manages to find his way, alone and unaided, into the House of Commons. This is the scene he knows best; this the place where he has spent so many breathless hours of his long life. He returns to it by instinct—to the stale air, the untidy benches, the drone of unmeant and unheeded speeches, the pallid Front Bench faces, the occasional exclamations of approval or dissent, the laughter so easily and so fatuously aroused, all the drab panoply of a mid-twentieth-century Parliament. When his bulky form appears, whoever may be speaking, whatever may be under discussion, the proceedings are, in effect, temporarily suspended. All eyes rest on him, in the galleries as on the floor of the House. With exaggerated obeisance, he makes his bow to Mr Speaker, and advances upon his old seat below the gangway. Then, after some long-drawn-out byplay with his handkerchief or a throat lozenge, he leans across to ask a neighbouring MP, in a sepulchral whisper, what the business is before the House, and who the Member is (pointing at him) on his feet. It may well be Macmillan or Gaitskell whom he cannot identify. His eyes seldom intimate recognition, and, when they do, it is from an old recollection. With the years, distant memories grow clearer. The present and the recent past are hidden from view under thick clouds of forgetfulness.

Attention remains fixed on him. As he well knows, no speech will be heard, no question receive other than desultory consideration while he is there. Honourable and Right Honourable Members, on both sides of the House, continue to be preoccupied with his strange, eerie presence among them. When he gets up to go, their eyes follow him, as they did when he came in. After he has gone, and they have resumed their business, it takes a little while for them to get back on to their own pedestrian wave-length. The atmospherics created by his incursion only gradually subside. What is it about him which makes him, even in his decrepitude, still tower above the others, and hold them in thrall? Not warmth of character—he is rather horrible. Not past services—in the House of Commons, of all places, it is true that (to use a phrase Shakespeare puts into the mouth of Timon of Athens) men bar their doors before the setting sun. Not famous orations—like all rhetoric, his wear badly. Few today can listen without squirming even to the wartime speeches, which were so stirring at the time, about blood, sweat and tears, and fighting on the beaches.

He has become a kind of totem. His continued existence provides a link with departed glory. Though the sun may have set, still, as long as he is there, some glow lingers about the western sky in which others may participate. He is produced, as totems are, to keep up tribal morale, which otherwise would sag under the weight of unfamiliar and disconcerting circumstances. Britannia no longer rules the waves, but did when Churchill was First Lord of the Admiralty . . .

An empty seat

Thomas Fanshawe Lindsay was born in India in 1910 and was educated at Corpus Christi College, Oxford. From 1947 to 1950 he was deputy director of Information Services at Conservative Central Office and in the 1950 general election he was attached to the personal staff of Winston Churchill. He was a leader-writer for the *Daily Telegraph* from 1955 until 1966, when he became an assistant editor of the paper.

T. F. Lindsay, *Daily Telegraph*, January 26, 1965

'The seat which, by the general wish of the House, should be left vacant this afternoon.' So said the Prime Minister, Mr Wilson, of the front-bench seat below the gangway, last occupied by Sir Winston Churchill before his retirement from the House.

It was indeed left vacant. Its vacancy dominated the solemn tributes paid in the Commons today by the leaders of all three parties and by Mr Turton, the senior back-bencher . . .

The Prime Minister hit exactly the right note when he said, 'In an atmosphere of quiet.'

'For now,' said Mr Wilson, 'the noise of hooves thundering over the veldt, the clamour of the hustings in a score of contests, the shots in Sidney Street, the angry guns of Gallipoli and Flanders, Coronel and the Falkland Islands, the sullen feet of the marching men in Tonypandy, the urgent warnings of the Nazi threat, the whine of the sirens and the dawn of the bombardment of the Normandy beaches; all these are silent.

'There is a stillness. And in that silence each has his memories . . .'

So the House parted as it had met, in silence, stillness and sorrow. All had been said that could be said, and the words were but the visible fraction of the iceberg . . .

Slowly and quietly the Members filed out of the Chamber. They were conscious, as were we all, of the descent of the early winter dusk.

1. *Daily Mail*, February 15, 1901.
2. Lady Violet Bonham-Carter, *Winston Churchill as I Knew Him* (1965), p. 81.
3. Earl Winterton, 'Churchill the Parliamentarian', in Charles Eade (ed.), *Churchill: By His Contemporaries* (1953), p. 95.
4. Quoted in David Cannadine, (ed.), *The Speeches of Winston Churchill* (Penguin edition, 1989), p. 8.
5. C. R. Attlee, 'Across the House', in Sir James Marchant (ed.), *Winston Spencer Churchill: Servant of Crown and Commonwealth* (1954), p. 75.
6. Woodrow Wyatt, 'Sir Winston Churchill in Parliament', in *Distinguished for Talent* (1958), pp. 200–1.
7. Indeed, Gladstone was a Secretary of State from December 1845 to July 1846 without having a seat in Parliament.
8. Winterton, op. cit., p. 86.
9. ibid., p. 88.
10. Attlee, op. cit., p. 74.
11. J. A. Gere and John Sparrow (eds.), *Geoffrey Madan's Notebooks* (1981), p. 14.
12. Margot Asquith, *Off the Record* (1943), p. 87.
13. Cannadine, op. cit., p. 10.
14. Winterton, op. cit., p. 89.
15. The Earl of Swinton, *Sixty Years of Power* (1966), p. 133.
16. Leo Amery, Diary, April 15, 1929.
17. See Chapter 16 ('How Churchill would have reformed Parliament') in Emrys Hughes, *Parliament and Mumbo-Jumbo* (1966), pp. 142–52.
18. Virginia Cowles, *Winston Churchill: The Era and the Man* (1953), p. 282.
19. Harold Nicolson, Letter to Vita Sackville-West, December 9, 1936.
20. Robert Rhodes James, *Churchill: A Study in Failure 1900–1939* (1970), p. 321.

21. Cannadine, op. cit., p. 10.
22. ibid., p. 6.
23. Harold Nicolson, Diary, January 20, 1940.
24. Harold Nicolson, Letter to Vita Sackville-West, June 5, 1940.
25. A. P. Herbert, 'The Master of Words', in Marchant, op. cit., p. 101.
26. Attlee, op. cit., pp. 75–6.
27. Herbert, op. cit., p. 113.
28. Cannadine, op. cit., p. 11.
29. Harold Nicolson, Letter to Ben and Nigel Nicolson, December 8, 1944.
30. Winterton, op. cit., pp. 90–1.
31. ibid., pp. 92–3.
32. Wyatt, op. cit., p. 205.
33. Attlee, op. cit., p. 74.
34. *Hansard*, June 23, 1953, col. 1689.
35. Colin Coote, 'The Politician', in Marchant, op. cit., p. 40.
36. Wyatt, op. cit., p. 208.
37. Churchill's memorandum on the rebuilding of the House of Commons Chamber; quoted in Wyatt, op. cit., p. 200.
38. Cannadine, op. cit., p. 13.
39. Dennis Bardens, *Churchill in Parliament* (1967), p. 357.
40. *Daily Chronicle*, May 19, 1927.
41. Hugh Dalton, *The Fateful Years: 1931–45* (1957), p. 93.
42. Emanuel Shinwell, 'Churchill as a Political Opponent', in Eade, op. cit., p. 124.
43. ibid., pp. 128–9.
44. Winterton, op. cit., pp. 94 and 89.
45. Wyatt, op. cit., p. 210.
46. Bardens, op. cit., pp. 334–5.
47. Wyatt, op. cit., p. 212.
48. Winterton, op. cit., p. 95.
49. Wyatt, op. cit., pp. 194–5.
50. Norman Shrapnel, *The Performers: Politics as Theatre* (1979), pp. 14–15.
51. ibid., p. 17.
52. Norman Wilding and Philip Laundy, *An Encyclopaedia of Parliament* (1961), p. 214.
53. *Punch*, February 27, 1901.
54. Quoted in Bonham-Carter, op. cit., p. 119.
55. Coote, op. cit., p. 39.
56. Attlee, op. cit., pp. 73–4.
57. Harold Macmillan, *Winds of Change, 1914–1939* (1966), p. 176.
58. David Margesson, MC (1890–1965), was the formidable Chief Government Whip from 1931 to 1940, thereafter becoming Churchill's Secretary of War for two years.
59. Sir John Sydney Wardlaw-Milne (1879–1967), the son of a banker, was educated privately and worked for several years in Bombay, where he was a member of the municipal corporation. He sat as Conservative MP for Kidderminster from November 1922 until he was defeated in 1945. Throughout World War II he was chairman of the Select Committee on National Expenditure.
60. Kingsley Wood had been Chancellor of the Exchequer since 1940.

12 A Sense of Place

The idea of making a pint-bottle hold what a quart would
not do is ridiculous. About 650 Gentlemen are
accommodated in a building which could only hold about
300. If the author of *Gulliver's Travels* had stated that
the wise Senate of some country he had visited had, in
the plenitude of its wisdom, declared that this was the
best arrangement which it could make for its own
accommodation, that would have been treated as the
best joke in the volume.

> A. M. Sullivan, Speech in the House of Commons,
> *Hansard*, July 12, 1880

In February 1771, when Sir George Saville's motion for a Bill concerning the rights of electors was proposed, another MP moved for Strangers to be excluded from the Chamber. When the House had been cleared of Strangers, Sir Joseph Mawbey pointed out that 'several hon. gentlemen complain of cold' and noticed that even Sir John Turner had 'got his great coat on'. The cold temperature in the Chamber gave rise to a joke. When Sir George Savile rose to bring in his Bill, the MPs belonging to the Court Party left the House for dinner. 'Counsellor Leigh said to Lord Clare as he was going out—"Fye, fye, my lord, is the House too hot for you?" while he was shivering with the cold and thrusting his hands up his great muff.'[1] One victim of these conditions was George Kinloch. 'Where I sit in the House,' he wrote to his wife Helen in early March 1833, 'there is a draft of air comes in from behind which is far from pleasant. I am obliged to sit with my hat on, as indeed most of the Members do.' The draught proved deadly: Kinloch died from a cold within a few days.

The old House of Commons, located in the St Stephen's Chapel, was not only cold and draughty, but also lined with dark wainscot, dimly lit by three chandeliers and infested with rats.[2] By virtue of its design and gloomy air, it lent itself to disruptive behaviour. The sketch-writer James Grant wrote that he had 'known members speak for half an hour at the time, without one single sentiment they uttered being known to one out of ten in the house. The house on such occasions is a scene of perfect confusion, and the noise is sometimes so great as to be heard distinctly in the street outside, a distance of forty or fifty yards, and this, too, though the doors are all shut.'[3] John O'Connell observed that 'the old House (St Stephen's Chapel) was much more favourable to the burking of a debate, or an orator, by noise and interruption, than the present. The recesses of the old gothic windows planked and wainscotted as they were in the most approved style of those veritable dark ages of England, the 17th and 18th centuries,

450

gave opportunities of concealment from the eye of the most vigilant Speaker or Sergeant-at-arms; whereas, in the present House there are no such convenient lurking places, and the guerilla warfare of interruptions and annoyances must be carried on without cover, and exposed to the heavy fire of the authorities.'[4]

The old Houses of Parliament as a whole were incommodious in the extreme. Gladstone, who took his seat in the House for the first time in 1833, commented: 'What I may term its corporeal conveniences were, I may observe in passing, marvellously small. I do not think that in any part of the building it afforded the means of so much as washing the hands. The residences of members were at that time less distant: but they were principally reached on foot. When a large House broke up after a considerable division, a copious dark stream found its way up Parliament Street, Whitehall and Charing Cross.'[5] A particular feature of the buildings was the lack of ventilation, as Macaulay complained in some verse he penned for his sisters: 'When the House is the coolest, as I am alive,/The thermometer stands at a hundred and five./We debate in a heat that seems likely to burn us,/Much like the three children who sang in the furnace.'[6]

The Radical MP Joseph Hume had for some time been urging Parliament to grant itself better accommodation and a witness of the conflagration was moved to remark that 'Mr Hume's motion for a new House is carried without a division'. King William IV saw the fire that destroyed the Houses of Parliament in 1834 as an opportunity for him to get shot of Buckingham Palace, which he evidently disliked, while Joseph Hume cast a beady eye towards the National Gallery. In the end, Parliament stuck to its old site. By February 1835 two temporary Houses of Parliament were in use at Westminster, the Commons meeting in the old Court of Requests and the Lords in the Painted Chamber, while a public competition was instituted to find the best design for the new Houses of Parliament in the Gothic style. The winning design was by Charles Barry, assisted in matters of decoration by his colleague Augustus Pugin. The history of the building of the new Houses of Parliament over the next fifteen years was beset with bureaucratic wrangling, disputes about the merits of design and decoration, delays, arguments about money and complaints about the final results. The Lords moved into their new Chamber in 1847 and the Commons followed suit in 1850. Although Barry had originally designed the Commons Chamber to accommodate all 600 MPs, the MPs themselves insisted that he reduce its size, then complained that it was not large enough.

There was a running battle between Dr David Reid, a ventilation expert whose designs introduced the means for creating strong upward draughts of air within the new Palace, and Barry, who felt that these ventilation shafts vitiated the fireproof aspect of his design. For years MPs had complained about the ghastly smells which wafted up from the sewage-ridden Thames. In 1846 'pestilential odours caused MPs to retreat from a committee and Disraeli referred to the Thames as "a Stygian pool, reeking with ineffable and unbearable horrors" '.[7] The extraordinary Victorian system of ventilation is described below by Sir Henry Lucy. However, when Parliament urged the replacement of a brick-built sewer, which had been constructed in 1838–9, with a flushable glazed pipe, it decided to allow the discharge of its own sewage into the Thames near to Westminster Bridge, with the the the consequence that at high tide the effluent was washed back against the Terrace.[8] Noxious odours were not confined to the river, however. In the 1860s it was discovered that the ammonia smell of horse dung was invading the Chamber. The inlet to the ventilation system was located near the door to the Ladies' Gallery. Horses would defecate there while coaches waited for several hours. Subsequently, it was decided that the coaches should wait in Speaker's Court until called.[9]

The heating and ventilation of the newly constructed Chamber were not satisfactory at first, and MPs refused to sit there permanently until 1852, in the meantime switching between the Chamber and the Court of Requests. However, the Chamber was occupied several times by human guinea-pigs: 'Companies of the Foot Guards were marched into the debating chamber and left there for hours at a time to see whether the ventilation system was beginning to work properly.'[10]

The squabbles about changes to Barry's plans for the subsequent development of the Palace, and the disputes about expenditure, continued into another generation with Edward Barry, Sir Charles's son, and Pugin's son, also Edward, engaging in protracted arguments about their fathers' respective contributions to the Palace, and with the Office of Works finally, in 1870, imposing such constraints and demands on Edward Barry as amounted to dismissal (he actually resigned).

Visiting Westminster for the first time in his late teens, Lloyd George was disappointed with what he found: '. . . great buildings outside, but inside they are crabbed, small and suffocating, especially the House of Commons'.[11] With the increase in the number of MPs from 632 to 670 following Gladstone's redistribution bill in 1885, there were noises about building a larger Chamber, but to no avail. Indeed, there were few significant changes from the 1890s until the 1940s. The interior of the Chamber remained the same, with the result that 'Sir Austen Chamberlain persisted in wearing his top-hat in the Chamber in the 1930s, long after the fashion for such headgear had diminished, so as to protect his eyes from the "top-lighting" '.[12] Gradually, rooms were taken away from ceremonial officials and re-allocated to Palace servants and members of the press and there was some encroachment on the inner courtyards, again to provide for servants, thus reducing the light and air created by Barry's plan.

At the beginning of the twentieth century, the Palace still had a reputation as a source of ill health. In 1902 when Sir Archibald Milman died, an MP attributed his demise to the cold, damp atmosphere of the House in the autumn and the failure to keep the building clean during the recesses: 'I suppose we shall have the usual sousing over of the tiles of the passages and meet the usual damp and steamy atmosphere which we as "human stoves" help to dry out at much risk to health. I have watched these proceedings for years, the House and its committee rooms and passages are full of poisonous dust, probably charged with influenza germs.'[13]

After the Commons Chamber was destroyed by an enemy bomb in 1941, MPs met at first in Church House, on the other side of Westminster Abbey, and thereafter in the Lords Chamber. In October 1943 Winston Churchill gave a speech in the House in which he argued that the Commons Chamber should be restored much as before. He was against enlarging it because 'if the House is big enough to contain all its Members, nine-tenths of the debates will be conducted in the depressing atmosphere of an almost empty or half-empty chamber . . . We wish to see our Parliament as a strong, easy, flexible instrument of free debate. For this purpose a small chamber and a sense of intimacy are indispensable . . . The conversational style requires a fairly small space, and there should be on great occasions a sense of crowd and urgency.' He was against adopting a semicircular chamber on the model of some continental countries and added that rebuilding the old chamber was the cheapest option. The left-wing Independent Labour MP James Maxton preferred a grand architectural design on a site 'in good English parkland' outside London, a suggestion mockingly dismissed by the Tory MP Captain Crookshank who said: 'I think it is one of the jests to which he sometimes treats the House. He outlined what seemed to be a glorified road-house somewhere, a cross between the late Crystal Palace, a civil airport and Waterloo Station, situated in the surroundings of Chatsworth.'

The House appointed a Select Commitee to consider plans for the rebuilding. The architect chosen, Sir Giles Gilbert Scott, was required to retain all the essential features of the old Chamber. Exactly the same number of seats (346 for a House with 600 Members) were provided, although there was greater accommodation in the galleries for strangers and members of the press. A new system of ventilation, dispensing with the vertical draughts favoured by the Victorians, was introduced, which relied on lateral currents of air; the lighting was changed to 'a delicate daffodil shade, designed to give the impression of a morning in early spring, but Members' faces took on a ghastly yellow hue as though they were seated in a charnel-house'; and the deficient acoustics were improved by little speakers 'cunningly concealed in the carved Tudor roses which decorated the backs of the benches', although 'as a result, listeners had to apply their ears to the back rail of each bench, giving a curiously contorted and soporific impression, rather remote from the Churchillian aim of "a sense of crowd and urgency" '.[14]

It has long been a part of the MP's role to show groups of constituents or schoolchildren around the Palace of Westminster. Indeed, after he resigned from Asquith's Cabinet in 1914, in protest against the war, John Burns showed 'half a million Colonial and American soldiers over the Houses of Parliament or Westminster Abbey'.[15] The Palace occupies eight acres and consists of 1,100 rooms and 100 staircases. As Alfred Bossom once wrote, 'it takes a lifetime to learn the House of Commons', illustrating this statement with an anecdote: 'One evening in the early thirties I had been dining with Sir Austen Chamberlain, and as we walked back to the Chamber along the corridor a part of the panelling suddenly opened and out came a mechanic. Sir Austen turned to me with a delighted look and said: "I've been in the House for over thirty years and I had not the slightest idea that that door existed!" '[16]

Associated with every modern image of Parliament is the Clock Tower known as Big Ben, after the bell with the distinctive tone contained within it. Originally, the light behind the clock-faces shone only while the House was sitting, though it now shines throughout the hours of darkness. In Victorian times the light only shone in the direction of the West End, because it was assumed that all MPs lived in that part of the city.[17] Big Ben had an additional peculiar appeal to Lord Randolph Churchill, who once bet that he could run across Westminster Bridge from the Surrey side to the steps under the Clock Tower between its first and twelfth chimes.[18]

Although the proximity of the Thames has not always been a boon, Barry's spacious Terrace overlooking the river was much appreciated by John Burns as a place to walk and discuss business ('One gets exercise, fresh air, and through both that sense of proportion of things generally that one fails to get in a room');[19] while Lord Frederic Hamilton (who had three brothers in the House in the 1885 Parliament) recalled how he used to while away the long hours after he had disposed of his daily correspondence: 'My youngest brother and I, both then well under thirty, used to hire tricycles from the dining-room attendants, and have races up and down the long river terrace, much to the interest of passers-by on Westminster Bridge.'[20]

However, of all the attractions of the Palace of Westminster the one most prized by the sketch-writer William Hale White was its atmosphere of peace and quiet: 'There is no more comfortable place in the world for a snooze than the House of Commons when the debate is dull, say upon an estimate night. In bed in London there is the chance of being disturbed by cabs, organs, brass bands, fowls kept in the mews or the area, or by the postman. But nothing extraneous save the voice of the big clock penetrates the House, and as for the noises inside when such a subject as the estimates are being discussed, they are soothing and somniferous.'[21]

Are steps deemed to be seats?

Anchitell Grey, *Debates of the House of Commons, 1667–94* (1769),
November 4, 1675

Mr Waller, who sat upon the steps, upon the Speaker's calling him to sit in his place, said: 'Cuts are made in the seats for steps here in the House. I know that in the Long Parliament, steps were seats, and seats were steps, as in an amphitheatre. The Rump put backs to our seats, and the steps, now new made, were seats. And I desire there may be some Order made in it, or steps must not be seats.'

Crammed

William Cobbett, *Weekly Register* (date unknown)

Why are we squeezed into so small a space that it is absolutely impossible that there should be calm and regular discussion, even from that circumstance alone? Why do we live in this hubbub? Why are we exposed to all these inconveniences? Why are 658 of us crammed into a space that allows to each of us no more than a foot and a half square, while, at the same time, each of the servants of the King, who we pay, has a palace to live in, and more unoccupied space in that palace than the little hole into which we are all crammed to make the laws by which this great kingdom is governed.

A deadly draught

George Kinloch, Letter to his wife Helen, March 1833

I have a cold in my head but, farther than making me blow my nose oftener than usual, I suffer no inconvenience from it. Where I sit in the House, there is a draft of air comes in from behind which is far from pleasant. I am obliged to sit with my hat on, as indeed most of the Members do.

The burning of Parliament

John Cam Hobhouse, Lord Broughton, *Recollections of a Long Life* (1911),
October 16, 1834

This was to me a memorable day; for, as I was sitting quietly at home with Lady Julia, I was roused by the intelligence that the House of Lords was on fire. As the care of the public buildings belonged to my department, I lost no time in going to St James's Palace. The whole building in front of Old Palace-yard was in flames, and the fire was gaining ground towards Bennett's Tower every instant; only a few soldiers and policemen were present, and three or four engines. A short time after more fire-engines came, but I thought the firemen were lamentably deficient in the knowledge of the best way to extinguish the flames.

I was with Melbourne, who was as usual very cool, and now and then inclined to be jocose. He could not help laughing when a man ran up to me and said, 'Sir John, we have saved King Charles's warrant'—meaning the original death-warrant, as if that document was particularly interesting to me.

The crowd behaved very well; only one man was taken up for huzzaing when the flames increased. I heard nothing of the exclamations recorded by the *Standard* newspaper, but I believe that one weaver did say, 'This comes of making the poor girls pay for their children'—alluding to the new Poor Law. A few persons attributed the fire to design, but, on the whole, it was impossible for any large assemblage of people to behave better.

John O'Connell, *Recollections and Experiences during a Parliamentary Career from 1833 to 1848* (1849)

It was during the recess of 1834–1835 that the old Houses of Parliament were burned. The common-sense motion of Mr Hume, to provide a more commodious place of assemblage, at least for the Commons, had been negatived but a few months before; and, as the crowd remarked during the fire, that motion was then carried 'without a division'.

His object, however, was but partially carried after all, as the fire could not altogether destroy and swallow up the site of the ancient palace of Westminster, as it did the buildings, ancient and modern, or modernised, which were upon that site. A most abominable smell from that *cloaca maxima* of London and Westminster, the Thames, used to be perceptible whenever the windows of the old Houses were opened; and although we are for the present a little less afflicted by this nuisance, in consequence of being shut out in the temporary House and library from the river by the interposition of two courts of the new buildings, with their lofty surrounding constructions, yet, when at length (if ever) we are to remove to the latter, the health-destroying nuisance will be renewed. Mr Hume and others were urgent for the removal to the site of the unhappy edifice called the National Gallery, in Trafalgar Square; but the majority of the House were of the opinion that '*les souvenirs valaient mieux que la santé!*' and so we are doomed to remain within the sphere of the incense-breathing Thames.

The old House of Commons had great interest about it. No doubt it was inconvenient, and scant of accommodation, but the present House had very little advantage over it in that or any other regard: and the House that we are told we shall get into at some remote future time in the new building will reproduce, if some reports speak true, several of the faults of St Stephen's; while all the great recollections which hallowed the latter, and made its defects to be almost forgotten, will of course be wanting to the new edifice; at least until it ceases to be new, and the Englishmen of 100 or 200 years hence (the Irishmen having been then for several generations in 'their own house at home') shall be sitting upon its benches.

Electric light in Parliament

T. P. O'Connor, *Gladstone's House of Commons* (1885)

June 10, 1881. When it reassembled at nine, a transformation had taken place in its appearance, for the electric light had been turned on. The effect on the House at first was unpleasant, for the light has a resemblance to the daylight that is ghastly and ungrateful to mind and eye. Familiar faces and figures seemed strange and weird: for instance, Mr Gladstone, sitting in a white waistcoat amid this new light, looked not festive and bright as he would under the gas and if one felt that it was real night, but worn and inopportune, as if he had been caught carousing by the early and mournful streaks of jocund day. The soft and mellow look of the glass roof, with the illumination bringing out its colours and squares, was lost; in its stead appeared a dark and dull mass, not relieved by the white and awkward-looking boxes in which the electric lamps are contained. Reporters, too, complained that the work of note-taking was rendered much more difficult. On the other hand, it must be said that after a while the light appeared more tolerable; features were more discernible, and the hideous grating in front of the Ladies' Gallery was less effectual in hiding whatever beauty of face or dress was there to be seen. The House, too, was or seemed to be cooler.

The havoc caused by the Fenian dynamitards

As part of a campaign of dynamite outrages in London, Irish Fenians planted two infernal machines in Parliament, one in the Chamber of the House of Commons and the other on a staircase near the inner lobby. A policeman named Cole discovered the first device on the staircase and coolly carried it, with its fuse hissing, into the cavernous space of Westminster Hall, where he threw it down. It gouged a crater out of the granite floor and ripped into the brickwork of the crypt below. Upon hearing the explosion of the first device, the sightseers in the vicinity of the chamber were evacuated. Cole was subsequently awarded the Albert medal, the civilian equivalent of the Victoria Cross.

G. W. Smalley, *New York Tribune*, January 28, 1885

The scene of the second explosion is on the left of the inner lobby, but Mr Denning [Inspector Denning] took us first to the right, to point out the exact spot corresponding to that where the dynamite is supposed to have been placed on the opposite side. The entrance to the House is in the centre. On either side, narrow passages with a step or two conduct to the seats under the Speaker's and distinguished strangers' galleries; where peers and other favoured personages may sit almost on a level with the members of the House itself. It was in the narrow passage to the left that the explosion took place; with the effect of making the passages less narrow; tearing away the walls, scooping out the floor, and rending the arches on which it rested. Workmen were clearing away the rubbish. A platform had been laid down, on which we could advance till we stood on the central site of the outrage.

The House of Commons itself was in full view. Benches that had been torn up lay about; broken timbers and fragments of all kinds strewed the place. Mr Denning asks us to look at the clock with its hands still marking 2.14, the moment of the explosion; at the uprooted cross bench, at the injury done to Mr Gladstone's seat opposite the corner of the clerk's table, at the marks on the Speaker's chair; and the other now familiar objects of interest. But it was the general aspect of the place which told us more of the story than all the details we could inspect . . .

The marks of the explosion were over it all; roof, walls, and floor had suffered. The actual structural damage is not very important, though it will take many weeks, and some thousands of pounds, to make good. But to the eye of the visitor on that morning, the chamber was a wreck . . . By the date fixed for the opening of the next session the chamber will be again to all appearance in good order.

It was evident from the account then given us, and from what we learned elsewhere, that the two explosions were meant to be simultaneous. But I am not sure that it is easy to realise what that means, until you have stood in the lobby and seen as well as heard what would have happened if the plan of the dynamitards had been carried out. A large party of sightseers would have been in the chamber but for the alarm given by the explosion in Westminster Hall. Another large party would have been in the lobbies, and in or over the staircase where the second case of dynamite was placed.

The ventilation system of the new House of Commons

Henry W. Lucy, *Memories of Eight Parliaments* (1908)

That the House of Commons is the Chamber with the best acoustical properties among its compeers is indisputable. Personally, with an experience exceeding that of most Members, I hold it to be also the best ventilated. This is a controversial point governed by idiosyncrasies. It is an old story, going back to a date beyond thirty years, how John Bright and Acton Smee Ayrton, sitting side by side on the Treasury Bench during the last years of Mr Gladstone's great Administration born in 1868, used to squabble over the temperature. While one declared it was intolerably cold, the other protested it was insufferable by reason of heat.

Dr Percy, then in charge of the ventilating machinery, was the recipient of angry letters from both statesmen. Ayrton was at the time First Commissioner of Works, and spent an appreciable portion of a useful, strenuous life in prowling round, closing up the air openings of the Chamber. 'Mr Ayrton was very susceptible to draughts,' Mr Prim, Resident Clerk of the Works in the Ventilation Department of the Houses of Parliament, subsequently Resident Engineer, confided to the Select Committee meeting in 1892. Mr Bright yearned for fresh air, from whatsoever quarter it came. Thus it came to pass that as they sat together watching the decadence of Gladstone's once vigorous Ministry, a coolness literally sprang up between the President of the Board of Trade and the First Commissioner of Works.

It is this difference in the temperature of statesmen and less important mortals that harries the life of those responsible for the ventilation of the House of Commons. What is one man's fresh air is another man's dangerous draught, leading to rheumatism and other direful consequences. The normal temperature of the House of Commons is, with infinite care and at considerable cost to the nation, kept at the level of 62°. That is the ideal temperature for healthy human beings. But so devotional is the care with which the priceless health and comfort of Members are watched over that varying circumstance leads to altered temperature. The thermometer is consulted every hour, the result being recorded in a book that will never be published. The inquiry is no mere slap-dash performance. Nothing is dealt with haphazard. An able-bodied man passes a useful life in perambulating the Chamber and its precincts, thermometer in hand, testing the temperature. No Member coming upon him by chance guesses his kindly errand. He may be seen flitting behind the Speaker's Chair at one end of the House, presently skirting the Chair of the Serjeant-at-Arms at the other, anxiously watching the thermometer and entering the record. Thence his parade leads him to the Division Lobbies, the retiring-rooms, the outer Lobbies, and all the places where Members congregate. His report is, hour by hour, carried to the Clerk of the Works, who, with a speed and decision unknown in Committee of Supply, deals accordingly with the ventilating apparatus.

I have mentioned the fact that the normal temperature aimed at is 62°. Having made profound study of human nature, the experts in charge of the ventilation of the House recognise that with a temperature 80° in the shade outside, members entering the chamber where it stood at 62° would feel it chilly. Accordingly, in such exceptional circumstances the temperature is nicely graduated, going up to 65°, or higher. The same infinite care watches over an all-night sitting. This *divertissement* taking place on a sultry summer night, a temperature of 62° is a luxury. With the dawn of early morning healthy animal nature grows chilly. The temperature of the Chamber is, accordingly, delicately doctored until, as far as possible, the anxious expert raises it to about the average of the blood heat of an Irish or Welsh Member.

In no other legislative assembly in the world is equal solicitude in the important matter of ventilation shown for the comfort of Members. The extreme Radical will feel some satisfaction in knowing that it is not extended to the House of Lords. The difference between the atmosphere of the two Chambers is strikingly disclosed on the rare occasions when the Lords sit late, carrying on debate in a crowded House. Ventilation is attempted by the vulgar process of opening windows. How ineffective this proves by comparison with the scientific, elaborate mechanism controlling ventilation in the House of Commons is brought home to the Member leaving his own House to sit for a while in the gallery overlooking the Peers. The air of cities contains an average of four volumes of carbonic acid per 10,000. In an ordinary room the ventilation is regarded as satisfactory as long as the proportion of carbonic acid in the atmosphere does not exceed six volumes per 10,000. The House of Commons, with some 350 people breathing its atmosphere, rarely exceeds four volumes, equivalent to breathing the fresh air outside. This simple matter of fact is a triumphant vindication of the success of its ventilation.

Doctors are agreed on the point that supply of fresh air should reach the proportions of fifty cubic feet per minute per head. That ideal is habitually exceeded in the House of Commons. Members who, like the oldest clubman, must grumble about something, complain that while the air is abundant it lacks freshness, inducing a feeling of lassitude. In fairness to the painstaking staff of the ventilation department it should be pointed out that this incontestable condition of constant attendance upon Parliamentary debate is due not to lack of freshness in the air supplied, but to the prodigious length of some speeches. As an incentive to a state of physical and mental lassitude, an hour's discourse from certain Members is equal to an increment of carbonic acid in the atmosphere of one volume per 10,000.

Two years ago careful experiments were carried out with desire to ascertain to what extent bacteria frequent the House. The results were curious—on the whole satisfactory. For reasons which Members familiar with its occupants may determine, the worst quarter of the House was, oddly enough, the bench immediately behind that on which His Majesty's Ministers sit. As the result of ten experiments made with infinite care, it was demonstrated that here bacteria revelled in proportion of 87 per cent, while the corresponding bench on the opposite side revealed the presence of only 65 per cent of undesirable visitors. On the back bench on the Government side the record ran as low as 57 per cent. Compared, as was done in the Select Committee's Report, with such representative congregations of innocents as gather in the town schools of Aberdeen and Dundee, where mechanical ventilation is in use, this incursion of microbes in the Ministerial stronghold is exceptionally high. The organisms were different in form. Happily, in no case was discovery made of the presence of any recognised as the cause of specific infectious diseases in man.

The unique privileges of Members of the House of Commons in respect of ventilation are secured by elaborate and costly machinery. When, after the destruction of the Houses of Parliament by fire in 1834, the structure was rebuilt, special attention was devoted to the subject. Dr Reid, the highest authority of the day, was entrusted with the care of this department. The process adopted by him was primarily based on the use of gigantic fans, which drove fresh air into the Chamber. While the supply of fresh air was an article of faith, the presence of a constant draught was a matter of fact. In this initial stage the main principle underlying the ventilation of the Chamber of today was adopted. Air was driven into the Chamber through the grating of the floor. Members, ever complaining, protested, with some reason, that while by this primitive process they were chilled in winter and scorched in summer, such air as was provided was served up strongly impregnated with pounded grit and road metal. A tradition lingers round this epoch, showing how a long-suffering Member secretly provided himself with a piece of paper freshly gummed. This, in the presence of sympathetic witnesses, he attached to one of the seats. On examination at the close of the sitting the paper was found to be covered with particles of fine dust projected by the ventilating apparatus. This was conclusive. Dr Reid and his system disappeared from Westminster.

After brief interval he was succeeded by Sir Goldsworthy Gurney, who, doing away with the primitive fans, adopted the principle familiar in collieries of a furnace at the base of an upcast. Dr Percy, following Sir Goldsworthy in care of the ventilating apparatus, maintained this principle, and with one or two improvements it is in practice at this day. The machinery is subterraneous.

There are many more vaults betwixt the foundations of Westminster Palace and the floor of the House of Commons than is dreamt of in the philosophy of honourable Members. Under the Octagon Hall lurks a vault whence the supply of air for the debating Chamber is drawn. Through doors and windows overlooking the river the balmy breeze of the Thames is indrawn.

This arrangement is accountable for an episode, threatening at the outset, farcical in the conclusion, that marked the reign of Mr David Plunket (now Lord Rathmore) at the Board of Works. One sultry summer night, the House being exceptionally crowded in anticipation of a division his private room was stormed by a mob of alarmed and angry Members. Even as the door opened to admit them the First Commissioner was conscious of a pestilential smell. This evidence confirmed their complaint that the corridors, the reading-room, the dining-room, and, to a modified extent, the lobby were permeated by malodour. The conclusion was obvious. Something had gone wrong with the drains, and the health of honourable and right honourable Members was in dire peril. Mr Plunket hastily summoned to consultation the chief engineers and the heads of his staff; hurried examination was made of the sanitary apparatus, without detecting a flaw. Even as the anxious work went forward the plague abated. The normal condition of the sedulously purified atmosphere was steadily, with increased rapidity, reasserting itself; the harried First Commissioner, going on to the Terrace with intent to cool his heated brow, came upon the heart of the mystery. Just passing the end of the Terrace, slowly making its way with the tide up the river, was a stately barge, with high deckload of fresh manure meant for riverside gardens. Drifting at slow pace past the Terrace of the House of Commons, the evening breeze, blowing off the heap, filled the ventilating bins with delectable air. Hence the scare.

The progress of the indraught is intercepted by a broad expanse of falling water, through which the air must needs pass, leaving behind it possible particles of undesirable dust. Inside the chamber are a couple of shafts worked by a large pair of wheels, which drive the air into what looks like a colossal corn bin. This is a chamber eight feet high extending the full breadth of the vault, a distance of thirteen feet. Inside this bin is a movable close-fitting shutter, which travels backwards and forwards. As it is pushed forward the air in the bin, having no other means of escape, passes upward through a funnel into another chamber prepared for its reception. The closely-fitting shutter advancing leaves a vacuum behind, into which the outer air comes rushing, in time to find itself driven upwards by return of the relentless shutter.

Thus through the long night, while tongues wag above, the almost silent shutter moves backward and forward, crushing the newly-come air out of the bin, only to find that a fresh supply has entered on the other side, making constant discovery that if the bin is to be emptied there is yet another journey to make.

The air thus dexterously trapped breathes itself out from the upper bin into a gallery, along which it courses till it finds itself under the legislative Chamber. Thirty feet above the lights of the House shine, twinkling through the close iron grating of the floor. It is so silent down there that one can distinctly hear the voice of the honourable Member addressing the Chair. Climbing a series of steep iron ladders the explorer comes upon a succession of gratings on which stand blocks of ice. Coursing round these the ambient air enters the House through the grating which serves as flooring, so cunningly hidden by twine matting that probably half the Members of the House are not aware of its existence.

The blocks of ice are for summer time. In wintry weather the air is comfortably heated before it enters the Chamber. When the fog lies low over London the outer air passes through layers of cotton wool six inches thick. The appearance of the cotton wool after a few hours' fog is a painful object-lesson for citizens. There was a memorable occasion when the fog prevailed unintermittedly for forty-eight hours, with the result that the cotton wool was as black as the black of a chimney. I have groped my way down to the House through a dense fog, and entering the legislative Chamber, have found it absolutely free from mist, the atmosphere in normal condition. That is the ultimate triumph of the patient, cultured care that watches over the lungs of the House of Commons.

By this elaborate process does fresh air get into the legislative Chamber in unbroken supply. How the vitiated atmosphere, occasionally tainted with strong language, escapes is a simpler process. By the marge of the ceiling are panels opening upon a space left between it and the roof. The air, rarified by use, ascends as the sparks fly upward, escapes by these open panels, is conducted by flues to the basement, and delivered in a gallery ending in a shaft opening up in the Clock Tower, a height of 230 feet. On the basement a great fire burns an open hearth. Drawing to it the inrushing air, it drives it up the shaft and so into the infinitude of spacious London.

The outbreak of World War II

Arthur Baker (1890–1962) was the son of a Somerset farmer who was also a county alderman, a lord of the manor and a chairman of the Bridgewater Divisional Liberal Association. He had a brother on the *Daily Telegraph*, who 'had been a frequenter of the Press Gallery for many years'.[22] Baker joined the *Tiverton Gazette* in 1910, a weekly paper published by his uncle. A stint on the *Western Morning News* in Plymouth was followed by service in the Somerset Light Infantry during World War I. He joined the Parliamentary Staff of *The Times* in 1919. Thereafter he spent almost thirty-seven years in the Press Gallery and for twenty-two of those years was Chief of *The Times* Parliamentary Staff. He became chairman of the Press Gallery in 1941.

Arthur Baker, *The House is Sitting* (1958)

Over that unforgettable week-end at the beginning of September 1939, when war was declared, poor Moyes was inundated with enquiries. I saw him two or three times, and the latest information on the Sunday evening was that evacuation would begin on the Tuesday, September 5, or the Wednesday, September 6. But, as the days passed, evacuation became less and less probable. The period of 'phoney war' made it unnecessary, and when Churchill became Prime Minister in May 1940 it was certain that we should never leave Westminster.

Though, looking back, the evacuation plans seem to have been quite needless, and would only have made confusion worse confounded, it must not be forgotten that there was a school of thought which believed that Hitler, immediately war was declared, would send over a thousand bombers in an attempt to wipe out London. Colour was certainly given to this view by the first air-raid warning which was sounded just before noon on Sunday, September 3. We were at war with Germany as from 11 a.m. on that Sunday morning. Our second and final ultimatum had expired. The Prime Minister (Neville Chamberlain) had spoken to the people on the radio at 11.15 a.m. I was on my way up to town from Wimbledon for the Sunday meeting of Parliament, which had been fixed for noon. As I walked across Westminster Bridge I heard the wailing note of the sirens—unfamiliar then, but soon to become such a part of our war-time existence. I went down the steps under Big Ben to walk along to the Press Gallery entrance as usual, but I was urged by the police and air-raid wardens to take shelter quickly.

I went straight into one of the rooms on the Terrace floor which was our shelter. (Of course, it was really no sort of shelter at all, but we did our best to imagine it was!) What a sight met my eyes! MPs, officials, newspapermen, were all gathered together, talking excitedly and wondering if this was Hitler's reply to the British ultimatum. Mr Speaker was there, in his court dress and knee-breeches: Lloyd George was there; and many others. It was an uncanny experience, unlike those experiences of a year later when real air raids made it inevitable that most of one's night life in London should be spent underground, unless on duty. We wondered how soon enemy aeroplanes would get through the balloon barrage, which we had seen a few minutes earlier rising over the roof-tops of London. We were soon to be put out of our suspense. In about ten minutes the sirens began to wail again, but this time it was the long, steady, piercing note of the 'All Clear'. We all trooped out of our 'shelter'. I went upstairs to *The Times* room to prepare for the meeting of the House.

What a week-end that was! Parliament sat on the Saturday and the Sunday, an unheard-of procedure. On the Saturday evening there was a short but bitter debate, following what some people thought was a feeble effort by the Prime Minister. We had been told privately that there had been 'a hitch with France', and that turned out to be true. It was during these angry exchanges in the Commons that Leo Amery shouted across to Arthur Greenwood (who, in the absence of Clem Attlee, was leading the Opposition), 'Speak for England!' Had we but known it, a last-minute effort was even then being made to preserve peace, and that accounted for the Prime Minister's hesitancy.

Parliament, when it liked, could act with lightning speed. It did so that week-end. Emergency legislation of all sorts was passed through both Houses without opposition. Where necessary, Standing Orders and Rules of Procedure were suspended. *The Times* Parliamentary report on Monday, September 4, occupied two whole pages.

The House is destroyed by an enemy bomb

Sir Henry Morris-Jones, *Doctor in the Whips' Room* (1955)

On the night of May 9–10, 1941, I was on Home Guard duty on the west turret of Westminster Hall from midnight to 4 a.m. It was a beautiful night with a clear moon. The constant activity of aeroplanes overhead, without the dropping of any bombs, caused us to comment on their unusual visitation. Lieut.-Colonel Mayhew, my fellow guard, although deaf, could identify 'planes better than I, and he was certain they were German. The next night, while I was off duty, the House of Commons was destroyed.

It was during the course of one of the exercises of the Home Guard against the effects of bombing that Patrick Munro, Member for Barry—an unassuming, hard-working Whip—died from his exertions.

The House of Commons resembled a darkened barracks; sand-bagged windows and doors, blacked-out rooms and corridors gave it a depressing appearance, and walking through some of the passages needed a wary tread. One evening, going home through Westminster Hall, I almost stumbled against a body lying on the bottom step, helpless and much distressed. It was the Earl of Lucan, a very elderly Peer. He had fallen and fractured his thigh. I accompanied him to Westminster Hospital, where he made a remarkable recovery and later returned to his official duties.

Harold Nicolson, Diary, May 16, 1941

I go to see the ruins of the old Chamber. It is impossible to get through the Members' Lobby which is a mass of twisted girders. So I went up by the staircase to the Ladies' Gallery and then suddenly, when I turned the corridor, there was the open air and a sort of Tintern Abbey gaping before me. The little Ministers' rooms to right and left of the Speaker's Lobby were still intact, but from there onwards there was absolutely nothing. No sign of anything but *murs calcinés* and twisted girders.

The Commons take possession of their new chamber in 1950

Harry Boardman, *The Glory of Parliament* (1960), October 21, 1950

After nine years' tenancy of the House of Lords, the Commons next Thursday will enter into possession of their new home. Or should one say their new-old home, since it is a replica of the old House built strictly within the limits of the old site? It is a great moment. During all the nine years, the Commons have never been entirely comfortable in their borrowed surroundings. It was under a full moon on the night of May 10–11, 1941, that the old Chamber crumpled under German bombs in one of the fiercest air raids on London of the war. All that survived, having any sort of coherence, was fragments of the outer walls. They provided an irregular frame round the chaos of tumbled masonry.

On the morning of May 12, Mr Churchill stood with Lord Reith, then Minister of Works, and Lord Beaverbrook, gazing at the epitome of the lunacy of modern war. The air was laden with dust and acrid with fumes of burning timber. Mr Churchill took in the grievous sight with hardly a word to his two colleagues. He must have been deeply moved, but for once he did not show it.

The old Chamber had played a great part in his life. It had been his stage for forty years, and for the last year he had been playing on it his most illustrious part. It was the first year of his Premiership, the most glorious of the five, as history may well pronounce. People are apt to forget that it was in the old House that he made the early and the greatest of his war speeches. Mr Churchill departed, and within a day or two the House assembled in what, looking back on it, was an amusing attempt to provide a reduced model of the old Chamber in flimsy timber and green baize in Church House. When the House of Lords had been made ship-shape again the peers gave up their Chamber to the Commons, and there they have been ever since—over nine years. Mr Churchill had been advised that the House of Commons might be rebuilt in eighteen months after the plans were passed!

No one who had sat in the old Chamber but had an affection for it. The place had its genius. There were its history and associations, but there were other intangible ways in which it had acquired a soul. There was an ingratiating intimacy about it. Mr Churchill has often extolled this virtue in it. No better testimony to its spell could be furnished than a remark of James Maxton, the humorous rebel. During the debate on the motion setting up the Select Committee on the rebuilding he claimed to have been every bit as fond as Mr Churchill of the old House, and then he said it was no mere affair of stones; it was a sentient place; and one can still recall Mr Churchill's sudden admiration for the imaginative stroke.

And yet the Chamber was not old. This part of Barry's Palace of Westminster was completed in 1852, and it was in that year that the Commons took possession of the Chamber. Its life, therefore, ran to eighty-nine years. That contrasts with nearly three hundred years spent in St Stephen's Chapel before the fire of 1834. But what an eighty-nine years! The period begins just twenty years after the passing of the Reform Bill. A score of years before 1941, complete Parliamentary democracy based on adult suffrage had arrived to crown the cautious beginning of 1832.

The history of these eighty-nine Parliamentary years is, of course, largely the history of the nation for the period. What impresses itself tremendously as you look over the era is the country's opulence in political genius and talent, and the wealth of public spirit that put it at the service of the House of Commons. Is it not most probable that Pitt, Burke, and Fox, if they could have seen the mid-Victorian Parliaments, would have decided that there had been no declension on their day in a House of Commons that contained at one and the same time Palmerston, Disraeli, and Gladstone? To come to a later day, would they not have found Balfour intellectually satisfying, and approved Asquith's Roman temper? And would they not have felt the fascination of Lloyd George's genius? As for Mr Churchill, they would have rushed to him as to a brother. But the Prime Ministers make only part of the story. There are the men of the front rank who crossed Barry's stage without reaching the first place, indisputably great forces in our politics like Cobden and Bright, and Joseph Chamberlain. And there is the legion of secondary figures not without renown. Parnell and the Irish chapter bulk large in the story; and historically of the greatest importance there is the arrival of Keir Hardie heralding the advent of an independent Parliamentary Labour party destined to attain office by 1924 and power with a great majority another twenty years later. But it is an inexhaustible roll.

The new House is the fourth home the Commons have had. The first was the Chapter House of Westminster Abbey; the second St Stephen's Chapel; and the third Barry's Chamber. They took to the Chapter House at Westminster when in Edward III's reign they formally separated from the Lords. The date when the Chapter House began to be used by the Commons is put about 1376. There they sat until 1547, though there are records of their meeting in Blackfriars in the reign of Henry VIII. In 1547 Edward VI allotted St Stephen's Chapel to them and there the House conducted its deliberations for 278 years, that is until St Stephen's went up in flames in 1834. All authorities treat this fortuitous transference to St Stephen's as of great importance for the future history of Parliament. First, the chapel was rectangular. Then there were the stalls on either side which obliged half the House to sit facing the other half (at least, this is the belief of Mr Maurice Hastings in his book, *Parliament House*). Later the stalls were replaced by benches. Thus, it is suggested, was the way prepared for the evolution of the two-party system. Also, the chapel was small and accordingly encouraged the formal conversational style of speech which has become the British tradition, contrasted with the full-blooded orations from the rostrum of Continental assemblies. The Speaker's chair was placed before the site of the altar, and the lectern in the middle of the choir gave way to the table on which the mace rested and at which the clerks sat. There then, in the middle of the sixteenth century, were the lineaments of the House of Commons we know today. They have remained unchanged throughout the centuries.

There was a small body of members that would have preferred a new House on a new site, but the great weight of opinion was behind Mr Churchill, who made the cause of reproducing the old Chamber very much his own. And there it now is, and the only change from the old House is that the Press Gallery has been enlarged, and a third row added for the public in the side galleries, though much additional accommodation is being provided for members elsewhere. There is, however, another difference that will at once strike anyone who knew the old House, and that is the light oak and the lighter green upholstery—a lighter green than that of the old benches—but the total effect is pleasing and harmonious.

The House of Commons Library

Tom Driberg, *The Best of Both Worlds: A Personal Diary* (1953), May 31, 1952

Court mourning for the late King ends tonight. In my mail today are a number of letters from Government departments, but only two with black edges: one from the Prime Minister, one from the Foreign Office. So far as I can recall, only the FO and Downing Street have followed this archaic usage in this period of mourning.

In the first few days after the King's death, a good deal of black-edged stationery—very thick, of fine quality, for it presumably dates from 1936, or even from 1910—was put out in the racks on the writing-tables in the Members' Library at the House of Commons; but I don't think many of us used it.

The real peace of the country is in delicious contrast to the merely 'hushed' and unreal 'seclusion' of the House of Commons library, where an MP learns all too well the truth of the old dictum that Parliament is 'a place where you can neither work nor rest'.

I described this library as follows in an article in the *Architectural Review* which contains the longest parenthesis I have ever written:

If the MP wants to do some writing or reading he goes into the library. This is a series of five lofty rooms stretching along the river front of the Palace one floor above the terrace level. It is, in its way, a splendid set of rooms; the carpets are thick; the chairs are covered in fine green leather, stamped in gold with the Westminster portcullis; the bookshelves run to within six feet of the ceiling; above them are panels of green brocade in heavily carved frames. The file of *The Times* rests on a mahogany table provided by Sir Christopher Wren. It is a quiet place to work in (but for the division-bells, the messenger with the green card indicating that someone has called to see you, the messenger with the pink slip indicating that someone wants you on the telephone, the periodic ticking of the annunciator recording that at 3.50 your colleagues in the Chamber had reached Clause 3, Page 3, Line 32, the honking of river traffic saluting you as it passes, the colleague who says: 'Excuse me, old boy, but who's PPS to the Financial Secretary to the War Office?' the colleague who says: 'Do come up to Room Twelve for half-an-hour—we've got Dr Jumbo-Mumbo speaking to the Tropical Malnutrition Group, and nobody's turned up,' and the agitated Whip who wants you to help 'make a House' because old So-and-so's 'up' and everyone's trooped out for a drink).

There is room for only a few score of the 625 MPs to sit at the massive tables (laden with artistic metal stationery-racks, green-shaded lamps, Pugin penwipers, letter-scales, flagons of gum, bottles of water for moistening stamps, and sealing-wax lamps always flickering behind their shields, like sanctuary-lamps beside a Tractarian aumbry). There are easy chairs for barely a dozen to read or snooze in. There is practically nowhere else in the whole building to rest during the purgatorial ordeal of an all-night sitting.

1. Michael MacDonagh, *The Reporters' Gallery* (1913), p. 190 and 190 n.
2. Harry Graham, *The Mother of Parliaments* (1911), p. 68.
3. James Grant, *Random Recollections of the House of Commons* (1836), pp. 61–2.
4. John O'Connell, *Recollections and Experiences during a Parliamentary Career from 1833 to 1848* (1849), p. 257.
5. John Morley, *The Life of William Ewart Gladstone* (1903), Vol. I, p. 101.
6. Lines written in a letter to his sisters Hannah and Margaret, July 18, 1832.
7. Barnett Cocks, *Mid-Victorian Masterpiece* (1977), p. 59.
8. ibid., pp. 48–9.
9. ibid., pp. 98–9.
10. Stanley Hyland, *Curiosities from Parliament* (1955), p. 205.
11. David Lloyd George, Diary, November 12, 1881.
12. A. P. Herbert, *Independent Member* (1950), p. 39.
13. Cocks, op. cit., pp. 109–10.
14. ibid., pp. 113–19.
15. Alexander Mackintosh, *Echoes of Big Ben: A Journalist's Parliamentary Diary, 1881–1940* (1945), p. 70.
16. Alfred C. Bossom, *Our House: An Introduction to Parliamentary Procedure* (1948), p. 146.
17. Robert Rhodes James, *An Introduction to the House of Commons* (1968), p. 91.
18. Henry W. Lucy, *A Diary of the Home Rule Parliament, 1892–1895* (1896), p. 46.
19. William Kent, *John Burns: Labour's Lost Leader* (1950), p. 58.
20. Lord Frederic Hamilton, *The Days Before Yesterday* (1920), p. 215.
21. Catherine Macdonald Maclean, *Mark Rutherford: A Biography of William Hale White* (1955), p. 204.
22. Arthur Baker, *The House is Sitting* (1958), p. 20.

13 Eating, Drinking and Smoking

> A Member in the House of Commons sneering at an
> oration given elsewhere as 'an after-dinner speech',
> Disraeli with real anger repeated the term: 'An after-
> dinner speech! An after-dinner speech! The Hon.
> Member sneers at an after-dinner speech! The greatest
> speeches ever delivered in this place have been after-
> dinner speeches.'
>
> Sir William Fraser, *Disraeli and his Day* (1891)

It was in 1773 that the Palace of Westminster first provided refreshment facilities for MPs. One John Bellamy was appointed as Deputy Housekeeper of the Lords and Commons. His kitchen and tavern provided MPs with meat, pies and port, and the facility became known simply as Bellamy's. Indeed, Pitt the Younger is supposed to have remembered the caterer on his deathbed in 1806 with the words: 'I think I could eat one of Bellamy's veal pies.'[1]

However, Bellamy's prices were high (he was a wine merchant on the side)[2] and a Select Committee in 1863 reported that only twelve MPs had used the facility on a daily basis. Bellamy's was destroyed in the fire which burned the Houses of Parliament in 1834, though Bellamy, the son of the original deputy housekeeper, was fortunate to have insured his personal effects. The new Houses of Parliament had larger, purpose-built kitchens and in 1848 the House appointed a Select Committee to look into 'proposed arrangements for the kitchen, eating and accommodation rooms for Members'. Thus was born the Kitchen Committee. By 1900 there were twenty cooks employed by the House and the extraordinary scale of the catering is rendered in detail below by Charles T. King. The Palace of Westminster today contains no fewer than twenty-six bars and restaurants.

The ennui engendered by the nature of parliamentary business and the presence in the Chamber of preachy speakers and bores was a spur to MPs to leave for their dinners. John Forster recalls a lunchtime in the mid-seventeenth century when MPs rushed out with such undignified alacrity that Mr Speaker Lenthal felt impelled to tell them 'they were unworthy to sit in this great and wise assembly in parliament, that would so run forth for their dinners'.[3] By the late eighteenth century the dinner hour had become institutionalised as the time of day when lesser speakers and bores (known as 'dinner-bells') would rise to their feet in the Chamber. By the mid-nineteenth century, one writer was referring to the Tories as being primarily the dining-out party and a House in which high spirits were in evidence was described as a 'well-dined House'.

Peel frequently dined in the House, as did Disraeli. Sir John Cam Hobhouse recalls an evening when he and Peel ate their mutton-chops at separate tables, alone in the room and silent, until they had finished their meals, when Peel spoke to Hobhouse about a proposed monument to Lord Byron.[4] Disraeli would often talk to his opponent John Bright in the dining-room, but he did not like to leave the precincts of the Chamber while Leader of the House: 'When the House, as was its usual practice in his time, sat through the dinner hour, he remained and took a hasty dinner at the Cabinet table; or sometimes joined his wife in her brougham drawn up in one of the courts at St Stephen's, and there in the carriage ate with her a daintier meal which her solicitude had brought down for him.'[5] Gathorne-Hardy was not given the job as Disraeli's successor in the Commons, in part because 'he incurred more than once the reproof of his chief for missing a critical division owing to his otherwise praiseworthy habit of going home, whenever possible, to dine with his wife'.[6]

Lord Rosebery was another for whom dinner took precedence. Lloyd George recalled (to Frances Stevenson) the occasion of an important debate in the House of Lords when he 'overheard Rosebery's valet say to him, "Your grouse is done to a turn, my lord," and Rosebery disappeared, leaving the Debate to take care of itself. "He was self-indulgent and everything could take second place to his own personal enjoyment", was D.'s comment. The fact that his grouse was waiting was the determining factor in the debate ... Lulu Harcourt was another, D. says, who always liked his food. He always ordered special food at the Ministerial table—a thing which no one else ever did.'[7] According to Parnell's mistress, Mrs O'Shea, she 'often went up to the House to fetch' Parnell 'out to dinner at a restaurant', because he 'hated dining in the House'.[8]

Lord William Pitt Lennox declared the coffee-room 'abominable',[9] while Sir John Sinclair wrote in 1872 that 'the dinner rooms are comfortable and spacious ... but it is somewhat more expensive, and very inferior to the Clubs; and very often, just as you are raising the first morsel to your lips, jingle, jingle, jingle goes the bell, and you have to rush off to vote, finding your hot joint tepid and your gravy congealed on your return'.[10] Sir Richard Temple, writing in 1886, noticed that 'the dining-rooms and all their belongings were quite inferior to what the Members would see in their clubs and their homes. I was not at all affected by this fault myself; but I was surprised at it, because the authorities should have been interested in inducing members to stay in the House through the dinner hour, and in obviating any discomfort which might cause them to go elsewhere.'[11] The stamina of some MPs was partly explained by the Victorian habit of consuming a hearty breakfast. Albert Pell wrote in his memoirs that he 'could go for a great many hours without food in the House of Commons, never touching anything between breakfast at ten at the Carlton and dinner there at half-past eight or nine'.[12]

Others have considered the presence of refreshment facilities to be a disadvantage to those seeking to get things done. 'I wish now and then that there was no such thing as a smoking-room at the House of Commons,' wrote T. P. O'Connor. 'It would be better if there were no dining-rooms and that the House, meeting at twelve in the day, allowed men to have a light lunch and sent them home at six o'clock in the evening to have their dinners at home.'[13] Indeed, it was the irregular hours of the House which necessitated the presence of such facilities. During the 41½-hour sitting in 1881, G. W. E. Russell remembered, 'the Refreshment-Rooms at the House were kept open all night, and we recruited our exhausted energies with grilled bones, oysters, and champagne, and went to bed at breakfast-time'.[14]

As for the fare itself, it has been frequently adapted over the years to reflect changing dietary habits. In Edwardian times, as Charles T. King recorded, a favourite dinner 'included oysters, clear turtle, fillet of sole, Virginia ham, boiled pheasant, and other things'. King added that 'the bill of fare of the House of Lords is a trifle simpler, although the House of Lords' cooking is not to be excelled, I think, anywhere'.[15] By the mid-1920s, the fare had been refined yet further. 'The Victorian Era, though an improvement on the Georgian, was undoubtedly rather indulgent in the matter of eating and drinking,' wrote Sir James Agg-Gardner, the chairman of the Kitchen Committee from 1917 to 1928. 'Today we dine more wisely. The "dinner of ceremony" in the House has been simplified, and the heavier wines formerly in vogue have been supplanted by light French and German wines, lager beer, and cider.'[16]

Disraeli complained late in his career that the parliamentary correspondent now related how MPs 'dine, even the wines and dishes which they favour', and that he followed them 'into the very mysteries of their smoking-room'. The *Illustrated London News*, for example, chose to illustrate the Irish Round Table in the Commons dining room in October 1909 and also the scene when German black bread was served for the first time in March 1910. There were other culinary innovations. A Scots Member called Kirkwood was responsible for the introduction of porridge as an evening meal 'prepared under his personal direction'.[17] During the session of 1908 the Kitchen Committee 'founded for the first time in history a vegetarian dinner for members. There were to be found a few MPs to eat it, but not many.'[18]

Towards the end of the eighteenth century, the Lutheran pastor Moritz observed that MPs were in the habit of cracking nuts or eating oranges or 'whatever else is in season' in the Chamber itself. The lobby of the House was frequented by an orange-seller who also provided hard biscuits (the latter were much favoured by Fox). Disraeli described how a Member faltering in his speech sent for oranges. When Brougham made his famous six-hour speech on law reform in 1828 he kept a hatful of oranges on the bench by his side for periodic refreshment.[19] E. M. Whitty described how Bulwer Lytton, after indulging in some high-flown oratory, 'sat down intensely satisfied, plunging into an orange with the avidity of a Demosthenes, after having upset a Philip for the sixth time—seeming, as he sucked it, and yellowed his pale face with it, supremely ludicrous'.[20]

Joseph Hume was an assiduous attender of the House in the 1820s and 1830s, regularly present in the Chamber 'from the moment the doors were opened . . . until the adjournment'. During wearisome debates he fortified himself with pears. 'Can it be that there are any peculiarly salubrious qualities in pears?' wrote James Grant, 'for, by his own admission, he always filled his pockets with this species of fruit when it was to be had, and ate the pears in the house, making them answer as a substitute for dinner.' Fruit was not the only foodstuff permitted in the Chamber. In August 1880, during a twenty-one hours' sitting, the Irish Member A. M. Sullivan brought in a bag of buns and ate what Labouchere called 'a palpable supper'.[21]

From the 1870s onwards, there was also the delightful institution of tea on the Terrace in the afternoons, which afforded the added pleasure of female company. Cress sandwiches and strawberries and cream were the usual fare. 'Sometimes as many as eight hundred teas were given on the Terrace on one day,' wrote Charles T. King of the summer of 1908. Joseph Chamberlain, the Radical-turned-Tory, could be seen entertaining duchesses, while Labour MPs like Keir Hardie and Will Thorne were also to be glimpsed entertaining friends.[22]

Drunkenness among MPs has been a problem down the centuries. 'I will suppose this fault was less frequent when Solon made it one of his laws that it was lawful to kill a magistrate if he was found drunk,' wrote George Savile, Marquis of Halifax, in a 1695 pamphlet warning about the bibulous tendencies of MPs. 'Such a liberty taken in this age, either in the Parliament or out of it, would do terrible execution.'[23] The earliest evidence of drunkenness in the Chamber is provided by Samuel Pepys, and we know that Pitt the Younger was obliged to vomit one night in Solomon's Porch, a doorway behind the Speaker's Chair, owing to an excessive intake of port. This was a precursor to a respectable parliamentary performance, so contemporaries tell us; whereas a later premier, Asquith, became unravelled in the House through drink. 'The practice of seeing double in the house, after a certain hour, is not new,' wrote James Grant in 1836. 'It was quite common as far back as the days of Pitt and Dundas. They were in the habit of dialoguing each other after having dined together, as follows: Pitt—"I can't see the Speaker, Hal; can you?" Dundas—"Not see the Speaker, Billy!—I see two!" '[24]

On one occasion in the early nineteenth century, Sir George Rose, a country member, arrived in the Chamber drunk and asked Mr Speaker for a comic song. He was taken into custody by the Serjeant-at-Arms and brought to the Bar of the House, where he was invited to beg the Speaker's pardon. His condition, however, led him to declare that he would beg no man's pardon, not even King George's, and certainly not that of the little man in a big wig. He was locked up for the night and the next day expressed his contrition. He was duly reprimanded and ordered to pay the Serjeant-at-Arms's costs.[25] When Sir Charles Wetherell attacked the administration in which he was serving as attorney-general over its policy of Catholic emancipation, his speech was so violent 'that he was currently reported to have been drunk when he made it'.[26] Disraeli's letters in the late 1830s contain several references to drunkenness in the House. 'No one cheered me more vehemently than Hobhouse, who was a little drunk,' he wrote;[27] and of another Member: 'We thought he was drunk, but the Whigs say the fault was he was not, and that when he is tipsy and is not prepared he is very good.'[28]

Lord Brougham spoke for four hours on the second reading of the Reform Bill in 1831, keeping himself going with mulled port. When he reached his peroration he went down on his knees and begged the Lords to pass the Bill. He 'remained in this attitude so long that his friends, fearing that he was suffering as much from mulled port as emotion, picked him up and replaced him on the Woolsack'.[29] Mr Speaker Cornwall (who held the office from 1780 to 1789) was notorious for keeping a flagon of porter beside the Chair, and even Mr Gladstone had his pomatum-pot in which a *mélange* of sherry and egg was stored for his periodic sustenance during long speeches. Disraeli favoured a stronger mixture: brandy and water. 'On a memorable night Mr Gladstone said Disraeli had access to sources of inspiration not given to Her Majesty's Ministers,' wrote the free-thinker George Holyoake, who had seen Lord John Manners bring Disraeli five glasses of brandy and water during the course of his speech and averred that the Tory leader clutched the Table for support.[30]

Justin McCarthy recalled that in the House in the early 1850s 'there hardly ever took place a night's debate then and for many Sessions after during which some members did not make it evident by the manner of their speeches that they had been stimulating their nerves and screwing up their courage a good deal too much at the expense of the bottle or the decanter ... In the former days it might be said without exaggeration that hardly a night passed without giving the public some exhibition of a drunken member amusing his audience by trying to take part in a debate. We all know that in the days of Pitt and Fox and Sheridan such exhibitions were much more common...'[31] A refreshment bar providing alcoholic beverages was constructed in a corner of the Members' Lobby, but a Liberal Member, Edward Morton, who was a churchwarden, objected. 'The first sound that greets a stranger visiting the House of Commons', he pointed out, 'is the clinking of glasses and the popping of corks.' The bar was moved into a poky room opening off the lobby, which had previously served as a post office, and sales of alcohol declined.[32]

'Those who were in Parliament 30 or 40 years ago will, I am sure, corroborate my assertion', wrote Sir James Agg-Gardner in the late 1920s, 'that rare as was then the appearance of inebriety, of recent years there has never been the slightest sign.'[33]

However, in the opinion of Fenner Brockway, new Labour MPs were particularly susceptible to the perils of drink:

The inevitable deterioration of their existence was hastened by the ease with which drink could be obtained. The Houses of Parliament are classed as a Royal Palace and accordingly there are no licensed hours; drink can be had all day and night. I do not wish to exaggerate the drunkenness which occurred at the House, but it was rare during my period in Parliament for one or more members not to be intoxicated after nine o'clock at night; the temper of the debates always rose after this hour and unseemly interruptions were common. One Member had the habit when he drank too much of maintaining an unceasing 'hear, hear' like a small machine gun. There was one occasion when the Cabinet Minister responsible for winding up a debate on Unemployment could stand only with difficulty. By this I was utterly shocked and left the Chamber, remarking to Dr Marion Phillips, beside whom I was sitting, that a workman would be sacked if he were found drunk at his bench . . . In his day Keir Hardie laid down the rule that no MP should touch drink during Parliamentary hours, and most of the Members of our Group [the ILP] carried out this practice.[34]

This self-denying ordinance was known as the Keir Hardie pledge, and in 1935 one Labour MP, the temperance campaigner Dr Alfred Salter, was pressing for the pledge to be re-instituted, although he was able to declare proudly that 74 out of the 154 official Labour MPs were teetotal.[35] Nevertheless, Harry Boardman, the *Manchester Guardian* sketch-writer, paid tribute in 1953 to 'Rose and Annie, who, in their famous bars, have attended, for more than a generation, to the lubrication of Members' throats with tea and not-tea'.[36]

The phenomenon of the well-dined House has persisted in modern times, though only rarely has it been so pronounced as to invite criticism. In 1965 Labour MP Patrick Duffy caused a row when the press reported some remarks he made at a meeting of his constituents claiming that some Tories had been drunk during censure debates. 'The deliberate and insistent obstruction, involving synthetic points of order and the baying, to prevent Government Front Benchers from being heard,' Duffy said, 'was due to the fact that some of the Opposition members came straight from the bar and created virtual chaos.'[37] Again, during the debate on Labour's Aircraft and Shipbuilding Bill in 1976, which resulted in a tied vote, Michael Foot asserted that the jobs of workers in these industries were being put in jeopardy by a 'semi-drunken Tory brawl', which caused one Tory MP to respond that to be accused of being 'semi-drunk is as bad as being drunk'. Foot was forced to revise his opinion: 'Yesterday many Opposition members tried to stop me speaking in the House when they were sober,' he explained, 'and tonight some have tried to stop me speaking when they were in a different condition.'[38]

When smoking was first introduced to Britain in the late sixteenth century, it was tolerated in the Chamber, but as it became more and more fashionable, an order was made for its prohibition: 'Ordered, that no member of the House do presume to smoke tobacco in the gallery, or at the table of the House, sitting as Committee'. When the Palace was rebuilt in the 1840s, provision was made for special smoking-rooms, though even here a form of prohibition was applied. One writer noted 'how largely the smoking of short pipes prevails in the smoking-room of the House of Commons. The cigar and cigarette smokers seem to feel their isolation and the awkwardness of their position.'[39] Aside from this there was the social demarcation that was enforced, though not rigidly, between MPs of differing party allegiance. 'There is a tendency', noted Fenner Brockway, 'for different parties to appropriate particular smoking-rooms: in my day the Labour loyalists crowded the Map Room of the Library, the Conservatives occupied the smoking-room on the ground floor, and the Liberals monopolised the Chess Room.'[40] In the 1920s one MP was so lost in a reverie in the Chamber that he casually lit his pipe, forgetting that he was not in his own sitting-room at home. Sir James Agg-Gardner wrote in the mid-1920s that 'smoking is becoming more extensively cultivated, and permeates nearly all the libraries and adjacent rooms. I am afraid the day is not far distant when it will be introduced in the lobbies surrounding the Chamber and possibly, as has been suggested, into the Chamber itself.'[41]

One indulgence that was permitted in the Chamber for many years was the consumption of snuff. 'Churchill still takes a pinch from the box traditionally kept by the principal door-keeper,' wrote Alexander Mackintosh in 1945, 'but there are no addicts now like T. P. O'Connor or the great lawyer Charles Russell who "first his snuff-box opened, then his case".'[42]

Two drunken Members cause a disturbance

Samuel Pepys, Diary, 1666

December 19. [Sir R. Ford] did tell me how Sir Allan Broderick and Sir Allan Apsley did come drunk the other day into the House, and did both speak for half an hour together, and could not be laughed, or pulled, or bid to sit down and hold their peace, to the great contempt of the King's servants and cause; which I am grieved at with all my heart.

The Earl of Carnarvon inspired by claret

Parliamentary Debates, 1668–1741

He is said never to have spoken before in that House, but having been heated with wine, and more excited to display his abilities by the Duke of Buckingham (who meant no favour to the treasurer but only ridicule), was resolved before he went up to speak upon any subject that would offer itself. Accordingly he stood up, and delivered himself to this effect:—'My Lords, I understand but little of Latin, but a good deal of English, and not a little of English history; from which I have learnt the mischiefs of such kind of prosecutions as these, and the ill fate of the prosecutors. I could bring many instances, and those very ancient; but, my lords, I shall go no further back than the latter end of Queen Elizabeth's reign: At which time the Earl of Essex was run down by Sir Walter Rawleigh, and your lordships very well know what became of Sir Walter Rawleigh. My Lord Bacon, he ran down Sir Walter Rawleigh, and your lordships know what became of my Lord Bacon. The Duke of Buckingham, he ran down my Lord Bacon, and your lordships know what happened to the Duke of Buckingham. Sir Thomas Wentworth, afterwards Earl of Strafford, ran down the Duke of Buckingham, and you all know what became of him. Sir Harry Vane, he ran down the Earl of Strafford, and your lordships know what became of Sir Harry Vane. Chancellor Hyde, he ran down Sir Harry Vane, and your lordships know what became of the Chancellor. Sir Thomas Osbourn, now Earl of Danby, ran down Chancellor Hyde; but what will become of the Earl of Danby your lordships best can tell. But let me see that man that dare run the Earl of Danby down, and we shall soon see what will become of him.'—This being pronounced with a remarkable humour and tone, the Duke of Buckingham, both surprised and disappointed, after his way cried out, 'The man is inspired! and claret has done the business.'

A drunken Member insults the Speaker

Lord John Townshend, 1810

The member for Sussex, Mr Fuller, entered the House in a state of inebriety, and too audibly mistook the Speaker for an owl in an ivy-bush. He was at once named, and handed over to the Serjeant.

The next day the Speaker administered a severe but dignified rebuke.

Pearson on refreshments

Joseph Pearson, *Pearson's Political Dictionary* (1793)

ALICE'S—A Coffee-House, frequented by the Members for *soups*, which Bellamy can't make, and other *refreshments*, while Burke is speaking.—*Mem*. He never rises but I have directly to open the door to let the Members out.—N.B. *Frank*, who has lately had his hair tied up, and powdered, would never have any custom at all but for his *soups*; for the stupid dog can neither *write*, nor *read*, and ha'nt a word to say.

BELLAMY'S—A damn'd good house, up stairs, where I have drunk many a pipe of red port. Here the Members, who cannot say more than *Yes* or *No* below, can speechify for hours to Mother Bellamy about beef steaks and pork chops. Sir Watkin Lewes always dresses them there himself—and I'll be curst if he ben't a choice hand at a beef steak and a bottle, as well as a pot and a pipe.

BRANDY—A comfortable liquor, as hot as Pepper Arden, as strong as Harry Dundas, as clear as Charles Fox, as red as Alderman Curtis, when he's blushing at getting a biscuit contract—ha! ha! ha!—It's a liquor, in short, that makes me at first as lively as Billy Butler—but if I take too much of it I feel myself as dull as Dolben, and stupid as Hawkins Brown.

DINNER-BELL—A bell rung upon the winding up of a debate, for the Members up stairs at Bellamy's to come down, and do as they are bid—N.B. A good excuse for some to leave their bills unpaid.

DRYBUTTER—The name of a woman attending the lobby with oranges, who knows more of the Members' private *affairs* than all the old bawds in Christendom put together.

SANDWICHES—Two small slices of bread and butter, almost transparent, with a thin piece of stale ham, or beef, between them, and used to keep the people in the gallery from famishing, from Eleven o'clock, till six the next morning.— N.B. *Bellamy* charges a shilling for them, and they don't stand him in above two-pence. I once had one from him, and his wife made me pay for it. By the bye, I ought to have had a *feeling* there. *Bellamy's* profit, notwithstanding the Serjeant at Arms, or his Deputy, as Dick Rigby once said, when Cooke was appointed Pay-Master General with him, may be *put to bed to him*, is a damn'd deal more than my *Guineas*.

❖

Bellamy's Kitchen

Charles Dickens, 'Bellamy's', *Evening Chronicle*, April 11, 1835

But let us not omit to notice Bellamy's kitchen, or, in other words, the refreshment-room common to both Houses of Parliament, where Ministerialists and Oppositionists, Whigs and Tories, Radicals, Peers, and Destructives, strangers from the gallery, and the more favoured strangers from below the bar, are alike at liberty to resort; where divers honourable members prove their perfect independence by remaining during the whole of a heavy debate, solacing themselves with the creature comforts; and whence they are summoned by whippers-in, when the House is on the point of dividing; either to give their 'conscientious votes' on questions of which they are conscientiously innocent of knowing anything whatever, or to find a vent for the playful exuberance of their wine-inspired fancies, in boisterous shouts of 'Divide,' occasionally varied with a little howling, barking, crowing, or other ebullitions of senatorial pleasantry.

When you have ascended the narrow staircase which, in the present temporary House of Commons, leads to the place we are describing, you will probably observe a couple of rooms on your right hand, with tables spread for dining. Neither of these is the kitchen, although they are both devoted to the same purpose; the kitchen is further on to our left, up these half-dozen stairs. Before we ascend the staircase, however, we must request you to pause in front of this little bar-place with the sash-windows; and beg your particular attention to the steady honest-looking old fellow in black, who is its sole occupant. Nicholas (we do not mind mentioning the old fellow's name, for if Nicholas be not a public man, who is?—and public men's names are public property)— Nicholas is the butler of Bellamy's, and has held the same place, dressed exactly in the same manner, and said precisely the same things, ever since the oldest of its present visitors can remember. An excellent servant Nicholas is—an unrivalled compounder of salad-dressing—an admirable preparer of soda-water and lemon—a special mixer of cold grog and punch—and, above all, an unequalled judge of cheese. If the old man have such a thing as vanity in his composition, this is certainly his pride; and if it be possible to imagine that anything in this world could disturb his impenetrable calmness, we should say it would be the doubting his judgement on this important point.

We needn't tell you all this, however, for if you have an atom of observation, one glance at his sleek, knowing-looking head and face—his prim white neckerchief, with the wooden tie into which it has been regularly folded for twenty years past, merging by imperceptible degrees into a small-plaited shirt-frill—and his comfortable-looking form encased in a well-brushed suit of black—would give you a better idea of his real character than a column of our poor description could convey.

Nicholas is rather out of his element now; he cannot see the kitchen as he used to in the old House; there, one window of his glass-case opened into the room, and then, for the edification and behoof of more juvenile questioners, he would stand for an hour together, answering deferential questions about Sheridan, and Percival, and Castlereagh, and Heaven knows who beside, with manifest delight, always inserting a 'Mister' before every commoner's name.

Nicholas, like all men of his age and standing, has a great idea of the degeneracy of the times. He seldom expresses any political opinions, but we managed to ascertain, just before the passing of the Reform Bill, that Nicholas was a thorough Reformer. What was our astonishment to discover shortly after the meeting of the first reformed Parliament, that he was a most inveterate and decided Tory! It was very odd: some men change their opinions from necessity, others from expediency, others from inspiration; but that Nicholas should undergo any change in any respect was an event we had never contemplated, and should have considered impossible. His strong opinion against the clause which empowered the metropolitan districts to return Members to Parliament, too, was perfectly unaccountable.

We discovered the secret at last; the metropolitan Members always dined at home. The rascals! As for giving additional Members to Ireland, it was even worse—decidedly unconstitutional. Why, sir, an Irish Member would go up there, and eat more dinner than three English Members put together. He took no wine; drank table-beer by the half-gallon; and went home to Manchester-buildings, or Millbank street, for his whiskey-and-water. And what was the consequence? Why the concern lost—actually lost, sir—by his patronage. A queer old fellow is Nicholas, and as completely a part of the building as the house itself. We wonder he ever left the old place, and fully expected to see in the papers, the morning after the fire, a pathetic account of an old gentleman in black, of decent appearance, who was seen at one of the upper windows when the flames were at their height, and declared his resolute intention of falling with the floor. He must have been got out by force. However, he was got out—here he is again, looking as he always does, as if he had been in a

477

handbox ever since the last session. There he is, at his old post every night, just as we have described him: and, as characters are scarce, and faithful servants scarcer, long may he be there, say we!

Now, when you have taken your seat in the kitchen, and duly noticed the large fire and roasting-jack at one end of the room—the little table for washing glasses and draining jugs at the other—the clock over the window opposite St Margaret's Church—the deal tables and wax candles—the damask table-cloths and bare floor—the plate and china on the tables, and the gridiron on the fire; and a few other anomalies peculiar to the place—we will point out to your notice two or three of the people present, whose station or absurdities render them the most worthy of remark.

It is half-past twelve o'clock, and as the division is not expected for an hour or two, a few Members are lounging away the time here in preference to standing at the bar of the House, or sleeping on one of the side galleries. That singularly awkward and ungainly looking man, in the brownish-white hat, with the straggling black trousers which reach about half-way down the leg of his boots, who is leaning against the meat-screen, apparently deluding himself into the belief that he is thinking about something, is a splendid sample of a Member of the House of Commons concentrating in his own person the wisdom of a constituency. Observe the wig, of a dark hue but indescribable colour, for if it be naturally brown, it has acquired a black tint by long service, and if it be naturally black, the same cause has imparted to it a tinge of rusty brown; and remark how very materially the great blinker-like spectacles assist the expression of that most intelligent face. Seriously speaking, did you ever see a countenance so expressive of the most hopeless extreme of heavy dullness, or behold a form so strangely put together? He is no great speaker: but when he does address the House, the effect is absolutely irresistible.

The small gentleman with the sharp nose, who has just saluted him, is a Member of Parliament, an ex-Alderman, and a sort of amateur fireman. He, and the celebrated fireman's dog, were observed to be remarkably active at the conflagration of the two Houses of Parliament—they both ran up and down, and in and out, getting under people's feet, and into everybody's way, fully impressed with the belief that they were doing a great deal of good, and barking tremendously. The dog went quietly back to his kennel with the engine, but the gentleman kept up such an incessant noise for some weeks after the occurrence, that he became a positive nuisance. As no more parliamentary fires have occurred, however, and as he has consequently had no more opportunities of writing to the newspapers to relate how, by way of preserving pictures he cut them out of their frames, and performed other great national services, he has gradually relapsed into his old state of calmness.

That female in black—not the one whom the Lord's-Day-Bill Baronet has just chucked under the chin; the shorter of the two—is 'Jane' the Hebe of Bellamy's. Jane is as great a character as Nicholas, in her way. Her leading features are a thorough contempt for the great majority of her visitors; her predominant quality, love of admiration, as you cannot fail to observe, if you mark the glee with which she listens to something the young Member near her mutters somewhat unintelligibly in her ear (for his speech is rather thick from some cause or other), and how playfully she digs the handle of a fork into the arm with which he detains her, by way of reply.

Jane is no bad hand at repartees, and showers them about, with a degree of liberality and total absence of reserve or constraint, which occasionally excites no small amazement in the minds of strangers. She cuts jokes with Nicholas, too, but looks up to him with a great deal of respect; the immovable stolidity with which Nicholas receives the aforesaid jokes, and looks on, at certain pastoral friskings and rompings (Jane's only recreations, and they are very innocent too) which occasionally take place in the passage, is not the least amusing part of his character.

The two persons who are seated at the table in the corner, at the farther end of the room, have been constant guests here, for many years past; and one of them has feasted within these walls, many a time, with the most brilliant characters of a brilliant period. He has gone up to the other House since then; the greater part of his boon companions have shared Yorick's fate, and his visits to Bellamy's are comparatively few.

If he really be eating his supper now, at what hour can he possibly have dined! A second solid mass of rump-steak has disappeared, and he eats the first in four minutes and three quarters, by the clock over the window. Was there ever such a personification of Falstaff! Mark the air with which he gloats over that Stilton, as he removes the napkin which has been placed beneath his chin to catch the superfluous gravy of the steak, and with what gusto he imbibes the porter which has been fetched, expressly for him, in the pewter pot. Listen to the hoarse sound of that voice, kept down as it is by layers of solids, and deep draughts of rich wine, and tell us if you ever saw such a perfect picture of a regular gourmand; and whether he is not exactly the man whom you would pitch upon as having been the partner of Sheridan's parliamentary carouses, the volunteer driver of the hackney-coach that took him home, and the involuntary upsetter of the whole party?

What an amusing contrast between his voice and appearance, and that of the spare, squeaking old man, who sits at the same table, and who, elevating a little cracked bantam sort of voice to its highest pitch, invokes damnation upon his own eyes or somebody else's at the commencement of every sentence he utters. 'The Captain', as they call him, is a very old frequenter of Bellamy's; much addicted to stopping 'after the House is up' (an inexpiable crime in Jane's eyes), and a complete walking reservoir of spirits and water.

The old Peer—or rather, the old man—for his peerage is of comparatively recent date—has a huge tumbler of hot punch brought him; and the other damns and drinks, and drinks and damns, and smokes. Members arrive every moment in a great bustle to report that 'The Chancellor of the Exchequer's up,' and to get glasses of brandy-and-water to sustain them during the division; people who have ordered supper, countermand it, and prepare to go downstairs, when suddenly a bell is heard to ring with tremendous violence, and a cry of 'Di-vi-sion!' is heard in the passage. This is enough; away rush the members pell-mell. The room is cleared in an instant; the noise rapidly dies away; you hear the creaking of the last boot on the last stair, and are left alone with the leviathan of rump-steaks.

William Lockey Harle, *A Career in the Commons: or Letters to a Young Member of Parliament* (1850)

You dine very frequently in that singular apartment, in the vicinity of the House of Commons, called the 'kitchen'. Mr Bellamy's beer may be unexceptionable, and his chops and steaks may be unrivalled; but why do the legislators of England delight in eating a dinner in the place where it is cooked, and in the presence of the very fire where the beef hisses and the gravy runs? Explain this, I pray you, to my unsophisticated understanding.

Bellamy's Kitchen seems, in fact, a portion of the British constitution. A foreigner—be he a Frenchman, American, or Dutchman—if introduced to the 'kitchen', would stare with astonishment if you told him that in this plain apartment—with its immense fire, meat-screen, gridirons, and small tub under the window for washing the glasses—the statesmen of England very often dine; and men possessed of wealth untold, and with palaces of their own, in which luxury and splendour are visible in every part, are willing to leave their stately dining-halls and powdered attendants, to be waited upon while eating a chop in Bellamy's Kitchen, by two very unpretending old women. Bellamy's Kitchen is part and parcel, I repeat, of the British constitution. Baronets, who date from the Conquest, and squires of every degree, care nothing for the unassuming character of the 'kitchen', if the steak be hot and good, if it can be quickly and conveniently dispatched, and the tinkle of the division bell can be heard while the dinner proceeds. Call England a proud nation, forsooth! Say that the House of Commons is aristocratic! Both the nation and its representatives must be and are unquestionable patterns of republican humility, if all the pomp and circumstance of dining can be forgotten in Bellamy's Kitchen! . . .

I do not wish to disparage Mr Bellamy—his cooking apparatus, Jane, or any other person or thing—but I hope, most sincerely, that when the new houses are finished, the Commons of England will be able to dine in a place less hot in the month of June, than 'Bellamy's Kitchen'!

Mr Alpheus Cleophas Morton and the Dinner Question

Sir Alpheus Cleophas Morton (1840–1923) was educated privately in Canada and became an architect and surveyor. He was prominent in the affairs of the Corporation of the City of London and various other metropolitan bodies, and sat as Liberal MP for Peterborough, 1889–95; and for Sutherlandshire, from 1906 until his retirement in 1918.

Henry W. Lucy, *A Diary of the Home Rule Parliament, 1892–1895* (1896)

May 25, 1894. As soon as the House got into Committee of Supply on the Civil Service Estimates, Mr Alpheus Cleophas Morton moved to diminish the vote of £4,897,350 by the sum of £2,000, being the subvention granted by the State to the Commissariat Department of the House of Commons. Dr Clark in his genial way put the matter in another form, declaring that the House was 'sponging on the nation to the amount of £2,000 a year, in order that members' dinners might come a little cheaper'. Colonel Nolan took what, at the outset, appeared higher ground. From a personal point of view, he had only to lament a tendency, Batavian in its impulse, to clap on 40 per cent to the price of wines—a process, it should be said, in some cases necessary to give the article even an appearance of value. That was unprincipled conduct on the part of the Committee from which members personally suffered. Colonel Nolan's generous soul bled for the waiter. He drew a graphic picture of 'Robert' with a large family (possibly a bedridden mother) looking on, whilst a member luxuriated in the rich spring soup that bubbles up from the House of Commons kitchen, or made-believe to crunch between his teeth the limp and lukewarm whitebait, the waiter meanwhile steeped in gloomy reflection upon his inadequate wage and the strong improbability of its being supplemented by a tip from Lucullus.

'How can a man dine in comfort in such circumstances?' Colonel Nolan asked, personally addressing the Chairman of Committees, whose acquaintance with the House of Commons cuisine is extensive and peculiar.

Perhaps this parenthetical remark was a mistake. The House listened with sympathy whilst the Colonel, speaking two hundred words a minute, piled up the agony of the waiter. It was kindly meant, unselfishly done. But when, even in an aside, he turned the light on the pampered diner, and with swift touch pictured his disappointment with the asparagus because the woes of the waiter vulgarly obtruded themselves at the feast, the selfish Sybarite stood confessed.

Mr Alpheus Cleophas Morton was not influenced in his action either by consideration of the hard lot of the waiter, who, it seems, for five days' work gets from 29s to 35s in wages and meals worth 12s 6d, or by the distress which overwhelms a man accustomed to a decent meal when he sits down to the scramble of a House of Commons dinner. The member for Peterborough is always wanting to know, and of late his curiosity has been excited by the mystery that broods over the receipts and expenditure of the Kitchen Committee. All the members who constitute that body are well-dressed, most of them wear watches, chains, and rings. Some have of late taken to coming down to the House in private carriages. Mr Morton makes no accusation, refrains even from the echo of a note of imputation. Only, why do not the Committee set forth in parallel columns details of their income and expenditure, and frankly state what becomes of the enormous profits they must make from a monopoly of commissariat supply for 670 gentlemen, with glass and crockery, coals and gas free, and a subvention of £2,000 a year taken out of the pocket of the working man? The Kitchen Committee declining to produce a return setting forth these particulars, Mr Morton now proposed to fine them for their contumacy by withdrawal of the annual grant.

The opportunity was seized by Mr Sydney Herbert, who graces the chair of the Kitchen Committee, to make a statement that casts a final pall of gloom over the whole business. It appears that not only are the House of Commons dinners disappointing, badly cooked, and rampageously served, but, even with extraneous advantages possessed by no other club in London, the financial result is as often a deficit as it shows an immaterial surplus. The experiment of placing the commissariat arrangements under the direction of a Committee of Members on the basis of a club arrangement has been tried now for some years. For the Committee, who give up much time and thought to the work, it has proved a thankless task. For members the result is a matter of perpetual and occasionally petulant complaint. The House of Commons has been likened to a Nasmyth hammer, that can, with nicely adjusted stroke, disestablish a church or sanction by its vote the annual payment to the rat-catcher at Buckingham Palace. Today's debate brought into strong light the fact, patent to some members on four nights in every week, that it has not yet been able to devise a scheme whereby it can provide itself with a simple dinner at a reasonable price.

❖

The ingenuity of Colonel Mark Lockwood

Amelius Richard Mark Lockwood (1847–1928), the son of a general, was educated at Eton and served in the Coldstream Guards, retiring with the rank of Lieutenant-Colonel in 1883. He sat as Unionist MP for West Sussex from 1892 until 1917, when he was created Baron Lambourne. He was also president of the Royal Horticultural Society and a railway company director.

Henry W. Lucy, *The Balfourian Parliament, 1901–1905* (1906)

June 26, 1902. The calamity to the King that eclipsed the gaiety of the nation, a touch of sorrow that made the whole world kin, fell on the House of Commons Kitchen Committee as a bolt out of the blue. In common with other joyous preparations for the Coronation, the luncheon in Westminster Hall was abandoned. It would be impossible to exaggerate the consequent inconvenience. Waiters had been engaged regardless of expense; wholesale orders for comestibles had been irrevocably placed; the tables were already spread in Westminster Hall. Worse still—or was this the best of it?—something like thirteen hundred twelve and sixpences jingled in the coffers of the Kitchen Committee. The waiters might be bought off by simple process of paying them. The mountains of roast beef, the plains of cold lamb, the thickets of three-legged chickens, were easily disposed of. There was, close by, the Westminster Hospital; not far off the Little Sisters of the Poor, whose capacity for cold meat is notoriously incommensurate with their physical proportions. But what about foodless members clamouring for restitution of their five half-crowns?

The Kitchen Committee even in this parlous case soared to the height of circumstance. They met and drafted a proclamation after the manner of Napoleon I on the burning of Moscow. It is a masterpiece of mingled firmness and pathos.

'The Kitchen Committee of the House of Commons,' thus it ran, 'deeply lament the unfortunate circumstances that have led to the abandonment of the Coronation festivities in Westminster Hall.' That is, to use a culinary metaphor perhaps not inapplicable, serving out of the milk of human kindness. Honourable members reading so far would bow their heads and murmur, 'Yes, yes, quite right; those Kitchen Committee fellows aren't such a bad lot after all.'

The next sentence led to marked revulsion of feeling. 'It would be impossible, they find, to refund the money which has been paid for the proposed breakfast and luncheon. While acknowledging the hardship thus inflicted upon purchasers of tickets, they rely upon the good feeling of the House to place a favourable construction on their action.'

As a literary production this leaves nothing to be desired. It has the dignity of a Speech from the Throne, and something more than its average grammar. Note the subtle touch of the parenthetical words 'they find'. Here, for the least imaginative mind, is conjured up a picture of the Kitchen Committee spending a laborious day in looking up some means of refunding the money and finding none. Then follows the appeal to the higher nature of the mere twelve-and-sixpenny luncher. 'The Kitchen Committee rely upon the good feeling of the House to place a favourable construction on their action.'

Old Parliamentarians will note in the closing words of this sentence a literal quotation from the consecrated speech a long line of newly elected Speakers make when they stand at the Bar of the House to receive the Sovereign's seal on the choice of the House of Commons.

These sentences lead up to the finest stroke of the masterpiece. 'The only return they' (the lachrymose Kitchen Committee) 'can make is to allow members to partake of luncheon and dinner today (Thursday) and tomorrow at the House gratuitously.'

It is not unwarrantably betraying the secrets of the Kitchen if it be told that this sublime touch was due to the chairman, Colonel Mark Lockwood. It was for some time resisted by unimaginative members of the Committee. They had pouched the twelve-and-sixpences; why unload a stray half-crown? The Colonel chuckled, shook his knowingly, even winked.

'You leave it to me,' he said. 'Put your trust in your chairman, and your chairman will pull you through.'

Throughout yesterday the Colonel was much in evidence in the lobby and on the terrace. With hands in his trousers pockets, his hat pitched back on his head at an angle more miraculous than ever, the light of hospitality literally blazing on his war-bronzed face and his home-grown carnation, he stopped members by the way.

'Come down to lunch here tomorrow, dear boy; also on Friday. Dine, too, on both nights. Won't cost you a stiver. Kitchen Committee pay everything.'

His colleagues were increasingly alarmed till today dawned and brought its secret. The Scotch Estimates were down for consideration in Committee at both afternoon and evening sitting. As usual, the attendance was limited to some thirty or forty Scotch members, and though their appetites are healthy and it was understood most of them cannily refrained from joining in the family home breakfast, the demand on the resources of the commissariat was comparatively trifling.

As for tomorrow, the House adjourns at six o'clock, and no one, not even an Irish member, stays for dinner.

Having set everything in train, the chairman of the Kitchen Committee last night secretly left London for Bishop's Hall, Romford, Essex, and won't be back for a few days.

The smoking-room

Charles Wallwyn Radcliffe Cooke (1841–1911) was born in Herefordshire and educated at Emmanuel College, Cambridge, where he won a couple of university prizes. He was called to the bar in 1872. He wrote a book about the Agricultural Holdings Act of 1875, as well as this humorous volume about Parliament. Active in Herefordshire politics, he was Conservative MP for West Newington from 1885 until he retired in 1892; and for Hereford from August 1893 until he retired from the House in 1900. He was also president and founder of the National Association of English Cider Makers.

C. W. Radcliffe Cooke, *Four Years in Parliament with Hard Labour* (1890)

I have now arrived at a period of the night's labours when I must allow my pen to linger over the most agreeable, and I might add most influential of institutions, the smoking-room of the House of Commons, whither I now repair in order to enjoy an after-dinner whiff. In point of fact there are two smoking-rooms, one on the basement, which opens on to the Terrace, and one next the dining-rooms, on a level with the House and its surroundings. It is of the latter alone that I shall speak. The lower smoking-room is a bleak, comfortless chamber, well enough in summer as a shelter from a shower, should one happen to be on the Terrace. But there its merits, such as they are, end. The true smoking-room is the upper one, sacred to members only. The apartment itself is not remarkable. It is, I should suppose, some thirty feet or so square, and lofty in proportion . . .

The general appearance of the apartment is that of a second-class waiting room at a railway station, so there is none of the cosiness of the domestic snuggery about it. Still, a creditable attempt is made to meet the wants of the after-dinner lounger. In order to accentuate a sense of ease, there should ever be gradations of comfort, descending from luxurious repose to mere stiff-backed unrest; and here we have variety enough, from the armchair in the chimney corner, which by a long course of incubation is accommodated to the exuberance of the human frame, the abiding place of the oldest, the wittiest, or the worthiest, down through a sliding-scale to the clerkly cane-bottom, fit repository for the humbler or hardier limbs of the young or the unconsidered. One feature of the room should not pass unnoticed. This is a rhomboidal space, fenced off in one corner and flanked on the outer side by cases of cigars. One is disappointed at first not to see a wooden Highlander on guard outside, and, within, a young lady with towzled hair, it looks so like a section of a tobacco shop. Inspection reveals the fact that, though there is no young lady in the space in question, it is, nevertheless, tenanted. For a while a mystery clung round the spot which puzzled me. From a kind of recess or cupboard noises, perpetually recurring, proceeded, in part resembling the clashing of crockery; whereupon, after an interval, a being in the garb of a waiter, but with the mien and air of a conjuror or medium, would produce, apparently from nowhere, a cup of coffee, tasting appropriately enough of nothing. In time I discovered that this magic cave answered the purpose of a refreshment bar, whence, by some occult process, the drinks that smokers mostly affect could be supplied to them. On one occasion I rashly asked for bread and butter with my coffee. The presiding genius mentioned above muttered words sounding so weird and incantation-like that I fully looked for a spirit hand to waft me from mid-air the object of my desire. It seems, however, that I had demanded something which it was beyond even his art to procure. He vanished, and after long absence reappeared, and, with a contemptuous gesture, as of one who would signify that a request for food in a smoking-room where good liquor abounded was foolishness, proffered me a currant bun of antique mould, stale and unpalatable, a remanet from past Parliaments, which, had it been a thing of life, would have babbled of Peel and Palmerston, and demanded therefore a fabulous price as for a curiosity in breadstuffs.

485

Were the smoking-room the legislative chamber, what laws we should pass, what reforms we should effect, and how the people would rejoice and sing! . . .

Of late I am bound to admit that a change, not altogether satisfactory, has been wrought in the social aspect of the smoking-room by the introduction of the game of chess. Instead of the small coteries of friends who used to while away the half hour after dinner, or the interval from business when the Speaker left the Chair, with anecdote and repartee, you have some half dozen or so of chess-players, each pair surrounded by a circle of onlookers, silent but critical. Two years ago, before chess was thought of, we had the temporary use, as an addition to the smoking-room of the House of Lords which opened out of the latter apartment. The convenience of the arrangement, which was appreciated then, would be enhanced if we could obtain the room again, since it would enable us to give to the chess-players the accommodation they need, and at the same time to restore some of the social geniality of the smoking-room proper which the absorbing attractions of the game have in a measure checked.

The new Parliament wining and dining

Charles T. King, *The Asquith Parliament (1906–1909)* (1910)

One of the pleasantest memories I have of this Parliament is of the spectacle of the late Sir Alfred Jacoby, the Chairman of the Kitchen Committee, called by an ancient and well-worn joke, 'The Minister of the Interior', standing up in his place at the front Liberal bench below the gangway, holding a big magnifying glass about the size of a platter, and solemnly reading out some trifling answer to a question about the dining arrangements with the air of a great Minister announcing an international crisis. The House did not laugh as a rule; it simply beamed with quiet enjoyment. The late Sir Alfred was succeeded in this distinguished post by Colonel Lockwood, who is affectionately known in the 'inner circle' as 'Uncle Mark'. One of Colonel Lockwood's political opponents down in the Epping division of Essex tried to belittle the Colonel by saying to voters: 'Oh, the idea of voting for Colonel Lockwood; he is nobody. They only put him in charge of the kitchen.'

But let no man run away with the idea that the Chairman of the Kitchen Committee of the House of Commons is a mere nobody. On the contrary, he is a great man. Lord Stanley went from the membership of the Kitchen Committee to a membership of the Government of the day. Colonel Lockwood was able to reign over the Kitchen Committee and adorn his Majesty's Privy Council, as well as to earn respect and admiration, and what is, perhaps, more to the point, the whole-hearted gratitude of his fellow-members of the House of Commons. When there came on that unparalleled contest by night and day over the Budget of 1909, Colonel Lockwood sustained the fighters. Popping about briskly with his hat on the back of his head and a big carnation in his buttonhole, the Colonel saw that if members were to carry on this fight without dropping from sheer exhaustion, the Kitchen Committee must rise to this unprecedented occasion. So it rose. The Colonel set up a special methylated spirit apparatus, by which soups, chopped kidneys, and all sorts of other more or less light and sustaining things could be kept hot all night. In the hot weather Mr Lloyd George was able many a time during the Budget debates to slip off the Treasury bench about two or three in the morning and plunge into the delicious coolnesses of a big slice of juicy melon. One night, so did the good grace of the Kitchen Committee rise above mere party barriers, that soon after Mr Lloyd George had refreshed himself in the sultry night with melon, Mr Balfour with steps long and slow, wandered out of the Chamber and took melon also.

That was for the sultry nights, but the Budget fight went on and on, and Colonel Lockwood was as capable of sustaining them in the nights of frost and cold. Not only did he keep the appetising *entrées* hot, with plenty of cups of soup for the sustenance of the Budget fighters, but he caused what soon became in the autumn of 1909 quite a craze for basins of hot bread and milk. There was a curious little scene one night over this bread and milk. It was in the small hours. The House of Commons, jaded by the hard fight, had fallen into the trough of misery. There lounged into the dining-rooms five Liberals. One of them was an enthusiast over bread and milk. Another of them was apparently new to this sustaining dish. He was one of the 'young bloods' of the Liberal Social Reform party, a man of high tone, of extremely polished demeanour, of correct West End garb, generally adorned by a bunch of violets. One of the MPs 'stood treat'. He launched out with prodigal recklessness on five basins of bread and milk at threepence each. Although a Liberal pledged to retrenchment as well as reform, money seemed to him as nothing. The polished gentleman took up his spoon, and looked at it as one waiting to be initiated. They showed him how to eat his bread and milk. He plunged the spoon with sudden resolution into the bowl. He took half a spoonful. He tried it. He hesitated. He squared his shoulders, threw his hat to the back of his head, and tried again. But it was no use. He put down the spoon and turned round. 'Here, waiter,' he said, 'bring me a coffee and liqueur brandy.' To show that he was no mere *dilettante* politician, I may mention that he was that strenuous Liberal land reformer, Mr Agar Robartes.

The Colonel never let the enormous responsibilities of his office depress his sunny good humour. He reigned over a gargantuan feeding apparatus. For instance, the Valentia Vat itself is a mighty wooden vessel which is never allowed to get lower than about three hundred and fifty gallons of old Scotch whisky. Its full capacity is seven hundred and eight gallons. When the Valentia Vat gets a little low, but still with a good many gallons in it, they pour in some more ten-year-old whisky, so that the blend, continually maturing in the wood, is held by experts to be very good indeed. Then there is a smaller vat of

Highland whisky, which holds an enormous quantity—enough, one would think, to refresh and enliven all the MPs in the House without its mighty neighbour. Then there is a trifle in the way of a vat of Irish whisky, which holds many gallons, but on which there is never very much of a run compared with the broad thirst for Scotch.[43] Then there is a very interesting cabinet with all sorts of compartments in it. This is not a set of pigeon-holes or documents of State or measures of social reform. It contains about ten thousand cigars, and they are all carefully divided up according to quality and price. An MP can have out of this great cabinet a more or less fragrant weed at a penny, or a big thick one at sixpence, or princely cigars at half-a-crown. In fact, there are cigars here of nearly every price between these two extremes.

As to the wines, there are generally over six thousand pounds' worth of wine in stock, and it is a common thing for the yearly sale of wines in the House of Common to come to four or five thousand pounds. What with the wines and the whiskies, the claret cups, the Plantagenet cups, the hock cups, the shilling dinners of the ordinary rank and file, the two-shilling dinners with which the Labour member will sometimes regale Labour delegates from a distance, the sovereign dinners with which sometimes the rich Liberal or Unionist will entertain distinguished men of science, art, or letters, the money taken comes altogether to something like twenty thousand pounds a year.

Let us take a glance at some simple *menus* of the House of Commons. To begin with, there is a very big shilling's worth. For the sum of one shilling an MP can get a cut from a hot joint, a couple of vegetables, the choice of sweets, and bread, cheese and butter without stint. It is a dinner which, for quality and quantity combined, can hardly, I think, be got for the money anywhere else in this country.

The resources of the Kitchen Committee of the House of Commons are so wide that a member can have almost anything, from a threepenny basin of bread and milk to a superb seven-course dinner costing two or three pounds. One of the finest efforts of the Kitchen Committee which I have had the pleasure of enjoying was the occasion on which the British Parliament entertained the officers of the French Fleet in Westminster Hall in August, 1905.

On that day luncheon was served (and a very able luncheon it was) to fifteen hundred persons. There were gay doings on the Terrace, with tea for the ladies, and the Kitchen Committee did it all with ease and smoothness. On that occasion the French guests were regaled with the sight of two heroic barons of beef placed on tables at the two ends of the great hall. The attack on those mighty barons was made with such excellent effect that very soon there was nothing left but the bare bones to tell the story.

As soon as this C.B.–Asquith Parliament had been in existence a few months the Kitchen Committee had a curious experience. They found some reductions in the sales of wine, but an enormous reduction in the consumption of food. In the early part of the final Session something like depression fell on the business of the Kitchen Committee, for so bad was trade, so little were members spending in March, 1909, on dinners and wines, and so heavy is the cost of keeping up the army of waiters and the other staff, that for a time the Kitchen Committee, in spite of the fact that it receives a special grant of one or two thousand pounds a year out of Imperial taxation, was making a loss of about fifty pounds a week. This slump was brought about largely by the closing of the galleries to ladies, owing to the misbehaviour of a couple of women who had got into the Ladies' gallery, on the usual understanding on the part of the MP who introduced them that they would be of good conduct. This sudden event helped to change the laughing, fashionable throngs in the House of Commons' dining-rooms into a dull and meagre attendance of a few lugubrious members, and an order for a bottle of wine at anything much above a shilling was, for a time, a rare experience indeed.

It was not long after this when another crisis threatened the Kitchen Committee. Almost as soon as the Budget was introduced, and six months before it passed even the Commons, the price of whisky was raised in the members' drinking bars and lounges of the House of Commons. It was at this time that Colonel Lockwood created a good deal of laughter in the House of Commons by the exalted tone and supreme gravity of his answer to Sir Robert Hobart on this question. Sir Robert is a descendant of Oliver Cromwell, and it was not to be expected that he could brook anything in the shape of tyranny without having something to say. So Sir Robert Hobart, Liberal Member for the New Forest division of Hampshire, asked the Chairman of the Kitchen Committee whether he was aware that the charges in the refreshment room for whisky were recently raised from threepence to fourpence for the half-glass and from sixpence to sevenpence for the full glass; that these charges had now been reduced to threepence-halfpenny for the half-glass and sixpence-halfpenny for the full glass, and whether he would state on what grounds these charges had been raised and then lowered.

Colonel Lockwood, adorned with a draught-board bow tie, an enormous carnation of the latest pink, and an air of European gravity, replied: 'With the idea of meeting a deficit and a falling revenue by taxing luxuries, and perhaps with the hope of increasing temperance by limiting the expenditure of honourable members, my esteemed colleague the Member for Mid-Derbyshire (Sir Alfred Jacoby) placed a super-tax on whisky of a penny a portion, raising the price from threepence to fourpence and from sixpence to sevenpence. The increase of a halfpenny on each portion would show a slight profit on the increased duty. There is probably enough whisky, Irish and Scotch, to last this Session. (Cheerful laughter.)

'In order, however,' added the Colonel, 'to meet the wishes of members, and in view of an arduous Session, the Kitchen Committee agreed to remit a halfpenny of the super-tax, leaving only an increased price of a halfpenny per measure, threepence-halfpenny and sixpence-halfpenny respectively. Members can avoid paying the odd halfpenny by purchasing two portions of whisky instead of one.' (Laughter.)

It soon became evident that if the great Liberal House of Commons went down to fame for no other feature, it would do so for breaking the Parliamentary record for catering, and for its comparatively large consumption of beverages other than wines. Now the House of Commons is about the easiest place I know of in which to drink wine. I have known men whose outlook on life and the conditions of their own purse is such that they had always resolved (before coming to the House of Commons) that wine was a luxury beyond their means. But there are two forces which enable a man to drink wine in the House of Commons. First of all, an MP who takes a serious view of his Parliamentary duties must spend a very large amount of time indeed within the closed-up walls of the Palace of Westminster. If you have spent long hours indoors without a breath of fresh air and are jaded with much mental labour, and you find that wine is cheaper here than it is in the outside world, and that you can get a fairly sound claret for tenpence per bottle, the chances are that you will begin to experience a sort of reckless feeling that you are really able to afford half a bottle with your wing of chicken or your grilled sole.

It was found before this Parliament had been in existence long that the consumption of wine went down, and that many new members were taking either beer or some such temperance drink as ginger ale, ginger beer and lemonade. They ate, however, more than the ordinary amount of food. As a matter of fact, this did not bring much money into the coffers of the State, and it made a heavy run on that money which is voted by the House of Commons every year out of the strong-boxes of the Treasury. The fact is in that wonderful shilling dinner an MP with a healthy appetite, who has not been too long shut up in the House of Commons, can often do justice to a second cut of sirloin. The shilling covers the meal whether he has one cut or two, one potato or ten or whether he take a little nibble of the cheapest Cheddar or a large dig of it. It was stated early in this Parliament that the Kitchen Committee were losing on some of the bountiful shilling meals something like threepence or fourpence per repast. No doubt some of this was got back when richer members ordered a dinner at half-a-guinea or a sovereign. Thus we have the great principle of Socialism, which it will be seen lies not only in many of the great Bills, but also in the hearth and the groaning board of the House of Commons itself.

In the Session of 1908, in spite of the looming shadow of the great Budget, which is said to have tightened many of the purse-strings of the fearful, £863 worth of cigars were smoked, and members and their guests at the House consumed nearly £10,000 worth of food. Faithful records of the Kitchen Committee reported that there were served in the House of Commons portion of the Palace of Westminster 25,764 luncheons, 37,697 dinners, 61,376 teas, and 3,727 meals at the bars.

Here is the gastronomic record of the all-night sitting which took place on March 20th–21st, 1907. The House of Commons fought for twenty-seven hours. The morning had peeped in at the windows on a wearied assembly of contending men, pale as to face, dishevelled as to hair, wan as to features, drooping as to eyelids, but stout still of heart. It was the longest sitting there had been for about a quarter of a century. The House was tired, feverish, nervous, excited, putting out an unthinkable amount of nervous energy, but really doing very little . . .

Small wonder then that on such an exhausting night as this there should be great demand for refreshment. Here is a rough estimate, given to me by a high official of the department concerned, of the refreshment consumed:—

Dinners, etc. . . .	1,500
Bacon cut up for breakfast rashers . . .	224 lbs.
Eggs fried, boiled and poached . . .	2,000
Dozens of oysters eaten . . .	25
Cups of coffee . . .	525
Glasses of whisky and soda . . .	680
Brandies and sodas . . .	175
Bottles of dry ginger ale . . .	38
Devilled bones . . .	160
Cuts of ham, tongue, roast beef, pressed beef, and the like . . .	Countless.

Most of the dining and wining, however, is carried on under pleasanter conditions. Very soon after the Liberals came into power in 1906 Mr Lewis Harcourt, as First Commissioner of Works, commandeered a room from the Lords, added it to the premises of the Commons, did it up, put palms and panels into it, and made it a fine special dining-room. This place, christened 'The Harcourt Room', formed a feasting-place throughout this Parliament for members of all parties and their fair guests. In the height of the London season the Harcourt Room of the House of Commons soon formed one of the gayest and most fashionable scenes in London—with angry antagonists fresh from fight in the Chamber sitting down together amid the glint of silver and the chatter of pretty women, to forget for an hour the clash of controversy.

Doing the staff a favour

Fenner Brockway, *Towards Tomorrow* (1977)

I get on well with the staff of the House. There was an amusing occasion when a waitress in the cafeteria expressed concern because the adjournment debate, permitted for half an hour, had commenced at 11.15 p.m. If it finished a minute before 11.45 p.m. the staff could not be taken home by car. I went into the

Chamber. There were only three MPs there—a Welshman speaking eloquently about a constituency grievance, the Minister whose responsibility it was, and his Parliamentary secretary. The Minister concluded his reply at 11.43 and the Speaker rose to adjourn the House. I also rose and the Speaker called me. To the surprise of the Welshman I backed him enthusiastically; to this day he doesn't know why. Big Ben struck 11.45. The staff had their cars home.

1. Norman Wilding and Philip Laundy say that this story was related by an old waiter of the House of Commons to Disraeli, soon after he entered Parliament, and emphasise its apocryphal nature; *An Encyclopaedia of Parliament* (1961), p. 33.
2. Factsheet No. 53, House of Commons Public Information Office, p. 2.
3. George Henry Jennings, *An Anecdotal History of the British Parliament from the Earliest Periods to the Present Time* (1880), p. 451.
4. Lord Broughton, *Recollections of a Long Life* (1911), pp. 92–3.
5. W. F. Monypenny and G. E. Buckle, *The Life of Benjamin Disraeli, Earl of Beaconsfield* (1910–12), Vol. II, pp. 840–1.
6. ibid., p. 868.
7. Frances Stevenson, Diary, November 16, 1934.
8. Katherine O'Shea, *Charles Stewart Parnell: His Love Story and Political Life* (1914), Vol. I, p. 122.
9. Lord William Pitt Lennox, *My Recollections 1806–13*, Vol. I, p. 232.
10. Quoted in Factsheet No. 53, House of Commons Public Information Office, p. 4.
11. Sir Richard Temple, Bt., *The Story of My Life* (1896), p. 230.
12. Thomas Mackay (ed.), *The Reminiscences of Albert Pell, Sometime MP for South Leicestershire* (1908), p. 231.
13. Hamilton Fyfe, *T. P. O'Connor* (1934), p. 184.
14. G. W. E. Russell, *One Look Back* (1912), p. 211.
15. Charles. T. King, *The Asquith Parliament (1906–1909): A Popular History of its Men and Measures* (1910), p. 288.
16. Sir James T. Agg-Gardner, *Some Parliamentary Recollections* (1927), p. 86.
17. ibid., p. 88.
18. King, op. cit., p. 239.
19. Michael MacDonagh, *Parliament: Its Romance; Its Comedy; Its Pathos* (1902), p. 119.
20. E. M. Whitty, *St Stephen's in the Fifties: The Session 1852–3, A Parliamentary Retrospect* (1906), p. 70.
21. T. P. O'Connor, *Gladstone's House of Commons* (1885), p. 88.
22. Henry W. Lucy, *A Diary of the Home Rule Parliament, 1892–1895* (1896), p. 156; King, op., cit., pp. 253–4.
23. George Savile, Marquis of Halifax, *Some Cautions Offered to the Consideration of Those Who are to Choose Members to Serve in the Ensuing Parliament* (1695).
24. James Grant, *Random Recollections of the House of Commons* (1836), pp. 378–9.
25. MacDonagh, op. cit., pp. 118–19.
26. *Dictionary of National Biography*, Vol. LX, p. 386.
27. Benjamin Disraeli, Letter to Sarah Disraeli, March 16, 1838.
28. Benjamin Disraeli, Letter to Sarah Disraeli, January 31, 1840.
29. Harry Graham, *The Mother of Parliaments* (1911) p. 149 n.
30. G. J. Holyoake, *Bygones Worth Remembering* (1905), Vol. II, pp. 45–6.
31. Justin McCarthy, Introduction to Whitty, op. cit., pp. x–xi.
32. *Parliamentary Pictures and Personalities: 'Graphic' Illustrations of Parliament, 1890–1893* (1893), p. 61.
33. Agg-Gardner, op. cit., p. 87.
34. Fenner Brockway, *Inside the Left: Thirty Years of Platform, Press, Prison and Parliament* (1942), pp. 221–2.
35. *The Times*, December 13, 1935.
36. Harry Boardman, 'Ian in the Lobby', in Trevor Evans (ed.), *The Great Bohunkus: Tributes to Ian McKay* (1953), p. 108.
37. *Sunday Express*, February 14, 1965.
38. George Thomas, *George Thomas, Mr Speaker: The Memoirs of Viscount Tonypandy* (1985), p. 151.
39. C. W. Radcliffe Cooke, *Four Years in Parliament with Hard Labour* (1890), p. 16.

40. Brockway, op. cit., p. 222.
41. Agg-Gardner, op. cit., p. 94.
42. Alexander Mackintosh, *Echoes of Big Ben: A Journalist's Parliamentary Diary, 1881–1940* (1945), p. 164.
43. The Valentia Vats were named after Viscount Valentia (1845–1927), who sat as Conservative MP for Oxford City from 1895 until 1905, when he became Baron Annesley.

14 Comedy and Wit

The House warmly welcomes any excuse for a roar of
good-humoured laughter in which all can join, which
does good to all and hurts the feelings of no one.

Spencer Leigh Hughes, *Press, Platform
and Parliament* (1918)

Colonel George Onslow, the MP who in the late 1760s harried those printers who
published the proceedings of Parliament, was described by Horace Walpole as one 'of
those burlesque orators who are favoured in all public assemblies, and to whom one or
two happy sallies of impudence secure a constant attention, though their voice and
manner are often their only patents, and who, being laughed at for absurdity as frequently
as for humour, obtain a licence for what they please'.[1] Every generation has had such
licensed clowns and exhibitionists, whether they be a Colonel Sibthorp, from the 1830s
to 1850s, or a Gerald Nabarro, from the 1950s to 1970s (although, while Sibthorp
opposed all forms of progress, Nabarro initiated helpful legislation as a back-bencher).

Sir Thomas Fowell Buxton once wrote that the House likes 'good sense and joking'
above all else, and the tension of many an austere or hostile debate has been lessened
by humour. 'During the contests of Home Rule, often protracted and angry,' recalled Sir
James Agg-Gardner, 'the situation was relieved by the wit and repartee of Irish Members
of both parties . . . One of the disasters of the Home Rule victory has been the loss
inflicted on the vivacity and humour of the House of Commons.'[2]

These displays, however, appeal primarily to initiates. 'Parliament humour is a very
special thing,' wrote a former *Times* parliamentary correspondent in 1966. 'The jokes
tend to be simple, yet so frequently based on the personal foibles of members or quirks
of past policy that they are completely unintelligible to the outsider. Just study the faces
in the public gallery as the Commons collapse in knee-slapping, rib-tickling, aisle-rolling
mirth. Nine out of ten of them will be completely baffled; the tenth will be laughing
politely because he always laughs at other people's jokes. Not one in a hundred will find
the thing funny.'[3] Fewer things are funnier than the grave and perplexed expression
on the face of an MP who fails to understand why his remarks or manner are causing
his colleagues to laugh—something, of course, that it is impossible for an outsider to
glean from a verbatim report of the proceedings.

Indeed, parliamentary humour tends to be a deflating humour. In 1792, during the
French Revolution, an order to buy three thousand daggers from a Birmingham armourer
came to the attention of Edmund Burke, who borrowed the sample dagger from the
Secretary of State. During a speech in the House he hurled the dagger to the floor and
exclaimed, 'Let us keep French principles from our heads, and French daggers from our

hearts!' This melodramatic gesture elicited laughter and caused Sheridan to whisper to a neighbour, 'The gentleman has brought us the knife, but where is the fork?'[4] Earl Winterton remembers a quip that humbled Lloyd George, who had been associated with the Marconi shares scandal as well as the selling of honours: 'L.G. was aggressive and provocative; he got a nasty retort from "Wedgy" [Mr Wedgwood Benn, Secretary of State for India], whom he described as "Moses dancing before the Ark"; the latter immediately sprang to his feet and said "I have never worshipped the golden calf!" The House roared with laughter for several minutes . . .'[5]

The receptiveness of the House to certain types of humour varies according to the time of day and the nature of the occasion. Lord Broughton recalls how during a debate on a grave incident an MP, a senior military man, told the House how his cousin had been shot through the jaw at the Battle of Busaço (in the Peninsular War) and had 'borne "the pain of extracting the bullet without a groan, though it was as bad as pulling out a tooth" . . . The bathos caused a loud laugh. The House catches anything ludicrous in the midst of the deepest distress.'[6] During one all-night sitting a bald MP complained in a speech that the helmets worn by the yeomanry were unhealthy. He was followed by Dr Tanner, the Home Ruler, who sat behind him and elaborated upon this subject, frequently indicating the bald pate beneath him. As Spencer Leigh Hughes pointed out, 'a performance of this sort may be a huge success at four in the morning, but it would be quite a failure at four in the afternoon'.[7]

Some comic incidents are appreciated only by an individual and have only become known after the event. Speaker Manners Sutton said that the only time he had ever laughed while in the Chair was when, during a debate which had featured acrimonious in-fighting among the Opposition, a large rat had walked from the Opposition to the Treasury benches in apparent disgust.[8] Feargus O'Connor, the Chartist MP, was engaged in a dispute in the dining-room of the House with The O'Gorman Mahon as to whether a beetroot on the table before them was actually a mangelwurzel. O'Connor dashed into the House and demanded a ruling from the Speaker, who said it was not part of his duties. The following night the Speaker found himself trapped in the Chamber by a loquacious speaker at the time when he normally went for his chop and claret in a room behind the Chair. When he was finally able to extricate himself from the debate, he discovered that someone else had consumed his meal. O'Connor was the culprit. Soon afterwards, his behaviour became even more peculiar and he was committed to a private asylum.[9]

Parliamentary humour also crosses the party political divide. A witty performer will attract the admiration of most MPs just as an unintentionally comical character will provoke their laughter. 'Any member who can relieve by his wit and humour the seriousness and monotony of debate is certain of a full House,' observed the reporter Michael MacDonagh;[10] while John Burns wrote of 'the shout of laughter which goes up at some comical incident which wells party feeling into a sense of common human humour'.[11]

Yet professional jokesmiths are not necessarily adept when it comes to parliamentary humour. Sir Henry Morris-Jones observed that 'funny men do not do well in Parliament. A. P. Herbert was an exception in his exhibition of this trait. He had other over-riding qualities and he was sparing in his use of humour.'[12]

Henry Martin

Henry Martin (1602–80) was a Member of the Short and Long Parliaments and a convinced anti-Royalist whom Charles I wanted to have tried for high treason. During the Civil War he gave £1,200 to the Parliamentary cause and was made Parliamentary Governor of Reading. He was one of the King's judges and it was said that when Cromwell signed Charles I's death warrant he laughingly wiped the ink from his pen across Martin's face. He came close to forfeiting his life when he attacked those MPs who had pledged their support for Richard Cromwell when he briefly succeeded his father as Protector in 1659. After the Restoration in 1660, Martin surrendered himself to the authorities and again came close to being executed along with other Regicides. Lord Falkland persuaded the House that they would be making a sacrifice of a 'rotten old rascal' if they bothered to execute him. Instead, he was imprisoned for the remaining twenty years of his life.

John Aubrey (1626–97) was the son of a Wiltshire squire who was diverted from a career at the bar by the Civil War and the need to manage his family estates. He was a keen antiquarian and his *Brief Lives* of contemporaries was never intended for publication in its entirety. (The papers were deposited in the Ashmolean Museum by the author in 1693.)

John Aubrey, *Brief Lives* [1669–96] (1898)

He was a great and faithful lover of his country, and never got a farthing by the Parliament. He was of an incomparable wit for repartees; not at all covetous; humble, not at all arrogant, as most of them were; a great cultor of Justice, and did always in the House take the part of the oppressed.

His speeches in the House were not long, but wondrous poignant, pertinent, and witty. He was exceedingly happy in apt instances. He alone has sometimes turned the whole House. Making an invective speech one time against old Sir Henry Vane; when he had done with him, he said, But for young Sir Harry Vane; and so sat him down. Several cried out, What have you got to say to young Sir Harry? He rises up: Why! if young Sir Harry lives to be old, he will be old Sir Harry! and so sat down, and set the House a-laughing, as he oftentimes did. Oliver Cromwell once in the House called him, jestingly and scoffingly, Sir Harry Martin. H.M. rises and bows; I thank your *Majesty*. I always thought when you were a King I should be knighted. A godly member made a Motion to have all profane and unsanctified persons expelled the Houses. H.M. stood up and moved that all Fools might be put out likewise, and then there would be a thin House. He was wont to sleep much in the House (at least dog-sleep). Alderman Atkins made a Motion that such scandalous members as slept, and minded not the business of the House, should be put out. H.M. starts up: Mr Speaker, a motion has been to turn out the Nodders, I desire the Noddees may also be turned out.

❖

Lord North

Frederick North (1732–92), styled Lord North from 1752, was the eldest son of the 1st Earl of Guilford, and was educated at Eton; at Trinity College, Oxford; and on Grand Tour. He was MP for Banbury from 1754 to 1790, first elected as a supporter of the Duke of Newcastle, and he rose to become Prime Minister, from 1770 to 1782, presiding over the King's disastrous policy towards the American Colonies. Always George III's favourite minister, he returned to office in coalition with Fox, though without the King's approval. The coalition soon fell and Lord North remained in the Commons in opposition to Pitt until 1790, though he rarely attended owing to blindness. He inherited his father's seat in the Lords and from 1773 until his death he was Chancellor of Oxford University.

Charles Greville, Diary, September 7, 1834

Tommy Townshend, a violent, foolish fellow, who was always talking strong language, said in some debate, 'Nothing will satisfy me but to have the noble Lord [North]'s head; I will have his head.' Lord North said, 'The honourable gentleman says he will have my head. I bear him no malice in return, for though the honourable gentleman says he will have my head, I can assure him I would on no account have his.'

George Henry Jennings, *An Anecdotal History of the British Parliament from the Earliest Periods to the Present Time* (1880)

Once, when speaking in the House, Lord North was interrupted by the barking of a dog which had crept in. He turned, and archly said, 'Mr Speaker, I am interrupted by a new member.' The dog was driven out, but got in again, and recommenced, when Lord North, in his dry way, added, 'Spoke once.'

Sylvester Douglas (Lord Glenbervie), Journal, July 16, 1801
[an anecdote related to Douglas by a Mr Williams]

Early in his administration George Grenville on the Opposition Bench was then speaking against the state of the public finances, and Lord North had fallen asleep, but towards what Robinson or Sir G—— A—— supposed the end of the speech, they awakened him just as Grenville was saying, 'I shall draw the attention of the House to the revenues and expenditure of the country in 1689.' Upon which Lord North said to the person who had jogged him, 'Zounds, you have wakened me near one hundred years too soon.'

Abraham Hayward, *Biographical and Critical Essays* (1874)

The noble lord's figure was certainly ill-fitted for oratorical effect; but by dint of tact, temper, and wit, he converted even his personal disadvantages into means of persuasion or conciliation. 'One member,' he once said, 'who spoke of me, called me "that thing called a minister". To be sure,' he said, patting his large form. 'I am a thing; the member, therefore, when he called me a "thing", said what was true; and I could not be angry with him. But when he added "that thing called a minister", he called me that thing which of all things he himself most wished to be, and therefore I took it as a compliment.'

With equal adroitness Lord North turned his incurable sleepiness to account.

When a fiery declaimer, after calling for his head, denounced him for sleeping, he complained how cruel it was to be denied a solace which other criminals so often enjoyed—that of having a night's rest before their execution. And when a dull prosy speaker made a similar charge, he retorted that it was somewhat unjust in the gentleman to blame him for taking the remedy which he himself had been so considerate as to administer. Alderman Sawbridge having accompanied the presentation of a petition from Billingsgate with an invective of more than ordinary coarseness, Lord North began his reply in the following words: 'I cannot deny that the hon. alderman speaks not only the sentiments but the very language of his constituents.'

❖

Unwigging Members

J. S. Harford, *Recollections of William Wilberforce* (1864)

[Elwes] wore a wig; it looked as if it might have been picked off a hedge or a scare-crow. At that time we used to wear dress swords occasionally at the House; for instance, if going to the opera. One day, Bankes, whose carriage is stiff and lofty, had on his sword, and was seated next to Elwes, who leant his head forward just as Bankes was rising up to leave his place, when the hilt of his sword came in contact with Elwes' wig, which it whisked off and bore away. The House was instantly in a roar of laughter. I never shall forget the scene. There was old Elwes, without his wig, darting forward to reclaim it; and Bankes marching on quite unconscious of the sword-knot which he wore, and wondering what the laugh was about.

❖

The impudence of John Wilkes

John Wilkes (1725–97) was the son of a wealthy London malt distiller. He was educated at Lincoln's Inn and at Leyden University, and was Sheriff of Buckinghamshire, 1754–5. He was MP for Aylesbury from 1757 to 1764, during which time he founded the *North Briton*, a radical newspaper. He was prosecuted for a libel of the King, but managed to turn this around and win damages from the ministers concerned for illegal arrest. However, in 1764 he was expelled from the House for allegedly writing a blasphemous and licentious poem. After a period of exile in Paris, he returned in 1768 and fought three successful elections for Middlesex, though he was each time barred from taking his seat. The following year he was elected an Alderman of London, and thereafter served as Sheriff of London, 1771–2; Lord Mayor, 1774–5; and City Chamberlain, 1779–97. He was eventually allowed to sit in the Commons, representing Middlesex from 1774 until 1790, when he retired rather than face the judgement of his constituents, with whom he had become unpopular for supporting Ministers. A supporter of the rebellious American colonists in earlier years, he was renowned for being cross-eyed and debauched, though infinitely good-humoured. 'To laugh and riot and scatter firebrands with him was liberty,' wrote Horace Walpole.[13]

George Pellew, *The Life of the Rt Hon. Henry Addington, First Lord Sidmouth*
(1847)

On the 28th of May, in this year [1790], it became the Speaker's duty publicly
to reprimand Major Scott, a member of parliament, for having published a
statement relating to the trial of Mr Hastings, which was considered disrespectful
to the House. Before the public business commenced, the Speaker had observed
Mr Wilkes conferring with Major Scott; and he subsequently ascertained from
a friend, who happened to be within hearing, that the subject of their conversation was as follows:—*Wilkes.* 'I give you joy. I am glad to see you in full dress.
It is an occasion on which a man should appear to the best advantage.' *Scott.*
'Joy! what do you mean? Why I am here to be reprimanded.' *Wilkes.* 'Exactly;
and therefore I congratulate you. When the Speaker has finished, abuse them
all confoundedly, for which you will be sent either to Newgate or the Tower,
and then you may be member for Middlesex or Westminster, whichever you
please.' . . .

At some other time Mr Wilkes came up to the Speaker in the chair, and
told him that he had a petition to present the House from a set of the greatest
scoundrels and miscreants upon earth: when called upon, however, shortly
afterwards, to present it, he said, with the gravest possible face, 'Sir, I hold in
my hand a petition from a most intelligent, independent, and enlightened body
of men.' On another occasion when there was much confusion in the House,
the Speaker observing that his call of 'Order, order!' was not attended to,
especially by Mr Wilkes, repeated the expression, coupling it with that gentleman's name; upon which Mr Wilkes said very deliberately, ' "Order! Mr Wilkes"?
That is a singular association. Wilkes and treason, and Wilkes and rebellion,
have often been coupled together; but Wilkes and order never.'

The lace ruffles

John Timbs, *A Century of Anecdote from 1760 to 1860* (1864)

Upon the change of Ministry in 1782, great was the change in the aspect of
the House of Commons. The Treasury Bench and places behind it were now
occupied by the new Ministry, emerged from their obscure lodgings, or from
Brookes's, having thrown off their blue and buff uniforms, and being now in
court-dresses, decorated with swords, lace, and hair-powder. Some degree of
ridicule attached to this extraordinary metamorphosis. It happened that just
then Lord Nugent's house in Great George-street had been broken open, and
robbed of a variety of articles; among others, of a number of pairs of laced
ruffles. He caused the particulars of the stolen articles to be advertised in the
newspapers, where they were minutely specified. Coming down to the House
of Commons, a gentleman, who accidentally sat next to him, asked his Lordship

if he had yet discovered any of the articles recently lost. 'I can't say that I have,' answered he, 'but I shrewdly suspect that I have seen some of my lace ruffles on the hands of the gentlemen who now occupy the Treasury Bench.' This reply, the effect of which was infinitely increased by the presence of Fox and Burke, occasioned much laughter.

❖

Saying Jack Robinson

John Robinson (1727–1802) was the son of a Westmorland merchant and became a barrister. He was MP for Westmorland from 1764 to 1774 and for Harwich from 1774 to 1802. He became a Secretary in the Treasury in 1770 and from this date until 1782 was Lord North's faithful agent and fixer. He subsequently declined to follow North into coalition and later became a supporter of Pitt. From 1786 to 1802 he was Surveyor of Woods and Forests.

John Timbs, A *Century of Anecdote from 1760 to 1860* (1864)

During the debate on the India Bill, at which period John Robinson was secretary to the Treasury, Sheridan, one evening when Fox's majorities were decreasing, said, 'Mr Speaker, this is not at all to be wondered at, when a member is employed to corrupt every body in order to obtain votes.' Upon this there was a great outcry made by almost every body in the House. 'Who is it? Name him! name him!' 'Sir,' said Sheridan to the Speaker, 'I shall not name the person. It is unpleasant and invidious to do so, and therefore I shall not name him. But don't suppose, Sir, that I abstain because there is any difficulty in naming him; I could do that, Sir, *as soon as you could say Jack Robinson.*'

❖

Lord Mahon

Charles Stanhope (1753–1816), styled Lord Mahon from 1763 (he became 3rd Earl of Stanhope in 1786), was educated at Eton and at Geneva, where he studied science. He served as a major of dragoons in the Swiss army and married first a daughter of the Earl of Chatham, and later a daughter of another prominent MP, Henry Grenville. An eccentric radical, he was MP for Chipping Wycombe from 1780 to 1786, opposing Lord North's administration and supporting Pitt until they differed over the French Revolution. During his six years in the Commons he spoke no fewer than ninety times. He was also a successful inventor.

Sir Nathaniel Wraxall, Bt., *Posthumous Memoirs of My Own Time* (1836)

This eccentric nobleman, who, as Earl Stanhope, has acted a conspicuous as well as a very useful part in the discussions of the House of Peers during a long period of time, and whose recent death may, in my opinion, be considered as a public misfortune, was brought up principally by his father at Geneva. He had there imbibed very strong republican, or rather levelling principles, ill adapted to a man whose high birth and prospects should naturally have inspired him with sentiments more favourable to a monarchy. If he had flourished a century and a half earlier, under Charles I instead of under George III, he would unquestionably have rivalled Ludlow or Algernon Sydney in their attachment to a commonwealth. His person was tall and thin, his countenance expressive of ardour and impetuosity, as were all his movements. Over his whole figure, and even his dress, an air of puritanism reminded the beholder of the sectaries under Cromwell, rather than a young man of quality in an age of refinement and elegance. He possessed stentorian lungs and a powerful voice, always accompanied with violent gesticulation. The 'Rolliad' describes him as— 'Mahon, outroaring torrents in their course.' So strongly did he always enforce his arguments by his gestures, as to become indeed sometimes a troublesome neighbour when greatly animated by his subject. He commonly spoke from the row behind the Treasury bench. In the course of one of his harangues, respecting a measure that he himself had suggested, the object of which was the suppression of smuggling, impelled by the warmth of his feelings, just as he was commending his friend and relation the First Minister for 'his endeavours to knock smuggling on the head at one blow', he actually dealt Mr Pitt who sat below him a smart stroke on the head.[14] This manual application of his metaphor convulsed the House with laughter, and not a little surprised the Chancellor of the Exchequer; but it seemed neither to disconcert nor to arrest the impetuosity of Lord Mahon's eloquence. Since the ludicrous circumstance of Lord North's taking off Welbore Ellis's wig on the chafe of his scabbard, no scene more comic had been acted within the walls of the House of Commons. The same satirical production which I before cited, when alluding to Lord Mahon, says—

> 'This Quixote of the nation
> Beats his own windmills in gesticulation.
> To strike, not please, his utmost force he bends,
> And all his sense is at his fingers' ends.'

An apologetic Orangeman

Frederick Shaw (1799–1876) was called to the Irish bar in 1822. He was a Conservative MP for Dublin in 1830 and for Dublin University from 1832 until 1848, when he retired. He opposed agricultural protection in 1846.

T. B. Macaulay, Letter to his sisters Hannah and Margaret,
August 16, 1832

I did not reach home till four this morning, after a most fatiguing and yet rather amusing night. What passed will not find its way into the papers, as the gallery was locked during most of the time. So I will tell you the story.

There is a bill before the House prohibiting those processions of Orangemen which have excited a good deal of irritation in Ireland. This bill was committed yesterday night. Shaw, the Recorder of Dublin, an honest man enough, but a bitter Protestant fanatic, complained that it should be brought forward so late in the Session. Several of his friends, he said, had left London believing that the measure had been abandoned. It appeared, however, that Stanley and Lord Althorp had given fair notice of their intention; so that, if the absent members had been mistaken, the fault was their own; and the House was for going on. Shaw said warmly that he would resort to all the means of delay in his power, and moved that the chairman should leave the chair. The motion was negatived by forty votes to two. Then the first clause was read. Shaw divided the House again on that clause. He was beaten by the same majority. He moved again that the chairman should leave the chair. He was beaten again. He divided on the second clause. He was beaten again. He then said that he was sensible that he was doing very wrong; that his conduct was unhandsome and vexatious; that he heartily begged our pardons; but that he had said that he would delay the bill as far as the forms of the House would permit; and that he must keep his word. Now came a discussion by which Nancy, if she had been in the ventilator, might have been greatly edified, touching the nature of vows; whether a man's promise given to himself,—a promise from which nobody could reap any advantage, and which everybody wished him to violate,— constituted an obligation. Jeptha's daughter was a case in point, and was cited by somebody sitting near me. Peregrine Courtenay on one side of the House, and Lord Palmerston on the other, attempted to enlighten the poor Orangeman on the question of casuistry. They might as well have preached to any madman out of St Luke's. 'I feel,' said the silly creature, 'that I am doing wrong, and acting very unjustifiably. If gentlemen will forgive me, I will never do so again. But I must keep my word.' We roared with laughter every time he repeated his apologies. The orders of the House do not enable any person absolutely to stop the progress of a bill in Committee, but they enable him to delay it grievously. We divided seventeen times, and between every division this vexatious Irishman made us a speech of apologies and self-condemnation. Of the two who had supported him at the beginning of his freak one soon sneaked away. The other, Sibthorpe, stayed to the last, not expressing remorse like Shaw, but glorying in the unaccommodating temper he showed and in the delay which he produced. At last the bill went through. Then Shaw rose; congratulated himself that his vow was accomplished; said that the only atonement he could make for conduct so unjustifiable was to vow that he would never make such a vow again; promised to let the bill go through its future stages without any more divisions; and contented himself with suggesting one or two alterations in details. 'I hint at these amendments,' he said. 'If the Secretary for Ireland approves of them, I hope he will not refrain from introducing them because they are brought forward by me. I am sensible that I have forfeited all claim to the favour of the House. I will not divide on any future stage of the bill.' We were all heartily pleased with these events: for the truth was that the seventeen divisions occupied less time than a real hard debate would have done, and were infinitely more amusing. The oddest part of the business is that Shaw's frank good-natured way of proceeding, absurd as it was, has made him popular. He was never so great a favourite with the most frivolous opposition. This is a curious trait of the House of Commons.

The missing amendment

Daniel Whittle Harvey (1786–1863) was a retired solicitor who had married an heiress and become the proprietor of the *True Sun* and *Weekly True Sun* newspapers. He was refused admittance to the bar on account of evidence against his character, but eventually obtained a verdict in his favour from a House of Commons committee in 1834. Meanwhile, he sat as Radical MP for Colchester from 1818 to 1834, and for Southwark from 1834 to 1840, when he was made Commissioner of the Metropolitan Police.

Thomas Spring-Rice (1790–1866) was MP for Limerick from 1820 to 1832 (his father-in-law was the Earl of Limerick), and for Cambridge from 1832 to 1839, when he was elevated to the peerage as Baron Monteagle. He had served as an Under-Secretary of State in the short-lived Canning Administration, and was a Secretary of the Treasury in 1830. He was briefly Secretary of State for the Colonies, and from 1835 to 1839 he was Chancellor of the Exchequer.

James Grant, *Random Recollections of the Lords and Commons* (1838)

The occasion was that of the Chancellor of the Exchequer bringing the question of the Civil List under the consideration of the House. It will be remembered, that Mr Daniel Whittle Harvey gave previous notice of his intention to propose an amendment to the motion of the right honourable gentleman. As is usual on such occasions, as a matter of courtesy, Mr Harvey, before commencing his speech, handed to Mr Spring Rice the amendment he meant to propose; but instead of giving the right honourable gentleman a copy of the amendment in question, Mr Harvey handed him the original itself, and this, too, without providing himself with a copy.

There can be no doubt Mr Harvey's intention was to have asked his amendment back from Mr Spring Rice before beginning his own speech; but having forgotten to do this, and also forgetting for the moment that the Chancellor of the Exchequer had his amendment in his possession, Mr Harvey concluded an able and luminous speech by observing, with his usual volubility, that he now begged 'leave to propose the following amendment'. Mr Harvey immediately leaned down to 'pick up' his 'following amendment' from among a quantity of papers which were lying on his seat; but no 'following amendment' was to be found.

It was then that the fact flashed across his mind, that he had handed it to the Chancellor of the Exchequer, and that the latter gentleman had not had the politeness to return it. 'My amendment,' exclaimed Mr Harvey, with some tartness of manner, 'is in the custody of the Chancellor of the Exchequer. Be pleased to hand it over to me.' As the honourable gentleman uttered the last sentence, he looked anxiously towards Mr Spring Rice, who was five or six yards from him, at the same time stretching out his hand to receive the document, when it should be returned to him, through the means of some of the intervening honourable gentlemen. Mr Spring Rice looked amazed and confounded when the honourable member for Southwark so pointedly apostrophised him, as being the custodier of his amendment. To be sure, he said nothing in the first instance; but it was very easy to see that he was inwardly ejaculating, 'Me, your amendment!' The fact was, that he also had become oblivious of the circumstance of the document being in his possession.

However, in a few moments the conviction was brought home to his mind, that he was a defaulter in this respect; and forthwith he commenced a most vigorous search for the amendment; Mr Harvey all the while standing in his place, with his eyes as steadily fixed on the Chancellor of the Exchequer as if he had been about to play the cannibal with him. Mr Spring Rice searched his pockets: the missing amendment was not there. He eagerly and hastily turned over a miniature mountain of documents, erected by his side, on the seat on which he sat: still there was no appearance of the lost amendment. He then rose up, and advancing to the table, rummaged for some time among a heap of papers there: the search was still in vain. He resumed his seat, and enquired of Lord Morpeth, who was sitting beside him, whether he knew anything of the mysterious disappearance of Mr Harvey's amendment. Lord Morpeth significantly shook his head, being just as ignorant on the matter as the Chancellor of the Exchequer himself.

Lord Morpeth, however, kindly consented to assist in the search for the missing amendment; and great was the activity he displayed in turning and returning over, after Mr Spring Rice, the various documents that lay on the seat and on the table.

Long before this time, Mr Harvey, tired of holding out his hand to receive that which was not likely to be forthcoming in 'a hurry', had drawn it in, and, as if determined to take the thing as coolly as possible, folded his arms on his breasts, and stood in that attitude with all the seeming resignation of a philosopher who patiently submits to a calamity which it is not in his power to avert. In the mean time, however, though thus motionless in one sense, he was not so in another. His tongue was occasionally set agoing.

He remarked on one occasion, with that bitter sarcasm of manner which is peculiar to himself, that this was the first document of his which had ever been taken so much care of by a cabinet minister. Roars of laughter, to the manifest mortification of Mr Spring Rice, followed from both sides of the house. On another occasion, he observed that he was quite delighted to see that his amendment was so safe in the keeping of the Chancellor of the Exchequer as that no one could have any chance of abstracting it. All this time Mr Spring Rice and Lord Morpeth were most exemplary, as regarded the eagerness with which they prosecuted their search for the lost document. It is worthy of remark, that no one joined with them; but all, even the liberal members, seemed to enjoy the sport.

To the Conservatives, the affair was a rare piece of amusement. I observed some of them laughing heartily who were never seen to laugh within the walls of the house before, and in whose existence, even out of doors, a hearty laugh might be said to be quite an era. Mr Spring Rice, after 'turning about and wheeling about', in search of an amendment, with an agility worthy of his namesake of Jim Crow notoriety, at length bethought himself of unlocking a small tin box, in which he keeps the more valuable of his papers; when, to his infinite joy, after rummaging for a few seconds among its contents, he discovered the missing amendment. He pounced upon it just as a Bow-street officer would on some offender, for whom he had been on a vexatious search, when alighting on him; and dragging the innocent amendment out of its place of concealment, held it up in his hand to the gaze of the House, exclaiming, as loud as his lungs would permit, and with an air of triumph, 'Here it is! here it is!'

'I'm happy to see that the right honourable gentleman prizes it so highly,' said Mr Harvey, in the sarcastic way to which I have alluded, 'as to place it among his most valuable papers, and to lock it up in his box.' Peals of laughter followed, and during their continuance the amendment was handed over, through the assistance of two or three intermediate members, to the honourable gentleman whose property it was; who, as soon it had reached him, read it amidst renewed peals of laughter. The bursts of laughter which were thus resounding through the house, was much increased by the circumstance of Colonel Sibthorp, who sat directly opposite to Mr Spring Rice, rising with all his imperturbable gravity, and with his huge mustachios looking unusually large, to second the amendment. It certainly was a novelty in the proceedings of the House of Commons to witness the most ultra Tory, perhaps, in the house, rising to second an amendment on a vital question, moved by one of the greatest Radicals.

The shouts of laughter which followed the circumstance, had their origin in the impression that the gallant mustachioed Colonel had seconded the amendment in a mistake; but when it was understood that there was no mistake in the matter, and that the gallant gentleman was perfectly aware of what he was about, the Liberal members looked unutterable things at one another. It was at last understood that the Tories were, from factious motives, about to join the extreme section of the Reformers on that particular occasion, not doubting that in the event of a division ministers would be in a minority, and consequently be compelled to resign office. The circumstance, however, of the Chancellor of the Exchequer giving Mr Harvey certain specific pledges in reference to the treatment of the Pension List, induced the latter gentleman to withdraw his amendment, which of course prevented any division taking place.

The Speaker at a loss

John Evelyn Denison (1800–73) was educated at Eton and at Christ Church, Oxford. He sat, as a Whig and later as a Liberal, for various seats from 1823 until he was created Viscount Ossington in 1872, being out of the House for only a few years in the 1830s. He was first elected Speaker in 1857 and was three times re-elected.

Sir William Fraser, *Disraeli and his Day* (1891)

Speaker Denison was not conspicuous for his readiness of resource in dealing with the very complicated rules and practice of the House of Commons. A difficult question on Order arose. Speaker Denison, as was his wont, touched the Senior Clerk, Sir Thomas Erskine May. Sir Thomas, rising, was asked by the Speaker what on earth he recommended him to do. The legend tells that Sir Thomas whispered, 'I recommend you, Sir, to be very cautious': then vanished through the door at the back of the Chair.

George Dempster MP

George Dempster (1732–1818) was the son of a Dundee merchant and was educated at St Andrews, at Edinburgh University, and at the Royal Academy, Brussels. He became a Scots advocate and founded the first bank in Dundee. He sat as an independent Whig MP for Perth Burghs, 1761–8 and 1769–90. A director of the East India Company, he opposed continental wars and was hostile to Lord North.

Mark Boyd, *Reminiscences of Fifty Years* (1871)

I have heard my father say that when he was a young man in London he was in the habit of meeting in society Mr Dempster, member for the Burghs of Forfar, Perth, Dundee, Cupar, and the learned city of St Andrews, who had entered the House of Commons in 1762, two years after the accession of George III, and did not retire from Parliament until 1790. He was a man much respected in and out of Parliament; and as little more than half a century had elapsed when he became an MP since the union of Scotland with England, and less than a quarter of a century since the battle of Culloden and the executions on Tower Hill, following the rebellion of 1745, he was peculiarly sensitive and tenacious in respect to the maintenance and vindication of Scottish rights: and his national susceptibilities were well known on both sides of the House.

One evening an English member, in his peroration, in some humorous remarks respecting Scotland, had given sad offence to Mr Dempster, who was no exception to Sydney Smith's charge against Scotchmen of not understanding a joke, for the moment he concluded, up rose the aggrieved member, and in a loud voice addressed the Speaker, being resolved that his pithy rejoinder should be heard distinctly throughout St Stephen's: 'Sir, I beg to inform the honourable member, in reply to those most illiberal remarks with which he has concluded his speech, that I am proud of having been born a Scotchman and brought up a Presbyterian,' and down he sat; when his honourable opponent rose and said, 'Mr Speaker—All I have to say is that I consider the honourable member very thankful for extremely small mercies.'

The confusion of Colonel Wilson, the Member for the Ceety of York

Colonel James Wilson was a magistrate and Deputy-Lieutenant of Yorkshire, and a lieutenant-colonel in the Army. Earlier in his life he had been a member of the Council of the Island of St Vincent in the West Indies. He served as a Tory MP for the City of York from 1826 to 1830.

Mark Boyd, *Reminiscences of Fifty Years* (1871)

My friend, the late Mr Simon Cock, was a man of high mental capacity, so much so, in fact, as to have attracted when a youth the notice of William Pitt. In after years, from his great commercial and financial abilities, he was on different occasions employed by the Government of the day in negotiating with foreign powers on commercial matters, such as the removal and modification of restrictive duties, and had his career been in Parliament and his party been in power, he must have attained to the Chancellorship of the Exchequer or the Presidency of the Board of Trade.

He was a man of benign and intellectual aspect, reminding me both in height and appearance of a former prime minister, Earl Grey. In latter years he was a sad martyr to asthma, but when relieved for a time of his sufferings was one of the most delightful and cheerful companions at the head of his own table or at the table of a friend. I remember a very laughable incident, in which Mr Cock was the chief actor and exponent.

We had met at the table of a most hospitable countryman of mine in Portland Place, where there was a fairly balanced proportion of the English, Irish, and Scotch element, represented respectively by Sir John Lowther, the late Lord Keane, and Colin Campbell (afterwards Lord Clyde). One of the party, a Scotchman, and acknowledged on all sides to be one of the strangest specimens of the Caledonian to be met with, had gone out to the West Indies from the village of Moffat some forty years previously, and evidently long before he had finished his education. Fortune, however, had favoured him, as he was enabled to return to England with a handsome fortune a little over middle life, and the first investment he made of a portion of it was in the purchase of a castle and estate in Yorkshire, becoming very shortly afterwards one of the representatives for York in Parliament. Finding that I was from Scotland, he communicated to me the fact that he also was from that part of the world, and imparted to me the high senatorial position he held, as well as his former military rank, a colonel of West India militia. He then touched upon the important annual motion approaching in Parliament for the repeal of the Corn Laws, on which subject he considered it incumbent that he should lay his opinions, through the medium of the House of Commons, before the country. 'You must keep in mind the position I hold, as one of the two members for the second *ceety* in England. It is absolutely *requeered o'* me that I should speak; *ma* constituents will expect it, and I would not like to disappoint them. I should further tell you, Mr Boyd, that I am an auld Tory, what they *ca noo* a Conservative, and that the Harewoods, and in fact *a'* the Lascelles family, and the Lowthers there—Sir John Lowther was sitting opposite—will look *oot* for me speaking on the motion; but I should just tell you that I am *vera* far *frae* being *weel* up on the subject.' 'Then, colonel, as you have made up your mind to join in the debate, the very ablest man you could consult on so important a matter is our friend there, Mr Simon Cock.' 'That's a *vera* good suggestion, Mr Boyd.' Although it was our first time of meeting each other, he was by no means reticent on the important political attitude he was about to assume in the *Hoose*, therefore, so soon after dinner as the opportunity offered, he at my suggestion addressed Mr Cock, or rather Mr *Koke*, the name he gave him throughout the evening. 'Mr *Koke*, you are aware that the annual motion for the repeal *o'* the Corn Laws, which is *a' nonsense*, is coming on, and I think as I am member for the second *ceety* in the kingdom, and never yet having *spokken* in the *Hoose*, I must do so *noo*. But, Mr *Koke*, I should tell you that I *hae* never *thocht ower* (over) the subject, and therefore should feel greatly *obleeged* to you if you would kindly write *oot* a bit *o'* a speech for me.' All eyes were directed to Mr Cock, whose gravity and dry humour were now to be tested. 'Well, colonel, you must first inform me what your precise views are.' 'Noo, Mr *Koke*, there's exactly where you might assist me, for I tell you candidly, I ken (know) far *mair aboot* West India sugar than English corn.' 'Then am I to understand that you will oppose Mr Villier's views on corn law repeal?' 'Oh, certainly, and I should like to speak early in the debate.' This we all highly approved of. 'Noo, Mr *Koke*, understand me, when I tell you that I am for the *mainteenance o'* the Corn Laws, I *tak'* the same view with Lord Harewood, and *a'* the Lascelles clique, and with *ma frien'* there, Sir John Lowther.' 'Well, colonel, you have made it quite clear what I have to do for you, but as you hold the prominent position of member of Parliament for the ancient and historical city of

York—' 'Quite true, Mr *Koke.*' 'Would you not like to bring forward, which you could introduce in the course of your argument, a scale of protective duties of your own—something different from the present scale—an original idea and suggestion coming from yourself?' 'That's excellent, Mr *Koke*, it would be the *vera makin' o'* me as a politician, and there's no man that would be better pleased than *ma frien'*, Sir John Lowther, for there's *nae* jealousy between us.' 'Colonel, I shall be delighted.' It may easily be conceived the amusement all this afforded, with the accompaniment of Mr Cock's humorous remarks. '*Noo*, Mr *Koke*, ye *maun mak* (must make) the *hale o'* the speech for me, and I promise you to get *mysel' weel* up *in't.*'

Accordingly Mr Cock a day or two afterwards fulfilled his promise *verbatim et literatim*, for he wrote out in plain and distinct language a most excellent speech for the honourable member for the *ceety o' York* or for any other honourable member advocating non-repeal principles. Unfortunately for the colonel, the speech was written on half sheets of paper on one side only, to which he had not been accustomed. But the great misfortune to which he was exposed was an omission on Mr Cock's part in not numbering his leaves. Hence the catastrophe that ensued, otherwise the colonel might have gone down to posterity as famous as 'Single-speech Hamilton'.[15] The night of debate arrived, but I had been unsuccessful in getting my name on the Speaker's list, or an admission to the gallery. I was told that a fair muster of the gallant colonel's political admirers were in their places as he was to speak early, who were much amused to witness the assiduity with which he was perusing his lesson and turning over the half dozen sheets of manuscript. That he had got the speech by heart *in cumulo* there is no reason to doubt, as he delivered the first page of the *exordium* with great fluency, and in a vernacular so pure as to bring back to the House of Commons, in the recollection of one or two members who still survived, the days of Pitt's famous minister, Dundas. Had the leaves of his brief only been paged, so excellent was the colonel's memory that those who heard him, and were in the secret, felt convinced that although 'they came to laugh they would have stayed to praise'; but as he delivered the contents of page 4 where 2 should have come, and 5 instead of 3, etc., he produced a medley such as seldom had been served up in the House of Commons.

Sir Robert Peel

Abraham Hayward, *Biographical and Critical Essays* (1874)

Peel shone where such a man would be least expected to shine, in humour. He also excelled in quiet sarcasm. In the debate on commercial distress (Dec. 3, 1847), Alderman Reynolds, one of the members for Dublin, had asked, 'Did not everybody know that the profit and advantage of banking consisted very much in trading on your credit in contradistinction to your capital?' In the course of the masterly reply with which Peel closed the debate he said: 'I have the greatest respect for bankers in general, and Irish bankers in particular, and among Irish bankers I well know the position enjoyed by the honourable gentleman. Now, with all the respect to which he is entitled, and with all suavity and courtesy, I will tell him that, in his banking capacity, I would rather have his capital than his credit.' . . .

In 1848 Feargus O'Connor was charged in the House with being a Republican. He denied it, and said he did not care whether the Queen or the Devil was on the throne. Peel replied: 'When the honourable gentleman sees the sovereign of his choice on the throne of these realms, I hope he'll enjoy, and I'm sure he'll deserve, the confidence of the Crown.' . . .

Sheil had learnt and forgotten the exordium of a speech which began with the word 'necessity'. This word he had repeated three times, when Sir R. Peel broke in—'is not *always* the mother of invention'.

O'Connell deals with an Anti-Papist

Michael MacDonagh, *Irish Life and Character* (1898)

A certain member, named Thomas Massey, who had his eye always on the Pope, brought in a Bill to obliterate the Popish affix 'mas' or 'mass', and substitute the good old Saxon word 'tide' in all such instances as Christmas and Michaelmas, so that they should read 'Christ-tide and Michael-tide', respectively. O'Connell listened attentively to all the member had to advance in favour of his scheme, and then got up and said, 'Since the honourable gentleman is so anxious to wipe out the obnoxious "mass" from the English vocabulary, why does he not make a commencement by Saxonising his own name? In that case he would be known as Thotide Tidey.' The Bill was fairly laughed out of the House.

Disraeli puts down another Anti-Papist

Justin McCarthy, *Reminiscences* (1899)

One night, when the Conservatives were in office, Whalley put a question to Disraeli, demanding to know whether the Government had received any recent information with regard to certain machinations of the Jesuits against the security of the Established Church in England, and whether the Government were taking any steps to resist these insidious enterprises. Disraeli arose and leaning on the table in front of him, began, with a manner of portentous gravity and a countenance of almost funereal gloom, to give his answer. 'Her Majesty's Ministers,' he said, 'had not been informed of any absolutely new machinations of the Jesuits, but they would continue to watch, as they had hitherto watched, for any indication of such insidious enterprises. One of the favourite machinations of the Jesuits,' he went on to say, with deepening solemnity, 'had always been understood to be a plan for sending into this country disguised emissaries of their own, who, by expressing extravagant and ridiculous alarm about Jesuit plots, might bring public derision on the efforts of the genuine supporters of the State Church. He would not venture to say whether the Honourable Member had knowledge of any such plans as that—'; but here a roar of laughter from the whole House rendered further explanation impossible, and Disraeli composedly resumed his seat.

The 'chaff' of Ralph Bernal Osborne

Ralph Bernal Osborne (1802–82) was the son of Ralph Bernal, a landowner of Jewish descent who sat in the House of Commons as a Whig from 1818 to 1852 and was chairman of Committees for a number of years. Ralph Bernal Osborne, the eldest son, was educated at Charterhouse and at Trinity College, Cambridge. He took a commission in the Army and stayed there until elected to Parliament in 1841. After the dissolution of that year he became the Liberal Member for Chipping Wycombe and a few years later married the daughter of an Irish baronet, Sir Thomas Osborne, and assumed her name, being known thereafter as Bernal Osborne. In 1847 he was elected as MP for Middlesex and from 1852 to 1858 served as Secretary of the Admiralty in the successive ministries of Aberdeen and Palmerston. From 1857 to 1859 he represented Dover and from 1859 until 1865 he sat for Liskeard, resigning two weeks before the dissolution of that latter year because his constituency had chosen another sitting Member to represent them. In 1866 he was elected in a close-run contest for Nottingham, though he lost the seat at the general election of 1868. The following year he fought Watford and lost, but the sitting Member was unseated on petition and Bernal Osborne was returned. His parliamentary career ended when he was defeated in 1874. Bernal Osborne was regarded as a great wit, who entertained audiences both in the House and on the hustings, but he was felt to be too much of a lightweight for high office. Disraeli once provoked the House to laughter by saying that Mr Bernal Osborne had sat for so many places that he forgot at that moment which of them he represented.

Sir William Fraser, *Disraeli and his Day* (1891)

Bernal Osborne, in a speech of some length, was summing up the demerits of Sir Robert Peel and his followers; among others, he mentioned Mr Goulburn; and artfully induced the House of Commons to believe that he intended to praise Sir Robert's Chancellor of the Exchequer. He said that while at various times Sir Robert Peel had been deserted by his friends, there was one who had adhered to him with chivalrous tenacity; looking at Mr Goulburn. The House cheered, with the sympathy which it always feels, or at any rate shows, to loyal political devotion. They did not know what was coming; nor, no doubt, did the hero of the moment, who looked so chivalrous as he could. Bernal Osborne then added these words, 'Of whatever changes the Right Honourable Baronet (Sir Robert Peel) showed himself capable; amidst all the vagaries of his life;

511

whenever the Right Honourable Baronet changed from one side of this House to the other, there,' pointing at Goulburn, 'was that miserable old tin kettle still fastened to his tail.'

Two distinguished Members of the Government, one Member for a County, the other for a very snug Borough, the property of Lord Egmont, seceded from the Tory Government; they gave their reasons, which were honest, for their secession. The latter addressed the House at great length on the subject of Reform in the abstract: and explained the cause of his leaving the high position which he had lately occupied. The House listened with an attention worthy of the gravity of the character of him who addressed it. A most elaborate and carefully prepared essay was given to us. No smile lighted the face of any Member: in fact the situation was serious in the extreme. Sitting opposite to the orator, not on a seat, but on the floor of the gangway, the path which divides the House of Commons in half laterally, sat Bernal Osborne, watching Mr W., and listening to his words with real, or affected, interest. His attitude was that of a jackdaw, or any bird with a long beak, who is compelled to hold his head sideways to obtain a clear view of his object. After an hour's description of the good and evil of Reform in the abstract, Mr W. uttered these words:

'Now, Mr Speaker, I approach another, and most important branch of this great subject. I shall have to use a term; frequent in the vernacular; familiar to the ears of all whom I am now addressing; but, when I do so, it will be in no mocking spirit; but with all the solemnity that such a great subject requires. Before I enter upon it, I will ask the House seriously to answer this question "How will you define the terms 'rotten' and 'pocket borough'?"'

Quick as lightning Bernal Osborne said distinctly 'Midhurst'. Mr W.'s own seat! The effect was an instant and deafening roar through the whole House.

In one of the first speeches that I heard of Bernal Osborne, George Hudson, the 'Railway King', of whom might be said, as of Cato, sometimes *'mero caluisse virtus'*, attracted his attention by some inarticulate sounds, expressive of doubts of the fact uttered by the orator: it was about six p.m.: turning upon Hudson, he said, 'I must beg the Member for Sunderland not to interrupt me: at this *early* period of the evening, he has no excuse for making a noise.' This of course did not diminish the wrath of Hudson; who sprang to his feet; and endeavoured to address the House. Bernal Osborne, however, continued: 'Sit down, pray! I accept your apology: say no more!'

On another occasion he was very neat: It was on the vote for the Royal Academy of Music; the House being in Committee. Bernal Osborne said, 'We heard in former years of the merits of the English Opera: Now, Sir, one of the most popular of English Operas has always been "Artaxerxes": In that Opera is a well-known song; it begins, "In Infancy our hopes and fears". Sir, this vote is in its infancy; and I propose that we put an end to its hopes and fears; and strangle it at once.'

❖

Lord Palmerston

Sir William Fraser, *Disraeli and his Day* (1891)

There was no comparison in matters of fence between Disraeli and other Members of the House. His sword was at least a foot longer than that of others: he very rarely laid himself open to a retort. On one occasion he did so: and so obviously that even Lord Palmerston could ripost with effect. Someone had mentioned an anomaly in a projected measure of the Government. Disraeli replied that in this country many things were anomalous: that the British Constitution was anomalous. He was standing next to Sir Edward Bulwer Lytton. 'For instance,' said he, 'the question may be asked, why is one man made a Minister because he can make a speech? Why is another man made a Minister because he has written a book?' Lord Palmerston in answer naturally said, after repeating these words, 'These are questions that, when I look opposite, I frequently ask myself.'

❖

Benjamin Disraeli

Sir William Fraser, *Disraeli and his Day* (1891)

Many of the sarcasms and invectives, which Disraeli poured out upon Sir Robert Peel, have become part of the British language: I do not repeat them; I am unwilling to vex any member of a family from whom I have received life-long kindness: but there is one so good, and so completely within the rules of Parliamentary satire, that I must quote it. It was on the evening on which Sir Robert Peel announced his change of views on the Corn Laws: he prudently made a very long speech: exhausted the House: and by the time he made his announcement the atmosphere had become loaded: and the House fatigued. Disraeli, however, roused them by a few words; amidst loud, vociferous cheering. The words were these. 'What has occurred tonight reminds me, Sir, of what occurred in the late war between Turkey and Russia: if I err in my facts the gallant Admiral opposite (Sir Charles Napier) will correct me. An expedition against Russia was projected: the grandest fleet ever manned by the Turks floated on the waters of the Bosphorus: the Sultan reviewed the fleet: he gave the command of it to his favourite Vizier: a man to whose hands the destiny of Turkey had been entrusted for years. The fleet set sail, amidst the enthusiasm of the Turks: the Muftis of Constantinople prayed for its success; as the Muftis of England did at the last General Election. What was the dismay of the Turks! What was the horror of the Sultan! When his favourite Vizier

513

led the fleet straight into the enemies' port! (loud laughter). He too was maligned: he too was called a traitor: but he said, No! his political opinions had changed: and his conscience would no longer permit him to remain in the service of the Sultan!'

❖

Joseph Hume

Joseph Hume (1777–1855) was a Radical MP for Aberdeen, 1818–30; for Middlesex, 1830–7; and Kilkenny, 1837–41. He was a stickler for controlling public expenditure and was much admired by Gladstone for this reason.

Sir William Fraser, *Disraeli and his Day* (1891)

The special object, in my early days, of Disraeli's derision was Joseph Hume; the 'unco guid' Member for Montrose: Either the recollections of Wycombe, or the affected solemnity of Hume, roused Disraeli's spleen: he was never tired of gibing at him, whom he invariably called his 'Hon. Friend'. Cobden having read a very abusive letter, we called out 'Name! name!' Cobden would not give the name of the writer: but handed the letter to Hume, who was sitting immediately below him. Hume at once nodded his head in a portentous manner of approval; and Cobden continued, 'My Hon. Friend below me will guarantee the respectability of the writer.' Disraeli, who followed, said, 'My Hon. Friend, the Member for Montrose, with that frankness which characterises him, guarantees the respectability of a writer whom two minutes before he had never heard of.' At another time, Disraeli said of Hume, 'My Hon. Friend, the Member for Montrose, has spoken this evening with that perspicuity of expression, and that accuracy of detail, which he always shows: particularly on subjects as to which he is profoundly ignorant.'

The great moment, however, of Hume's life, from a House of Commons point of view, was when, replying to the frequent taunts of Members opposite, and particularly to one member who constantly tormented him, he said, in broad Scotch, 'You are perpetually worrying me about my imputations, and allegations; I have long known you: it is time that I should tell you, to your face, that you are yourself the greatest allegator in the House.'

❖

The Scull and the Monkey

Michael MacDonagh, *Irish Life and Character* (1898)

Lord Monck, at one time Governor of Canada, sat in the House of Commons for an English constituency. An Irishman himself, he was very patronising to the Irish members. Meeting Vincent Scully, the Member for Tipperary, in the Lobby one night, he slapped him on the shoulder, and said familiarly, 'Well,

Scull, how are you?' The other, annoyed by this form of address, rejoined: 'I will thank you, my lord, not to deprive my name of the last letter. Or, if you do, pray add it to your own and call yourself—Monkey.'

Christopher Sykes

Christopher Sykes (1831–98), the son of a Yorkshire baronet, was educated at Rugby and at Trinity College, Cambridge. A traditional Conservative, he was MP for Beverley, 1865–8; for the East Riding of Yorkshire, 1868–85; and for the Buckrose division of the Riding of Yorkshire from 1885 until his retirement in 1892.

Henry W. Lucy, *Strand Magazine*, April 1899

At the time of his death Mr Christopher Sykes was not a member of the House of Commons. But he lived there through many Sessions, and has left behind him deathless memories. Few men equally silent gave the House larger measure of delight. To behold him was a liberal education in deportment. Perhaps no one could be so proper or so wise as he habitually looked. But it is something for mortals to have at hand a model, even if it be unattainably high.

One night in the Session of 1884 Mr Christopher Sykes startled the House by bringing in a Bill. If any member boldly imaginative had in advance associated the Yorkshire magnate with such an undertaking, he would instinctively have conjured up a question of enormous gravity—say the repeal of the Union, or the re-establishment of the Heptarchy. When it was discovered that Mr Sykes's bantling was to a Bill to amend the Fisheries (Oysters, Crabs, and Lobsters) Act 1877, the House shook with Homeric laughter.

Circumstances were favourable to the high comedy that followed. Ordinary members bring in Bills in the prosaic opening hour of a sitting. Mr Sykes selected the alternative opportunity presented at its close. At that hour the House is always ready for a lark. The discovery of Mr Sykes standing behind the empty Front Opposition Bench, grave, white-waistcoated, wearing in the buttonhole of his dinner-coat the white flower of a blameless life, promised sport. He held a paper in his hand, but said never a word, staring blankly at the Speaker, who was also on his legs, running through the Orders of the Day. For a member to remain on his feet whilst the Speaker is upstanding is a breach of order of which Mr Sykes was riotously reminded. For all answer, he looked around with the air of a stolid man surveying, without understanding, the capering of a cage of monkeys.

The Speaker, charitably concluding that the hon. member was moving for leave to bring in the Bill, put the question. Sir Wilfrid Lawson observed that the Bill was evidently one of great importance. It was usual in such circumstances for the member in charge to explain its scope. Would Mr Sykes favour the House with a few observations?

Mr Sykes took no notice of this appeal or of the uproarious applause with which it was sustained. Leave being given to bring in the Bill, Christopher, who had evidently carefully rehearsed the procedure, rose and with a long stride made his way to the Bar. Members in charge of Bills, having obtained leave to introduce them, stand at the Bar till, the list completed, the Speaker calls upon them by name to bring up their Bill, which they hand to the Clerk at the table. To the consternation of the Speaker and the uncontrollable amusement of the House, Mr Sykes, having reached the Bar, straightway turned about, walked up the floor, Bill in hand, and stood at the table solemnly gazing on the Speaker. As nothing seemed to come of this, he, after a while, retired a few paces, bowed to the Mace, again, advanced, halted at the foot of the table, and again stared at the Speaker. The Solicitor-General and another Minister who happened to be on the Treasury Bench took him by each arm, gently but firmly leading him back to the Bar, standing sentry beside him in preparation for any further unauthorised movement.

Other business disposed of, the Speaker called him by name. Mr Sykes, whose unruffled visage and attitude of funereal gravity were in striking contrast with the uproarious merriment that prevailed on both sides, again advanced, handed the Bill to the waiting Clerk, and forthwith departed. This was a fresh and final breach of Parliamentary rules. It is ordered that a member, having brought in a Bill, shall stand at the table whilst the Clerk reads out its title. In reply to a question from the Speaker he names a day for the second reading. Swift messengers caught Mr Sykes as he was crossing the Bar and hauled him back to the table, where at last, preserving amid shouts of laughter his impregnable air of gravity, he completed his work.

But he never brought in another Bill, and, though he did not immediately retire from Parliamentary life, he withdrew closely in his shell, even as the perturbed periwinkle or the alarmed cockle shrink from the rude advance of man.

❖

Sir Wilfrid Lawson

Sir Wilfrid Lawson, Bt. (1829–1906), the son of a baronet, was educated privately. He was president of the United Kingdom Alliance for the Suppression of the Liquor Traffic; he was a Liberal MP for Carlisle, 1859–65 and 1868–85; for the Cockermouth division of Cumberland, 1886–1900; for the Camborne division of Cornwall, 1903–6; and for Cockermouth again, briefly, in 1906.

Alfred H. Miles, *The New Anecdote Book* (1906)

In the discussion on the Sunday Closing Bill in 1888 Sir Wilfrid remarked of a brother member who was well known not to be an abstainer: 'I have no doubt the Hon. member is about to make a speech on this question of drink, for I see him sitting there evidently full of his subject.'

Saying 'Boo' to a goose

Michael MacDonagh, *Irish Life and Character* (1898)

A ready retort is also highly appreciated at St Stephen's. The happiest and most crushing one I ever heard was given about ten years ago. In the course of a rather acrimonious political debate an Irish member taunted his opponents on the other side of the House with their want of knowledge. 'At least we are not stupid,' said one of the members subsequently. 'Can that be said of the hon. gentleman? For my part, I do not believe he could say "boo" to a goose.' The Irish member at whom this taunt was cast immediately sprang to his feet, and in a loud voice shouted across the floor, 'Boo, boo!'

Major O'Gorman

Michael MacDonagh, *Irish Life and Character* (1898)

'Why are Irishmen always laying bare their grievances?' asked an irritated English member who had lost his patience during a long Irish debate. 'Because they want them redressed,' shouted the Major across the floor of the House.

Parnell's one joke

Michael MacDonagh, *Irish Life and Character* (1898)

Parnell only made one joke in the House of Commons. Ward Hunt was First Lord of the Admiralty in the last Disraelian administration. He was remarkable for a propensity to fall asleep on the Treasury Bench. One session, during the consideration of the Mutiny Bill, a motion was made from the Irish benches for the abolition of 'the cat' in the Navy. Ward Hunt opposed the motion on the ground that flogging was administered only in cases of serious crime. Parnell pointed out that among the offences for which 'the cat' might be used was that of a man sleeping at his post whilst on duty. 'Now,' continued Parnell, 'I should like to know whether the First Lord of the Admiralty regards *that* as a serious offence?'

Chamberlain winded

C. F. G. Masterman, *Daily News*, 1906

The cleverest repartee—now historic—was at Mr Chamberlain's expense. It was early in the Session, immediately after the famous 'surrender' letter of the City Election. It was an Irish debate. Everyone was in a bad temper. Mr Chamberlain, in scornful and bitter accents, was setting himself to exacerbate the feelings of the great majority opposite him, and especially of the Irishmen at his side. The tension was extreme when he rose to his climax. 'When the hon. member for East Mayo,' he drawled out slowly, 'congratulates and praises the new Chief Secretary for his brave speech, I am reminded of the boa constrictor who first slavers his prey before he devours it.' He paused for a moment of dramatic silence; and in that pause a still small voice enquired from the Irish benches, 'Is that what yer did to Bhalfour?' The tension suddenly snapped—in Homeric laughter—and the rest of that speech was very hastily concluded.

Balfour's insolence to the Irish

Frances Stevenson, Diary, May 11, 1919

Mr Balfour came down to tea, and stayed to dinner. He was most entertaining, being in a jovial mood, and reminisced freely. D. [Lloyd George] told him of the first time he heard him (Balfour) in the House, during an Irish Debate, and chaffed him on his insolence to the Irish members who were attacking him about one of their party who was said to be wasting away in prison. For answer Mr Balfour simply pulled a paper out of his pockets, and read a record of the man's daily increase in weight since he had been in prison.

Balfour's wit

Lord Willoughby de Broke, *The Passing Years* (1924)

One phrase that Mr Balfour delivered in reply, and therefore on the spur of the moment, remains in my memory. A versatile member had been excusing himself for a more than usually quick change of mind by a reference to his conscience. In his reply Mr Balfour spoke of 'a conscience yielding rapidly to treatment'. Surely the polished rapier of Parliamentary fence has seldom been more effectively used. It was a palpable hit.

Sir Henry Campbell-Bannerman

Sir Henry Campbell-Bannerman (1836–1908) was educated at Glasgow University and was Liberal MP for Stirling district from 1868 until his death. He first held office in Gladstone's first administration as Financial Secretary for War and he was Chief Secretary for Ireland (1884–5). Thereafter, he was Secretary of State for War (1886 and 1892–5) and was chosen as Leader of the Opposition in 1899. He was Prime Minister from 1905 to 1908 and Father of the House from 1907 to 1908.

George Leveson-Gower, *Years of Endeavour 1886–1907* (1942)

The late Alpheus Cleophas Morton, who sat for Peterborough from 1889 to 1895 and was subsequently knighted, added to a certain ungainliness of appearance a corresponding occasional infelicity of expression. Once when criticising methods of administration in Egypt as arbitrary and giving too little scope for native talent, he made the following extraordinary remark: 'In fact, Mr Speaker, things will never improve in Egypt until the Khedive is able to stand upon his own bottom.' When Campbell-Bannerman rose to reply, he observed, with great gravity, that 'his honourable friend had indicated a method for the regeneration of Egypt which he feared it would be difficult to fulfil. However desirous the Khedive of that country might be to forward the well-being of its inhabitants, he thought it scarcely fair to expect a potentate of middle age and of sedentary habits to indulge in acrobatics of so difficult and complicated a nature.'

A copious Peer

Margot Asquith, *More Memories* (1933)

In all the debates that I have attended I have never been fortunate enough to hear any very witty interruption, and wish I had been in the House of Lords when Lord Haversham told me their Lordships had been bored to extinction at some copious Peer who usually opened his speeches with: 'And now, my Lords!—I ask myself this question—'

At which, a young peer said in a loud voice: 'And a *damned dull* answer you'll get!'

Quips and repartee

Colin Brooks, *More Tavern Talk* (1952)

I have never been, to my great regret, a notebook-keeping man. I say to my great regret for I often wish I had compiled a commonplace book of Parliamentary quips and repartee. Many I easily remember but forget the utterers. One of the most famous was said by Lloyd George, when he was accusing that great Imperialist Joe Chamberlain of instigating or promoting the Boer war because the Chamberlains had holdings in Kynochs, the explosives and armaments manufacturers. 'We see how it is, Mr Speaker, sir,' he purred, 'the more the Empire expands, the more this family contracts.' Another memorable quip came from Tim Healy about the same period, when the Gvt. had made a fool of itself by replying to offers of troops for South Africa with the incredible reservation 'unmounted men preferred'. It was the time of disasters and 'regrettable incidents'. Someone at question time had asked how many horses Britain had sent to South Africa. The answer was given, and Tim rose to ask a supplementary. 'Will the Government say how many asses have been sent to South Africa?' Perhaps the quickest bit of interplay was when the young Winston Churchill, just after the war, had returned from an African visit on which he had written a book. A Tory member in a speech said he feared that the Under-Secretary for the Colonies on that visit had contracted a native disease called Beri-beri, the symptom of which was a swelling of the head. 'No, no,' said Mr Churchill, 'a swelling of the feet.' Said the member, unabashed, 'That, Mr Speaker, is exactly what I meant. The honourable member is too big for his boots.' In my own time the most pleasing quip came from Maurice Petherwick, known to all his friends as Bobbie. Bobbie was in the midst of a speech when there came a sound of dissent from Lord Winterton, known to all *his* friends as Eddie. Bobbie paused. 'Mr Speaker, sir, I had expected from this side of the house a tide of support. All I can discern is a backward eddy.' There is one other quip which I treasure, though it may not have been uttered in Parliament. Randolph Churchill recently reminded me of it. When his father, Winston, sat for Dundee, 'F.E.' in the course of a speech said, with that dripping contempt with which he could instil his languid, leisurely voice: 'I see from the *Dundee Advertiser*— I mean the newspaper, not the politician . . .' The Victorians were not without the art. When that great master of flouts, gibes and jeers, Lord Salisbury, accused Her Majesty's Prime Minister, Gladstone, of using the methods of a pettifogging attorney, the House of Lords called on him for a withdrawal and apology. He rose and said, 'I am willing to apologise, to the members of what I cannot doubt is a hard-working and deserving profession.'

Jack Jones

John Joseph Jones (1873–1941) was born in Ireland and educated at Christian Brothers' schools there. A builder's labourer by occupation, he served as a councillor in West Ham and in 1911 he became an organiser for the National Union of General and Municipal Workers. He was elected for the Silvertown division of West Ham in 1918 as a National Socialist, but took the Labour Whip, holding his seat until he retired in 1940.

Patrick Hastings, *The Autobiography of Patrick Hastings* (1948)

My only really pleasant recollection of my first Parliament arises from the memory of the interjections of Jack Jones, for many years the Member for Silvertown. Poor Jack! I often thought he might have done so much better than he did. He was a great, if somewhat bitter, humorist. I can see him now, listening with bored disapproval from his stand at the back of the Labour benches. It is said of him that on one occasion a lady member was declaiming against the evils of intemperance, and with passionate intensity announced that she would rather commit adultery than drink a glass of beer. 'Who wouldn't?' interposed Jack politely. But he was not always so polite, though I must confess that his lapses from perfect taste were generally justified. A notoriously wearisome gentleman was making an oration of inordinate length upon nothing in particular, in the course of which he remarked: 'What I really want, Mr Speaker, for the purpose of my argument is a moratorium.' 'You are quite wrong, sir,' came the reply. 'What you want is a crematorium.'

Willie Adamson

William Murdoch Adamson (1881–1945) was born in Scotland and became National Officer of the Transport and General Workers' Union. He was Labour MP for the Cannock division of Staffordshire from 1922 until he was defeated in 1931, regaining the seat in 1935 and holding it until he retired a few months before his death. He was a Government Whip from 1941 to 1944. His wife, Jennie Adamson, was MP for the Dartford division of Kent, 1938–45, and for Boxley, 1945–6, and also served as Minister of Pensions during World War II.

Herbert Morrison, *The Autobiography of Herbert Morrison* (1960)

Willie Adamson, leader of the Fife miners, was the popular first Labour Secretary of State for Scotland. He knew and loved his Scotland and championed its cause inside the government. He also had his own dour technique for answering supplementary questions. He gave the same answer every time:

'Muster Speaker, I'll gie the matter ma due conseederation.'

He got away with this charming and disarming answer for about six weeks; then a Scots Liberal got up and put another supplementary immediately after Willie had finished answering the previous one.

'Mr Speaker,' he asked, 'can the right honourable gentleman give no other answer to a supplementary question but that he will give it his due consideration?'

Willie Adamson stood up, blinked and paused for a moment. Then he said:

'Muster Speaker, I'll gie tha' matter ma due conseederation as weel.' The House roared and he got away with it.

Ernest Brown

Alfred Ernest Brown (1881–1962) was educated at Torquay. He won the Military Cross during World War I and briefly represented Rugby as a Liberal (December 1923–October 1924). From 1927 to 1945 he was MP for Leith, first as a Liberal, then as a Liberal National after 1931. He held various ministerial posts in the National Government, and during World War II was successively Secretary of State for Scotland, Minister of Health, Chancellor of the Duchy of Lancaster, and Minister of Aircraft Production. He led the Liberal National Group throughout the war, but was defeated in 1945.

Arthur Baker, *The House is Sitting* (1958)

There was a well-known story prevalent in the Gallery and Lobby about Ernest. It has been published elsewhere, and repeated many times. But it may be worth repeating once more. One evening Baldwin was sitting on the Treasury Bench, screwing up his eyes and nose as he browsed happily through the pages of *Dod's Parliamentary Companion* (a favourite pastime of his), when he heard a tremendous noise from outside the Chamber. It seemed to come from somewhere behind the Speaker's Chair. Baldwin was for once roused to some appearance of animation. Turning to the Chief Whip, who happened to be sitting beside him, he exclaimed, 'What the devil is that row?' 'Oh,' replied the Chief Whip, 'don't worry; it's only Ernest Brown telephoning to his constituents at Leith!' Like a flash the answer came back from S.B., 'What does he want to use a telephone for?'

Winston Churchill

Harold Balfour, *Wings over Westminster* (1973)

One day in the early thirties when he was back-bencher in the political wilderness, Churchill was surrounded in the Smoking Room by a ring of younger members hanging on to his words. The name of the speaker in the Chamber came up on the ticker-tape. Someone asked Churchill if he was going to listen. 'No,' he replied, 'I am tired of listening to the dreary drip of dilatory declamation.' A long pause then—'I have been keeping that for three weeks.' Churchill was shown a photograph in the *Evening Standard* of a Member well-known for his unfortunate homosexual tendencies. The picture showed the Member arm-in-arm with a stout middle-aged lady as they were coming out of the Registry Office after their marriage. 'Look, so-and-so got married today.' Winston's reply—'Very peculiar, very peculiar—but buggers can't be choosers!'

At the time of the Mount Everest expedition Winston joined in the Smoking Room talk. He was asked what he thought about it. 'I do not wish to overrate chastity,' he replied, 'but there is much to be said for virgin mountains.' During the final years of his Premiership, Churchill became very deaf. The most respected and worthy member for Maidstone, Alfred Bossom, was speaking. Churchill turned to David Margesson, Chief Whip, sitting beside him on the Treasury Bench. 'Who is that speaking?' he asked very slowly and audibly.

'Bossom,' replied David.

Leaning towards him with hand to ear, 'What did you say, David? Say it again.'

With emphasis Margesson repeated, 'Bossom, Alfred Bossom.'

Winston pondered for a moment. 'Bossom? Bossom? What a *very* peculiar name—neither one thing or the other.'

Churchill came on to the Treasury Bench when a young Secretary of State was presenting his Service Estimates. It was very unusual for the Prime Minister to come in on such an occasion and the Minister felt extremely flattered. When he sat down Winston turned to him and said, 'I came to test a new hearing aid. It does not work.'

Nye Bevan

Woodrow Lyle Wyatt (b. 1918), Baron Wyatt of Weeford, was educated at Eastbourne College and at Worcester College, Oxford. He served in the Army during World War II, attaining the rank of major. He sat twice as a Labour MP, for the Aston division of Birmingham from 1945 to 1955, and for the Bosworth division of Leicestershire from 1959 to 1970; and he briefly held junior ministerial office towards the end of the Attlee premiership. He later became a vigorous Thatcherite commentator, notably for the *News of the World*. Apart from his journalism, he has held the chairmanship of the Horserace Totalisator Board since 1976.

Woodrow Wyatt, *Confessions of an Optimist* (1985)

In the Members' Smoking Room I sat happily in the circle round Nye Bevan. He was a clubbable man who liked to drink, gossip and pour out his comments among a group of admirers. Michael Foot, John Strachey, Tom Driberg and Geoffrey Bing, descendant of a Chinese sea captain, were among them. The conversation was brisk and funny, the jokes frequently provided by Nye Bevan. There was a veteran Labour MP called Seymour Cocks. Once when his name came up on the indicator as speaking in the Chamber Nye looked up and said, 'Oh yes, Seymour Cocks and hear more balls.'

An exchange from the Official Report

Sir Gerald David Nunes Nabarro (1913–73) was educated at London County Council School, served in the Army from 1930 to 1943, and then worked as a businessman in engineering and road transport. He was chairman of the West Midlands Young Conservatives from 1946 to 1948 and its president, 1948–50, and he sat as Conservative MP for

Kidderminster from 1950 until 1964, when he stood down for health reasons. He recovered sufficiently, however, to become MP for South Worcestershire in 1966. Recognisable by his handlebar moustache, he was an eccentric, much loved as a broadcaster, and a champion of Private Members' legislation. He was the prime mover of Clean Air Bills, 1955–6. He was also parliamentary adviser and consultant to the National Tyre Distributors Association.

Hansard, House of Commons Debates (1957–8)

54. Mr Nabarro asked the Chancellor of the Exchequer whether he is aware that a manufacturer of key holders was recently informed by the Customs and Excise authorities that a holder for the pocket, designed in such a way that the flap closing it would prevent the keys from falling out and damaging the pocket, would be subject to 60 per cent Purchase Tax, but if the size of the flap could be reduced to $\frac{1}{2}$ inch in size, the holder would be free of Purchase Tax; and whether, in view of the fact that the holder with the $\frac{1}{2}$-inch flap would be ineffective from the point of view of protecting the user's pocket, he will instruct the officials to reconsider the matter.

The Financial Secretary to the Treasury (Mr J. E. S. Simon): Yes, Sir. The matter has been reconsidered and, as my hon. Friend is aware, the anomaly has been rectified.

Mr Nabarro: I think it will be agreed that good progress is now being made in this field. Will my hon. and learned Friend now deal with the matter sensibly and objectively and give instructions to the Customs and Excise authorities to endeavour conscientiously to abolish all these quite ridiculous anomalies that are wasting so much of the nation's trade and time?

Mr Simon: I cannot accept the implications of that supplementary question, but we should be grateful to my hon. Friend for drawing attention to the anomalies which unquestionably exist.

55. Mr Nabarro asked the Chancellor of the Exchequer when the regulation was introduced laying down that doorknockers 5 inches or more in length shall be free of tax whereas doorknockers under that length carry 30 per cent Purchase Tax; and what has been the revenue from Purchase Tax on doorknockers for each of the past five years for which figures are available.

Mr Simon: Following consultation with the trade, doorknockers over $4\frac{3}{4}$ inches long have been treated as free of tax under a relief for builders' hardware introduced in 1948. On the second part of the Question, I would refer my hon. Friend to the reply which my right hon. Friend the Member for Monmouth (Mr P. Thorneycroft) gave him on 17th December.

Mr Nabarro: Why is there this invidious distinction between doorknocking nutcrackers and nutcracking doorknockers—

Mr Speaker: Order.

Mr Nabarro: This is an invidious distinction, Mr Speaker.

Mr Speaker: It may be an invidious distinction, as the hon. Member says, but I rather think he is now anticipating Question No. 56. Is not that about nutcrackers?

Mr Nabarro: I understood the Financial Secretary to say that he was answering the Questions together. It is a quite understandable mistake, because that is how the Chancellor of the Exchequer generally rides off these difficulties. Will my hon. and learned Friend put this matter into good order?

Mr Speaker: The hon. Member should ask Question No. 56 if he wants to get on to the subject of nutcrackers.

56. Mr Nabarro asked the Chancellor of the Exchequer whether he is aware that, in view of the fact that a nutcracker is liable to Purchase Tax at 15 per cent whereas a doorknocker over 5 inches in length is free of tax, there is an increasing practice of supplying nutcrackers with screw holes so that they could theoretically be used as doorknockers, with the result that with such modification these nutcrackers become free of tax; and what instructions have been issued to Customs and Excise staff with regard to this matter.

Mr Simon: No, Sir; I do not think Customs staff need instructions to help them distinguish a nutcracker from a doorknocker.

Mr Nabarro: Now will my hon. and learned Friend apply himself to the Question that I have put to him? Why is there this invidious distinction between doorknocking nutcrackers and nutcracking doorknockers? Is he aware that this is a perfectly well-known device, practised by manufacturers? I have evidence of it in my hand. Is he aware that this ridiculous position, which was mentioned in a leading article in *The Times* on 11th February, is bringing the whole of the Purchase Tax Schedules into disrepute? Is it not time that the matter was drastically overhauled by abolition of the Purchase Tax and substitution of a sales turnover tax at a very small and uniform rate over the whole field?

Mr Simon: My hon. Friend tempts me to reply in the words of the conductor Richter to the second flute at Covent Garden—'Your damned nonsense can I stand twice or once, but sometimes always, by God, never.'

1. Horace Walpole, *Memoirs of the Reign of King George III* (1845), Vol. II, p. 286.
2. Sir James T. Agg-Gardner, *Some Parliamentary Recollections* (1927), p. 227.
3. William Norris, *One from Seven Hundred* (1966), p. 120.
4. Harry Graham, *The Mother of Parliaments* (1911), p. 148 n.
5. Earl Winterton, Diary, November 7, 1929; *Orders of the Day* (1953), p. 160.
6. Lord Broughton, *Recollections of a Long Life* (1911), p. 92.
7. Spencer Leigh Hughes, *Press, Platform and Parliament* (1918), pp. 151–2.
8. Thomas Moore, *Memoirs, Journal and Correspondence of Thomas Moore* (1853–6), Vol. II, p. 320.
9. Michael MacDonagh, *Irish Life and Character* (1898), pp. 275–6.
10. ibid., p. 268.
11. Quoted in Arthur Page Grubb, *The Life Story of the Right Hon. John Burns, PC, MP* (1908), pp. 154–5.
12. Sir Henry Morris-Jones, *Doctor in the Whips' Room* (1955), p. 165.

13. Alan Valentine, *The British Establishment 1760–1784* (1970), pp. 929–30.

14. There have been similar instances. In 1763, Richard Rigby attacked Lord Temple as the sinister influence behind Wilkes and the mob. Temple's brother, James Grenville, 'rose, in amazing heat, to defend his brother and vomited out a torrent of invectives on Rigby . . . the bitterest terms flowing spontaneously from him who had ever been the most obscure and unready speaker; and what added to the outrage of the diction was, that sitting on the bench immediately above Rigby, and darting about his arm in the air, he seemed to aim blows at the latter, who was forced to crouch lest he should receive them' (Walpole, op. cit., Vol. I, p. 260). During his maiden speech, George Canning's 'violent and theatrical action' meant that 'people about me were apprehensive of some mischief from me' (see Chapter 1). In 1853 William Ewart in emphasising a point brought down his fist on the hat of the solemn Joseph Hume. This hat, which had a broad brim and a long nap, 'descended below Hume's chin, and his heavy, unintelligent features were completely obscured'; the result was uproarious laughter. Again, Edwin James QC, a red-faced blusterer, became so agitated while delivering his maiden speech that one of his fists kept flying close to Lord John Russell, whose 'dodgings to avoid the fist were exquisite'. (Both the previous anecdotes are taken from Sir William Fraser, *Disraeli and his Day* (1891), pp. 38–41.) On another occasion, in June 1890, William O'Brien, in the course of wild gesticulation, accidentally thumped the hat of Tom Sutherland (the chairman of the P&O) with his rolled-up order paper.

15. 'Single-speech Hamilton' was the nickname given to William Gerard Hamilton, secretary of Lord Halifax, who in 1755 delivered himself of a vigorous and remarkable speech. According to Walpole, he 'broke out like the Irish rebellion, three-score thousand strong, when nobody was aware or in the least suspected it'. (Quoted in George Henry Jennings, *An Anecdotal History of the British Parliament from the Earliest Periods to the Present Time* (1880), p. 365.)

15 Friends and Enemies

'It has long been the boast of the House of Commons,' remarked Disraeli, 'that even when political passions run high and party warmth becomes somewhat intense, there should exist between those members of both parties who take any considerable share in the conduct of business, sentiments of courtesy and, when the public interest requires it, even of confidence.'[1] Indeed, it could be argued that the capacity of parliamentary life for engendering friendships across the political divide has been one of the principal factors behind the stability of the British political system.

George Canning wrote to a friend and political ally to explain that his intimacy with a member of the Opposition, Sheridan—a childhood friend—would not compromise his public sentiments.[2] On the other hand, Sir Samuel Romilly ceased to be a friend of Spencer Perceval, because he hated Perceval as a minister.[3] However, such qualms are unusual, as the sketch-writer James Grant observed:

> When Sir Charles Wetherell and the late Henry Hunt, men whose policies were wide as the poles asunder, were both in Parliament, it was no uncommon thing to see them sitting in close juxtaposition with each other, often, too, engaged in most earnest conversation together, as if the utmost cordiality and the most perfect unanimity of political feeling existed between them. In the Reformed Parliament might be seen Sir Robert Peel and Mr Cobbett sitting cheek-by-jowl, while close by them were to be found Sir Robert Inglis, the great advocate of the Church of England and ecclesiastical establishments in general, and Mr Gillon, the sworn foe of both, apparently as friendly together as if of one heart and one soul in such matters.[4]

Sir William Fraser was surprised to see Disraeli and Lord John Russell, 'very shortly after an embittered controversy in the House, chatting together with good-humoured familiarity', while George Smythe told him that when he had been Under-Secretary for Foreign Affairs and the Earl of Derby had been regularly attacking his chief, Lord Aberdeen, in the most extravagant terms, yet he and Derby had nonetheless dined together every night.[5] When Bright resigned from Gladstone's Cabinet in 1882 over the bombardment of Alexandria, 'Bright's resignation speech from the second bench below the gangway on the Ministerial side was brief and sorrowful, and so was Gladstone's reply. The two men, while differing on the application of the moral law to the Egyptian issue, were careful of one another's feelings. Their mutual esteem remained.'[6] The Labour left-winger Fenner Brockway also received encouragement from Winston Churchill: 'When in 1929 I was elected to Parliament he sent me a note: "I hate your policies but you deserve to be here" . . .'[7]

After their rift during the 1791 Canada Bill, Burke and Fox, who had been fast friends for twenty-five years, never recovered their former intimacy. Both were prominent leaders of the Opposition, but whereas Fox had recommended the new French constitution as a model, Burke had excoriated it. Fox's supporters, and even Fox himself, had persistently interrupted Burke when he was speaking and although Fox whispered to Burke when he sat down that there was no loss of friends, Burke replied that their friendship was at an end. 'There are not many lasting friendships in politics that stand the test of adversity,'

Sir Henry Morris-Jones has pointed out. 'Fewer still in your own Party. The friendship between Joseph Chamberlain and Charles Dilke was notable and singular. The dead are quickly forgotten. This is partly attributable to the intensity and concentration of political life—its rivalry and ambition.'[8] Another Radical, Henry Labouchere, never forgave Chamberlain for splitting from Gladstone over Home Rule, though Gladstone himself behaved with courtesy towards his former Cabinet colleague, congratulating him on the maiden speech of his son, Austen.

H. H. Asquith identified two schools of thought in the matter of friendships between politicians of different party affiliations: '. . . those who think that friendly and, still more, familiar intercourse between the combatants when they are off the battlefield impairs the sincerity of public life; and those who think that political differences may without any lack of honesty be ignored in private'.[9] John Bright 'always tended towards the sterner view of familiarity between political opponents,' his biographer, G. M. Trevelyan, has written, 'namely that it is difficult to attack in public a man with whom the orator consorts much in private'. As is shown in his diaries, however, Bright would occasionally enjoy friendly intercourse with Disraeli over dinner in the Commons, even though he scorned Disraeli's political character. One commentator felt that Bright's attitude was to the detriment of his cause: 'Mr Bright carries his inexorable detestation of Toryism into the lobby: whence he is shunned in the green-room and hooted on the stage'.[10]

Joseph Chamberlain, on the other hand, believed that 'there is a large space in the field of politics, and a still greater space in our social life, which is altogether free from any taint of party bitterness; and foreigners have told me that what has struck them most in their experience of this country is the fact that political opponents, even in the bitterest controversy, can still remain firm personal friends'. Gladstone always forgave Lord Salisbury his barbs, because he had had fond memories of Salisbury's mother and had first encountered the Tory leader 'as a little fellow in a red frock rolling about on the ottoman'. In his tribute to the Liberal politician William Harcourt, A. J. Balfour pointed out that 'he never allowed party differences to mar the perfection of personal friendship . . . I am proud to say that he honoured me with his friendship for many years, and never was that friendship clouded even when our political differences were in their most acute stage'.[11] A more recent judgement has come from Nigel Nicolson, who has averred that Parliament 'is one of the few places where the bore is forced to recognise himself as such, and one of the marks of a parliamentary bore is to allow his political attitude to affect his personal relationships'.[12]

The club-like atmosphere of the Palace of Westminster in modern times has no doubt encouraged good relations between political opponents and has isolated the obsessives. A Tory MP, writing in 1890, insisted that 'one of the chief attractions of the smoking-room is that there we sink political differences . . . although opinions freely expressed and without any tinge of party rancour on a vast variety of subjects, men with mere fads—the peculiar people of the House—seldom turn up in the smoking-room, or, if they do, keep their views on their respective fads to themselves'.[13] Even so, the paradox of MPs sinking their differences in private has continued to perplex some witnesses. 'Parliamentary life would, it is said, become impossible if Members did not learn to live amicably with one another in the smoking-room, once they have shot off their mouths in the Chamber,' wrote an experienced member of the Press Gallery. 'An excellent convention—but is it a convention? Here we have 630 men and women, friendly—except for normal human antipathies—in private, and fighting like Kilkenny cats in public.'[14]

Although Churchill vehemently opposed the Labour Party in the early 1920s—Manny Shinwell recalled that Labour MPs bitterly resented Churchill's slur that their party was unfit to govern—he endeavoured to maintain friendly relations with individual Labour MPs. In 1924 the formation of the first Labour Government elicited a friendly letter from Churchill to Ramsay MacDonald. 'No letter received by me at this time has given me more pleasure than yours,' MacDonald replied. 'I wish we did not agree so much! . . . I have always held you personally in much esteem, and I hope, whatever fortune may have in store for us, that personal relationship will never be broken.'[15] It seems difficult to believe that, a decade or so later, the personal relationship survived Churchill's famous jibe against MacDonald—that he resembled a circus exhibit called 'The Boneless Wonder', which Churchill had seen as a child—but Churchill continued to be a benevolent patron of MacDonald's son, Malcolm. Again, Churchill frequently harried Philip Snowden, Labour's Chancellor of the Exchequer from 1929 to 1931, but when Snowden died his widow wrote to say: 'Your generosity to a political opponent marks you for ever in my eyes the "great gentleman" I have always thought you.'[16]

Towards the end of World War II, Churchill encountered one of *his* most scourge-like critics, Richard Stokes, the Labour MP for Ipswich, at the entrance to the Smoking Room. He put a hand on Stokes's shoulder and said he forgave him. 'Such hatred as I have left in me, and it is not much, I would rather reserve for the future,' he told him, adding as he moved away, 'H'mm. A judicious and thrifty disposition of bile.'[17] Another Tory leader, Macmillan, described Bevan in private as 'my friend for many years'.[18]

In the House of Lords the atmosphere has traditionally been more conducive to restraint in manners, since with the passage of time enmities have often been dissipated and ambitions exhausted, yet some never manage to suppress their bile. 'My sixty-fifth birthday,' wrote Lord Reith in his diary on July 20, 1954. 'Sat in the House of Lords for about twenty minutes, report stage of TV bill. Absolutely nauseating; Jowitt asking courteously and cogently for a change in the title of the Independent Television Authority and De la Warr just feebly saying it couldn't be done and giving no reasons. And the three palsied old hags, Woolton, Swinton and Salisbury, yapping away on the front bench. I left in disgust.'

❖

John Pym and the Earl of Strafford

Sir Thomas Wentworth (1593–1641), 1st Earl of Strafford, was from a Yorkshire land-owning family and was educated at Cambridge. He was knighted in 1611 and elected as MP for Yorkshire a few years later. Although at first a critic of Charles I, he was converted to the King's cause in 1628 by the bestowal of a peerage and thereafter became the King's most faithful and ruthless counsellor. Later, he was further elevated to an earldom and made Lord-Lieutenant of Ireland. Strafford and Archbishop Laud were eventually impeached by Parliament under the leadership of John Pym; despite the questionable legality of the indictment, Strafford's tyrannical policies were punished with a sentence of death which Charles I, for fear of open rebellion, approved.

George Henry Jennings, *An Anecdotal History of the British Parliament* (1880)

A few weeks after the prorogation of 1628, Wentworth was made a peer; and it is said that on the eve of his elevation an accidental meeting took place between himself and Pym, when the latter remarked, 'You are going to leave us, but I will never leave you while your head is upon your shoulders.' They did not meet again until the great occasion in Westminster Hall, when Pym set forth the Earl's impeachment on behalf of the Commons of England. At one critical point, in Pym's final address, where he was replying to Strafford's defence, 'If the law hath not been put in execution, as he allegeth, these two hundred and forty years, it was not for want of law, but that all that time hath not bred a man bold enough to commit such crimes as these,' the speaker turned and met the haggard look of his old comrade, who had been intently regarding him; and for the moment Pym is said to have been deprived of his self-possession. 'His papers he looked on,' says one present, 'but they could not help him to a point or two, so he behooved to pass them.' Strafford had anticipated in his defence the feeling he must have experienced at the moment, saying, 'That I am charged with treason by the honourable Commons is my greatest grief. It pierces my heart, though not with guilt, yet with sorrow, that in my grey hairs I should be so misunderstood by the companions of my youth, with whom I have formerly spent so much time.'

❖

George Canning and Henry Addington

Henry Addington (1757–1844), 1st Viscount Sidmouth, was educated at Winchester and at Brasenose College, Oxford. In 1783 he was elected as MP for Devizes. He served as Speaker from 1789 to 1801, and then, following the resignation of Pitt (compared to whose lustre he glowed but faintly) as Prime Minister from 1801 to 1804. His administration was avowed a failure, but he went on to serve as an illiberal Home Secretary from 1812 to 1821. Canning sneeringly nicknamed him 'the Doctor' because his father had been Pitt the Elder's family physician, although Canning was 'himself the son of an actress', as one of his biographers has noted.[19] Canning was also responsible for that cruel quip against him, 'London is to Paddington,/As Pitt is to Addington.'

George Canning, Letter to his wife Joan, 1802

The Dr was cruelly laughed at last night, upon the accidental use of some equivocal medical term which fell from him. So much so, as to appeal to the Chair for protection. I am glad of it, and glad that it was in my absence, because when I am by, they lay the ridicule of him on me and mine. And it is well that he should see that the contempt into which he is fallen is universal. It does not signify. A man so despised cannot stand. How he is to fall, when, whither, by his own consent—by the King's desiring him to go—or forced out by Parlt. I cannot tell—but he is too low in the opinion of the world to go on for many weeks longer. This may be perhaps in some measure the work of me and mine: but he has helped it himself—and it be it whom it may the work is done.—The laugh at his blue and gold coat the other day was enough to drive a man of sensibility crazy.[20]

Sir Robert Peel and George Canning

Sir William Fraser, *Disraeli and his Day* (1891)

Sir Robert Peel produced considerable effect upon the House, by quoting the lines from Canning's admirable poem, 'The New Morality'. It was believed by many that Canning's death was owing to the persecution which he had met with from Sir Robert Peel, and other of his former friends:

> 'Give me the avowed, the erect, the manly foe!
> Straight I may meet: perchance may turn his blow.
> But of all plagues that Heaven in wrath may send,
> Save! Save! Oh save me from a candid friend!'

Disraeli replied, 'The Scene the House of Commons! the Poet Mr Canning! the Orator the Right Hon. Baronet! I congratulate him upon his retentive Memory! and his courageous Conscience!'

Arm-in-arm

James Grant, *Random Recollections of the House of Commons* (1836)

Those unacquainted with the secrets of the prison-house would naturally infer that those members of the opposite politics whom they see night after night heartily abusing each other were not on friendly terms together. There are some cases in which the conclusion might be just: in the great majority it would not. Before and after the dissolution of Sir Robert Peel's Government, the Right Honourable Baronet and Lord John Russell were often seen in most friendly conversation together. Some weeks after the meeting of the present Parliament, Mr Hughes Hughes, the member for Oxford, made a most violent attack on Mr O'Connell, pointedly referring, among other things, to his ordering death's heads and cross-bones to be painted over the doors of those electors who would not vote for his nominee in the county of Cork. Mr O'Connell repelled the attack with equal violence, and retorted, as he did to Mr Shaw, the member for the University of Dublin, on another occasion, that Mr Hughes' head was a calf's-head. Some nights afterward both gentlemen were seen walking arm-in-arm up Parliament-street, on their way home from the house.

❖

Benjamin Disraeli and Sir Robert Peel reconciled

It is not clear whether Disraeli understood correctly that he had been reconciled with his former leader Sir Robert Peel. Robert Blake, Disraeli's biographer, is sceptical about the claim.

Benjamin Disraeli, Memorandum (1860s)[21]

A day or two after Peel's death Gladstone was at the Carlton and said: 'Peel died at peace with all mankind; even with Disraeli. The last thing he did was to cheer Disraeli. It was not a very loud cheer, but it was a cheer; it was distinct. I sat next to him.'

I had concluded the great debate on the Greek (Pacifico) business at four o'clock in the morning. It was the first, and the only time, in which, the Protectionist party acting again with Sir Robert Peel, or rather he acting again with them, I had to assume, and fulfil, the duties of leader in his presence. I wished to avoid it, as I thought it might be distressing to him, and I shrink from anything presumptuous. I had means of communicating with him, through Forbes Mackenzie, who was one of my Whips and who had been a Lord of the Treasury under Peel. Though Mackenzie had resigned his office on the Repeal of the Corn Laws, he still maintained his friendly relations with Sir R. Peel and his old colleagues. Sir Robert answered Mackenzie that he certainly meant to speak, but had no wish to close the debate. And he thought that Mr Disraeli, from his position, ought to close it.

The majority in favour of Lord Palmerston was unexpectedly large: 46. Mackenzie went to tell Sir Robert the numbers before they were declared. Sir Robert looked disappointed, and said: 'I had thought it would not have exceeded 20.' I heard this myself, for, in that strange state of affairs, I was only removed on the front bench by two persons from Peel, during the latter years of his life. He was very conciliatory to me. Partly because his was not a nature that bore rancour; partly because, as he esteemed success in the House of Commons the greatest of human possessions, he respected a triumphant adversary; and partly, as I know, because he wished to bring back his followers into office under Lord Derby by an arrangement which would have, of course, omitted himself . . .

. . . The majority, however, dispelled these dreams. It was caused by a section of the Tories, who saw through the affair and looked upon it as a plot to bring the Peelites back, and put them at the head of the party, and they acted accordingly. Next morning Peel was dead, or as good! He seemed quite well in the House, and spoke well—with none of the bitterness of his followers against Palmerston. (By the bye, Lord P. met me shortly after the debate, and said: 'You and Peel treated me like a gentleman: which no one else did.')

Although he could not have been in bed before 5 o'clock, devoted to the Prince, he rose early to attend a Council about the projected 'Great Exhibition'.

There was some financial question. He took it up, but not with his usual lucidity. Then he put pen to paper, but seemed confused, and finally said he would think over the matter, and send his results to the Prince. He went home, and afterwards went out to ride, and it happened. Was it a fit? If so, it was brought on by unnecessary want of rest and repose. I know, as well as most men, what it is to get home at 4 or 5 in the morning after an exciting division. Sleep is not commanded under such circumstances, even by the philosophical. Had Peel taken his fair rest, would he have been saved? Bulwer Lytton thought not when we talked over these matters. 'He had done his work,' he said. 'No man lives who has done his work. There was nothing left for him to do.'

I did not rise, that fatal day, so early as Sir Robert Peel. And in the afternoon my guardian angel persuaded me, instead of going to Clubs and Houses of Commons, to take a drive in our agreeable environs. We were returning through the Regent's Park, and two gentlemen on horseback, strangers, stopped our carriage. 'Mr D.,' they said, 'you will be interested to hear that Sir Robert Peel has been thrown from his horse, and has been carried home in a dangerous state.'

'Dangerous?' I enquired. 'I hope not. His loss would be a great misfortune for this country.'

They seemed a little surprised, but I spoke what I felt . . .

Gladstone offered a different version of the circumstances surrounding the Pacifico debate when he wrote the following recollection towards the end of his life.[22]

W. E. Gladstone, 1897

A very curious incident on this occasion evinced the extreme reluctance of Sir R. Peel to appear in any ostensible relation with Disraeli . . . Disraeli, not yet fully recognised as leader of the Protectionists, was working hard for that position, and assumed the manners of it, with Beresford, a kind of whipper-in, for his right-hand man. After the Palmerston speech, he asked me on the next night whether I would undertake to answer it. I said that I was incompetent to do it, from want of knowledge and otherwise. He answered that in that case he must do it. As the debate was not to close that evening, this left another night free for Peel when he might speak and *not* be in Disraeli's *neighbourhood*. I told Peel what Disraeli had arranged. He was very well satisfied. But, shortly afterwards, I received from Disraeli a message through Beresford, that he had changed his mind, and would not speak until the next and closing night, when Peel would have to speak also. I had to make known to Peel this alteration. He received the tidings with extreme annoyance: thinking, I suppose, that if the two spoke on the same side and in the late hour just before the division it would convey the idea of some concert or co-operation between them, which it was evident that he was most anxious to avoid.

❖

Disraeli and Ralph Earle

Sir William Fraser, *Disraeli and his Day* (1891)

Ralph Earle, MP, who had been for many years confidential private secretary to Disraeli, quarrelled with him for some reason that has not been explained; and which may never be known. He considered himself to have been harshly treated in being dismissed from Disraeli's confidence on receiving an official appointment; and, though possessing much cleverness, and a considerable amount of good sense, made the great error of attacking Disraeli in the House of Commons just before a Division, when it is always impatient; pouring out his invectives against his late master in a feeble manner, and producing, as might be supposed, the effect of rendering himself absurd. The House knew nothing of the circumstances of the quarrel; and cared as little. Earle had, of course, plenty of enemies, who turned upon him, and upbraided him for what appeared to be an act of unprovoked ingratitude.

♣

A crushed hat

Sir William Fraser, *Disraeli and his Day* (1891)

Hats play a conspicuous part in the House of Commons. Sitting covered is probably permitted as taking away an easy means of insubordination and dis-order, if the rule were to sit uncovered. A good hat is not frequently seen there. No one can secure a place unless its owner be there at prayer-time; Members now do not scruple to secure their places with a second hat before prayers; even early in the morning. It seems extraordinary that in a country like ours there should not be room in the Senate-House for all the Members. Speaking from the side-galleries ought to be encouraged: not only would the Member addressing the House be better heard, but he would be at a decided advantage in speaking from the gallery. One little incident relating to a hat I must relate. Sitting next to an esteemed friend, a distinguished member of the legal profession, he rose to address the House on a subject of considerable interest. The Tory party were at the time in opposition: I was distressed to observe that his whole line of argument was in favour of a proposal of the actual Government. I noticed that he had in close proximity to his person a perfectly new hat. It was an exquisite hat: and must have cost from twenty-three to twenty-five shillings. I placed this hat immediately behind him; so that when he sat down he would crush it. Not only did he continue his argument, but he positively began to attack his own side. This my sense of justice convinced me would never do. I may mention that a Judgeship was at the time vacant. I felt that this terrible dereliction from party duty must be punished. I deliberately changed the position of the beautiful hat, exquisite in its glossy freshness, from vertical to horizontal: my worst hopes were realised. After a peroration, in which he denounced the want of good sense of his own leaders, he sat down amid the cheering of our opponents. Crash into hopeless ruin went the hat! Placed vertically, it might have been restored: laterally, it was annihilated. I can see him now, holding up the hat with a look which reminded me of Macbeth glancing at his bloody fingers. 'This is a sorry sight.' He never knew, and I believe never suspected, who had done this. When he reads this work, as he will, it may remind him that there is an earthly retribution. I ought to add that he obtained a Judgeship.

❧

Justin McCarthy and Sir John Mowbray

Justin McCarthy, *Reminiscences* (1899)

No man has been more popular in the Lobby during my time, as, indeed, no man has been more popular in the House itself, than Sir John Mowbray. If I were set to describe the finest type of English Conservative country gentleman, I should try to paint a picture of Sir John Mowbray. Settled and strong in his own political convictions, he was happy in the possession of that too rare faculty which enables a man to understand that others may have totally different opinions and yet be honest men and worthy citizens, and good fellows too. I always think that Sir John Mowbray and Sir Roger de Coverley would have been steady and congenial friends, if the destinies had only allowed Sir Roger to be born just about the time of the Battle of Waterloo, and to sit for a Conservative constituency in the House of Commons . . . Everybody remembers the time when the Pigott forgeries were published, and the charges were made against the Irish Nationalist Members which led to the appointment of the Parnell Commission. Just at the time when the charges were made, and the political air was full of commotion, I went down one day to the House of Commons, and I met Sir John Mowbray in the Lobby. He had a group of friends around him whom I mentally set down as Conservative constituents from the University of Oxford. The House had not yet assembled, and up to that time no opportunity had arisen for any authoritative denial of the charges made against Parnell and his Party. As I was passing the group in the Lobby Sir John Mowbray's quick eye lighted on me. 'Mr Justin McCarthy,' he said, in a tone of amazing solemnity, 'I want my friends here to see how we Conservative gentlemen treat Irish Members publicly accused of favouring conspiracies to murder.' Then, in an instant, the solemn manner was changed, and Sir John's eye beamed with its wonted animation and kindliness. 'Give me your hand, my dear McCarthy,' he exclaimed, 'and let me present you to my friends here, who will all be delighted to know you.' No words of mine could tell how deeply I was touched by such a welcome from such a man at such a moment.

Charles Bradlaugh and Annie Thornton

Mrs Thornton was a House of Commons carpet-mender and was interviewed on her retirement.

Edinburgh Evening Dispatch, April 27, 1931

'But the kindest of all men was Mr Bradlaugh. He was once locked up in the Clock Tower all night, and if we had our way, we servants of the House would have made him more comfortable. For he deserved to be happy if ever a man did. He was considerate in every little action, even in the smallest things. For instance, he never flung his cigar ends away, but put them on a ledge for Charlie the road-sweeper. What could be kinder than that?'

Lloyd George and Sir John Henniker Heaton

Sir John Henniker Heaton (1848–1914) was educated at Kent House School and at King's College, London. He owned land through his mother in Australia as well as several Australian newspapers. Having represented the Governments of New South Wales and Tasmania on international missions, he sat as 'Progressive Conservative' MP for Canterbury from 1885 until 1910, when he retired. He was responsible for instituting the Imperial Penny Postage in 1898.

David Lloyd George, Letter to his family, August 9, 1890

Talking of Puleston a very interesting thing happened last night.[23] Whilst I was listening to some dreary debate or other about 110-ton guns a Conservative MP called Mr Henniker Heaton with whom I am rather chummy, and a very decent fellow he is too, beckoned me to come over to sit by his side on the Conservative benches. This I did and I found by the aroma of his breath that he had imbibed just a sufficient quantity of the wine which maketh glad the heart of man to make him communicative. It was after dinner and that's the time to get at an Englishman's secrets. He told me that he was very sorry for what the Government had done with Carnarvon Castle. That it was an act of gross jobbery and that all the members sitting around him on the Tory side were very disgusted over it. He said he hoped it would do me no harm for he went on to say 'although I am a Tory I have a sneaking sort of regard for you'. He then told me something about Puleston. He didn't think much of him.

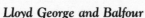

Lloyd George and Balfour

David Lloyd George, Letter to his brother William George, July 25, 1905

Balfour tried to smile pleasantly at me today. He doesn't want to quarrel with me. As one man on our side said 'You are so obviously one of his favourites—he was very upset by your speech yesterday, but still he didn't hit you hard.'

❖

Lloyd George's preference for Tories

Frances Stevenson, Diary, April 17, 1935

D. held forth about the mean-mindedness of Liberals as a race. They are frightened of reforms that will mean increased taxes—always have been. He remembers when as a very young boy the news came of the Education Act. A leading local Liberal opposed it, saying it would mean heavier rates. The local Tory agent supported it, saying that the boys of the neighbourhood should be properly educated. D. has never forgotten the difference in attitude of the two men. I cannot understand how D. ever became a Liberal, but for the fact that he would in his then circumstances have had no chance as a Tory. But he is instinctively drawn towards Tories for his friendships, and hates the sanctimonious humbug which seems to characterise the majority of successful Liberals. His great friends have been people like Winston, F.E., Horne, Geddes and Riddell. He always said there are no Liberals who would make a jolly dinner party such as we used to have in the days of the old Coalition.

❖

Lloyd George and the Speaker discuss William Gallacher

A. J. Sylvester, Diary, November 8, 1936

The Speaker said: 'The one man I hate in the House is Gallacher.' L.G. went on: 'So do I. He affects me physically.' The Speaker said: 'Yes, but you can go out and I can't.'[24]

❖

Baldwin and Churchill

Harold Balfour, *Wings over Westminster* (1973)

The India battle raged on. Baldwin and Churchill met in somewhat different circumstances to the Chamber. Both found themselves standing beside each other in the stalls of a lavatory off one of the lobbies. Said Baldwin, leaning towards his companion in occupation, 'At last, my dear Winston, we meet on a common platform for a common purpose.'

Sir Henry 'Chips' Channon, Diary, March 22, 1937

At the House of Commons, nothing much, except that I was startled to see Mr Baldwin and Winston drinking together, and alone in the Smoking Room; this is unheard of, and no one has seen them sitting together for ten years. Is it Baldwin's valedictory policy to be conciliatory to everyone, or is it a genuine reconciliation, or just mere chance? Churchill's stocks will now rise. They were like kittens in a basket, but they were certainly not drinking milk.

Lloyd George and Ramsay MacDonald

A. J. Sylvester, Diary, November 10, 1937

The adjournment of the House was to be moved in order to pay tribute to Ramsay MacDonald. The Prime Minister, Attlee and Sinclair were to speak, and I was asked to enquire whether L.G. would speak as Father of the House. I had to make an excuse. He disliked Ramsay MacDonald intensely.

Lloyd George and Neville Chamberlain

A. J. Sylvester, Diary, May 2, 1938

L.G. listened to Neville opening the debate. L.G. spoke for forty-five minutes. Not only did he do well, but, what was more important today, he did well in his own estimation. Since the row with the Prime Minister in the House, he had lost confidence in himself. Coming out of the Chamber, he met Winston. 'A magnificent speech,' said Winston. Neville passed at that moment. Winston said: 'You are having a quiet time.' 'Yes,' said Neville, looking at L.G., 'I did have until just now.' The Prime Minister does not like L.G.: it is mutual.

Harold Balfour and Jimmy Maxton

Harold Balfour, *Wings over Westminster* (1973)

The Clydesiders, ILP Jimmy Maxton, Geordie Buchanan, Campbell Stephen, Wheatley and, later, McGovern, gave the most effective Parliamentary opposition first to their own Labour Government and after 1931 to the National Government. Not until the '35 Parliament did I get to know well Jimmy Maxton and his fellow members of the Independent Labour Party. By then the Tories were so numerous that we almost encircled the Chamber. I found myself sharing the front bench below the gangway on the Opposition side with two Conservative friends, Peter Macdonald, who sat for the Isle of Wight, and the right-wing stalwart Henry Page-Croft, who sat for Bournemouth for many years. He finally became Lord Croft, Under-Secretary for War in the Lords in Churchill's 1940 Government where he made his famous speech on the Home Guard equipped with pikes to repel the then threatened invasion. On the same bench were Jimmy Maxton, Geordie Buchanan and McGovern.

When day after day you sit alongside, you get to know neighbours pretty well. Although politically we were poles apart we were a happy bunch. Jimmy Maxton, 'The Pirate' as he was called because of his long black hair with forelock falling over forehead, dark eyes and sallow skin, was a proud man. In the Smoking Room he would never take a drink or a cup of coffee from you because he quite literally could not afford to repay even such modest hospitality. In those days the pay of an MP was £400, later raised to £600 a year. The Clydesiders shared a small flat in Battersea where they took it in turns to cook and do the household chores. Also they shared a decrepit little Ford saloon to carry them across Westminster Bridge. One evening I came back to the House after a day's shooting. I had some pheasants in the back of the car and I knew that if I tried to make a gift of them to Jimmy he would certainly refuse. I asked the policeman in Palace Yard which was Mr Maxton's car. He pointed out the battered Ford and I threw a brace of pheasants into the back. Jimmy's thanks the next day were typical and quite unembarrassing to both parties. 'Harrold,' he said in his rolling Glasgow accent, 'you have one claim to fame. You can say that you are the only man who has fed a whole political party.'

One day I had two questions on the order paper dealing with Ramsgate harbour, owned by the Ministry of Transport. One of these was on navigational aids to the harbour entrance and the other on the inadequate public lavatories. After the Minister had replied Jimmy turned to me and said, 'Harrold, indeed you do cover the waterfront.' If I were asked who would have won a House of Commons popularity poll in the '31–'38 Parliament I guess my reply would be Jimmy Maxton.

W. J. Brown

So Far . . . (1943)

In the Chamber, Members are divided along Party lines. In the Smoking Room the divisions, or if you will the groupings, are on lines of interest and choice, quite other than Party groupings; often indeed cutting right across Party groupings. But whether in public, in the Chamber, or behind the scenes in the Smoking Room, the play of personalities goes fascinatingly on.

My particular associates in the House consisted partly of political friends and partly of political foes. Of the political friends, Maxton, Oliver Baldwin, Strachey, Frank Wise and Aneurin Bevan were the more remarkable. Of the political foes, John Buchan is the one of whom I think most affectionately.

Maxton had a genius for friendship: still has, indeed. He was perhaps the most popular man with MPs of all Parties in that House. He looks a tragic figure, with the long black hair—silvering now!—and the sad eyes, with the heavy black eyebrows, and the lined face and the sensitive mouth. And indeed, he has known tragedy. But his chief characteristic is a rippling sense of fun, and a whimsical, Barrie-like humour. He is never happier than when poking fun at himself. In those days he lived in a strange bachelor establishment—to which women did not penetrate—with Campbell Stephen and George Buchanan, where they did their own cooking, made their own beds, and took turns at the washing up, all to the accompaniment of never-ending political discussion! Now that partnership is broken. Maxton married the Secretary who had looked after him politically for so long. Campbell Stephen lives at a hotel, and Georgie I know not where. At this Battersea flat I spent many an evening and heard from, and of, Maxton many a good story.

The one about him I like best was that of his retort to a Tory who said to him one day: 'James, you have the manners of a prince and you dress like one of the unemployed!' Maxton's reply was, *'Naturally—I dress like my friends!'*

Oliver Baldwin was a queer fellow! He was much interested at that time in Spiritualism, and would have sessions with mediums, with a shorthand writer to take a record of the proceedings. One or two such sittings I attended with him, but am bound to say never heard anything which could not be accounted for on purely natural grounds. Oliver himself had a queer sixth sense, a capacity for divination, of which I will quote two examples.

One day we were in the Lobby outside the Chamber, talking. Inside the Chamber, the ballot for 'Private Members' Motions' was being taken. Suddenly Oliver said: 'Excuse me, Bill, I must go in. The next name they call will be mine.' I went in with him. It was!

On another occasion, in the Harcourt Dining Room, at the other end of the room from that at which Oliver was sitting, a man collapsed and slid from his chair to the floor. There was an immediate movement of the folk at Oliver's table to go to his aid. 'Don't bother,' said Oliver, 'you can do nothing! The man is dead.' And, believe it or not, he was . . .

Oliver lost his seat in 1931; but he looms up on my horizon from time to time, usually from some out of the way corner of the earth.

Frank Wise, who sat for Leicester, had had a remarkable career. He was, so far as I know, the only Clerk in the House of Commons who ever subsequently became a Member of that Assembly. Frank had an inexhaustible capacity for hard work, and if there was a statement to be drafted or a resolution to be worded, it was usually Frank who did it. His death, from a stroke, a few years after he had lost his seat, was a grievous loss. Aneurin Bevan, whose first Parliament this also was, was a fascinating talker, one of the best conversationalists, I should say, in all Britain. He was a Welsh miner, and in those days possessed an air of enquiring innocence which was most deceptive. He had a slight stammer which excited sympathy, but the brain behind the stammer was lightning-like in its movement, and was used on occasion with the precision of a steam-hammer. In Parliamentary performance he was very uneven, sometimes brilliant, sometimes badly missing fire. He was the only man in Parliament whom I ever saw put Mr Lloyd George to complete discomfiture. It was as if the ghost of Lloyd George of thirty years earlier had risen to confront the living man. When in a recent debate Bevan said of Mr Winston Churchill that 'he mistook verbal felicities for intellectual inspirations', he gave a first-rate example of the kind of polished invective of which he was and is capable.

John Buchan, the distinguished novelist—late Lord Tweedsmuir and Governor-General of Canada—had a curious sing-song way of speaking in the House. His intonation was rather like that of the music-hall parody of a curate, but his matter was always first-rate. In the Smoking Room he was a friendly, genial soul, full of good stories and a dry Scottish wit. I grew to like him very much . . . His fine series of novels remain to tell of his warm humanity and zest for life: and his *Cromwell* and other studies to tell of the deeper interests of his heart. If you want an example of his innate charity of judgement you will find it in his chapter on Ramsay MacDonald, in *Memory-Hold-the-Door*. A great and a good man!

❧

Churchill and Attlee

Sir Henry 'Chips' Channon, Diary, February 20, 1951

As I was walking in the Smoking Room corridor, I saw Winston, immaculately dressed, pleased with himself and puffing a cigar, approach: immediately in front of us walked Attlee and Arthur Moyle, his PPS. There was almost a collision; Winston did not make way (Attlee did, slightly) but made them one of his little courtly half-bows which he reserves for people he does not like. I was fascinated; as he passed me a second later he smiled, winked and passed on.

❧

Fenner Brockway

Inside the Left: Thirty Years of Platform, Press, Prison and Parliament (1942)

The best side of Parliamentary life was the friendships it developed. One such was my own friendship with Charles Trevelyan, Minister of Education. Every Thursday I used to have a meal with him in his delightful house in Great College Street, within a stone's throw of Parliament, so near that Charles had a division bell in his hall: on many occasions we scrambled across, via subterranean passages under the House of Lords, and voted in divisions on the summons of the bell. Trevelyan was very conscientious about not passing on Cabinet secrets to me, but he sympathised with the ILP desire for a more courageous policy, and we co-operated a good deal within the limits of our respective positions. Another friend I made was Oliver Baldwin, son of the Conservative Leader. Oliver had a great respect for his father, despite the difference of political views, and one often saw them chatting together in the smoking rooms. Oliver was a curious mixture in character: half mystic, half man of the world. He soon became disillusioned with Parliament, and one met him wandering the passages with eyes on distant things or found him sitting on the edge of the most distant bench of the House, as though to emphasise his apartness. Then he would give way to the mood of devil-may-care. He would turn to young Conservative friends in the House and forget the serious side of life, until some issue pulled him up sharply. He generally voted with the ILP Group but spoke little, though on one occasion he delivered a startlingly frank speech against war preparations, illustrating it with graphic stories of his own experiences in the Services.

Macmillan and Gaitskell

Harold Macmillan, interviewed by Alistair Horne for his *Macmillan 1957–1986* (1989)

He might have been a lecturer in Economics. He made the mistake, which Lloyd George warned me about, of making too many points . . . he would ask ten, or fourteen, questions—one of which was unanswerable, without telling him a direct lie . . . I soon learned that you only answered the easy ones . . . If he had asked one question which he knew I couldn't give the answer to truthfully, it would have been much more effective. But he asked so many questions, it was like one of those exams where you know that the candidate need not attempt more than any four! So you attempted the four easy ones. Poor man. I did it over and over again to him; he never spotted it . . .

Macmillan and Harold Wilson

Harold Wilson, interviewed by Alistair Horne for his *Macmillan 1957–1986* (1989)

There was absolutely no malice. After we had savaged each other in the House, we would then meet for a drink . . . I think he liked my crack about his being 'First in, first out' at Suez, and when he was moving in for the kill in the House he invariably kicked the table under the dispatch box with his right foot. Such courteous intimations have become rare since then!

1. Alexander Mackintosh, *Echoes of Big Ben: A Journalist's Parliamentary Diary, 1881–1940* (1945), pp. 163–4.
2. George Canning, Letter to Henry John Richman, 1793; quoted in George Henry Jennings, *An Anecdotal History of the British Parliament from the Earliest Periods to the Present Time* (1880), pp. 207–8.
3. R. G. Thorne (ed.), *The History of Parliament: The House of Commons 1790–1820* (1986), Vol. V, p. 82.
4. James Grant, *Random Recollections of the House of Commons* (1836), p. 5.
5. Sir William Fraser, *Disraeli and his Day* (1891), pp. 316–17.
6. ibid., p. 13.
7. Fenner Brockway, *Towards Tomorrow* (1977), p. 68.
8. Sir Henry Morris-Jones, *Doctor in the Whips' Room* (1955), pp. 164–5.
9. The Earl of Oxford and Asquith, *Memories and Reflections 1852–1927* (1928), Vol. I, p. 116.
10. E. M. Whitty, *St Stephen's in the Fifties: The Session 1852–3, A Parliamentary Retrospect* (1906), p. 35.
11. A. G. Gardiner, *The Life of Sir William Harcourt* (1923), Vol. II, p. 591.
12. Nigel Nicolson, *People and Parliament* (1958), p. 63.
13. C. W. Radcliffe Cooke, *Four Years in Parliament with Hard Labour* (1890), p. 17.
14. T. F. Lindsay, *Parliament from the Press Gallery* (1967), p. 75.
15. Martin Gilbert, *Churchill's Political Philosophy* (1981), pp. 101–2.
16. ibid., p. 102.
17. A. P. Herbert, *Independent Member* (1950), pp. 106–7.
18. George Hutchinson, *The Last Edwardian at No. 10: An Impression of Harold Macmillan* (1980), p. 13.
19. Sir Charles Petrie, *Life of Canning* (1930), p. 36.
20. Addington had made the mistake of appearing in elaborate court dress.
21. Disraeli's biographers, W. F. Monypenny and G. E. Buckle, say that the memorandum was 'written apparently in the sixties': *The Life of Benjamin Disraeli, Earl of Beaconsfield* (1910–12), Vol. I, p. 1074.
22. John Morley, *The Life of William Ewart Gladstone* (1903), Vol. III, ch. 4.
23. Puleston was a Tory MP who had stood against Lloyd George for the Caernarvon Boroughs seat.
24. The Speaker in question was Captain FitzRoy.

16 Strangers and Foreigners

On the whole, the Members were fine-looking men,
though some were of very ordinary mien; countenances
marked by nothing, except in one or two instances by
the small-pox.

Anon. (An American lady), *Change for the American
Notes: In Letters from London
to New York* (1843)

Strangers were regarded with suspicion and disapproval by Members for a couple of centuries and the privilege of excluding strangers was much invoked. 'When the debates in Parliament began to excite the interest of the public, and to attract an eager audience,' wrote Erskine May, 'the presence of strangers was connived at. They could be dismissed in a moment, at the instance of any member; but the Speaker was not often called upon to enforce the orders of the House.'[1] Although strangers included members of the press and female observers, the specific experience of these groups is dealt with in two subsequent chapters. Here, we are concerned with those strangers, several of them foreigners, who do not belong to either category.

Originally, it was feared somehow that the presence of strangers would endanger or denigrate the proceedings of Parliament. In 1584 a stranger who had sat in the House for two hours before he was apprehended as such, was stripped and searched and made to swear secrecy.[2] In 1740 Lord Chancellor Hardwicke stated in the House of Lords that the dignity of the House was diminished by 'admitting all kinds of auditors to your debates', because it 'makes them be what they ought not to be, and gives occasion to saying things which else would not be said'.[3] The actor-manager David Garrick was spotted in the Gallery in 1777 by an MP who demanded his expulsion—the next day this MP complained that a mere player should not be allowed to hear the debates, but was opposed by Burke, who claimed that he had learned much eloquence from Garrick's playing.[4]

At first, a stranger had to obtain an order from an MP and also had to pay a half-crown fee to a door-keeper. In 1837 a Member suggested that the public should be allowed to attend without an order from an MP, because such a requirement tended to disqualify the masses who were not represented in Parliament. Lord John Russell, however, argued that such a relaxation of the rules would invite the attendance of pickpockets and the proposal was rejected. For many years, strangers would be obliged to queue for several hours before gaining admittance. A system of balloting for seats in the Strangers' Gallery was instituted in 1867 and after two Fenian dynamiters were discovered to have been admitted to the Gallery a formal application had to be made to the Speaker's secretary in advance.

Owing to the chaotic organisation of the old Palace of Westminster before the fire of 1834, with the law courts located in Westminster Hall, strangers could mistakenly wander into the Chamber of the House of Commons. In 1771 a stranger was accidentally counted in a division and even long after the new Palace had been built, in 1875, two strangers entered the Chamber during a debate and remained there when the House was cleared for a division, at which point their presence was discovered. Even animals sometimes invaded the House: a young jackdaw flew into the House in 1604, a mouse-coloured spaniel wandered in the following year.[5]

Special provision of seats was made for distinguished strangers, such as peers and foreign ambassadors or aristocrats. The former Tory Lord Chancellor, Lord Lyndhurst, received a warmer welcome than he had bargained for when he entered the House and sat below the bar as an Irish Member was speaking. The moment he was noticed the Irish Members set to barracking him. Sir Almeric Fitzroy asked Sir Henry Wilson, FM, the Deputy Chief of Staff in 1922, how he liked the House of Commons, 'upon which he smiled grimly and said, "I go and look at them sometimes," as if they were a collection of curious animals'.[6] In 1956, when Marshal Bulganin and Nikita Khrushchev, who were visiting Britain in an official capacity, sat in the Distinguished Strangers' Gallery alongside a Russian-speaking Tory MP, Harry Boardman devoted that day's *Manchester Guardian* sketch to their presence and their apparent bemusement at the proceedings.[7] Sometimes a famous stranger would even be admitted to the Reporters' Gallery. The *News Chronicle* reporter Ian McKay 'found Charlie Chaplin sitting in my seat in the Press Gallery listening to Baldwin telling us our frontier was on the Rhine'.[8]

Foreign visitors have often found Parliament a disappointment. Alexis de Toqueville was expecting great pearls of wisdom, eloquently expressed, to fall from the lips of the Duke of Wellington. 'The Duke began his speech with difficulty and hesitation and was never completely at ease,' he recorded. 'It was the strangest sight to see the man who had won so many battles and defeated Bonaparte as embarrassed as a child reciting its lesson before a pitiless pedagogue. The hero of Waterloo did not know where to put his arms or legs, nor how to balance his long body. He picked up and put down his hat, turned to the left and the right, ceaselessly buttoned and unbuttoned the pocket of his breeches as if he wanted to seek his words there, words to be sure that did not flow easily from his mind.' Still, a stranger lucky enough to attend the House on the day of an anxious debate which threatened to bring down the Government was enthused by the experience: Count de Montalembert attended the debate on Cardwell's Motion in 1858 and wrote a pamphlet, *Un débat sur l'Inde au Parlement Anglais*, in which he drew unfavourable comparison between the French and English legislatures and for which the French Government prosecuted him.[9] The writer who assumed the character of a Russian noble from St Petersburg, Count Paul Vasili, was more cynical about the nature of this democratic assembly. 'The labours of the English Parliament are very severe,' he explained; 'two hours of each sitting are wasted in questions asked by members who are longing to read their names next morning in the local newspaper, and want to prove to their constituents that they are something more than voting machines.'[10] A future American president, Congressman James A. Garfield, visited the Commons to watch one of the debates on the 1867 Reform Bill and admired the 'un-English style' of speaking exhibited by Gladstone and Bright, which had 'little of that distressful hobbling which marks the mass of Parliamentary speakers'.[11]

Americans in particular have wanted Parliament to be more awesome than it was. One American visitor told Frederick Moir Bussy, an editor of *Hansard*, how shocked he was to see the Prime Minister, Mr Balfour, put his feet on the table, not on 'his own bright particular centre-piece of furniture' in 'his own private room', but on the table presided over by the Speaker of the House of Commons: 'The reckless bravado and the flouting of universal etiquette involved is emphasised by the fact that to "get there" he has to slither down on the cushioned bench until the nape of his neck rests upon the oak frame of it, where his back ought to be; the middle of his spine occupies the actual seat. The position is not only inelegant, it is shocking to the tender susceptibilities of all who have regard for what you Britishers call the amenities of polite society.'[12]

On another occasion, Bussy obtained a standard voucher for admission to the Strangers' Gallery of the House of Lords on behalf of two American merchant princes and persuaded the Duke of Marlborough (who had married a Vanderbilt) to sign it, but the foreign visitors, rather than surrender the voucher and thereby gain admittance to the Gilded Chamber, preferred to retain the piece of paper 'to show the people back home'.[13]

❖

'Mr Pepys, Speaker of the Parliament-house'

Samuel Pepys (1633–1703), the renowned diarist, was the son of a London tailor and was educated at St Paul's School and at Trinity Hall and Magdalene College, Cambridge. He was never a Member of Parliament, but in his capacity as an Admiralty official it fell upon him to defend the management of the Navy before the House of Commons.

Samuel Pepys, Diary, 1668

March 4–5. . . . So we all up to the Lobby; and between 11 and 12 o'clock were called in, with the Mace before us, into the House; where a mighty full House, and we stood at the Bar—viz., Brouncker, Sir J. Mennes, Sir T. Harvey and myself—W. Penn being in the House as a Member. I perceive the whole House was full, and full of expectation of our defence what it would be, and with great prejudice. After the Speaker had told us the dissatisfaction of the House, and read the report of the Committee, I begin our defence most acceptably and smoothly, and continued at it without any hesitation or loss but with full scope and all my reason free about me, as if it had been at my own table, from that time till past 3 in the afternoon; and so ended without any interruption from the Speaker, but we withdrew. And there my fellow-officers, and all the world that was within hearing, did congratulate me and cry up my speech as the best thing they ever heard, and my fellow-officers overjoyed in it. We were called in again by and by to answer only one question, touching our paying tickets to ticket-mongers—and so out; and we were in hopes to have had a vote this day in our favour, and so the generality of the House was; but my speech being so long, many had gone out to dinner and come in again half drunk, and then there are two or three that are professed enemies to us and everybody else; among others, Sir T. Littleton, Sir Tho. Lee, Mr Wiles (the coxcomb whom I saw heretofore at the cockfighting), and a few others; I saw these did rise up and speak against the coming to a vote now, the House not being full, by reason of several being at dinner but most because the House was to attend the King this afternoon about the business of Religion (wherein they pray him to put in force all the laws against nonconformists and papists); and this prevented it, so that they put it off to tomorrow come sennit. However, it is plain we have got great ground; and everybody says I have got the most honour that any could have had opportunity of getting.

March 6. Up betimes, and with Sir D. Gawden to Sir W. Coventry's chamber, where the first word he said to me was, 'Goodmorrow Mr Pepys, that must be Speaker of the Parliament-house'—and did protest I had got honour for ever in Parliament. He said that his brother, that sat by him, admires me; and another gentleman said that I could not get less than 1000*l* a year if I would put on a gown and plead at the Chancery bar. But what pleases me most, he tells me that the Solicitor general did protest that he thought I spoke the best of any man in England. After several talks with him alone touching his own business, he carried me to Whitehall and there parted; and I to the Duke of York's lodging and find him going to the park, it being a very fine morning; and I after him, and as soon as he saw me, he told me with great satisfaction that I had converted a great many yesterday, and did with great praise of me go on with the discourse with me. And by and by overtaking the King, the King and the Duke of York came up to me both, and he said, 'Mr Pepys, I am very glad of your success yesterday'; and fell to talk of my well speaking; and many of the Lords there, my Lord Berkely did cry me up for what they had heard of it; and others, Parliament[-men] there about the King, did say that they never heard such a speech in their lives delivered in that manner. Progers of the Bedchamber swore to me afterward before Brouncker in the afternoon, that he did tell the King that he thought I might teach the Solicitor general. Everybody that saw me almost came to me, as Joseph Williamson and others, with such eulogy as cannot be expressed. From thence I went to Westminster hall, where I met Mr G. Montagu; who came to me and kissed me, and told me that he had often heretofore kissed my hands, but now he would kiss my lips, protesting that I was another Cicero, and said all the world said the same of me. Mr Ashburnham, and every creature I met there of the Parliament or that knew anything of the Parliament's actings, did salute me with this honour— Mr Godolphin, Mr Sands, who swore he would go twenty mile at any time to hear the like again, and that he never saw so many sit four hours together to hear any man in his life as there did to hear me. Mr Chichly, Sir J. Duncom, and everybody doth say that the Kingdom will ring of my ability, and that I have done myself right for my whole life; and so Capt. Cocke, and other of my friends, say that no man had ever such opportunity of making his abilities known. And, that I may cite all at once, Mr Lieutenant of the Tower did tell me that Mr Vaughan did protest to him, and that in his hearing it, said so to the Duke of Albemarle and afterward to W. Coventry, that he had sat 26 years in Parliament and never heard such a speech before—for which the Lord God made me thankful, and that I may make use of it not to pride and vainglory, but that now I have this esteem, I may do nothing that may lessen it.

A Prussian view

Carl Philip Moritz was a Prussian pastor who travelled to England in 1782, publishing his *Travels, chiefly on Foot, through several parts of England in 1782, described in Letters to a Friend* back in his native land later that year. Although an English translation was published in 1795, I have taken this excerpt from the 1965 translation by Reinald Nettel.

C. P. Moritz, Letter to a friend, June 13, 1782

One afternoon, about three o'clock, which is about the time when parliamentary sittings start, I asked the way to Westminster Hall and an Englishman very courteously directed me there. In this manner one may easily find one's way all over London, for anyone who has the ability to make himself understood may ask whom he pleases.

Westminster Hall is a huge Gothic building, its roof supported not by pillars but by misshapen angels' heads carved in wood and projecting from each side-wall.

Going through this long hall and mounting a few steps at the end, you may pass down a dark passage and finally arrive at the House of Commons. This chamber has a pair of great double doors at floor level. Ascending a little staircase, however, you come to the strangers' Gallery overhead.

When I mounted these stairs for the first time and arrived at the parapet, I saw a very respectable man standing there dressed all in black, whom I asked if I might be allowed to go into the gallery. He replied that unless I were introduced by a Member of Parliament I could not be admitted. As I had not the honour of knowing a Member of Parliament, however, I turned and began to descend the stairs much disappointed. On the way down I heard something about a bottle of wine, apparently addressed to me but which I was utterly unable to comprehend until I arrived home, when my landlady explained that the well-dressed man wanted me to slip two shillings or half-a-crown into his hand to buy a bottle of wine.

This I did on the following day, when that very same man who had previously turned me away now opened the door—after I had pressed a mere couple of shillings in his hand—and personally recommended me to a place in the gallery with the utmost courtesy.

Then, in this rather unimposing building, rather like a chapel, I saw for the first time the whole English nation gathered together by representation. The Speaker, an elderly man, sat right opposite to me in a raised chair. He wore a full-bottomed wig, a black gown, and had his hat on his head; the chair much

resembled a small pulpit except that it had no reading-desk upon it. In front
of this chair stood a table, like an altar, at which sat two black-gowned men
called clerks, and on this table lay a great gilded sceptre near the rolls of
parchment which contained the Acts of Parliament. This sceptre is removed
to a place under the table whenever the Speaker leaves his chair, which he
does every time the House resolves itself into committee by which they mean
an inquiry or discussion; during this time he lays aside his power and authority.
As soon as the discussion is over, however, someone tells the Speaker, 'Now
you can take the chair again,' and the sceptre is replaced on the table before
him.

The benches for the members of Parliament stand round the sides of the
chamber under the gallery. They are covered with green cloth and so arranged
that back benches are raised higher than those in front, like the choir-stalls in
our churches, so that anyone addressing the House can always see over the
heads of those sitting in front of him. Similarly with the benches in the gallery.
Members keep their hats on but spectators in the gallery remove theirs.

Members of the House of Commons wear no special clothing. They enter
the House in greatcoats, boots and spurs! It is not unusual to see a Member
stretched out on one of the benches while the rest are in debate. One
Member may be cracking nuts, another eating an orange or whatever fruit may
be in season; they are constantly going in and out. Whenever one of them
wishes to leave the chamber he stands first before the Speaker and makes him
a bow, just like a schoolboy begging permission of his teacher.

Members address the House without any stiffness of speech. One of them
simply rises from his seat, takes off his hat, turns towards the Speaker (to whom
all speeches are directed), holds his hat and stick in one hand while he
gesticulates with the other.

Whenever one of them speaks badly or the matter of his speech lacks interest
for the majority, the noise and laughter are such that the Member can hardly
hear his own words. This must be a very fearful time for him. It is amusing
when the Speaker calls out from his chair, like a schoolmaster appealing against
disorder: 'To order! To order!' Often without attracting much attention.

During the course of a good, purposive speech, however, absolute stillness
reigns, and one Member after another shows his approval by shouting 'Hear
him!'—a cry often taken up by the whole House, making so much noise
that the Speaker is often again interrupted by this shout of approval. Yet
notwithstanding its inconvenience this shout is always a great encouragement
and I have often observed how a Member who had begun with little confidence,
speaking without much spirit, would warm up under such incitement and end
with a flashing display of oratory.

As all speeches are addressed to the Speaker they begin with the word 'sir',
whereupon the Speaker lifts his hat slightly but immediately puts it on again.
This 'sir' is often used also in the course of the address and serves to help

anyone who has lost his memory; for if he says 'sir' and with it makes a short pause, he can think of what is to follow. I have seen one obliged to draw a sort of plan out of his pocket, as at a loss, like a candidate hesitating in his sermon, but otherwise a parliamentary speech is never read. These speeches have their stock phrases, as 'whereof first consideration must be taken in this House', and the like.

On the first day I was there an Englishman who sat next to me in the gallery pointed out to me the best-known Members of Parliament, such as Fox, Burke, Rigby, etc, all of whom I heard address the House. They were debating whether some material reward should be given to Admiral Rodney in addition to his elevation to the peerage. In the course of the debate young Lord Fielding took Mr Fox to task for having, as a Minister of State, opposed the election of Admiral Hood as Member for Westminster.

Fox was sitting on the Speaker's right, not far from the table whereupon the gilded sceptre lies. He now took his stand so near the table that he could reach it with his hand and was able to bang his fist on it with many a violent blow, thus giving force to his speech. He defended himself against Lord Fielding by insisting that he voted in the election referred to, not as a Minister, but in his capacity as a private citizen, in which capacity he had given his vote to another candidate—Mr Cecil Wray. When the King appointed him—Fox—Secretary of State, they made no bargain regarding his rights as a private voter, nor would he have engaged in such a barter anyway. I cannot describe to you with what fire and eloquence he spoke, and how the Speaker in his chair continually nodded approval with his great bewigged poll while all shouted 'Hear him! Hear him!' and when it seemed he was about to come to an end called out 'Speak yet!', and in this wise he continued nearly two hours.

Rigby thereupon made a short but witty speech to point out how little provision the bare title of Lord or Lady made without money, and closed with the Latin phrase: *infelis pauperas quia ridiculos miseros facit*, after having observed however that inquiry should first be made to ascertain if Admiral Rodney had recently received any considerable prize-money, for in that event he would not need a further grant of money. Since then I have been to the Houses of Parliament almost every day and find the entertainment there to be satisfying beyond most other.

Fox is still much beloved of the people, despite his having been the cause of Admiral Rodney's recall. Yet I have myself heard Fox speak in highest praise of the Admiral. Charles James Fox is dark, small, thickset, generally ill-groomed and looks rather like a Jew; nevertheless he is well-informed and his political sagacity is evident in his eyes. I have often heard it said here: 'Mr Fox is cunning like a fox.' Burke is a well-built man, tall and straight but already looking somewhat elderly. Rigby is very fat, with a hearty red complexion.

I was much shocked by the open abuse which Members of Parliament flung at each other. For example, one Member ended his speech and another rose immediately and commenced with the phrase: 'It is quite absurd', etc, 'what the Right Honourable Gentleman has argued.' (For with this title do Members of the Lower House honour each other.) In conformity with parliamentary procedure, however, nobody says to another Member's face that he has spoken like a fool, but turns to the Speaker in the customary way and says, as though addressing the Speaker: 'The Right Honourable Gentleman has talked a lot of nonsense.'

It is very funny to see one Member speaking and another making the appropriate gestures, as I noted being done on one occasion by a worthy old burgess afraid to speak himself but who emphasised his neighbour's sentences with so many gestures that his whole body was in motion.

The gist of the debate is often lost in bickering and misunderstanding between each other. If they go on too long and become tiresome a general cry goes up: 'The question! The question!' which must often be repeated many times because both parties invariably want to have the last word. However, the question is at last put and the Speaker says: 'All in favour say "Ay"; all against say "No".' Then one hears a confused shriek of 'ay' and 'no' together and the Speaker says: 'It seems to me there are more "ayes" than "noes",' or vice versa. Then all spectators must leave the gallery and voting starts in earnest. Members look up at the gallery and shout, 'Withdraw!' until all spectators have left the room. Then they are locked in a room downstairs until the voting is over, after which they may return to the gallery. It greatly surprised me to see apparently well-conducted Englishmen pushing and shoving as soon as the door was reopened after the voting, in order to get the best seats in the gallery. Two or three times we were sent out of the gallery in this way and later allowed to return.

The spectators include people of all ranks and there are always ladies among them. A couple of shorthand-writers sat not far from me, trying stealthily to take down the words of the speakers, which can be read in print the same night. These reporters are presumably paid by the editors of the newspapers. There are a few regular visitors to Parliament who pay the doorman a guinea for the whole session. I have seen some Members of Parliament also take one of their young sons to sit with them in the House.

It has been proposed that a gallery should be erected in the House of Lords, but this has not been put into effect. There the business is conducted with more ceremony and decorum. Anyone who wishes to observe mankind, however, and study human nature in the raw, should go to the House of Commons.

❖

Erik Gustaf Geijer

Impressions of England 1809–1810 (1932)

February 2. Was for the first time in Parliament. The chamber is small, and although without any kind of grandeur may yet be called splendid compared with what it must formerly have been. It was enlarged on the occasion of the Union between Ireland and England, when the Lords, too, were removed to a more convenient place. It is interesting to see this carelessness of every kind of display in all which touches the public. To work without ostentation and without fuss belongs to this nation's character. The House of Commons where, if one comes some hours before the members are assembled, one may see the custodian's girls dusting and tidying, where the very smallness of the chamber and its appointments removes all sense of ceremony, where the members walk, stand, sit (read the papers and chat, too, when the debates are not interesting) during the debates as best suits their convenience, in top-boots, with hats on and in great-coats, or go up into their gallery and lie at full length on the benches to listen to the speeches, this House has rather a domestic aspect than the appearance of a ceremonial meeting-place for the nation's representatives. The House meets at four o'clock, when the Speaker takes his chair. The Gallery was already full at one o'clock. I came there at twelve. The English have in such respects an exemplary patience. One must come to the Gallery in time to get a place, for it accommodates only a hundred and fifty persons.

The debates in the House sometimes continue till five o'clock in the morning. At about eight o'clock in the evening the House went into Committee of Inquiry on the Walcheren Expedition—and in order to suppress the uncertain and incomplete or biased accounts in the newspapers, which in the Duke of York's case are considered to have done much harm, it was moved that all strangers should withdraw. Consequently I was only able to hear a small part of the sitting, during which nothing noteworthy occurred. There was much hissing in the Gallery when they cried that strangers must withdraw.

My neighbour became so troublesome to me that I had to change my place. His dress, his speech and the aroma of gin around him showed to what class he belonged. He had never before been in Parliament; attacked me at once with the declaration that this place affords the greatest spectacle that the world can produce, that he as an Englishman was proud of it, that for the rest the whole House was corrupt, that reform was necessary, that principles were the chief thing, and more of such rubbish, which he had heard repeated and had learned by heart. He asked if I had seen Sir Francis,[14] said of Bonaparte, that he laughed at the English ministry, that no ministry was worth anything, they were all alike, that reform, etc; that he feared—although he did not desire—that the French, in the absence of reform, would annex England to France and so forth. All these are opinions which distinguish the party, which here is called independent, which always clamours for reform, but for the rest displays little enough intelligence. The conversation was only worth notice in that it confirmed what I have heard before and proved, that the independent party has a large mob-following. It is natural that it should have. That this pot-house politician was, moreover, a *Freeholder* appeared from the fact that when he attacked all mankind with his republican catchwords and no one took any notice of him, he shouted at the top of his voice: 'The freeholders of this country are not to be insulted.' My man then slept through the whole debate.

The House is reconciled to Warren Hastings

Warren Hastings (1732–1818) joined the East India Company in 1750 and was made Governor-General of Bengal in 1774. After ruling for ten years, during which he introduced important reforms and fought the Mahrattas for control of large areas of territory, he returned to England only to find that the Whig Opposition, led by Burke, Fox and Sheridan, were engineering the House of Commons to bring impeachment proceedings against him on charges of maladministration and corruption. There was a period in the mid-1780s when scarcely a day went by without some parliamentary initiative on the part of either his champions or detractors. His trial lasted for seven years and resulted in his acquittal, though at a cost to him of £80,000—virtually the entire fortune he had made in India. However, the East India Company provided him with the money needed to live as a country gentleman. A few years after his acquittal, he was invited to give evidence about Indian affairs before the Commons (meeting in Committee) and the Lords.

George Thompson, Letter to Sir John D'Oyley, May 17, 1813

I accompanied him to the House of Commons when he went to give his evidence. Whilst we were sitting in the Speaker's room preparatory to his examination, Sir Thomas Plumer came to us, and I congratulated him on the very different auspices under which we now assembled from those which formerly brought us there. He heartily participated in this feeling, and earnestly said, 'Did you not hear just now a great noise in the House?' Upon our answering in the negative, he added, 'I made sure you must, for when Mr Hastings's name was mentioned, and a motion made that he might be offered a chair, a louder acclamation followed than I ever remember to have heard within its walls.' At the close of his evidence the members, influenced by one common feeling of respect, rose spontaneously, and taking off their hats, stood whilst he retired. You who know the warmth and generosity of his heart will readily conceive how forcibly it was touched, and how delightfully affected by so unequivocal, unlooked for, and rare a testimony of public esteem. His reception before the Lords was hardly less flattering. The Duke of Gloucester, at his own request, called upon him and took him in his chariot to the House, waited with him in one of the chambers till he was summoned, accompanied him into the committee room, attended whilst he gave evidence, and at its close conducted him back again to his Royal Highness's chariot. Whilst before the Lords he was accommodated with a seat, an honour which I am told is almost unprecedented. Throughout the whole investigation the most marked attention has been paid, both to his person and his opinions. The very officers of both houses, even to the printers of their proceedings, as well as the persons employed by the

Company, seem to have vied with each other in manifesting their respect for him.

❧

Visiting the House as a Stranger

Anon. (A Member of the Upper Benches), *The Collective Wisdom: or, Sights and Sketches of the Chapel of St Stephen's* (1824)

Imagine, then, courteous reader, that some mighty field day has come round—some day, which has stood rubric for weeks in the notices, and been put off thrice, in order that it might lick up importance like a snowball, that the 'petitioning tools' throughout the country have been set to work pro and con, till the skins of as many calves are upon and below the table as are purchased in Smithfield in a week; that the leading speakers have been drudging at their orations for a month, that the followers and fencers have got their points, and that the mutes are divided, and have been told, 'how many glasses' (of wine of course, not of sand) each speaker is to run: imagine that it is about two o'clock, and that you, who have come from a distance, and are most anxious to be enlightened by the wisdom and warmed by the eloquence of the Senate, have stuffed your pocket with sandwiches, and are elbowing through the crowd in Westminster-hall. You of course take no time to admire the admirable proportions of that most splendid barn in the three kingdoms; you do not heed the exquisite taste with which the towers and entrance have been restored, nor do you utter a single curse at the bad taste which is erecting the filthy pile, the new courts, upon the old building—like a barnacle on a ship's bottom. You pass all these things, and come bump upon the dark passage, through which a Briton must grope toward either House of Parliament. You squeeze into the lobby, and look at the place where Perceval was shot, and the form upon which Bellingham the assassin sat down cool and unconcerned after he had perpetrated the atrocious deed; and if you have enough of brass and of curiosity, you poke your nose half-way in at the door, by which the 'Collective' are dropping in, to stick upon the benches bits of paper expressing the name and quality of the wisdom which is to occupy them for the night; but before you have seen anything more than three windows with heads most emblematically round, and the top of an old black chair, not unlike (saving that the royal beast bear a greater proportion to the whole) that of the Right Worshipful in your own Mason lodge, the door keeper most unceremoniously drives you away from matting which must be trod only by the Collective feet. Being, haply, a person of weak, or at least irritable nerves, the fear of the serjeant-at-arms, and the paying of your fees, comes upon you, and you retreat as fast you can, and in your retreat kick by accident the basket of an old Jewess, and set the oranges spinning all over the lobby. Having achieved these exploits, you assail the staircase; and if you be strong in the legs, and clever at the elbows, work your way to the door of the Messengers' lobby,—not, however, till your sandwiches get a fair offer of entering your stomach laterally. You stand there for full two hours; and while your ribs are elbowed and your toes trod upon, you see the ample bald sconce of Mr Wright moving to and fro, as he admits by the private door those who have more newly worked keys than your half-crown. The speaker enters, the door opens, and you are shot away from the landing place across the steps, and up to the gallery door, as if a goodly charge of gunpowder were at your heels! You get into the gallery; and the front rows are full, excepting just room for one gentleman in the middle. Some wag invites you there, and you squat yourself down under the shade of the clock-case, where you can see nothing. Before you find your mistake, the seats are all filled save the backmost; and you sit down there, but ere you have got time to draw your breath, the *Times* or the *Chronicle* ejects you, but obligingly gives you a berth in the next row, and whispers you from time to time the names of the members who are pulling up their breeches, conning their notes, or kicking their heels upon the benches below.

You have now time to look about you; and the first things that strikes you is the mean and sombre appearance of the House. 'The Chapel of St Stephen— the scene of so many great sayings—the theatre of the "Collective Wisdom", why it is not half as large, or one-third as tasteful, as my own parish church.' Its walls are dull and dingy, and the roof is so near you, that you feel as if you were to be suffocated. You look to the right and left, and wonder at the small space allotted for strangers; and ignorant that they are for the lolling and lounging members, you wonder why there is nobody in the side galleries. Just before you is the table, upon the near end of which lies the mace, and at the far end sit the clerks. Beyond that is the Speaker, with a most graceful wig and manner, and some young lay Member chatting with him, just to shew to a random constituent in the gallery (haply yourself) that he can approach the chair. To your left are the Ministers upon the bench next the table; behind them the ministerial seconders; then the 'country Gentlemen', behind whom sit a mixed multitude: to your right, upon the first bench, are the heavy artillery of the Opposition, and behind them the light troops. The benches on both sides are rounded away, and mingle and are lost behind the Speaker's Chair; where, as at neutral ground, Tories and Whigs exchange civilities and snuff-boxes.

Behind you sit 'the morning papers' pointing pens and pencils, and complimenting the anticipated speakers of the night in the inverse ratio of their anticipated speeches. You are amazed that any set of men, especially a set of men whose words and faces evince so much intelligence, should treat not with indifference only, but with absolute dislike, that which you have come so far, and wished so fondly to hear; but you will be pleased to bear in mind that their eyes and fingers must ache at the writing of speeches which to you are mere matter of amusement, and that their memories must be on the rack recollecting, and their judgements untwisting and piecing together the bones and muscles of this body of eloquence,—that, in short, they have to arrest the wind which is sweeping in gales, breathing in zephyrs, roaring in tempests, or whirling in tornadoes, give it body and permanence, and send it abroad all over the world. When you have finished your survey, and are listening to some piece of criticism or end of wit upon the seat behind you, you hear the names of the numbers repeated in a very melodious but solemn voice, and fancy that some one has come to give the House a lesson in arithmetic; but upon lending your other ear, you find that it is nothing more than the Speaker going through the routine of counting the house. When he comes to thirty-nine he makes one himself, takes the chair, and business commences.

Jehangeer Nowrojee and Hirjeebhoy Merwanjee

Nowrojee and Merwanjee were naval architects, the son and nephew of the master builder in the East India Company's dockyard in Bombay. The fifth generation of their family to serve the East India Company, they had been sent to England to learn the new skill of constructing steam vessels under the patronage of Sir Charles Forbes, the Bombay merchant.

Journal of a Residence of Two Years and a Half in Great Britain (1841)

On the 25th of February, 1841, accompanied by our kind friend Thomas Baldock, Esq, who procured for us admission, we paid a visit to the House of Commons, and were allowed to sit in the body of the house, under the Strangers' Gallery, and were separated from the members only by a slight rod of iron. We had previously paid a visit to the House of Commons, through the kindness of our friend Sir Charles Forbes, but as we then had nobody with us to tell us the names of the members, our first visit lost much of its interest.

This night was a very important night, as it was to be a trial of strength between the Liberals and the Conservatives; and out of six hundred and fifty-eight members, five hundred and ninety-seven were that night present. The question under discussion was a Bill introduced by Lord Morpeth, a member of the Whig administration, relative to Irish Parliamentary Voters. A Bill of the same name, introduced by Lord Stanley, now a Conservative, but who had been, a short time since, a minister of the Whig government, was so different in some of its clauses, that it appeared all the Conservatives had agreed to vote against the second reading of this Bill, and of course all the Ministerialists were gathered together to vote for it; and almost all the sixty-one members who were not present to vote this evening had, what is called, paired off: that is, a Conservative who wished to be away agreed with a Liberal who also wished to be away that neither of them would vote, and this neutralising of each other's votes is called pairing off. We were admitted into the body of the house somewhere about six o'clock on Thursday evening, and there we sat until half-past two on Friday morning, about eight hours and a half. Shortly after we entered the house an influential gentleman among the Conservatives told our friend that the Ministers would have a majority of six, and about eight o'clock he said another ministerial member had posted home from Vienna, and that the majority of votes would most probably be seven; and to prove how accurately he made his calculation, the Ministers had a majority of five; one of the persons who was expected to vote with the Ministerialists voted with the Opposition, and thus accounted for the variation. The gentleman in question is sometimes called the whipper-in of the Conservatives, that is to say, he urges all to vote, knows where every member is, and if he intends to be in the house or not. This must be a troublesome office.

The present House of Commons is a temporary affair only. The former place where they met was destroyed by fire a few years since; and a magnificent erection for the House of Lords and Commons is now building close to the Westminster Hall, and very near to the present building. The Speaker, who is one of the members, is the chairman; he is seated in a raised chair near the extremity of the large room, and where he can see all the members. On his right hand, on seats raised one above the other, the ministers of the day and their friends sit; the most influential on the upper front seat, called the treasury benches, nearest to the Speaker. The opposition members sit on the left hand of the Speaker, and are arranged according to their importance to their party, similar to their opponents opposite. The Speaker is much disfigured by wearing an immense wig of whitish hair and a black gown, and, seated at a table before him, are three persons similarly attired in wigs and gowns, who *are not members*, but are Clerks of the House, and keep the records. And upon the table is laid a beautiful silver gilt ornament, three or four feet long, called the mace. When the house is in what is called Committee of the House, Mr Bernal, member for Rochester, sits at the table, and the Speaker does not sit in the chair; but Mr Bernal, who is called Chairman of the Committees, acts then exactly as if he was the Speaker. In a raised chair, at the opposite end to the Speaker, is seated Sir William Gossett, the serjeant-at-arms, who is to preserve order below the bar, and to take into custody any member, or other person, upon the command of the Speaker, who may do anything contrary to the usages of Parliament; when he wishes to withdraw for a short time, John Clement Esq, deputy serjeant-at-arms, takes his seat. When we entered the house Mr Gisborne was addressing the house from the ministerial side, and there were not then perhaps one hundred members in the house, and then Mr Cholmondeley answered from the opposition; Mr M. J. O'Connell replied to him, and Mr Tennent opposed the second reading, and Mr W. Roche spoke in favour of it. This was all what soldiers would call light skirmishing; and now what they call the big guns began to go off. Mr Shaw, the Recorder of Dublin, from the opposition benches, in a very lengthy but good speech spoke against the Bill, and this called up the great Irish agitator, Mr Daniel O'Connell. He spoke upwards of two hours, addressed the house in most energetic terms, imploring the members, for the safety and welfare of England and Ireland, 'to do justice to Ireland', by placing her upon the same footing as England in all things. He spoke most feelingly—most forcibly, and with his large figure, clear distinct voice, and peculiar Irish pronunciation, he attracted much of our attention, particularly when he said very loudly,—'Grant this Bill, and you will take away much of my powerful influence: I call upon you to disarm me by doing justice to my country.' He was very many times loudly cheered by the members who sat on his side of the house.

Strangers are not allowed to be present in the House of Commons by the strict rules of the house; and, in fact, they are *supposed* never to be present: but in a gallery behind the Speaker's chair are forty or fifty reporters for the different newspapers, who are writing down in short-hand all that is said, and who go out and are relieved at stated periods; and it is a fact that although on the morning of the 26th of February, the debate did not close nor was the division declared, until near three o'clock, every speech that was made in the house was printed just as delivered, in the several newspapers, and, soon after eight o'clock, was laid upon the breakfast tables of the inhabitants of London. The Speaker is supposed to be ignorant of these people being present, as they are behind him; and the strangers admitted by the members into the gallery over which we sat, and the persons near us who were admitted by the Speaker, would be ordered immediately out of the house if any member were to rise and say, 'Mr Speaker there are strangers in the house,' he would then call out, 'Strangers must withdraw.' And whenever any member chooses to divide the house, that is, to request persons to *vote* upon any subject, all visitors have to go out instantly.

We were, as a matter of course, dressed in our costume; and, sitting in the foremost seat allowed for strangers, we had a capital view of all the members, and could hear remarkably well nearly everything that was said; and consequently every member could see us. We fancied once, when Mr O'Connell was speaking, that he observed and alluded to us. He was looking towards us, and at that time in his most forcible manner he said, 'Mind what you are doing, the eyes of the whole world are upon you'; or words to that effect. It might be fancy, but such was our impression at the time.

After Mr O'Connell had finished his speech, Sir Robert Peel (who was formerly first minister of the crown, and who has been for some time leading man of the Tory party) rose, and, looking very angrily at Mr O'Connell, attacked him for sometime for the threats that he (Mr O'Connell) had indulged in towards England; he said 'He has spoken in a tone totally unworthy of the representative of the Irish people. In a tone and temper unworthy of that character; such as I never heard. I do not complain of the high tone which that honourable and learned gentleman takes, but I do complain of the apparent delight with which he gloated on the past animosities between two peoples.'

Sir Robert also said, 'I believe you libel your country; you libel your country when you insinuate that they would not join us in repulsing the attacks, either of France or America.' In making these observations, he seemed as if he was much angry and could not control his feelings. We think a good debater should never lose his temper; if he does, we think he may sometimes lose sight of his argument. After a little more than a quarter of an hour, the violence of Sir Robert Peel towards Mr O'Connell appeared to abate, and he then went into the merits of the proposed measure, and calmly stated his views and opinions in very fluent language. Mr O'Connell, after Sir Robert had finished his personalities, packed up his papers, made his bow to the Speaker, and left him to his two hours' speech. And we think him a great speaker, but his actions were odd, as he kept thrusting one of his hands out between the flaps of his coat, and swinging himself round. We should have called him an orator, but for his losing his temper. Still we should say he reasoned well, and his speech appeared to make a great impression upon his side of the house. The cheers were loud and often, and he appealed in very strong language to the Ministers of the Crown, who sat opposite to him, as to what they would do upon certain other questions with their now sworn friends, Mr O'Connell and his partisans. At all events, Sir Robert Peel seemed determined again to go at length into the details of the question, and to oppose it with all his power. We could but smile at the loud cheers and the enthusiasm that was shewn then to him by his party, among whom, we were informed, he was a short time since rather unpopular, in consequence of his not having moved quite so quickly or violently as they wished, so that we fancied the mass within doors were almost as fickle in their minds as the mob without doors.

Lord John Russell, a minister of the crown, and the political ministerial leader of the House of Commons, then rose, and we were surprised to find that he did not speak fluently; he appeared to have an impediment in his speech, but after a little while he shook off his apparent impediment, and he, for nearly two hours, spoke principally in explanation of the question before the House. His side of the House cheered him quite as loudly as Sir Robert Peel had been cheered. We looked at him, he was a little pale-looking man, with a tolerably loud voice, but not harmonious, and his action, although energetic, was not altogether pleasing.

But after all these people had spoken, and argued, to gain converts as it were, the result was nearly as it had been foretold at an earlier hour in the evening. For upon a division the ministers of the crown had only a majority of five. So that all these long speeches might have been spared, and all the members of the House, the messengers, and the reporters, might for all the good effect the debate had had, all of them been quietly enjoying their night's rest. We were told that this was a grand trial of strength, and if the ministers had not had most votes with them, conservatives would have changed sides in the house, and the liberals would no longer have been ministers. We saw in addition to those who spoke, several members of whom we had heard much—Sir James Graham, Lord Stanley, Lord Morpeth, Lord Howick, Mr Hume, Mr Byng, who has been more than fifty years member for Middlesex, Sir John Hobhouse, Mr Bernal, Sir Charles Adam, and a host of others. This is an evening that we shall never forget. We consider it the most exciting eight or nine hours that we ever spent, and yet upon the whole we were disappointed. We had expected to have seen the representatives of all the wealth, all the talent, all the resources of the country, better dressed and a different looking set of men. We saw them with their hats upon their heads for the last two or three hours sleeping in all directions, and only opening their eyes now and then, when a cheer louder than common struck upon their ears; still such an assemblage of men holding the destinies of millions in their hands, we may never again see.

Carlyle is not impressed

Thomas Carlyle (1795–1881), the Scottish historian, critic and essayist, was born in Dumfries and educated at Annan Grammar School and at the University of Edinburgh (although he left without a degree). In 1822–3 he was tutor to Charles and Arthur Buller, the sons of an East India Company civil servant. Years later he was taken to the House by the mother of his old pupils, to hear Charles Buller speak, who was by then the Radical Reform MP for Liskeard.

Letter to his mother, Margaret A. Carlyle, June 17, 1842

It struck me as the strangest place I had ever sat in, that same House! There was a humming and bustling, so that you could hear nothing for most part; the Members all sitting with their hats on, talking to one another, coming and going: you only saw the Speaker (a man with an immense powdered wig, in an old-fashioned elevated chair) and half heard him mumbling, 'Say Aye, say No; the Ayes have it!—passing Bills, which nobody except one or two, specially concerned, cared a fig about, or was at pains to listen to! When a good speaker rose, or an important man, they grew a little more silent, and you could hear.

A non-elected laird taking his seat in the House

Mark Boyd, *Reminiscences of Fifty Years* (1871)

The following anecdote I heard from Mr Cutlar Fergusson, MP, as well as from the laird himself the day after the occurrence. I wrote it out at the time, and it appeared shortly afterwards in a London magazine. A worthy Scotch proprietor whose estate was in Kirkcudbrightshire, then represented by the Right Hon. R. Cutlar Fergusson, the Judge-Advocate in Lord Melbourne's Government, came up to London for a few weeks shortly after the assembling of a new Parliament. He called upon his Right Hon. friend, who asked him what he could do for him in town; the laird said that nothing he would like so much during his stay as being present at the debates in the House of Commons. 'That being the case,' said the Judge-Advocate, 'I will have your name placed on the Speaker's list.' The following evening the laird was early in his attendance at the House, found his name on the list, and was told by the door-keeper to enter. Where the Speaker's privileged friends sat he knew not, but up the body of the House he walked, and took his seat on the second bench of the opposition close behind Sir Robert Peel. An interesting debate came on, and the laird sat undisturbed until the House adjourned at midnight. Fortunately for him there was no division, and equally fortunately it was a new Parliament. Next day he called upon Mr Fergusson, whose first enquiry was: 'What became of you, as I looked for you in vain?' 'Oh,' said the laird, 'I saw you moving about the House, and tried to catch your eye. I was delighted with the debate, and I shall now be a constant attendant.' From the laird's vernacular he was supposed to be a recently elected Scotch member, and being a tall, portly, gentlemanly-looking man, so far as appearance went, passed muster very well. Next night found the laird occupying his former seat. However, about nine o'clock Lord Granville Somerset, who the previous evening had his doubts as to the genuineness of the reputed Scotch MP, went to the serjeant-at-arms and asked who was that tall man sitting behind Sir Robert Peel? 'Oh, he is a Scotch member, one of yourselves, Lord Granville.' 'I doubt that exceedingly,' said his lordship, 'and I doubt his being a member at all.'

The serjeant-at-arms, all excitement, flew round behind the opposition benches and gave the laird a sharp tap on the shoulder, desiring him to come to him. The laird so far complied, but not being accustomed to being treated unceremoniously, asked the stern official what he meant? 'Why, sir, you were in the House last night?' 'I was.' 'You sat in the same place you have been now occupying?' 'Yes, the very same, and what right have you to disturb me?' 'You are in my custody.' 'In your custody! for what? Hands off!' exclaimed the laird in any other tone than a mild one. 'Who are you?' asked the serjeant. 'Who am I! go and ask Mr Cutlar Fergusson; he placed my name on the Speaker's list, and if there is any mistake'—the laird being now very angry—'it was your duty, as the servant of the House, to have shown me where to sit.' The serjeant-at-arms was so far relieved; but still holding the laird's arm, the latter again exclaimed 'Hands off!' and being a powerful man, soon wrested himself from the official's grasp. 'Tell me where my place is.' This he was only too happy to do, and the laird now took his fresh seat in St Stephen's under considerable excitement, muttering to the serjeant-at-arms, that it was a matter of indifference to him where he sat, provided he heard the speeches, but he must beg not to be again disturbed.

This escapade of my countryman in the House of Commons used to amuse a hospitable friend of mine in town beyond measure, the more so from the fact of his coming from his own and my part of Scotland. One day, after dinner, I was asked by my friend to tell the story, and finding myself sitting next to Mr William Holmes, MP, the Conservative 'whip', I remarked that Mr Holmes would correct me if I went wrong. The Hon. gentleman was kind enough afterwards to say that I had told it *right* well.

Mr Holmes then proceeded in a vein of dry humour to tell us, that such an occurrence had never before happened in the House of Commons, and that the 'actor' could only be a Scotchman. 'Ah, you Scotchmen do like to get things *chape*, but it is the first time there was ever *soch a chape sate* had in St *Staven's*. The fact is, your friend and countryman intended to keep his *sate* during the rest of the session, and being a clever fellow had discovered that all he had to do to avoid detection was to slip out of the House a few minutes before a division, and when that was over to come back to his place. I told Lord Granville Somerset that he had made a mistake in sending the serjeant-at-arms to look after your friend, as we were in desperate want of some more Scotchmen on our side the House.'

Nathaniel Hawthorne

Nathaniel Hawthorne (1804–64), the American novelist, was born in Salem, Massachusetts, and was educated at Bowdoin College. He wrote numerous short stories and several novels, including *The Scarlet Letter* (1850) and *The House of Seven Gables* (1851). He had been a Boston customs official, 1839–41, and was Surveyor of the Port of Salem, 1845–9. From 1853 to 1858 he was US consul in Liverpool, having been appointed by President Franklin Pierce, an old college classmate.

Passages from the English Note-Books of Nathaniel Hawthorne (1870)

From Downing Street we crossed over and entered Westminster Hall, and passed through it, and up the flight of steps at its farthest end, and along the avenue of statues, into the vestibule of the House of Commons. It was now somewhat past five, and we stood at the inner entrance of the House, to see the members pass in, B——h pointing out to me the distinguished ones. I was not much impressed with the appearance of the members generally; they seemed to me rather shabbier than English gentlemen usually, and I saw or fancied in many of them a certain self-importance, as they passed into the interior, betokening them to be very full of their dignity. Some of them looked more American—more like American politicians—than most Englishmen do. There was now and then a grey-headed country gentleman, the very type of stupidity; and two or three City members came up and spoke to B——h, and showed themselves quite as dull, in their aldermanic way, as the country squires . . . B——h pointed out Lord John Russell, a small, very short, elderly gentleman, in a brown coat, and so large a hat—not large of brim, but large like a peck measure—that I saw really no face beneath it. By-and-by came a rather tall, slender person, in a black frock-coat, buttoned up, and black pantaloons, taking long steps, but I thought rather feebly or listlessly. His shoulders were round, or else he had a habitual stoop in them. He had a prominent nose, a thin face, and a sallow, very sallow complexion; . . . and had I seen him in America, I should have taken him for a hard-worked editor of a newspaper, weary and worn with night labour and want of exercise,—aged before his time. It was Disraeli, and I never saw any other Englishman look in the least like him; though, in America, his appearance would not attract notice as being unusual. I do not remember any other noteworthy person whom we saw enter; in fact, the House had already been some time in session, and most of the members were in their places.

We were to dine at the Refectory of the House with the new member for Boston; and, meanwhile, B——h obtained admittance for us into the Speaker's gallery, where we had a view of the members, and could hear what was going on. A Mr Muntz was speaking on the Income Tax, and he was followed by Sir George Cornewall Lewis and others; but it was all very uninteresting, without the slightest animation or attempt at oratory,—which, indeed, would have been quite out of place. We saw Lord Palmerston; but at too great a distance to distinguish anything but a grey head. The House had daylight in it when we entered, and for some time afterwards; but, by-and-by, the roof, which I had taken to be a solid and opaque ceiling, suddenly brightened, and showed itself to be transparent; a vast expanse of tinted and figured glass, through which came down a great, mild radiance on the members below. The character of the debate, however, did not grow more luminous or vivacious; so we went down into the vestibule, and there waited for Mr ——, who soon came and led us into the Refectory. It was very much like the coffee-room of a club. The strict rule forbids the entrance of any but members of Parliament; but it seems to be winked at, although there is another room, opening beyond this, where the law of seclusion is strictly enforced.

The dinner was good, not remarkably so, but good enough,—a soup, some turbot or salmon, cutlets, and I know not what else, and claret, sherry, and port; for, as Mr —— said, 'he did not wish to be stingy.' Mr —— is a self-made man, and a strong instance of the difference between the Englishman and the American, when self-made, and without early education. He is no more a gentleman now than when he began life,—not a whit more refined, either outwardly or inwardly; while the American would have been, after the same experience, not distinguishable outwardly and perhaps as refined within, as nine-tenths of the gentlemen born, in the House of Commons. And, besides, an American comes naturally to any distinctions to which success in life may bring him; he takes them as if they were his proper inheritance, and in nowise to be wondered at. Mr ——, on the other hand, took evidently a childish delight in his position, and felt a childish wonder in having arrived at it; nor did it seem real to him, after all . . .

We again saw Disraeli, who has risen from the people by modes perhaps somewhat like those of Mr ——. He came and stood near our table, looking at the bill of fare, and then sat down on the opposite side of the room with another gentleman, and ate his dinner. The story of his marriage does him much credit; and indeed I am inclined to like Disraeli, as a man who has made his own place good among a hostile aristocracy, and leads instead of following them.

Hippolyte Adolphe Taine

Hippolyte Adolphe Taine (1828–93), the French critic and historian, was educated at the École Normale Supérieure, where he learnt to speak English, Latin and German, as well as studying philosophy, theology, literature and music. Thereafter he devoted his life to scholarship. His *History of English Literature* (1871) and his *Notes on England* are considered to be his finest works.

Notes on England (1872)

The Lords' chamber is fine, comfortable, and well-adapted for its purpose. Seats in red leather, deep and rich wainscoting, Gothic gilding in dull gold; an impression of serious opulence is produced by this. The members present are not numerous; I was told there are sometimes five or six; save on great political occasions they stay away; besides, discussion is frequently useless, each vote being known before hand. The leading members were named to me, and I heard enormous fortunes mentioned, the largest are £300,000 a year. The Duke of Bedford has an income from landed property of £220,000; the Duke of Richmond has 300,000 acres in one holding; the Marquis of Westminster, proprietor of a district of London, will have a revenue of £1,000,000 on the expiration of the long leases. The Marquis of Breadalbane, it is said, can ride on horseback for thirty leagues in a straight line without quitting his estate; the Duke of Sutherland possesses an entire shire of that name in the north of Scotland. Three Bishops in white surplices occupy their places. But the outsides of the assembly are scarcely imposing. One peer has the face of an old diplomatic machine, another that of an amiable and worn-out librarian; the minister who rises resembles an intelligent attorney. Some young peers are dandies and have their hair parted in the middle; others, hugely bearded, remind one of commercial travellers. Lord C—— alone has the fatigued, penetrating, and fine physiognomy of an artist. Their ways are very simple; they might be called ordinary men at their club; they keep their tall chimney-pot hats on their heads, speak from their places, without fuss, in a conversational tone. This absence of stiffness is excellent; an embroidered uniform like that of our senators or of our peers is a pomp and a superfluity which re-acts within from without and renders the thought as artificial as the appearance. These persons do business and do not make phrases.

In the House of Commons from ten o'clock till midnight. There is still greater freedom from constraint; the House is full, and all have their hats on their heads; some wear them far back and pressed down. Several wear white hats, fancy trousers and coat, are leaning back, half-lying on their seats, one of them is entirely lolling on his, and two or three are rather free and easy. They enter, go out, talk with a wearied and unceremonious air; certainly a club in which one were to behave in this style would be moderately respectable.

The ministers were pointed out to me—Lord Palmerston, Mr Milner Gibson, Lord John Russell, Sir Charles Wood, Mr Gladstone. Alongside of us, in the gallery, several members of the Upper House came and seated themselves, one young immensely rich duke, all had bad cravats, and he had a shabby coat. Below us there is silence. The members, tightly packed on their benches, have not even a desk on which to write. They take notes upon their knees, drink a glass of water which they afterwards put on their seat. Each one speaks standing in his place, in a natural tone and with few gestures. Certainly a chamber arranged in this way, and so narrow, is incommodious, and even unhealthy, too warm in summer and for the night sittings; a man must be quickly worn out there. But this simplicity denotes a business-like people, who suppress ceremonial in order to get through their task. On the contrary, a raised tribune, isolated like that of our Legislative Assembly, leads to theatrical eloquence.

The business of the day related to the encroachment of the Lords, who had voted a money bill without the assent of the Commons; the debate, it is said, is one of the most important of the year; the House is full and attentive. After Mr Seymour, Mr Horsman rises. Very distinct pronunciation, a perfectly just and convinced tone, energy without emphasis. His thesis is that the Lords are not a body of simple, privileged personages; though not elected, they represent the people. They are country gentlemen, like the others, holding lands and shares like the others, having the same interests, the same education, the same ideas, being as well situated as themselves to decide about the common interests. Election is but one means only for naming the representatives of the nation; there were others, for example the possession of a certain dignity, which is the case of the Bishops, inheritance, which is the case of the Queen and the lay Lords. Besides, since 1832, the Commons have had a marked preponderance; the control of a second body is required, without which they would fall into pure democracy, etc. Rather long, he repeated himself; however, he made an impression; cries of 'hear, hear' arose at nearly every sentence. After him, and in the opposite sense, spoke Mr Bright, an accomplished orator. But I had seen too many things these days; my nerves are not as strong as those of a member of Parliament, and I left the House.

A Stranger takes part in a Division

Richard Henry Dana (1851–1931), the son of the author of *Two Years Before the Mast*, was born in Cambridge, Massachusetts, and educated at Harvard. He qualified at the bar and became a civil servant, drafting the Civil Service Reform Act, Massachusetts (1884). He was an active campaigner for civil service reform from the 1880s to the 1920s.

Richard Henry Dana, *Hospitable England in the Seventies: The Diary of a Young American, 1875–1876* (1921)

July 22, 1875. In the afternoon I went down to the House of Commons at Sir William Vernon Harcourt's invitation. I sent in my card to him and was shown into the inner lobby, which I had hardly entered when out rushed a member in a state of wild excitement, throwing his arms about and shaking his fists and making short ejaculations such as, 'I will expose the villains, all of them!' I heard the word 'cheats' and I think 'liars'. The man's excitement was great and he spoke hurriedly and disconnectedly. For my part I was astonished at the scene. I knew nothing whatsoever of the situation or what he was talking about. The general impression on me was that I never had seen an educated man so thoroughly given up to the passion of the moment. At the French Assembly, or even at Washington, I should not have been so much surprised, but it was very strange to see all this in the decorous House of Commons. I was told that it was Mr Plimsoll. Good blind Fawcett, the political economist, and other members tried to calm Plimsoll, but all to no purpose. He would not be led away nor even allow a hand to be put on him. The lobby was soon cleared of strangers by the officers of the House, so I did not see how they managed to get the honorable member calmed and away. Soon I learned that the Government had announced the 'slaughter of the innocents', and the Merchants' Shipping Bill, which was Plimsoll's pet measure, and which the Government had practically promised him would be carried out at this session, had been included in the slaughter. This bill provided for the ship load-mark and for giving sailors a right to claim from public authorities a survey of the vessel and its food so as to prevent their being sent to the bottom in unseaworthy vessels for the sake of the insurance which the owners might get, or be forced to rely on insufficient, old, or musty food . . .

To come back to the 'episode': it turned out that, in the House, Plimsoll had denounced Disraeli in the most violent terms as not being a man of his word and 'a liar', and when called to order by the Speaker, would not retract. Some of his friends at the time went so far as to say that he had lost his mind from brooding over his bill. The tragedy of Ajax naturally occurred to me, where the old hero became demented while brooding over the loss of the armor of Achilles.

Soon after Sir William came out and took me into the House, but it was evidently in a very unnatural state. The 'Hears' were weak or forced. There was no disturbance, yet no one was listened to, and the speakers spoke as one might speak after a deafening clap of thunder. All were evidently under great nervous tension. (This was before the times of Parnell's leadership of the Irish Home Rule group, when the House became accustomed to violent scenes.) This tension continued for some time, and even Disraeli failed to 'amuse' the House. But not long after Mr Gladstone got up and made a short but earnest speech against the Government's arranging their plans and debating measures in caucus instead of publicly in the House and then not telling the House the results of their deliberations. After this the members settled down to their usual state of mind. The 'Hears' were loud and natural, and I think I am not mistaken in saying that it was because they recognised an old leader in whom they had confidence and he, though in the minority, alone set them right. It had a magic effect like the sudden appearance of Sheridan at the Battle of Winchester in the Civil War.

Sir William took me into the Members' Dining-Room. It was against the rule to take strangers there. They had to go to the Strangers' Room. It was just like Sir William to ignore such rules. He goes to the heart of matters and prefers not to be bound by formalities. Besides, he is large and physically powerful, a prominent member in line for being Prime Minister some day, and has such a 'blinking smile' as to intimidate any too officious waiter. Sir William belongs to one of the oldest families in Great Britain. He gained first-class honors at Cambridge and has been Solicitor-General (later, 1880, he was Secretary of State for the Home Department and Chancellor of the Exchequer, 1885–86, and again, 1892–95) . . .

I have not so far mentioned that in the House of Commons the members wear their tall silk hats except when addressing the House. You sometimes see these hats pulled over their eyes, and whether they are sleeping or pondering over debate is a matter only of conjecture. They do not wear gloves as they did when my great-uncle, Edmund Dana, was present about 1801.

Friday, July 23. I returned to London with the two young members of Parliament, who took me with them into the House of Commons, and I saw the procedure of 'complaints on motion to go into committee on supplies'. The House of Commons, having the sole power over supplies, takes the opportunity, whenever a motion is made to bring up a question of supplies, to slander the Government in every way. The complaints were very general and on all sorts of matters. It is customary to give the broadest license at these times, not keeping the members in the slightest degree to the motion or to any of the items of the contemplated appropriations. One of these members of Parliament who took me in was a young Irishman, and knowing that I wanted to see all the procedure in the House and noticing that there was no quorum present, said: 'If you have never seen it before, I will call the Speaker's attention to the lack of quorum and have a counting out.' This he did for my special benefit. When the counting began there were only thirty-eight, but one zealous member dragged in three of his friends so as to bring the number above the necessary forty and business continued.

Saturday, July 24. Harcourt invited me to the House of Commons to hear the Plimsoll settlement or apology or whatever it might turn out to be, which is to take place tomorrow. The general opinion in the club seemed to be that Plimsoll intended to create a sensation and even contemplated being put into confinement. He certainly did succeed in creating a great deal more sympathy from his disorderly conduct than he could have aroused in any other way. It was, however, clearly not all of it acting; he was really very much excited. The truth probably lies between the two extremes. He was doubtless greatly worked up, took advantage of his opportunity, and let his passion have pretty full sway. Disraeli intimated, but avoided directly asserting it, that he allowed all this scene to come off so as to secure the public backing outside necessary to enable him to pass the bill inside the House of Commons. Many doubted the truth of this intimation and believed it to be but an adroit way of turning an actual blunder to his own benefit. I believed it was nothing but a bit of 'Dizzy's' humor. (The main part of Plimsoll's bill passed this session and was perfected the next, in 1876.)

❖

The House cheers some Indian officers

T. P. O'Connor, 'The House of Commons, its Structure, Rules, and Habits', *Harper's New Monthly Magazine*, December 1893

I remember one occasion which made a great impression upon me. There was a contingent of Indian soldiers in England. A few of their officers—in uniform strange and picturesque—were brought into the Distinguished Strangers' Gallery. There was something very striking in this outward and visible presentation of the greatness, vastness, and, if the word be permissible, weirdness of an empire that is the ruler of countless millions, foreign in creed, race, and custom, separated by centuries and continents and oceans from the English people at home. The House, by a sudden and irresistible impulse, gave vent to the curiously profound emotion which such a scene was calculated to elicit. There immediately rose from all parts a cheer that was long, hearty, charged with emotion, and though it took no more eloquent form than 'Hear, hear!' very loud and very prolonged, it had the same stimulating effect as the loud hurrah of a regiment charging at the double. The Indian soldiers certainly appreciated it, for they started to their feet, and standing with the professional straightness and stiffness of the soldier, they brought their hands in salute to their turbans.

'Buffalo Bill' visits the House

William Frederick Cody (1846–1917), the American Wild West hero, had been a pony express rider, a cavalry scout and a supplier of buffalo meat to workers on the Kansas Pacific Railway. In eighteen months (1867–8) he killed 4,280 buffaloes. He also killed Yellow Hand, the Cheyenne chief, in a hand-to-hand fight. Later, he ran the Wild West Show and became Judge-advocate-general in Wyoming.

The date of Buffalo Bill's visit was sometime in April 1887. According to a letter from Justin McCarthy MP to his friend Mrs Campbell-Praed: 'The parliamentary sensation this evening so far has been the presence of Buffalo Bill in our dining-room. He was entertained by Lord Charles Beresford.'[15]

Sir James T. Agg-Gardner, *Some Parliamentary Recollections* (1927)

A popular hero of the Far West known as 'Buffalo Bill' was, I remember, introduced to the Gallery of the House while he was performing at the White City. Asked afterwards what he thought of the proceedings he confessed to finding the debates, of which he could not understand a word, and the general proceedings somewhat dull. One thing he admitted had excited his keenest interest. In his early days he had been a scalp-hunter, and he observed, sitting on the bench below him, a member with a mass of thick curly white hair. He said it would have been the delight of his life to have 'tomahawked' the scalp to add to his collection. The remark was repeated to the gentleman referred to— a genial and popular Member for Manchester, John McClure—who highly appreciated the compliment thus conveyed.

In the secret of the House

Virginia Woolf (1882–1941), the novelist, was the daughter of Leslie Stephen, the jurisprudentialist. She was privately educated and married Leonard Woolf, her business partner in the Hogarth Press. They formed the core of the Bloomsbury Group of liberal intellectuals. In addition to her novels, the most important of which were published in the 1920s, she wrote critical essays and occasional journalism. This extract is from one of a series of articles she wrote for *Good Housekeeping* about British institutions.

Virginia Woolf, 'This is the House of Commons', *Good Housekeeping*, October 1932

Certainly our own House of Commons from inside is not in the least noble or majestic or even dignified. It is as shiny and as ugly as any other moderate-sized public hall. The oak, of course, is grained yellow. The windows, of course, are painted with ugly coats of arms. The floor, of course, is laid with strips of red matting. The benches, of course, are covered with serviceable leather. Wherever one looks one says, 'of course'. It is an untidy, informal-looking assembly. Sheets of white paper seem to be always fluttering to the floor. People

569

are always coming in and out incessantly. Men are whispering and gossiping and cracking jokes over each other's shoulders. The swing doors are perpetually swinging. Even the central island of control, where the Speaker sits under his canopy, is a perching ground for casual members who seem to be taking a peep at the proceedings at their ease. Legs rest on the edge of the table where the mace lies suspended; and the secrets which repose in the two brass-bound chests on either side of the table are not immune from the prod of an occasional toe. Dipping and rising, moving and settling, the Commons remind one of a flock of birds settling on a stretch of ploughed land. They never alight for more than a few minutes; some are always flying off, others are always settling again. And from the flock rises the gabbling, the cawing, the croaking of a flock of birds, disputing merrily and with occasional vivacity over some seed, worm, or buried grain.

One has to say to oneself severely, 'But this is the House of Commons. Here the destinies of the world are altered. Here Gladstone fought, and Palmerston and Disraeli. It is by these men that we are governed. We obey their orders every day of the year. Our purses are at their mercy. They decide how fast we shall drive our cars in Hyde Park; also whether we shall have war or peace.' But we have to remind ourselves; for to look at, they do not differ much from other people. The standard of dress is perhaps rather high. We look down upon some of the glossiest top hats still to be seen in England. A magnificent scarlet button-hole blazes here and there. Everybody has been well fed and given a good education doubtless. But what with their chatter and laughter, their high spirits, and impatience and irreverence, they are not a whit more judicious, or more dignified, or more respectable-looking than any other assembly of citizens met to debate parish business or to give prizes for fat oxen. This is true; but after a time some curious difference makes itself suspected. We feel that the Commons is a body of a certain character; it has been in existence for a long time; it has its own laws and licences. It is irreverent in a way of its own; and so, presumably, reverent too in its own way. It has somehow a code of its own. People who disregard this code will be unmercifully chastened; those who are in accord with it will be easily condoned. But what it condemns and what it condones, only those who are in the secret of the House can say. All we can be sure of is that a secret there is. Perched up high as we are, under the rule of an official who follows the prevailing informality by crossing his legs and scribbling notes on his knee, we feel sure that nothing could be easier than to say the wrong thing, either with the wrong levity or the wrong seriousness, and that no assurance of virtue, genius, valour is here sure of success if something else—some indefinable quality—is omitted.

A mangy, forgotten look

George Orwell was the pseudonym of Eric Arthur Blair (1903–50), who was born into an Anglo-Indian family, and educated at Eton. He did a variety of jobs before settling down to live as a writer of novels and essays during the 1930s; he fought as a Republican during the Spanish Civil War and was wounded. He was a Socialist, and his most famous novels, *Animal Farm* (1945) and *1984* (1949), were dystopian critiques of totalitarianism. This is an extract from one of his regular 'London Letter' columns for the *Partisan Review*. Although he attended the House on behalf of the BBC, Orwell was not there to report parliamentary proceedings.

George Orwell, *Partisan Review*, Spring 1944

When I was working with the BBC I sometimes had to go and listen to a debate in the Commons. The last time I had been there was about ten years previously, and I was very much struck by the deterioration that seemed to have taken place. The whole thing now has a mangy, forgotten look. Even the ushers' shirt fronts are grimy. And it is noticeable now that, except from the places they sit in (the Opposition always sits on the Speaker's left), you can't tell one party from another. It is just a collection of mediocre-looking men in dingy, dark suits, nearly all speaking in the same accent and all laughing at the same jokes. I may say, however, that they don't look such a set of crooks as the French Deputies used to look. The most striking thing of all is the lack of attendance. It would be very rare indeed for 400 members out of the 640 to turn up. The House of Lords, where they are now sitting, only has seating accommodation for about 250, and the old House of Commons (it was blitzed) cannot have been much larger. I attended the big debate on India after Cripps came back. At the start there were a little over 200 members present, which rapidly shrank to about 45. It seems to be the custom to clear out, presumably to the bar, as soon as any important speech begins, but the House fills up again when there are questions or anything else that promises a bit of fun. There is a marked family atmosphere. Everyone shouts with laughter over jokes and allusions which are unintelligible to anyone not an MP, nicknames are used freely, violent political opponents pal up over drinks. Nearly any member of long standing is corrupted by this kind of thing sooner or later. Maxton, the ILP MP, twenty years ago an inflammatory orator whom the ruling classes hated like poison, is now the pet of the House, and Gallacher, the Communist MP, is going the same road. Each time I have been in the House recently I have found myself thinking the same thought—that the Roman Senate still existed under the later Empire.

---

1. Quoted in George Henry Jennings, *An Anecdotal History of the British Parliament from the Earliest Periods to the Present Time* (1880), p. 414.

2. Harry Graham, *The Mother of Parliaments* (1911), p. 259.

3. ibid., pp. 263–4.

4. Jennings, op. cit., p. 415.

5. *Journals of the House of Commons*, May 31, 1604; May 14, 1605.

6. Sir Almeric Fitzroy, *Memoirs*, Vol. II, p. 775.

7. *Manchester Guardian*, April 25, 1956.

8. Ian Mackay, 'My Greatest Moments', *News Chronicle*, July 29, 1947.

9. Justin McCarthy, A History of Our Own Times (1910), Vol. III, pp. 123–4.

10. Count Paul Vasili (pseud.), *The World of London (La Société de Londres)* (1885), p. 95.

11. James A. Garfield, Journal, August 8, 1867; quoted in Henry Steele Commager (ed.), *Britain Through American Eyes* (1974), p. 407.

12. Frederick Moir Bussy, *Irish Conspiracies: Recollections of John Mallon and Other Reminiscences* (1910), pp. 245–6.

13. ibid., pp. 247–50.

14. Sir Francis Burdett (1770–1844) was the Radical MP for Boroughbridge, a seat bought for him by his father-in-law in the hope that it might make him a more faithful husband. In 1810 he was committed to the Tower for challenging the authority of the House of Commons to imprison a man who had attacked it for excluding the public from its debates.

15. Justin McCarthy and Mrs Campbell Praed, *Our Book of Memories* (1912), p. 103.

17 The Fourth Estate

A common toast of reporters at social meetings was
'Joseph Hume getting up, and George Canning sitting
down'. The meaning was this: the reporter who had to
report the one so abridged his task that a quarter of an
hour's subsequent work was all that was required of him,
while to have an hour of Canning implied three or four
hours' toil at the office.

Samuel Carter Hall, *Retrospect of a Long Life* (1883)

It was Macaulay, in his essay on Hallam's *Constitutional History*, who coined the phrase
'the fourth estate' to denote the pressmen who reported Parliament: 'The gallery in
which the reporters sit has become a fourth estate of the realm. The publication of the
debates, a practice which seemed to the most liberal statesmen of the old school full of
danger to the great safeguards of public liberty, is now regarded by many persons as a
safeguard tantamount, and more than tantamount, to all the rest together.'[1]

In earlier times, before the Revolution of 1688, it had principally been fear of a
sovereign's wrath that impelled MPs to insist that the proceedings of the House of
Commons, in particular its debates, be kept secret. The Clerk of the House of Commons,
John Rushworth, was ordered 'not to take any notes there without the precedent
directions and commands of the House, but only of the orders and reports made in this
House'. Members, too, surreptitiously took notes of debates, and the diaries and journals
of MPs such as Sir Symonds D'Ewes, Anchitell Grey, Cavendish, Townsend and others
provide a valuable source for historians. Even at the time the gleanings of some such
MPs 'found their way into the coffee-houses and news-letters of the day'. From the mid-
seventeenth century until 1771 there was a parade of news-writers brought to the Bar
of the House and made to kneel and receive the reprimand of the Speaker in addition
to being fined. Some reporters, it is true, were guilty of misrepresenting what was said
in the Chamber, but for the most part the MPs feared being made accountable for what
they said in the course of debates. In 1771 several London newspapers challenged the
power of the House, which ordered their printers to come to the Bar. However,
the miscreants defied the Serjeant-at-Arms and were given succour by the Mayor and
Aldermen of the City of London, who were promptly committed to the Tower. These
were treated as heroes during their six weeks' imprisonment and thereafter the House
of Commons never sought to prevent the publication of debates, although individual
offenders found to be guilty of misrepresentation were still censured in the traditional
manner.

It was not until 1803 that the efforts of the pressmen were officially recognised by the Speaker granting them the right to occupy the back bench of the Strangers' Gallery. However, the odious practice was continued by some MPs of invoking the Standing Order for excluding strangers. In 1810 Sheridan argued in a debate on this matter that a Member should give his reason for wishing to exclude strangers and that a vote should be taken. He was opposed by William Windham, who stated that the profession of parliamentary reporter included 'men of all descriptions—bankrupts, lottery-office keepers, footmen and decayed tradesmen'. One reporter who had written for the *Morning Post* responded to this by sending a letter to that paper claiming that on one occasion an MP had offered both him and another colleague a bribe to report his speech. The reporters as a body chose to boycott the reporting of Windham's speeches, while Sheridan pointed out that of twenty-three parliamentary reporters eighteen had been 'educated at the Universities of Oxford or Cambridge, Edinburgh or Dublin' and many of them had been scholars of distinction.

After the Houses of Parliament were consumed by fire in 1834 a special gallery was afforded to reporters in the temporary Chamber in which MPs met until Barry rebuilt the Palace of Westminster. In May 1865 Charles Dickens addressed the annual dinner of the Newspaper Press Fund, recalling the privations of his former profession of parliamentary reporter. 'I have worn my knees by writing on them on the old back row of the old Gallery of the old House of Commons,' he said, 'and I have worn my feet standing to write in a preposterous pen in the old House of Lords, where we used to be huddled together like so many sheep, kept in waiting, say, until the Woolsack [the Lord Chancellor's seat] might want restuffing.'[2] Charles A. Cooper, who later edited the *Scotsman*, served a spell in the Reporters' Gallery in 1861. He later wrote that, while the Gallery itself was no worse in its conditions for journalists than the Chamber was for MPs, nonetheless 'when you got out of the Gallery you went into cells ... All the rooms were low-ceilinged, dark and dismal. If you remained in them for half an hour you were tortured with headache, if you had a head that could ache. To get to these rooms you had first to climb a narrow winding stair from Palace Yard below, then to pass through a sort of anteroom, and then along a dark passage.' For refreshment the reporters could obtain ham, corned beef, bread, tea and coffee, and alcoholic beverages, but no sit-down dinner.[3]

In 1880 the Gallery was enlarged to accommodate the representatives of the leading provincial papers. Sir Alexander Mackintosh, the greatest of the provincial parliamentary reporters, arrived in 1881 as representative for the *Aberdeen Free Press*. Other facilities, such as larger writing rooms, a library, a dining-room and a tea-room, smoking-rooms and a bar, were soon provided. By 1897 there were no fewer than 260 journalists, reporters and descriptive writers who belonged to the Reporters' Gallery.

Successive administrations decreed that the taxpayer should pay for the creature comforts of members of the Reporters' Gallery. One of the last acts of the outgoing Unionist Government in 1905, for example, was to furnish the pressmen with a lift to convey them from Palace Yard to their working quarters, while a few years later the Liberal Government gave the journalists 'a bath and a big new writing-room large enough for a small concert hall'.[4] Inside the Chamber, too, there were improvements. When the House met to hear Lloyd George's 1909 Budget statement, the press were allotted a line of seats in the Strangers' Gallery in addition to their usual accommodation, and the Chancellor agreed to send up every quarter of an hour 'the section of his notes dealing with the portion of his speech just concluded'.[5] However, there were still problems caused by the normal physical arrangements. 'Vision ... is poor; the position of the Gallery in both Houses makes it impossible to see some speakers,' wrote Charles Gayton, 'and they have to be identified at first by their voices.' Acoustically, the Commons was adjudged to be better than the Lords—'with a good seat in the Press

Gallery, one could hear nearly every speaker in more or less comfort', while 'in the Lords Gallery nearly all speakers were more or less inaudible' until microphones were installed.[6]

Strict standards of dress were expected from the Gallery men. 'Black coats and top hats were the thing' when Frederick Peppiatt joined the Gallery and he later remembered how the door-keepers 'frowned upon a journalist (I believe he was the nephew of A. J. Mundella, a one-time Cabinet Minister) who came into the Gallery in knickerbockers. They were to have further shocks when two other journalists came in wearing velvet jackets . . . In my earlier days nearly all Gallery men wore beards as well as top hats.'[7] By the early 1960s the rules had been relaxed somewhat. 'In summer journalists were allowed to appear in shirt-sleeves,' T. F. Lindsay has since recalled, 'but only if they were not wearing braces.'[8]

Saving seconds

Frederick Moir Bussy, *Irish Conspiracies: Recollections of John Mallon and Other Reminiscences* (1910)

The advent of the halfpenny morning press has been signalised by an entire revolution in the amount of importance exhibited in the minutiae of Parliamentary proceedings—from a reportorial point of view. Whether this is due to the exigencies of space or to a want of proper respect on the part of the bantlings of the Fourth Estate for the heavy fathers of debate, it is not for me to say. Suffice it that the elect of the people and the favoured of the gods, engaged in talking statutes and tariffs, obtain but scant courtesy at the hands of the modern Press, except on occasions when, by reason of their backslidings or eccentricities, they become really interesting. Nowadays the legislative assemblies are judged solely by the importance of their measures or the entertaining attributes of their men, rather than by that special glamour which used to attach to mere membership of the 'best clubs', or 'talking shops', as they are variously described. In the very recent days that are dead things were far different. The whole scheme of journalistic enterprise was wont to centre around Parliament and Parliamentarians. The importance and dignity of the penny papers used to be estimated by the length and accuracy of their parliamentary reports, and all that was best and brightest on their reportorial staffs was turned on to such enthralling material as could be provided by Mr Galloway Weir on the restricted elbow-room allotted to Scottish crofters or by Mr Love Jones-Parry on the toothsomeness of rook pie. The evening papers vied with each other in their efforts to bring the proceedings of the 'faithful Commons' up to the latest possible moment before going to press, and the 'tapeworms'—as the mechanical news-distributing instruments were styled in those days—spluttered and groaned and bubbled in their efforts to beat each other with the dissemination of the momentous information that Mr Wharton was 'still speaking', or that Mr Bowles had twitted the Government with want of proper interest in the religious training and physical culture of the Rhodesian aborigines. Such was the competition, in fact, that the organisation I represented in that Mecca of reportorial journalists, the Press Gallery of the Commons, provided me with a kind of brass coffee-pot arrangement on my desk within the very precincts of the House itself. In reality, it formed one end of a pneumatic tube, at the other extremity of which a telegraph clerk sat in a cupboard at the foot of the stairs leading out into Palace Yard. As each announcement of the slightest moment was made, it was my duty to dash it down on a slip of paper, jamb it into a chunk of baize-covered gutta-percha tubing, and then and there dump it in the 'coffee-pot', close the lid and press an electric bell. Then there came a weird sound from within the 'coffee-pot', as though some unhappy infant were being throt-tled. Members on the floor of the House below would irritably exclaim: 'Sh!' the Sergeant-at-Arms would scowl up at the gallery with an expression of indignant horror at the sacredness of the popular chamber being outraged by such uncanny noises; the ladies behind the 'gridiron' above would crane their necks to catch a glimpse of the domestic tragedy they were perfectly satisfied was taking place somewhere at hand, and Mr Speaker would command: 'Order, order!' in his most severe and authoritative tones. Then there would come an almost equally gruesome tapping of a tiny hammer on a lump of boxwood, which was substituted and did service for a bell, and which indicated to me that my message had been successfully sucked to its destination and was in process of being telegraphed around to all the clubs and most of the evening papers in London. That scheme constituted a most laudable effort to economise time in the conveyance of Parliamentary news to the public, but owing to its eccentricities and the disadvantages I have indicated, it had a short and not over-glorious existence.

Correcting the record

Bussy, who edited Hansard's *Parliamentary Debates* for a while, objected not only to attempts by MPs to alter the record of their speeches but also to their habit of failing to use sufficient postage stamps when returning proofs. When he refused to accept the parcels he was carpeted by the Secretary to the Treasury, but when he pointed out that five ex-Postmasters-General were among the culprits the matter was dropped and free postage for such correspondence was obtained.

Frederick Moir Bussy, *Irish Conspiracies: Recollections of John Mallon and Other Reminiscences* (1910)

The scheme for the production of 'Hansard', before the two Houses commenced to do the work for themselves, authorised, on the one hand, the boiling down of speeches until the residuum was either wholly important or interesting, except in the case of the plutocracy of the 'talking shop', who are lumped up as Ministers and ex-Ministers. Then, on the other hand, by way of topsy-turvying that eminently sensible arrangement, the contract provided that members should be permitted to revise the 'proofs' of their own utterances—which they did by rehabilitating all the ornamental verbiage which had been judiciously eliminated, and by adding much that had not been spoken at all, if there were any apparent possibility of turning the delivery into an essay. It was just the men who ought to be cut down who spent hours in writing up their speeches, and it required the constant vigilance of an editor and several assistants to see they did not tamper with any foolishness they had been guilty of—there is plenty of it in the House of Commons—and at which the House had laughed; that they did not work off platitudes on posterity which their modesty, or their timidity, or—more likely—the temper of the House had prevented them inflicting upon that particular assembly, at all events. I remember the case of one gentleman in particular, who in a speech after dinner had made some observations which were considered to be an undue reflection upon the conduct of the Crown. Mr Gladstone had jumped up in a tremendous heat of virtuous indignation and castigated the honourable member, and Mr Speaker Peel had severely rebuked him from the Chair. When the report appeared in type the member came to me, declaring he had never said the things attributed to him, and attempted to bully and browbeat me into leaving them out. He even threatened to bring my conduct before the House if I refused him, and this notwithstanding that to leave him out would have made the remarks of Mr Gladstone altogether ridiculous and uncalled-for, and have rendered the Speaker's 'ruling' altogether pointless and inane. I had to seek the protection of the Speaker, and as Mr Peel kindly initialled the proof for me as being entirely accurate, the lapses of the honourable gentleman were duly preserved for those who may care to search for them. On another occasion the late Sir Ellis Ashmead-Bartlett sent me a printed slip of a three-column speech he had failed to floor the 'faithful Commons' with, because it was late at night when he attempted it and the House had successfully howled him down. My editorial instincts prompted me to carefully mislay the precious document as the most reasonable and least ostentatious way out of the difficulty. Poor Ashmead-Bartlett fumed and flustered, but it was too late once the 'Debates' was published, so I recommended him to print the whole thing in his own weekly paper, called *England*, which he did, with all the 'Hear, hears', 'Cheers' and 'Laughter' it ought to have evoked.

Arthur Baker, *The House is Sitting* (1958)

I always dealt firmly with any attempt by a Minister or member to persuade me to alter anything that had been said in his speech; it was our job to 'give what the man says'. If a mistake were made by an MP, there were two legitimate ways in which it could be corrected. The MP or Minister could make the correction publicly in the House the next day (Mr Speaker always permitted 'personal explanations' to be made); or the correction could be made in a letter to the Editor.

It was easy to dispose of back-benchers who wished corrections to be made, but Ministers were sometimes more difficult, and especially Prime Ministers. Ramsay MacDonald was one of the worst offenders. His failings in this respect were watched very carefully by some of his own followers, especially by Geordie Buchanan when he was member for the Gorbals division of Glasgow. But Ramsay never prevailed on me to alter the report.

Another Prime Minister who once made a determined effort to induce me to make him say what he intended to say rather than what he did say was Neville Chamberlain. It was while the Spanish civil war was still raging, and Neville was taking on himself the responsibility of answering major questions on foreign policy in the Commons. His reply concerned Franco's attitude in a certain eventuality. My reporter gave a verbatim of what Neville said, and, as I happened to be sitting in the Gallery at the time, I knew that the report was accurate. It was a surprise therefore when, an hour or so later, a telephone call came from downstairs stating that the Prime Minister had made a mistake in his reply, that he meant to say something quite different, and would we alter what he actually had said to what he meant to say. I refused this request and pointed out that the Prime Minister had other means of correcting his error. A little later, a junior Minister (Sir Geoffrey Shakespeare), who was a warm friend of mine, and had himself been a member of the Press Gallery for a time when he was out of the House, came up to my room. He had been sent by the Chief Whip, and he pleaded with me to make the alteration, even trying to make my flesh creep by declaring that the reply as it stood might lead to an international crisis. I did my best to be courteous, but I remained adamant. (In this I had been strengthened by a private talk with my Editor a little earlier.) Eventually the Minister admitted that, of course, my attitude was right, and departed. I heard no more about it officially; but privately I was told that, when Neville heard that I had refused his request, he was asked, 'What will you do if the matter is raised in the House tomorrow?' His reply was alleged to be, 'I shall deny that I ever said it.'

Sixty Budgets

Alexander Mackintosh, *Echoes of Big Ben: A Journalist's Parliamentary Diary, 1881–1940* (1945)

When I retired from regular work in 1938 I was the antique doyen of the Parliamentary journalists. 'Mac!' my Press Gallery colleagues would call out to me when Edward VIII left the Throne, 'tell us how this compares with James II's abdication!' It was familiar banter that I should be asked 'What did Gladstone say?' For forty years, from 1881, I represented the *Aberdeen Free Press*, and after a year on the *Aberdeen Press and Journal*, I became Parliamentary correspondent of the *Liverpool Daily Post*. For some forty years without a break I wrote the Parliamentary letter for the *British Weekly*.

Gallery life changed as greatly as anything else. Long ago when the House of Commons sat very late there were no all-night trams or trains, and groups of journalists going the same way home would share a four-wheeler or take the first morning train from Victoria (about 4 o'clock). Or walk miles home.

Scanty provision was made in my early years for the comfort of the Press Gallery men, scarcely any for their recreation. Food could be had only in a small tea-and-reading room and at a bar where we got a slice of cold beef. Successive generations enjoyed growing facilities until eventually with a score of rooms we reached the comforts and conveniences of a well-equipped club. The time came when we were able to have a bath.

Another relief. Annunciators in our writing-room saved sketch-writers from constant attendance in the Gallery. We could miss the dull men and go in again when the annunciator said that somebody interesting was 'up'. Telephones took the place of the boys on ponies or bicycles who used to speed the news to Fleet Street, and from my own special telephone box I could speak to my head office. Typewriters invaded the rooms after the first German War.

Parliamentary reporting has changed a lot in my time. Early this century, a Cabinet Minister, a distinguished Liberal, said to me with ill-concealed petulance that it was the duty of the Press to report the speeches, not to comment on the manners and idiosyncrasies of the members. Old-fashioned reporters regarded the strictly accurate transcript as their whole duty. I asked one why he did not insert the name of the 'honourable gentleman' to whom Gladstone had referred in a scathing passage? The report left the reader in doubt of the gentleman's identity. 'It is not my duty,' observed the old-fashioned reporter, 'to add to Gladstone's words.'

Since that time—when long columns of speeches were unrelieved by as much as a sub-heading—the seeing eye has played a larger part along with the hearing ear, and the descriptive pen has come largely into vogue. Summaries are freer in style and the Parliamentary sketch as a rule is more given to highlights and personal touches. The most remarkable new development is the sketch-report which sometimes supplements the ordinary report, sometimes takes its place. In its own way it can adequately draw public attention to Parliament, though straight reporting of Parliamentary speeches should not be allowed to die out. Modern MPs are by no means generally displeased by picturesque references to themselves in the up-to-date style of journalism. But the MP has not been born who is not mighty proud to read a substantial straight report of what he was saying . . .

Silence is enjoined upon the Gallery in the interests of the men there themselves as well as the orators downstairs. I was in the French Chamber during an exceedingly stormy scene when frenzied comment passed between deputy and journalist. Such irregularity was inconceivable at Westminster. Even when an MP came up to the side of the Gallery to speak to a reporter the conversation was carried on in a whisper. But we did not live under a system of tyranny. It is true that when I entered the Gallery we received little consideration from the Authorities. But gradually we received more and more the rights of self-government, until we enjoyed a sort of Home-rule under the Speaker and the Serjeant-at-Arms. The consideration we enjoyed ultimately from them and the First Commissioner of Works I acknowledged as Chairman of the Committee when Baldwin came upstairs to unveil a panel in our Library.

I received the honour of Knighthood in 1932 after my half-century of Parliamentary journalism. I was gratified on my retirement six years later by gifts from colleagues in and out of Parliament and from MPs with whom I had been specially associated. From the Gallery Committee I received a Memorial, framed in Westminster Palace oak, extolling the assistance I had given by my services and 'high standard of professional conduct' to the development of the Parliamentary Press Gallery into an essential and respected part of British democratic machinery.

A word more—on my record of Budgets. My second broadcast on changes in Parliament was given at the opening of the Budget in 1940. That was the sixtieth annual financial statement I had heard, besides many supplementary Budgets, and I lived to hear several more. I don't think anybody else has an equal record.

1. Thomas Babington Macaulay, *Edinburgh Review*, September 1828.
2. Quoted in Michael MacDonagh, *The Reporters' Gallery* (1913), p. 345.
3. Charles A. Cooper, *An Editor's Retrospect: Fifty Years of Newspaper Work* (1896), pp. 76–7.
4. Charles T. King, *The Asquith Parliament, (1906–1909); A Popular History of its Men and Measures* (1910), p. 241.
5. Frank Dilnot, *The Old Order Changeth* (1911), pp. 38–9.
6. Charles Gayton, 'Reporting Parliament', *The Kemsley Manual of Journalism* (1950), p. 257.
7. Frederick Peppiatt, memorandum quoted in Arthur Baker, *The House is Sitting* (1958), pp. 162–3.
8. T. F. Lindsay, *Parliament from the Press Gallery* (1967), p. 7.

18 Ladies Last

Disraeli held the theory that no man was regular in his
attendance at the House of Commons until he was
married.

Sir William Fraser, *Disraeli and his Day* (1891)

Some MPs have enjoyed attending the House because it offered an opportunity to escape
from their wives. Others have wished to escape from the masculine atmosphere of the
House. George Goschen, writing to Lady Randolph Churchill from the Commons,
agreed with her suggestion that he wanted 'a "rest from the House and all its inmates".
We hang on here in a deplorable condition without amusements and without ladies,
without any interests except the dying interests of a dull Session. Sometimes a stray
woman appears on the terrace, but what is that among so many?'[1]

In 1675 the Speaker saw some ladies in the Gallery who were partly hidden by the
MPs sitting in front of them. 'What borough do those ladies serve for?' asked the Speaker.
'They serve for the Speaker's Chamber,' replied Sir William Coventry, to which Sir
Thomas Littleton added, 'The Speaker might mistake them for gentlemen with fine
sleeves dressed like ladies.' The Speaker, though not convinced, let the matter drop,
remarking, 'I am sure I saw petticoats.'[2]

Watching MPs in action was a fashionable pursuit for women in the late eighteenth
century. 'In the House of Commons every boy who can articulate is a speaker, to the
great dispatch of business and solidity of councils,' wrote Mrs Montagu to one of her
friends in February 1762. 'They sit late every night, as every young gentleman who has
a handsome person, a fine coat, a well-shaped leg, or a clear voice, is to exhibit these
advantages. To this kind of beau-oratory and tea-table-talk, the ladies, as is reasonable,
resort very constantly.'[3]

After ladies were banned from the Gallery of the House in 1778, they were nonetheless
permitted to observe the proceedings of the House from a more discreet vantage. They
were smuggled into the subfuce space between the roof and the false ceiling that had
been installed in St Stephen's Chapel by Wren at the end of the seventeenth century,
and from there they gazed down through the holes in an octagonal grille, or ventilator,
above the large central chandelier in the Chamber.

During the session of 1834, the sister of an MP accidentally wandered into a side
gallery instead of proceeding to the ventilator. 'The Speaker [Sir Charles Manners
Sutton] seemed quite delighted with the novelty of a politician in petticoats; he never
withdrew his eye from the fair intruder an instant during the short time she remained
in the house.'[4] The ventilator certainly had its drawbacks. Virtually all that could be
seen were the tops of the legislators' heads. A few ladies deliberately avoided the

humiliating ordeal of the ventilator. The Duchess of Gordon, according to Wraxhall, donned men's clothing and obtained access to the Strangers' Gallery. Sheridan's wife, too, is said to have disguised herself as a man so as to hear one of her husband's speeches.[5]

Mrs Gladstone rarely missed one of her husband's important speeches and was therefore a constant presence in the Ladies' Gallery. Mrs Disraeli, too, knew her duty, as related by Sir William Fraser: 'Driving to the House of Commons with her husband, who was about to make a speech of great importance, by the clumsiness of the servant in closing the door, Mrs Disraeli's hand was severely injured: the pain must have been extreme; but not a groan escaped her: she bore all the suffering without a word, fearing lest it might disturb her husband's equanimity at the time when it was required to address the House of Commons.'[6]

The journalist Alexander Mackintosh pointed out that the phenomenon of tea on the Terrace of the House of Commons had become one of London's social highlights. 'Miss Ellen Wilkinson has handsomely described it [the House of Commons] in *The Division Bell Mystery*, as probably the best mixed club in the world,' he wrote in the early 1940s. 'It has many of the amenities of a club and in peace time tea on the Terrace on a summer afternoon with ladies as guests was singularly pleasing. Terrace tea became fashionable at the end of last century, and there was a hubbub in the lobbies when one member's wife sent a card to her friends: "At home on the Terrace from 5 to 7 p.m." That social pretension was frowned upon. One old-fashioned journal stood abashed before the introduction of waitresses on the Terrace; it feared this might lead to flirtations and scandals!'[7] Indeed, the Terrace was becoming so much the province of the ladies in the summer of 1893 that the Speaker issued an edict declaring that the area to the left of the door giving access to the Terrace would be reserved for men only. MPs and their male guests could cross over and visit ladies in the area to the right of the doorway, but the ladies were not allowed to venture into the male preserve.[8] Nor was the Terrace the only area of the Palace that was affected by an influx of ladies. In the summer of 1892, wrote Henry Lucy, the 'terrace, corridor, and lobbies were as full of fashionably dressed ladies as is the Park at church parade on fine Sundays. After being everywhere else, the ladies generally finished up by peeping at the House through a glass window within the main entrance. The regulation hitherto has been that a member may conduct two ladies at a time to this coign of vantage. The consequence was that there was a shifting crowd of ladies blocking up the lobby, waiting their turn.' The Speaker soon declared that the ladies could only enjoy this privilege after seven o'clock in the evening, and since this was the time when they must dress for dinner it proved 'practically prohibitive'.[9]

The Ladies' Gallery above the Speaker's Chair was the sole accommodation for women (they were not allowed to sit with men in the Strangers' Gallery) until 1917. When the House discussed the proposal that ladies should be officially allowed to hear the debates, one MP expressed the hope that 'every honourable Member who is blessed with daughters will negative this idle and ridiculous proposition'.[10] However, when Barry rebuilt the Houses of Parliament it was decided to provide better accommodation for lady visitors than the ventilator, although the suggestion that ladies should sit in the open galleries of the Commons was rejected. Instead a special gallery was allocated to them with a protective metal lattice grille which had the effect of restricting the view in both directions, but principally for the MPs. 'This [grating in front of the Ladies' Gallery] only exists in the House of Commons,' observed a foreign visitor who added that 'the Lords are not so easily agitated by the sight of fair faces'.[11] Even an advanced reformer like Harriet Martineau felt that accommodation for ladies in the House would attract the wrong sort who would prove 'a nuisance to the Legislature and a serious disadvantage to the wiser of their own sex'.[12]

In 1880 two Irish Nationalist Members complained about the Ladies' Gallery. A. M. Sullivan called it 'a mere den', adding that he had 'taken ladies from foreign countries there and Englishmen should see the way in which American ladies turned up their noses—at the Ladies' Gallery in the House of Commons'. J. C. McCoan considered it 'simply a disgrace to the House and it reminds me of nothing I have ever seen except the stage-box in the Cairo Theatre, where the ladies of the Khedive's harem are screened off from the profane view'.[13]

Yet, according to Alexander Mackintosh, the grille was often favoured by the ladies themselves: 'Some Victorian women defended it because "it enables us to sit as we like, to talk together, to hang up our shawls and bonnets and dress as we please".'[14] As First Commissioner of Works, Herbert Gladstone proposed in 1894 that the grille should be done away with, but discovered that both the Members and ladies were divided on the issue. There was one distinct advantage for the ladies in having the grille. Since the Ladies' Gallery was deemed to be outside the House, it did not have to be cleared when strangers were obliged to withdraw for a division.

Lady Violet Bonham-Carter recalled an occasion when she visited the Ladies' Gallery as a young girl during the period of her father's premiership. She overheard Lady Londonderry, then the doyenne of London society, make some disparaging comments about a Liberal MP who was speaking, not realising that the man's wife was sitting within earshot. Lady Violet sent a note of complaint to Mr Speaker Lowther, who replied as follows: 'Dear Miss Asquith, I am so sorry, but I am so busy at this moment dealing with the devils below that I really cannot cope with the angels above.'[15]

The angels were not otherwise invariably angelic, however. In 1888 Mr Speaker Peel was shocked to hear applause for a speech emanate from the Ladies' Gallery. In 1908 two suffragettes chained themselves to the grille of the Ladies' Gallery and shouted 'Votes for Women!', causing Mr Speaker Lowther to close the Gallery to all but the Speaker's personal guests. After a woman rushed on to the floor of the House and shouted the same slogan, the Speaker banned ladies from the inner lobby as well. 'The pleasure with which the House of Commons saw the Ladies and Strangers' galleries remain empty', wrote Charles T. King, 'may be judged from the fact that when about this time Mr Speaker suggested re-opening these galleries next Session groans loud and deep went up from all parts of the House.'[16] In 1909 the Ladies' Gallery was reopened, but only for relatives of MPs, who were obliged to ballot for tickets a week in advance. A later display of feeling by the ladies went unpunished, though. When on June 28, 1919, Lloyd George announced that Germany had signed the Treaty of Versailles, Members sang 'God Save the King', in which only Neil Maclean, MP, refused to join; but the Ladies' Gallery made up for this defection by adding, contrary to the rules of the House, their voices to the anthem.[17]

The grille was finally removed in 1917, the year that women were awarded suffrage. However, some ridiculous, discriminatory rules still applied to female strangers. Lloyd George's secretary and mistress, Frances Stevenson, recorded in her diary that she was unable to hear one of his speeches the whole way through 'as we were all turned out of the Ladies' Gallery at 7.30 in accordance with an absurd rule to that effect.'[18]

The first woman to be elected to Parliament was Countess Markiewicz, a Sinn Fein representative, in 1918, but she refused to take her seat, and so it was Lady Astor who became the first woman MP to be introduced into the Chamber the following year. Frances Stevenson was hurt to discover that Nancy Astor had been saying spiteful things about her and Lloyd George while affecting to be friendly: 'Anyhow, she will get her reward in the House of Commons! I do not think any *wise* woman would choose to sit in the House!'[19] Her prediction was fulfilled. Lady Astor did indeed have an uncomfortable time. She later recalled meeting Churchill at a dinner about two years after she had entered the House and 'he said "It's a very remarkable performance" and I said "What?" and he said "Your staying where you are" and I said "Well, Winston, why on earth didn't you speak to me?" He said "We hoped to freeze you out" and then he added: "When you entered the House of Commons, I felt like a woman had entered my bathroom and I had nothing to protect myself with except a sponge".'[20] Lady Astor tended to provoke an unfavourable reaction in many MPs, such as the Speaker, Captain FitzRoy: 'It is stated that during a Garden Party at Cliveden, Lady Astor said to him: "Listening to the bores in the House you must often, Captain Fitzroy, wish you were dead." "On the contrary," he replied, "I have often wished *you* were." '[21]

It was during Baldwin's premiership that a woman MP, Florence Horsbrugh, moved the Address in reply to the King's Speech for the first time. 'It was gallantly—and truly—said by men that she performed her new duty better than many members of their own sex,'[22] recorded Alexander Mackintosh; though she was expected to appear in evening dress, whereas the male MPs were permitted to appear in lounge suits.[23]

The early women members tended to be feisty characters. Writing in 1950, A. P. Herbert reflected that the women Members of the inter-war period 'were a better vintage than the women of today. They wasted fewer words than the men, worked hard and fought like tigresses. Lady Astor, Mrs Tate, made battling speeches with wit and fire: Miss Rathbone feared nothing and never gave up, though she had a sad knack of making the men laugh in the wrong place. On the subject of the official statistics concerning maternal and infant mortality, they tell me, she said: "Mr Speaker, Sir, we have ante-natal treatment and we have post-natal treatment: but we still have these appalling figures." Megan Lloyd George (still there, I am glad to say) speaks with gentle and persuasive grace.'[24]

How the ladies obtained access to the House of Lords

Lady Mary Wortley Montagu (1689–1762), daughter of Evelyn Pierrepont, married Edward Wortley Montagu, for many years MP for Huntingdon.

Lady Mary Wortley Montagu, Letter to Lady Pomfret, March 1739

The ladies have shown their zeal and appetite for knowledge in a most glorious manner. At the last warm debate in the House of Lords, it was unanimously resolved that there should be no crowd of unnecessary auditors; consequently the fair sex were excluded, and the gallery destined to the sole use of the House of Commons. Notwithstanding which determination, a tribe of dames resolved to show on this occasion that neither men nor laws could resist them. These heroines were Lady Huntingdon, the Duchess of Queensberry, the Duchess of Ancaster, Lady Westmorland, Lady Cobham, Lady Charlotte Edwin, Lady Archibald Hamilton and her daughter, Mrs Scott, Mrs Pendarvis, and Lady Francis Saunderson. I am thus particular in their names, since I look upon them to be the boldest assertors and most resigned sufferers for liberty I ever heard of. They presented themselves at the door at nine o'clock in the morning, where Sir William Saunderson respectfully informed them that the Chancellor had made an order against their admittance. The Duchess of Queensberry, as head of the squadron, pished at the ill-breeding of a mere lawyer, and desired him to let them up the stairs privately. After some modest refusals, he swore by G—— he would not let them in. Her grace, with a noble warmth, answered by G—— they would come in, in spite of the Chancellor and the whole House. This being reported, the peers resolved to starve them out; an order was made that the doors should not be opened till they had raised their siege. These amazons now showed themselves qualified for the duty even of foot soldiers; they stood there till five in the afternoon, without either sustenance or intermission, every now and then playing volleys of thumps, kicks, and raps against the door, with so much violence that the speakers in the house were scarce heard. When the Lords were not conquered by this, the two duchesses (very well apprised of the use of stratagems in war) commanded a dead silence of half an hour; and the Chancellor, who thought this a certain proof of absence (the Commons also being very impatient to enter), gave order for the opening of the door; upon which they all rushed in, pushed aside their competitors, and placed themselves in the front rows of the gallery. They stayed there till after eleven, when the House rose, and during the debate gave applause, and showed marks of dislike, not only by smiles and winks (which have always been allowed in these cases), but by noisy laughs and apparent contempts; which is supposed the true reason why Lord Hervey spoke miserably.

Ladies removed from the gallery of the Commons

London Chronicle, February 2, 1778

This day a vast multitude assembled in the lobby and environs of the House of Commons, but not being able to gain admission by either entreaty or interest, they forced their way into the gallery in spite of the doorkeepers. The House considered the intrusion in a heinous light, and a motion was directly made for clearing the gallery. A partial clearing only took place; the gentlemen were obliged to withdraw; the ladies, through complaisance, were suffered to remain; but Governor Johnstone observing that if the motive for clearing the House was a supposed propriety, to keep the state of the nation concealed from our enemies, he saw no reason to indulge the ladies so far as to make them acquainted with the arcana of the State, as he did not think them more capable of keeping secrets than the men. Upon which, they were likewise ordered to leave the House. The Duchess of Devonshire, Lady Norton, and nearly sixty other ladies were obliged to obey the mandate.

John Hatsell (1743–1820) was educated at Queens' College, Cambridge, and studied law in the Middle Temple. He became a Clerk Assistant in the House of Commons and was Chief Clerk from 1768 until 1797, when he retired with the thanks of the House.

John Hatsell, *Precedents of Proceedings in the House of Commons* (1781)

When a member in his place takes notice to the Speaker of strangers being in the House or gallery, it is the Speaker's duty immediately to order the Serjeant to execute the orders of the House, and to clear the House of all but members, and this without permitting any debate or question to be moved upon the execution of the order. It very seldom happens that this can be done without a violent struggle from some quarter of the House, that strangers may remain. Members often move for the order to be read, endeavour to explain it, and debate upon it, and the House as often runs into great heats upon this subject; but in a short time the confusion subsides, and the dispute ends by clearing the House, for if any one member insists upon it, the Speaker must enforce the order, and the House must be cleared.

The most remarkable instance of this that has occurred in my memory was at a time when the whole gallery and the seats under the front gallery were filled with ladies. Captain Johnstone, of the Navy (commonly called Governor Johnstone), being angry that the House was cleared of all the 'men strangers', amongst whom were some friends he had introduced, insisted that 'all strangers' should withdraw. This produced a violent ferment for a long time; the ladies showing great reluctance to comply with the order of the House; so that by their perseverance business was interrupted for nearly two hours. But at length they were compelled to submit. Since that time ladies, many of the highest rank, have made several efforts to be again admitted. But Mr Cornwall and Mr Addington have as constantly declined to permit them to come in. Indeed, were this privilege allowed to any one individual, however high her rank, or respectable her character and manners, the galleries must soon be open to all women, who from curiosity, amusement, or any other motive, wish to hear the debates. And this to the exclusion of many young men, and of merchants and others, whose commercial interests render their attendance necessary to them, and of real use and importance to the public.

❖

Mullins the Orange Woman

Joseph Pearson, *Pearson's Political Dictionary* (1793)

ORANGE WOMAN—A young, plump, crummy, rosy-looking wench, with clean white silk stockings, Turkey leather shoes, pink silk short petticoat, to show her ankle and calf to the young bulls and old goats of the House. The jade has always a clean nice light cotton, or sometimes, towards the end of the Sessions, a sprigg'd, pencil'd, Members muslin gown, with a thin gauze neckerchief, by way of enamel, as blunt black Norfolk calls it, to display the swelling pencil of Nature's herald office to more advantage. With her black eyes, and black hair, covered by a slight curtain'd bonnet, used to sit that young b——h Mullins, with a basket of oranges on one hand, and hard biscuits on the other, chiefly for the use of my friend Charley Fox, who seems more relieved by a biscuit, in a hot debate, than I am by a bumper of brandy. Thus accoutr'd, as Lisburne used to say, did that young slut kill more Members with her eyes, and her damn'd sighs, than ever all his brother's soldiers did men in America. Out comes a Member, shoving me aside, and knocking the tobacco-box out of Barwell's hand, brush-up he gets to Mullins—Mother Dry, her mistress, leers aside, pretending, the brim, to be warming herself at the brazier—Old Griffin, whispering the young one, puts an orange in his pocket, tells her it is a damn'd dull debate—the House will sit all night—in a whisper requests her to follow him into the Court of Requests, or meet him near the Exchequer Coffee-house, Palace-yard, where he has two or three shillings worth of coach in the Yard, beside gold for the girl, or, as good old Burgoyne calls it, Hesperian fruit for her oranges. Trig and demure, the b—— comes back—mother Dry leaves the basket to meet the old Peers—and this orange woman's business is nothing more than to blind the lobby-loungers by her hard biscuits and her sour fruit, while she takes care, in private, to handle the affairs of most of the National Representatives, in order to relieve and shorten the drowsy fatigues of long debate.—*Mem.* She never shortened me! although she has Clementson! *mum!*

Watching the proceedings of the Commons through 'the ventilator'

Alicia Bayne, *Autobiographic Recollections of George Pryme Esq.*, MA (1870)[25]

Only the lower half of St Stephen's Chapel had been used by the Commons. The upper part, with its vaulted roof and unglazed windows, was a large vacant chamber. In the centre of this was a wooden lantern called 'the ventilator'. This had eight small openings in it, just large enough to admit a head, and was surrounded by a circular bench. By this means ladies who were privileged to go there could catch a glimpse of speakers within a certain radius. When tired of peering through these pigeon-holes we roamed about our prison, and it was very refreshing to look out on a summer's evening upon the Thames. We were locked up, and every now and then our custodian came to tell us who was 'on his legs'. Sometimes members came up; Mr Stanley, now Lord Derby, often when Mrs Stanley was there. The present gilded cage which is so complained of is a paradise to the draughty dusty room I speak of, but we liked it nevertheless, and it was a great treat to have tea in a Committee-room. I remember Mr T. B. Macaulay joining our party there on one of the evenings of an anti-slavery debate.

Maria Edgeworth (1767–1849), the Irish novelist, was born in England, and educated by her father, returning to the family estate in Longford County as a teenager. In 1798 she published her first book, *Practical Education*, co-written with her father, who had been an MP in the Irish Parliament. Her first novel, *Castle Rackrent* (1800), was a success and was admired by Walter Scott; several other novels followed. She visited Parliament again for the state opening in 1844, the same year that she was made an honorary member of the Irish Academy.

Maria Edgeworth, Letter to Mrs Ruxton, March 9, 1822

A garret the whole size of the room—the former chapel—now the House of Commons; below, *kitcats* of Gothic chapel windows stopped up appear on each side above the floor: above, roof-beams. One lantern with one farthing candle, in a tin candlestick, all the light. In the middle of the garret is what seemed like a sentry box of deal boards, and old chairs placed round it; on these we got and stood and peeped over the top of the boards. Saw large chandelier with lights blazing immediately below; a grating of iron across veiled the light so that we could look down and beyond it. We saw half the Table and the Mace lying on it, and papers, and, by peering hard, two figures of clubs at the farther end; but no eye could see the Speaker or his chair—only his feet; his voice and terrible 'Order' was soon heard. We could see part of the Treasury Bench and the Opposition in their places—the tops of their heads, profiles and gestures perfectly. There was not any interesting debate,—the Knightsbridge affair and the Salt Tax,—but it was entertaining to us because we were curious to see and hear the principal speakers on each side. We heard Lord Londonderry, Mr Peel and Mr Vansittart; and on the other side, Denman, Brougham, and Bennett, and several hesitating country gentlemen, who seemed to be speaking to please their constituents only. Sir John Sebright was as much at ease as in his own drawing-room at Beechwood: Mr Brougham we thought the best speaker we heard, Mr Peel next; Mr Vansittart the best language, and most correct English, though there was little in what he said. The Speaker, we were told, had made this observation on Mr Vansittart, that he never makes a mistake in grammar. Lord Londonderry makes the most extraordinary blunders and *mal-à-propos*. Mr Denman speaks well. The whole, the speaking and the interest of the scene surpassed our expectations, and we felt proud to mark the vast difference between the English House of Commons and the French Chambre des Députés.

❖

A Member recalls how he tried to improve the Ladies' Gallery

Grantley Berkeley, *My Life and Recollections* (1866)

I must not forget the attempt made by me to procure a better gallery, whence the ladies might listen to the debates, nor the fun we had in the House when some of the oldest members in it rose to oppose the leave I asked for, and assured the Speaker that 'if ladies were permitted to sit undisguised in the gallery, the feelings of these gallant old soldiers and gentlemen would be so excited and turned from political affairs that they would not be able to do their duty to their country'.

To prevent my elders being thus led astray, I proposed a trellis-work, or partial screen, betwixt the collective gaze of the House and the assembled beauty, and tenderly alluded to a certain incident that took place in the old dark hole, or 'lantern', when the late Maurice O'Connell expected his charming wife to be there to hear one of his first speeches. By some accident her arrival was delayed. The place being quite dark, and the affectionate husband expecting and thinking of but one female, was led by his ear to the flutter made by flowing drapery, when on offering a conjugal embrace, he had his arms much fuller than he expected with the then Dowager Duchess of Richmond.

In spite of all the opposition, leave was obtained to appoint a Committee to consider the best way of carrying out the resolution of the House for an alteration in the gallery; having achieved this I mounted my horse and rode into the Park, where the news had spread before me. On entering on the grass by the water, several groups of ladies and gentlemen who were riding together cheered me.

We had very good fun on the Committee, and one dear, gallant old soldier, now no more, who served on it, asked me 'what I could be thinking of to propose a gallery for women; you're married,' he continued, 'and you ought to have remembered that when a man is in Parliament the business of the House is always an excellent excuse for not being at home. If you get a comfortable gallery, and make an attendance at the debates a fashion among women, we shall have our wives looking us up.'

'Then why don't you move for a skulking-room for men?' I retorted. 'But at all events you have got the library, where you can be supposed to be reading or writing, if your better half should be scanning the benches and not see you; so, old boy, you may do 'em yet.'

We studied an alteration in the ladies' gallery and got it through, but when I moved its adoption in the House, Lord John Russell rose, and was dead against it, and on a division I was beaten on the question of supply. However, the attempt, though openly defeated, covertly worked some good, and improvements, though not to the extent I wanted, were made.

A subscription was then set on foot by the ladies for the presentation to me of a piece of plate, in token of their approbation; but certain of their lords and masters thought proper to put a veto against it, and the amount collected was much circumscribed. It did not prevent a fund being raised, however, nor many ladies who were forbidden to contribute to it, doing so, and I had several letters telling me to look at certain initial letters on the subscription list, explaining who they really represented.

A very pretty figure of one of the graces, bearing a basket of flowers, was then purchased and presented to me, with the following inscription:—

'Presented, AD 1841, to the Hon. Grantley Berkeley, MP, by some ladies, in token of their appreciation of his having advocated their claim to admission to hear the debates in the House of Commons, and obtained, by a majority of 153 to 104, a resolution that ladies should have access to a gallery, the carrying into effect of which resolution was afterwards opposed by Lord John Russell, and defeated by him on a question of supply.'

It went much against my inclinations thus to have the measure defeated, as it were, by a side wind, so I set about looking into the real state of affairs, which, according to the express rules of the House prevented ladies from at any time taking their places in the strangers' gallery, and I found that no law of the House affected the sex of the 'strangers' named for exclusion, but that 'all strangers', 'reporters' and all, were merely there on sufferance. Custom alone prevented ladies from applying for, or gaining admission to the 'Strangers' Gallery'. An idea struck me that would at least create some fun, and it was to get a large party of ladies together, who would put on long military cloaks, such as I used to wear when in the Guards, over their dresses, and men's hats, and in that attire ascend to the Strangers' Gallery, and passing the porters, which, mingled with gentlemen, they could easily have done, take their seats in the gallery, and then, by doffing their hats and cloaks, disclose their sex to the astonished eyes of the Speaker.

I would have been in my place, with plenty of supporters to have defended their position, and as the gallery, by any 'standing rule of the House', could only have 'been cleared of strangers', we could have insisted that if the ladies 'must withdraw', so must all the men, and every one of the 'reporters of the press'. The ayes and noes thus in antagonism would have made, as Sir Lucius O'Trigger says, 'a very pretty quarrel' as they would have stood, and the matter for the time have been scarcely within any prospect of settlement. An enactment of the House could only have ended the business, by thereafter defining the sex of the strangers.

At first I thought that this attempt would have been made, for very many women in society, amused with the idea, agreed to put themselves under my direction, but, alas! that old and terribly true saying that 'anything known to more than two never is a secret', told against me in this instance. My female volunteers let the affair escape their camp before I had said a word of it to mortal man, and the rumour getting abroad, the supposed-to-be wiser heads prevailed, and the experiment was abandoned.

The campaign to repeal the Contagious Diseases Acts

The social reformer Josephine Butler (1828–1906) campaigned against the white-slave trade and the Contagious Diseases Acts which required women who resided in seaports or garrison towns to undergo regular examinations for venereal disease. She was married to George Butler, who was the Canon of Winchester.

Josephine Butler, Letter to her son Stanley, February 28, 1883

We went to the House at four o'clock yesterday. Justin McCarthy was speaking. There was still to the last a chance of Mr Hopwood's resolution coming on, but perhaps not till midnight. I did not remain in the Ladies' Gallery, but came and went from the prayer-meeting to the Lobby of the House. We saw John Morley take the oath and his seat. The first thing he did after taking the oath was to sit down by Mr Hopwood and say, 'Now tell me what I can do to help you tonight, for the thing our Newcastle electors were most persistent about was that I should oppose this legislation.' I then went to the Westminster Palace Hotel, where we had taken a large room for our devotional meeting. There were well-dressed ladies, some even of high rank, kneeling together (almost side by side) with the poorest, and some of the outcast women of the purlieus of Westminster. Many were weeping, but when I first went in they were singing, and I never heard a sweeter sound. There were some cultivated voices amongst them, and the hymns were well chosen. I felt ready to cry, but I did not; for I long ago rejected the old ideal of the 'division of labour', that 'men must work and women must weep'. A venerable lady from America rose and said, 'Tears are good, prayers are better, but we should get on better if behind every tear there was a vote at the ballot box.' Every soul in that room responded to that sentiment. I never saw a meeting more moved. The occasion and the circumstances were certainly pathetic. As we continued to pray we all felt, I think, a great pity come into our hearts for those men who were at that moment in the House so near to us, who wield so great a responsibility, and so many of whom will have a sad account to give of their use of it.

Charles Parker told me the next day that at that time several MPs were walking about the Lobby, and that two young men, not long in Parliament, said to him, 'Have you heard, Parker, that the ladies were to hold a prayer meeting tonight to pray for us? But I suppose it is given up, as this debate is to be postponed.' Mr Parker, better informed, said, 'On the contrary, that is just what they are doing now, praying for us. It throws a great responsibility on *us*.' The young men, he said, looked very grave, Father had to return home, I went back to the House, while other women remained and continued their intercessions. All Westminster was wrapped in a haze, out of which glared only the great light on the clock tower. I walked through the mist, feeling rather sad, and wondering how much longer this horrible yoke would remain fastened on the neck of a people who wish to get rid of it, and how long women will be refused a voice in the representation of the country. I climbed up the wearisome gallery stairs, and from the grating saw a crowd of our gentlemen friends from the country sitting in the Strangers' Gallery opposite. How patiently they sat through those long hours. Some of them had come even from Scotland for the purpose. Father had gone home, but just above the clock I saw George, and tried to catch his eye, but he, believing that I was at the other meeting, did not look towards our gallery or see me. I sat on till midnight for the chance of our resolution coming on. By and by Mr Hopwood asked the Speaker's leave to make a statement. He then made a very good speech, explaining, rather to the country than to the House, how it was he was prevented from bringing on his resolution, and saying that Parliament and the Government should have no peace on the question, for the country was aroused, and nothing could lessen their present determination. He called them to witness to the needless waste of time there had been in talking and recriminations before midnight. Mr Trevelyan told me he thought our opponents had purposely prolonged the debate on the Address . . .

After another half hour at the meeting, I returned once more to the Lobby of the House, and found some of our friends waiting about. They took me on the terrace along the river front. The fog had cleared away, and it was very calm under the starlit sky. All the bustle of the city was stilled, and the only sound was that of the dark water lapping against the buttresses of the broad stone terrace, the water into which so many despairing women have flung themselves.

I forgot to tell you that before the debate began I ventured into the circular hall or lobby next to the House itself, having caught sight of the venerable face of Mr Whitwell. He remembered me, and shook hands. I stood near him in a corner, as if he had taken me under his protection. The first word he said to me was, 'Has it ever struck you that there is no one thing in the whole of Christ's discourses to which He has given such emphasis as that of the certainty of prayer being answered? Now you may be sure our persevering prayers will be answered in this matter.' I saw several other friends, among them your member, Mr Williamson, who said, 'Tell your son that I have presented his petition from St Andrews, and that I support the prayer of it with all my heart.' I am glad to tell you Albert Grey and Robert Reid, father's old pupil at Cheltenham, are with us on the question. I met Cardinal Manning in the Lobby, and had a pleasant talk with him. He is much in earnest about all good movements. He has been ill, and looked even thinner than a spider! He said he would do all he could for us, through his influence, on the Irish Catholic vote.

Although Hopwood failed to bring on his resolution, another Member, Mr Stansfeld, moved a resolution on April 20 condemning compulsory examination. This was carried by 182 votes to 110 and the Government suspended the operation of the Acts in May. However, it dragged its heels over repeal of the legislation. There was further campaigning in 1885 and the Repeal Bill was finally given Royal Assent in April 1886. This is Josephine Butler's account of the crucial debate in April 1883.

Josephine Butler, Letter to her sister Harriet, April 1883

Some day I trust I shall be able to tell you in detail of the events of the last few days. I longed for your presence during the debate; it was for us a very solemn time. All day long groups had met for prayer—some in the houses of MPs, some in churches, some in halls, where the poorest people came. Meetings were being held also all over the kingdom, and telegraphic messages of sympathy came to us continually from Scotland and Ireland, France, Switzerland and Italy. There was something in the air like the approach of victory. As men and women prayed they suddenly burst forth into praise, thanking God for the answer, as if it had already been granted. It was a long debate. The tone of the speeches, both for and against, was remarkably purified, and with one exception they were altogether on a higher plane than in former debates. Many of us ladies sat through the whole evening till after midnight; then came the division. A few minutes previously Mr Gerard, the steward of the Ladies' Gallery, crept quietly in and whispered to me, 'I think you are going to win!' That reserved official, of course, never betrays sympathy with any party; nevertheless I could see the irrepressible pleasure in his face when he said this.

Never can I forget the expression on the faces of our MPs in the House when they all streamed back from the division lobby. The interval during their absence had seemed very long, and we could hear each other's breathing, so deep was the silence. We did not require to wait to hear the announcement of the division by the tellers; the faces of our friends told the tale. Slowly and steadily they pressed in, headed by Mr Stansfeld and Mr Hopwood, the tellers on our side. Mr Fowler's face was beaming with joy and a kind of humble triumph. I thought of the words: 'Say unto Jerusalem that her warfare is accomplished.' It was a victory of righteousness over gross selfishness, injustice, and deceit, and for the moment we were all elevated by it. When the figures were given out a long-continued cheer arose, which sounded like a psalm of praise. Then we ran quickly down from the gallery, and met a number of our friends coming out from Westminster Hall.

It was half-past one in the morning, and the stars were shining in a clear sky. I felt at that silent hour in the morning in the spirit of the Psalmist, who said: 'When the Lord turned against the captivity of Zion we were like unto them that dream.' It almost seemed like a dream.

When Mr Cavendish Bentinck was speaking against us I noticed an expression of pain on Mr Gladstone's face. He seemed to be pretending to read a letter, but at last passed his hand over his eyes and left the House. He returned before Mr Stansfeld made his noble speech, to which he listened attentively.

A lady novelist in the environs of the Chamber

Mrs Rosa Caroline (Murray-Prior) Praed (1851–1935), the Anglo-Australian novelist who wrote under the name of Mrs Campbell Praed, was born in Queensland, Australia, where her father was Postmaster-General. She was fascinated by literature and politics and spent much time in the Ladies' Gallery of the Queensland House of Legislators. While on a tour of the United States with her husband (Campbell Mackworth Praed), she encountered the writer and Irish Nationalist MP Justin McCarthy, who was over there on a lecture tour. With McCarthy's assistance she became a regular visitor to the Ladies' Gallery of the House of Commons; and together they wrote three novels of English political life: '*The Right Honourable*' (1886), *The Ladies' Gallery* (1888) and *The Rebel Rose* (1888). She also wrote several novels about middle-class colonial life.

Mrs Campbell Praed, Introduction to *Our Book of Memories* (1912)

The writing of our political novels made it necessary for me to study the activities of the House of Commons, from every standpoint available to an outsider, for planning the scenery of the story, arranging the exits and entrances of its chief characters and the general stage effects. To me it was a renewal, in fuller and more vital measure, of the old political flavouring of my Australian girlhood when I had often spent hours in the Ladies' Gallery of the House of Legislature listening to debates on which hung the fate of a Ministry, and my own poor little immediate fate as well—the retirement again into Bush cloisterdom, or the enjoyment of a season in town. That past experience was like a rehearsal in the provinces by an untrained company of the great Empire drama. *This* was the real thing, the Big Play, performed in the metropolitan theatre by the original actors.

In those days of the House of Commons, there were not the tiresome restrictions which have prevailed since the Female Suffragists made precautions necessary against feminine entrance.

A woman under the wing of her special law-maker might loiter in the Inner Lobby, might stand on the perch outside the sacred, brazen doors, and watch what was going on in the Debating Chamber. She might pass through the long Library—though not for an instant might she sit down therein except under condign penalty: she might walk along the upstairs lobbies—where Mr McCarthy showed me the special desk at which so many of his letters to me were penned: she might roam the vestibules, study the frescoes, be shown the windows on the great staircase, beneath which the standard weights and measures of England are embedded. She might be taken past the historic statues into the Great Hall of Westminster where Warren Hastings was impeached and down which, at former coronations, the Champion of England rode. She might pace the cloistral-like garden beside the House of Lords, might, upon certain days, inspect that hallowed chamber. And then, after quite an excursion, she would find herself taking tea on the Terrace—to my mind the most fascinating part of the whole business.

The Terrace was less crowded and the company more select in the eighties than I have since known it. Tea and strawberries in June upon the Terrace of the House of Commons was, among the political set, one of the pleasantest features of London life. These loiterings and explorations generally took place when the debates were not expected to be lively or when no seat had been procured for the Ladies' Gallery. It was not so difficult to get one in the beginning of our collaboration. Later, the increased demand obliged members to ballot for their lady-guests. It was the simplest thing in the world to drive down to the inner courtyard, go through the small door and climb the rather steep and gloomy staircase which led to the Ladies' Gallery. Sometimes I would meet Mr Gladstone on that staircase, escorting Mrs Gladstone up to her place, usually in the Speaker's Gallery: and, almost before I recognised him in the dimness of the staircase, would receive the kindly greeting he invariably stopped to give me on our chance encounters. Then, to slip into the front row behind the *grille*—if one were lucky—where, by and by, Mr McCarthy would find me and explain the debate and who was going to speak and what was likely to happen down below. I learned a good deal about party intrigue and parliamentary underplay from my literary colleague, who would talk to me *en bon camarade* about the latest political developments and his own hopes and disappointments and perplexities.

❖

A *wifely concern*

Jennie Jerome (1854–1921), Lady Randolph Churchill, was born in Brooklyn, New York, the daughter of Leonard Jerome, who had made his fortune on the New York stock exchange. She was brought up in New York and Paris. It was at the Cowes regatta in 1873 that she met Lord Randolph Churchill, a son of the 7th Duke of Marlborough, whom she later married and by whom she had two sons, Winston and John. Following her husband's death from a wasting disease (believed by some historians to have been syphilis), she later married a Guards officer, George Cornwallis-West, who was the same age as Winston. The marriage lasted from 1900 to 1914, during which time she became a playwright and author. In 1917 she married for a third time, to Montagu Porch, a member of the landed gentry who had worked in the colonies.

Lady Randolph Churchill, *Reminiscences* (1908)

Randolph, whose interest in politics had become very keen during his stay in Ireland, was now entirely absorbed by them. During this session the Bradlaugh incident arose, in which he took so prominent a part. I, too, caught the fever, and went frequently to the House of Commons, listening with growing interest to the debates. The Ladies' Gallery, for which one ballots, and the Speaker's Gallery, to which one is invited by the Speaker's wife, were not in those days the fashionable places of resort they have since become. Only a few ultra-political ladies frequented them. In the Speaker's Gallery Mrs Gladstone, picturesque and dignified, always occupied a reserved seat, from which she was seldom absent. Miss Balfour, too, was generally there. Mrs Cavendish Bentinck, a tall, handsome woman, whose flashing eyes and raven locks had gained for her among her friends the name of 'Britannia', and whose son married Miss Livingstone, of New York, was also an *habituée*, and literally seemed to live there. Later, Mrs Chamberlain joined the group. But the gay butterflies of society thought it too serious a place for them. Now, however, this has quite changed. The present generation are full of the desire of being, or appearing to be, serious. To be beautiful and rich is not sufficient; the real social leaders of today are not content with these accidents of birth and fortune. They aspire to political influence, or to be thought literary and artistic; and society follows the lead. For an interesting debate or to hear a popular politician they will make strenuous efforts to get into the Speaker's Gallery. On such an occasion many of the youngest and prettiest women in London can be found there. Hidden in Eastern fashion from masculine sight, fifty or more will sometimes crowd into the small, dark cage to which the ungallant British legislators have relegated them. The ladies in the first row, in a cramped attitude, with their knees against the grille, their necks craned forward, and their ears painfully on the alert if they wish to hear anything, are supposed to enjoy a great privilege. Those in the second row, by the courtesy of the first, may get a peep of the gods below. The rest have to fall back on their imagination or retire to a small room in the rear, where they can whisper and have tea. Some take the opportunity to polish off their correspondence, hoping, perhaps, that the letters, written on House of Commons paper, may convey a political flavour to the unpolitical recipients. Silence is supposed to be *de rigueur*, but the thread of many an interesting speech has been lost in the buzz of stage whispers and the coming and going of restless ones. 'Is that Mr ——?' exclaims a pretty blonde to her neighbour. 'Do lend me your glasses. Yes, it is he. I wonder if he would dine with me tonight?' ('Sh!' comes from a relative of the man who is speaking.) 'We are thirteen—so tiresome. I think I must send him a note by the usher.' ('Sh!') 'I can get the answer at once—*so* convenient.' ('Sh! sh!') 'Who is that odious woman hushing me? *Darling*, keep my chair; I will return in a moment'; and amid a jingling of beads and chains and a *frou-frou* of silk petticoats the fair one flies to scribble her note. Meanwhile the front row settles down once more to the speech to which they are listening. 'What an immoral argument! Just like a Radical's impudence to say such things!' exclaims in no dulcet tones a Conservative peeress, who would be better occupied waking up her lord in the Upper House than crowding out the wife of some Member of Parliament in the Lower. 'Be careful!' says her neighbour; 'his wife is next to you.' These are specimens of the remarks one sometimes hears. I remember an enthusiastic wife whose husband was making an important speech, betraying her too intimate knowledge of it by giving her unwilling listener the best points beforehand. Next to speaking in public oneself, there is nothing which produces such feelings of nervousness and apprehension as to hear one's husband or son doing so. There is no doubt, however, that the frequent recurrence of it minimises the ordeal, particularly if the speakers are sure of themselves. In this respect I can claim to being specially favoured, though Randolph, even after years of practice and experience, was always nervous before a speech until he actually stood up. This subject reminds me of a painful sight I once saw at a big political meeting. A young Member of Parliament with more acres than brains, who sat for a family pocket-borough, was making his yearly address to his constituents. Shutting his eyes tight and clenching his hands, he began in a high falsetto voice: 'Brothers and sisters, Conservatives!' and for thirty minutes he recited, or rather gabbled, the speech he had learned by heart, while his wife, with her eyes riveted on him, and with tears pouring down her cheeks from nervousness, unconsciously, with trembling lips, repeated the words he was uttering.

Mrs O'Shea in the Ladies' Gallery

Katherine O'Shea (1845–1921) was born Katherine Wood in Essex and married Captain O'Shea, a financially feckless ex-Army officer, in 1867. They lived with her wealthy aunt from 1875, and Captain O'Shea became Home Rule MP for Clare in 1880. Kitty met Parnell in the same year and fell in love with him, becoming his mistress and confidante. Her husband quickly became aware of their relationship but was at first prepared to tolerate it, even acknowledging three of Parnell's children by Kitty as his own, because he was hoping to obtain an income from her aunt's estate and because Kitty persuaded Parnell to give him another parliamentary seat after he had lost Clare. During the Kilmainham Treaty negotiations, Mrs O'Shea acted as a conduit between her lover and Gladstone. In 1889 Captain O'Shea sued for divorce, citing Parnell as co-respondent, which led to the Nationalist leader's downfall. Kitty married Parnell in June 1891, fourteen weeks before he died in her arms.

Katherine O'Shea, *Charles Stewart Parnell: His Love Story and Political Life* (1914)

Parnell had a most beautiful and harmonious voice when speaking in public. Very clear it was, even in moments of passion against his own and his country's foes—passion modulated and suppressed until I have seen, from the Ladies' Gallery, his hand clenched until the 'Orders of the Day' which he held were crushed into pulp, and only that prevented his nails piercing his hand. Often I have taken the 'Orders' out of his pocket, twisted into shreds—a fate that also overtook the slips of notes and the occasional quotations he had got me to look out for him.

Sometimes when he was going to speak I could not leave my aunt long enough to be sure of getting to the Ladies' Gallery in time to hear him; or we might think it inexpedient that I should be seen to arrive so soon after him at the House. On these occasions, when I was able, I would arrive perhaps in the middle of his speech and look down upon him, saying in my heart, 'I have come!'; and invariably I would see the answering signal—the lift of the head and the lingering touch of the white rose in his coat, which told me, 'I know, my Queen!'

This telepathy of the soul, intuition, or what you will, was so strong between us that, whatever the business before the House, whether Parnell was speaking or not, in spite of the absolute impossibility of distinguishing any face or form behind the grille of the Ladies' Gallery, Parnell was aware of my presence, even though often he did not expect me, as soon as I came in, and answered my wordless message by the signal that I knew.

Sometimes he would wish to speak to me before I went home, and would signal by certain manipulations of his handkerchief to me to go and await him at Charing Cross, or another of our meeting-places, and there he would come to tell me how things were going, or to chat for a few minutes, or get from me the replies to messages sent through me to Mr Gladstone.

Suffragette protests in the House

By coincidence, Emillie Peacocke, a female journalist for the *Tribune*, the Liberal daily, was present in the Ladies' Gallery when Sam Evans tried to talk out Keir Hardie's resolution on women's suffrage. According to her judgement, the ensuing protest was 'a spontaneous thing' provoked by the way in which their cause was 'lightly dismissed in a few cursory and unsympathetic words'.[26]

Charles T. King, *The Asquith Parliament (1906–1909)* (1910)

Among the futile things, at any rate, so far as this Parliament is concerned, was the series of amusing discussions on 'Votes for Women'. Only a few Members of this Parliament took the matter seriously, in the House, at any rate. One amusing evening there was a women's suffrage resolution before the House of Commons. It was on April 25th, 1906. Men knew no party on this question; a Liberal and a Conservative would get up and speak for women's suffrage, and a Liberal and a Conservative would get up and attack it. About a quarter to eleven that evening, Mr Samuel Evans, afterwards Sir Samuel, was attacking the women's suffrage motion. He seemed to me to present—physically, I mean— a good picture of a cross between the illustrations of Mr Tulkinghorn and those of Mr Pecksniff in the good editions of Dickens. There was nothing of the character of either, however, about 'Sir Sam'. I was looking down at the mildly amused assembly, and with my back, of course, to the Ladies' Gallery. All of a sudden there came from somewhere behind us one of the strangest screams I ever heard. It was not like a woman's shout, it hardly seemed like a woman's voice at all; it was shrill and nervous, intensely excited. Afterwards the owner of the voice got, so to speak, into her stride, and she became coherent and indignant. Several women began shouting through the metal grille of the Ladies' gallery. They poured scorn on Mr Sam Evans; they called for 'Votes for Women'.

'You will take it out,' screamed one shrill voice. 'Justice for women,' was another shout, and then the half-startled but intensely amused House of Commons looked up and saw a white flag flutter through the grille. It had on it in black letters the inscription: 'Votes for Women'. The first thought that came to one's mind while the police and attendants were clearing the Ladies' gallery was that if these women had been there long, how they must have writhed and chafed at the things the men down below had been saying about the sort of woman who says she wants a vote.

'Gurr-r-r-r! you liberty-loving Liberals!' screamed one of these ladies as she was bundled out. That was the beginning . . .

After this April night in 1906, when the screams came through the grille and women chirruped amusingly of a desire for votes, there were several other little disturbances, but Inspector Scantlebury and his merry men handed the ladies with remarkable kindness and patience into the street.

One night some women belonging to a certain suffrage organisation decided to make 'a real big demonstration'. They would get into the Ladies' gallery by promising a member that they would be of good behaviour, and then with girdles round their waists and little chains all ready they would chain themselves to the grille. Then, they reflected, they would be able to keep on addressing the House and shrieking for votes while the attendants would tug vainly at the chains unable to remove the demonstrators.

This they carried out. What I can never understand is why these women should choose to do it at the one time in all the proceedings of the House when there is next to nobody present. Mr Remnant, I remember, was continuing a debate, addressing two or three little knots of members who reclined, tiny islands of men, on broad spaces of empty green bench. It was the middle of the dinner-hour, when even on important nights there is next to nobody in the House. The 'demonstration' was fixed for half-past eight. Big Ben chimed the half-hour. I heard a little shuffle up in the Ladies' gallery. Then, looking up, I saw a couple of hands poked through the open ironwork of the grille. The chain was passed round, the lock snapped to. She was fast. Two young women did this. They were persons of no importance, but the incident is important because it was the crowning disturbance which led to both the public galleries being closed for a long time, and which led also to all women who were not relatives of a Member of Parliament being deprived of the privilege of listening to the debates during the rest of this Parliament.

The shrieking did not go on very long. The two girls chirruped funnily about 'justice'. Some officials fetched tools and took out a small section of the metal work. Then carefully carrying the detached portions of the grille so as not to hurt the girls, the officials conducted them to a committee room and filed off the chains. Inspector Scantlebury and his men gently escorted the girls out to Bridge Street, bade them a cheery 'Good-night', and disgusted them by declining to take them into custody.

'Never mind,' said one of the girls to me, brightening up, 'I am going to have another go. They will have to arrest me.' So she crept round to the St Stephen's entrance, where the police were keeping back a little crowd, and flung herself against a row of big constables. They told her to go away. She ran back and flung herself at one of the biggest. He pushed her back. She had another attempt, and they swung her round and round to calm her down. She leaned against the stone wall for a moment, got her breath, and threw her light form against a long heavy row of constables for the last time.

Then they simply had to take her away.

It was not only in the Ladies' gallery that lady guests of Members of Parliament thus abused hospitality. There is a little square of glass in the swinging doors between the House of Commons and the Members' lobby. It had been for a long time the privilege of MPs to bring their fair guests to these swinging doors to look through the glass and watch the House of Commons at work. Through these swinging doors was but a step. One night a woman took this step. She ran in a few yards, the easiest thing in the world. She did not, of course, ask permission of the MP who had brought her in. She was caught by an official and taken out. Then the privilege of the little peephole, as it was called, at the swinging doors was taken away, not merely from this one weird woman but from all women.

James William Lowther (1855–1949) was the son and grandson of MPs and was educated at Eton; at King's College, London; and at Trinity College, Cambridge. He was called to the bar in 1879 and was a Conservative (later Unionist) MP for Rutland, 1883–5; for the Penrith division of Cumberland, 1886–1918; and for the Penrith and Cockermouth division of Cumberland from 1918 until 1921, when he was created Viscount Ullswater. Having served as Deputy Chairman of Ways and Means for ten years, he was Speaker of the House of Commons from 1905 to 1921.

Viscount Ullswater (James Lowther), *A Speaker's Commentaries* (1925)

So far as the House of Commons was concerned, an amusing incident occurred when a number of the militant Suffragettes having chartered a steam launch and got it moored close to the terrace, addressed the Members, who happened to be indulging in five o'clock tea there, and showered upon them cards of invitation to an afternoon party, purporting to come from myself. The invitation cards were gilt-edged and elaborately got up, with the Royal Arms at the top and inscribed as follows:

The Speaker of the House of Commons
requests the pleasure of the company of the
President, Executive Committee and Members
of the Women's Freedom League
at Tea in the
Garden of the Speaker's Residence, House of Commons
on Tuesday, July 22nd, at 6 p.m.
Music and Speeches. RSVP.

On this I will only observe that the Speaker is not entitled to use the Royal Arms and that there is no such place as the garden of the Speaker's residence.

On another occasion, whilst Mr Asquith was addressing the House on the second reading of the Finance Bill, a man in the Strangers' Gallery threw a bag of flour at him. The missile missed the Prime Minister and burst on the steps of the Speaker's chair, but did no harm to anybody beyond making a great mess. If Sir Courtenay Ilbert had happened to have been in his seat at the table, it might just have hit him full in the face. The same individual threw some leaflets into the House headed 'Grace before Meat', and with a picture representing Mr McKenna forcibly feeding a woman in prison dress bound to a chair and with the following lines below the drawing:

> Observe how we treat every case
> With the chivalrous tact of our race
> How before we proceed
> To forcibly feed,
> We never omit to say our grace

One Monday morning a woman was discovered by the police hidden in a cupboard in a lobby of the House. She was as black as a chimney-sweep and in an exhausted condition. It appeared that she had by some means secreted herself on the roof and obtained entrance to a flue, from which hunger had at last compelled her to escape. What she had hoped to do there or how her action could assist her cause are unsolved mysteries. She only succeeded in making herself very uncomfortable and somewhat ridiculous.

❖

Mrs Lloyd George keeps vigil alone in the Ladies' Gallery

Charles T. King, *The Asquith Parliament (1906–1909)* (1910)

One night I looked up at the ladies' grille about midnight. Quite a number of wives and relatives of MPs were there. At one o'clock most of them had gone. A little later there was a flutter of feminine dress, the passing glimpse of a fashionable hat, and all the women had gone—save one. Up in the gallery one devoted woman kept the vigil. Down on the floor of the House was a worn man, fighting hour by hour with the end of the fight still weeks and perhaps months ahead. With a given point nearly through, with a clause almost finished, with a division on an amendment apparently within a minute's reach, fresh arguments or the repetition of old ones, fresh cross-examiners, fresh streams of hostile facts, would be poured on this spare figure. The woman up in the Ladies' gallery still gazed down. Here on the floor of the House a man after long years in Opposition was making the greatest fight of his life, and the lone woman, regardless of the approaching dawn, was watching the contest. Two o'clock, three o'clock, four o'clock, and the wife still gazing down, the husband still carrying on the fight undaunted. It was not until the Chancellor of the Exchequer some time towards the morning thrust his papers wearily into a red dispatch-box, snapped the fastening with a little click and vanished in the shadows behind the Speaker's chair that the silent watcher above broke her lonely vigil.

The arrival of the first woman MP

Nancy, Viscountess Astor (1879–1964), was born of wealthy parents in Virginia, in the United States. She married William Waldorf Astor and upon his death followed in his footsteps and was elected as Conservative MP for Plymouth.

Mr Speaker Lowther had been consulted by Lady Astor about whether she would wear a hat for the day of her introduction as a Member. He advised against it on the grounds that 'fashions in ladies' hats varies frequently: a constant change of headgear would become the subject of remark equally with the absence of any change'. Lady Astor declined his advice and wore a toque. She later recalled that it had been an 'alarming' experience 'to walk up the House of Commons between Arthur Balfour and Lloyd George, both of whom had said they believed in women but who would rather have had a rattlesnake in the House than me at the time'.[27] On the same day, the Speaker gave permission for the first lady reporter to take her seat in the Reporters' Gallery. (A previous attempt by Charles Bradlaugh to have a female reporter admitted in 1890 had been refused by Mr Speaker Peel on the grounds that 'it might lead to all manner of unforeseen consequences'.)[28]

Arthur Baker, *The House is Sitting* (1958)

1 December 1919 was a great day for the women of Britain and the Common-wealth. The Outer Lobby at Westminster was crowded with women, all eager to see Lady Astor take her seat. But, as it happened, she entered by the members' entrance and walked through the Lobby practically unnoticed. For the first time the door-keeper of the House of Commons allowed a woman to cross the threshold which no one of her sex had passed before during the sittings of the House, save at her peril. I remember that there were more women than men in the Strangers' Gallery. At the other end we could look up from the Press Gallery at the Ladies' Gallery above and at the back of us. There, from behind the hated grille, still more women, many of them Lady Astor's personal friends, looked down on the historic scene. Lord Astor smiled at his wife from the Distinguished Strangers' Gallery, where the American Ambassador and the High Commissioner for Canada were also seated.

The Peers' Gallery was quite full. Two women journalists, greatly daring, sought and secured admission to the Press Gallery. I forget their names, but I believe one of them represented the *Daily Mail*. This invasion was unexpected, but the Serjeant at Arms held that, as the House and the public galleries were now open to women, he could not prevent duly accredited women representa-tives of newspapers which had the entree from enjoying a similar privilege. Hence women were admitted as members of the House of Commons and of the Press Gallery on the same day.

Lady Astor, after her introduction, took the corner seat on the second bench below the gangway on the Opposition side among a group of young Conservatives. She and they were officially designated 'Coalition Unionists' and supported the Lloyd George Administration, but there were so many Coalition members that they had to overflow to the Opposition side of the Chamber.

Though Lady Astor was wise enough not to make her maiden speech on the night of her introduction, she recorded her first vote. It was against premium bonds.

I have often thought how well-equipped she was to be the pioneer for her sex in Parliament. The House of Commons was then a very conservative assembly, not only in the political sense. The entry of a woman to those sacred precincts was a real revolution. Fortunately, that particular woman was possessed of any amount of courage. She needed every bit of it. She was no respecter of persons, and expressed her views freely and frankly—perhaps too frankly for the peace of mind of some of the older members of her party. She was a convinced total abstainer, and made no secret of her dislike of the use of alcohol. Nor could she suffer fools gladly. In her early years in the Commons, she was wont to show her impatience with the ponderous utterances of some elderly Conservatives. Frequently I have seen her throw up her hands in utter despair at some reactionary remark from her own side of the House. Her comments on such occasions were made quite freely, and were often audible in the Press Gallery. They were not always flattering. The late Sir William Davison, the member for South Kensington, who afterwards went to the Lords as Lord Broughshane, seemed to annoy her greatly.

I remember a priceless incident little more than a year after Lady Astor came into the House. It was during the report stage of the Juvenile Courts Bill, which Lady Astor strongly supported, but which was not so popular with some 'die-hards'. Reference had been made to 'two talking women', and Lady Astor retorted fiercely, 'I do not believe any woman would talk more nonsense than some of the old women in this House!' She went on to criticise the members who were opposing the Bill. 'It is no good saying they are opposing this on legal grounds because really the opposition is against women, and all this legal ground is camouflage. All I ask is that you look at the hon. members who are opposed to it. Look at them and their past and you will see——'

At this there were shouts of 'Withdraw!', and Lady Astor was unable to complete her sentence. When order had been restored, the House dissolved in laughter as she remarked, with an air of injured innocence: 'I am not referring to their past outside this House; I am talking about it inside this House, so they need not get so nervous.'

Frances Stevenson, Diary, December 1, 1919

Went to see the first lady MP take her place in the House. It really was a thrilling moment, not from the personal point of view, but from the fact that after all these hundreds of years, this was the first time that a woman had set foot upon that floor to represent the people—or a certain number of them. I had a lump in my throat as I saw her come in at the far end—a very graceful, neat figure—and wait for her turn to walk up the floor. The PM [Bonar Law] was very self-conscious and nervous and made a false start in his anxiety to get it over. He was obviously relieved when he reached his seat, and the House was much amused.

❧

How to describe the lavatories for women Members

Tom Driberg, *The Best of Both Worlds: A Personal Diary* (1953), June 2, 1951

There is still discrimination against women in the Houses of Parliament—and women MPs are angry about it. It concerns a delicate subject—the whereabouts of 'the ladies'.

Wherever men MPs are, however long they may have to remain in the debating chamber, there is always a toilet within a minute's walk. Not so for the women; but ever since 1941, while MPs have been using the Lords', the women have been assured that this need would be attended to when the Commons was rebuilt.

They say it hasn't been adequately . . . and their fury is aggravated by learning that during the expensive refurbishing of the Lords, room and money have been found for a convenient women's convenience for peers' wives and guests just where they were always told there couldn't be one.

Continuing male dominance in Parliament is, indeed, illustrated not only by such major absurdities as that peeresses in their own right cannot sit in the Lords, or that no woman, however distinguished, can be allowed a ticket for the Distinguished Strangers' Gallery of the Commons, but also by these mundane trivialities. Most of the MPs' lavatories around the place are not labelled *Men* or *Gentlemen*, but *Members Only*, as if there were no women MPs.

At least, thank goodness, the Palace of Westminster will never be disfigured by those whimsical lavatory signs which are, in some secular establishments, the most painful of humour. The Lads and Lasses of Butlin's camps are mild in comparison with some on the other side of the Atlantic—for instance (in a smart New York restaurant) *Little Boys' Room* and *Little Girls' Room*; and (at a golf club) *Mr Golfer* and *Mrs Golfer*; and (at a yacht club) *Buoys* and *Gulls*; and (perhaps worst of all, in antique Gothic lettering, at a sham-olde-English 'tavern' in Hollywood) *Milord* and *Milady*.

The wrong tone

Oliver Lyttelton (Viscount Chandos), *The Memoirs of Lord Chandos* (1962)

I must say that during my fourteen years in the House of Commons there was not an effective lady parliamentarian. As a rule, in the House women are too earnest, and seem apologetic and on the defensive. This is hardly surprising when their handicap is weighed up. They are no more than a handful, perhaps twenty-five or thirty in all, out of a House of 630. They do not use the Smoking Room, and necessarily are out of touch with the current opinion of Members. They find it difficult to distinguish between the smart Members whom no one is willing to listen to, and the solid, sincere bores, who will always get a hearing because the House likes sincerity. One very popular Member, who had a fierce and burning faith in personal liberty, never spoke, as far as I can remember, a word of sense in any debate which I heard. Yet the House would fill up and listen to him with respect. The ladies would not have known his qualities, which were only manifested in private. Smoking-room stories are also bandied about in the House of Commons and usually, from their nature, the lady Members do not hear them.

In short, the lady Members seldom get the tone or mood of the House right. A small number tried to assert the equality of the sexes by being ruder and more unruly than the worst of their male colleagues.

1. George G. Goschen, Letter to Lady Randolph Churchill: quoted in *The Reminiscences of Lady Randolph Churchill* (1908), pp. 96–7.
2. George Henry Jennings, *An Anecdotal History of the British Parliament from the Earliest Periods to the Present Time* (1880), p. 420.
3. ibid.
4. James Grant, *Random Recollections of the House of Commons* (1836), p. 17.
5. Michael MacDonagh, *Parliament: Its Romance; Its Comedy; Its Pathos* (1902), p. 110.
6. Sir William Fraser, *Disraeli and his Day* (1891), p. 286.
7. Alexander Mackintosh, *Echoes of Big Ben: A Journalist's Parliamentary Diary, 1881–1940* (1945), p. 164.
8. Henry W. Lucy, *A Diary of the Home Rule Parliament, 1892–1895* (1896), pp. 156–7.
9. ibid., p. 62.
10. Patrick Howarth, *Questions in the House: The History of a Unique British Institution* (1956), p. 100.
11. Count Paul Vasili (pseud.), *The World of London (La Société de Londres)* (1885), p. 96.
12. Harry Graham, *The Mother of Parliaments* (1911), p. 272.
13. Stephen King-Hall and Ann Dewar, *History in Hansard 1803–1900* (1952), p. 197.
14. Mackintosh, op. cit., p. 82.
15. *The Times*, January 12, 1968.
16. Charles T. King, *The Asquith Parliament (1906–1909): A Popular History of its Men and Measures* (1910), p. 285.
17. Earl Winterton, *Orders of the Day* (1953), p. 93.
18. Frances Stevenson, Diary, November 30, 1934.
19. Frances Stevenson, Diary, November 29, 1919.
20. Anthony King and Anne Sloman, *Westminster and Beyond* (1973), p. 55.
21. Sir Henry Morris-Jones, *Doctor in the Whips' Room* (1955), pp. 158–9.

22. Mackintosh, op. cit., p. 139.
23. Harold Nicolson, Diary, October 29, 1936.
24. A. P. Herbert, *Independent Member* (1950), p. 39.
25. Alicia Bayne was the daughter of Professor Pryme and the editor of his *Recollections*.
26. Anne Sebba, *Battling for News: The Rise of the Woman Reporter* (1994), p. 54.
27. King and Sloman, op. cit., p. 55.
28. James Lowther (Viscount Ullswater), *A Speaker's Commentaries* (1925), p. 271.

INDEX